LIVESTOCK AND MEAT MARKETING

THIRD EDITION

LIVESTOCK AND MEAT MARKETING

THIRD EDITION

John H. McCoy, Ph.D.
Emeritus
Kansas State University

and

M.E. Sarhan, Ph.D.
Sigma One Corporation
Raleigh, North Carolina

An **avi** Book
Published by Van Nostrand Reinhold Company
New York

To
Margaret, Monica, Anthony, and Michael

An AVI Book
(AVI is an imprint of Van Nostrand Reinhold Company Inc.)
Copyright © 1988 by Van Nostrand Reinhold Company Inc.

Library of Congress Catalog Card Number 87-23136

Printed in the United States of America

Van Nostrand Reinhold Company Inc.
115 Fifth Avenue
New York, New York 10003

Van Nostrand Reinhold Company Limited
Molly Millars Lane
Wokingham, Berkshire RG11 2PY, England

Van Nostrand Reinhold
480 La Trobe Street
Melbourne, Victoria 3000, Australia

Macmillan of Canada
Division of Canada Publishing Corporation
164 Commander Boulevard
Agincourt, Ontario M1S 3C7, Canada

16 15 14 13 12 11 10 9 8 7 6 5 4 3 2 1

Library of Congress Cataloging-in-Publication Data

McCoy, John Henry, 1912–
    Livestock and meat marketing.

    "An AVI book."
    Includes index.
    1. Meat industry and trade—United States.
I. Sarhan, M. E. II. Title.
HD9415.M25 1988   381'.416'00973   87-23136
ISBN 0-442-20488-4

Preface

The major purpose of this book remains unchanged. It is presented, this time with a co-author, as a basic text and as a general reference in the area of livestock and meat marketing. However, whether we like it or not, major changes have occurred in the red meat industry in recent years with significant impact on the marketing sector. The vigorous, rapidly expanding red meat industry of the pre-1980 period ran into serious trouble during the 1980s. Demand for red meat slacked off coincident with a general farm crisis. The pace of concentration in cattle feedlots and hog production quickened. Numerous small meat-packing plants ceased operation. New developments occurred in futures market hedging, use of options, forward contracting, meat packing and processing, electronic marketing, export potential, and world-wide government policy considerations. These are some of the changes necessitating a major revision of many sections and the addition of three new chapters.

It is more obvious than ever before that success in this industry requires more than efficiency in production. It is hoped that the material presented here will contribute not only to a better understanding of markets and marketing, but also to more profitable marketing strategies. Entirely new sections have been added and all tables and figures have been updated where possible. We have drawn upon numerous new research offerings, and we express appreciation to those authors. We also owe a debt of gratitude to the many students, teachers, industry representatives, and reviewers for suggestions which we trust will improve this edition.

John H. McCoy, Ph.D.
M. E. Sarhan, Ph.D.

Contents

LIVESTOCK AND MEAT MARKETING

THIRD EDITION

Introduction

LIVESTOCK–MEAT, AN IMPORTANT INDUSTRY

The production and marketing of livestock and related products comprise one of the largest and most important industries in the world. In both developed and developing countries, millions of producers depend upon raising livestock for a livelihood. Although the degree of meat processing and the sophistication of distribution systems vary directly with a country's economic development, vast amounts of resources— manpower, land, and capital—are devoted to the industry on a global basis.

Marketing systems differ from country to country, and variations occur within each of the latter, but all have one primary purpose—to move products from producer to consumer as efficiently as possible. That can become a staggering responsibility because the quantities involved are enormous, distances are often great, and most of the products are highly perishable.

The importance of an industry can be viewed in many different ways. In an economic sense, importance may be related to such factors as the number of people employed (directly and indirectly), the amount of investment, the quantities of physical resources used, and the quantities of products produced. From the standpoint of the physical health of the nation, concern attaches to the safety, wholesomeness, and nutritive aspects of the products of the industry in question. Governmental agencies are concerned with the contributions an industry may make to tax revenues. Importance also may be attached to an industry's contribution to national defense. In recent years, concern has become pronounced over social issues such as environmental pollution and the costs involved in dealing with them. Some aspects of importance are capable of quantitative measurement; others are not. Some could be measured, but appropriate data have not been assembled. Enough information is available, however, to show that, by any reasonable standards, livestock and meat are big business in the United States.

1

Product Output

Products of the livestock industry are essential to the comfort, health, and well-being of countless millions the world over. Meat, of course, is the primary product. Lean meat is prized as a basic source of high-quality protein. As strange as it may seem to a majority of Americans, the fat component of meat is equally desired by many peoples.

In the U.S. alone, approximately 17.82 billion kilograms (39.27 billion pounds)[1] of red meat were produced during 1984. Beginning stocks were 293 million kilograms (646 million pounds), and about 1.23 billion kilograms (2.721 billion pounds) were imported. Exports were 309 million kilograms (682 million pounds) during the year. That was an average net availability of 77.1 kilograms (169.9 pounds) for every man, woman, and child in the country. A greater total tonnage of meat is consumed in the U.S. than in any other country, but, on a per capita basis, U.S. is outranked by Argentina, New Zealand, Uruguay, and several others.

An often overlooked and sometimes unappreciated output of the industry is the wide array of products that are derived from livestock in addition to carcass meat. These products may be classified as edible by-products, inedible by-products, pharmaceuticals, and variety meats. The following is only a partial listing of such products. Among the better known variety meats are liver, heart, tongue, kidneys, brains, and sweetbreads. Edible by-products include oleo stock, oleo oil gelatin, suet, and sausage casings. Among the more commonly recognized inedible by-products are leather, wool, mohair, inedible fats, fatty acids, glues and adhesives, animal feeds, fertilizers, combs, buttons, paper, bone charcoal, and surgical sutures. Livestock are walking factories of more than 100 pharmaceutical products. Insulin is perhaps the best known. Not so well known are heparin, epinephrine, thrombin, fibrinolysin, chymotrypsin, glucogon, trypsin, parathyroid hormone, corticotropin (ACTH), thyrotropin (TSH), and vasopressen. The importance to mankind of this type of product is far beyond any monetary value.

Assets

Total assets of U.S. farmers and ranchers were $1.031 trillion at the beginning of 1984 (Table 1.1), a figure that reflects the current value of all equipment, livestock, land, buildings, and savings of farmers and

---

[1]Carcass weight. One kilogram = 2.2046 pounds.

Table 1.1. U.S. Farm and Ranch Assets on January 1, 1981–1984
(From USDA, 1984).

Item	Year			
	1981	1982	1983	1984*
Physical assets				
Real-estate	828,442	818,862	769,198	764,539
Non-real-estate	218,584	219,476	228,176	216,532
Financial assets	42,749	45,140	47,796	50,055
Total†	1,089,775	1,083,479	1,045,170	1,031,127

*Preliminary.
†May not add because of rounding.

ranchers. The magnitude of this figure dwarfs that of even the largest industrial corporation in the world.

Information is not available to indicate the proportion of farm and ranch assets applicable to livestock. Any such determination would show that, in addition to assets used directly in livestock production, the bulk of those assets devoted to forage and feed grain production are indirectly an integral part of the industry.

In addition to farm and ranch assets, the total industry includes the packing, processing, and distribution sectors. Beyond these are numerous associated, or supplementary, sectors that are entirely or partially devoted to functions of the industry, including substantial assets in facilities for transportation (truck and railroad), marketing (auctions, terminals, concentration yards, futures markets, etc.), banking and credit, veterinary services, manufacturing of veterinary equipment and supplies, feed manufacturing, livestock and meat processing-equipment manufacturing, insurance companies, publication of numerous magazines and newspapers, etc. No one has ever calculated the combined value of assets vested in livestock and meat, but there is no doubt that this industry, if not the leader, is near the top for all U.S. industries.

Cash Receipts. Cash receipts from farm and ranch marketings totaled $138.7 billion (exclusive of government payments) in 1983 (Table 1.2). Of this total, $38.8 billion was from meat animals. The share of cash receipts from meat animals increased until the early 1970s, then decreased as stepped-up world-wide demand for grain coincided with a cyclical slump in cattle prices. In recent years, the share of cash receipts from meat animals, wool, and mohair has remained relatively constant.

The importance of meat animals and wool varies considerably among

Table 1.2. U.S. Cash Farm and Ranch Receipts, 1980–1983

Product	1980	1981	1982	1983*
		(Million $)		
Cattle and calves	31,464	29,579	29,893	28,694
Hogs	8,921	9,785	10,623	9,714
Sheep and Lambs	470	416	447	418
Total meat animals	40,855	39,780	40,963	38,826
Wool and mohair	93	104	72	NA†
Dairy products	16,587	18,128	18,354	18,808
Poultry and eggs	9,158	9,951	9,542	9,701
Other livestock items	1,103	1,240	1,268	1,868
Total livestock and products	67,795	69,202	70,199	69,203
Crops	72,706	73,071	74,353	69,516
All commodities	140,501	142,273	144,551	138,719

Source: USDA, 1983, and USDA, 1984A.
*Preliminary.
†NA = Not Available.

the states—both in absolute amount and as a percentage of farm and ranch cash receipts (see Table 1.3). Iowa was high in total dollar receipts in 1983 with slightly over $4.6 billion, whereas Wyoming was tops in the percentage of receipts, with a combined meat-animal and wool total of over 77.1 percent.

A large share of income received by farmers and ranchers is pumped back into the economy in payment for production expenses, and most of the remainder is spent for household and personal items. As meat and wool moves through marketing channels, value is added by slaughtering, processing, and distribution. Sales of red meat at retail were estimated at $61.5 billion in 1983. Since cash receipts to farmers and merchants were $38.8 billion, the value added in slaughtering, processing, and distribution pumped an additional $22.7 billion ($61.5 − $38.8 = $27.7) into the economy, and this does not take into consideration the impact on it of wool, mohair, and exports. In light of such figures, it is apparent that the livestock-meat industry is an important component not only of U.S. agriculture, but in the national economy as well.

Interrelationships with Other Industries

Livestock is important not only in absolute terms—that is, from the standpoint of the number of dollars turned over by the industry—but even more so in the additional business activity generated in other economic sectors that service livestock and meat producers. This is com-

Table 1.3. Cash Farm and Ranch Receipts from Meat Animals and Wool for Selected States, 1983

State	Meat animals ($1,000)	Wool ($1,000)	All commodities ($1,000)	From meat animals (%)	From wool (%)
Illinois	1,874,756	486	8,143,616	23.0	*
Iowa	4,680,070	1,485	9,334,873	50.1	*
Missouri	1,626,699	384	3,588,002	40.8	*
Kansas	2,954,554	869	5,397,867	54.7	*
N. Carolina	479,987	22	3,783,925	12.7	*
Georgia	474,012	NA†	3,310,099	14.3	NA
Alabama	421,546	NA	2,112,348	20.0	NA
Mississippi	260,903	NA	2,291,119	11.4	NA
Arkansas	315,966	NA	2,999,467	10.5	NA
Oklahoma	1,369,776	301	2,691,515	50.9	*
Texas	4,347,952	15,438	8,970,399	48.5	0.2
Montana	583,285	3,731	1,503,303	38.8	0.2
Wyoming	450,774	6,574	592,887	76.0	1.1
Colorado	1,757,638	4,426	2,926,988	60.0	0.2
N. Mexico	469,385	3,673	962,055	48.8	0.4
Arizona	535,054	934	1,643,630	32.6	0.1
California	1,337,515	5,875	13,493,731	9.9	*
Nebraska	3,768,404	639	6,010,352	62.7	*
Idaho	546,115	2,197	2,015,523	27.1	0.1
Indiana	1,176,637	260	4,009,442	29.3	*
Kentucky	572,914	70	2,798,147	20.5	*
Michigan	404,708	361	3,001,461	13.5	*
Minnesota	1,584,603	823	6,277,407	25.2	*
Nevada	121,038	565	224,177	54.0	0.3
N. Dakota	493,836	836	2,691,133	18.4	*
S. Dakota	1,375,801	3,835	2,586,148	53.2	0.1
Ohio	702,457	680	3,673,664	19.1	*
Oregon	287,841	1,703	1,700,115	16.9	0.1
Utah	207,778	3,271	578,707	35.9	0.6

Source: USDA 1985.
*Less than 0.5%.
†NA = Not Available.

monly referred to as the "multiplier effect." It applies to income generated in other sectors, as well as the output of goods and services and employment in the other sectors. No sufficiently disaggregated national studies have been made comparing the multiplier effect of meat-animal sectors with other sectors, but this has been done in individual states, for example, Emerson *et al.* (1973 and 1982) in Kansas; Wright *et al.* (1983) in Texas; and Otto and Futrell (1984) in Iowa.

Multipliers. Particular multipliers of the several studies cited are not presented here because the periods and sectors chosen are not identical and valid comparisons may not be possible. Each of the studies produced output and income multipliers, and, in addition, the Iowa study produced employment multipliers. Results of all four studies showed that livestock, meat, and related sectors were characterized by significant interrelationships with other sectors of the economy. An additional dollar's worth of output and/or income in a livestock-related sector created a rippling effect by generating output, income, and employment in other sectors of a magnitude greater than that in the originating sector. This effect emphasizes the importance of livestock in the economic development of an area. It lends credence to the proposition that public and private policies that enhance development in livestock-related sectors will simultaneously boost output, employment, and income of associated sectors. At the same time, it points to unfortunate consequences to the economy of an area upon the decline of that area's livestock and meat industries. This relationship holds whether the decline is of a secular (long-run) nature, as appears to be the case of beef cattle feeding in the Corn Belt, or a short-time disruption, such as that which occurred throughout the United States during the mid-1980s. At such times, multipliers work in reverse. A decline in livestock sectors works to the detriment, not only of livestock producers, but also of related business and industry.

It is readily apparent from the data that the livestock and meat sectors are highly interrelated with other industries in Kansas, Texas, and Iowa. Logically, comparable relationships would be expected in other important livestock states or regions. The significance of these relationships lies in the indicated importance of these sectors in the economy of their state or region. They provide a clue that economic development of a state may be enhanced by research and extension activities that provide for the development of livestock and meat production.

Land Utilization

Livestock production utilizes a far greater area of land than any other activity. On a worldwide basis, it is estimated that about two-thirds of the land devoted to agriculture is range land, meadow, or permanent pasture (National Research Council 1977). In the United States, 69 percent of the agricultural land was grazed in 1969 (Nix, 1975). Even if one includes nonagricultural land, more than one-half of its total land area is devoted to range, "consisting of grassland, shrublands, and open forests. . . . " (USDA, 1974). In the western states, a much higher percentage is devoted to grazing. The production of supplementary pastures, forages, and feed grains necessitate additional vast acreages.

A major share of the feed used by western livestock comes from native range, pastures, and meadows on land that, under present conditions, has virtually no other feasible alternative to food production use. The same situation prevails through the Flint Hills and Osage Pasture areas of Kansas and Oklahoma, and many other localized areas in all parts of the United States.[2] Livestock (primarily cattle and sheep) utilize this native vegetation and enormous quantities of roughage, crop aftermath, etc., which otherwise would contribute nothing to the food supply. Forages, both native and cultivated, provide an economical means of growing livestock preparatory to finishing for slaughter. Requirements of the grain finishing operation support a major share of the feed grain industry which in itself is the prime user of much of the best land in the United States.[3] Consumers spend more for meat than for any other food item, a fact attesting to the importance placed upon the end product.

Employment

Published data are not available on the number of people employed in the production, processing, and marketing of livestock and meat. Directly or indirectly, nearly all farmers and ranchers have a hand in it. Most of those who do not produce livestock are involved in feed production to a greater or lesser degree. The relationship is obvious for those in feed grain and forage production. It is less obvious in such crops as cotton and sugar beets, but even many of these crops do have feed by-products, such as cottonseed meal and beet pulp. Even fruit and vegetable producers are involved in a minor way because limited quantities of their pulp and refuse are used for livestock feed. In 1984, there were 3.50 million persons employed in farming (USDA, 1986). According to USDA statistics, about 40 percent of the total labor hours spent in farm work were used directly in livestock, feed, and hay production. Since a substantial part (more than 70 percent) of the remaining labor hours must have had some indirect input to enterprises related to livestock feed, it can be assumed that about 85 percent of this effort had some input to either direct livestock production or feed production. Thus, there are approximately 2.98 million persons (85 percent of 3 million) engaged in livestock production phases. In all

---

[2]Some of the lands, of course, have other uses such as recreation, wildlife habitat, mining, and watersheds for hydroelectric, irrigation, and urban water supplies

[3]It is recognized that exports of feed grains have accounted for a significant, but variable, proportion of feed grain disposition in recent years, but domestic feed utilization is the major support of that industry.

of agriculture, there are about eight people in marketing for every six engaged in production. If that same ratio holds true for the livestock sector, some 3.97 million people would be engaged in the marketing of livestock and meat. In total, then, there would be 6.95 million people employed in production and marketing. And if all service and complementary employment were included, such as veterinarians, insurance agents, publishers, equipment manufacturers, etc., it is possible that the total amounts to about 10 million. It was estimated by Otto and Futrell (1984) that some 34,800 persons were employed in beef cattle production and related sectors in Iowa alone.

MARKETS AND MARKETING

Marketing—the Concept

Marketing is that area of economics concerned with the exchange and valuation of goods and services.[4] This definition encompasses (1) activities associated with the physical movement and transformation of goods, and (2) the pricing of goods and services. In some aspects, the physical functions of marketing are related to production. In economic jargon, production, is defined as the creation of "utility," or usefulness. Utility may be created by changing the form, location, availability over time, or possession (ownership) of a product. In a narrow sense, marketing is sometimes construed to apply only to exchange of title (Bakken, 1953)—a definition that would limit it to problems of possession utility, including pricing and the activities associated with buying and selling. By long tradition, however, marketing has been considered to be a broader activity than this. By the so-called "functional" approach to the study of marketing, it would include, in addition to buying and selling, such functions as transporting, storing, processing, packaging, advertising, collecting and disseminating market news, standardizing and grading, inspecting, financing, and risk bearing. This definition would appear to include the creation of all types of utility listed under the definition of production and prompts the question of whether there is a difference between production and marketing.

There is little to be gained belaboring this point. For administrative purposes, the USDA considers marketing to be limited to those activities that take place from the time products leave the farm gate. Activi-

---

[4]Agreement is not universal on an acceptable definition of marketing (or of the term "market"). The usefulness and validity of a definition is associated with its application. A different definition may be perfectly proper and correct depending upon the use made of it.

ties performed prior to that time are considered to be production. Clearly, however, there can be a direct relationship between the two. A marketing program may be influenced by prior decisions that determine the quantity, quality, or timing of production. Even prior to that, a decision that determines the quality of feeder livestock purchased may directly affect the feeding program. Since marketing and production are so closely intertwined, there is a growing awareness that efficiencies may be gained by considering production and marketing as one integrated or coordinated system. This is one application of the so-called "systems" approach to economic as well as noneconomic problems. We will not attempt to draw a firm distinction between marketing and production here.

What Is a Market?

At first thought, the concept of a market may appear rather straight-forward. The livestock auction building and pens on the outskirts of one's home town or the big office building and yards of public terminal livestock markets at such places as Kansas City or Omaha are quite evident. It is also rather common, however, to hear references to the "cattle" market, the "corn" market, the "automobile" market. On other occasions, the reference may be to the "futures" market or the "cash" or "spot" market. In the first instance, a market was associated with a particular place; in the second, the association was with a commodity; and in the third, with an element of time. In other cases, a market may be defined as a particular group of people, an institution, a mechanism for facilitating exchange, or as a "perfect" or "imperfect" market. The market concept also has been linked to the degree of communication among buyers and sellers and the degree of substitutability among goods. Although there are differences among these concepts, any one of them might be correct for a particular purpose. The concept of a perfect market, for example, is an abstraction used by economists as a benchmark for evaluating the performance of market situations that deviate from its specifications. Further reference will be made to the perfect market in later sections.

Our application here of the term "market" does not necessitate a single choice of definitions. Depending upon the particular context, reference will sometimes be to certain geographically located markets; on other occasions, to markets for a particular class, grade, or weight of livestock. Various aspects of the cash and futures markets, as well as the agencies and institutions that make up these markets, will be analyzed at some length. In other words, a comprehensive concept of the market will be used.

It is generally agreed that a viable, competitive market requires more than physical facilities. The assembly and concentration of salable livestock and meat may tend to promote competition, but the essential ingredients are people and a communication system—people who are adequately informed with respect to (1) the quality of livestock or meat being offered, (2) the current or prospective value of that quality of animals, and (3) bargaining techniques. If all parties interested in transacting business are adequately informed and have an efficient communication system, it is apparent that the concept of a market would need little reference to geographical location or space. Some recent developments in livestock marketing have made this more and more obvious (e.g., electronic markets).

Role of Markets and Marketing in the Economy

It was implied in previous paragraphs that we are concerned with marketing under competitive conditions. This is normally taken for granted because we live in a "market economy"—sometimes also called an "exchange economy," a "competitive economy," or "capitalism," where competitive forces are "relatively" free to exert their influence in the formulation of prices and in direction of the economy. Needless to say, this is not the case throughout the world. Although all countries have some degree of government regulation or control over marketing activities, the situation is one of degree. The United States is at one end of the spectrum, with a relatively low degree of government control. Such countries as the Soviet Union, Peoples Republic of China, Albania, and Cuba are at the other end, with a relatively high degree of central planning.

Regardless of the economic system in question, certain functions must be performed. Goods must be produced and distributed. Income must be distributed among the participants. In a market economy, competitively determined prices are the guiding force that gives direction to what is produced, what technologies are used in production, where production takes place, when production is carried out, when and where consumption takes place and who gets the proceeds from the whole process. In a completely centralized economy, such decisions as these would be dictated by the government through administrators, committees, boards, etc., responsible for operation of the economy. The attainment of an optimum that meets or approaches economic, social, and political objectives is an extremely complex problem. The problem is no less complex in a market economy, but the approach is vastly different. Here, chief dependence is placed upon impersonal, competitive market forces that generate prices that give direction to the economy—again with the expectation that economic, social, and political objectives will be met to a satisfactory degree. This freedom places a tremendous burden on the markets. If markets do not operate efficiently, resources used in production may be misallocated; consumers may not have goods available in the form, quantity, quality, place, and time desired; and inequalities may occur in the distribution of income among individuals. Departure from generally desired objectives or goals prompts government intervention in the name of the public interest or general welfare. Intervention may take many forms, e.g., inspection, licenses, regulations designed to curb monopoly or enhance competition.

REFERENCES

American National Cattlemen's Association. 1965. Proc. 3rd Coordinated Beef Improvement Conf., Texas A & M University, July.

Bakken, H. 1953. Theory of Markets and Marketing. Madison, WI: Mimir Press.

Emerson, J. et al. 1973. The interindustry structures of Kansas. Dept. Econ. Analysis, State of Kansas, Topeka.

Emerson, J. et al. 1982. Ogallala aquifier study in Kansas. Kansas Water Office, State of Kansas, Topeka.

Fowler, S. H. 1961. An introduction to livestock marketing. In The Marketing of Livestock and Meat, 2nd ed. Danville, IL: Interstate Printers & Publishers.

National Science Council. 1977. World food and nutrition study, the potential contributions of research. National Academy of Science, Washington, D. C., June.

Nix, J. E. 1975. Grain-fed versus grass-fed beef production. USDA Econ. Res. Serv. Circular 602, April.

Otto, D., and Futrell, G. 1984. Economic contributions and impacts of changes in Iowa's livestock and meat processing industries. Legislative Extended Assistance Group, Institute of Urban and Regional Research, Univ. of Iowa, LEAG Series 84-4.

USDA. 1955. Guide to agriculture, USA. USDA Econ. Res. Serv., Agr. Econ. Rept. 95.

USDA. 1974. Opportunities to increase red meat production from ranges of the United States. Six Agencies: Econ. Res. Serv., Ext Ser., Forest Serv., Soil Cons. Serv., Agr. Res. Serv., Co-op. State Res. Serv. (unnumbered), June.

USDA. 1984A. Agricultural Statistics 1984, U.S. Govt. Printing Office.

USDA. 1984B. Economic indicators of the farm sector, state income and balance sheet statistics. USDA Econ. Res. Serv. ECIFS3-3, September.

USDA. 1985. Economic indicators of the farm sector, state income and balance sheet statistics. USDA Econ. Res. Serv. ECIFS3-4, January.

USDA. 1986. Economic indicators of the farm sector, production and efficiency statistics 1984. USDA, ERS ECIFS4-4.

2

Historical Perspective

Many changes have occurred in methods of marketing livestock and meat in the United States, and the dynamic nature of the industry practically assures that changes will continue. The following thumbnail sketch of historical development is presented, not so much in the interests of history per se, but rather to point out the factors that have been responsible for changes in the marketing system. Understanding the history and the factors and their influence will help us to understand current as well as future developments. In many respects, the marketing system developed in conjunction with, and as an integral part of, the production process. For both, it has been a gradual, but steady evolution.[1]

Among the more important factors influencing market development have been shifting geographical centers of livestock production and population; shifting import–export opportunities; changes in the technology of transportation and refrigeration; changes in the structural characteristics of the producing, packing, wholesaling, and retailing components of the industry; and developments in grading livestock and meat and the collection and dissemination of market intelligence.

Marketing was of little significance in the self-sufficient, subsistence economy of the early settlers. Meager surpluses of livestock and meat were readily bartered for other necessities. In time, a continuous influx of immigrants gave rise to population concentrations in cities in the present Central Atlantic states. Simultaneously, livestock production expanded in the eastern coastal region and slowly pushed westward and southward. Cattle were introduced in the southwest—through Spanish influence and largely by missionaries—as early, if not earlier, than on the East Coast, but the pattern of the marketing system that was to emerge as the prevailing model had its origins in East Coast livestock development. As specialization of labor increased, a need quickly developed for trade. Barter between producers and consumers

---

[1]The introduction and subsequent development of domestic meat animals is an extremely important and interesting chapter in U.S. annals. For those who may be interested, a considerable body of literature is available on the subject. Examples include Clemen (1923), Duddy and Revzan (1938), Thompson (1942), Wentworth (1948), and Williams and Stout (1964).

soon was replaced by merchants (middlemen) who, for a fee, acted as the go-between for producers and consumers. As long as distances were not too great, most slaughtering was done by the producers themselves, who then delivered dressed carcasses to local retail merchants. As both distances and demand for meat increased, the feasibility arose for another intermediary—a merchant who would buy live animals. This person might slaughter the animals and retail the meat himself or slaughter and sell dressed carcasses to a retail merchant. Thus, in our earliest period, direct marketing—producer to slaughter—was the rule. As will be pointed out later, the trend for some years has been back to direct marketing of slaughter livestock.

At first, all movement of livestock was on foot. No other means were available. In time, limited river and coastal water transport was introduced. Slaughtering was confined to winter months. Meat preservation was crude, being limited to smoking, salting, and pickling, the meat then being packed in barrels for storage and shipment. It was these techniques that gave rise to the term meat "packer," a term that has persisted and is now used synonymously with "slaughterer." Commercial trade in "packed" meats got underway around the mid-1600s with shipments to the British West Indies and the provisioning of sailing vessels (Clemen, 1923). The West Indies trade was initiated by New England colonies, but in time the geographical advantage of Virginia and the Carolinas gave the latter the competitive edge—an early U.S. example of regional competitive advantage. (Probably the latest analogous example is the development and introduction of hybrid grain sorghum in the Southern Plains states, which gave that region a competitive advantage over others in cattle feeding.)

As a rule, curing and packing was done by individuals, farmers or merchants, until about 1662. At that time, William Pynchon launched what is purported to be the first commercial venture in meat packing (Clemen, 1923). The plant was located at Springfield, Massachusetts. Prior to that, Pynchon had been a cattle drover. According to Webster's New World Dictionary, the word "drover" has two meanings: (1) a person who takes a drove of cattle to market, and (2) a cattle dealer. This occupation is worthy of mention because at that time, and for some time later, it was an important element in the marketing system. Many farmers drove their own livestock, but, as distances lengthened, this became more of a problem. Additionally, some preferred to sell at home for a known price and let the professional drover carry the risk from there on. As the definition indicates, drovers would drive farmers' livestock to market for a fee, or, acting as dealers, they would buy livestock from farmers and market them on their own account. The definition given above implies that droving applied only to cattle. Although used most extensively for cattle, it also was used to some extent for hogs and sheep and, in some cases, even for turkeys.

From a dealer's standpoint, droving was a risky profession. Market information was almost nonexistent; there were physical hazards on the trail; and marketing consisted basically of locating a slaughterer who wanted livestock at that particular time—at best an uncertain proposition. Nevertheless, drovers continued to be a significant link in the marketing system until the advent of railroads and emergence of terminal markets.

Marketing apparently continued on an informal, unorganized basis until the mid-1700s although there is no question that the pace of activities and the volume of trading increased significantly with the passing years. Although a number of cities emerged as market centers, Boston was particularly active, and it was there, or nearby, that the formalities of organized marketing were first reported. This happened for meat a few years prior to live animals. In 1742 in Boston, a meat market known as Faneuil Hall was erected. Here " . . . the old-fashioned ways came to an end . . . Regulations were . . . voted regarding the quality of meat sold and as a result both the producer and consumer were greatly aided" (Clemen, 1923). The thriving meat market bolstered the meat packing business and this, in turn, bolstered livestock marketing in the vicinity (or possibly the order of causation was reversed). In any event, the Brighton, Massachusetts market is cited as a leader. Brighton is now a part of the Greater Boston area. This market was established by Jonathan Winship, who

. . . established a large slaughter house there, and producers of beef cattle soon began to find their way to this place to effect a sale. Other butchers came here to compete with him in making purchases, and in a short time the business became centered here, Mr. Winship having wisely encouraged and fostered it. This is believed to have occurred at the time of the old French War (1756) or very soon after. From that time this was the cattle market of New England. . . .

Brighton Market was the model for many others in the East and later in the West. [It was] . . . an example of the old-fashioned market institution which was the forerunner of the great, modern centralized livestock market . . . (Clemen, 1923).

Following the War of Indenpendence, settlement rapidly spread westward over the Allegheny Mountains and into the rich Ohio Valley.

Shortly after the beginning of the nineteenth Century, the center of livestock production shifted to that region. Droving continued as a means of transporting cattle to eastern markets. The great distances, however, necessitated development of the packing industry, particularly for hogs. The activity originally centered at Cincinnati, which became known as "Porkopolis." Not only was Cincinnati in the heart of a rich production area, but it also was on the Ohio River. River transport down the Ohio and Mississippi provided an outlet for livestock and meat to southern cities and for export. As livestock production spread westward, the packing industry also spread, and the packing of beef increased with the westward movement, although at this stage beef packing was limited. As production spread into Illinois and beyond, the distances to eastern markets became too great for the droving of fat cattle. This necessitated the movement of stock cattle eastward for finishing in Ohio or further east. New England no longer could successfully compete with the West in fattening cattle, however, and was rapidly being industrialized. Simultaneously, the South was specializing in cotton.

The region now known as the Corn Belt virtually took over livestock production. When the southern meat market soon proved to be the most lucrative, the movement of meat and livestock down the Ohio and Mississippi rivers increased to the detriment of eastern markets, thus provided a stimulus for eastern interests to promote improved transportation to the east. Canal construction was greatly expanded during the first half of the 1800s and canals became important links in the transport system. Private toll roads and public roads were pushed throughout the settled area. More important, the drive for trade gave a great impetus to railroad construction. By the 1850s, railroads had reopened the eastern meat trade and quickened the pace of expansion of the livestock-meat industry.

It was about this time that livestock auctions gained recognition. The auction method, of course, was not new. It had been used in Great Britain for centuries. Early American colonists trafficked in auctions to some extent, but apparently they were not used extensively for livestock. Auction marketing was reported along with other development in the Ohio Valley. The first mentioned—in 1836 (Henlein, 1959)—was the Ohio Company for Importing English Cattle. Others were organized in the following 25 years or so in Ohio and Kentucky in connection with the sale of imported purebred cattle (Henlein, 1959). Clemen (1923) reported that they were used for cattle, mules, jacks, jennies, horses, sheep and swine, but the extent of auction marketing was not specifically recorded. After a relatively short period of growth however, this method of business waned, for new factors were shaping the marketing system. Among these were the influence of railroads in association with regional shifts of production and the growing need for yarding facilities at points of assembly.

Railroads were being pushed through the Ohio, Mississippi, and Missouri River Valleys. With an ever-growing volume of livestock, drovers and yards became available for holding stock until its sale. Earlier, this had been a minor problem since stock could usually be sold upon arrival. One privately operated yard, the Bull's Head Market, was reported in Chicago as early as 1848. By the early 1860s, each of the five major railroads serving Chicago had individually constructed yards as an enticement to business. Livestock was a major source of freight revenue. A multiplicity of railroads converging in Chicago from the heavy production areas to the west and south soon made Chicago the major market center.

Another simultaneous development of major significance was the emergence of the livestock commission agent. Prior to this time the owner (drover or farmer) acted as his own agent in selling. This was a time-consuming job, and owners were often ill-informed on market conditions. Drovers undoubtedly could see that use of an agent would relieve them of the expense of accompanying livestock to market and allow them more time to solicit business. Another advantage to drovers and farmers lay in financing. Commission firms were able to remit full receipts upon sale of livestock, whereas drovers formerly bought on credit and sold on credit with delayed payments all down the line. The first bona fide livestock commission firm began operation in Chicago in 1857 (Clemen, 1923), a development that must be considered a major milestone in livestock marketing.

The Civil War (1861–1865) brought on unprecedented demands for meat. Many retail-oriented markets were operating by that time, but Chicago's was the greatest in volume. It became painfully apparent, however, that individually railway-owned stockyards, scattered about the city, were inadequate and inefficient from both an operational and pricing standpoint. Buyers could be at only one yard at a time. Shippers often had only one choice of rail line and ran the risk of arrival at a yard devoid of buyers. This dilemma was soon remedied. At the urging of virtually all interests—although a trifle belatedly on the part of railroad officials—the Illinois legislature in 1865 incorporated the Union Stockyards and Transit Company. This provided for a single facility to accommodate all rail lines and came to serve as the model of public terminal livestock markets for many other cities.

Thus, the tendency toward centralization of marketing which had begun under individual auspices received a shot-in-the-arm through public sponsorship. At that time, Chicago had all the ingredients for a great market, a position it held for many years. Railroads converged on the city from the tremendously productive regions to the west and south, directing livestock there as into an enormous funnel. The Union Stockyards provided the physical facilities for handling the stock, and rapid expansion of slaughtering and processing plants provided the packing capacity. Outgoing rail and water transportation facilitated shipments of meat and reshipment of live animals credit resources were available to finance necessary investments and operations.

Other centrally located cities also possessed certain advantageous attributes and quickly came to prominence as terminal markets. Among these were East St. Louis, Kansas City, Wichita, St. Joseph, Omaha, St. Paul, Sioux City, and Indianapolis, to mention only a few. The stream of cattle flowing into these markets by this time had gained additional sources of supply. These were the vast range lands of the Southern Plains states and the Southwest. The Northern Plains states followed in a short time. Droving continued to be a vital link, for the railroads had not yet penetrated that far. Figure 2.1 shows the principal trails over which thousands of cattle were driven to reach these markets.

Fig. 2.1. Map of the principal cattle drives. (*Courtesy,* Arizona Highways.)

Prior to the Civil War, cattle production in Texas had expanded faster than available markets warranted. Southern coastal cities provided about the only outlets beyond the state itself, and these outlets were severely restricted by the monopoly tactics of shipping interests. With the outbreak of the Civil War, these markets were virtually eliminated, and cattle industry of Texas suffered a severe depression. Wartime demands inflated the price of cattle in eastern markets even as range prices dropped. That, of course, provided a tremendous incentive for range cattlemen to reach the lucrative eastern markets. The only alternative was to move the cattle on foot to a rail head. Many obstacles lay in the way, but in time these were overcome. Trails were established and thousands of cattle began to be delivered. As the rails were extended, the drives progressively shortened, until, by about 1880, this era ended. In the process, however, some of the loading points (which also were market points, like Abilene and Dodge City) gained fame and a sort of notoriety that seems destined to continue.[2]

The year 1857, mentioned earlier as the beginning of commission firm operation, also marked the inauguration of another innovation of incalculable significance. Summer meat packing made its debut as a result of the use of natural ice refrigeration. The use of natural ice had obvious limitations, but it was soon augmented by artificially produced ice and this, in turn, by mechanical refrigeration. The use of mechanical refrigeration was well established by 1880 (Ives, 1966). The use of refrigeration revolutionized the meat packing industry since it could now be a year-round business, which added greatly to operational efficiency. Storage and shipment of fresh meat became feasible. Not only was the quantity of meat available on an annual basis increased, but the quality also was enhanced, a consideration that undoubtedly boosted demand. Recognition of quality, however, did not come about automatically. Eastern packers were averse to inshipment of fresh western beef. Railroads had cattle cars, but not refrigerated box cars, and they resisted change. Rumors were spread of the objectionable quality and unwholesomeness of refrigerated meat. There may have been some basis for this at the beginning, but techniques were soon perfected. Year-round markets were opened for producers, although the seasonality of production was to continue—and continues to this day although at an abating rate.

Centralized terminal marketing remained the dominant method until

---

[2]For an interesting account of this period, see *Historic Sketches of the Cattle Trade of the West and Southwest* by Joseph G. McCoy, published in 1874 by Ramsey, Millet and Hudson of Kansas City and reprinted in 1932 by the Rare Book Shop, Washington, D.C.

after World War I. Even before that, however, other factors were at work which were to verify the proposition that, in the world of economics, "things never stay put for long." Improved varieties permitted the northwesterly expansion of corn production. Consistent with previous tendencies, the packing industry was prone to follow livestock production. A number of other factors were involved in this movement, but probably the most significant was expanded use of motor trucks and improvements of roads and highways. A sharp drop in livestock prices following World War I made farmers relatively cost-conscious and more critical of marketing charges and practices at terminals. Improvements in market news services and adoption of grade standards made possible a wider dissemination of market information (Duddy and Revzan, 1938). The trend toward decentralization of markets became obvious following the close of World War II and is continuing to date. As packing plants were constructed nearer to the point of production, producers tended to revert to direct marketing of slaughter livestock. The movement initially was much more extensive with hogs than with cattle or sheep. In later years, it has spread more and more to cattle and sheep. It is particularly apparent with the expansion of finished cattle production in the Southwest, on the West Coast, and in the Southern Plains states. It is significant that in May, 1970, Chicago, the former "hog butcher of the world," stopped accepting hogs at the Union Stockyards. Trading in cattle and sheep ceased in August, 1971.

Auction markets that were known in colonial times and came on with a flurry about the mid-1800s, only to fade into obscurity, came back in a big way following World War I. Although of only limited use for slaughter livestock (there are exceptions to this), auctions assumed significant proportions in the marketing of feeder livestock and cull cows. The 1930s were a period of very rapid expansion, with a slowing of the growth rate during the 1940s, and a slight decline in the number of auctions during the 1950s. Annual data are not available, but it appears that the number of livestock marketed through auctions has tended to stabilize in recent years.

During the period since World War I, structural changes at the retail level have materially changed the wholesale and retail system of meat marketing. These changes have come about with the emergence of large chain supermarkets and their influence on the relative competitive position of retailers versus packers. Their atempts to obtain a steady supply of uniform quality meat have reverberated back through channels—through packers all the way to the producer level. In fact, the increase in bargaining power of the retail sector, as exemplified by chain stores, is a near reversal of the situation prior to World War I.

Producers have always been concerned with their relative position in bargaining—a concern that has come to the foreground with particular emphasis during the last 25 years. Farm groups are attempting, by various means, to improve their bargaining position—a subject that will be discussed in some detail in Chap. 7.

Over the years, the import–export balance has also reversed itself. Although considerable variation was experienced in earlier periods, exports were an important element in the livestock-meat industry during the latter half of the 1800s. From that time on, however, exports dwindled and, with the exception of war periods, constituted a minor fraction of total meat production, although remaining of major proportions for certain items such as lard, variety meats, and hides. In recent years, the United States has become a major importer of meat and has continued to be a substantial exporter of lard, fats (both edible and inedible), hides, and variety meats. Livestock interests have been instrumental in the passage of national legislation designed to limit imports. Although exports of live animals are growing in importance, imports continue to be a matter of national concern.

REFERENCES

Clemsen, R. A. 1923. *The American Livestock and Meat Industry.* New York: Ronald Press.

Duddy, E. E., and Revzan, D. A. 1938. *The Changing Relative Importance of the Central Livestock Market.* Chicago: University of Chicago Press.

Henlein, P. C. 1959. *Cattle Kingdom on the Ohio Valley, 1783–1860.* Lexington: University of Kentucky Press.

Ives, J. R. 1966. *The Livestock and Meat Economy of the United States.* Chicago: American Meat Institute.

Thompson, J. W. 1942. A history of livestock raising in the United States, 1607–1860. USDA Agr. History Ser. 5,1,14–15, 37, 108.

USDA. 1966. Agricultural markets in change. USDA, Econ. Res. Serv., Agr. Econ, Rept. 95, July.

Wentworth, E. M. 1948. America's Sheep Trails. Ames, IA: Iowa State College Press.

Williams, W. F., and Stout, T. T. 1964. *Economics of the Livestock-Meat Industry.* New York: Macmillan Co.

3

Economic and Marketing Principles

MARKETING PROBLEMS

Problems that have arisen in the free-market system stem directly from the functions markets are expected to perform in directing the economy. These may be grouped under four general classifications: (1) determination of consumer demands, (2) reflection of these demands back through market channels to processors and producers, (3) equitable distribution of the income generated, and (4) physical movement of goods through market channels to consumers. Problems arise with respect to the efficiency with which these functions are performed. From an analytical standpoint, the first three are encompassed in the study of problems of "pricing efficiency" and the latter under problems of "operational efficiency." In actual operation, the two are often interrelated.

Operational Efficiency

Operational efficiency in marketing is analogous to the engineer's concept of physical efficiency, i.e., it is concerned with measuring input–output relationships. In marketing, the relevant relationships are either in the physical movement of products from point of production to point of consumption, or in transformation of products from one form to another. An improvement in technology that permits an increase in quantity of goods processed or moved into the market without a proportional increase in resources or—what amounts to the same thing—a decrease in resources used in marketing without a proportional decrease in quantity of goods handled—either of these possibilities would represent an increase in operational efficiency. In either case, it is assumed that unit costs of marketing would be lower with improvement in operational efficiency. There are many examples of this. Studies have revealed that labor requirements per unit of livestock handled can be reduced at many livestock auctions by improvements in pens, alleys, gates, scales, and sale ring layouts that facilitate the movement and sale of livestock (McNeeley et al. 1953). Modernized methods and office equipment can reduce bookkeeping costs per live-stock unit handled in larger marketing operations. Another example is the use of multiple-deck and drop-center trucks, which lead to a reduction in unit costs of transportation.

Not all types of operational efficiency lend themselves to such straightforward measurement, however. Suppose the output were marketing services instead of physical quantities. Service cannot be measured in physical units, yet services most certainly are an output of the marketing system. The commission agent engaged to sell livestock on a terminal market is expected to perform a service, as is the order buyer engaged to purchase feeder cattle. One approach would be to consider that the value of the commission agent's services is the additional value he obtains for livestock over that which could have been obtained without his services. Likewise, the value of the order buyer's services may be presumed to be the difference between the value (cost to you) of feeder cattle purchased by the order buyer as compared to the value (cost to you) if you had not used his services. The principle of added value is clear enough, but quantification can sometimes be difficult.

In a broader sense, value added in manufacturing can be used as an imputed value of services performed by the firm engaged in manufacturing. Calculated marketing margins of farm products, defined as the margin between farm prices and retail prices, is an approximation of the value of services performed in processing and moving goods from farm to consumer. Both value added and marketing margin are crude measures of operational efficiency. The general assumption involved is that competition will be great enough to prevent the inclusion of excess profits in value added and/or in marketing margins. Although this may be a valid assumption, conclusive evidence is hard to come by. In spite of recent investigations that failed to uncover the existence of unreasonable profits in food industries,[1] many farmers and ranchers feel that they are disadvantaged in bargaining for the sale of their products and suspect excess profits in the processing and distributing sectors.

Farmers and ranchers are interested in marketing livestock at the lowest cost consistent with price received (i.e., as long as marketing economies enhance the net price). Over the years, producers have usually questioned whether gains in operational marketing efficiency accrue to them, to the market agencies, or to consumers. In a competitive economy, any reduction in marketing costs that results in above nor-

---

[1]Investigations were carried out by the National Commission on Food Marketing, an investigating agency formed by Congressional action in 1964. Relevant reports by this and other commissions are discussed in later chapters.

mal profits will attract additional competitors. With the possibility of increased profits, competition for products to handle tends to enhance prices paid to producers. Competition by buyers, farther down the marketing channels, to get products as cheaply as possible will also tend to lower selling price. Lack of adequate competition anywhere in the system may permit above normal profits for some time, but if competition is keen, an improvement in operational efficiency will benefit all parties in the long run.

Nevertheless, farmers and ranchers on more than one occasion have been dissatisfied with what they considered exorbitant marketing costs. Probably the most extensive counteraction has been the organization of farmer-owned marketing agencies, such as cooperatives.[2] There are examples of cooperative livestock commission agencies, cooperatively operated auctions, various types of cooperative livestock and wool pooling arrangements, and cooperative packing plants. Early history is replete with examples of farmer agitation for the lowering of freight rates. And, largely as a result of farmer dissatisfaction, the Packers and Stockyards Administration of the USDA currently exerts a degree of control over the level of commission, yardage, and feed charges at public livestock markets.

PRICING EFFICIENCY

The traditional sense of pricing efficiency has been described by Phillips (1961):

> Pricing efficiency . . . is concerned with the price-making role of the market system. It concerns how accurately, how effectively, how rapidly, and how freely the marketing system makes prices which measure product values to the ultimate consumer and reflects these values through the various stages of the marketing system to the producer . . .
>
> Economic theory suggests that prices which reflect more accurately the preferences of consumers will do a more efficient job in allocating productive resources to maximize consumer satisfaction and producer incomes.

Thus, pricing efficiency is concerned with such questions as how well the price system interprets changes in consumer demands, how well prices transmit changing demands back to producers and induce a proper allocation of resources among alternative productive uses, and

---

[2]Not all cooperatives are organized solely in the interest of operational efficiency. Cooperatives may also be designed to improve pricing efficiency or to act in dual capacity for both operational and pricing objectives.

how well the price system distributes income among producers and marketers.

If consumers have a preference for meat with certain quality specifications, it is presumed that competitive market forces, acting through the pricing mechanism, will transmit this message through market channels back to producers and induce an increase in production of meat with those specifications—and vice versa with meat of less desirable qualities. A much-discussed example of this is consumer reaction to overfat pork. An efficient pricing system would be expected to record this situation in consumer willingness to pay more for leaner pork. Thus, a price differential would be transmitted from the retail level back through distribution channels—processors, packers, and market agencies to the producers. The differential, if it were of significant magnitude, would be expected to induce swine producers to increase production of lean, meat-type hogs relative to the production of lard-type hogs. This assumes that the increase in price equals or exceeds any associated increase in production costs and provides an example of prices directing a reallocation of resources. Presumably producers and consumers both would benefit from such a change. Whether market agencies or packers and processors would benefit would require an analysis of their costs and returns. In spite of considerable criticism over the speed and effectiveness of pricing efficiency in the hog market, a substantial increase has occurred in the production of leaner hogs over a period of years (Agnew, 1969; Van Arsdall and Gilliam, 1979). This is not to say that the market exhibited perfect pricing efficiency, but it serves as an example of the principle. Further improvement undoubtedly can be made, and if consumer preferences change, the market will be expected to transmit these changes.

Classical economic theory, built around a model of perfect competition, was able to show that self-generating competitive forces would optimize the allocation of resources, the production and distribution of goods, and returns to factors of production, i.e., wages, rent, and interest. There would be no pure profits, but management would receive a minimal, normal profit. From the beginning, the prevailing economic philosophy in the United States has been no relatively free and competitive markets. However, it was also apparent from the beginning that unbridled competition produced some undesirable social results, and regulations of many sorts have been incorporated into the system.

The attributes of perfect competition have never existed, and no one has argued that they ever did. It always has been obvious that from the private, individual standpoint, advantage could be gained by introducing or developing an imperfection in the system, e.g., developing inequality in bargaining power. In other words, private interest is not necessarily compatible with the general interest. As a member of society, each person is presumed to be cognizant of social responsibility. At the same time, experience has shown, by and large, that individuals or firms will go about as far as the law allows (or as far as personal moral convictions allow) in the enhancement of profit.

Concern about farmer bargining power is, in reality, concern about pricing efficiency. A term used in this connection is "market performance." Farmers have shown dissatisfaction with the distribution of returns. Some would resort to greater governmental intervention, directly or indirectly. Others recommend voluntary farmer organization with the exercise of self-discipline in marketing. This area will be discussed later in relevant chapters, but it should be noted here that market organization (the structure that gives rise to the behavior or conduct of firms and their performance in terms of pricing efficiency) is not a static phenomenon. As noted by Farris (1965), producers of most farm products " . . . traditionally have readily available to them markets in which prices, though subject to various kinds and degrees of imperfections, were generated in a relatively impersonal manner. This is changing; such markets are fading from the scene."

As the traditional, relatively impersonal market structure fades away, the system tends to drift towards a situation where more prices and terms of trade are being set by negotiation, formula, or some other institutional arrangement. The markets for a number of agricultural commodities already have faded considerably from the traditional, impersonal, free, and open market structure. Examples are milk, eggs, and a number of fruits, vegetables, and specialty crops. These are commodities marketed under federal or state marketing orders and agreements. To a degree, farm price support programs have altered the working of the traditional market, too. This is an example of an attempt to set up an institutional arrangement (i.e., the support program) within the traditional market—to supplement without eliminating or replacing it.

Livestock marketing is influenced to a lesser degree by personal or institutional arrangements than are other major agricultural commodities. Even here, however, contracting is being done by farm organizations and individuals under negotiated conditions. Vertically integrated operations are becoming more commonplace in the production, processing, and marketing of all species—cattle, swine, and sheep. Some farm groups continue to lobby for government-guaranteed prices. In the wholesale meat trade, substantial quantities are sold by formula. Arrangements such as these deviate from the open competitive market system, but they do not lessen the need for a knowledge of economic principles. When negotiators sit down around the bargaining table or individuals take it upon themselves to do their own buying and selling, the need for an understanding of economic theory and principles is as great as it is in the free and open market, if not more so. When legislators and their staffs formulate price policy, and when administrative agencies implement the associated programs, a thorough knowledge of theory and principles is essential. Foremost among marketing theories are those that explain the relationships between demand and supply.

ORGANIZATIONAL CHARACTERISTICS

An area of market research that has received increasing attention in recent years is the study of market organization or market structure analysis. This approach holds that relationships exist between structural characteristics of an industry and the competitive behavior of firms in that industry, and beyond that, that these attributes are associated with economic performance.

Performance is the critical issue here, as was touched upon in the discussion of pricing efficiency and operational efficiency. Individual producers as well as the general public have a stake in this matter because the degree of efficiency attained affects producer prices and profits. It affects the costs to consumers, and thereby their real income, and it affects general resource utilization. Society as a whole has an interest in optimum utilization of resources. Performance has many other facets, of course, such as the degree of price stability in the industry, equitability of income distribution among people, degree of economic progress, and level of employment.

There has been substantial evidence for decades that farmers have been dissatisfied with the economic performance of markets for farm products. Of recent origin are the National Farmers Organization (NFO) and the American Agricultural Movement, both of which were organized in an attempt to improve farm income. Dissatisfaction reached a high pitch in early and mid 1980 with protest demonstrations, including tractorcades to state capitals and the national capital. The inauguration of the National Cattlemen's Association CATTLE-FAX program and the introduction of electronic marketing and market information networks in many sectors are examples of an attempt to improve prices and incomes but with a different approach. Through the years, history is replete with other examples including both private and public attempts to alleviate farm problems. To the extent that these problems are associated with structural characteristics and firm conduct or behavior, market structure analysis is a legitimate area of marketing.

Market Structure

Among the major structural characteristics of a firm or an industry are the following:

1. *Degree of concentration*—This refers to the number of firms, the size of firms, and their size-distribution. Is the industry composed of only a few large firms—such as automobile manufacturing? Is the industry composed of many firms, but dominated by a few large ones? Is the industry composed of many small firms? Economic theory indicates that such characteristics can influence output and profit rates. They also may influence income distribution, progressiveness of the industry, and other measures of performance. The multitude of relatively small farmers does not have the control over output or of profits that the steel industry has, for example.

2. *Product differentiation*—Do individual firms have the power, by advertising or otherwise, to convince consumers that their products are different from those of competitors? Is there a relation between the degree of concentration and the ability of firms to differentiate their products? Not only is farming characterized by a low degree of concentration, but its products are relatively homogenous. There is little opportunity for individual farmers to differentiate products. Exceptions occur such as purebred livestock breeders who have been able to show excellence in their stock. Citrus growers have been able to show excellence in their stock. Citrus growers have been successful in differentiating "Sunkist" oranges as have walnut growers in marketing "Diamond" brand walnuts. Processors of farm products, of course, make extensive use of brand names. This is particularly true in marketing canned vegetables and fruits. Some large meat packers have successfully identified their brands of processed meat, but progress has been slow in differentiating fresh meat. Swift & Co. has attempted to differentiate its beef under the tradename Proten.[3] Other packers began a concerted effort to brand retail cuts of both beef and pork during the mid 1980's. Only time will tell whether they will be successful. In the boxed-beef trade, packers have some ability to differentiate by cutting style and private grades. Although a few examples of differentiating agricultural products at the farm level exist (accomplished largely by

---

[3]Registered trademark of Swift & Co.

farmer cooperatives), the vast bulk leaves the farm unbranded and undifferentiated. Outside of agriculture, differentiation is the rule.

3. *Barriers to entry into an industry*—The relative ease (or difficulty) with which a firm gains entry into an industry is closely associated with degree of concentration. Traditionally, farming has been an industry with easy entry. Nearly anyone who wished could start farming. This no longer is true for commercial-sized farms. Capital requirements associated with economies of size necessitate large-scale financing that is not available to everyone. In nonfarm sectors, successful differentiation of product by already established firms may be an effective barrier to entry by new firms. In other instances, absolute cost advantages and/or economies of scale already obtained by existing firms may prevent new firms from entering that industry. Firms in an industry with effective barriers against new competitors exercize a different sort of behavior than firms in a highly competitive industry.

Market Conduct

Market conduct refers to the behavior of firms—the strategy they use (1) individually in competition with other firms, in purchasing inputs and selling output, and (2) in conjunction with other firms, which may take the form of informal cooperation or collusion. In the early decades of the 1900s, a few large U.S. meat packers were alleged to have used collusive practices. Practices arising out of market strategy are usually related to price or product manipulation. The objective usually is to optimize profits.

For all practical purposes, farmers acting individually can exercise no positive market strategy. No one individual can exert any effective control over price, industry output, or differentiation of product. In contrast, where a few firms dominate an industry, they can, by informal agreement or through collusion (explicit or tacit), exercise some degree of control over output and prices. They can differentiate products; they can divide the market; they can carry out advertising and promotional programs.

MARKET PERFORMANCE

It has been apparent for years in the market arena that farmers have been operating at a competitive disadvantage relative to other economic sectors (Clodius, 1959). The implication is that market structural characteristics are associated with differences in conduct and performance. It follows that there are two logical approaches available to alleviate the situation: (1) make the nonagricultural sectors more like agriculture, i.e., make them conform more to the structure, conduct, and performance of the more highly competitive model that typifies agriculture, or (2) make agriculture more like the nonagricultural sectors, i.e., allow agriculture a degree of economic power more commensurate with that of nonagricultural sectors. There is nothing new or novel in these approaches. They have been discussed for decades.

Over the years numerous actions to implement both approaches have been taken by both private and public (government) means. Among the public actions are freight rate regulations, antitrust laws, legislation aimed at unfair competition and price discrimination, farm price and income support legislation, specific legislation designed to regulate livestock marketing charges and to promote competition on public markets, laws providing for standardization in grading, laws that implement market news reporting, specific restrictions on certain large meat packers under a "Consent Decree," and legislation to facilitate the organization of farmers' cooperatives. This is merely a sample of public actions presumably aimed at correcting or alleviating unsatisfactory conduct and performance of firms and industries. There are many more, some of them directly related to agriculture and some not.

Private efforts on these problems probably are best exemplified by cooperatives. The organization of a farmer cooperative is recognition that a joint effort may provide farmers with some economic power where individually they have none. There are many types of cooperatives including some devoted exclusively to livestock marketing. The activities of the National Farmer's Organization are conducted as a cooperative effort.

A number of commodity-oriented organizations also illustrate private efforts. Among these are the National Pork Producer's Council with a check-off program for financing promotional programs for pork, the American Sheep Producers Council with a similar program, the National Cattlemen's Association with its subscription-financed CATTLE-FAX, and a Federal government-approved check-off program for financing research and promotional programs for beef.

There appears to be a growing recognition among livestock producers (and other farm sectors) that the eventual attainment of economic power (bargaining power) necessitates a joint effort in order to gain "countervailing power" (Galbraith, 1952) in the market place. If this is an indication of the trend, it will mean a further fading of the impersonal open markets. Opportunities for joint efforts increase as the number of producers becomes smaller (and operations become larger)—a trend which has been in evidence for many years.

ECONOMIC PRINCIPLES

Use of the word "theory" has a tendency to disturb many people who have only a layman's concept of its meaning. One way to avoid an issue on the point would be to avoid use of the word. But it is a perfectly legitimate word and in an academic setting, at least, there is justification for coming to common agreement on its meaning. In the vernacular, theory has come to be synonymous with "impractical" or "nonfactual." That is a totally distorted view from the standpoint of a scientist, and this would hold for scientists of any discipline, be it economics, chemistry, animal science, physics, etc. In briefest terms, "theory" to a scientist is a "systematic explanation." It is an explanation " . . . which describes the workings and interrelationships of the various aspects of some phenomenon" (Baumol, 1961). Used in this sense, it would be contradictory to label theory as impractical, per se. If a theory gives an accurate explanation, it by definition cannot be classed as nonfactual. A determination of whether it is practical or feasible may require additional analysis.

There is no guarantee, of course, that every theory is going to provide a satisfactory or adequate explanation. In some instances, it may simply be bad theory—an inaccurate explanation—but that is not equivalent to being impractical or nonfactual. In other cases, a theory may appear to be an adequate explanation of a phenomenon, given the state of knowledge at a particular point in time, but turn out to be inaccurate or inadequate at a later time when additional knowledge becomes available. Many such examples exist in the physical and biological sciences. Before man landed on the moon, various "theories" had been advanced regarding the nature of its matter and origin. The moon landings produced evidence showing some of them wrong.

In economics, it is recognized that some of the theoretical models of various market situations do not precisely correspond to the real world. The widely used "perfectly competitive" model is an example.[4] It is an abstraction of the real world—a simplified model used as an illustration of certain principles and as a guideline or benchmark with which other market situations may be compared.

---

[4]It is assumed that readers have a knowledge of elementary economics. Readers who have not had recent work in economics should review a modern elementary text on price theory.

THEORY OF DEMAND

Demand—the Concept

"Demand" is another word that means different things to different people. During periods when prices of, say slaughter steers, are increasing or are at a relatively high level, one often hears the comment that "demand is high." Conversely, when prices are low, the comment may be that "demand is low" or "demand is dropping." Under certain circumstances, these comments may be partially correct, but they are loose, nontechnical concepts of demand. For effective communication among market analysts and for consistent use in economic analysis, we need a precise, rigorous meaning. Fortunately, there is an accepted definition: Demand is the functional relationship between prices and quantities of a product that buyers will purchase in a specified market, *ceteris paribus*. Note that "prices" and "quantities" are used in the plural. *"Ceteris paribus"* (literally, Latin for "other things being equal") refers to the assumption that all other factors—in addition to price—that can influence the quantity purchased remain unchanged. Under this definition, demand is a series of prices and quantities, not just the quantity at a particular price or the amount of money spent for some particular quantity.

The "functional relationship" may be expressed (1) in table form often referred to as a schedule, (2) as a mathematical function, or (3) in graphic form. For example, the prices at which consumers will purchase various quantities of a hypothetical product may be expressed in schedule form as follows:

Price per Unit ($)	Quantity
1.00	180
2.00	160
3.00	140
4.00	120
5.00	100
6.00	80
7.00	60
8.00	40
9.00	20

If we consider that the quantity consumed is a function of price (i.e., that quantity purchased depends upon price), we can, by rather elementary mathematical calculations "fit" a function to the above data as follows:

In general form, $Q = f(P)$

In specific form, $Q = 200 - 20\,P$

where:

Q = quantity

P = price

This series of prices and quantities can also be shown in graphic form, as in Fig. 3.1, where line D1–D1 is a demand curve illustrating this functional relationship. Notice that this follows the tradition in demand analysis of using quantity as the dependent varible.[5]

The above three forms of expression are simply different ways of presenting the same data—the same functional relationship. All three are used extensively in economics.

Conceptually, we speak of individual demand and aggregate or market demand. The latter is simply the sum of the demands of individuals who make up the market.

The ceteris paribus condition requires some clarification. It is obvious that price is not the only factor that determines the quantity of goods consumers buy. Among the more important "other factors" are population (the number of buyers); income levels (the purchasing power of buyers); personal preferences or tastes; the price, quality, and availability of substitute or complementary products that compete with the product under consideration for the buyer's dollar; buyer's expectations of future prices of the product under consideration and of prices for substitute or complementary products. What we mean by the ceteris paribus assumption is that at a given time in a given market these things will be at some observable level. Their effect upon quantities purchased will be incorporated in the price–quantity relationship, but at that time the only thing that is considered to vary is price. We want to know the effect on quantity purchased that is brought about solely by price variation when everything else is constant.

This does not mean that we are uninterested in the effect "other factors" may have on the quantity purchased. On the contrary, we are intensely interested and also try hard to determine the relationships between these factors and quantity purchased. In economic parlance, they are called "demand shifters" for it may be said that a change in

---

[5]It may be noted that in graphic analysis the vertical axis traditionally is used for the dependent variable. In graphing demand curves, however, it is conventional to put price on the vertical axis. In a sense this is inconsistent, but there is nothing sacred about these conventions. The graph would be equally valid one way as the other. Our major concern is with the relationship between variables—not which one is the dependent variable and which axis is used for one or the other.

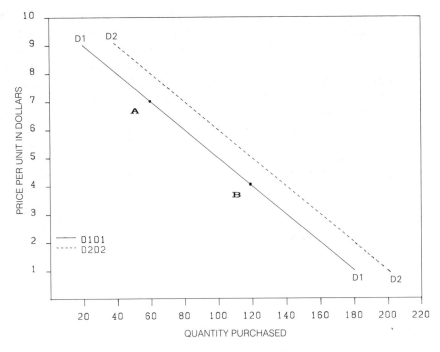

Fig. 3.1.   Hypothetical demand curve.

one (or more) of these factors results in a "change in demand" or a "shift in demand." A change in the factor implies that some time elapses between one set of ceteris paribus conditions and another.

Using the same data presented in the previous illustrations, let curve D1–D1 in Fig. 3.1 represent a demand curve where all the so-called demand shifters are at some given level. Points A and B do *not* represent different demands, nor do the different locations of A and B represent a change in demand. Both are on the same demand curve, and what they mean is that at $7.00 per unit, buyers will purchase 60 units, but *if* the price were $4.00 they would purchase 120 units. They simply represent two, among an infinite number of price-quantity relationships on that demand curve, only one of which can be realized in a given market at any one time. Now, assume that some time elapses and incomes of buyers increase. With higher incomes, buyers would be expected to pay higher prices for any specified quantity (or what amounts to the same thing, purchase a greater quantity at any specified price). Buyers may now purchase 80 units at $7.00 per unit where originally they would have purchased only 60 units; or, at $4.00 per unit, they may now purchase 130 units where originally they would have purchased only 120—and so on at other price levels. Thus, the change in income (the increase in income) shifted the entire demand curve from D1–D1 to D2–D2. The changed demand shows that greater quantities would be taken at all possible prices (or what amounts to the same thing, higher prices would now be paid for all possible quantities). In this example, it was considered that only income increased, but the same reaction could occur from changes in any one, or any combination, of the demand shifters. (An increase in demand is indicated by shift to the right on the graph; a decrease would show up as a shift to the left.)

Population in the United States has increased year by year, providing one of the most stable and important shifters (increasers) in the demand for farm products. On the average, per capita personal disposable incomes have increased fairly consistently for a number of years. Studies show that consumers have a strong tendency to increase purchases of beef as incomes increase, but the same relationship has not always held for pork. These relationships will be discussed in some detail at a later point.

Derived Demand

Consumer demand for meat makes itself felt at the retail level—at the supermarket. To be more specific, a demand exists for each separate cut of meat. How is this demand transmitted to livestock producers? From the farmer's standpoint, the demand for slaughter steers, for example, is a "derived demand"—that is, the demand derived from consumers' demand for beef. The aggregate retail value of all retail cuts establishes a value for the carcass at the packer level. The carcass value, in turn, establishes the value of the live steer. The same sort of derived demand exists for hogs and lamb and, as a matter of fact, for the various classes, grades, and weights of animals within each species.

This is an oversimplified statement, but it contains the essential features of the concept of derived demand. It is obvious in this situation that the degree of pricing efficiency throughout market channels is of considerable importance in transmitting to producers the demands of consumers.

Elasticity of Demand

A knowledge of the functional relationship that exists between prices and quantities of a particular product is valuable to market analysts, but probably of even more importance is a measure of the degree of sensitivity of change in quantity purchased that is occasioned by a change of price. This is what is meant by elasticity. In the study of price elasticity, we are interested in determining the percentage change in quantity purchased, occasioned by (or associated with) a specified percentage (say 1 percent, or 10 percent) change in the relative price of that commodity (own-price elasticity) or to a change in the price of another commodity (cross elasticity). An excellent example of cross elasticity of direct interest among livestock producers would be the following:

What effect would a decrease in pork prices have on the quantity of beef purchased by consumers, assuming beef prices remain unchanged? Of major importance, also, is income elasticity, which is the percentage change in expenditures for a product (or quantity purchased, depending upon the model used by the researcher) associated with a specified change in income. Thus, there are three concepts of elasticity to be noted:

1. Own-price elasticity, which if written fully and more precisely would read, "price elasticity of demand," but normally is shortened to price elasticity
2. Income elasticity, which again more precisely would be written as "income elasticity of demand"
3. Cross elasticity, a cross-price elasticity.

Price Elasticity.   The importance of price elasticity lies in its association with total revenue (i.e., total expenditures of purchasers). Total revenue is the total amount of money spent by consumers for a product as calculated by the total of the quantity purchased (or sold) multiplied by the price. If, for the moment, we ignored costs of production, it would be apparent that the sellers of a product would want to maximize total revenue received. It readily can be shown that under conditions of an elastic demand, total revenue can be increased by cutting price (or by increasing the quantity for sale, which amounts to the same thing viewed from a different angle). If demand is elastic, a given cut in price will result in a more than proportionate increase in quantity sold, and hence, an increase in revenue.

Before proceeding, we must present methods of calculating elasticity and clarify some terms. Price elasticity is calculated as a numerical measure that is referred to as the "coefficient of price elasticity." It is calculated by dividing percentage change in quantity by the associated percentage change in price, or

$$e_{D/P} = \frac{\% \, \Delta \, Q}{\% \, \Delta \, P}$$

where:

$e_{D/P}$ = coefficient of price elasticity of demand

Δ = change

Q = quantity

P = price

Thus, $^eD/P$ is a ratio of the two percentage changes. The sign of the ratio normally is expected to be negative since price and quantity usually move in opposite directions; this was referred to earlier as an inverse relationship. Some authors omit the sign of the elasticity coefficient since it is universally understood to be negative for all goods except Giffen goods. (Giffen goods—named after Sir Robert Giffen, a Victorian economist—are goods subject to exceptional circumstances in which a rise in price may lead to an increase in the quantity purchased; such cases are rare.) The magnitude of the coefficient can range from zero to infinity (negative infinity).

If price changes were associated with no change in quantity purchased, elasticity would be zero, or perfectly inelastic. Graphically, this would be a vertical line (curve), such as D_1 in Fig. 3.2, that might be visualized as some unique, absolutely necessary product. Such an extreme case, however, is unlikely. If an unlimited quantity were to be purchased at a given price, elasticity would be infinite, or perfectly elastic, and this would show up as a horizontal curve (see D_2 in Fig. 3.2). This is the situation the individual farmer faces in selling most products. No individual hog producer, for example, sells enough hogs to influence the price of the product. For all practical purposes, any one farmer can sell all the hogs he owns without depressing prices. In the aggregate, however, prices and quantities normally move in opposite directions.[6]

Most demand curves fall somewhere between the limiting extremes—sloping downward to the right on a graph, such as D_3 in Fig. 3.2. Within this in-between area is a dividing line that separates the "relatively elastic" (often shortened simply to "elastic") from the "relatively inelastic" (often shortened to "inelastic"). The separation occurs at an elasticity of -1.0, or unit elasticity. This point occurs where the percentage change in quantity is exactly equal to the percentage change in price. Demand here would be unitarily elastic. For example,

---

[6]There are exceptions to the normal situation. Some goods with high "snob" or "prestige" appeal sell greater quantities at higher prices than at lower prices. These cases are rare and of no concern to this discussion.

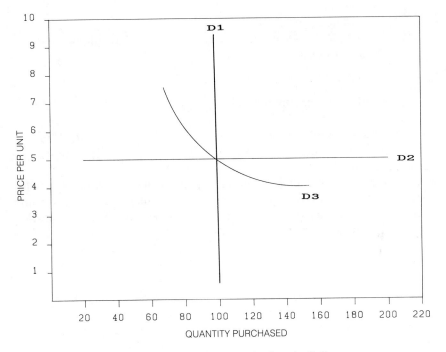

Fig. 3.2. Different degrees of price elasticity.

if a 5-percent decrease in quantity was associated with a 5-percent increase in price, the price elasticity would be -1.0; that is,

$$e_{D/P} = \frac{-5.0}{5.0} = -1.0$$

The change in price in this case is exactly offset by the change in quantity purchased, a situation that can occur where a firm or family budgets a certain amount of money for a given item and sticks to the budget whether prices rise or fall.

For those with a knowledge of the calculus, determination of the coefficient of price elasticity is a simple calculation, providing the mathematical function is known. For illustrative purposes, we will use the demand function presented earlier, i.e., $Q = 200 - 20P$. The formula for calculating elasticity is then:

$$e_{D/P} = \frac{dQ}{dP} \frac{P}{Q}$$

where:

$\dfrac{dQ}{dP}$ = the first derivative of Q with respect to P (from the demand function)

P = price (any relevant, specified price)

Q = quantity consumers would purchase at the specified price

For the demand function used here, $dQ/dP = -20$. With this, the formula becomes $^eD/P = -20\,P/Q$, and we simply plug in applicable pairs of P and Q.

A number of relevant price–quantity pairs were shown earlier. Others may be calculated by inserting any relevant price in the demand function and calculating its associated Q. We complete the illustration by calculating $^eD/P$ where $P = \$6.00$ and $Q = 80$:

$$e_{D/P} = -20\,\frac{6.00}{80} = -1.50$$

Thus, $^eD/P$ is -1.50 at the point on the demand curve when $P = \$6.00$ and $Q = 80$.

To calculate $^eD/P$ at another point, we take $P = \$2.00$ and $Q = 160$. Then,

$$e_{D/P} = -20\,\frac{2.00}{160} = -0.25$$

These two calculations should serve to show that the coefficient of elasticity may vary at different points on the same demand curve, a fact that is further illustrated in Table 3.1 where the coefficient of elasticity is shown for nine points. The coefficient varies from one point to another. On only one unique type of demand curve—the rectangular

Table 3.1. Hypothetical Price, Quantity, Elasticity, and Total Value Relationships.

Price ($)	Quantity	Coefficient of elasticity	Total revenue ($)
9.00	20	−9.00	180
8.00	40	−4.00	320
7.00	60	−2.33	420
6.00	80	−1.50	480
5.00	100	−1.00	500
4.00	120	−0.67	480
3.00	140	−0.43	420
2.00	160	−0.25	320
1.00	180	−0.11	180

hyperbola—does elasticity remain constant throughout the entire curve.

For those who do not have a knowledge of the calculus, the coefficients can be calculated by elementary arithmetic, again providing the demand schedule is known. For illustrative purposes we will use the schedule of prices and quantities in Table 3.1, which is the same schedule presented earlier. In this case, we assume a movement from one point on the demand schedule to another point, calculate the percentage change in price and the percentage change in quantity, then divide percentage change in quantity by percentage change in price. This is the ratio that produces the coefficient of price elasticity. The formula is as follows:

$$e_{D/P} = \frac{\dfrac{Q2 - Q1}{Q2 + Q1}}{\dfrac{P2 - P1}{P2 + P1}} = \frac{\% \, \Delta \, Q}{\% \, \Delta \, P}$$

where:

$Q1$ = quantity before change

$Q2$ = quantity after change

$P1$ = price before change

$P2$ = price after change

Δ = change

To complete this illustration, we shall assume that price and quantity were $6.00 and 80 units, respectively, before change; the price then drops to $5.00, which has a corresponding quantity of 100 units, and the coefficient becomes

$$e_{D/P} = \frac{\dfrac{100 - 80}{100 + 80}}{\dfrac{5.00 - 6.00}{5.00 + 6.00}} = \frac{\dfrac{20}{180}}{\dfrac{-1.00}{11.00}} = -1.22$$

The same procedure could be repeated at alternative places on the demand schedule to obtain measures of price elasticity throughout the schedule.

As pointed out in elementary economics, this is a measure of "arc elasticity." It represents an arc, or area, of the demand curve rather than a point as was obtained by the method involving the calculus.

The method involving calculus is considered to be preferable being more precise, but is not necessary for an understanding of the concept. Any coefficient of elasticity within the range, 0 to −1.0, (noninclusive) is classified as relatively inelastic. Any coefficient greater than −1.0 is classifed as relatively elastic. These two categories encompass virtually all goods and services that enter market transactions. Some elementary graphic explanations of elasticity purport to show that a steeply sloped demand curve is inelastic and that a gently sloped curve is elastic. This interpretation can be misleading since the slope of a curve is not equivalent to elasticity. As was shown earlier, the formula for price elasticity equals the reciprocal of the slope of the demand curve at a certain point on the demand curve multiplied by the ratio of price at that point to the quantity at the same point. Thus, slope and elasticity cannot be the same and elasticity slope should not be confused with elasticity. The linear (straight line) demand curve drawn on arithmetic graph paper will have the same slope throughout its entire length, but when elasticity is calculated at various points along that demand curve, it will be found that the coefficient changes continuously throughout the length. Again do not confuse slope with elasticity.

It was mentioned earlier that total revenue is associated with elasticity. The price–quantity schedule presented earlier is repeated in Table 3.1, along with calculations of the coefficient of elasticity and total revenue at various points throughout the demand schedule. Note that the coefficient of elasticity varies throughout the demand scheduling, ranging from −9.00 to −0.11. The schedule became less elastic with movement from higher prices (lower quantities) to lower prices (higher quantities). Total revenue also varies, rising from $180 to a peak at $500 and then declines to $180 again. Note that total revenue rises until elasticity reaches unity. As the coefficient becomes less than unity, total revenue decreases.

The lesson to be learned here is that a firm, or an industry, which has (or which can obtain) sufficient control over prices or production can maximize total revenue by proper manipulation of these variables. If demand is relatively elastic, it can, by cutting prices, increases sales and total revenue up to the point where demand becomes unitarily elastic. If it is operating in an inelastic demand, it can increase total revenue by raising the price and cutting back the quantity offered for sale to the point that demand becomes unitarily elastic.

Maximization of total revenue does not automatically maximize profits. The firm or industry would also need a knowledge of cost behavior to maximize profits. Generally, a reduction in production would not increase per-unit costs. An increase in production could lead to higher, lower, or constant per-unit costs depending upon the characteristics of the cost functions of that particular firm or industry. The price elasticity faced by individual firms is greater than that faced by an entire industry, a case that is clearly true for farmers. Individual farmers face a perfectly elastic demand for hogs, or cattle, or corn, etc., but the demand faced by any one of these sectors of the entire industry is substantially less. Elasticity at retail ordinarily is greater than at any earlier stage in the marketing–production process. For instance, the price elasticity for ham or pork chops is greater than for hogs at the farm level.

Demand theory indicates that, for a given change in price, the resulting change in quantity demanded is larger in the long run than in the short run. For example, the theory states that with a real increase of price of a commodity, the quantity demanded will immediately decrease as people adjust their budgets and spending. If the higher price persists, further reductions will take place in the quantity demanded. This may be explained by the facts that it takes time for consumers to adjust their purchasing habits, and to some extent it may also take time for the information to reach all people.

Income Elasticity.   The concept of income elasticity is analogous to that of price elasticity in that it refers to sensitivity of change in expenditures for a product associated with a change in income, everything else remaining constant. It is known that as incomes increase, consumers will buy more of some products, but less of others. Products that fall in the former category are classed as superior products, whereas those in the latter category are classed as inferior products. Hamburger may be considered an inferior product by people who already have relatively high incomes, that is, they probably would eat less hamburger with further increases in income, but people in low income brackets likely would increase hamburger consumption if their incomes were increased. To the latter, hamburger is a superior product.

Studies several years ago showed pork to be an inferior product on the basis of average incomes in the United States. This presumably was associated with an image (at that time) of pork as a relatively fat cut of meat, a perception that meant that consumers would spend less for pork as their average income increased. With substantial improvement in the quality of pork in recent years, however, there is evidence that consumers now react differently than they did in an earlier period. Roy and Young (1977) found a positive income elasticity for pork beginning with the 1956–1965 period.

Livestock producers and meat marketers obviously have no direct control over consumer incomes. Indirectly, they have some control in fostering (or opposing) national economic policy that may have an impact on employment and wage rates. On the other hand, producers and marketers do have direct control in the improvement of the quality of a product, which may, in turn, improve its income elasticity. In a sense, this may mean changing the product rather than changing the income elasticity, but the net result to producers and marketers may be the same.

The coefficient of income elasticity is calculated in a manner similar to that for price elasticity. The formula for income elasticity by the arithmetic method is as follows:

$$e_{D/I} = \frac{\% \, \Delta \, Q}{\% \, \Delta \, I}$$

where:

$e_{D/I}$ = coefficient of income elasticity of demand

Δ = change

E = expenditures (for a specified product)

I = income

By use of the calculus, the formula is

$$e_{D/I} = \left(\frac{dE}{dI} \right) \left(\frac{I}{E} \right)$$

The sign of the coefficient is positive for superior products and negative for inferior products.

Cross Elasticity. Cross elasticity refers to price–quantity relationships between or among different products. For example, beef and pork are "substitutes" for one another, or, in other words, they are competing products. It is not enough simply to know that a drop in pork prices will hurt beef consumption and cause a lowering of beef prices. A market analyst needs to know in quantitative terms how much a specified drop in hog prices, and subsequently pork prices, will affect beef consumption and beef prices. The general relationship between substitute products is shown by curve A in Fig. 3.3. If products are substitutes, an increase in the price of product Y will result in increased purchases of product X, assuming no change in the price of product X or real income.

Although the vast majority of products are substitutes to a greater or lesser degree, this is not true of all. Some products are "complementary." In this case, an increase in the price of product Y will be associ-

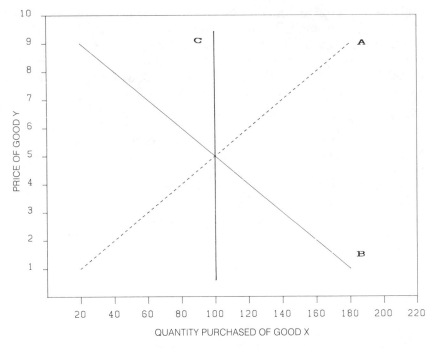

Fig. 3.3.   Cross relationships between good X and good Y.

ated with a decrease in the purchase of product X (see curve B, Fig.
3.3). Automobiles and gasoline provide an example. An increase in the
price of automobiles would be expected to result in decreased sales of
gasoline, because fewer autos would be sold and hence less gasoline
would be needed. A decrease in the price of sweet corn probably would
lead to an increase in purchases of butter (or margarine). More sweet
corn would be sold, and since most people butter sweet corn, more butter would be purchased.

Included in this category also are "joint" products. Beef and cattle
hides are joint products. An increase in the price of beef (assuming this
would result in fewer cattle being purchased) would lead to fewer hides
being sold. This could, of course, bring about a longer term effect. If
the increased price of beef persisted, farmers and ranchers would be
induced to produce more beef cattle and thus lead to increased sales
(and purchases) of hides, though prices of both might decline in the
process.

In another class are "supplementary" products. Supplements are
products whose demands are unrelated. This means that the quantity
purchased of product X has no relation to the price of product Y (curve

C in Fig. 3.3). Products that comprise a minor element in the purchases of a firm likely would fall into this category (for example, the quantity of salt purchased by a sausage manufacturer has virtually no relationship to the price of sausage). Supplementary products are not of particular importance in this study of livestock and meat marketing.

The Concept of Price Flexibility

Price flexibility is the relative responsiveness of the price of a commodity associated with a change in the quantity consumed/marketed of that commodity (own-price flexibility) or the quantity of another commodity (cross-price flexibility). If own-price elasticity is known, price flexibility can be approximated by calculating the reciprocal, i.e., percent change in price divided by the percent change in quantity marketed/demanded. It follows that own-price flexibility increases as elasticity decreases. In other words, the more inelastic the demand, the greater effect a given change in quantity will have upon price received. For most food commodities in the United States (which usually have low price elasticities), a 1-percent change in the quantity marketed/consumed will result in more than 1-percent change in price. For example, a price flexibility for beef of -1.50 is interpreted to mean that a 10-percent change in the quantity of beef consumed/marketed will result in a change in price in the opposite direction by 15 percent in order to move the additional quantity in the market.

Although it is possible to approximate own-price flexibility coefficients by calculating the reciprocal of own-price elasticity, it is appropriate only in the unique situation of a single demand function having price as its only independent variable. It is not appropriate if the demand function includes other variables such as income and other prices.

Cross-flexibilities cannot be approximated under any circumstances by calculating the reciprocal of cross-elasticity coefficients. Flexibilities are usually estimated by taking the inverse of the price elasticity matrix after estimating a system of demand equations. Once the inverse is calculated, the diagonal elements give the own-flexibility coefficients and the off-diagnoal elements are the cross-flexibility coefficients.

Supply—The Concept

In a technical sense, supply is the functional relationship between prices and the quantites of a product that producers are willing to place on a market. Like demand, this concept envisions a schedule of alternative prices and quantities that can be shown in table form, as a mathematical function, or in graphic form. It also envisions the situation in which the quantity marketed is a function of price alone, all other factors that could influence the quantity marketed having been assumed to be constant. In the calculations by which supply (and demand) functions are determined, these other factors are held constant by statistical processes. We logically expect a supply curve to have a positive slope, i.e., we expect producers to place more of a given product on the market at relatively high prices than at lower prices. Figure 3.4 illustrates a supply curve.

A supply function looks like a demand function except for its algebraic sign. Following is a hypothetical example:

$$Q = 1.45\ P$$

The constant is omitted in this function to indicate that at zero prices nothing would be marketed. The similarity of supply and demand functions may prompt the question of how one differentiates between the two. This is the so-called problem of "identification," which was defined by Breimyer (1961) as follows:

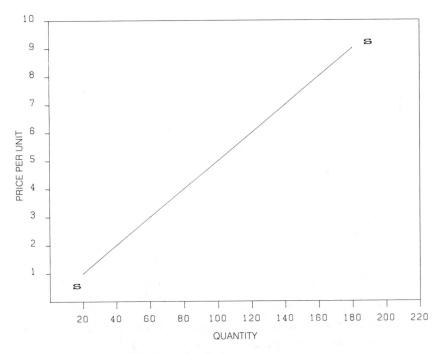

Fig. 3.4. Hypothetical supply curve.

"Identification is the term given to the principle that few observed values are of either pure supply or pure demand. Price changes in the market place do not carry any labels accommodating to analysts which explain whether they were due to demand forces or supply forces." Elmer Working's (1927) article of more than 30 years ago remains the basic reference. Working concerned himself with how to identify supply and demand forces as represented in statistical data, and with how to separate slopes of demand and supply curves from shifts in their positions.

... as Working (1927) pointed out in his article on identification, it is not necessary that true demand and true supply curves be constructed if the analyst only wants a method that will help him forecast future trends in prices.

Elasticity of Supply

The concept of elasticity of supply is comparable in meaning to that of elasticity of demand. Supply elasticity refers to the sensitivity of change in quantity marketed to specified changes in price. The formula for calculating elasticity of supply is the same as that for demand, as follows:

$$e_{S/P} = \frac{\% \, \Delta \, Q}{\% \, \Delta \, P}$$

where:

$e_{S/P}$ = coefficient of elasticity of supply

Δ = change

Q = quantity

P = price

By use of calculus, the formula is

$$e_{S/P} = \left(\frac{dQ}{dP} \right) \left(\frac{P}{Q} \right)$$

The coefficient of supply elasticity normally carries a positive sign, but in some instances, $^{e}S/P = 0$. This would be the case, for example, if a certain stock of a product were available for a market and no more could be made available at any price. Here, the supply would be perfectly inelastic, When $^{e}S/P$ is less than 1 but greater than zero (i.e., $0 < {}^{e}S/P < 1$), supply is said to be relatively inelastic—usually referred to simply as "inelastic." When $^{e}S/P = 1$, the supply is unitarily elastic, and, when $\infty {}^{e}S/P > 1$, the supply is said to be relatively elastic, or simply "elastic." The limiting case on the upper end is $^{e}S/P = \infty$, or infinitely elastic. In this limiting case, the quantity offered has no relation to price.

Although the notion of supply abstracts from the effects of everything that can affect the quantity offered for sale except price, it is well known that "other factors" do affect the quantity offered. These other factors, called "supply shifters," are conceptualized and handled in a manner comparable to demand shifters. Among the supply shifters are (1) technical innovations (improvements in physical input-output conditions), (2) changes in factor prices (changes in prices of inputs), (3) development of new technology, and (4) changes in opportunity costs.

PRICE FORMATION

It is important to distinguish between two concepts: price determination and price discovery. Price determination refers to the interaction of the forces of supply and demand to establish a market clearing price level. Price discovery, on the other hand, refers to the process by which buyers and sellers arive at a particular price. The price discovery process may take place through private negotiations, public bidding (in person, or using an electronic device), closed bids, or administrated pricing.

Price formation is related to the degree of competition in the market. A considerable body of price theory has been developed covering perfect competition, oligopoly, monopolistic competition, and monopoly. The available theory is generally satisfactory except for the case of oligopoly, i.e., an industry dominated by a relatively few large firms. Under these conditions, it is difficult to generalize because the action one firm takes will depend upon the action its competitor takes. This can make price and output indeterminate except for special cases governed by rigid assumptions.

We present here only the basic concept of price formation as generated by the interaction of forces of demand and supply in a highly competitive market situation. It is noted, however, that institutional factors, such as structural characteristics and market conduct as discussed in the previous section, may permit price modification or manipulation, particularly in the short term.

It sometimes is argued that the supply of livestock is relatively fixed for any given day or even for longer periods.[7] This theory is based on

---

[7]The fixed-supply assumption may be appropriate for a commodity harvested at one particular time, thereby setting the quantity available for the subsequent year.

the assumption that, for a short period, a certain number of livestock is on hand and price cannot influence that number. If this were the case, supply would show up on a graph as a perfectly inelastic, i.e., vertical curve, as illustrated in Fig. 3.5. The aggregate demand will almost always be a negatively sloped curve (as D-D in Fig. 3.5) that will intersect the supply curve at some point representing the market clearing price for that number of livestock.

The assumption of fixed supply, however, is not very realistic for livestock. Producers can withhold or rush livestock to some degree. Given some time they can make animals heavier or lighter depending on timing of marketing and variations in feeding programs. A positively sloping supply curve, even for the short period, is probably normal for livestock markets.

Normal, short-period industry supply-and-demand curves are shown in Fig. 3.6. Industries, of course, are made up of individual firms, and these industry supply–demand functions are derived from firm supply–demand functions. The intersection of D-D and S_1-S_1 mark the short-period equilibrium price, P_1, at which quantiy Q_1 would clear the market. Demand and supply can shift, as was discussed earlier. An

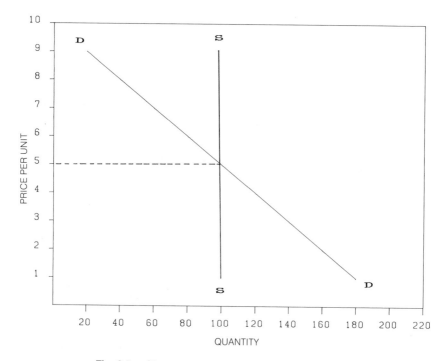

Fig. 3.5. Short-run equilibrium price, fixed supply.

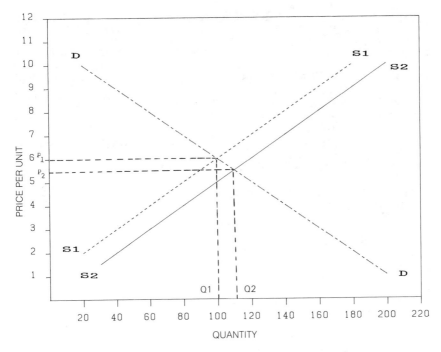

Fig. 3.6.   Short-run equilibrium price, normal supply function.

increase in supply would shift the entire curve to the right, as shown by S_2-S_2. If demand remained unchanged, the new point of intersection with D-D would be at a lower price, P_2, and an increased quantity, Q_2. A simultaneous increase in demand and supply can have offsetting effects on price, and an increase in demand without a proportionate increase in supply can result in a higher price. It should be readily apparent that the effect on price of a change in either supply or demand will be related to the degree of elasticity associated with supply and demand.

Over the long run, prices under highly competitive conditions are associated with long-run costs. Costs must be covered in the long run for firms to stay in business. Any profits above normal would attract new firms, but it takes time for adjustments to be made. There are lags between the time decisions are made and carried out, and uncertainties exist even in the most competitive markets. Imperfections in the market system result in continuous price variations about a moving long-period equilibrium. Moving equilibrium has been compared to " . . . a man riding a bicycle" (Shepherd and Futrell, 1969).

REFERENCES

Baumol, W. J. 1961. *Economic Theory and Operations Analysis.* Englewood Cliffs, NJ: Prentice-Hall.

Breimyer, H. F. 1961. Demand and prices for meat. USDA Econ. Res. Serv. Tech. Bull. 1253.

Clodius, R. L. 1959. Opportunities and limitations of improving bargaining power of farmers. *In Problems and Policies of American Agriculture.* Ames, IA: Iowa State University Press.

Dahl, D. C., and Hammond, J. W. 1977. *Market and Price Analysis, the Agricultural Industries.* New York: McGraw-Hill Company.

Farris, P. L. 1965. Talk given at 3rd Coordianted Beef Improvement Conf., Texas A & M University, July.

Galbraith, J. K. 1952. *American Capitalism—the Concept of Countervailing Power.* Boston: Houghton Mifflin Co.

McNeeley, J. *et al.* 1953. Texas livestock auction markets—methods and facilities. Texas Agr. Experiment Sta. Misc. Publ. 93.

Phillips, V. B. 1961. Price formation and pricing efficiency in marketing agricultural products: The role of market news and grade standards. Proc. 26th Ann. Conf. Nat. Assoc. Social Sci. Teachers, Econ. Sect., Howard Univ., Washington, D.C., April 20.

Roy, S. K., and Young, R. D. 1977. Demand for pork: a long-run analysis. Texas Tech University, College of Agriculture Sciences Publication No. T-1-153.

Shepherd, G. S., and Futrell, G. A. 1969. *Marketing Farm Products.* 5th ed. Ames, IA: Iowa State University Press.

Tomek, W. G., and Robinson, K. L. 1972. Agricultural Product Prices. Ithaca, NY: Cornell Univ. Press.

Williams, W. F., and Stout, T. T. 1964. *Economics of the Livestock-Meat Industry.* New York. Macmillan Co.

Working, E. J. 1927. What do statistical demand curves show? Quart.

4

Livestock Production and Supply

It is readily observable that livestock and meat prices rise and fall over time. It is only to be expected that the financial fortunes of producers rise and fall with them. Occasionally, psychological and/or emotional disturbances trigger short-run price fluctuations, and sometimes institutional factors affect the market, but the factors that establish its basic direction are changes in supply and demand. This market is global; no country with trade connections can isolate itself from world conditions.

As mentioned in the last chapter, more and more imperfections are being introduced into the competitive open market system in the ever-present struggle to gain economic power. Some groups have suggested price control by private means; others have suggested government programs. In essence, either approach would necessitate control of supply and/or demand. Individuals have no hope of supply or demand control, but, by astute management, may take advantage of favorable price movements and avoid unfavorable movements. Regardless of the approach or the objective, a thorough knowledge of supply and demand factors is essential. This chapter examines livestock production and supply. The following chapter presents production and price movements, and Chap. 6 discusses demand.

WORLD LIVESTOCK AND MEAT PRODUCTION

Leading Livestock Producers

Accurate livestock inventory records are not available for a number of Asian and African countries. A notable omission among larger countries is the Peoples Republic of China, which is known to produce substantial numbers of hogs. Until recently, inventory statistics for that country were not available to the public. The Food and Agriculture

Table 4.1. World Livestock Numbers, Leading Countries, Jan. 1, 1984.*

Cattle†		Hogs		Sheep	
Country	Mil. Hd.	Country	Mil. Hd.	Country	Mil. Hd.
U.S.S.R.	119.4	U.S.S.R	78.5	U.S.S.R.	144.8
U.S.A.	113.7	U.S.A.	56.7‡	Australia	134.5
Brazil	93.3	Brazil	33.0	New Zealand	70.2
Argentina	58.3	W. Germany	23.4	Turkey	50.5
Mexico	33.9	Mexico	15.8	India	40.9
Colombia	24.4	Poland	15.8	S. Africa	31.9
France	23.9	Spain	14.7	Argentina	28.0
Australia	21.7	Romania	14.4	Uruguay	23.3
Turkey	17.2	E. Germany	12.8	U. Kingdom	23.2
W. Germany	15.6	France	11.2	Romania	18.6

Source: USDA (1984A—Updated for the U.S.).
*Various dates of enumeration are used by the countries reporting animal numbers. Data presented in this table approximate Jan. 1 as closely as possible.
†In 1984, India reported 248.7 million cattle and buffalo, making it the leading country in total bovine numbers. Because of the relative insignificance of cattle production as a source of meat in India, however, this country was excluded from the leading cattle-producing countries shown here.
‡As of Dec. 1, 1983.

Organization of the United Nations (FAO), however, is currently reporting combined (for PRC and Taiwan) livestock estimates. Recent reports suggest that China is a major livestock producer.[1] Table 4.1 shows the 10 leading producers of each specie for which 1984 USDA data are available. The Soviet Union (USSR) leads the world in number of cattle. The United States is second, with Brazil a strong third. In world livestock statistics, water buffalo are counted with cattle in many countries. Among the top 10 leaders, however, water buffalo are not important. Figure 4.1 shows cattle inventory in selected major beef-producing countries for the period 1975–1986.

The USSR also outranks all other countries in number of hogs and sheep. The United States is second in hogs, followed by Brazil, which again is a strong third. Australia holds second place in sheep production and is not far from first place. New Zealand is third in sheep production. World livestock numbers vary from year to year, due primarily to economic factors and weather conditions.

---

[1] For example, FAO (1985) estimated that China (including both the PRC and Taiwan) had 58.6 million cattle, 19.2 million buffalo, 304.4 million hogs and pigs, 98.9 million sheep, and 68.2 million goats in 1984.

Million head

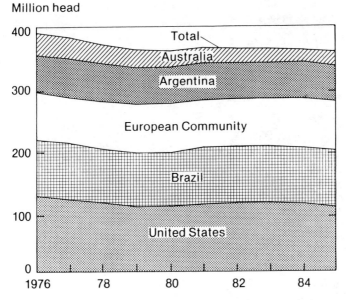

Fig. 4.1. January 1 cattle inventory in major beef-producing countries, 1976–1985 (inventory taken as close to Jan. 1 as possible). [*Courtesy*, USDA Exten. Serv. (undated).]

Leading Meat Producers

The United States is unquestionably the largest producer of meats, producing almost twice as much as the nearest competitor, the Soviet Union. In 1983, the United States led in beef, veal, and pork, but was ninth in lamb, mutton, and goat meat production. The first-place ranking by the United States in pork production at the same time it ranked second in hog numbers is an indication of a highly efficient swine industry. Tables 4.2, 4.3, and 4.4 show average red meat production by continent and for specified countries for the several species during 1975–79 and annual production for the years 1980 through 1983.

World meat production has increased in response to a growing demand and largely reflects increases in population and gains in spendable incomes. Production gains were greatest in beef and veal, which constituted about one-half of the total world red meat supply. Pork production increased 13 percent, whereas lamb, mutton, and goat meat increased 8 percent. It may be noted that European countries are heavy producers of pork. Japan, which appeared to be reducing pork

Table 4.2. Beef and Veal Production* in Specified Countries—Average, 1975-79; Annual, 1980-83.

Region and country	Avg. 1975-79 (1,000 metric tons)	1980 (1,000 metric tons)	1981 (1,000 metric tons)	1982 (1,000 metric tons)	1983 (1,000 metric tons)
North America:					
Canada	1,072	971	1,015	1,029	1,035
Costa Rica	73	67	75	77	67
Dom. Repub.	38	43	46	49	49
El Salvador	32	32	29	30	30
Guatemala	80	90	91	75	67
Honduras	49	62	64	68	63
Mexico	840	1,065	1,129	1,200	975
Nicaragua	74	61	47	48	54
Panama	45	43	49	55	55
United States	11,298	9,999	10,533	10,425	10,705
Subtotal	13,601	12,433	12,898	13,056	13,100
South America:					
Argentina	2,890	2,822	2,955	2,579	2,300
Brazil	2,226	2,150	2,250	2,400	2,500
Colombia	548	664	715	682	653
Uruguay	347	336	407	383	418
Venezuela	284	298	279	348	359
Subtotal	6,295	6,270	6,606	6,392	6,230
Europe:					
EEC-10					
Belgium-Lux.	291	311	319	287	300
Denmark	242	245	238	231	228
France	1,737	1,836	1,839	1,698	1,760
W. Germany	1,418	1,564	1,532	1,471	1,460
Greece	110	100	94	89	90
Ireland	381	444	315	344	360
Italy	1,034	1,148	1,111	1,107	1,130
Netherlands	363	376	428	413	440
United Kingdom	1,072	1,102	1,059	960	1,010
Subtotal	6,648	7,126	6,935	6,600	6,778
Austria	186	200	199	200	199
Finland	110	112	120	115	119
Portugal	86	97	105	116	116
Spain	418	422	418	420	410
Sweden	148	157	158	160	160
Switzerland	150	169	156	161	156
Subtotal	1,098	1,157	1,156	1,172	1,160

Table 4.2. *(continued)*

Region and country	Avg. 1975–79 (1,000 metric tons)	1980 (1,000 metric tons)	1981 (1,000 metric tons)	1982 (1,000 metric tons)	1983 (1,000 metric tons)
Bulgaria	132	153	150	155	155
Czechoslovakia	423	442	428	429	410
E. Germany	427	386	445	427	425
Hungary	152	161	151	150	147
Romania	289	299	284	220	230
Poland	836	800	600	757	605
Yugoslavia	332	335	323	343	342
Subtotal†	2,591	2,576	2,381	2,481	2,314
Soviet Untion‡	6,780	6,645	6,600	6,600	6,800
Africa:					
Egypt	55	259	278	286	290
South Africa	550	619	542	582	582
Subtotal	605	878	820	868	872
Asia:					
China (Taiwan)	9	5	5	6	6
Israel	22	16	12	13	16
Japan	363	418	471	481	485
S. Korea	100	127	94	83	98
Philippines	118	127	180	186	188
Turkey	196	200	201	210	220
Subtotal	808	893	963	979	1,013
Oceania:					
Australia:	1,930	1,533	1,420	1,680	1,386
New Zealand	554	496	498	516	500
Subtotal	2,484	2,029	1,918	2,196	1,886
Total Specified Countries	40,910	40,007	40,277	40,344	40,153

Source: USDA (1984C).
*Carcass weight basis.
†Based on official CEMA data (includes fats and offals), with adjustments for live animal trade.
‡Slaughter weight basis (including fats and offals) used in official USSR statistics.

Table 4.3. Pork Production* in Specified Countries—Average, 1975-79; Annual, 1980-83.

Region and country	Avg. 1975-79 (1,000 metric tons)	1980 (1,000 metric tons)	1981 (1,000 metric tons)	1982 (1,000 metric tons)	1983 (1,000 metric tons)
North America:					
Canada	593	877	869	833	850
Mexico	995	905	1,088	1,200	1,075
United States	6,038	7,537	7,199	6,454	6,843
Subtotal	7,626	9,319	9,156	8,487	8,768
South America:					
Brazil	826	980	980	970	970
Colombia	108	113	105	101	106
Venezuela	76	78	83	87	96
Subtotal	1,010	1,171	1,168	1,158	1,172
Europe:					
EEC-10					
Belgium-Lux.	640	700	716	700	670
Denmark	781	971	992	983	990
France	1,539	1,597	1,640	1,610	1,610
W. Germany	2,518	2,726	2,700	2,673	2,700
Greece	121	144	152	154	155
Ireland	127	157	153	152	156
Italy	828	981	992	994	1,005
Netherlands	936	1,062	1,149	1,165	1,195
United Kingdom	892	947	972	977	1,037
Subtotal	8,382	9,285	9,466	9,408	9,518
Austria	335	358	353	375	376
Finland	147	167	178	183	185
Portugal	136	155	178	177	177
Spain	746	986	1,021	1,115	1,273
Sweden	299	317	321	325	313
Switzerland	253	279	275	290	298
Subtotal	1,916	2,262	2,326	2,465	2,622
Bulgaria	341	372	380	400	420
Czechoslovakia	780	852	889	778	777
E. Germany	1,142	1,253	1,329	1,210	1,220
Hungary	871	944	943	984	1,033
Romania	823	915	925	820	875
Poland	1,748	1,787	1,384	1,510	1,285
Yugoslavia	732	740	784	785	755
Subtotal†	6,437	6,863	6,634	6,487	6,365
Soviet Union‡	5,103	5,183	5,204	5,200	5,600

Table 4.3. (*continued*)

Region and country	Avg. 1975–79 (1,000 metric tons)	1980 (1,000 metric tons)	1981 (1,000 metric tons)	1982 (1,000 metric tons)	1983 (1,000 metric tons)
Asia:					
China (Taiwan)	451	537	537	525	588
Japan	1,196	1,475	1,396	1,427	1,450
S. Korea	147	235	209	238	268
Philippines	326	412	450	457	498
Subtotal	2,120	2,659	2,592	2,647	2,804
Oceania:					
Australia	190	232	231	229	234
New Zealand	38	38	39	40	40
Subtotal	228	270	270	269	274
Total Specified Countries	32,822	37,012	36,817	36,121	37,129

Source: USDA (1984C).
*Carcass weight basis.
†Based on official CEMA data (includes fats and offals), with adjustments for live animal trade.
‡Slaughter weight basis (including fats and offals) used in official USSR statistics.

production during the late 1960s, returned to a strong increasing trend during the 1970s and into the 1980s.

LIVESTOCK PRODUCTION IN THE UNITED STATES

Annual livestock inventory is a good indicator of the changes, relative importance, and characteristics of the livestock industry. The annual inventory of the various species published by USDA gives the number of animals in all classes as of January 1 for cattle and sheep and as of December 1 for hogs. Examination of changes in the inventory and its composition can indicate changes or shifts in the production mix. It also provides essential information for producers and market analysts in forecasting supply and prices and assists them in developing production and marketing strategies. For example, beef cow numbers may be the best indicator of underlying herd size. The supply of slaughter beef animals is largely determined by the number of heifers not kept for replacement, by steers 500 lb and over, and all steers and heifers under 500 lb. Similarly, the number of market hogs in the 180- to 219-lb

Table 4.4.   Lamb, Mutton, and Goat Meat Production* Specified Countries—
Average, 1975-79; Annual, 1980-83.

Region and country	Avg. 1975-79 (1,000 metric tons)	1980 (1,000 metric tons)	1981 (1,000 metric tons)	1982 (1,000 metric tons)	1983 (1,000 metric tons)
North America:					
United States†	157	144	153	166	170
South America:					
Argentina	128	112	114	112	110
Europe:					
EEC-10					
Belgium-Lux.	3	4	4	5	6
Denmark	1	1	1	1	1
France	154	179	173	180	176
W. Germany	26	30	28	27	27
Greece	118	120	121	120	119
Ireland	42	42	44	40	41
Italy	56	72	69	68	69
Netherlands	15	21	16	12	11
United Kingdom	239	278	263	268	281
Subtotal	654	747	719	721	731
Portugal	22	24	23	24	25
Spain	143	138	140	141	150
Subtotal	165	162	163	165	175
Bulgaria	76	83	93	96	95
Czechoslovakia	7	9	7	7	8
E. Germany	14	16	20	21	22
Hungary	7	5	9	9	9
Poland	22	22	17	16	16
Romania	53	64	58	62	65
Yugoslavia	59	58	57	59	60
Subtotal‡	238	257	261	270	275
Soviet Union**	915	894	900	800	825
Africa:					
Egypt	8	48	50	49	49
South Africa	160	159	162	180	185
Subtotal	168	207	212	229	234
Asia:					
S. Korea	1	1	1	1	1
India	368	380	482	488	492
Israel	5	6	5	6	4
Japan	0	0	0	0	0
Turkey	349	292	354	356	370
Subtotal	723	679	842	851	867

Table 4.4 *(continued)*

Region and country	Avg. 1975–79 (1,000 metric tons)	1980 (1,000 metric tons)	1981 (1,000 metric tons)	1982 (1,000 metric tons)	1983 (1,000 metric tons)
Oceania:					
Australia	542	548	517	554	479
New Zealand	504	560	626	619	653
Subtotal	1,046	1,108	1,143	1,173	1,132
Total Specified Countries	4,194	4,310	4,507	4,487	4,519

Source: USDA (1984C).
*Carcass weight basis.
†Lamb and Mutton only.
‡Official CEMA data (includes fats and offals), with adjustments for live animal trade.
**Slaughter weight basis (including fats and offals) used in official USSR statistics.

weight category is the best indicator of hog slaughter in the immediate future, whereas those under 60 lb indicate the size of slaughter several months in the future. Tables 4.5, 4.6, and 4.7 present the annual U.S. inventories for cattle and calves, hogs and pigs, and sheep and lambs, respectively, along with inventory composition according to standard USDA classification for 1970–1985.

Leading Livestock Producing States

The location of areas of livestock concentration follows the principle that governs industrial location. As a general rule, an area of concentrated production develops where an industry has a comparative advantage, or where it has the least comparative disadvantage. The availability and cost of inputs, transport charges on both inputs and outputs, and the location of existing and potential demand are controlling factors in industry location. Feed is by far the major input in livestock production. It almost is axiomatic that a region that possesses a comparative advantage in producing feed of a particular type also will have a comparative advantage in producing the specie and class of livestock adapted to the consumption of that feed.

Cattle, hogs, and sheep are produced in every state, but the geographical distribution is not uniform. Not only is the distribution different for each of the three species, but the density of production varies substantially for a given specie. The density of human population also varies. It is not surprising that the human population density does

Table 4.5. Cattle and Calves: Number by Class, United States, Jan. 1, 1970–1985.

Year	Cows and heifers that have calved		Heifers 500 lb and over		Other heifers 500 lb & over	Steers 500 lb & over	Bulls 500 lb & over	Calves Under 500 lb	Total cattle and calves
	Beef cows	Milk cows	Replacement for Beef	Milk					
			(1,000 Head)						
1970	36,689	12,091	6,431	3,880	6,132	15,265	2,272	26,609	112,369
1971	37,878	11,909	6,664	3,843	6,113	15,610	2,328	30,235	114,578
1972	38,810	11,776	6,987	3,828	6,399	15,999	2,377	31,688	117,862
1973	40,932	11,622	7,434	3,872	6,432	16,553	2,467	32,229	121,539
1974	43,182	11,297	8,193	3,941	6,852	17,760	2,643	33,922	127,788
1975	45,712	11,220	8,884	4,087	6,518	16,333	2,985	36,291	132,028
1976	43,901	11,071	7,192	3,956	7,391	17,094	2,845	34,531	127,980
1977	41,443	10,998	6,527	3,887	8,048	16,884	2,664	32,360	122,810
1978	38,738	10,896	5,858	3,886	7,949	16,868	2,538	29,643	116,375
1979	37,062	10,790	5,527	3,932	7,445	16,442	2,403	27,263	110,864
1980	37,086	10,779	5,939	4,158	7,130	16,019	2,492	27,590	111,192
1981	38,726	10,860	6,136	4,345	7,285	15,519	2,547	28,904	114,321
1982	39,319	11,012	6,615	4,532	7,181	15,501	2,618	28,827	115,604
1983	37,940	11,047	6,336	4,545	7,965	16,214	2,609	28,346	115,001
1984	37,494	11,109	6,183	4,532	7,851	16,371	2,549	27,611	113,700
1985	35,393	10,819	5,536	4,757	8,036	16,399	2,411	26,450	109,801

Source: USDA (1984B) for 1970–82 and USDA (1985A) for 1982–85.

Table 4.6. Hogs and Pigs: Number Kept for Breeding and Market, By Weight Group, United States, Dec. 1, 1969-1984.

Year	All hogs and pigs	For breeding	Market					
			Total	Under 60 lb	60–119 lb	120–179 lb	180–219 lb	220 lb & over
			(1,000 Head)					
1969	57,046	9,189	47,857	17,522	13,004	9,666	5,775	1,890
1970	67,285	9,645	57,640	21,288	15,612	11,424	6,925	2,391
1971	62,412	8,475	53,937	19,912	14,359	10,835	6,626	2,205
1972	59,017	8,650	50,367	19,303	13,395	10,187	5,783	1,699
1973	60,614	8,605	52,009	20,142	13,715	10,223	6,103	1,826
1974	54,693	7,389	47,304	17,732	12,495	9,685	5,740	1,652
1975	49,267	7,574	41,693	16,255	11,047	8,049	4,837	1,505
1976	54,934	8,011	46,923	18,714	12,307	8,932	5,292	1,678
1977	56,539	8,604	47,936	19,424	12,399	9,111	5,495	1,507
1978	60,356	9,605	50,751	21,244	13,086	9,443	6,979*	
1979	67,353	9,655	57,699	22,845	15,437	11,287	8,133	
1980	64,512	9,148	55,364	22,139	13,982	11,000	8,243	
1981	58,688	7,843	50,845	19,487	12,923	10,437	7,998	
1982	53,935	7,415	46,519	18,628	11,808	9,282	6,802	
1983	55,819	7,352	48,467	18,753	12,333	9,771	7,610	
1984	54,073	6,933	47,140	18,071	12,013	9,610	7,446	

Source: USDA (1984B) for 1969–1982, and USDA (1985B) for 1983–84.
*The 180- to 219-lb and 220-lb and over market-hog-weight groups combined into 180-lb and over weight groups starting 1978.

Table 4.7. Sheep and Lambs: Number by Class, United States, Jan. 1, 1970–85.

Year	Stock sheep					Sheep and lambs on feed	All sheep and lambs
	Lambs		One year old and over		Total		
	Ewes	Wethers	Ewes	Rams and wethers			
	(1,000 Head)						
1970	2,422	475	13,923	613	17,433	2,990	20,423
1971	2,280	463	13,609	594	16,946	2,785	19,731
1972	1,974	402	12,909	560	15,845	2,894	18,739
1973	1,883	354	12,049	482	14,768	2,873	17,641
1974	1,804	359	11,058	464	13,685	2,625	16,310
1975	1,510	404	10,083	437	12,436	2,079	14,515
1976	1,345	350	9,314	418	11,427	1,884	13,311
1977	1,401	379	8,850	361	10,991	1,731	12,722
1978	1,508	328	8,588	374	10,798	1,623	12,421
1979	1,684	356	8,366	380	10,786	1,579	12,365
1980	1,807	368	8,524	366	11,065	1,622	12,687
1981	1,788	357	8,771	370	11,287	1,649	12,936
1982	1,805	422	8,788	388	11,402	1,564	12,966
1983	1,407	340	8,267	372	10,385	1,641	12,026
1984	1,237	318	7,874	340	9,769	1,718	11,487
1985	1,016	284	7,233	314	8,847	1,596	10,443

Source: USDA (1984B) for 1970–1983 and USDA (1986B) for 1984–75.

not correspond with livestock production, but the fact that this is so complicates the marketing system.

The livestock inventories of the states can be used to rank each one in terms of its relative importance as a producer of a particular species. Table 4.8 presents the 10 top states according to January 1, 1985 inventories of cattle and sheep and December 1, 1984 inventory of hogs. The data indicate that hog and sheep production is more concentrated than cattle production. For example, although the top 10 cattle producing states accounted for 53.7 percent of all cattle on U.S. farms on Jan. 1, 1985, the top 10 states in hog inventory accounted for 79.2 percent of all hogs and pigs, and the 10 leading states in sheep inventory accounted for 71.1 percent.

Livestock Production Systems

In the absence of irrigation, vast areas of range and pasture land are adapted only to indigenous vegetation. The native forage of the Plains and Mountain States is suitable only for cow herds, cattle growing programs, and ewe flocks. Most of this land has no other feasible commercial use.[2] The density of cattle and sheep production in these areas is relatively light, but this should not obscure the fact that the areas are rather fully utilized. The nature of the livestock production systems adapted to these areas is classified, from the standpoint of land use, as extensive (in contrast to intensive).

In order to develop successful livestock marketing programs, producers and professional analysts must have some knowledge of the production system. This is important since the type of system used in production determines the type of animal produced, its probable market, and hence the market channel to be used.

Market channels for live animals are defined as the routes, or paths, in the marketing system through which livestock pass as they move from farm or ranch to slaughter or other purposes. For example, for finished livestock (i.e., those intended for slaughter), production consists of three stages or phases. The phases are (1) the basic cow-herd, sow-herd, and ewe flock operations from which arise increases in livestock numbers and the initial growth that takes place prior to weaning; (2) a growing phase—that period during which the chief objective is growth, involving liberal consumption of roughages and grass and

---

[2] It is recognized that with increasing affluence of an increasing population, pressures are mounting for both commercial and public recreational use of land suitable for those purposes. In some areas, residential development is taking substantial acreage. With the passage of time, nonagricultural demands will take additional acreage.

Table 4.8. Ten Leading States in Cattle and Sheep, Jan. 1, 1985, and in Hogs and Pigs, Dec. 1, 1984; Inventories and Percentage Contributions of U.S. Totals.

Rank	State	Cattle and calves (1,000 hd)	Percentage of U.S.	State	Sheep and lambs (1,000 hd)	Percentage of U.S.	State	Hogs and Pigs (1,000 hd)	Percentage of U.S.
1	Tex.	14,100	12.85	Tex.	1,810	17.33	Iowa	14,200	26.26
2	Neb.	6,100	5.56	Calif.	1,065	10.20	Ill.	5,400	10.00
3	Kans.	5,860	5.34	Wyo.	860	8.24	Ind.	4,300	7.95
4	Iowa	5,600	5.10	Colo.	675	6.46	Minn.	4,300	7.95
5	Okl.	5,300	4.83	S. Dak.	639	6.12	Neb.	3,700	6.84
6	Calif.	4,960	4.52	N. Mex.	538	5.15	Mo.	3,450	6.38
7	Mo.	4,850	4.42	Mont.	515	4.93	N. Car.	2,300	4.25
8	Wisc.	4,440	4.05	Utah	515	4.93	Ohio	1,970	3.65
9	S. Dak.	4,160	3.80	Oreg.	445	4.26	S. Dak.	1,600	2.96
10	Minn.	3,550	2.23	Iowa	360	3.45	Kans.	1,600	2.96
Ten States		58,920	53.70		7,422	71.07		42,820	79.20

Source: USDA (1986A). Percentages calculated by the authors.

sometimes limited quantities of grain; (3) a finishing phase—that a period of relatively heavy grain feeding during which the chief objective is finishing or fattening; and (4) the slaughtering of the animals. It is recognized that the first three stages in the production programs are not entirely separate or distinct. For example, young animals may be creep fed prior to weaning. This is the normal process for producing spring lambs and baby beef. Hog production often is more or less a continuous full-feeding process from weaning to slaughter. Cattle are sometimes fed grain while still on grass. Lambs and cattle may go directly to slaughter off wheat pasture. Lambs often go to slaughter upon weaning at the end of the grazing season.

Cull livestock normally are not put through a finishing stage. As Fowler (1961) reports, however, feeders in the Beet Belt (western Nebraska, through northern Colorado, Wyoming, and Montana) follow a practice of buying broken-mouth ewes and fattening them. Also, cull cows sometimes are fattened on wheat pasture or in feedlots.

Although the above list of exceptions and modifications may appear to be large, the bulk of meat produced from each of the three species is finished. A relatively large proportion of cattle and lambs change ownership during the production process, whereas a large proportion of hogs are grown out and finished without a change of ownership. Change in ownership necessitates the use of markets. The least complicated channel arises when the original herd or flock owner grows and finishes his own output and then sells the finished animals directly to a packer. The following discussion presents a brief description of the various livestock production systems for the three species.

Cattle Production Systems.   The emphasis and characteristics of U.S. cattle raising are affected by climate (through its impact on the availability of forage) and by the comparative advantage in feed grain or other crop production opportunities. Martin (1979) divided the United States into seven different cattle-raising regions and stated that changes in beef raising differed significantly among these regions. In contrast, Boykin *et al* (1980) defined four different production systems in cattle raising: (1) cow–calf–feeder system, (2) cow–calf–slaughter system, (3) stocker purchase–slaughter sales system, and (4) the stocker purchase–feeder sales system, as follows:

1. *Cow–calf–feeder:* This system includes the cow–calf and cow–yearling subsystems. The cow–calf subsystem includes the maintenance of a cow breeding stock and the selling of calves at weaning or shortly thereafter. Under the cow–yearling subsystem, calves are carried longer into the stocker phase. Availability of forage is the most important factor in determining whether or not to carry the calves to the

yearling stage. Yearlings may either go from pasture to feedlots for further feeding or directly to slaughter.

2. *Cow–calf–slaughter:* In this system, producers carry calves on range or pasture as stockers. Animals are either sold as slaughter calves or kept a little longer and sold as grass-fed cattle. Some producers may place stocker calves in feedlots and then sell them as grain-fed cattle.

3. *Stocker purchase–slaughter sales:* Stockers are weaned steer and heifer calves that are fed in a way to promote growth rather than fattening. In the stocker purchase–slaughter system, stockers are raised in the area where they were produced or are shipped into grazing areas where small grains, stock fields, and other feed sources are available. At a later stage, these stockers are placed in feedlots for finishing and then sold for slaughter.

4. *Stocker purchase–feeder sales:* In this system, the operator purchases weaned calves, carries them on range or pasture to the stocker phase, and then sells them to feedlots for finishing.

In a recent survey of U.S. cattle-raising systems (Boykin *et al.*, 1980) found that approximately 70 percent of U.S. cattle producers follow the cow–calf–feeder system. Only one-third of the operators in the North Central region sell feeder cattle, however, compared with over 75 percent of the operators in other regions.

Hog Production Systems. Hog production in the United States is carried out under different systems that can be characterized by size, types of hogs produced, degree of vertical integration, and degree of industrialization. Hog production is spread over a large and diverse geographical area, but the North Central Region dominates.

There are many ways to raise hogs and consequently many types of hog operations. Most, however, can be grouped as low- moderate- or high-investment operations. A hog operation may be only one of several enterprises in a farm business, it can be a part-time business with the operator employed elsewhere, or it can be a specialized business with a high volume of production and marketing. The following is a brief discussion of the types of operations and production systems.

1. *Low-investment operations:* These are usually built around existing facilities, farm-produced feed, and available family labor. Such operations usually involve herds of up to 50 sows, although some larger herds are operated with small investments where pasture is available.

2. *Moderate-investment operations:* These usually have modern farrowing houses and nurseries, with other facilities similar to those found in low-investment operations. A moderate-investment operation

can handle a moderately large volume of production and typically involves herds with 50 or more sows.

3. *High-investment operations:* These typically have several hundred sows and are specialized businesses. More investment capital is required for both facilities and equipment, but once that investment is made, the relatively large volume of production reduces cost per head to an amount equivalent to or less than that encountered with smaller investments.

Hog production systems may be classified into three basic types: the farrow-to-finish system, the feeder-pig production system, and the feeder-pig finishing system, all of which can be carried out under any of the above three types of operations.

1. *Farrow-to-finish:* This is the predominant system in the United States and involves the integrated operation of breeding and farrowing the sows, nursing the pigs up to weaning weight, and finish-feeding the weaned pigs to market weight. The breeding herd is maintained or expanded through a replacement-culling program.

2. *Feeder-pig production:* This system which is usually a common practice in grain-deficient areas, involves selling weaned pigs to operators in grain-surplus areas for finishing. Typically, feeder-pig operations are small-scale, although there are some indications that large units have developed in recent years (Crom and Duewer, 1980).

3. *Feeder-pig finishing:* This system is a feeding operation only and does not involve breeding and farrowing. Some farrow-to-finish operators buy feeder pigs for finishing purposes, usually to maximize the utilization of their facilities.

Sheep and Lamb Production Systems: Sheep and lamb production is concentrated in the states west of the Mississippi River, especially in Texa꜓ and California. More than 75 percent of the nation's sheep are raised in the West, where plentiful feed resources, both private and public ranges, are available.

Gee *et al.* (1976) indicated that about 40 percent of the sheep production in the West is from commercial-scale operations of 500 head or more. In comparison, Gee and Van Arsdall (1978) found that in the North Central Region sheep and lamb production is considered a supplementary operation by most producers, whose flocks usually average less than 100 head. About 89 percent of the region's producers surveyed operate as sole proprietors; the other 11 percent are involved in partnerships (9 percent) or family operations (2 percent).

Gee and Van Arsdall (1978) identified two types of sheep production systems: the breeding-ewes system and the lamb-feeding system. The breeding-ewes system involves breeding ewes, nursing the lambs up to weaning weight, and then selling or feeding the weaned lambs. The lamb-feeding system, on the other hand, involves purchasing feeder lambs and finish-feeding them to a slaughter weight. Wool is a secondary product from sheep enterprises.

CHANGES IN THE U.S. LIVESTOCK INDUSTRY

Farm and ranch production of cattle and calves in the United States, as measured by the live-weight quantity produced and adjusted for changes in inventory and inshipments, increased at a faster rate than inventory.

This increase resulted primarily because of an increase in the proportion of cattle that were grain-fed and a decrease in the number of usually lighter-weight range cattle that were sold. Hog and sheep production, on the other hand, has followed trends in inventories since the early 1960s. Thus, hogs have held steady, with only cyclical changes, whereas sheep production has been declining, with a few exceptions.

Changes in the Cattle Industry

Areas of highly concentrated red-meat animal-feeding (finishing) programs mirror areas of highly concentrated feed-grain production. It was pointed out in Chap. 1 that livestock feeding followed feed grain (corn) production as farming spread westward.[3] Feeding activities are still following geographic changes in feed-grain production that have resulted from recent developments in hybrid feed grains, irrigation, and government crop restriction programs. The Corn Belt has become the Corn–Hog Belt. In an earlier period, this region was also a major cattle-finishing area. This was a logical step from an economic standpoint. The demand from population concentrations in the East required an eastward flow of livestock and meat. The Corn Belt is strategically located from a geographical (freight cost) standpoint. Subsequently, population concentration increased on the West Coast. Coincident with this growth was increased irrigated feed-grain production in California, Arizona, and especially the Milo Belt, which resulted

---

[3] The location of broiler production is not oriented to feed-grain production to the same extent as that of red-meat animals. Feed inputs are significant in broiler production but relatively less important. The feed-conversion ratio is more favorable for broilers than for red-meat animals, and other factors—e.g., labor requirements—can be more easily satisfied in areas other than feed-grain-producing regions.

in a shift of cattle finishing to the central and southern Plains States. Farm program acreage restrictions on wheat have also encouraged increased production of grain sorghum, especially in the winter-wheat region.

Statistics from USDA reveal that while all cattle marketings in the United States increased by 42 percent from 1960 to 1984, fed-cattle marketings almost doubled during the same period. Table 4.9 summarizes changes in fed cattle marketed in 1960 and in the 1970–1985 period. Grain-fed cattle represented 39 percent of the total U.S. cattle marketings in 1960; by 1970, however, they accounted for 55 percent of the total. During 1974 to 1977, the percentages declined to under 50 percent, and in 1985 the grain-fed cattle marketed accounted for 54 percent of total marketings.

The USDA statistics also reveal that the North Central states market a larger percentage of their cattle in the form of grain-fed animals than does the U.S. as a whole and accounts for more than one-half of all U.S. fed cattle marketed. Although the region's contribution has declined, Kansas and Nebraska have actually increased their relative

Table 4.9. Cattle and Calves: Marketings, Fed Cattle Marketed, and Fed Cattle Marketed as a Percentage of Total Marketings, U.S. 1960 and 1970–85.

Year	Total cattle and calves marketings* (1,000 hd)	Fed cattle marketed (1,000 hd)	Percentage of total marketings
1960	34,378	13,496	39.3
1970	49,926	25,725	54.8
1971	49,143	26,127	53.2
1972	51,043	27,728	53.3
1973	48,369	26,083	53.9
1974	48,383	23,994	49.6
1975	54,315	21,260	39.1
1976	55,394	25,125	45.4
1977	56,378	25,969	46.1
1978	54,737	27,850	50.9
1979	47,656	25,566	53.7
1980	45,561	24,004	52.7
1981	46,739	23,818	51.0
1982	49,727	24,902	50.1
1983	48,037	25,752	53.6
1984	50,862	25,741	50.6
1985	48,739	26,095	53.5

Source: USDA (1984B and 1986C) and unpublished USDA data.
*Includes animals for slaughter market, as well as younger animals shipped to other states for feeding or breeding purposes. Includes custom slaughter for use on farms where produced.

importance. The decline in the relative importance of the cattle-feeding industry in most of the states in the North Central Region, and in the region as a whole, can be attributed to the significant geographical shift in production towards the Plains and the West, to the increased opportunity of feed-grain exports, and to technological changes during the past 25 years. The geographical shift is evidenced by the rapid feedlot construction and expansion in the West and Southwest during the early 1970s. Meisner and Rhodes (1974) discussed this structural evolution and listed the following three reasons for the change: (1) an increase in fed-beef demand as a result of growth in population and personal income, (2) greater availability of feed-grain supplies, associated with the development of new hybrid milo, particularly in the high Plains, and (3) increased use of new technology by large commercial feedlots and associated economies of scale. During this expansionary period, feeder-cattle supplies and capital were generally available to many feedlot operators. The animals were fed in increasingly larger feedlots, and producers, in order to achieve greater utilization rates in these larger lots, placed additional cattle on feed. Stout (1979), Martin (1979), and Van Arsdall and Nelson (1983) provide further discussion of such changes in the cattle-feeding industry.

Cattle feedlots may be divided into two types: (1) feedlots with a one-time capacity of less than 1,000 head, also called "farm feedlots," and (2) feedlots with a one-time capacity of more than 1,000 head, also called "commercial feedlots." Farm (or family) feedlots, usually a supplementary enterprise, are dominant in the Corn Belt. In the mid 1960s, farm feedlots sold more than 61 percent of all fed cattle marketed. Their number has dropped by half, however, and their share fallen below 30 percent. On the other hand, commercial feedlots, typically highly-mechanized primary enterprises found mostly in the Western and Plains (primarily southern Plains) States, became more important in spite of their relatively small number. For example, although the number of commercial feedlots represents only a small percentage of total feedlots, they have dominated marketings since the early 1970s (Fig. 4.2). In 1984, 1,898 commercial feedlots in the 13 leading states in cattle feeding, as reported by USDA, accounted for 78 percent of the fed cattle marketed from these states in 1984 (Table 4.10 and Fig 4.2). In contrast, the 61,813 small feedlots in the 13 states accounted for the remaining 22 percent during the same year. Van Arsdall and Nelson (1983) stated that since the mid 1960s "farmers cattle feeding has not declined relative to commercial cattle feeding, but has decreased in absolute terms in the traditional farmer feeding areas in states dominated by commercial feedlots."

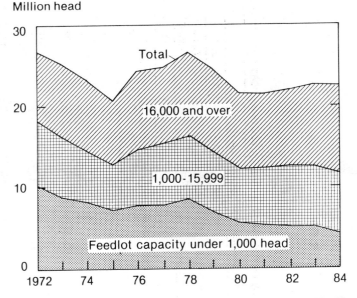

Fig. 4.2.   Fed cattle marketed by feedlot capacity in 13 states, 1972–1984. [Courtesy, USDA Exten. Serv. (undated).]

Although it is almost certain that the United States will continue to produce more feed grains that it consumes in the foreseeable future, these grains will be allocated to their highest end use by the market system. Because of the great world demand for grains for both livestock and human consumption, a large portion of the surplus will be exported. The availability of export markets coupled with increased transportation costs makes feed prices higher in areas with easy access to export points (for example, Illinois) than in areas without easy access (for example, the western part of the North Central Region). Thus, any increase in feeding in this region is likely to take place in the areas with less access to export points, as is evidenced in development in recent years.

It has been suggested by several groups that cattle feeders should feed cattle less grain and more roughage and produce leaner beef animals. Many argue that such a shift in feeding practices would not change meat quality but would reduce feeding costs and at the same time release some grain and other resources for other uses. Although these arguments appear plausible, it should be noted that cattle are ruminant animals, able to consume forages grown on low-quality noncrop lands and thus have an inherent advantage over hogs and broilers

Table 4.10. Number of Cattle Feedlots and Feed Cattle Marketed, by Size of Feedlot Capacity, 13 States, 1983.*

State	Under 1,000 feedlot		1,000 head and over feedlot capacity					
			1,000–1,999		2,000–3,999		4,000–7,999	
	Lots	Cattle marketed	Lots	Cattle marketed	Lots	Cattle marketed	Lots	Cattle marketed
	No.	(1,000 hd)	No.	(1,000 hd)	No.	(1,000 hd)	No.	(1,000 hd)
Ariz.	10†	28	‡	‡	‡	‡	‡	‡
Calif.	15	3	8	6	11	14	17	50
Colo.	135	135	70	112	65	247	31	247
Idaho	120	10	16	18	15	35	11	54
Ill.	10,950	865	40	60	10	30	‡	‡
Iowa	22,418	1,246	440	598	105	299	25	150
Kans.	2,491	88	60	100	35	105	35	308
Minn.	8,946	567	41	68	13	30	‡	‡
Nebr.	10,620	1,500	170	350	97	450	56	510
Okla.	246†	17†	‡	‡	7	16	6	20
S. Dak.	4,943	446	37	51	10	24	10†	144†
Tex.	862	100	9	20	14	80	19	130
Wash.	68	6	4	4	7	10	5	39
13 States**	61,813	4,982	899	1,392	391	1,342	215	1,575

State	8,000–15,999		16,000 and over		Total over 1,000 feedlots		Total all feedlots	
	Lots	Cattle marketed	Lots	Cattle marketed	Lots	Cattle marketed	Lots	Cattle marketed
	No.	(1,000 hd)	No.	(1,000 hd)	No.	(1,000 hd)	No.	(1,000 hd)
Ariz.	‡	‡	16	505	25	532	26	533
Calif.	21	140	21	815	78	1,025	93	1,028
Colo.	27	292	22	1,212	215	2,110	350	2,245
Idaho	8	137	5†‡	225†‡	55	469	175	479
Ill.	‡	‡			50	90	11,000	955
Iowa	8	125	4‡	75‡	582	1,247	23,000	2,493
Kans.	45	1,040	34	1,760	209	3,313	2,700	3,401
Minn.	‡	‡		‡	54	98	9,000	665
Nebr.	39	740	18	1,030	380	3,080	11,000	4,580
Okla.	8	87	8	495	31	620	275	635
S. Dak.	‡	‡		‡	57	219	5,000	665
Tex.	30	490	66	3,580	138	4,300	1,000	4,400
Wash.	3	33	5†‡	357†‡	24	443	92	449
13 States**	192	3,106	201	10,131	1,898	17,546	63,711	22,528

Source: USDA (1984B).

*Number of feedlots with 1,000 head or more capacity is number of lots operating anytime during year. Number under 1,000 head capacity is number at end of year.

†Lots and marketings from other size groups are included to avoid disclosing individual operations.

‡Included with other size groups to avoid disclosing individual operations.

**The 13 state total show actual number of feedlots and number of animals marketed in each size group. The sum of numbers shown by states under a specified size group may not add to 13 state total for that size group, since for some states size groups are combined to avoid disclosing individual operations.

(nonruminant species). In addition, it is argued that life-long beef-cattle rations include much smaller percentages of concentrates compared with life-long hog and broiler rations—about 16 percent for cattle, 85 percent for hogs, and 100 percent for broilers (Van Arsdall *et al.*, 1978).

Changes in the Hog Industry

Studies by Van Arsdall and Giliman (1979) and Van Arsdall and Nelson (1984) examining changes in the hog industry indicate a shift in the number and size of operations since the end of World War II. Forty-eight percent of all hogs in 1982 were produced in operations with annual sale of 1,000 head or more. In contrast, only 7 percent of hogs sold in 1964 came from operations of that size (Fig. 4.3). Van Arsdall and Nelson (1985) stated that "The most rapid shift to larger volume hog operations has occurred mostly since 1980 when total production was excessive relative to demand, and returns to producers were poor. Thousands of small producers gave way to larger ones between 1980 and 1984. The number of hog operations during this period dropped 34 percent nationally and 41 percent in the Southeast. By the end of 1984, the 6 percent of all producers who had 500 or more hogs in inventory (approximately equal to minimum annual sales of 1,000 head) held 52 percent of the total U.S. hog inventory." Figure 4.4 shows a summary of the relative importance of the various size groups in hog production in 1983.

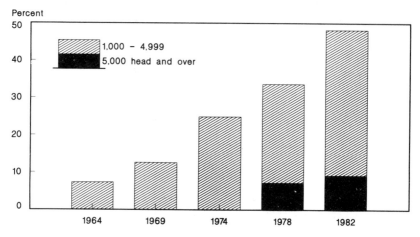

Fig. 4.3.   Hogs and pigs sold by size of operation, U.S. [*Courtesy,* Van Arsdall and Nelson (1985).]

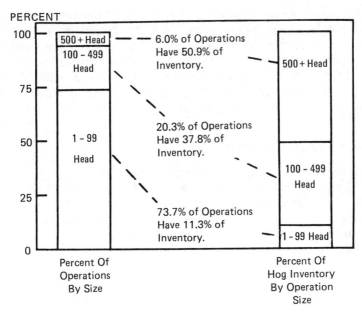

Fig. 4.4. Hogs and pigs: United States percent of hog operations and inventory by size group, 1983. [*Courtesy,* USDA (1984A).]

Most studies identified the following forces behind the changes and the factors that will continue to effect them: (1) technological developments in nutrition, disease control, production facilities, and equipment, (2) changes in crop production technologies that have resulted in more feed-grain production, (3) availability of credit and the producers' willingness to use investment capital for facilities and equipment, (4) tax and other public policies encouraging capital-intensive technologies, and (5) economies of size of operations, particularly in the use of capital-intensive or labor-saving equipment.

The hog industry continues to be concentrated near feed grain production in the Corn Belt and Southeast. About 430,000 hog production operations were reported in the United States in 1984, compared with over 2 million in the early 1950s. The trend towards larger hog production units has been accomplished largely through individual ownership and some family corporations. Van Arsdall and Nelson (1985) indicated that "Economies of size in hog production are substantial and continue to increase for operations producing up to 10,000 head, although performance varies among producers of all sizes." They concluded, "Hog production will likely continue to shift toward a smaller number of large, industrialized, and highly specialized operations, increasingly separate from crop production." Very little vertical integration exists in the hog industry. As Crom and Duewer (1980) have suggested, however, a substantial shift toward vertical integration is possible because of the potential economies of scale and the large initial investment required for modern facilities. Because of the close association between hog production and the availability of feed grains, no drastic regional changes in production location are expected.

Changes in the Sheep Industry

There has been a general downward trend in sheep inventories since World War II, attributable to several factors among them the difficulty in obtaining labor, availability of more attractive investment alternatives, predator problems, and reduction in grazing permits on federal lands. The decline in numbers, however, was partially offset by increased productivity.

REFERENCES

Boykin, C. C., et al. 1980. Structural characteristics of beef cattle raising in the United States. USDA, ESS Agr. Econ. Rept. 450.

Crom, R., and Duewer, L. 1980. Trends and developments in the hog-pork industry. USDA, ESS Staff Paper No. AGESSB1027, October.

Food and Agriculture Organization of the United Nations. 1985. FAO production yearbook 1984. FAO, vol. 38, Rome.

Gee, C. K., and Magleby, R. S. 1976. Characteristics of sheep production in the western United States. USDA, ERS Agr. Econ. Rept. 345.

Gee, C. K., and Van Arsdall, R. 1978. Structural characteristics and costs of producing sheep in the North Central states, 1975. USDA, ESCS-19.

Martin, J. R. 1979. Livestock production: Beef. In Another revolution in U.S. farming? Schertz, L. P. ed. USDA, ESS Part II. Agr. Econ. Rept. 441 85–118.

Meisner, J. C., and Rhodes, V. J. 1974. The changing structures of U. S. cattle feeding. Dept of Agr. Econ., Univ. of Mo., Columbia. Special Rept. 167.

Stout, T. T. 1979. The future of the livestock industry. Dept of Agr. Econ., Ohio State University. AERS, ESS 580.

Van Arsdall, R., et al. 1978. The future of livestock, poultry production. Feed stuffs 50 (24):22–26.

Van Arsdall R., and Gilliam, H. C. 1979. Livestock production: Pork. In Another revolution in U. S. Farming? Schertz, L. P. ed. USDA, ESS Part II. Agr. Econ. Rept. 441 190–254.

Van Arsdall, R., and Nelson, K. E. 1983. Characteristics of farmer cattle feeding. USDA, ERS Agr. Econ. Rept. 503.

Van Arsdall, R., and Nelson, K. E. 1984. U. S. hog industry. USDA, ERS Agr. Econ. Rept. 511.

Van Arsdall, R., and Nelson, K. E. 1985. Economics of size in hog production. USDA, Tech. Bull. 1712.

USDA. 1984A. Agricultural statistics 1984. USDA, SRS. U. S. Government Printing Office.

USDA. 1984B. Livestock and meat statistics, 1983. USDA, ERS Stat. Bull. 715.

USDA. 1985A. Cattle. USDA, Crop Reporting Board, SRS LvGn 1 (2-85). Released Feb.

USDA. 1985B. Hogs and pigs. USDA, Crop Reporting Board, SRS MtAn 3 (12-85). Released Dec. 23.

USDA. 1986A. Meat animals production, disposition, and income, 1985 summary. USDA SRS MtAn 1-1(86).

USDA. 1986B. Sheep and goats, USDA, Crop Reporting Board, SRS LvGn 1(1-86). Released Jan. 29.

USDA. 1986C. Packers and Stockyards' Statistical Resume 1984 Reporting year. USDA, P&S Admin., P&S Stat. Rept. 86-1.

USDA. 1985. Agricultural Chartbook Enlargements. USDA Extension Service (undated).

5

Production and Price Movements

Three types of production and price movements are of concern to live-stock market analysis: (1) secular, (2) cyclical, and (3) seasonal. Such movements are observable in inventories, market supplies, and prices.

Seasonal variations are those that tend to follow a more or less uniform pattern within the year (i.e., a 12-month period, but not necessarily one starting in January) and that conform to this pattern, furthermore, over a period of years. Consequently, peaks and troughs tend to come at about the same time each year.

A cyclical movement, as the name implies, is one that tends to follow a self-repeating pattern.[1] As defined here, therefore, a cycle extends for more than one year (it tends to repeat itself over a period of years).

Secular trends are long-time trends that persist over a period of several cycles.

Yet a fourth type of production and price movement is referred to as random, or erratic, variation. This type of movement has no uniformity and hence little or no predictability. Over a period of time, it is expected that random variations will cancel out and, hence, are usually ignored.

Price and production data as generated and reported in the markets at any given time represent the combined effects of secular trend, cyclical movement, seasonal movement, and random variation. As just mentioned, the random variations are usually ignored. A first task in a study of the remaining movements is the problem of isolating the effects of each from the effects of the others. Statistical techniques are available to do this job, but no attempt will be made here to present a statistical treatment. In the discussion that follows, the notion of secular trend is fairly obvious. Figure 5.1 is presented as an aid in visualizing the concept of cyclical and seasonal movements. Line A represents original data, adjusted only for secular trend and incorporating both cyclic and seasonal influences. In line B, the cyclical effect is isolated, i.e., seasonal influences have been removed. Line C represents the iso-

---

[1] The term "cycle" implies a degree of regularity that is not actually found in livestock raising. Cyclical tendencies exist, but successive movements are not identical.

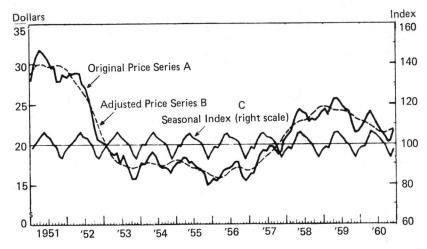

Fig. 5.1. Original, adjusted, and seasonal changes in average prices of all cattle slaughtered under Federal inspection. [*Courtesy,* Federal Reserve Bank of Kansas City (1962).]

lated effect of seasonal variation only. The following sections present the three types of movements as applied to cattle, hogs, and sheep, respectively—information that should facilitate comparison among the three species.

SECULAR TRENDS

Cattle—Secular Trends

The totals of all cattle and calves on hand as of January 1 of each year since 1870 (annual records were begun in 1867) are shown in Fig. 5.2. These figures include both beef and dairy cattle, both of which should be considered for purposes of this discussion. The breakdown by class for the period 1966-1983 is shown in Fig. 5.3. Over the years, the slaughter of dairy stock has contributed substantial quantities of beef, although this stock has been of declining importance since about the mid-1940s. From this table it is obvious that the secular, or long-time, trend in cattle numbers was upward until the 1970s. It is too early to tell with certainty at present, but there is some indication that the secular trend peaked at that time. Superimposed on the secular (long-run) trend are cyclical variations. Although the secular trend is upward, the rate of growth has not been uniform. The total period can be

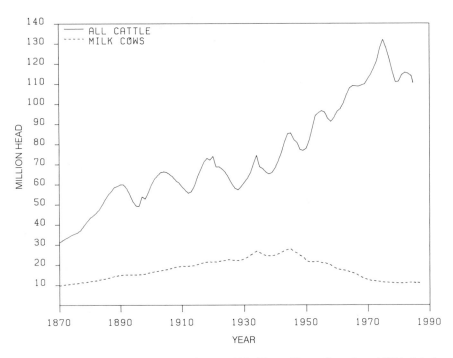

Fig. 5.2. Cattle on farms, Jan. 1, 1870 to 1985. (Plotted by authors from USDA data.)

Million head

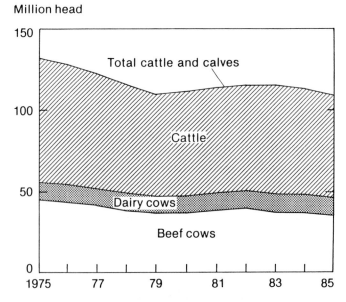

Fig. 5.3. Cattle on farms as of Jan. 1 by class, 1975–1985 (beef cows are those that have calved). [*Courtesy,* USDA Exten. Serv. (undated).]

logically broken into two segments, with the breaking point in the late 1920s, as shown in Fig. 5.4. (DeGraff, 1960)

Production per head has also increased so that the secular trend in production has increased at a faster rate than the numbers of cattle have (see Fig. 5.5). A number of factors have contributed to the increase in productivity. Among the more important are the following:

1. An increasing proportion of the cattle population is composed of beef cattle, and meat output per head is greater for beef cattle than for dairy cattle. The ratio of beef cows to dairy cows has changed rapidly since the early 1950s. A generally overlooked fact is that dairy cows outnumbered beef cows by more than 2 to 1 during the 1930s. By the early 1950s, beef cows equaled dairy cows, and in 1985 beef cows outnumbered dairy cows by more than 3 to 1. By almost any standard, this has been a very rapid change. The number of dairy cows reached a peak about the mid–1940s and has been declining steadily ever since, whereas beef cows have been on an increasing trend since the 1930s (see Fig. 5.6).

2. An increasing proportion of slaughtered cattle is composed of grain-fed cattle. The slaughter of vealers and calves declined steadily,

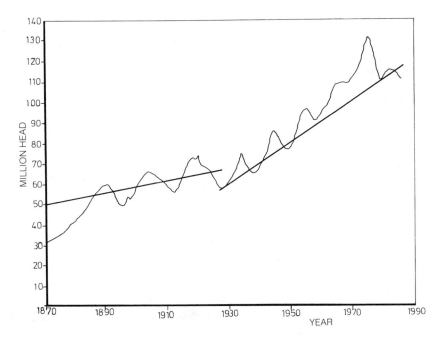

Fig. 5.4. Trends in number of cattle on farms, Jan. 1, 1870–1985. [Plotted by authors from USDA data and DeGraff (1960).]

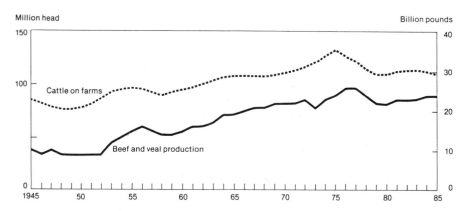

Fig. 5.5. Number of cattle and calves on farms Jan. 1, 1945–1985, and beef and veal production 1945–1985. [*Courtesy,* USDA Exten. Serv. (undated).]

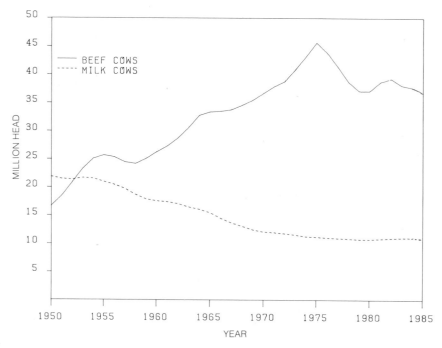

Fig. 5.6. Number of beef and milk cows on farms and ranches, Jan. 1, 1950–1985. (Plotted by authors from USDA data.)

and the slaughter of "grass-fat" cattle disappeared until a short period of relatively high grain prices in the mid 1970s temporarily halted that trend. Included in the increased numbers and proportion of cattle being grain fed are substantially more heifers than previously. Output of meat per head, of course, is increased substantially by holding cattle through the growing period and finishing them out on grain.

3. Improved breeding, feeding, and management are factors in increased productivity. The effects of these improvements show up in many ways, such as size of animal, conformation, carcass yield, yield of lean meat, feed efficiency, rate of gain, death loss, and percentage calf crop.

The net effect of these factors is not only an increasing trend in average dressed weight (Fig. 5.7), but also an improvement in beef quality. In 1980, approximately 80 percent of the total cattle slaughter was composed of grain-fed beef. It was half that much 35 years ago.

In an analysis of slaughter cattle prices, Franzmann (1967) calculated an average secular increase of $0.0063 per cwt per month for the period, Jan. 1921–Aug. 1967. This was based on monthly prices that

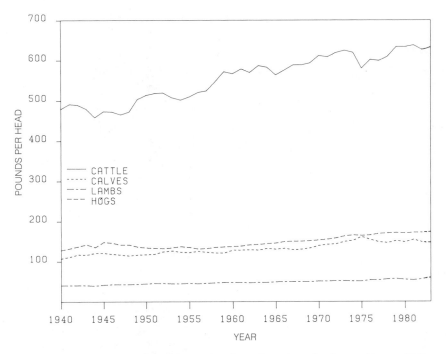

Fig. 5.7. Average dressed weight per head, cattle, calves, lambs, and hogs, 1940–1983. (Plotted by authors from USDA data.)

had been deflated—a process whereby the effects of inflation and deflation are removed. This long-run increase in price occurred during the time that the quantity of beef supplied (consumed) per person also was increasing. When prices increase simultaneously with quantity over a period of years, it is apparent that demand has increased, and at a faster rate than supply. Development occuring in the 1980s cast some uncertainty on the continuation of this trend.

Hogs—Secular Trends

The long-run trend in hog numbers makes an interesting comparison with that of cattle. As may be observed in Fig. 5.8, growth in the hog inventory was steadily upward (ignoring the effect of cyclical variations) from 1867 to the early 1920s. A comparison with the trend in cattle numbers (Fig. 5.2) shows that the rate of growth was about the same for both cattle and hogs up to that point and, furthermore, that the number of each species was not greatly different. A significant change occurred during the 1920s. The growth pattern for hogs be-

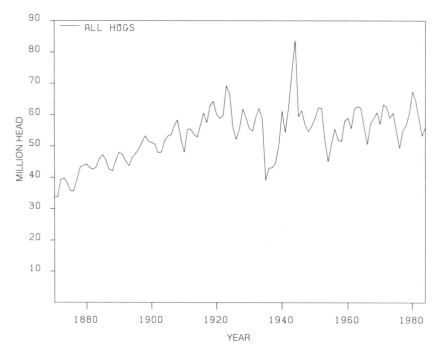

Fig. 5.8. Number of hogs on U.S. farms, Jan. 1, prior to 1962; Beginning 1962, the number on farms, Dec. 1. (Plotted by authors from USDA data.)

came irregular, with a severe drop during the drouth-depression period of the 1930s, a sharp increase during World War II, and a sharp decline following the Korean War of early 1950s. A secular trend line through the 1920–1984 period is essentially horizontal. It will be recalled that the rate of growth in cattle numbers increased during that period.

The long-time trend in pork production (this is tonnage of pork produced) shows a different picture (see Fig. 5.9). The drouth-depression effect and World War II effect can be logically ignored on the grounds that they were abnormal occurrences. The secular trend in pork production from 1900 to 1984 comes close to a linear trend with a growth rate of slightly less than 100,000,000 lb of pork per year. Even if one broke the trend around 1930 to obtain a better fit to the two separate periods, the trend during the latter definitely would be upward.

The apparent difference between the trend in pork production and hog numbers during the latter period is due to several factors. Improved breeding and production practices have increased productivity per head. In addition, improved feeding and management practices have speeded up the production and marketing process by finishing

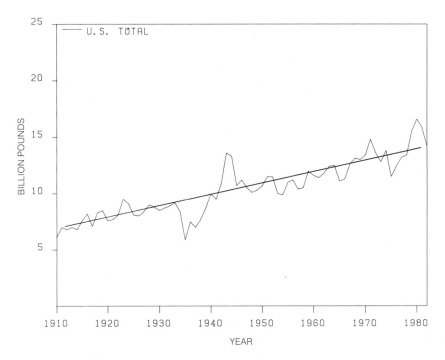

Fig. 5.9. Total pork production, dressed weight, 1910–1982. (Plotted by authors from USDA data.)

hogs at a lower age than formerly, i.e., increased rate of offturn. In spite of these increases in production, supplies of pork per person have trended slightly downward (due to human population increases) on a pork-excluding-lard basis (Fig. 5.10). This is the so-called "old consumption series" published by USDA until 1977. A new series of pork consumption "including lard" was initiated in 1977 and calculated for back years. That series shows a decided downward trend, largely as a result of the development of hogs with a progressively lower fat-to-lean ratio.

Hog prices over the long period have followed the general trend of cattle and lamb prices, and prices of all three species have followed the pattern of the "all commodity" wholesale price index (see Fig. 5.11). The effects of inflation and deflation, however, camouflage the trend in "real" prices. Figure 5.12 shows the trend in "real" hog prices, compared with prices of cattle and lambs (adjusted for price level changes). Visual appraisal of the secular trend may be made by ignoring the short-period ups and downs (which are cyclical variations). It is apparent that the trend has been persistently upward although the rate of

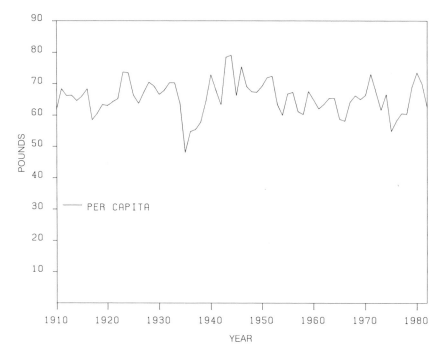

Fig. 5.10. Pork supplies (consumption) per capita, carcass weight, 1910–1982. (Plotted by authors from USDA data.)

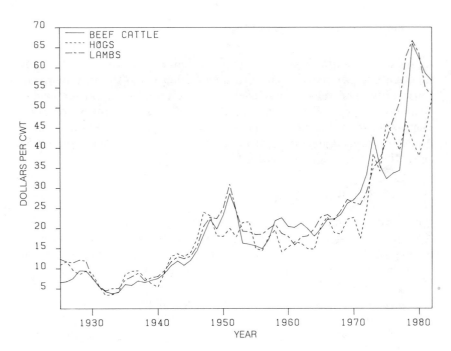

Fig. 5.11. Beef cattle prices compared with prices of hogs and lambs, 1925–1982. (Plotted by authors from USDA data.)

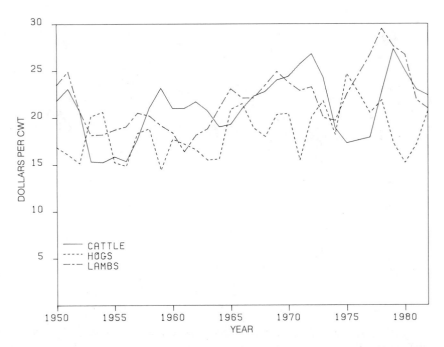

Fig. 5.12. Hog, cattle and lamb prices adjusted for price level changes, 1950–1983, 1967 = base year. (Plotted by authors from USDA data.)

increase was slight. Real prices increased an average of approximately $0.0025 per cwt per month until about 1960 when the rate increased noticeably. The recent increased rate is attributed to an increase in demand for pork. Producers have made significant improvements in the leanness and quality of pork, as will be pointed out in Chap. 6. Much promotional work has been done to increase the demand for pork. Their efforts have paid off.

Sheep—Secular Trends

The long-time pattern of growth in sheep inventory is shown in Fig. 5.13. The pattern illustrated here is a contrast to that of either cattle or hogs. Sheep numbers were substantially greater than cattle and slightly greater than hog numbers when annual records first became available (1867). The overall trend since 1867 may be described as irregular, with no decidedly general upward or downward tendency until World War II. At that time, inventories began a precipitous drop that continued until the 1950s. After a minor recovery, numbers again

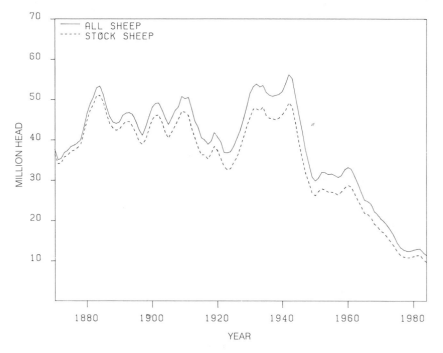

Fig. 5.13. Stock sheep and lambs on farms, Jan. 1, 1870–1983. (Plotted by authors from USDA data.)

turned downward. The number of sheep in the United States in 1984 was the lowest in more than 100 years.

The trend in total numbers conceals some definite changes within the sheep industry. For example, sheep numbers in the "native" sheep states declined generally throughout the period, whereas numbers increased in the western states until the 1930s. The drop during the 1940s hit all areas but was relatively greater in the western states. The reasons for this decline were varied, but the ones most usually cited were (1) the difficulty in obtaining labor, particularly sheepherders; (2) more attractive alternatives (in some cases, a more profitable alternative enterprise; in other cases, a less profitable enterprise but with offsetting noneconomic amenities); (3) problems in predator control (partially related to the labor problem); (4) difficulty in obtaining good quality breeding stock; (5) reductions in grazing permits on federal lands; and (6) general decline in demand for sheep meat following World War II, allegedly the result of unpleasant experience serving mutton to troops during the war.

Increases have been made in sheep productivity that have partially offset declining numbers, as shown in Fig. 5.14. Death losses have been reduced, the percentage lamb crop has improved, and average slaughter weight has increased. The latter has been accompanied by packer and merchandiser criticism and price discounts. Research by animal and meat scientists at Kansas State University, however, has shown that weight alone is not a valid criterion of lamb values. Improved meat-type lambs can be fed to heavier weights without undesirable marketing characteristics.

Increasing imports of lamb and mutton have also partially offset

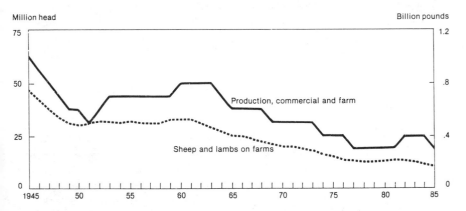

Fig. 5.14. Sheep numbers, lamb and mutton production, 1945–1985 (sheep and lambs on farms as of Jan. 1). [*Courtesy*, USDA Exten. Serv. (undated).]

declining U.S. production. During 1984, imported lamb and mutton amounted to slightly over 5 percent of U.S. lamb and mutton production. The importation of foreign wool and foreign fabrics, moreover, together with the increased domestic production of synthetic fibers, have kept competitive pressures on the domestic wool market.

The U.S. sheep industry appears to be at a critical point, if not necessarily a life-or-death matter. It would take a massive effort to turn production around to the extent that lamb again became generally available on a regular basis throughout the United States. The sheep industry is aware of the situation (Anon. 1976). In 1976, the American Sheep Producers Council was instrumental in developing a "Blueprint for Expansion." The rate of decrease in sheep numbers has tapered off, and a slight increase in sheep and lambs on farms and ranches were registered during 1980–1982 period, indicating a degree of success with the plan.

From a practical standpoint, lamb is a specialty product. The slump will not mark the end of the sheep industry. Lamb is preferred among certain people and in certain areas, thus assuring a market, however limited in volume.

CYCLICAL VARIATIONS

As mentioned earlier, cyclical variations are movements in livestock inventories and prices that tend to follow a pattern that repeats itself. A cycle must extend for more than one year. Livestock cycles have been observed since the late nineteenth century. The cyclical nature of the livestock industry may be observed in inventory numbers, in slaughter, and in prices. Coincident with cycles in the inventory are cyclial trends in prices. Typically, the latter are the inverse of inventory cycles, but the turning points do not occur at identical times. Analysts have used biological facts, economic theory, and statistical methods to explain the causes and behavior of cyclical movements. Before examining cycles of the three species, we will present a brief discussion of these analytical aspects.

Theory of Self-Generating Cycles. No two livestock cycles have been identical, but a remarkable similarity exists. This degree of consistency and uniformity suggests some underlying casual forces. There are underlying causes, no doubt, but analysts have never reached unanimous agreement on them. The major difference in opinion centers on whether the forces are self-generating within the industry (i.e., endogenous) or arise from forces outside the industry (i.e., exogenous). Analysts in the former camp hold that farmers' and ranchers' price expectations are the key.

For example, Walters (1965) indicated that in the case of cattle, "The industry seems to be seized periodically with 'spontaneous optimism.'" During these periods, usually following favorable prices, the growth rate of cattle numbers exceeds an equilibrium growth rate. Cattle numbers in the optimistic periods are increased by adding cows to the basic breeding herds and by keeping feeder cattle longer than usual, consequently to heavier weights. This increasing production finally exceeds the increasing demand, causing first slaughter prices and then feeder prices to decrease.

"With the advent of lower prices, the industry becomes subject to a kind of 'simultaneous pessimism.' The pessimistic cattle producers then reduce the size of their basic breeding herds (because they are less profitable) by selling cows from these herds and not replacing them with heifers. This adds even more to total production and further lowers slaughter prices. Feeders retain the cattle that they are feeding in hopes of better prices. However, after it becomes apparent that prices have stabilized at the lower levels, the fed-cattle producer must then sell his cattle at heavier weights than usual. These cattle are heavier because they have been retained for a longer time on a concentrated ration. Again this adds to the already towering production." The hog and sheep industries face similar experience with similar results, except for the length of the period.

The notion of self-generating cycles has prompted various attempts to explain them in terms of economic behavior. One such effort is the "cobweb" theorem, with original work done by Ezekiel (1938) and later applications developed by Harlow (1962) and by Ehrich (1966). The cobweb theorem provides an explanation of how, under certain conditions, prices and quantities supplied and demanded move around the hypothesized equilibrium point specified by the intersection of demand and supply curves as producers and consumers react to price changes. One of the conditions inherent in the theorem is a time lag in the response of production (quantity) change to price change. The livestock industry seems to provide such an example. In the case of hogs, it takes a year or more before a production change gets on the market as a result of a price change. With cattle, the lag is considerably greater.

An abbreviated description of the theorem is as follows. It may be assumed that a system at one point in time is in disequilibrium. In the real world, this would not be unusual. We assume a given supply curve, SS, and a demand curve, DD, as in Fig. 5.15, with price out of equilibrium at point A. This represents a price at which producers are willing to produce a considerably larger quantity, as would be indicated by a

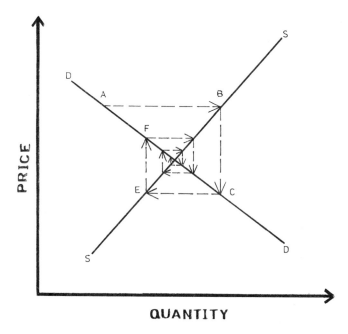

Fig. 5.15. "Cobweb" price and output movements.

horizontal movement to the right until intersection with the supply curve (point B). With a sufficient time lag, it may be assumed that producers would respond in that manner. This output will be taken by consumers, however, only at a substantially lower price, indicated by a vertical movement downward until intersection with the demand curve (point C). At that price, however, producers are off their supply curve and, in an effort to get back on it, they reduce production (to point E). Consumers, however, will pay a higher price (point F) for that quantity, and at the higher price producers will increase production; and so the system goes off on another round. The cobweb appearance is apparent, and hence the name. As drawn in Fig. 5.15, the movements are converging toward an equilibrium. It can be shown very easily that, by changing the shape of the curves (a rough indication or relative degree of elasticity), the movements can be changed to either an explosive or a divergent system.

In a somewhat sophisticated model, Ehrich (1966) concludes that the cobweb theorem is an inadequate model of dynamic economic behavior for either the hog or cattle economy. He states:

The characteristic behavior of production and prices suggests that harmonic motion is an appropriate model of cycle-generating forces in the U.S. beef economy. Essentially, true harmonic motion involves stimulus, response, and 'feed-back' which serves to alter the stimulus after a fixed delay. It appears that the physical characteristics of beef-cattle growth, uncertainty regarding future prices, and producers' behavior in the face of uncertainty, combine to produce harmonic behavior in annual fluctuations in cattle prices and numbers. In particular, producers respond to prices (stimulus) by changing the rate of planned production (increasing or decreasing the breeding herd incrementally), the change in production is realized after a delay (physical growth limitations), and the price stimulus is altered by realized production (prices are unilaterally affected by predetermined supplies).

Statistical estimates of the relationships among prices, inventory adjustments, and annual production of beef were consistent with the basic model. Of primary importance, the evidence supports the view that producers respond incrementally to deviations of price from equilibrium and it serves to deny the existence of a conventional supply function for beef cattle. For, of course, the conventional concept of a supply function presupposes that producers adjust to a new level of planned output which is independent of the present level of output, in response to a change in price levels, rather than seeking to change the rate of planned output from current levels.

Parenthetically, other evidence supports harmonic motion as a model of behavior for the hog economy as well as for the cattle economy. The cobweb theorem, which depends on the existence of a conventional supply curve, is then an inadequate model of dynamic economic behavior in either the hog or cattle economy (Ehrich, 1966).

Exogenous Factors Affecting Livestock Cycles. Others have contended that cycles are generated by stimuli outside the livestock industry. Among the factors cited are wars, social, political, and economic problems, situation with other livestock cycles, changes in taste and preference, inflationary and deflationary price trends, and variation in feed supplies (Hopkins, 1926; Burmeister, 1949; and Simpson and Farris, 1982). Most emphasis has been placed on the availability of feed, including, of course, range and pasture forage, especially in the case of beef cattle and sheep. There is some historical evidence that droughts have coincided with downturns in cattle numbers on occasion, but this is not true of all cycles.

In the case of cattle, Breimyer (1954) sums up the situation as follows:

The feed supply may be an important factor at all stages of the cattle cycle. Some think it is. Approximate overall indices of range and pasture condition and crop feed supply have been included in correlation analyses of cattle production, occasionally with positive results. As a rule, though, the supply of feed is not a restraining influence at early stages of expansion because any increase in feed prices is far overshadowed by soaring prices of cattle. Only after the typical cyclical decline in cattle prices has begun are feed supplies and prices watched more closely. From then on the supply of feed can be a controlling factor.

DeGraff (1960) recognizes the effects of livestock and feed prices in generating cycles but relates them to the biological timetable of animal reproduction. For example, he refers to cattle cycles as follows:

> While such influences as a change in demand or in feed supplies may initate a cycle, they do not explain the sequence of events which follows. The reason why a cycle follows its standardized pattern is found, not in economics, but in biology. Changes in cattle production, whatever caused their beginnings, are converted into a cyclical pattern by the natural biology of the cattle species.
>
> The life-span of cattle is long. They reproduce and grow slowly. If a bred heifer is kept for breeding instead of being sent to slaughter, her first calf does not reach the market until nearly three years later. This is indeed a long delay in economic response. To say that cycles in cattle originate largely within the industry itself is not to say that producers are either ignorant or indifferent to the consequences of their decisions. The slow moving biology of the species is the factor that extends the period between decision and consequence and leads to the patterned nature of the cattle cycle.

Cattle—Cyclical Variations

Cattle Inventory Cycles. Many economists and members of the cattle industry commonly define a full cycle as the period from one low point to the next low point in numbers. This definition may be used for other species of livestock as well. Over the entire period since cattle cycles were observed, cycles have averaged about 12 years in length, but earlier cycles were longer than later ones. Each cycle may be divided into two phases: (1) the upward or accumulation phase, and (2) the downward or liquidation phase. Even a casual observation of Fig. 5.2 reveals the upswings and downswings in cattle numbers. It also can be seen that the peak of each succeeding cycle was higher than the preceding peak and each trough higher than the preceding trough until the peak of 1981, which fell below the preceding peak (Table 5.1). Figure 5.16 is an alternative means of illustrating the cycles; here they are shown separately. Cycles may be observed in inventory numbers, in slaughter, and in prices.

Hasbargen and Egerston (1976) suggested that upswings and downswings of cattle cycles may be separated into three stages: (1) turn-

Table 5.1. Periods of Expansion and Contraction in Cattle Numbers for All Cattle and Calves on U.S. Farms, 1896–1984.

Year	No. on hand Jan 1. of indicated year (1,000 head)	Increase or decrease during year (1,000 head)	Increase or decrease during year (%)	Period increase or decrease (%)
		Accumulation		
1896	49,205	1,242	2.5	
1897	50,447	2,421	4.8	
1898	52,868	3,059	5.8	
1899	55,927	3,812	6.8	
1900	59,739	2,837	4.7	
1901	62,576	1,842	2.9	
1902	64,418	1,586	2.5	
1903	66,004	438	0.7	
Period total		17,347		35.0
		Liquidation		
1904	66,442	−331	−0.5	
1905	66,111	−1,102	−1.7	
1906	65,009	−1,255	−1.9	
1907	63,754	−1,765	−2.8	
1908	61,989	−1,215	−2.0	
1909	60,774	−1,781	−2.9	
1910	58,993	−1,768	−3.0	
1911	57,225	−1,550	−2.7	
Period total		−10,767		−16.2
		Accumulation		
1912	55,675	917	1.6	
1913	56,592	2,869	5.1	
1914	59,461	4,388	7.4	
1915	63,849	3,589	5.6	
1916	67,438	3,541	5.3	
1917	70,979	2,061	2.9	
Period total		17,365		31.2
		Liquidation		
1918	73,040	−946	−1.3	
1919	72,094	−1,694	−2.3	
1920	70,400	−1,686	−2.4	
1921	68,714	81	0.1	
1922	68,795	−1,249	−1.8	
1923	67,546	−1,550	−2.3	
1924	65,996	−2,623	−4.0	
1925	63,373	−2,797	−4.4	
1926	60,576	−2,398	−4.0	
1927	58,178	−856	−1.5	
Period total		−15,718		−21.5

(continued)

Table 5.1. (*continued*)

Year	No. on hand Jan 1. of indicated year (1,000 head)	Increase or decrease during year (1,000 head)	Increase or decrease during year (%)	Period increase or decrease (%)
		Accumulation		
1928	57,322	1,555	2.7	
1929	58,877	2,126	3.6	
1930	61,003	2,027	3.3	
1931	63,003	2,771	4.4	
1932	65,801	4,479	6.8	
1933	70,280	4,089	5.8	
Period total		17,047		29.7
		Liquidation		
1934	74,369	−5,523	−7.4	
1935	68,846	− 999	−1.5	
1936	67,847	−1,749	−2.6	
1937	66,098	− 849	−1.3	
Period total		−9,120		−12.3
		Accumulation		
1938	65,249	780	1.2	
1939	66,029	2,280	3.5	
1940	68,309	3,446	5.0	
1941	71,755	4,270	6.0	
1942	76,025	5,179	6.8	
1943	81,204	4,130	5.1	
1944	85,334	239	0.3	
Period total		20,324		31.1
		Liquidation		
1945	85,573	−3,338	−3.9	
1946	82,235	−1,681	−2.0	
1947	80,554	−3,383	−4.2	
1948	77,171	− 341	−0.4	
Period total		−8,743		−10.2
		Accumulation		
1949	76,830	1,133	1.5	
1950	77,963	4,120	5.3	
1951	82,083	5,989	7.3	
1952	88,072	6,169	7.0	
1953	94,241	1,438	1.5	
1954	95,679	913	1.0	
Period total		19,762		25.7
		Liquidation		
1955	96,592	− 692	−0.7	
1956	95,900	−3,040	−3.2	
1957	92,860	−1,684	−1.8	
Period total		−5,416		−5.6

Table 5.1. (*continued*)

Year	No. on hand Jan 1. of indicated year (1,000 head)	Increase or decrease during year (1,000 head)	Increase or decrease during year (%)	Period increase or decrease (%)
		Accumulation		
1958	91,176	2,146	2.4	
1959	93,322	2,914	3.1	
1960	96,236	764	0.8	
1961	97,000	3,369	3.5	
1962	100,369	4,119	4.1	
1963	104,488	3,415	3.3	
1964	107,903	1,097	1.0	
Period total		17,824		19.5
		Liquidation		
1965	109,000	− 138	−0.1	
1966	108,862	− 217	−0.2	
Period total		−355		−0.3
		Accumulation		
1967	108,783	588	0.5	
1968	109,371	644	0.6	
1969	110,015	2,354	2.1	
1970	112,369	2,209	2.0	
1971	114,578	3,284	2.9	
1972	117,862	3,677	3.1	
1973	121,539	6,249	5.1	
1974	127,788	4,240	3.3	
Period total		23,245		21.4
		Liquidation		
1975	132,028	−4,048	−3.1	
1976	127,980	−5,170	−4.0	
1977	122,810	−6,435	−5.2	
1978	116,375	−5,511	−4.7	
Period total		−26,164		−16.0
		Accumulation		
1979	110,864	328	.3	
1980	111,192	3,129	2.8	
1981	114,321	1,283	1.1	
Period total		4,740		4.3
		Liquidation		
1982	115,604	− 603	−.5	
1983	115,001	−1,301	−1.1	
1984	113,700	−3,951	−3.4	
1985	109,749			
Period total		−5,855		

(*continued*)

Table 5.1. (continued)

		Summary	
Years (inclusive)	No. years	Increase or decrease (1,000 head)	Percent
Accumulation phases			
1896–1903	8	17,237	35.0
1912–1917	6	17,365	31.2
1928–1933	6	17,047	29.7
1938–1944	7	20,324	31.1
1949–1954	6	19,762	25.7
1958–1964	7	17,824	19.5
1967–1974	8	23,245	21.4
1979–1981	3	4,740	4.3
Liquidation phases			
1904–1911	8	−10,767	−16.2
1918–1927	10	−15,718	−21.5
1934–1937	4	− 9,120	−12.3
1945–1948	4	− 8,743	−10.2
1955–1957	3	− 5,416	−5.6
1965–1966	2	− 355	−0.3
1975–1978	4	−21,164	−16.0
1982–			

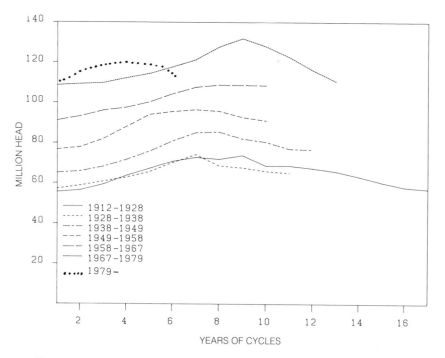

Fig. 5.16. Cattle on farms by cycles. (Plotted by authors from USDA data.)

around, (2) rapid growth, and (3) deceleration. Separating cycles into three stages and associating the stages with certain economic and behavioral factors provides a better understanding of cattle as well as other livestock cycles. Table 5.2 summarizes the general characteristics of the three stages. It should be pointed out that the upswing (accumulation) phase in cattle inventory includes the turnaround and rapid-growth stages and the first part of deceleration under the Hasbargen-Egerston system. The remaining part of the deceleration stage represents the liquidation phase in the two-phase system.

There was some evidence that cattle inventory cycles were dampening until the liquidation of 1975–78. In previous cycles, the liquidation phase had shortened, and the magnitude of decline had lessened. The consequences of a cyclical variation have been serious enough to warrant a brief review of the characteristics of past cycles.

The seven cycles that have occurred since 1896 are shown graphically in Fig. 5.16. Annual data for the years 1896–1985 are shown in Table 5.1, with a period divided into alternating accumulation and liquidation phases. Except for the seventh (1967–1978) and the eighth cycle (1979–present), two characteristics of the accumulation phases are apparent: (1) The length of accumulation phases has been remarkably uniform. Accumulation lasted six years during three cycles, seven years during two cycles, and eight years during two cycles—a range of six to eight years. (2) The number of head of cattle added to the inventory was also remarkably uniform. All were within the range of 17.2 to 21.2 million head. The percentage increase in cattle has declined with successive cycles, ranging from 35 percent in the first cycle down to

Table 5.2. Characteristics of the Turnaround, Rapid Growth, and Deceleration Stages of Cattle Cycles.

Item	Stage		
	Turnaround	Rapid Growth	Deceleration
Slaughter relative to inventory	Normal	Low	Increasing
Animal numbers	Stabilize then increase at normal rate	Increasing rapidly	1. Increasing at sharply declining rate 2. Actual drop
Cattle prices	Recover from low during deceleration	At their highest	Relatively low
Returns to producers	About average	Above average	Below average, especially to feeder producers

Source: Developed by authors from information in Hasbargen and Egertson (1976).

19.5 percent in the sixth. These figures follow from the fact that a fairly constant increase in absolute number has been added to an increasing base.

Until the unusually severe reduction of 1975–1978, liquidation phases were characterized by (1) a declining trend in the length of the phase; (2) a declining trend in the number of head liquidated; and (3) a declining trend in the percentage of the inventory liquidated. During early cycles, the liquidation phases lasted eight to ten years and in later cycles, two to three years. During early cycles, the liquidations amounted to 11 to 16 million head, whereas in 1965–66 it was less than 1/2 million head. Liquidation during that cycle was so small it can hardly be called a true downturn. Considering limitations on the accuracy of reported inventories (reported numbers are estimates, not actual counts), it appears that cattle numbers about leveled off in 1965 and held approximately constant until 1969, then started another accumulation phase that ended in 1974.

In 1978/1979, a relatively strong consumer demand for red meat while supply was relatively low gave cattle feeders and cow–calf operators their highest returns in many years. This resulted in the rebuilding of cow herds during 1979, and beef supplies during that year were the lowest since 1973. A stagnant demand for beef caused by economic and climatic problems during the 1980–1981 period—including drought, high interest rates, rising feed costs, and surpluses of poultry and other meat supplies—put the beef industry under a severe cost-price squeeze. These pressures eventually put an end to the accumulation phase in 1982, making it the shortest in history (only three years). Furthermore, the number of head added was the smallest on record (see Table 5.1).

Cattle Price Cycles. As stated earlier, price cycles are typically the inverse of inventory cycles (as numbers advance, prices tend to decline and vice versa), but the turning points do not occur at identical times. Studies of cattle cycles have shown that the turning point in beef production (slaughter) lags the turning point in cattle numbers by about two years (McCoy, 1959; Ehrich, 1966). Some lag is to be expected. For example, if cattle numbers are declining and prices rising, the decline in numbers will be halted by a withholding of heifers from market (the heifers to be retained for breeding purposes). This withholding will initiate an increase in inventory, but another immediate effect will be a further reduction in already-declining meat supplies and a continued strengthening of prices. When it becomes apparent from the build-up in cattle numbers that beef supplies are (or will be) increasing, prices turn downward, but this does not occur as soon as the build-up begins.

The turning point in cyclical changes in cow numbers also lags the turning point in feeder cattle prices by zero to two years (Ehrich, 1966). Thus, beef production (slaughter) turning points lag prices by zero to four years. The reverse situation has occurred with increasing phases of the cattle cycle.

The inverse relation between cattle numbers and prices may be seen in Fig. 5.17. During war periods (World War I, World War II, the Korean War, the Vietnamese War) and the period 1972–1974 associated with heavy USSR grain purchases, cattle prices moved upward along with increasing cattle numbers because of exceptionally strong inflationary pressures. At other times, however, prices and numbers generally moved in opposite directions. The cyclical nature of cattle prices is more readily observable when prices are adjusted for effects of price-level changes. When prices are deflated, as shown in Fig. 5.12, it should be noted that the price line here still shows the effect of a long-time gentle upward trend and the effect of seasonal ups and downs. The latter give the price line its jagged, saw-toothed appearance. In calcu-

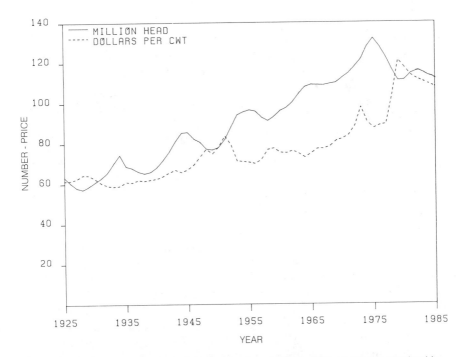

Fig. 5.17. Number of cattle on U.S. Farms, Jan. 1, 1925–1985, and price received by farmers for cattle. (Plotted by authors from USDA data.)

lating the true cycle, both secular and seasonal trend effects are statistically removed.

Franzman (1967) reported that, "On the average, the adjusted price paid decreased $2.35 per cwt as the industry progressed from a peak to a trough in the cycle. Conversely, when the industry went from trough to a peak, price increased by $2.35 per cwt."

The alternating economic booms and busts that have accompanied cattle cycles have been a matter of great concern in the cattle industry. Usually, members of the industry subscribe to the proposition that one of the functions of price in a market economy is to guide production. The biological lag, however, together with lack of precise market knowledge and other market imperfections, have resulted in drastic variations in income—frequently from prosperity to bankruptcy in individual cases. For a number of years, the industry has championed self-discipline as a means of smoothing drastic price variations.

To handle uncertainty and instability in production and profits more successfully, cattle industry trade associations and university and government researchers have developed a set of warning signals, or indicators. These can provide individual producers and the industry as a whole with some insight into the future direction of a cycle and assist them in adjusting/developing their production and marketing strategies accordingly. For example, signals may indicate possible turning points in cycles and help predict certain price movements. The seven indicators that are considered most important, and their significance, are shown in Table 5.3. It should be noted that no single indicator can provide sufficient information on the direction of a cycle. Many observers believe that information from several of them can enable producers to formulate a relatively accurate expectation of the direction of inventory and price cycles.

Hogs—Cyclical Variations

Over the years, hog inventories, slaughter, and prices have followed cyclical patterns (see Figs. 5.8 and 5.12). A comparison of Fig. 5.2 with Fig. 5.8 indicates that cycles in hog production have been less regular than in cattle production. Prior to World War I, the cycles occurred with greater regularity than they have ever since. Hog cycles average about four years, and this cycle holds whether based on earlier or later years, with averages of two years of expansion and two years of liquidation. The period 1941–1984 encompassed nine complete cycles (Fig. 5.18), which varied from three to seven years. It is obvious that the cycle has limited usefulness for market planning or price forecasting,

Table 5.3. Warning Signals of Direction of the Cattle Cycle.

Signal/indicator	Significance
Year of cycle	May indicate time of price break; in normal cycles, fifth to seventh year of expansion.
Percent of annual expansion in total cattle and calf inventory	If growth rate exceeds 2 percent for two to three years in a row, oversupply of beef and price problems are likely to arise.
Percent of annual expansion in cow inventory	If a cow herd is increasing at more than a 2-percent rate for several years, there is risk of overproduction and imminent price decline.
Ratio of annual cattle and calf slaughter to Jan. 1 inventory	Cattle herd is increasing too fast if this ratio drops below 37 percent; low prices would not be far off.
Ratio of annual cattle and calf slaughter to previous year's calf crop	A ratio below or above 88 percent warns that the herd is building too fast or too slow, respectively.
Ratio of annual cow slaughter to Jan. 1 inventory of all cows (i.e. beef cows plus dairy cows)	A ratio of 14 percent or less indicates expansion. A ratio less than 13 percent indicates overexpansion and signals price problems ahead.
Ratio of cow and heifer slaughter to steer slaughter	A ratio of 90 percent or less indicates that too many heifers are being held back for herd expansion.

Source: Developed by authors from information in Beale *et al.* (1983) and industry sources.

but when used with supplemental information, a knowledge of hog cycles can be a useful tool.

Hog cycles have been characterized to some extent by alternating major and minor peaks; that is, there is a tendency for a high peak to be followed by a low peak. This may be seen in the price line of Figs. 5.8 and 5.12, especially during the decades from 1890 to 1940. It shows up again in the first two inventory cycles shown in Fig. 5.18.

Figure 5.19 illustrates that prices and production move in opposite directions. Because of the relatively inelastic nature of the demand for pork (i.e., high price flexibilities), the variation in prices is proportionately greater than the variation in production. In other words, a given change in quantity produced (and marketed) will precipitate a relatively greater change in price.

The theory of the cyclical nature of hog production and prices is based on the supposition that producers respond to prices and prices

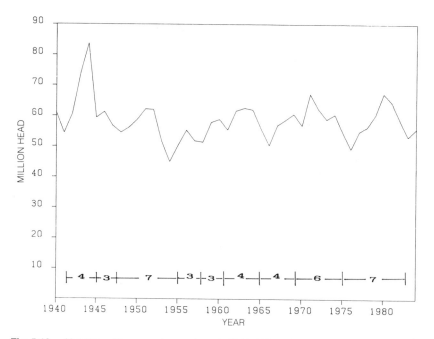

Fig. 5.18. Number of hogs on farms Jan. 1, 1940–1984 with length of cycle indicated; beginning 1969, the number on farms Dec. 1 of previous year. (Plotted by authors from USDA data.)

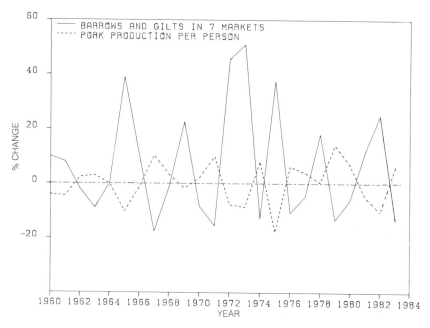

Fig. 5.19. Changes in hog prices and pork production, 1960–1983. (Plotted by authors from USDA data.)

reflect quantity produced—an interaction process. When hog prices are relatively high (profitable), farmers respond by increasing production. As production increases, prices tend to decline. Inherent lags in the biology of the production process, delays in the reactions of producers, and imperfect knowledge of the overall situation result in overreaction—an overshooting of equilibrium on both upturn and downturn.

The "hog–corn price ratio," usually shortened to hog–corn ratio, has been used for many years as an indicator of profitability in hog production and as a tool in forecasting turning points in production and price cycles. The hog–corn ratio is the ratio between the price of hogs and the price of corn, i.e., the price per hundredweight of live hogs divided by the price per bushel of corn. The quotient (ratio) actually represents the number of bushels of corn that are equal in value to 100 lb of hog:

$$\frac{\text{Price per cwt live hogs}}{\text{Price per bu corn}}$$

It is necessary to specify (1) the grade and weight of hogs, (2) the grade of corn, and (3) the market for which the prices apply. The needed information is usually easy to obtain and calculations are simple. For many years, the USDA has calculated and reported hog–corn ratios (steer–corn ratios are also reported). One that was widely used on a weekly basis as representative of the Corn Belt was the ratio for No. 1–3 hogs (220 lb) and No. 2 yellow corn at Chicago markets. Since closing of the Chicago public terminal market (hogs in May 1970; cattle and sheep in August 1971), USDA has used Omaha prices—a weighted average price of barrows and gilts and a simple average of No. 2 yellow corn. Both hog–corn and steer–corn price ratios are published weekly in USDA's *Livestock, Meat, Wool Market News*. In other publications, average hog–corn ratios are quoted for the U.S. farm level and for designated areas. Any producer can calculate a hog–corn ratio by using applicable market prices for his location.

The hog–corn ratio is only a rough approximation of the profitability of raising hogs. It is based on the notion that feed is the most important production cost and that corn is the most important feed. This undoubtedly is the case, but it does not reflect the situation as well as it did in former years since corn (or for that matter, any grain used in the ration) now comprises a smaller proportion of total production costs.

The hog–corn ratio in recent years has averaged around 18. Prior to World War II, it averaged about 12. The records show that in this earlier period a ratio higher than 12 tended to induce an expansion in hog production; a ratio less than 12 induced a cutback in production—

with a lag in both cases. Analyses typically compare, for example, the number of sows farrowed in the spring with the hog–corn ratio during the previous fall. At that time, the ratio was a reliable indicator of the direction of change in farrowing (Harolow, 1962), a statistic observable in Fig. 5.20. In the upper part of the chart, a horizontal line is drawn at a ratio of about 12, which was the average for the period shown— 1924 to 1960. The actual fall hog–corn ratio is plotted as it varied above and below this average. When above average, the area is cross-hatched; when below, it is left blank. The lower part of the chart shows change in sow farrowing during the spring to follow. It is readily apparent that above-average fall hog–corn ratios were followed by increases in the number of sows farrowed the next spring, and vice versa for periods of below-average hog–corn ratios. The logic of this type of analysis is that it is not the absolute price of hogs or corn that is associated with changes in the number produced, but the relation between prices of hogs and corn.

In recent years, the relationship between the hog–corn ratio and sow farrowings has not been as consistent as formerly. This is due in part to the declining relative importance of grain in the economics of production, as mentioned above. In addition, government price-support programs have tended to reduce (but not eliminate) variations in corn prices that formerly were associated with variations in production. Another factor is the changing structural characteristics of the hog industry. Many small producers still raise hogs, but the trend is toward larger and fewer operators. The investment required in larger and more specialized units makes those operators more inclined to maintain production near the optimum levels designed for their unit. Producers still make some adjustments in hog production according to the degree of profitability, but output is not as sensitive to relative changes in corn prices as in former years. There is evidence that producers now respond more than formerly to absolute hog-price and corn-price changes. It is also likely that progressive producers attempt to gear production to long-run expectations of supply-and-demand conditions.

Sheep—Cyclical Variations

A semblance of cyclical movements can be seen in Fig. 5.13, although they are not as obvious as in the case of cattle. Prior to World War II, there were seven discernible cycles, with an average length of about 10 years. The sheep cycle is longer than that of hogs, but shorter than that of cattle, a logical difference in view of the biological timetable of sheep relative to the other species.

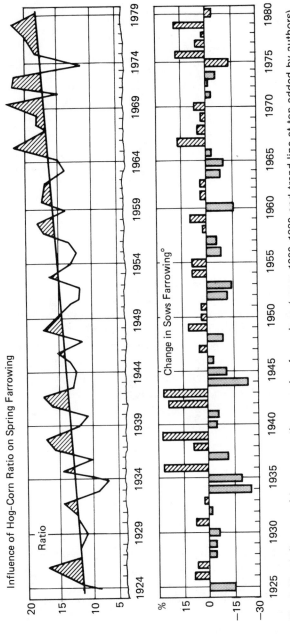

Fig. 5.20. Influence of hog corn ratio on spring farrowings (years 1960–1980 and trend line at top added by authors). (*Courtesy*, USDA.)

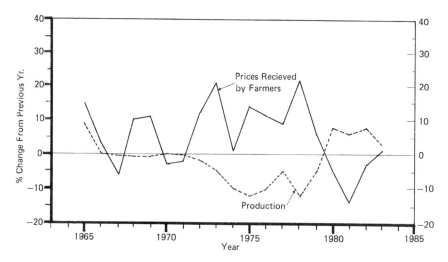

Fig. 5.21. Lamb production and prices. (Plotted by authors from USDA data.)

The rather drastic changes in sheep numbers since World War II have virtually obliterated cyclical trends. Nevertheless, the changes in production are reflected in corresponding price movements (see Fig. 5.21). If domestic production continues to decline and the importation of lamb increases, variation in domestic production will have less and less influence on prices—except when superior quality of domestically produced lamb may uphold a specialty market. For the foreseeable future, pronounced or definite cyclical movements are not likely, but variation in domestic production will continue to be the major factor offsetting prices.

SEASONAL VARIATIONS

As defined earlier, seasonal movements, or variations, are those that follow a more or less uniform pattern within the period of a year. Seasonal price movements are a direct reflection of seasonality in marketings and, to a lesser degree, seasonality in demand. Seasonality in marketings is related to biological factors and management practices. The latter are partially a matter of habit but more importantly are related to production costs.

Some classes of livestock have a relatively pronounced and consistent seasonal price pattern; some do not. It does not follow that the producer who adjusts his program to hit the seasonal high price will automatically maximize his profits. Some may be able to make profitable adjustments. For others, cost of production increases may more than offset higher prices. The producer must know the seasonality of his costs as well as the seasonality of prices.

Some producers may view prices with greater uncertainty in particular years. Even if future prices were certain, however, farmers and ranchers would still respond differently to given price situations because of differences in the amount and kind of resources available. Seasonal patterns can be broad guides in planning an individual business or marketing pogram. A producer can alter his marketing program to take advantage of certain favorable price periods without affecting the general seasonal pattern. If a large number of producers make the same adjustment to a seasonal trend, however, they may find the seasonal pattern changing. It will be shown later that such pattern changes have occurred.

Use of Index Numbers.   It will be noted in the following discussion of seasonal movements that the data are presented as index numbers. This is a particularly useful device since it can be used for both prices and production. It is possible to calculate average seasonal price patterns in dollars, and this sometimes is done, but the price level can change rather rapidly even though the pattern of movement may not change; in this case, calculations based on dollars would be of limited use. Conversion of data to index numbers is not a difficult process. Reconversion of index numbers to dollars is also a simple calculation, so that once the indices have been developed, they may be applied regardless of price level changes. If the seasonal pattern changes, then, of course, a new set of indices must be calculated.

Indices are convenient ways of showing the combined pattern of a large number of seasons. An average month is given an index of 100. High months then will have indices that are greater than 100, such as 105, 110, or 125. Months in which the seasonal lows occur will have indices of less than 100. One can get an idea of how to use a particular seasonal index by looking at a graph of the index, of which Fig. 5.22 is an example. On this graph the horizontal straight line represents an average (base line) for the entire year. In other words, the indices for the months of the year are all added together and divided by 12. This value is called 100 merely as a base to compare the indices for other months. The actual value of the index for each month is shown by the line going up or down from month to month. This is called the seasonal trend line, or, simply, the seasonal index.

Seasonal trends may be approximated simply by calculating a monthly average as a percent of overall average. There is a superior

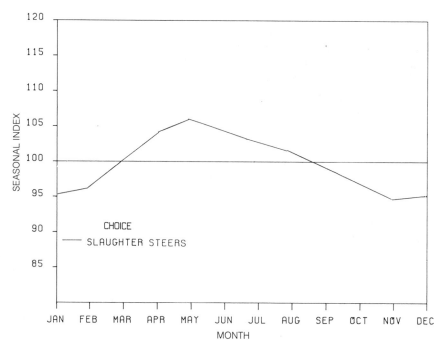

Fig. 5.22. Seasonal variation in prices of choice slaughter steers, 900–1,100 lb, Omaha, 1977–1982.

method used by many economists and analysts, however, that calculates the seasonal index as the 12-month moving average. Purcell (1979) indicated that this method, in addition to its simplicity, tends to remove cyclical and trend movements from the data, and, hence, to isolate seasonal movements. The following are the steps used to obtain seasonal indices with the centered 12-month moving-average method:

1. Arrange monthly prices from several years in chronological array. For example, the 72 price observations from a six-year data set are arranged from 1 to 72, where number 1 represents price in January of the first year and number 72 is the December observation of the sixth year.

2. Calculate a centered 12-month moving average of the data. (Readers may wish to consult an elementary statistics book for the steps used in calculating this.)

3. Divide each monthly price by the corresponding moving average to obtain an index value for each month.

4. Calculate the seasonal index by averaging the monthly indices for each month. For example, with 72 observations, only 60 monthly in-

dices will result, five for each month of the year, because the 12-month moving-average technique results in losing six observations at the beginning of the series and six at the end. For each month, the five indices are divided by 5 to obtain the month's average seasonal index.

Some analysts supplement the seasonal index with some measure of its uniformity or distribution, e.g., by reporting the standard deviation (S.D.) of the distribution of monthly indices around their mean, thus allowing more confidence in describing the trend. Two-thirds of the monthly seasonal indices are included above and below the average within one S.D. A band representing the S.D. may be drawn around the seasonal trend line. The width of the band gives some idea of the reliability that can be placed in a given seasonal trend. Other things being equal, the narrower the band, the more reliable the seasonal trend; that is, if the band is quite narrow, one can expect future prices to vary only slightly from the trend line.

Although a seasonal index gives an indication of the changes that can be expected throughout the year, a more direct application is made in estimating prices for some future month (for example) on the basis of current prices. The estimate is obtained by dividing the current price by the index for the current month and multiplying the results by the index for the future month. For example, if the present price for feeder steers is $65.00 per cwt and the current index is 92, then the estimated price three months from now (when the seasonal index is 105) would be

$$\frac{\$65.00}{92} \times 105 = \$74.18$$

This method of forecasting, of course, depends on the absence of disturbances that might seriously alter the general price level, the supply, or the demand situation and could lead to erroneous results in making estimates during times when conditions are changing rapidly.

Cattle—Seasonal Variations

The marketing of calves reaches a peak during the fall months at the close of the grazing season. The marketing of cull cows occurs at about the same time that farmers and ranchers cull their herds during roundups for calf weaning. These events are related to biological processes associated with the cow-calf production programs as well as the decline of range and pasture forage growth. As a rule, calf prices and cull cow prices are seasonally low during the period of heavy marketings.

Owners, of course, may hold their cull cows and calves for later sale, or they may sell them before the normal close of the range and pasture season. Some owners indeed do vary the time of sale, but most do not; they market about the same time each year from habit. The decision of those who do not rests on a market analysis of expected price changes versus associated costs and their effect on net profit. Herein lies the basis for our concern with seasonal analysis.

Choice Slaughter Steers. The seasonal price pattern for choice slaughter steers (900–1100 lb) at Omaha is shown in Fig. 5.22. The pattern shows a tendency for price strength during the spring and summer months and weakness during the fall months. It must be noted, however, that this pattern is relatively weak. The extent of variation (the amplitude) above the average line (i.e., the index = 100 line) at its highest point during May amounts to only 7 percentage points, and the variation below the average line at the lowest point during the period of weakness is just 9 percentage points. It can also be shown that choice-slaughter-steer prices in recent years have exhibited a weak, irregular seasonal tendency. Since little confidence can be placed in this seasonal trend, it is of limited use as a marketing tool. The pattern was influenced considerably by highly unstable prices during the 1973–75 period. The continued expansion of commercial feedlots, with a strong incentive for year-round feeding, tends to level out marketings. There is little doubt that this trend will continue, and with the leveling, there will be less irregularity in price movements and at the same time a reduction in the amplitude of seasonal trends.

The current pattern differs substantially from earlier periods. Wilson and Riley (1950), using the 1924–1941 period, reported a seasonal weakening of prices through spring and early summer, with prices declining to an index of about 94 in June. Their analysis showed a seasonal recovery from the June low to a high of 105.6 in mid-November. This pattern proved to be comparatively reliable at that time, and earlier. Prior to the era of commercial feedlots the customary procedure was to graze feeder cattle until the end of the grazing season. Some were slaughtered at that time as grass-fat cattle; the remainder went into feedlots—usually in the Corn Belt. The length of feeding period was geared to the quality of the cattle. So-called "plain" cattle were fed for the shortest period, and their marketings were bunched to take place just prior to the marketing of the next higher grade, and so on to the highest. Thus, the heaviest seasonal marketings and corresponding lowest seasonal prices for successively higher grades came in successive waves through the spring and summer. With the passing of marketing peaks for the particular grades, price recovery would begin. The peak for plain cattle would come in the spring or early summer and next would come the peaks for successively higher grades. This is a matter of only historical interest now, but it does illustrate the relationship between seasonality in marketings and prices. With present conditions tending to level out marketings, more and more there is reason to believe that the seasonal price pattern for slaughter steers will tend to flatten out in the future.

Medium Frame No. 1 Feeder Steers (Yearlings). The marketing of feeder steers historically has exhibited a relatively consistent seasonal pattern. Prices of yearling feeder steers exhibit a strong regular seasonal tendency, indicating that a considerable amount of confidence can be placed in expectations that prices in any given year will follow this pattern. As mentioned in the last section, sales were geared to the end of the grazing season. Purchases by graziers likewise were geared to the beginning of the grazing season. Consequently, a spring high and fall low could be depended upon with about as much reliability as the movements of a clock.

This basic pattern still persists, but at a somewhat reduced level. The increasing demand by feedlots for feeder cattle on a year-round basis has been instrumental in the change. Figure 5.23 shows the current seasonal pattern for Medium Frame No. 1 feeder steers (600–700 lb) at Kansas City. The spring high is followed by a drop in prices during June and July, a minor recovery in Aug.–Sept., followed by a fall low (Oct.–Dec.). The range from high to low is about 8 percentage points. With prices in the neighborhood of, say, $65.00 at the fall low, one could expect a price of about $70.00 for animals of that same weight and grade during spring. An animal purchased at a given weight in the fall usually will be in a different (heavier) weight classification by the following spring. Seasonal price patterns are based on a given weight and grade. To know the probable price differential applicable to animals as they progress through successive increases in weight, one needs an analysis of price margins. This subject will be gone into later.

Medium Frame No. 1 Steer Calves. Seasonal prices for steer calves follow essentially the same pattern as those for yearling feeder steers (Fig. 5.24). However, the range from low to high (referred to as the "amplitude") is greater and the regularity of the seasonal tendency slightly less. The evidence indicates that one can depend upon this pattern with a substantial amount of confidence.

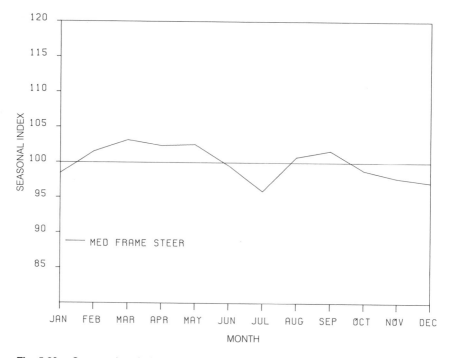

Fig. 5.23. Seasonal variation in prices of medium frame No. 1 feeder steers, 600–700 lb, Kansas City, 1977–1982.

Utility Slaughter Cows. The seasonal movement of utility slaughter cow prices is shown in Fig. 5.25. As mentioned earlier, this pattern is the inverse of seasonality in the marketing of cows. Cow prices range from a low index of about 92 in November to a high of around 106, which normally occurs about April. This can be classed as a pronounced seasonal variation. Again, substantial confidence can be placed in the occurrence of this price pattern.

Other Cattle and Calf Seasonals. Calculations have been made for many other classes, grades, and weights of cattle and calves. Figures 5.22 through 5.25 demonstrate the basic patterns to be found. It could be shown that prices of "good" grade slaughter steers have a slightly greater amplitude than those of choice steers, and that prices of "utility" grade slaughter steers have a higher amplitude than those of "good" grade steers, but the highs and lows of each occur at approximately the same time of year. This was not the case in earlier times, as was pointed out previously. The seasonal price pattern for heifers,

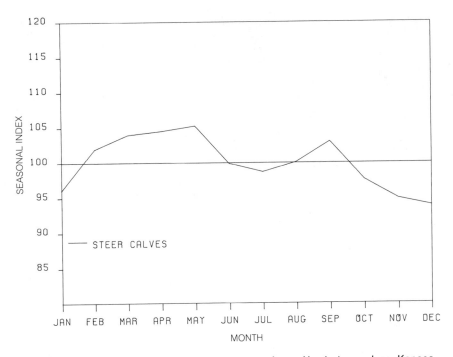

Fig. 5.24.   Seasonal variation in prices of medium-frame No. 1 steer calves, Kansas City, 1977–1982.

for both slaughter classes and feeder classes, follows the same general pattern as steer prices of comparable grade.

Hogs—Seasonal Variations

Hog prices follow a distinctive seasonal pattern that is directly related to the marketing of hogs. This, in turn, is related to the time of farrowing and to a lesser degree to feeding and breeding programs. Although farrowings are distributed throughout the year, they tend to be concentrated in certain months, thus leading to a concentration of marketings. The period of most pronounced concentration is during March and April for the spring pig crop and during September for the fall pig crop. The spring crop was formerly the larger of the two, but this difference also has lessened. Formerly 61 percent of the annual production during the early 1940s, the spring crop is now essentially equal to the fall crop.

Figure 5.26 shows the seasonal pattern of farrowings and market-

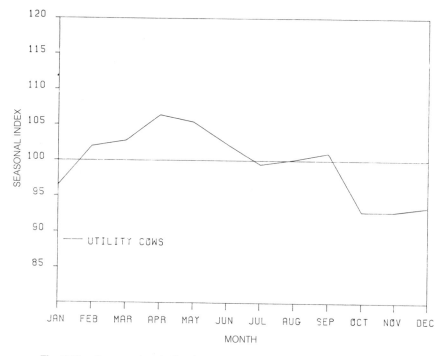

Fig. 5.25. Seasonal variation in prices of cull cows, Omaha, 1977–1982.

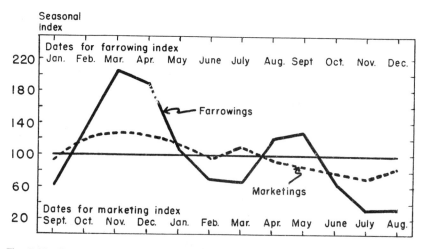

Fig. 5.26. Indexes of seasonal variation in sow farrowings and hog marketing for the United States, 1953–1957. [*Courtesy,* McCoy 1958).]

ings. Although the same scale is used for both, the index line for marketing lags (by seven months) so that the peak for marketings, which occurs in November, is matched with the peak for farrowings, which occurs in March. Monthly farrowings are not available for updating seasonal farrowings. Undoubtedly, the monthly seasonality has flattened out to a considerable degree, with increased year-round multiple farrowings, but spring and fall peaks still exist. It is clear that marketings are more evenly distributed than farrowings, but this is a relative matter. Marketings are far from uniform throughout the year.

Slaughter Barrows and Gilts, No. 1 (200–230 lb).   The seasonal price for barrows and gilts, shown in Fig. 5.27, is seen to be a movement of considerable proportions. The range is 14 percentage points. Prices reach a seasonal peak during the summer (July and August) when relatively few hogs are marketed. From that peak, prices decline to a fall low in November as marketings of hogs from the spring crop reach a peak. As this peak in marketings passes, prices recover to a minor peak in February, then decline as hogs from the previous fall crop are mar-

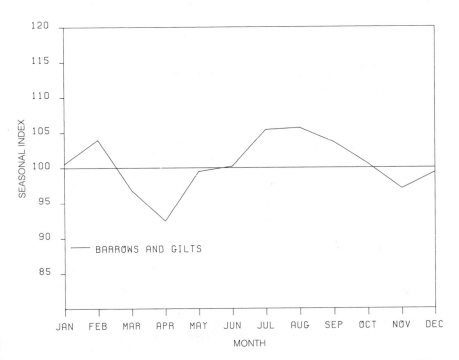

Fig. 5.27.   Seasonal variation in prices of U.S. No. 1 slaughter barrows and gilts, 200–230 lb, interior Iowa and southern Minnesota, 1977–1982.

keted, producing a second seasonal low in April. Seasonal highs and lows do not always hit the exact months indicated, since particular characteristics of individual years cause some minor shifting forward or backward. The seasonal pattern for hogs, however, is more consistent than that for most farm products. In earlier years, seasonal tendencies were relatively regular, but large, erratic price movements of recent years have changed this situation somewhat. From the standpoint of seasonality, however, it is a rare year when hog prices do not hit a high in the summer and a low in the fall. The winter and spring periods are less consistent.

The price pattern for barrows and gilts has changed over the years, as shown in Fig. 5.28. In the pre-World War II period, the summer peak occurred in September. During the immediate post-World War II period, it moved to August. Currently, it still tends to occur in August, although in some years it comes as early as June. This forward movement of the peak probably reflects changes made by hog producers in their attempts to cash in on higher summer prices. However, movement of the peak of the latest period shown (i.e., 1971–1975) back to August may indicate that there has been enough shifting of market-

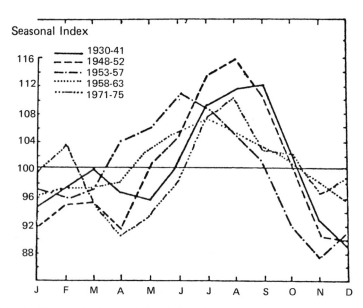

Fig. 5.28.   Seasonal price variation in U.S. No. 2 slaughter barrows and gilts, 200–220 lb, Kansas City, five periods.

ings to earlier months to depress those prices and simultaneously relieve pressure on the August period.

Another noticeable change in the seasonal price pattern is a decided reduction in amplitude—a tendency to flatten out. This undoubtedly has resulted from more uniform farrowings (increased multiple farrowings) and more uniform marketings. There is reason to believe that this trend will continue.

Slaughter Sows, No. 1 (300–400 lb).   The price pattern for sows is essentially the same as for barrows and gilts (Fig. 5.29), that is, it exhibits a summer high and a fall low. The summer high typically occurs in September; the fall low (which might more appropriately be called a winter low), in January. A secondary peak occurs in February, followed by a low in June. The amplitude is less than for barrows and gilts.

Feeder Pigs (40 lb).   Feeder pig prices, on the average, have a decided peak in early spring, then decline to a summer low, followed by partial recovery in fall and another dip during the winter. This general pattern

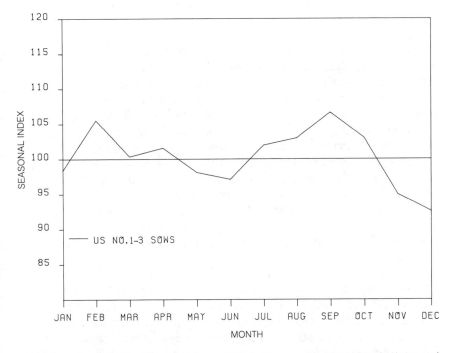

Fig. 5.29.   Seasonal variation in prices of No. 1–3 sows, 300–400 lb, interior Iowa and southern Minnesota, 1977–1982.

reflects the scarcity of feeder pigs on the market during early spring months, which, of course, is the main farrowing period. As the marketing of these pigs increases, prices decline. A second period of relative scarcity occurs in the fall about the time fall farrowings are highest. Although this seasonal variation has a high degree of amplitude, it also has a high degree of irregularity during the second half of the year.

SHEEP—SEASONAL VARIATIONS

There are two classifications of slaughter lambs: (1)spring lambs, and (2) fed lambs (also known in the trade as "old crop" lambs). In market quotation reports, USDA does not use the term "fed" lambs but quotes their prices under headings of "wooled and shorn lambs." None of these terms is entirely descriptive of the characteristics of the two classes of slaughter lambs. A major distinction between the classes is in the feeding programs (Cox, 1965).

"Spring lambs" are lambs marketed without having been weaned. They are milk-fat; in addition, many receive grain, usually by creep feeding arrangements. The production program is such that these lambs begin to reach markets in late spring, and marketings increase from that time into the summer.

"Old crop" or "fed" lambs are lambs that have been weaned and grain-fed in feedlots. Weaning normally takes place in late summer or fall at the end of the grazing season. These lambs may be "rough fed" for a period or placed in feedlots at weaning time. They normally are marketed in greatest volume during the winter months. The pattern of marketings for each class is instrumental in setting the pattern of seasonality in price movements of the respective classes.

There is some overlapping of marketings of spring lambs and fed lambs, which, if excessive in the spring months, can be detrimental to prices of both classes. The trade considers the two classes to be essentially two separate products. Other things being equal, consumers have a distinct preference for spring lamb. Merchandizers claim that it is difficult to move fed lambs once spring lambs arrive on the market in volume.

Choice Slaughter Lambs. The seasonal price patterns for both spring lambs and fed lambs are shown in Fig. 5.30. The period April–September is dominated by spring lambs and the remainder of the year by fed lambs. The peak in spring lamb prices usually occurs in May but occasionally varies one month forward or backward. A high at this time of year is very dependable, being the result of the relative scarcity

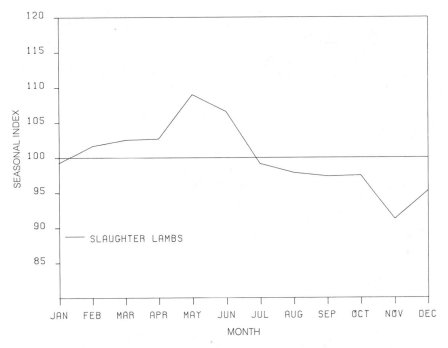

Fig. 5.30.   Seasonal variation in prices of choice slaughter lambs, Omaha, 1977–1982.

of marketings. Demand for lamb is also strong at this season. Almost invariably spring lamb prices decline throughout the summer months from the early high.

At the beginning of the season for fed lambs, prices usually start at a level that is about average for the season, then decline to a fall low. Following this, a moderate advance sets in as marketings taper off. The seasonal variation of fed-lamb prices is not as pronounced as that of spring lambs.

Choice Feeder Lambs.   Prices for feeder lambs follow a distinctive pattern (Fig. 5.31). Typically, a high occurs in the late-winter–early-spring period, followed by a rather drastic decline to early summer (May) and then by a minor recovery in June. Prices usually remain below average, with a definite rising trend (beginning in November) to the late winter high. Prices are considerably more irregular during late winter than the remainder of the year.

Seasonal price movements have not been calculated for slaughter ewes. Normally, culling takes place at the end of the grazing season.

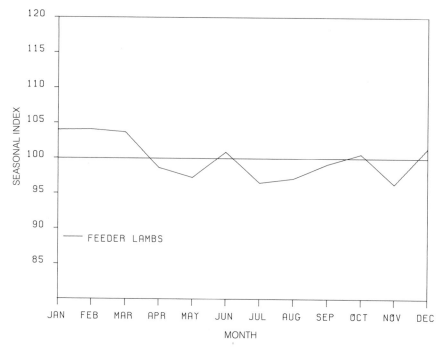

Fig. 5.31. Seasonal variation in prices of choice feeder lambs, South St. Paul, 1977–1982.

Substantial numbers go directly to slaughter, but many go to feedlots in the "Beet Belt" (western Nebraska, northern Colorado, Wyoming, and Montana) for fattening. It is a common practice to buy them by the head and sell them by the pound (Fowler, 1961)

EMPIRICAL SUPPLY STUDIES

The concept of supply—i.e., the quantities that producers stand willing to put on the market at various prices during a given time period—leaves considerable leeway in specifying that time period. For some purposes, analysts assume the quantity available for market—during, say, the current year—to be independent of current prices. The reasoning is that the number of animals available for current marketing was predetermined by prices (and possibly other factors) in a previous period. There is little doubt that greater flexibility—greater response to price—exists in the ability of producers to increase or decrease production as the time period is lengthened. The time required for reproduction constrains the domestic production response to price and to price changes. Imports, however, may take the place, within limits, of domestic production.

Within a period of anything less than a reproduction cycle, some supply changes, even though limited, can be made. Producers can (1) liquidate or add to their inventories, or (2) decrease or increase average slaughter weights by adjustments in feeding programs. It is generally assumed that the coefficient of price elasticity of supply is positive; that is, producers presumably will sell increased quantities as prices increase and reduced quantities as prices decrease. Given sufficient time, this probably is almost universally the case. In the short run, there are exceptions. Livestock feeders with animals approaching market grade and weight often react to a price decline by holding them longer than they otherwise would in hope that prices will rebound. Temporarily, the quantities marketed move in the expected direction, but the animals withheld gain weight, and the end result is an increase in quantity with decreased prices. After a period of unprofitable low prices, however, production will decline. Withholding to build up breeding herds, in response to a price rise, may also appear to be a contradiction to the law of supply. Several researchers have developed a theoretical explanation on the reasoning that, at the discretion of the owner, livestock are simultaneously capital goods and consumption goods (Reutlinger, 1966; Myers *et al.*, 1970; Marsh, 1977; and Nelson and Spreen, 1978). As a capital good, livestock may be kept for additional growth or herd expansion. If marketed immediately, they enter consumption channels. Marsh (1977) found that, "A priori, respective increases in livestock market prices in the current time period would reduce slaughter; the higher market price would induce additional buildup of beef and hog breeding herds. . . . The elasticities of supply for both are negative and very inelastic. If cattle and hog prices rise 10 percent, then cattle slaughter and hog slaughter are reduced 2 percent and .93 percent, respectively." This short-run phenomenon, however, is followed in time by increased tonnage from the growth of given animals or increased supplies from larger herds.

Derivation of a true supply function is complicated by the fact that farmers and ranchers respond to price increases over time, not only by increasing the quantity of inputs, but, usually, also by adopting new and improved technology. The observed production response may then be the result of a compounding, not only of price, but also of other factors. Some researchers make no attempt to isolate the effect of price change but instead calculate a "response function." In some respects, this is more descriptive of the real world, especially as the time span increases. It has been observed that after a prolonged price increase—

which is invariably followed by an increase in production that, in turn, precipitates a decline in prices—producers do not reduce production correspondingly to the equivalent decline in prices. That is a logical reaction under conditions where more or less fixed investments have been made in technological developments associated with the price rise. Thus, the response curve is not presumed to be reversible, whereas the supply curve *is* considered to be reversible.

Among the empirical livestock supply analyses is an Iowa study that reported an elasticity coefficient of 0.60–0.65 for spring farrowed pigs (Dean and Heady, 1959). This means that a 10-percent change in hog prices is associated with (in this case, it could be said "would result in") a 6- to 6 1/2-percent change (in the same direction) in pigs farrowed—all other factors being unchanged. This same study also indicated a higher degree of elasticity in post-World War II years than in prior years. A USDA study reported the supply elasticity for spring farrowings to be slightly higher (0.82) than did the Iowa study and confirmed an increase in supply elasticity in recent years. In addition, the USDA study noted lower elasticities for fall farrowings than for spring farrowings (Harlow, 1962). Tweeten (1970) estimated short-run elasticities of supply of 0.5 for beef and 0.6 for hogs.

Several researchers have investigated the relationship between feed supplies and livestock production. These are supply-related studies. Our previous discussion of the hog—corn ratio, with references cited, is an example. Swanson (1961) reported that a 1-percent change in the available quantity of feed concentrates (not counting government storage stocks) was associated with a 0.9-percent change (in the same direction) in feeds fed to livestock. Beyond that, he found that a 1-percent change in quantity of feed fed was associated with about 0.33-percent change (in the same direction) in livestock production.

Hassler (1962) found an inverse relationship between the quantity of feed concentrates fed and the price of feed concentrates. He reported that a 1-percent change in concentrate (grain) prices at the farm level was associated with an inverse change of about 0.2 percent in quantity of concentrates fed to beef cattle and about 0.1 percent in quantity feed to hogs—given sufficient time for producer response. These findings are consistent with the discussion presented in connection with producer response to the hog–corn ratio. In other words, as feed prices rise relative to livestock prices, fewer livestock will be produced; hence, less feed will be fed. It also is likely that producers will attempt to conserve concentrates as concentrate prices rise. The same argument applies to beef as well as hogs. The comparatively low coefficient found by Hassler, however, indicates that the feeding sector is not particularly sensitive to feed-concentrate prices.

Arzac *et al.* (1979) found, using an econometric model, that beef and pork production (supply) did not respond to current price. These results support the view that lag in response of supply to price contributes to cyclical behavior. The same study found that, in the long run, there is an inverse relationship between nonfed beef production and meat imports. Ospina and Shumway (1981) showed that corn prices have an impact on the composition and relative prices of slaughter beef cattle. An increase of corn prices was shown to reduce slaughter of choice beef cattle and increase slaughter of lower quality (utility) cattle. The results also suggested that, in the long run, as the average quality of beef marketed decreases, the observed average price also decreases. Trapp (1981) used estimated data for cattle on feed to forecast short-run fed-beef supplies. Incorporation of the estimated data resulted in improved accuracy of forecasting. He suggested that the methodology can be used, with some modifications, in forecasting production and supply of other types of livestock.

Dixon and Martin (1982) compared the ordinary least squares (OLS) method and a random and systematically varying coefficient model (RSVC) in forecasting U.S. hog production. It was shown that the RSVC technique is superior to OLS in forecasting quarterly production. The RSVC model results indicated that there is a dampening of seasonal effect and that feed prices are a relatively unimportant factor in production decisions. The model further supported the observation that the pork industry has gone through structural changes that were primarily the result of a lessening of seasonal effects. The results also indicated that because pork supply is responsive to current conditions, supply tends to fluctuate frequently. A recent study by Marsh (1983) employed a rational distributed lag model to describe the behavior of quarterly cattle prices. The results indicate that fed-cattle prices decline geometrically in response to changes in market supply. The results also showed that feeder-cattle prices move in a pattern that clearly reflects the beef-price cycle. Changes in input markets have less influence on price adjustment than do output markets.

REFERENCES

Anon, 1976. Blueprint clearing hurdle to profit with sheep. American Sheep Producers Council, Denver, CO, July.

Arzac, E. R., and Wilkinson, M. 1979. A quarterly econometric model of United States livestock and feed grain markets and some of its policy implications. *Amer. J. Agr. Econ.* 61: 297–308.

Askari, H., and Cummings, J. T. 1976. *Agricultural Supply Response, A Survey of the Econometric Evidence.* New York: Praeger.

Beale, Tommy, et al. 1983. Cattle cycles: How to profit from them. USDA, Ext. Serv. Misc. Pub. No. 1430.

Bickel, B. W. 1975. Seasonality of agricultural prices. Federal Reserve Bank of Kansas City. Monthly Review, June, pp.10–16.

Barksdale, H. C., et al. 1975. A cross-spectral analysis of beef prices. Amer. J. Agr. Econ. 57, No. E: 309–315.

Choi, W. 1977. The cattle cycle. European Review of Agr. Econ. 4(2): 119–136.

Cox, R. 1965. Private communication from Professor Emeritus, Dept. Animal Science and Industry, Kansas State University, Manhattan, KS.

Dahl, D. C., and Hammond, J. W. 1977. Market and Price Analysis, the Agricultural Industries. New York: McGraw-Hill Book Company.

Dean, G. W., and Ready, E. O. 1959. Changes in supply functions and supply elasticities in hog production. Iowa Agr. Expt. Sta. Res. Bull. 471.

DeGraff, H. 1960. Beef Production and Distribution. Norman, OK: University of Oklahoma Press.

Dixon, B. L., and Martin, L. J. 1982. Forecasting U. S. pork production using a random coefficient model. Amer. J. Agr. Econ. 63, 4: 530–538.

Ehrich, R. 1966. Economic analysis of the United States beef cattle cycle. Wyoming Agr. Exp. Sta. Sci. Monograph 1.

Ezekiel, M. 1938. The cobweb theorem. Quart. J. Econ. 52: 255–280.

Federal Reserve Bank of Kansas City. 1961. Is the cattle cycle changing? Monthly Review, Apr., pp. 3–9.

Fowler, S. H. 1961. Meat production and consumption. In The Marketing of Livestock Meat. 2nd ed. Danville, IL: Interstate Printers & Publishers.

Framzmam, J. R. 1967. The trend in slaughter cattle prices. Oklahoma Farm Econ., Oklahoma State University, Dec.

Gardner, B. L. 1976. Futures prices in supply analysis. Amer. J. Agr. Econ., Feb., pp. 81–84.

Gruber, J., and Heady, E. O. 1968. Econometric analysis of the cattle cycle in the United States. Iowa Agr. Expt. Sta. Res. Bull. 564.

Harlow, A. A. 1962. Factors affecting the price and supply of hogs. USDA Econ. Res. Serv. Tech. Bull. 1274.

Hasbargen, P., and Egerston, K. E. 1976. Beef cycles: A clue to current cattle outlook. Minnesota Agr. Economist. Agr. Ext. Ser. No. 579, Univ. of Minn., May.

Hassler, J. B. 1962. The U. S. feed concentrate-livestock economy's demand structure, 1949–59 (with projections for 1960–70). Nebraska Res. Bull. 203. A North Central Regional Pub. 138.

Hayenga, M. L., and Hacklander, D. 1970. Monthly supply-demand relationships for fed cattle and hogs. Amer. J. Agr. Econ. 52: 535–544.

Jones. G. T. 1965. The influence of prices on livestock population over the last decade. J. of Agr. Econ. 16: 420–432.

Jordan, W. J. 1975. The beef cattle cycle of the 1970's. Okla. Agr. Expt. Sta. Bull. B-271.

Kerr, T. C. 1968. Determinants of original livestock supply in Canada. Agr. Econ. Res. Council of Canada. Bull. 15.

Larson, A. B. 1964. The hog cycle as harmonic motion. J. Farm Econ., May: 375–386.

Maki, W. R. 1962. Decomposition of beef and pork cycles. J. Farm Econ., Aug.: 731–743.

Marsh, J. M. 1977. Effects of marketing costs on livestock and meat prices for beef pork. Montana Agr. Expt. Sta. Bull. 697.

Marsh, J. M.1983. A rational distributed lag model of quarterly live cattle prices. Amer. J. Agr. Econ. 63,3: 539–547.

Martin, L., and Zwaret, A. C. 1975. A spatial and temporal mode of the North America pork sector for the evaluation of policy alternatives. *Amer. J. Agr. Econ.* **57:** 55–56.

McCoy, J. H. 1958. Trends in hog prices. *Kansas Agr. Expt. Sta. Circ.* 368.

McCoy, J. H. 1959. Characteristics of cattle cycles. Unpublished data, Dept of Ag. Econ., Kansas State Univ., Manhattan, KA.

Meilke, K. D., *et al.* 1974. North American hog supply: a companion of geometric and polynomial lag models. *Canadian J. Agri. Econ.* **22:** 324–336.

Myers, L. H., *et al.* 1970. Short-term price structure of the hog-pork sector of the United States. *Indiana Agr. Expt. Sta. Res. Bull.* 855.

Nelson, G., and Spreen, T. 1978. Monthly steer and heifer supply. *Amer. J. Agr. Econ.* **60:** 117–125.

Neelove, M. 1958. *The Dynamics of Supply: Estimates of Farmer's Response to Prices.* Baltimore, MD: John Hopkins Univ. Press.

Ospina, Enrique, and Sumway, C. R. 1981. Impact of corn prices on slaughter beef consumption and prices. *Amer. J. Agr. Econ.* **63,** 3:700–703.

Powell, A. A., and Cruen, F. H. 1967. The estimation of production frontiers: The Australian livestock cereal complex. *Australian J. of Agr. Econ.* **11:** 63–81.

Purcell, J. C. 1965. Sources of beef and veal supplies and prices of cattle and calves. Georgia Agr. Expt. Sta. Mimeo Ser. N. S. 233.

Purcell, Wayne. 1979. *Agricultural Marketing: Systems, Coordination, Cash and Future Prices.* Reston, VA: Reston Publishing Co., Inc.

Reutlinger, S. 1966. Short run beef supply response. *Amer. J. Agr. Econ.* **48:** 909–91.

Simpson, J. R., and Farris, D. E. 1982. *The World's Beef Business.* Ames, IA: Iowa State Univ. Press.

Swanson, E. R. 1961. Supply response and the feed-livestock economy. In *Agricultural Supply Functions.* Ames, IA: Iowa State Univ. Press.

Tomek, W. G., and Robinson, K. L. 1972. *Agricultural Product Prices.* Ithaca, NY: Cornell Univ. Press.

Trapp, J. N., 1981. Forecasting short-run fed-beef supplies with estimated data. *Amer. J. Agr. Econ.* **56:** 107–113.

Trypos, P. 1974. Canadian supply functions for livestock and meat. *Amer. J. Agr. Econ.* **56:** 107–113.

Tweeten, L. G. 1970. *Foundations of Farm policy.* Lincoln, NE: Univ. of Nebr. Press.

6

Meat Consumption and Related Demand

In a technical sense, consumption is not synonymous with demand. As explained in Chap. 3, demand connotes a relationship between quantity and price. More specifically, demand is the schedule of quantities that purchasers are willing to buy at alternative prices during some given time period. Consumption is defined as the quantity of a product used (consumed) during a specified period without necessarily relating to price.

During a period of one year, for example, the quantity of meat consumed is essentially equal to the quantity available. The quantity available is primarily determined by current production. Storage stocks and net import-export balances are modifying factors. The quantity carried over in storage from one year to the next is only a negligible fraction of total consumption. Some meat is imported and some is exported. Although substantial for certain meats and at particular times, net import-export balances form, on the average, a relatively small fraction of total meat consumption. (International trade in livestock products will be covered in Chap. 18.)

The price consumers are willing to pay for a given quantity at any particular time is a function of their incomes, tastes, and preferences, expectations about future prices, and prices of competing products. Over the long period, the quantity made available by producers at a given time is a function of prices and profit expectations at a previous time.

Consumption trends will now be examined, as will factors that influence demand and consumption.

WORLD MEAT CONSUMPTION

Meat consumption in other countries is a matter of interest and economic importance to U.S. producers since the United States imports and exports substantial quantities of meat and animal products and our exports and imports are affected by consumption elsewhere. Within certain limits, the world may be considered one big market for meat. In the countries for which data are available, beef and veal accounted for almost 52 percent of the total red meat consumption during the 1975/79 period, pork accounted for 43 percent, and lamb, mutton, and goat meat accounted for 5 percent. The distribution among countries, however, varies to a great degree. The demand for meat is highly related to the income level and general affluence that is associated with economic development.

The United States ranks high among countries of the world in per-capita meat consumption but is far from the top. In 1982, Uraguay, historically the world leader in per-capita meat consumption, continued to be the leader, with 100 kilos (220-lb carcass weight basis) per person (Table 6.1). Following in order were New Zealand, 92 kilos (203 pounds), and Australia, 89 kilos (196 pounds). The United States was in seventh place with 76.4 kilos (168 pounds). Of the twelve leading meat-consuming countries, six increased consumption between the mid 1970s and early 1980s. The 105 kilos consumed by New Zealanders in 1978 was far from a record. In 1953, the people of Uraguay consumed 137 kilos (302 pounds) per capita. Argentina and Australia have exceeded 100 kilos in previous years. Figure 6.1 presents per-capita meat consumption in selected countries and the average for the European Economics Community (EEC) in 1982.

Total-red meat consumption by major consuming countries, includ-

Table 6.1. Leading Red Meat Consuming Countries, Average 1973–1977 and Annual 1978–1982.*

	Consumption per person, kg					
Country	Average 1973– 1977	1978	1979	1980	1981	1982†
Uraguay	98.8	102.8	81.5	90.8	101.1	99.7
New Zealand	101.6	104.6	100.2	93.1	88.5	92.2
Australia	103.5	103.4	88.8	88.6	81.6	87.8
Argentina	93.5	105.6	103.1	99.1	98.9	85.3
Hungary	59.1	86.2	85.0	83.3	81.8	83.8
Czechoslovakia	62.1	83.5	83.5	84.7	85.6	81.7
United States	85.3	84.3	81.3	81.6	80.3	76.4
Switzerland	65.9	69.3	69.1	74.5	75.0	76.1
Austria	67.4	72.0	73.2	73.7	75.2	75.5
Germany W.	67.9	72.7	74.1	75.1	73.5	73.2
Canada	74.2	74.0	70.8	74.3	74.7	72.4
France	66.1	70.4	70.3	71.5	71.2	71.2

Source: USDA (1983).
*Carcass-weight basis.
†Preliminary.

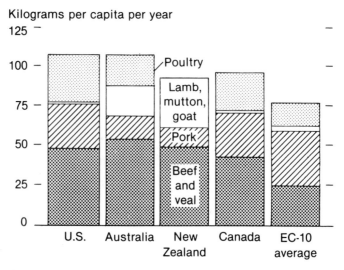

Fig. 6.1. Meat consumption in major producing countries, 1982 (meat consumption on carcass-weight basis; poultry consumption data not available for New Zealand). (Courtesy USDA Exten. Serv., undated)

ing those already mentioned, is shown in Table 6.2. Beef and veal consumption by country is given in Table 6.3. Uruguay and Argentina have been obvious leaders over the years. Cyclical factors tend to distort the trend effect in the short time period shown; however, Australia, New Zealand, and Japan have experienced an increasing trend since the 1960s. Japan has the greatest percentage increase. The longtime trend in the United States was upward until the mid–1970s. Severe financial losses by the cattle industry at that time and in the early 1980s, associated with cyclical liquidation, prompted serious questions about further per-capita gains, at least in the immediate future. Consumption of pork in 1982 in Hungary—the top consuming country of pork at 79.4 kilos (145 pounds) per person—is just slightly less than the consumption of beef in most of the top beef-consuming countries (Tables 6.3 and 6.4). Eastern and Northern European countries usually have the highest levels of pork consumption.

Although lamb, mutton, and goat meat are very important in some countries, world production and consumption of these products have declined in recent years. From the standpoint of per-capita consumption, New Zealand and Australia are in a class by themselves, averaging 31 kilos (68 pounds) and 19 kilos (42 pounds), respectively (Table 6.5). This is a substantial drop from previous levels in the mid 1960s. People of the Middle East have a traditional preference for these

Table 6.2. Total Red Meat Per-Capita Consumption in Specified Countries, Average 1973-1977 and Annual 1978-1982.*

Country	Consumption per person, kg					
	Average 1973-1977	1978	1979	1980	1981	1982†
North America						
Canada	74.2	74.0	70.8	74.3	74.7	72.4
United States	85.3	84.3	81.3	81.6	80.3	76.4
Mexico	23.2	29.3	31.3	30.0	32.7	35.1
South America						
Argentina	93.5	105.6	103.1	99.1	98.9	85.3
Brazil	28.0	26.7	25.8	25.2	23.5	24.3
Chile	25.6	22.3	22.2	22.1	24.9	26.0
Colombia	23.1	26.3	27.8	31.3	32.4	34.7
Peru	11.5	10.1	9.6	9.7	9.8	9.2
Uraguay	98.8	102.8	81.5	90.8	101.1	99.7
Venezuela	27.2	31.4	30.7	25.6	25.5	24.9
Europe Western (EEC)						
Belgium/Lux.	73.7	71.1	72.0	71.3	69.4	69.0
Denmark	55.1	66.6	66.5	70.7	63.5	63.8
France	66.1	70.4	70.3	71.5	71.2	71.2
Germany, FR	67.9	72.7	74.1	75.1	73.5	73.2
Ireland	63.3	63.6	64.3	64.3	64.7	62.9
Italy	43.2	45.3	46.6	49.9	48.9	48.5
Netherlands	53.3	52.7	55.6	54.1	57.8	59.6
United Kingdom	57.9	58.2	59.9	57.8	55.2	55.5
Austria	67.4	72.0	73.2	73.7	75.2	75.5
Finland	50.3	52.8	53.7	52.0	50.9	51.6
Greece	44.8	52.7	53.4	53.6	47.7	47.5
Norway	44.1	45.4	46.9	47.7	42.7	42.6
Portugal	29.9	28.5	26.9	27.5	28.7	29.6
Spain	36.6	39.4	42.9	41.4	41.7	42.7
Sweden	51.4	51.7	53.2	52.0	51.1	48.7
Switzerland	65.9	69.3	69.1	74.5	75.0	76.1
Europe Eastern						
Bulgaria	43.3	57.3	60.9	59.1	61.3	60.6
Czechoslovakia	62.1	83.5	83.5	84.7	85.6	81.7
Hungary	59.1	86.2	85.0	83.3	81.8	83.8
Poland	66.8	73.2	72.6	70.7	59.4	61.7
Yugoslavia	37.4	53.5	52.3	51.5	50.9	51.0
USSR	43.8	51.3	51.1	50.2	50.3	49.1
Africa						
South Africa	30.5	31.6	30.7	30.4	27.7	27.3

(*continued*)

Table 6.2.   (continued)

Country	Average 1973-1977	1978	1979	1980	1981	1982†
		Consumption per person, kg				
Asia						
Japan	17.5	19.4	20.6	21.0	20.8	20.9
Philippines	12.4	10.1	10.8	11.2	12.7	12.4
Oceania						
New Zealand	101.6	104.6	100.2	93.1	88.5	92.2

Source: USDA (1983).
*Carcass-weight basis.
†Preliminary.

Table 6.3.   Beef and Veal Per-Capita Consumption in Specified Countries, Average 1973-1977 and Annual 1978-1982.*

Country	Average 1973-1977	1978	1979	1980	1981	1982†
		Consumption per person, kg				
North America						
Canada	47.9	47.0	40.6	41.2	42.5	42.6
United States	56.1	55.9	49.2	47.8	48.2	48.1
Mexico	13.8	12.3	13.7	15.7	16.3	17.6
South America						
Argentina	80.4	94.1	89.7	85.8	86.6	73.4
Brazil	20.3	19.0	17.8	16.8	15.4	16.4
Chile	19.0	17.5	16.7	16.1	18.3	19.3
Colombia	18.6	21.4	22.8	26.3	27.7	25.8
Paraguay	—	—	—	—	—	—
Peru	5.8	5.0	4.5	4.4	4.9	4.6
Uruguay	76.1	86.4	67.3	77.7	82.7	83.8
Venezuela	21.3	25.3	24.6	20.3	19.8	19.3
Europe Western (EEC)						
Belgium/Lux.	29.4	27.9	27.8	26.8	25.6	25.0
Denmark	15.6	17.1	14.5	13.7	12.3	12.3
France	29.9	32.4	33.1	33.2	32.1	31.9
Germany, FR	23.6	24.1	24.2	24.1	22.9	22.5
Ireland	23.9	24.5	24.0	22.9	22.4	21.9
Italy	24.5	24.2	24.6	25.9	25.1	24.8
Netherlands	20.5	18.9	19.0	18.5	18.7	18.7
United Kingdom	24.8	25.4	25.3	23.9	22.9	22.6

Table 6.3.   (continued)

Country	Average 1973–1977	1978	1979	1980	1981	1982†
		Consumption per person, kg				
Europe Western (EEC)						
Austria	24.9	25.5	25.3	25.3	25.8	25.7
Finland	23.4	22.0	23.6	22.7	21.7	22.1
Greece	18.4	24.1	22.4	22.6	15.3	14.8
Norway	18.1	19.4	20.0	20.2	17.7	18.3
Portugal	12.8	11.3	9.7	9.8	10.0	9.6
Spain	12.9	12.6	12.8	11.6	11.0	11.0
Sweden	18.7	17.7	17.9	17.6	16.9	16.7
Switzerland	25.6	26.4	26.0	28.1	28.3	29.0
Europe Eastern						
Bulgaria	11.9	15.8	15.7	13.7	14.1	13.7
Czechoslovakia	25.7	28.1	28.6	28.6	27.2	26.7
Hungary	9.3	8.3	7.0	6.2	4.3	4.3
Poland	20.7	22.1	22.6	22.3	18.7	20.4
Yugoslavia	12.0	15.2	15.5	14.7	14.9	15.2
USSR	24.6	27.2	27.0	26.6	26.4	26.1
Africa						
South Africa	21.2	22.1	22.7	21.7	19.0	18.9
Asia						
Japan	3.8	4.7	4.9	5.1	5.3	5.5
Philippines	3.9	3.1	2.8	2.7	3.8	3.6
Oceania						
Australia	64.9	72.1	52.3	49.8	48.8	53.7
New Zealand	54.4	62.5	59.7	49.3	46.5	49.7

Source: USDA (1983).
*Carcass-weight basis.
†Preliminary.

meats. Residents of Greece consume about as much lamb, mutton, and goat meat as either beef or pork. Average consumption in the United States has declined for several decades and nationwide stands at 0.8 kilo (1.75 pounds). However, it is estimated that consumption in New York is about 5.5 kilos (12 pounds) and is almost at that level in large cities of California.

Horse meat is a minor component of world red-meat consumption. In recent years, however, people of the Belgium-Luxembourg area are reported to consume about 3.2 kilos (7 pounds) per person. That is as

Table 6.4.   Pork Per Capita Consumption in Specified Countries, Average 1973-1977 and Annual 1978-1982.*

Country	Average 1973-1977	1978	1979	1980	1981	1982†
	Consumption per person, kg					
North America						
Canada	25.0	25.9	29.2	32.3	31.5	29.1
United States	28.3	28.1	31.8	33.6	31.9	28.1
Mexico	8.3	16.3	16.9	13.5	15.8	17.0
South America						
Argentina	9.4	8.0	9.7	9.9	9.0	8.7
Brazil	7.1	7.3	7.6	8.0	7.8	7.6
Chile	3.9	3.3	4.1	5.0	5.7	5.8
Colombia	4.1	4.5	4.6	4.6	4.2	3.9
Peru	3.3	3.1	3.2	3.3	3.0	2.9
Uruguay	7.5	5.7	5.7	5.3	5.3	5.3
Venezuela	6.5	5.8	5.8	5.1	5.5	5.4
Europe Western (EEC)						
Belgium/Lux.	39.8	41.5	42.4	42.6	42.4	42.6
Denmark	38.9	48.9	51.2	56.4	50.6	50.9
France	31.2	34.2	33.3	34.3	34.9	35.1
Germany, FR	43.8	47.9	49.0	50.2	49.8	49.9
Ireland	28.8	29.5	32.3	33.5	33.8	32.9
Italy	16.8	19.7	20.5	22.5	22.3	22.2
Netherlands	30.5	33.6	36.2	35.0	38.5	40.4
United Kingdom	25.3	25.6	27.4	26.2	25.7	26.0
Austria	42.1	46.1	47.5	48.0	49.0	49.4
Finland	26.2	30.6	29.9	29.1	29.0	29.3
Greece	12.1	14.5	16.8	17.2	18.7	19.1
Norway	20.9	20.6	21.3	22.1	19.9	19.0
Portugal	14.5	14.8	14.9	15.4	16.4	17.7
Spain	19.3	22.9	26.5	26.1	27.0	28.1
Sweden	31.6	33.3	34.6	33.7	33.5	31.3
Switzerland	38.7	41.7	42.0	44.8	45.3	45.6
Europe Eastern						
Bulgaria	27.0	34.5	38.9	39.6	40.5	40.3
Czechoslovakia	46.3	54.9	54.4	55.5	57.8	54.5
Hungary	49.6	77.6	77.8	77.0	77.4	79.4
Poland	44.9	50.4	49.3	47.8	40.1	40.8
Yugoslavia	23.0	35.7	34.2	34.3	33.4	33.2
USSR	15.4	20.5	20.5	19.6	19.9	19.3
Africa						
South Africa	3.4	3.0	3.3	3.1	3.2	3.2

Table 6.4.   (*continued*)

Country	Consumption per person, kg					
	Average 1973–1977	1978	1979	1980	1981	1982†
Asia						
Japan	10.7	12.4	13.6	14.4	14.0	13.9
Philippines	8.3	6.9	7.9	8.4	8.8	8.7
Oceania						
Australia	13.9	14.2	14.3	15.9	15.7	15.0
New Zealand	11.6	12.5	11.3	11.4	11.7	11.5

Source: USDA (1983).
*Carcass-weight basis.
†Preliminary.

Table 6.5. **Mutton, Lamb, and Goat Meat Per-Capita Consumption in Specified Countries, Average 1973–1977 and Annual 1978-1982.***

Country	Consumption per person, kg					
	Average 1973–1977	1978	1979	1980	1981	1982†
North America						
Canada	1.2	1.1	1.0	0.8	0.7	0.7
United States	0.9	0.7	0.7	0.7	0.7	0.8
Mexico	0.9	0.7	0.7	0.8	0.6	0.5
South America						
Argentina	3.7	3.5	3.7	3.4	3.3	3.2
Brazil	0.5	0.4	0.4	0.4	0.3	0.3
Chile	2.5	1.5	1.4	1.0	0.9	0.9
Colombia	0.5	0.4	0.4	0.4	0.5	0.5
Peru	2.3	2.0	1.9	2.0	1.9	1.7
Uruguay	15.1	10.7	8.5	7.8	13.1	10.6
Venezuela	0.3	0.3	0.3	0.2	0.2	0.2
Europe Western (EEC)						
Belgium/Lux.	1.2	1.7	1.8	1.9	1.4	1.4
Denmark	0.4	0.6	0.8	0.6	0.6	0.6
France	3.6	3.8	3.9	4.0	4.2	4.2
Germany, FR	0.5	0.7	0.9	0.8	0.8	0.8
Ireland	10.6	9.6	8.0	7.9	8.5	8.1
Italy	1.1	1.4	1.5	1.5	1.5	1.5
Netherlands	0.2	0.2	0.4	0.6	0.6	0.5
United Kingdom	8.1	7.2	7.2	7.7	6.6	6.9

(*continued*)

Table 6.5. *(continued)*

Country	Consumption per person, kg					
	Average 1973–1977	1978	1979	1980	1981	1982†
Europe Western (EEC)						
Austria	0.3	0.4	0.4	0.4	0.4	0.4
Finland	0.2	0.2	0.2	0.2	0.2	0.2
Greece	14.3	14.1	14.2	13.8	13.7	13.6
Norway	5.0	5.4	5.6	5.4	5.1	5.3
Portugal	2.5	2.4	2.3	2.3	2.3	2.3
Spain	4.2	3.9	3.6	3.7	3.7	3.6
Sweden	0.6	0.7	0.7	0.7	0.7	0.7
Switzerland	1.2	1.2	1.1	1.6	1.4	1.5
Europe Eastern						
Bulgaria	8.4	7.0	6.3	5.8	6.7	6.6
Czechoslovakia	0.5	0.5	0.5	0.6	0.6	0.5
Hungary	0.2	0.3	0.2	0.1	0.1	0.1
Poland	0.6	0.7	0.7	0.6	0.6	0.6
Yugoslavia	2.4	2.6	2.6	2.5	2.5	2.6
USSR	3.8	3.6	3.6	4.0	4.0	3.7
Africa						
South Africa	5.9	6.5	5.7	5.6	5.5	5.2
Asia						
Japan	2.4	2.3	2.1	1.5	1.5	1.5
Philippines	0.1	0.1	0.1	0.1	0.1	0.1
Oceania						
Australia	24.7	17.1	22.2	22.9	17.1	19.1
New Zealand	35.6	29.6	29.2	32.4	30.3	31.0

Source: USDA (1983).
*Carcass-weight basis.
†Preliminary.

much total meat as is consumed by people of some less-developed countries.

In total pounds of meat consumed (that is, per-capita consumption times population), the United States leads all other countries. On the average during the past two decades, U.S. consumption accounted for approximately one-third of all beef and veal, slightly more than one-quarter of all pork, and about 4 percent of all lamb, mutton, and goat meat. These percentages have not changed substantially in recent years.

During the period from the mid 1970s to the early 1980s, all but 13 of the countries shown in Table 6.2 recorded gains in meat consumption. Four of the seven showing decreased consumption are in South America. Growth in meat consumption is closely associated with income level, and income level in turn is closely associated with economic development.

The Less-Developed Countries (LDC's) of Africa, Asia, and Central America hold vast numbers of people who consume only a few pounds of meat per person per year. Aside from those whose religion forbids the consumption of certain meats (e.g., Moslems, Jews, and Hindus), these people would purchase more meat if their incomes were higher. The potential of this immense latent market challenges the imagination, just as the formidable array of barriers to economic growth challenges those who are so vigorously pursuing it. Progress will be made and eventually these countries will be brought into the world market economy. Some Central American countries have made significant strides in exportation of beef in recent years. Additional efforts can be expected in the future. In the immediate future, however, foreseeable developments will not significantly affect meat consumption in the LDC's. This is a long-range situation.

U.S. MEAT CONSUMPTION

Per-capita consumption of red meat was high in the United States in the early days, which is typical of frontier countries. Around 1900, however, total meat consumption began a slight downturn as population increased faster than meat supplies. This trend was reversed following the drouth-depression period of the 1930s, and a definite upward trend was established. A decline in beef consumption from the early 1900s to the mid–1930s largely accounted for the decline in total meat consumption. In terms of absolute quantity, beef consumption now is far ahead, although this has not always been the case. It is not apparent from Fig. 6.2, but pork consumption was usually higher than beef consumption until the early 1950s. Prior to that, beef consumption had temporarily exceeded pork consumption on several occasions, but since the early 1950s beef has dominated. Since the 1950s, beef consumption has increased about 50 percent. U.S. consumers ate 128 lb (carcass weight) of beef per capita in 1976—the peak year since records have been kept. Pork consumption has varied around the 65-lb level most of the time since the early 1950s, and only in the most recent years has it shown a tendency to increase (USDA 1984A).

Veal, lamb, and mutton have always comprised a relatively minor

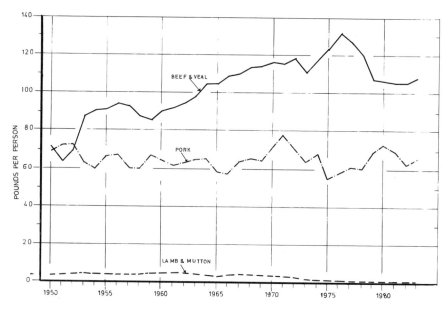

Fig. 6.2. Per capita meat consumption in the United States, carcass-weight basis, 1950–1984. (Plotted by authors from USDA data.)

fraction of total meat consumption. Consumption of each was on a slightly increasing trend until about the end of World War II. Since that time the trend of each has been decidedly downward. Consumption of veal amounted to only 2 pounds per person in 1983, and lamb and mutton consumption was about 1.7 pounds. Thus, the gain in total meat consumption since the early 1950s has been virtually all beef.

Although by far the bulk of meat consumed is fresh meat, Ives (1966) has pointed out that the share of total meat represented by sausage and canned meats has risen more than the overall trend. USDA data indicate that processed meats represented about 7 percent of per-capita meat consumption in the 1970s.

Meat Consumption Patterns in 1965 and 1977–78

Consumption data are reported on a regular annual basis for the United States as a whole, but regional or state information is available only from special studies, which are not made at regularly scheduled intervals. The USDA has carried out several nationwide household consumption surveys in the past 50 years. Except for the last survey—carried out over a one-year period covering four quarters beginning in the spring (April, 1977) and ending the following winter (March,

1978)—previous surveys were carried out to cover just one week and provided some information on regional meat-consumption characteristics by type of household and income level. Although the latest survey is not fully comparable with previous studies, the spring quarter data are comparable.[1]

Data from the 1977–78 Nationwide Food Consumption survey show that the meat group (red meat, poultry, fish, eggs, nuts, and peanut butter) accounted for 38 percent of home food dollars. Milk and milk products were a poor second, accounting for 12 percent of the at-home food dollars, followed by grain products and vegetables (at 12 percent each), and fruits (8 percent). Other food groups accounted for a lesser percentages (USDA 1984B).

USDA data indicate that consumers spent 4.2 percent of their income on red meat and poultry in 1979 but only 3.6 percent in 1982. The largest percent of income spent on meat is for beef (2 percent in 1982), followed by pork (1.1 percent).

Among all households interviewed in 1977–78, only 4 percent indicated that they did not consume red meat during the week in question. Only 9 percent did not consume beef compared to 20 percent of the families reporting no pork consumption. Based on the 1977–78 survey, Haidacher *et al.* (1982) estimated the proportion of total meat budget allocated to different meats and within each meat category. The results indicate that the budget allocated to red meat (as a percent of total meat budget) was 66.4 percent in 1977 compared to 70.1 percent in 1965. Changes have also occurred in the allocation within the red meat budget. For example, the percentage of at-home budget allocated for beef fell slightly from 1965 (42 percent) to 1977 (41 percent) of all meat budget, but, as a percentage of red meat budget, it has actually increased by 1.7 percent (from 60 to 61.7 percent in spring 1977). The percentage of total at-home meat budget allocated for pork decreased by 2 percent between the two surveys, and by 1 percent when only red meat budgets are considered. The share of the red meat budget spent on veal dropped from 2.1 to 1.8 percentage points between the two surveys, the same percentages as with lamb and mutton budget allocation.

By Region. For purposes of analysis of household surveys, the United States is divided into four regions—North Central, Northeast, South, and West. During the four-week period of the 1977–78 study, consumers in the North Central region used the most red meat—2.70

---

[1] This section draws heavily on a USDA national survey of household consumption of red meats, poultry, and fish (Haidacher *et al.* 1982).

pounds per person per week. But families in the Northeast had the largest per capita money value of meat consumed. Those in the South consumed 2.66 pounds of red meat; the Northeast, 2.62 pounds; whereas those in the West averaged 2.41 pounds (Table 6.6). These differences may appear to be minor, but on this basis, consumption in the North Central region would be 12 percent greater than in the West. Farm families were the biggest consumers of red meats, but farm consumption also varied considerably among regions. Urban households were the next biggest, and non farm rural households consumed the least, the same as in the 1965 survey (Table 6.7). As for the urban population, the 1977–78 survey showed that central city families were the biggest consumers of red meat, followed by nonmetropolitan and suburban families, respectively (Table 6.8).

Beef consumption was highest in the North Central region, with the Northeastern and Western regions tied for second place. The South was lowest in beef consumption, but highest in pork consumption. The Northeast and West were relatively low in pork consumption but exceeded the South and North Central in lamb and mutton consumption (Table 6.6).

By Season. Statistical analysis of the 1977–78 survey (Haidacher *et al.*, 1982) indicates that total meat consumption was not significantly influenced by season. The analysis indicated, however, that there was substantial variation among individual meat items that had been eliminated by "aggregation" (that is, by grouping the individual meat items

Table 6.6. Per-Capita Weekly Home Meat Consumption, by region 1977–1978.

	Consumption, lb				
Item	Northeast	North Central	South	West	U.S. total
Total meat	4.45	4.27	4.54	3.86	4.32
Red meat	2.62	2.70	2.66	2.41	2.61
Beef	1.67	1.77	1.63	1.67	1.69
Pork	0.82	0.89	0.99	0.67	0.86
Veal	0.07	0.02	0.02	0.02	0.03
Lamb, mutton, goat meat	0.06	0.01	0.01	0.05	0.03
Poultry	1.03	0.78	0.97	0.77	0.90
Fish and shellfish	0.32	0.26	0.42	0.30	0.34
Miscellaneous	0.43	0.52	0.49	0.37	0.48
Franks	0.15	0.16	0.14	0.12	0.15
Luncheon meats	0.21	0.29	0.23	0.19	0.24
Variety meats	0.07	0.08	0.12	0.06	0.09

Source: Haidacher *et al.* (1982).

Table 6.7. Per-Capita Weekly Home Meat Consumption, by Urbanization, Spring 1965 and 1977.

| Item | Urban | | Rural | | | |
| | | | Farm | | Non Farm | |
	1965	1977	1965	1977	1965	1977
Total meat	4.47	4.42	4.64	5.19	4.10	4.17
Red meat	2.74	2.67	2.95	3.75	2.49	2.59
Beef	1.61	1.71	1.79	2.59	1.46	1.66
Pork	1.01	0.88	1.15	1.13	0.99	0.90
Veal	0.06	0.04	0.01	*	0.02	0.01
Lamb, mutton, goat meat	0.07	0.04	0.01	0.03	0.02	0.02
Poultry	0.85	0.89	0.80	0.64	0.74	0.78
Fish and shellfish	0.35	0.39	0.37	0.37	0.37	0.33
Miscellaneous	0.52	0.47	0.52	0.43	0.51	0.47
Franks	0.16	0.14	0.15	0.12	0.18	0.17
Luncheon meats	0.25	0.24	0.26	0.21	0.25	0.24
Variety meats	0.11	0.09	0.11	0.10	0.08	0.06

Source: Haidacher et al. (1982).
*Less than 0.005.

Table 6.8. Per-Capita Weekly Home Meat Consumption, by Urbanization 1977–1978.

Item	Consumption, lb		
	Central city	Suburban	Nonmetropolitan
Total meat	4.76	4.14	4.15
Red meat	2.71	2.56	2.59
Beef	1.72	1.68	1.68
Pork	0.91	0.82	0.88
Veal	0.05	0.04	0.02
Lamb, mutton, goat meat	0.04	0.03	0.02
Poultry	1.06	0.85	0.81
Fish and shelfish	0.41	0.31	0.30
Miscellaneous	0.57	0.41	0.45
Franks	0.16	0.13	0.15
Luncheon meats	0.26	0.22	0.23
Variety meats	0.15	0.06	0.07

Source: Haidacher et al. (1982).

into a total of meat consumed). Seasonality in consumption is associated with weather conditions, holidays, and the cyclical nature of production. Estimates of seasonal variation relative to the spring quarter are shown in Table 6.9. As expected, the data indicate that ground beef and steak, franks, and poultry are consumed more heavily during the summer and spring, reflecting more outdoor cooking of items that require relatively short cooking time during these quarters. Whole tur-

Table 6.9. Seasonal Variation in Per-Capita Weekly Home Meat Consumption, 1977–1978.

Item	Spring	Summer	Fall	Winter
		Percent difference from spring		
Total meat	4.61	1	0	−1
Red meat	2.80	−1	−5	−2
Beef	1.78	2	−3	−2
Pork	0.95	−8	−8	−3
Veal	0.04	−10	−3	10
Lamb, mutton, goat meat	0.04	1	−3	−24
Poultry	0.90	6	21	12
Fish and shellfish	0.41	0	−14	−21
Franks	0.15	9	−15	−8
Luncheon meats	0.24	10	1	−1
Variety meats	0.10	−15	−2	−1

Source: Haidacher et al. (1982).

key and red meat items requiring long cooking time were consumed more in the fall and winter. In general, the 1977–78 study indicates that consumption of red meat and fish were highest in the spring and lowest in the winter, whereas turkey consumption was highest in the fall.

By Family Size.   Haidacher *et al.* (1982) reported that "generally, per capita consumption declines as household size increases. This may be due to inadequacies of the scale variables, interactions between household size and other variables (perhaps income) and/or more efficient use of food in larger households." It should be pointed out that larger households tend to include more children, who are small consumers and thus tend to lower per-capita meat consumption for the average person. Table 6.10 clearly supports the researcher's conclusions.

By Species.   Beef accounted for more than one-half of total red and miscellaneous meat consumption in all regions during 1977–78. The percentage was highest in the West (59 percent) and lowest in the south (54 percent), as shown in Table 6.11. It should be noted that these percentages increased between 1965 and 1977 in all regions. On the other hand, pork consumption (as a percentage of total red and miscellaneous meat) declined from 1965 to 1977 in all regions. Pork consumption in the South accounted for the highest percentage (32 percent) and the West, the lowest (26 percent).

Table 6.12 indicates that the total quantity of red meat consumed during spring 1977 was 1.5 percent below the 1965 level, with a larger decrease in veal and pork consumption. Figure 6.3 shows the relative importance of various meats in weekly at-home meat consumption in the springs of 1965 and 1977.

Average at-home beef consumption in the survey week increased

Table 6.10. Per-Capita Weekly Home Meat Consumption, by Family Size, 1977–1978, U.S.

Item	Consumption, lb					
	Number of persons					
	1	2	3	4	5	6 or more
Red meat	2.94	3.09	2.77	2.44	2.35	2.30
Beef	1.85	1.99	1.80	1.59	1.51	1.47
Pork	0.98	1.00	0.91	0.79	0.79	0.79
Veal	0.05	0.05	0.03	0.03	0.03	0.02
Lamb, mutton, goat meat	0.06	0.05	0.02	0.03	0.02	0.02

Source: Haidacher *et al.* (1982).

Table 6.11. Beef, Pork, and Other Meats as a Percentage of Total Red and Miscellanous Meat Consumption, all Households, by Region, for One Week in the Spring of 1965 and 1977.

	Percent consumption					
	Beef		Pork		Other Meats*	
Region	1965	1977	1965	1977	1965	1977
Northeast	49	55	29	27	22	18
North Central	51	54	32	29	17	17
South	45	53	38	32	17	15
West	55	59	27	26	18	15

Source: Calculated by the authors from Haidacher et al. (1982).
*Veal, lamb, mutton, goat, franks, luncheon, and variety meats.

from 1.59 pounds per capita in 1965 to 1.73 pounds in 1977. Pork consumption by farm families decreased slightly from 1965 to 1977, but a substantial decline in the consumption of other households resulted in a 15 percent decline for total pork consumption. The per-capita consumption of veal declined from 1965 to 1977. Lamb and mutton consumption by farm families increased from 1965 to 1977, but this was offset by a decline in other households, resulting in a relatively stable lamb and mutton consumption for the nation as a whole between the two surveys (Tables 6.7 and 6.12). As noted in Tables 6.13 and 6.14, however, consumption of lamb, mutton, and goat meat has dropped in all areas but the North Central region from spring 1965 to spring 1977.

For the United States as a whole in 1977–78, beef accounted for about 65 percent of all red meat (Table 6.6), but the figure was higher

Table 6.12. Per-Capita Weekly Home Meat Consumption, Spring 1965 and 1977.

Item	1965, lb	1977, lb	Change, %
Total meat	4.42	4.39	−0.7
Red meat	2.74	2.70	−1.5
Beef	1.59	1.73	8.8
Pork	1.06	0.90	−15.1
Veal	0.04	0.03	−25.0
Lamb, mutton, goat meat	0.04	0.04	0.0
Poultry	0.82	0.85	3.7
Fish and shellfish	0.36	0.37	2.8
Miscellaneous	0.51	0.47	−7.8
Franks	0.16	0.15	−6.3
Luncheon meats	0.25	0.24	−4.0
Variety meats	0.10	0.08	−20.0

Source: Haidacher et al. (1982).

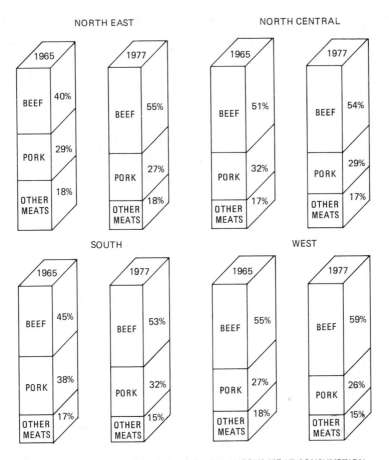

PERCENTAGE OF TOTAL RED AND MISCELLANEOUS MEAT CONSUMPTION

Fig. 6.3. Relative importance of various meats in home consumption during one week in spring 1965 and 1977.

in the West (69 percent) than in the Northeast (64 percent) North Central (66 percent) or, South (61 percent). The sharpest increase in beef consumption between spring 1965 and spring 1977 was in the South (see Table 6.13). It should be noted here that the quantity of weekly per-capita beef consumption has actually declined between the two surveys by 8 percent in the West and by a slight margin in the North Central region (Tables 6.13 and 6.14). Pork comprised one-third of the red meat consumed nationwide in 1977. In 1965, pork accounted for 34 percent of the red meat consumed in the South versus 59 percent for beef. By 1977, the percentages were 37 and 62 percent for pork and

Table 6.13. Per-Capita Weekly Home Meat Consumption, By Region Spring 1965 and 1977.

	Consumption, lb							
	Spring 1965				Spring 1977			
Item	NE	NC	S	W	NE	NC	S	W
Total meat	4.41	4.58	4.29	4.43	4.43	4.40	4.59	3.96
Red meat	2.68	3.00	2.50	2.86	2.62	2.79	2.77	2.54
Beef	1.57	1.81	1.33	1.85	1.69	1.80	1.72	1.70
Pork	0.92	1.14	1.13	0.91	0.81	0.95	1.02	0.73
Veal	0.09	0.03	0.02	0.02	0.06	0.02	0.02	0.03
Lamb, mutton,								
goat meat	0.10	0.02	0.02	0.08	0.06	0.02	0.01	0.07
Poultry	0.84	0.74	0.87	0.78	0.99	0.77	0.91	0.69
Fish and shellfish	0.36	0.28	0.45	0.30	0.41	0.31	0.43	0.31
Miscellaneous	0.52	0.56	0.47	0.49	0.43	0.53	0.47	0.32
Franks	0.18	0.18	0.14	0.16	0.16	0.15	0.14	0.13
Luncheon	0.24	0.30	0.22	0.23	0.20	0.30	0.22	0.21
Variety	0.10	0.08	0.11	0.10	0.07	0.08	0.11	0.08

Source: Haidacher et al. (1982).

beef, respectively. It should be noted that this was just about the reverse of the situation during the 1950s. Tables 6.12 through 6.14 indicate that per-capita pork consumption decreased from 1965 to 1977 in every region of the nation including the south.

Raunikar et al. (1970) found that ". . . . per capita demand (for pork)

Table 6.14. Per-Capita Weekly Home Meat Consumption in Spring 1977 as a Percent of Consumption in Spring 1965, by Region.

	Percent consumption			
Item	Northeast	North central	South	West
Total meat	100.5	96.1	107.0	89.4
Red meat	97.8	93.0	110.8	88.8
Beef	107.6	99.5	129.3	91.9
Pork	88.0	83.3	90.3	80.2
Veal	66.7	66.7	100.0	150.0
Lamb, mutton,				
goat meat	60.0	100.0	50.0	87.5
Poultry	117.9	104.1	104.6	88.5
Fish and shellfish	113.9	110.7	95.6	103.3
Miscellaneous	82.7	94.6	100.0	65.3
Franks	88.9	83.3	100.0	81.3
Luncheon meats	83.3	100.0	100.0	91.3
Variety meats	70.0	100.0	100.0	80.0

Source: Calculated by authors from data in Haidacher et al. (1982).

is relatively high in the Southern, Lower Mid-Atlantic, Lakes, and Central Plains regions, relatively low in the Middle Mid-Atlantic, New England, Rocky Mountain, and Pacific regions, and near the national average in the North Plains and Upper Mid-Atlantic regions." In a companion study, Raunikar et al. (1969) found that " . . . per capita demand (for beef) is relatively high in the Pacific and Mountain regions, relatively low in the South and near the national average in the Upper Mid-Atlantic and New England regions." For both pork and beef these studies projected a reduction in regional differences by 1980 and indicated that the most rapidly expanding markets are those located along the southern boundaries of the United States from Florida to California.

By Cut of Meat. When meat was shipped to retail outlets in carcass form, sales and consumption of the various cuts were in about the same ratio throughout the various regions. This was especially the case with beef in the early 1950s. By 1965, an increase had occurred in the shipment of primal-wholesale cuts of beef, a trend that continued into the 1980s. As a result, consumption of different cuts began to vary considerably by region and by type of household. For the United States as a whole, steaks (loin, rib, round, and chuck) comprised a larger percentage of total beef consumption in the spring of 1965 than of 1977—39 percent compared to 34 percent. In the spring of 1977, ground beef comprised the larger percentage of total beef consumption—36 percent compared to 26 percent in the spring of 1965 (Haidacher et al. 1982).[2] See Table 6.15 and Fig 6.4.

Consumption of steak decreased markedly (as a percentage of total beef consumption) in all regions and among all types of households, except farm families (Tables 6.16 and 6.17). The decrease was greater in the West and Northeast than the North Central and Southern regions. Relative declines also occurred in all but the Southern region for roasts and "other" beef cuts (see Tables 6.15-6.17).

Changes in consumption of various pork cuts by regions and type of household are shown in Tables 6.15-6.17. Here, wide differences are noted among regions in both 1965 and 1977. Consumption of fresh pork (as percent of total pork) increased in all regions except the Western. Consumption of processed pork decreased slightly in the three regions that experienced an increase in fresh pork consumption but increased in the West. Consumption of bacon and sausage was relatively low in the North, East, and North Central regions but remained rela-

---

[2] Part of this change is attributed to possible changes in retailing, including expansion of fast-food outlets, and to survey reporting procedures.

Table 6.15. Percentage of Beef and Pork Consumed as Various Cuts, by Season, 1977-1978 and Spring 1965.

	Spring 1965	Percent consumption 1977-1978				
		Spring	Summer	Fall	Winter	Average
Beef						
Loin and rib						
Steaks	18	18	16	15	16	16
Roasts	2	1	2	1	1	1
Round and chuck						
Steaks	21	16	16	15	14	15
Roasts	24	23	23	25	23	23
Ground	26	36	37	36	37	37
Other	9	6	6	8	9	8
Pork						
Fresh*	32	38	39	41	40	40
Processed*	33	29	25	23	26	26
Bacon and sausage	35	33	36	36	34	34

Source: Calculated by authors from Haidacher et al. (1982).
*Excluding bacon and sausage.

tively stable from 1965 to 1977 in all regions. It is worth noting that luncheon meats accounted for 6 percent of total meat consumption—8 percent if poultry and fish are excluded—for the United States as a whole (Table 6.6).

Table 6.16. Percentage of Beef and Pork Consumed as Various Cuts, by Region, Spring 1965 and 1977.

	Percent consumption							
	Spring 1965				Spring 1977			
	NE	NC	S	W	NE	NC	S	W
Beef								
Loin and rib								
Steaks	20	18	19	18	20	18	17	17
Roasts	3	2	2	3	2	1	2	2
Round and chuck								
Steaks	27	17	20	26	19	14	15	18
Roasts	24	25	23	23	22	24	23	21
Ground	19	31	28	22	32	39	37	35
Other	7	7	8	8	5	4	6	7
Pork								
Fresh*	37	35	27	36	44	39	35	34
Processed*	36	33	33	29	30	31	25	32
Bacon and sausage	27	32	40	35	26	30	40	34

Source: Calculated by authors from Haidacher et al. (1982).
*Excluding bacon and sausage.

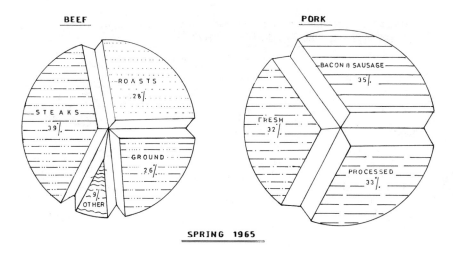

SPRING 1965

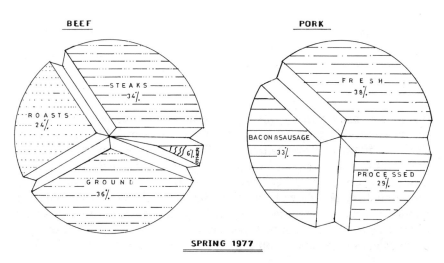

SPRING 1977

Fig. 6.4. Percentage of beef and pork consumed as various cuts, spring 1965 and 1977.

Factors Related to Meat Consumption

Many factors are related to the quantity of meat consumed and to the amount of money spent for meat. In previous sections, attention was called to differences in consumption among nations and among regions within the United States. These differences are largely reflections of more basic factors, of which the more important are price of product, level of family income, and prices of competing products. Other factors

Table 6.17. Percentage of Beef and Pork Consumed as Various Cuts, by Type of Household, Spring 1965 and 1977.

	Percent consumed					
	Urban		Rural			
			Farm		Nonfarm	
	1965	1977	1965	1977	1965	1977
Beef						
Loin and rib						
Steaks	19	19	18	24	16	14
Roasts	2	2	3	2	2	1
Round and chuck						
Steaks	24	16	17	14	19	16
Roasts	25	22	23	22	23	24
Ground	22	35	30	34	32	39
Other	8	6	9	4	8	6
Pork						
Fresh*	36	40	27	26	27	37
Processed*	32	28	37	38	33	29
Bacon and sausage	32	32	36	36	40	34

Source: Calculated by the authors from data in Haidacher et al. (1982).
*Excluding bacon and sausage.

are ethnic background, type of occupation, religious beliefs, personal tastes and preferences, diets, and food fads. In terms of total consumption, the number of people involved is obviously an important factor. The relationship between numbers of people and meat consumption needs little analysis. Other things being equal, a 1 percent increase in the number of people will result in about a 1 percent increase in the quantity of meat consumed. Our primary concern is with factors that affect the quantity consumed per person; emphasis is thus placed on product prices, incomes, and prices of competing products.

Price of Product. The relationship between consumption and price of product is explained by theories of demand. It is quite obvious to consumers with a limited budget that they can, and will, buy more meat at lower prices than at higher prices, and vice versa. Prices, of course, are established at various levels throughout the marketing system. An examination of the price–quantity relationship at the retail and farm levels follows.

Retail Demand. The relationship between prices and quantity consumed inolves the notion of price elasticity of demand, which was discussed in Chap. 3. A considerable amount of research has been done on price elasticity for various products, the results of which are not identical but reasonably consistent. Differences in research results on this problem can arise from differences in the time period upon which the study is based, on the one hand, and differences in research methodology, on the other.

Two general conclusions are as follows: (1) Demand is less elastic at the farm level than at retail, and (2) demand is less elastic for aggregates of food than for individual items. A number of excellent demand studies have been made. Three of the most comprehensive that involve meats are those of Brandow (1961), George and King (1971), and Haidacher et al. (1982). In an exhaustive study, Brandow found retail price elasticities to be as follows: beef, − 0.95; veal, − 1.60; pork, − 0.75; and lamb and mutton, − 2.35. George and King (1971) estimated retail price elasticities of − 0.64 for beef; − 1.72 for veal; − 0.41 for pork, and − 2.63 for lamb and mutton. The 1971 study derived somewhat lower (i.e., less elastic) estimates for beef and pork and slightly higher estimates for veal and lamb and mutton than those found by Brandow. Haidacher et al. (1982) estimated the cross-price and income elasticities for red meat, poultry, and fish in the U.S. The price elasticity was set at − 0.68 for red meat; − 0.89 for poultry; − 0.05 for fish; and − 1.03 for nonfood. These coefficients are shown in diagonal positions in Table 6.18. The last column of the table shows the estimated income elasticities; the off-diagonal cells are the cross-price elasticities. The researchers disaggregated the composite commodities of Table 6.18 to obtain more specific information on the individual meat. The results are shown in Table 6.19. The price elasticities, as shown in Table 6.19, were estimated as follows: beef and veal, − 0.66; pork, − 0.73; other red meats, − 0.69; chicken, − 0.58; and turkey, − 0.65.

Interpretation of the elasticity coefficients—taking beef and veal as an example from Table 6.19—is that a 1-percent increase in retail beef prices will result in a decrease in quantity purchased of 0.66 percent (or vice versa for price decrease). This, as well as George and King's estimate of price elasticity of beef, can be classed as moderately inelastic, whereas Brandow found it to be only slightly inelastic. In an earlier

Table 6.18.   Price and Income Elasticities of Red Meat, Poultry, and Fish.*

Item	Red meat	Poultry	Fish	Nonfood	Expenditure
Red meat	−0.6768	0.0984	0.0117	0.1033	0.6507
Poultry	0.5649	−0.8860	0.0522	−0.3560	0.7470
Fish	0.1590	0.1199	−0.0531	0.0833	0.5492
Nonfood	−0.0235	−0.0088	−0.0023	−1.0263	1.2064

Source: Haidacher et al. (1982).
*This table contains partial results of a composite food-demand system.

Table 6.19. Estimated Price Elasticities, Disaggregated Demand Model.*

Corresponding change in consumption of	Given a 1-percent change in the price of				
	Beef and veal	Pork	Other meats	Chicken	Turkey
Beef and veal	−0.6565	0.1171	0.0140	0.0409	−0.0056
Pork	0.1613	−0.7302	0.0353	0.1014	0.0202
Other red meat	0.0712	0.1373	−0.6898	−0.0494	0.0202
Chicken	0.1613	0.2796	−0.0327	−0.5804	0.0148
Turkey	−0.650	0.2320	0.0597	0.0626	−0.6485

Source: Haidacher et al. (1982).
*This table contains partial results of a disaggregated demand system containing 42 food commodities and nonfood.

pioneering study, Working (1954) reported that the demand for beef was more price elastic in the long run (five or ten years) than in the short run (one year). His calculation of short-run price elasticity was −0.90, which is reasonably close to Brandow's figure. Working determined the long-run price elasticity for beef to be −1.40 to −1.50. At this level, demand would definitely be elastic.

No one disagrees with the proposition that long-run demand can be more elastic than short-run demand, but not all researchers agree that Working's analysis proved the point. From the standpoint of market control, the degree of elasticity is an important consideration. Supply reduction programs are based on the supposition that demand is price inelastic (that is, that a reduction in quantity would result in a more than proportionate increase in price). This would mean an increase in seller's total revenue and (unless costs increased) presumably an increase in net revenue. If the demand is elastic, however, supply reduction would decrease rather than increase revenue. Whatever the degree of price elasticity, the beef-cattle industry, through the spokesmanship of its national organization, has never condoned a mandatory supply-control program. The opposition to such an approach has never been based on possible negative revenue effects as a result of an elastic demand. It is not known whether industry actions are the reflection of an intuitive feeling that revenue would decline, simply a reflection of rugged individualism, or some other aspect. Although the question of degree of price elasticity in the long run is not settled, there is general agreement that the short-run elasticity of demand for beef is less than unity. As mentioned, Brandow reported −0.95 and Working, −0.90. Others (Breimyer, 1961; Hassler, 1962) have reported somewhat lower elasticities, and there is some evidence that the degree of elasticity is decreasing with the passing of time.

George and King (1971) estimated the elasticity of demand for veal at −1.72, and for lamb and mutton at −2.62. No comparable estimates were made by Haidacher *et al.* (1982). It can be assumed that the coefficient for lamb and mutton represents primarily the demand for lamb, rather than mutton. Consumers are more sensitive (i.e., respond by adjusting purchases) to price changes of veal and lamb than to price changes of beef and pork.

Both Brandow (1961) and George and King (1971), as well as most studies, indicate that pork has the lowest degree of price elasticity of any meat. Although results of other studies range both higher and lower than this, most studies put the elasticity of pork less than unity and below that of beef. Haidacher *et al.* (1982) found the price elasticity of pork to be −0.73, as shown in Table 6.19. The authors acknowledged that the "magnitude of price elasticity for pork relative to beef and veal appears to be somewhat higher when compared to other estimates and experience, which usually show a slightly larger relative importance for beef and veal. Similar comments apply to the magnitude of the elasticity for pork relative to chicken and turkey." The researchers, however, citing the statistical tests of significance of their research results, concluded that "Nevertheless, except for fresh and frozen fish, the relatively small standard errors of these price elasticities suggest that they warrant a degree of confidence."

Price-elasticity coefficients for chicken (−0.58) and turkey (−0.65) are also shown in Table 6.19. The price-elasticity coefficient for turkey is relatively larger than for chicken, meaning that quantity purchased is relatively responsive to price change. Thus, according to the 1982 study, it appears that all major meats have a relatively inelastic demand at retail.

Farm-Level Demand.   Producers are usually more concerned with price-quantity relationships at the farm level. Most realize that demand for their products is derived from retail demand, but lags and market imperfections often screen the direct relationships.

Farm-level price-elasticity coefficients from Brandow's study (1961) are as follows: Cattle, −0.68; calves, −1.08; hogs, −0.46; and sheep and lambs, −1.78. George and King (1971) found farm-level price elasticities of −0.42 for beef, −0.24 for pork, and −1.67 for lamb and mutton. Since Haidacher *et al.* (1982) did not report farm-level elasticities, comparison with earlier studies is not possible. As expected, in all cases elasticity is less at farm level than at retail, which follows from the fact that marketing charges remain relatively fixed when prices vary. A price change at retail will be passed back through marketing channels to farmers in almost its entirety. Since farm prices are lower than retail prices (by the amount of marketing charges), a given price change has a greater percentage effect on farm prices (which is a lower absolute amount than retail price) than on retail prices. An example will make this clear. Assume that a retail price is $1.00 per lb and marketing charges are 40 cents per lb. The farm price equivalent would be 60 cents per lb (i.e., $1.00 − $0.40 = $0.60). Suppose that retail prices decrease 10 cents per lb. At the retail level, the change amounts to 10 percent. If the entire 10 cents decrease is taken from the farm price, the change amounts to almost 17 percent of the farm price. If it assumed that the percentage change in quantity marketed was the same at both levels, this translates to a lower degree of elasticity at the farm than at retail level. This situation appears to be verified by the evidence presented.

So far, we have discussed elasticity of demand in terms of the effect on quantity purchased of variations in price, which is the viewpoint of a merchandiser. The same situation viewed in the inverse may be put in the form of a question. What is the effect upon price of variations in quantity? This is more in line with the viewpoint of producers. There is evidence that more and more producers are becoming concerned. Various farm organizations have undertaken programs designed to gain some control over variations in quantity marketed, both in terms of total quantities and cyclial and seasonal variations. If price elasticity is known, this question can be answered by calculating its reciprocal, which gives an approximation of the "price flexibility" coefficient. It follows that price flexibility increases as elasticity decreases. In other words, the more inelastic the demand, the greater the effect a given change in quantity will have upon price received (a discussion of a different view on the priori assumption of this relationship will follow).

A knowledge of price elasticities, coupled with good estimates of impending changes in quantities available for market, provides one basis for forecasting price changes. Take the case of hogs as an example. George and King's (1971) estimated elasticities suggest that flexibility at the farm level may be approximated at −4.17 [the reciprocal of price elasticity, but see Haidache et al. (1982) and Chap. 3 for caution]. This is interpreted to mean that a 1-percent change in the quantity of hogs marketed will result in a change in price at the farm (in the opposite direction) of 4.17 percent. Thus, if one had a good estimate that hog marketing will increase 10 percent next year, he can predict that, other things being equal, prices will decline about 42 percent. It may be noted that hog price flexibility derived by Brandow's analysis would be substantially less than that. A tentative estimate of hog price flexibility used by many market analysts in past years was −2.5 to −3.0.

Haidacher et al. (1982) estimated price (i.e., "own-price") and cross-price flexibilities as shown in Table 6.20. The coefficients of price flexibility between the price of beef and veal and the quantity of beef, −0.37, indicates that a 1-percent increase in market quantity of beef would require a beef and veal price decrease of about 0.4 percent. Other price flexibilities can be interpreted in a similar way. The authors acknowledged the fact that all estimates of price flexibilities are less than unity "does contradict expectations based on conventional wisdom, which holds that own-price flexibilities for demand-inelastic commodities are greater than 1 in absolute value." They explained this discrepancy as follows: "However, this conventional view is based on the definition of the price flexibility as the reciprocal of the corresponding elasticity, a situation appropriate to the unique circumstance of a single demand relation in which quantity is solely a function of its own prices. In general, this concept is not appropriate for a demand function in which quantity is a function of all prices and income, or for a complete system of such demand equations. In the present context of a meat subsystem, there is no a priori reason for expecting these flexibilities to be greater than 1 (absolute value) nor does the fact that they are less than unity imply corresponding own price elasticities which are greater than 1 (absolute value)."

This type of information also can be used as a criterion for determining market strategy or market policy. An organization (or public agency) charged with developing a market program would be interested in knowing the effect upon price of reducing supplies some specified percentage. A knowledge of price elasticities is essential in such a situation. It might be noted in this connection, that an organization or agency will be interested not only in the immediate price and income effect but also in the longer period situation. This involves the possibility and probability of competitors coming in with alternate products which may be domestically produced substitutes or the same product imported from other countries.

The price elasticity of "all meats" taken as an aggregate is less than that of most individual meats. This arises from the reaction of most

Table 6.20. Estimated Price Flexibilities for Meat.*

Item	Beef	Veal	Pork	Lamb and mutton	Broilers	Turkey
Beef and veal	−0.3685	−0.0174	0.0081	−0.0029	0.1501	0.0048
Pork	0.1777	0.0001	−0.6001	−0.0120	0.2481	0.0239
Broilers	−0.1001	0.0075	−0.3627	−0.0017	−0.4094	0.0330
Other meats	−0.0850	−0.0065	−0.0891	−0.0063	0.1154	−0.0001

Source: Haidacher et al. (1982).
*This table contains partial results of a complex demand system.

consumers in general that "meat" in some form, is virtually a necessity. Price elasticity is lower on necessities than on luxuries. It is recognized, of course, that such foods as eggs, fish, cheese, etc., can replace meat to a degree, but to a smaller degree than one meat item can replace another. In addition, the quantity of total meat which consumers will purchase is somewhat limited by the capacity of the human stomach. Once a person's stomach is reasonably full it takes substantial price reductions to induce that person to purchase additional quantities. He/she will, however, substitute one meat for another as relative prices change.

Price of Competing Products. The quantity of a product consumed during a given time is affected by prices of competing products. Competing products are defined as goods that can be used as substitutes for the product in question. Most people prefer some change in the meat dish from day to day simply for the sake of variety and enjoyment. Here, however, we are concerned with the degree of response that purchasers will make in substituting one meat for another as a result of price changes. If the price of pork rises, consumers will purchase larger quantities of beef, lamb, chicken, etc.—assuming prices of the competing products remain unchanged. How much effect will a 1-percent increase in pork prices have upon the consumption of beef? This information is obtained from a determination of cross elasticities.

It will be recalled that the negative numbers in the diagonal of Table 6.19 are price elasticities. The off-diagonal numbers are cross elasticities.[3] Under the column headed "beef and veal," one finds 0.16 on the row titled "pork." This is interpreted as follows: a 1-percent increase in beef and veal (composite) prices will result, *cetris paribus*, in an increase of 0.16 of 1-percent in the quantity of pork purchased by consumers—or, as it is often stated, a 10-percent increase in beef and veal prices will result in an increase of 1.6 percent in the quantity of pork purchased.

The reaction of consumers in purchasing pork in response to a change in the beef and veal prices is relatively low. The coefficient is 0.12. It is noted that the reaction in purchasing beef and veal in response to a change in pork prices is the same (0.16). A change in pork prices has a greater effect on purchases of other red meats, turkey, and chicken than it does on purchase of beef and veal.

---

[3] All coefficients of own-price elasticities are, as expected, negative. Cross-price elasticities are expected to be positive for substitutable products. The negative signs for some of the turkey and chicken relationships were caused by statistical deficiencies in the data used in the estimation (Haidacher *et al.*, 1982).

In general, the cross elasticities between poultry and red meats are low (Table 6.18), which appears to belie a rather common assumption that a lowering of poultry prices will result in drastic switch from red meat. Over the years, a long-term declining trend in poultry prices has been associated with a long-term increasing trend in poultry consumption. It has been presumed this took place at the expense of red meat. The low degree of cross elasticity shown in Tables 6.18 and 6.19 might cast some doubt on this presumption. Over a long period of years, however, even a relatively low cross elasticity could have a considerable cumulative effect. It might also be possible that the degree of cross elasticity declines as consumption of poultry reaches higher and higher levels. If this should be the case, competition from poultry could taper off in the future.

Cross-price flexibilities are useful when viewed from the standpoint of the effect that a change in quantity of one meat will have on the price of another, on the one hand, or the effect that a change in quantity marketed of one species of live animals will have upon the price of another, on the other hand. The latter ordinarily is the more general concern of producers. For example, if during the fall of a given year it was forecast that broiler production would expand next year—say, by 10 percent—what effect would this have upon beef prices? Two things are obvious: (1) Increased production of broilers will result in lower broiler prices and possibly lower cattle and beef prices (assuming no change in other factors), and (2) the lower the degree of substitutibility, the less will be the effect on cattle and beef prices.

The off-diagonal coefficients in Table 6.20 are the cross-price flexibilities. For example, the figure between broilers and beef and veal, 0.15, indicates that a 1-percent change in the quantity of broilers would require a 0.15-percent change (in the opposite direction) in the price of beef and veal if consumers are to purchase the additional quantity of broilers. Other coefficients can be similarly interpreted.

Income.   The relationship of income changes to meat purchases can be expessed as (1) changes in quantity purchased, (2) changes in expenditures (or value), and/or (3) changes in price paid. A number of studies have developed this type of information. We will draw primarily from just four: (1) a USDA analysis that relied on a national household survey (Rizek and Rockwell, 1970); (2) Brandow's (1961) analysis mentioned earlier; and (3) George and King (1971) and Haidacher et al. (1982). Emphasis will be on comparison of the 1965 and 1977 surveys, with limited reference to selected aspects of the other studies.

Figure 6.5 is a graphic presentation of income–consumption relationships for all meats, red meats, beef, pork, veal, and for lamb and

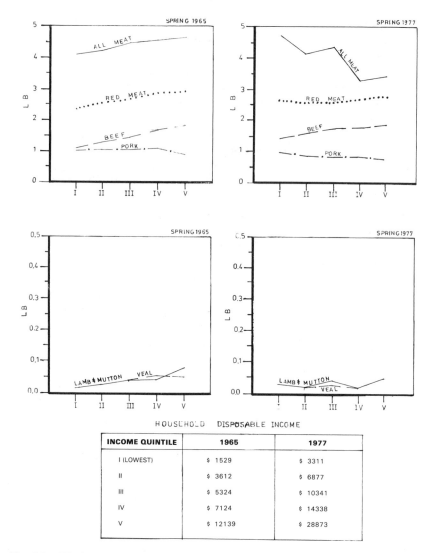

Fig. 6.5. Weekly home meat consumption per person by income, spring 1965 and 1977.

mutton for the United States as a whole in spring 1965 and 1977. It may be observed in Fig. 6.5 and Table 6.21 that in the spring of 1965 the weekly consumption of all meat increased as income increased but decreased as income increased in the 1977 survey. Haidacher *et al.* (1982) found that while lower-income households consumed more meat at home in 1977, the average value of weekly home consumption was

Table 6.21. Per-Capita Weekly Home Meat Consumption, by Income Quintile, Spring 1965 and 1977.

	Income Quintile									
	1965					1977				
Item	I	II	III	IV	V	I	II	III	IV	V
					Consumption, lb					
Total meat	4.11	4.19	4.47	4.58	4.61	4.71	4.19	4.40	3.38	4.37
Red meat	2.35	2.52	2.75	2.93	2.98	2.63	2.56	2.60	2.72	2.77
Beef	1.18	1.38	1.64	1.75	1.87	1.55	1.61	1.64	1.77	1.87
Pork	1.13	1.08	1.03	1.09	0.98	1.02	0.91	0.89	0.91	0.80
Veal	0.02	0.03	0.04	0.05	0.05	0.03	0.02	0.03	0.02	0.05
Lamb, mutton, goat	0.02	0.03	0.04	0.04	0.08	0.03	0.02	0.04	0.02	0.05
Poultry	0.85	0.82	0.81	0.81	0.80	1.00	0.82	0.73	0.80	0.86
Fish and shellfish	0.42	0.33	0.34	0.35	0.37	0.46	0.31	0.34	0.38	0.37
Miscellaneous	0.49	0.52	0.57	0.49	0.46	0.61	0.49	0.46	0.48	0.37
Franks	0.13	0.16	0.18	0.17	0.15	0.17	0.15	0.14	0.16	0.13
Luncheon	0.22	0.24	0.29	0.25	0.23	0.26	0.23	0.25	0.26	0.20
Variety	0.14	0.12	0.10	0.07	0.08	0.18	0.11	0.07	0.06	0.04

Source: Haidacher et al. (1982).

lower than for higher-income families. This may be explained by the fact that higher-income households purchase more expensive meats. Data in Table 6.21 and Fig 6.5 indicate that lower-income households consumed more pork, poultry, fish, and miscellaneous meats per person than higher-income households. Between the 1965 and 1977 surveys, households in the lowest income category increased per capita consumption level of all meat, whereas higher-income households decreased total consumption.

There was a 12-percent increase in per-capita red-meat consumption by lower-income households between spring 1965 and 1977, as compared to a 7.6-percent decrease by the higher-income families. In general, the difference in per-capita consumption of beef across the income quintiles narrowed between the two surveys. At-home pork consumption declined for all income levels. In fact, the negative relationship between income and pork consumption observed in 1965 was even more pronounced in 1977. Veal and lamb consumption was greater for higher-income households in both 1965 and 1977 surveys.

Haidacher *et al.* (1982) used the 1977–78 survey data to estimate regression equations for various relationships between consumption of different meats and selected variables. The results related to income are shown in Table 6.22. The coefficients show responses to income changes, presented in three forms of elasticities: expenditure, quantity, and quality. The expenditure (money-value) elasticities measure the percentage change in expenditure in response to a 1-percent change in disposable income. For example, the 0.14 expenditure elasticity for red meat (Table 6.22) means that a 1-percent increase in income is associated with a 0.14-percent increase in the money value of red meat consumed. The quantity elasticity coefficients shows the percentage

Table 6.22. Consumer At-Home Responses to Changes in Income, 1977–1978.

Item	Expenditure elasticity	Quantity elasticity	Quality elasticity*
Total meat	0.12	0.00	0.12
Red meat	0.14	0.04	0.10
Beef	0.18	0.07	0.11
Pork	0.02	−.06	0.08
Veal	0.54	0.41	0.13
Lamb, mutton, goat meat	0.79	0.62	0.17
Franks	−1.7	−.21	0.04
Luncheon meats	−.08	−.16	0.08
Variety meats	−.16	−.32	0.16

Source: Haidacher *et al.* (1982).
*Calculated as the difference between the expenditure elasticity and the quantity elasticity.

change in quantity consumed as a result of a 1-percent change in income (i.e., income elasticity). Quality elasticity measures the extent to which the average price paid varies with consumer income. Other studies (Breimyer, 1961) have shown a positive correlation between time and beef consumption. In a statistical sense, time is a rough indicator of change in personal tastes and preferences. These factors—income, tastes, and preferences—go a long way in explaining the increased demand for beef in recent decades.

Consumer purchases of veal and lamb are considerably more sensitive to income changes than of pork or beef, as indicated by the higher coefficients shown in Tables 6.22 and 6.23.

The persistent decline in lamb consumption appears to be a direct reflection of reduction in the available supply. Lamb ranks relatively high in both price and income elasticity. Consumers who eat any lamb at all usually have a distinct preference for it. There is a presumption that consumers who eat lamb when it is available lose their preference when it is unavailable and will not again purchase it. Evidence is lacking on this point, but it is a reasonable hypothesis. It is known that lamb consumption is highest on the East and West Coasts and extremely light in the heartland of the country.

Veal consumption has declined as the demand for feeder cattle has strengthened relative to the veal slaughter market. The demand for feeder cattle is strong enough to divert most vealers into feedlots for finishing. Consumption of veal will continue to decline, but most of the possible shift has already been accomplished.

Data in Table 6.22 show that pork consumption (i.e., quantity per person) does not bear the same relationship to income as does beef consumption. Incomes and quantity of pork consumed are negatively related (e.g., a quantity elasticity of −0.06 in Table 6.22). The negative relationship of incomes with respect to quantity purchased has serious

Table 6.23. Income Elasticity of Demand at Retail: Percentage Changes in Quantity Demand Resulting from 1-Percent Change in Income.

Quantities Demanded of	Income Elasticities		
	Brandow (1965)	George and King (1971)	Haidacher et al. (1982)
Beef	0.47	0.29	—
Veal	0.58	0.59	—
Beef and veal	—	—	0.23
Pork	0.32	0.13	0.48
Chicken	0.37	0.17	0.18
Turkey	0.49	0.77	−0.36

implications for the pork industry. It means that as average incomes increase, consumers cut back on the quantity of pork they purchase. Increasing average income is taken to be a symbol of economic progress. Average incomes have been increasing over the years, and national economic policy is designed so as to continue the trend.

Haidacher *et al.* (1982), Rizek and Rockwell (1970), and many others, including Brandow (1961) and George and King (1971), derived a positive relationship between expenditures for pork and average income—although the relationship is considerably weaker for pork than for other red meats. The income elasticity for pork has apparently changed over time. In a study covering the years 1950–1973, Ray and Young (1977) found that the elasticity value was "negative in the earlier periods of fit, then approached zero and finally became positive and statistically significant around 0.4 and 0.5 for the most recent periods of fit."

Income–chicken-consumption relationships fall in about the same patterns as that of pork, i.e., negative with relation to quantity, but positive with relation to value of purchases and price paid. In the case of turkey, the relationships are positive and at a higher level than for chicken.

Other Factors. In addition to income, meat prices, and prices of competing products, meat consumption is influenced by type of occupation, ethnic background, religious beliefs, diets and food fads, and perhaps other factors.

Mechanization and automation not only have influenced type of occupation but also have reduced the amount of heavy physical labor involved in given occupations. These factors were, and still are, instrumental in shifting large numbers of people from farm residencies and farm occupations to cities and, in many cases, less strenuous occupations. Farm households also tend to eat more beef than do urban and rural nonfarm households. Similarly, farm households typically consume more pork than do urban or rural nonfarm households. There was an exception to this in the 1965 survey that showed that farm families in the Northeast consumed less pork than other types of households. The decline in farm population has undoubtedly contributed to the decline in pork consumption experienced in recent decades.

Ethnic background shows up particularly in food habits of immigrants. For example, people from the Mediterranean and the Near East have a much higher preference for lamb and mutton than many other peoples. These preferences are especially strong during the lifetime of the immigrants. They carry over to a considerable extent to their children but gradually dissipate with succeeding generations. This phenomenon is considered to be a factor, though not a controlling one, in the decline in lamb consumption in the United States. People from certain areas in Europe, and especially eastern Europe, have a decided preference for rather highly seasoned sausages. This shows up not only as an ethnic characteristic, but also as a geographic characteristic because of the tendency of immigrants to settle near relatives and friends, thus developing geographic concentrations of certain nationalities in the United States. An area south of the Great Lakes at one time was known as the "dry sausage belt" largely for this reason.

Religious beliefs can influence meat consumption. Jewish and Moslem restrictons on pork consumption obviously reduce the average consumption of pork and enhance the consumption of beef, veal, mutton, and undoubtedly other foods. It is estimated that Orthodox Jews consume 40 to 50 percent more beef per capita than the national average (Anon., 1953).[4] Jewish kosher[5] as applied to meat necessitates the purchase of more pounds per person to get the same net pounds of beef as nonkosher meats. Only the forequarters are used for the kosher trade, and forequarters contain more waste in the form of bone and fat than do hindquarters. Prior to 1966, Roman Catholics were restricted in the consumption of meat on Fridays and during Lent. The lifting of this ban probably resulted in a small increase in meat consumption, but tradition still induces a considerable restraint on Friday meat consumption.

Widespread publicity and pronouncements from the medical profession on possible linkage of obesity and overweight to diseases of the heart and blood vessels have resulted in some shifting away from fatter to more lean cuts of meat and probably to some extent away from animal fats to vegetable fats. The question of animal fats versus vegetable fats is not resolved. Nevertheless, it has an impact on meat consumption. Pork consumption probably sustained the greatest adverse affect due to the public image of pork as a relatively fat meat, but that image has improved immeasurably in recent years.

REFERENCES

Anon. 1953. Armour's Livestock Bur., Chicago. April–May.
Brandow, G. E. 1961. Interrelationship among demands for farm products and implications for control of market supply. Penn. Agr. Expt. Sta. Bull. 680.

---

[4] An analysis of meat consumption in the Northeast, however, indicated no significant difference in beef consumption among members of Jewish, Catholic, and Protestant faiths.
[5] Kosher is a Hebrew word meaning "clean" or "fit to eat" according to Jewish dietary laws.

Breimyer, H. F. 1961. Demand and prices for meat. USDA Econ. Res. Serv. Tech. Bull. 1253.

Dahl, D. C., and Hammond, J. W. 1977. *Market and Price Analysis, the Agricultural Industries.* New York: McGraw-Hill Book Company.

Foote, R. L. 1956. Elasticities of demand for nondurable goods, with emphasis on food. USDA Agr. Marketing Serv. 96.

George, P. S., and King, G. A. 1971. Consumer demand for food commodities in the United States with projections for 1980. California Agr. Expt. Sta. Giannini Foundation Monograph Number 26.

Goodwin, J. W., *et al.* 1968. The irreversible demand function for beef. Oklahoma Agr. Expt. Sta. Tech. Bull. T–127.

Haidacher, Richard C., *et al.* 1982. Consumer Demand for Red Meats, Poultry, and Fish. USDA Agr. Res. Serv., AGES 820818, Washington, D. C.

Hassler, J. R. 1962. The U.S. feed concentrate-lifestock economy's demand structure, 1949–59 (with projections for 1960–70). Nebraska Res. Bull. 203. Also, North Central Regional Publ. 138.

Heimstra, S. J. 1970. Food consumption, prices, expenditures supplement for 1968. USDA Econ. Res. Serv., Agr. Econ. Rept. 138.

Ives, J. R. 1966. The livestock and meat economy of the United States. American Meat Institute, Chicago.

Langemeir, L., and Thompson, R. G. 1967. Demand, supply and price relationships for the beef sector, post World War II period. Amer. J. Agr. Econ. 49, 169–185.

Mann, J. S., and St. George, G. E. 1978. Estimates of elasticities of food demand in the United States, USDA Econ. Stat. and Co-op Serv. Tech Bull. No. 1580.

McDonald, R. F. 1966. Influence of selected socio-economic factors on red meat consumption patterns in the Northeast Region. Maryland Agr. Expt. Sta. Bull 477.

Raunikar, R., *et al.* 1969. Spatial and temporal aspects of demand for food in the United States. II. Beef. Georgia Agr. Expt. Sta. Res. Bull. 63.

Raunikar, R., *et al.* 1970. Spatial and temporal aspects of demand for food in the United States. III. Pork. Georgia Agr. Expt. Sta. Res. Bull. 85.

Rizek, R. L., and Rockwell, G. R. 1970. Household consumption patterns for meat and poultry, Spring 1965. USDA Econ. Res. Serv., Agr. Econ. Rept. 173.

Roy, S. K., and Young, R. D. 1977. Demand for pork: a long-run analysis. Texas Tech Univ., College of Agricultural Sciences Publication No. T-1-153.

Tomek, W. G., and Cochrane, W. W. 1962. Long-run demand: a concept and elasticity estimates for meats. *J. farm Econ.* 44: 717–730.

Tomek, W. G., and Robinson, K. L. 1972. Agricultural Products Prices. Cornell Univ. Press, Ithaca, N.Y.

USDA. 1969. World meat consumption. USDA Foreign Agr. Serv. Circ. FLM 12–69.

USDA. 1977. Per capita meat consumption. USDA Foreign Agr. Serv. Circ. FLM 2–77.

USDA. 1983. World Livestock and Meat Situation and Outlook. Foreign Agr. Circ. FL&P–183., Washington, D. C.

USDA. 1984A. Agricultural Statistics 1984. U.S. Gov. Printing Office, Washington, D.C.

USDA. 1984B. 1984 handbook of Agricultural Charts. USDA Agr. Handbook No. 637.

Walters, F. E., *et al.* 1975. Price and demand relationships for retail beef: 1947–1974. Colorado Agr. Expt. Sta. Tech. Bull. 125

Working, E. J. 1954. Demand for Meat. Inst. Meat Packing, Univ. of Chicago.

7

Types of Livestock Markets and Marketing

Marketing encompasses a wide range of functions. Among those most directly concerned with livestock are transporting, grading, financing, market news reporting, risk bearing, buying, and selling. This chapter is devoted primarily to the traditional institutional arrangements and agencies concerned with buying and selling. Certain aspects of other marketing functions are treated in subsequent chapters. In terms of producer problems, doubts, frustrations, and dissatisfaction, however, it is the pricing of the product—the outcome of the buying-selling function—that stands out above all others.

It was pointed out in Chap. 2 that growth and development of the marketing system followed an historical pattern of adaptation to evolving geographical settlements and to technological developments in transportation and meat preservation. Producer dissatisfaction with alleged lack of competition among buyers and lack of market information were other factors that helped shape market development. Many changes have occurred in the system over the years. A number of modifications and innovations have been introduced, but the changes have been of an evolutionary nature. Although the basic organizational arrangement of earlier days continues to provide the predominant market framework, innovations (electronic marketing is an example) have been introduced.

Producer concern with deficiencies in the system varies with economic conditions, which in turn are associated with production cycles. During recent years, much attention has been given to alternative marketing systems and to possible modifications of the present system (Black and Uvacek, 1972; Farris and Dietrick, 1975; Forker, et al., 1976; Wohlgenant and Greer, 1974). Extreme financial stress sustained by the industry during the mid-1970s gave considerable impetus to these studies. A period of even greater stress during the 1980s is sure to stimulate research in additional alternative market arrangements. A persistent upward spiral of production costs coupled with extreme instability of livestock prices leads to a high risk factor, and the latter provides a powerful incentive for change. In this chapter, we examine present markets and marketing arrangements and discuss selected alternatives that have been suggested to replace or modify the present system. One such alternative—electronic markets and marketing—has generated much interest in recent years and appears to have great potential. Chapter 12 is devoted to it.

TYPES OF LIVESTOCK MARKETS

Producers in most of the United States have access to several types of markets. From the standpoint of competition among markets, this is a desirable situation. A producer who is dissatisfied with a particular market can patronize another. This option tends to generate competition among markets, but if the locality is dominated by one or a few buyers, the degree of competition may still be less than satisfactory (Armstrong, 1976). At the same time, some researchers have pointed out the operational inefficiencies of duplicative, small-scale markets in certain parts of the country (Broadbent, 1970). These are aspects of market organization that have implications for both pricing efficiency and operational efficiency.

Newberg (1959) distinguished 13 types of livestock markets, as follows: (1) stockyards, central public markets, or terminal markets; (2) auction markets; (3) local markets, concentration yards; (4) country dealers; (5) packer buyers; (6) packing plants and packers' buying stations; (7) order buyers; (8) other farmers; (9) locker plants and retailers (usually a few head are sold to a local retailer or locker plant); (10) pools, where livestock (mostly lambs) are pooled and sorted and producers are paid according to the grade they supply; (11) special type auctions (held infrequently, mostly for feeder and breeder cattle); (12) cooperative shipping associations; and (13) cooperative selling associations.

All of these types are still on the scene, although many changes have taken place in the use of the various markets. Commercial feedlots, country commission-men, electronic markets, and producer bargaining associations can be added to the list.

There is no completely satisfactory nomenclature of market types that serves all purposes. Some would object to ambiguity and duplication in the above list. For example, order buyers operate at terminal public markets and auctions as well as carry out free-lance country operations. Many terminal public markets have incorporated auctions in their operations. Packer buyers operate at terminal public markets and auctions and also buy directly from feeders in the country.

The most commonly cited reasons for selecting a certain market outlet by producers are as follows: (1) price and the competitive nature of the pricing process, (2) convenience, (3) habit, (4) knowledge of the market or market personnel, (5) available services, (6) transportation cost, (7) type of livestock sold (some markets are more advantageous for particular class or grade of livestock), (8) net returns, and (9) importance of livestock in the production enterprise (if livestock sale accounts for most of the seller's income, he is likely to select a market based on price and competition; if it is not significant, convenience is probably more important). Although there is no single criterion for sellers' choice of a particular market outlet, price and convenience are probably the most important.

TYPES OF MARKETING

In addition to classifying markets, there is merit in a two-way classification of marketing. The differentiation rests on whether the principals to the transaction (sellers and buyers) utilize the services of a professional intermediary, i.e., a market agency or middleman. From the producer's standpoint, public terminal markets, auctions, country commission-men, bargaining associations on the selling side, and order buyers on the buying side, all are clearly in the class of markets providing or utilizing intermediaries. Other types of markets ordinarily do not use professional intermediaries. In essence, this differentiation of the market process involves the issue of "direct" versus "indirect" marketing—a controversial issue for decades. It involves the question of whether a livestock producer engages the services of a professional to make the sale or purchase transaction or does the job himself. The issue revolves around the question of whether a professional marketer can obtain a net return for the producer over and above what the producer himself could get, one that will at least pay for the services of the marketer and, hopefully, something in excess of that. In deciding whether to engage such services, the producer must weigh additional costs against additional revenue. The additional costs may include commission, shrinkage, trucking, yardage, feed, insurance, etc.

Trends in the use of various channels over the years reflect a combination of forces, such as changes in technology (communication, transportation, refrigeration) that have spurred decentralization of the packing industry and producer dissatisfaction with existing market channels. It is not the intent here to pass judgment on whether producers should do their own selling and buying. The operator of a commercial cattle feedlot who is buying and selling cattle every day undoubtedly is in a different situation from the many farmer feeders who buy only one lot of feeder cattle a year. Yet even in the latter case, much depends upon the qualifications of the individual.

ATTRIBUTES OF A GOOD MARKETER

The qualifications of a livestock marketer—whether he be a commission agent, an order buyer, a packer buyer, or a producer doing his own selling and buying—include three major attributes:

1. He must have the ability to judge livestock. In this he must be able to evaluate all the characteristics that affect price, grade (including both quality grade and yield grade), carcass yield (including fill and shrinkage factors), and weight.
2. He must know the market value of the particular class, grade, and weight of livestock under consideration—at the time in question. In other words, he must be up-to-date on the market situation.
3. He must have the ability to bargain. In the bargaining process it is imperative to know livestock and the current market situation, but that is not enough. Bargaining involves personality traits, attitude toward the other party, knowledge of trade language, persuasiveness without antagonizing the other party, and ability to leave the impression that the other party obtained full value in the bargain.

In developing the attributes of a livestock marketer, training can be important but does not completely substitute for experience. Market evaluation fo quality characteristics changes over time. Demand and supply factors change. To stay abreast of the changing situation requires continuous attention. Many professional marketers upon returning from a vacation will spend time up-dating themselves on the current situation before attempting to carry out transactions.

Analogies seldom portray a situation perfectly. Producers in day-to-day problems, however, find themselves faced with many decisions about whether to hire a professional or to do the job themselves. Few producers hesitate to make routine carpenter, plumbing, electrical, or mechanical repairs. On the matter of personal health and legal problems, operators almost invariably utilize services of doctors and lawyers. It would frequently be possible for an individual to handle his own legal matters, but few attempt it, and few would consider attempting to doctor themselves. The question of doing one's own marketing probably lies somewhere in between these extremes. Just as some individuals can do better than others in carpentering and plumbing, and some can come closer to handling their own legal problems than others, some livestock producers have the knowledge and ability to do their own marketing. Others undoubtedly would come out ahead financially by hiring the services of professionals.

MARKET CHANNELS AND OUTLETS

The routes or paths in the marketing system through which livestock pass as they move from farm or ranch to slaughter are known as *market channels*. Changes in ownership as livestock moves through successive production phases (as discussed in Chap. 4) necessitate the use of markets. Figure 7.1 presents a simplified diagram of market channels. The least complicated channel arises whenever the original herd or flock owner grows out and finishes his own output and then sells the finished animals directly to a packer. In many cases, however, the channels are more complicated than any combination shown. Livestock may pass through the ownership of a number of dealers, for example, as they move from one phase to another. There also may be a change of ownership during a given phase of production. Nevertheless, the diagram gives a general picture of types of markets and a number of connecting linkages that, taken together, portray the bulk of channels used. It also shows the links where professional intermediaries ordinarily are used.

Data on market outlets used by livestock producers in a particular state or in the nation as a whole are not collected or reported on a regular basis. Rather, information on outlets is obtained through a limited number of surveys by the USDA, the department of agriculture of the various states, or land grant universities. Several studies were published in the 1960s and 1970s on the market channels through which livestock was marketed (e.g., Newberg, 1963, and Illinois Cooperative Reporting Service, 1965.)

A more recent indication of the market outlets used by producers is found in a 1977 marketing channel survey conducted by the U.S. Department of Agriculture (USDA 1979). The survey classified market outlets into the following:

1. Local auctions and commission firms
2. Packers and butchers
3. Other farmers and ranchers
4. Commercial feedlots
5. Other sources (such as pools and cooperatives)

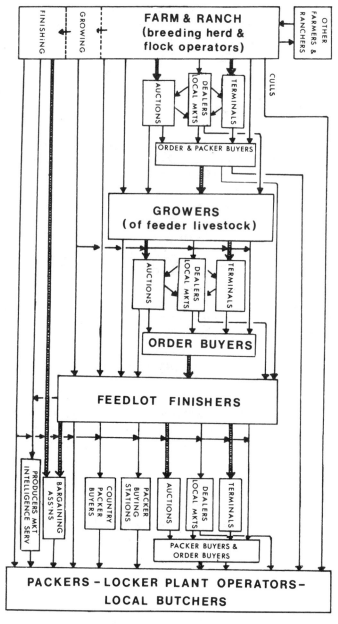

Fig. 7.1.   Schematic of livestock market channels: Wide arrows are channels on which professional marketing assistance is resorted to by livestock producers. (Plotted by authors from USDA data.)

The survey results are shown in Table 7.1 for the United States. The survey indicated that producers in the various states may differ from the average U.S. producer in methods by which they market their livestock. For example, producers who participated in the survey in Illinois indicated that 87 percent of their steers and heifers were sold through local auctions and commission firms as compared with 42 percent in the United States, where packers purchased 47 percent of the steers and heifers (compared with 12 percent in Illinois). Other farmers purchased smaller percentages of Illinois calves (13 percent) than the U.S. average of 30 percent. The survey also showed that 3 percent of the steers and heifers and 8 percent of the lambs were sold to commercial feedlots in the U.S., but, for example, none were sold through these lots in Illinois. The extent of the use of various methods varied from species to species, as shown in Table 7.1.

The results of a special survey of western United States sheep producers showed that commercial sheep producers (selling 50 or more head) sold 43 and 32 percent of their sheep to packer buyers and order

Table 7.1. Market Outlets Used By Producers in the United States, 1977.

Species	Local auctions and commission firms (%)	Packers and butchers (%)	Other farmers and ranchers (%)	Commerical feedlots (%)	Other (%)
Cows (38 states)	77	14	8	—	1
Steers and heifers (38 states)	42	47	3	3	1
Calves (38 states)					
201–499 lb	83	3	13	—	1
200 lb and under	76	4	18	—	2
Barrows and gilts (22 states)	42	56	—	—	—
Sows and boars (22 states)	64	34	2	—	—
Feeder pigs (22 states)	50	15	34	—	1
Stock sheep (22 states)	47	16	35	—	2
Lambs (22 states)	44	40	6	8	2

Source: USDA (1979).

buyers, repectively. Dealers and auctions accounted for 10 percent each and the remaining 5 percent was divided about equally between pool and other market outlets (Gee and Magleby, 1976). Boykin *et al.* (1980) reported that sales through auctions were the most prevalent market outlet used by cow–calf operators in all beef-raising regions of the United States. Auctions were followed in importance by direct sales, order buyers, commission firms, and other outlets, respectively. The same study showed that fewer stocker-feeder operators sold cattle through auctions than cow–calf producers did, yet, auctions remained the most frequently used outlet followed by order buyers, direct sales, and commission firms. The study also showed that marketing through order buyers and selling directly increase with stocker-feeder herd size.

Hass and Hogeland (1980) reported that hog producers in 10 Midwestern states during 1977 sold 17 percent of their animals through terminals, 10 percent through auctions, 36 percent to dealers, and 37 percent directly to meatpackers. Van Arsdal and Nelson (1984) reported that feeder pig producers in the U.S. in 1980 sold about 75 percent of their pigs either through auctions or directly to feeder pig finishers. Direct sales were most common in the North Central Region (NCR), whereas auctions were the dominant outlet in the Southeast. Other outlets used less frequently were (1) order buyers or dealers at farm, (2) delivery to cooperative markets, (3) delivery to contractors, (4) direct sale to buyer but livestock retained on farm and fed by producer with profit (or loss) to be split at specified shares, and (5) terminal markets. In comparison, direct sale to packers was the most commonly used channel for slaughter hogs, followed by terminal markets (particularly in the NCR) and then by auction markets.

INDIRECT MARKETING

Indirect marketing is the marketing of livestock with the services of an intermediary (i.e., with the services of commission agents). Six indirect marketing outlets are examined here: (1) terminal markets, (2) auction markets, (3) board-selling and call markets, (4) country commissionmen, (5) order buyers, and (6) bargaining associations.

Public Terminal Markets

For brevity, public terminal markets will be referred to simply as "terminal markets." Key elements in the definition indicate that this is a public market. Anyone has the privilege of buying or selling on a terminal market. As will be pointed out later, however, patrons usually find it advantageous to engage commission firms or order buyers to make the transactions. The necessary physicial facilities—e.g., yards, scales, loading and unloading docks, office building—are owned and maintained by a stockyard company.

A brief sketch of the evolution of terminal markets was given in Chap. 2. They were a logical outgrowth of the pattern of railroad transportation and the concentration of packing plants at rail terminal points. In 1984 there were 24 terminal livestock markets in operation, a number that has declined persistently from a high of 80 in the 1930s. Terminals are located primarily in the North Central states. For example, of the 24 terminals operating in 16 of the 50 states during 1984, 15 (63 percent) were in that region). Other regions with terminals were Southern Plains, North Atlantic, South Central, and Pacific (Table 7.2). Decentralization of the packing industry and technological developments in communication and transportation have had an adverse effect on terminals. The impacts are still being felt and undoubtedly will be for some time to come. After more than a century of operation, the Chicago Union Stockyards—a landmark in the history of terminal markets—stopped marketing hogs in May 1970 and in August 1971 closed for all livestock. For decades, Chicago had been the prime example of terminal marketing. Its organization and operation were cited in textbooks, research publications, and popular articles as the pattern for terminals. Its shutdown does not necessarily mean the end of terminal

Table 7.2. Number of Livestock Markets, Dealers and Order Buyers, by Region, End of 1984.

Region*	Livestock markets			Dealers and order buyers[‡]
	Terminals[†]	Auctions	Total[†]	
North Atlantic	2	92	94	620
East N. Central	5	181	86	1,244
West N. Central	10	450	460	1,679
South Atlantic	0	198	198	415
South Central	2	277	279	577
Southern Plains	4	224	228	445
Mountain	0	96	96	595
Pacific	1	90	91	458
Alaska and Hawaii	0	0	0	0
United States	24	1,608	1,632	6,033

Source: USDA (1986).
*Locations of markets and business addresses for dealers and order buyers (dealers and order buyers may operate in more than one state).
[†]Terminals have more than one market agency selling on commission; auctions have only one.
[‡]Dealers purchase slaughter and nonslaughter livestock for resale for their own accounts; order buyers purchase livestock on a commission basis for others.

markets in general. Receipts had been declining for a number of years, and the yards were located on relatively high-priced land—land that had other, and more lucrative, uses. Some other terminals in this same situation may in time succumb to declining receipts.

Powers and Bendt (1968) make the following observation:

Technological changes have made obsolete the idea that space is an important element in the definition of a market. Today, widely scattered buyers and sellers can be in instant communication with each other via telephone, radio, and television. Transportation facilities are such that supplies can be quickly and easily distributed to areas of greatest demand. In short, there is less need for large centralized markets to serve as collection points for livestock and there is less need for buyers and sellers to be in close physical proximity to have keen competition in a market system . . .

. . . the terminals must now adjust to the new realities, the new demands of a changed marketing system operated by new participants with new technologies and new demands.

The trend in receipts of livestock at terminal markets is shown in Fig. 7.2. Recent data on packer purchases from terminals and livestock marketed through posted markets are shown in Tables 7.3 and 7.4, respectively. Historically, the decline in terminal hog marketings has been greater than for other species in both absolute numbers and in percentage of total marketings. Numbers of calves and sheep have dropped, but total numbers slaughtered also have dropped. The number of head of cattle marketed through terminals held fairly constant until recent years. However, the total number slaughtered has been on an inclining trend so the percentage of total slaughter cattle moving through terminal markets has steadily declined. Terminal markets remain important to many producers and packers as an outlet and also as a source of livestock prices and other market information.

There is no question of the declining relative importance of terminals as a class. Considerable differences exist among the remaining markets, however, as some are holding their own very well and will be in the picture for the foreseeable future.

Organizational Arrangements   The organizational set-up at all terminals is similar but not identical. The physical facilities are owned by a stockyards company—usually a corporation. The stockyards company does not engage in buying and selling of livestock. Its remuneration is derived from charges for use of the yards, sale of feed, office rental, and charges for various services such as branding, castrating, dehorning, vaccinating, and dipping livestock.

The yards physically are divided into divisions by species, i.e., cattle,

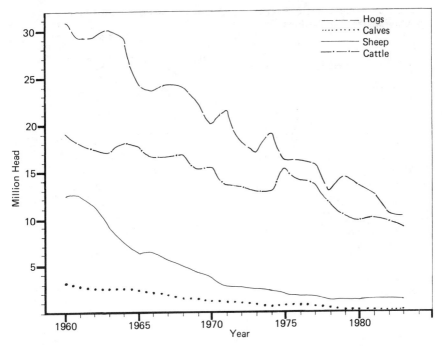

Fig. 7.2   Total livestock receipts at terminal markets, 1960–1984. (Plotted by authors from USDA data.)

hogs, and sheep. The stockyards company assigns certain pens to specific commission firms for their exclusive use. Scales are owned by the stockyards company and operated by its employees. The scales, however, are inspected and tested from time to time, being under the supervision of government personnel of the Packers and Stockyards Administration, an agency of the Agricultural Marketing Service (AMS) of the USDA. It is commonly known simply as P&S.

Although buying and selling is open to the public, the selling of patrons' livestock is done almost exclusively by personnel of commission firms. Individuals, partnerships, cooperatives, corporations may operate these firms. Buying is done by a wide range of types of buyers: packer buyers, order buyers, yard dealers, wholesale provisioners, local butchers, farmers, ranchers, and feedlot operators.

Packer buyers are employed by a particular packing firm (usually located in relatively close proximity to the market) and receive a salary from the employer.

Order buyers are not salaried. They buy livestock that normally is to be shipped to some more or less distant point. Order buyers usually

Table 7.3. Percentages of Packers Purchases of Livestock from Terminal and Auction Markets, 1974–1984.

Year and market outlet	Cattle (%)	Calves (%)	Hogs (%)	Sheep (%)
1974				
Terminals	13.9	6.5	17.6	11.5
Auctions	16.4	63.1	12.4	13.5
1975				
Terminals	14.4	8.3	16.3	10.0
Auctions	19.7	59.2	12.2	15.6
1976				
Terminals	12.9	7.7	17.1	9.8
Auctions	20.8	62.3	11.5	15.0
1977				
Terminals	12.0	7.3	15.6	11.0
Auctions	18.6	57.2	12.7	13.2
1978				
Terminals	10.6	8.9	15.8	9.9
Auctions	15.5	52.1	11.5	11.1
1979				
Terminals	8.7	6.5	14.9	9.1
Auctions	13.7	51.6	10.3	9.3
1980				
Terminals	8.6	6.4	13.5	7.6
Auctions	14.3	49.9	9.8	12.0
1981				
Terminals	8.1	9.0	11.6	7.0
Auctions	14.5	48.2	10.0	15.0
1982				
Terminals	7.0	4.3	12.0	7.7
Auctions	14.9	52.9	8.9	11.0
1983				
Terminals	7.1	4.5	14.2	6.0
Auctions	15.3	47.2	9.0	11.6
1984				
Terminals	6.6	2.9	10.3	8.9
Auctions	14.7	46.9	6.8	12.2

Source: USDA (1986 and earlier issues).

specialize in a particular class of livestock and have clientele who phone them orders for both slaughter and feeder livestock that meet certain specifications. Order buyers do not take title (ownership) to the livestock they purchase but simply act as agents in filling the orders.

Table 7.4. Livestock Marketed Through Posted Public Markets in the U.S., 1973–75 and 1980–84.

Year	Number of head*			Percentage	
	Terminals (1,000)	Auctions (1,000)	Total (1,000)	Terminals (%)	Auctions (%)
Cattle and calves					
1973	9,091	44,748	53,839	16.9	83.1
1974	9,391	40,219	49,610	18.9	81.1
1975	10,731	47,257	57,988	18.5	81.5
1980	7,111	40.159	47,270	15.0	85.0
1981	6,589	39,618	46,207	14.2	85.8
1982	6,348	41,118	47,466	13.4	86.6
1983	5,998	42,617	48,615	12.3	87.7
1984	5,884	43,552	49,450	11.9	88.1
Hogs and Pigs					
1973	12,777	20,483	33,260	38.4	61.6
1974	14,384	21,203	35,587	40.4	59.6
1975	11,781	20,101	31,882	37.0	10.0
1980	12,005	26,122	38,127	31.5	68.5
1981	10,752	22,534	33,286	32.3	67.7
1982	9,065	19,393	28,458	31.9	68.1
1983	9,029	19,652	28,681	31.4	68.6
1984	8,780	19,836	28,616	30.6	69.4
Sheep and lambs					
1973	1,343	5,126	6,469	20.8	79.2
1974	1,256	4,792	6,048	20.8	79.2
1975	1,062	4,500	5,562	19.1	80.9
1980	488	4,536	5,024	9.7	90.3
1981	557	4,522	5,079	10.9	89.1
1982	558	4,704	5,262	10.6	89.4
1983	495	5,269	5,764	8.5	91.5
1984	462	5,277	5,739	8.0	92.0

Source: USDA (1986 and earlier issues).
*Numbers may not add as a result of rounding.

Their remuneration is a commission received from the parties who place the orders.

Yard dealers (also known as yard traders, speculators, and scalpers) buy livestock with the objective of reselling at a higher price. The term "yard trader" has, for some people at some times, carried a derogatory connotation. To a large extent, this is a misunderstanding. Yard dealers perform the function of always being present in the market. At certain times other buyers may be relatively scarce or inactive, particularly on odd lots. In the absence of yard dealers, these odds and ends might be stranded in distress situations. Yard dealers often can accumulate enough livestock through a number of such transactions to form larger lots of uniform quality. Such lots then become attractive to buyers, and enhanced price for the larger, more uniform lot provides a profit incentive for yard dealers.

Wholesale provisioners often like to go into the yards personally to select slaughter livestock for a specific trade and have the livestock slaughtered on a custom basis. Local butchers, who may operate a retail store or locker plant, buy limited numbers of slaughter livestock. Farmers, ranchers, and feedlot operators do some buying at terminals, but most purchasing for this group is done through their order buyers.

From an organizational standpoint, sellers and buyers (including primarily commission firms, order buyers, packer buyers, and, sometimes, yard dealers) often form a "livestock exchange." In some cases, yard dealers form a separate "dealers exchange." The livestock exchange serves as a self-regulatory organization that makes recommendations on changes in commission-rate charges, promotes various public relations activities, and cooperates with conservation organizations in the interest of reducing livestock loss from bruising, crippling, disease, and death.

An original distinction of terminal markets was the transacting of business by "private treaty." Private treaty simply means that price is arrived at by buyer and seller bargaining in privacy. The outcome (price or other terms of the transaction) is known only to the participants. This is in contrast to an auction where bidding is done by public outcry and terms of the transaction are known to everyone in attendance. With the introduction of auction selling at a number of terminals, private treaty is no longer a distinctive attribute of terminal markets.

Operational Features. Terminals ordinarily are open for business Monday through Saturday, although activity is light late in the week (Cramer, 1958). The markets are open seven days a week to receive livestock. Hog receipts are relatively uniform Monday through Friday, although some markets deviate from this pattern. Cattle receipts at terminals traditionally have been concentrated early in the week—with more than 40 percent of the week's receipts on Monday and about 20 percent on Tuesday. Among factors associated with early week concentrations are more active buying by packers and order buyers, influence of truckers, and tendency on some markets for prices to be higher early in the week (Cramer, 1958). From an operational standpoint, this is an inefficient underutilization of physical facilities and manpower during the latter part of the week. In order to reduce this inefficiency and underutilization, most terminal markets added auctions to their operations late in the week (few are held more than once a week) for a single specie or for a single class for certain animals. By holding an auction late in the week, some terminals have attempted to spread out receipts of feeder cattle.

Many commission agents are not opposed to early receipts since they like to spend the latter part of the week in the country visiting patrons and soliciting business.

A producer who wishes to sell livestock at a terminal market ordinarily consigns his livestock to a commission firm. Most producers who patronize terminals have such acquaintanceship. Any producer who has not established a contact probably should visit the market for this expressed purpose prior to shipping livestock. Most commission firms send their personnel to the country several days a week to solicit business and consult with patrons about the condition of their livestock, the market situation, and the probable value of the livestock.

The number of commission firms at a market varies with its size, but at least two firms must operate there (Newberg, 1959). Most terminals have enough firms for shippers to have some choice. Competition among commission firms for producer patronage is the major force that makes a market go. Likewise, competition among markets makes the market system effective.

Some commission firms specialize in certain species; others handle all species; larger firms have specialists who devote their time exclusively to a single class of a given specie.

A shipper ordinarily notifies the commission firm in advance of his intentions to ship—giving approximate time of arrival. He also should give any special instructions he may have regarding feeding or handling of the livestock at the market. Upon loading of the livestock at the feedlot, farm, or ranch, the trucker is given the name of the commission firm. The name of this firm, together with a count and description of the livestock, is entered on a ticket by the trucker. This ticket serves several purposes. Upon arrival at the market, it indicates the commission firm to which the animals are to be delivered. It also provides a check on the livestock count and description, and it provides the commission firm with the name of the trucker. When the livestock are sold, trucking charges are deducted from the proceeds and remitted directly to the trucker by the commission firm.

In this process, the shipper of the livestock "consigns" his livestock to the specified commission firm. The shipper, in effect, authorizes personnel of that commission firm to act as his agent in selling the livestock. For this service, the firm charges a fee or "commission." Each market has its specified schedule of charges for selling and buying live-stock. These schedules are known as "tariffs." There can be differences in selling and buying charges among terminal markets, but there is no difference in charges among commission firms at a given market, a rule enforced by federal government regulation. The logic of this arrange-ment is that competition among firms at a given market must be on the basis of services performed rather than on the amount of commis-sion charged. It is presumed this enhances the services received by producers.

In 1978, P&S ruled that commission charges could be on either a per head basis or a percentage of the proceeds. While commissions based on proceeds are widely used at auctions, most terminals by choice charge commissions on a per head basis. From time to time, it had been argued that, logically, a difference should exist in the commission on, say, a choice slaughter steer selling for $500 and a canner cow sell-ing for $200. While there are points pro and con, the basic rationale is that the time, effort, and knowledge required to handle the various classes are reasonably equivalent, and a charge by the head keeps com-petition on the basis of service performed. The courts have upheld this ruling on the principle that charges based on value of the animals are unfair and discriminatory and bear no relation to the costs of providing services.

Upon notification by a customer of an impending shipment, the com-mission agent issues a feeding order to stockyard company personnel in accordance with instructions received from the consignor (shipper). In the absence of instructions, the commission agent issues feeding instructions in accordance with his own judgment.

Livestock delivered before opening of the market is sorted for uni-formity in weight, grade, color, etc., by the commission agent, if, in his judgment, that will enhance their sale. When the market opens, the commission agent stays at his pens, shows the livestock to prospective buyers, offers them for sale, and attempts to sell them at the most advantageous terms from the standpoint of the seller. This involves considerable bargaining over a single price for the entire lot versus sale of the majority at an agreed price with the privilege of cutting back specified animals at a lower price.

The skill and expertise of a commission agent comes in knowing when he has the best possible offer for a pen of livestock on that partic-ular day. If he is unable to obtain a reasonable offer, he may hold the livestock over for the following day's market, but this involves some expense and risk and is not common operating procedure.

It is possible for a shipper to have the agent notify him of bids before consummating a sale, but he ordinarily does not do so. It tends to restrict the actions of the commission agent severely unless the shipper is at the pen when the bargaining takes place. A bid by a prospective buyer is good only at the time it is made. Once the bidder leaves the pen, his bid, so to speak, "goes with him." An owner who has specified that the commission agent must call him for an approval on bids could lose a sale from a bidder who will not wait for the commission agent to place a long-distance telephone call.

Upon completion of sale, the livestock are weighed and delivered to pens of the buyer, or holding pens, pending shipping instructions. Title of ownership passes to the buyer upon the weighing.

Details of the transaction (price, weight, and name of buyer) are transmitted to the commission firm's office. An "account of sale" is prepared for the shipper giving this information and calculation of gross proceeds, itemized charges, and net proceeds. This, along with a check for the net proceeds, is transmitted to the shipper. Itemized charges include the trucking charge (which, as mentioned earlier, is forwarded directly to the trucker); commission charges, which are retained by the commission firm for its selling services; a small deduction per head, which is transmitted to the National Livestock and Meat Board and used for industry promotional purposes; brand inspection charges (applicable in some states); a small charge for transit insurance; and charges assessed by the stockyards company. Included in the latter are yardage (a small fee for use of the stockyards), feed, and insurance applicable at the yards. The deduction for the National Livestock and Meat Board will be refunded to a consignor upon request; otherwise it is forwarded to the Board's central office in Chicago. All commission firms are required by federal regulation to carry bond, which helps assure a shipper that he will receive payment.

A shipper who prefers to have his livestock sold by auction at a terminal would consign the livestock to a commission firm in the manner described above (for private treaty) but would specify he wanted them sold at auction. The commission agent again would short and shape up lots that in his judgment would enhance the sale. At most terminal auctions, a member of each commission firm provides the starting price for livestock consigned to that firm. Some terminals assess a "ring fee" in addition to yardage on livestock sold through the auction.

An individual who wishes to purchase livestock at a terminal may, if he chooses, deal directly with a commission agent by private treaty or by personal bidding at the auction. On the other hand, if he wishes to engage the services of an order buyer, he simply conveys to the latter his specifications for the particular class of livestock he desires, including price constraints. In addition to firms and individuals who limit their activities exclusively to order buying, most commission firms also act as order buyers in filling the requests of their patrons.

Types of Receipts. Three different types of livestock receipts are handled at terminal stockyards: (1) saleable, (2) direct, and (3) through receipts.

"Saleable receipts" are livestock delivered to the market for sale at that market.

"Direct receipts" are livestock which have been purchased elsewhere by a local packing plant without sufficient holding pen space. They are delivered to the terminal yards for temporary holding prior to slaughter. A yardage fee, somewhat smaller than the regular charge, is assessed for direct receipts.

"Through receipts" are livestock which are unloaded for feed, water, and rest, then reloaded for further shipment. Ordinarily, "throughs" are not assessed yardage but are charged for feed.

Regulation and Supervision. Terminal markets are subject to regulation at two levels: (1) self-regulation imposed by the rules of livestock (and dealers) exchanges, and (2) federal regulations as specified by the Packers and Stockyards Act of 1921 and amendments.

Rules and regulations of livestock exchanges are drawn up voluntarily by members in accordance with the constitution and by-laws of the exchanges. The overall objective is a matter of self-interest in maintaining a viable and progressive market. Rules are designed to maintain a high level of ethical business activity and provide a mechanism for settling controversies.

Prior to 1958, only stockyards involved in interstate trade and having 200,000 or more square feet of pen space came under jurisdiction of P&S. The P&S Act was amended in 1958 to include all persons and firms engaged in marketing and meat packing in interstate or foreign commerce. This amendment substantially expanded the number of markets covered. The Act prescribes rules of fair competition and fair trade practices. Terminal markets (and auctions) are "posted," which means that a notice is posted in three conspicuous places at the market by P&S personnel giving notice that this is a posted market and setting forth a schedule of charges for services performed.

Posting gives P&S jurisdiction over the following:

1. Changes in charges and fees of agencies operating at that market. (This applies to commission charges, yardage, etc. To change the

established rates, agencies concerned must file recommended changes in writing with P&S at least 10 days before the change is to be effective, and present evidence substantiating reasons for the change.)[1]

2. Trade practices that may be construed as fraudulent or unfair competition.
3. Maintenance of reasonable and adequate facilities.
4. Testing of scales to the capacity used, at least twice a year.
5. A requirement that individuals and agencies operating on the market carry a prescribed minimum bond and report annually all transactions of livestock and payments as well as all other operating accounts.

Auction Markets

Although the auction method of selling livestock has a long history, it was not until the 1920s and 1930s that auction marketing really caught on. As illustrated in Fig. 7.3, growth during the 1930s was especially pronounced. Expansion continued through the 1940s and early 1950s, though the rate of increase gradually tapered off. Because of the exclusion of public markets with less than 200,000 square feet of pen space from the P&S Act prior to 1958, the actual number of auctions was not known or reported. Special surveys reported the numbers for 1930, 1937, 1949, and 1955 to be 2,000, 1,345, 2,472, and 2,322 markets, respectively (Engleman and Pence, 1975). Since the peak number of 2,472 auctions that was reached in 1949, a decline in number has occurred, but, generally speaking, the volume of livestock handled by the average auction has increased. The volume of livestock (and percentages) purchased by packers from auctions has declined, however, as shown in Tables 7.3 and 7.4. At the end of 1984, there was 1,608 auctions operating throughout the country (Table 7.2).

Auction markets are distributed fairly uniformly throughout the United States relative to the density of livestock production. The proportion of livestock handled by acutions varies considerably by region, however, as shown in Table 7.5. Although this table shows marketing through posted markets only, it reveals a high level of auctioneering in the South Altantic, Mountain, and Pacific regions.

---

[1]A series of public hearings in 1978 produced a recommendation from the Packers and Stockyards Administration that market operators be allowed to change selling charges after 30-day notice without the previously required clearance from that agency.

LIVESTOCK AUCTION MARKETS

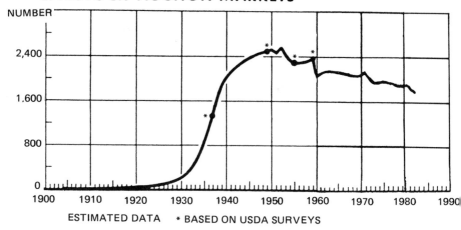

Fig. 7.3. Livestock auction markets, 1930–1984.

Organization. From a business standpoint, auctions may be organized as corporations, partnerships, or individual proprietorships. A limited number are organized by cooperatives (e.g., Interstate Producers Livestock Association—IPLA—operates auctions in three states: Illinois, Missouri, and Iowa). Most of the larger ones are corporations and many small ones are owned and operated by individuals. In contrast to terminals, where ownership and operation of yards, scales, building, etc., are separate from the selling agencies, both the ownership of the physical facilities and the selling function of auctions are under the same management. As discussed earlier, most terminals also operate auctions to increase labor and facility utilization and, hence, improve their operational efficiency.

Auction markets are used primarily, but not exclusively, for selling feeder livestock and cull animals. Although not a major avenue for slaughter livestock sales, packers nevertheless obtain substantial numbers through them. As was shown in Table 7.3, packer purchases through auctions in 1984 amounted to 14.7 percent of the cattle, about 46.9 percent of the calves, 6.8 percent of the hogs, and 12.2 percent of the sheep.

Table 7.5. Livestock Marketed Through Posted Public Markets, By Type of Market and By Region, 1984.

Kind of livestock region*	Number of head			Percentage		
	Terminal Markets† (1,000)	Auction Markets† (1,000)	Total‡	Terminal	Auction	Total
Cattle and Calves						
North Atlantic	112	1,571	1,683	6.7	93.0	100.0
East N. Central	940	3,531	4,471	21.0	79.0	100.0
West N. Central	3,005	13,542	16,547	18.1	81.9	100.0
South Atlantic	0	3,640	3,640	0.0	100.0	100.0
South Central	320	6,020	6,340	5.0	95.0	100.0
Southern Plains	1,507	8,816	10,323	14.5	85.5	100.0
Mountain	0	4,260	4,260	0.0	100.0	100.0
Pacific	0	2,162	2,162	0.0	100.0	100.0
Alaska and Hawaii	0	0	0	0.0	0.0	0.0
United States	5,884	43,552	49,540	11.9	88.1	100.0
Hogs and Pigs						
North Atlantic	168	514	682	24.6	75.4	100.0
East N. Central	2,767	3,815	6,582	42.0	58.0	100.0
West N. Central	5,519	9,971	15,490	35.6	64.4	100.0
South Atlantic	0	2,779	2,779	0.0	100.0	100.0
South Central	135	1,825	1,960	6.8	93.2	100.0
Southern Plains	193	470	663	29.1	70.9	100.0
Mountain	0	235	235	0.0	100.0	100.0
Pacific	0	227	227	0.0	100.0	100.0
Alaska and Hawaii	0	0	0	0.0	0.0	0.0
United States	8,780	19,836	28,616	30.6	69.4	100.0
Sheep and Lambs						
North Atlantic	38	153	191	19.9	80.1	100.0
East N. Central	62	615	677	9.1	90.9	100.0
West N. Central	374	1,335	1,729	21.6	78.4	100.0
South Atlantic	0	422	422	0.0	100.0	100.0
South Central	7	133	140	5.0	95.0	100.0
Southern Plains	19	1,591	1,610	1.1	98.9	100.0
Mountain	0	666	666	0.0	100.0	100.0
Pacific	0	342	342	0.0	100.0	100.0
Alaska and Hawaii	0	0	0	0.0	0.0	0.0
United States	462	5,277	5,739	8.0	92.0	100.0

Source: USDA (1986).
*Livestock marketed through a market in one region may be move to other regions for further feeding, breeding or slaughter.
†Terminals have more than one market agency selling on commission; auctions have one.
‡Totals may not add as a result of rounding.

Operation of Auctions. Most auctions sell livestock just one day a week, although a few operate on two or more days. A 1982 survey of Illinois' auctions indicated that 21 percent of the auctions operated more than once a week, and that all markets operate every week during the year. The most frequent day of the week for an auction was Wednesday, followed by Thursday. As expected, because of the nature of livestock production practices winter and fall were the busiest seasons whereas summer was the least busy (Sarhan and Kunda, 1982).

A livestock owner who wishes to sell his animals through an auction market consigns his livestock much in the way he would for terminals. Though not a requirement, it is good business practice for an owner to contact the auction manager several days prior to sale and notify him of intentions to deliver. It is a common practice for auction managers or their representative to visit patrons on request, inspect their livestock, and advise the patron regarding that inspection, market conditions, and probable value of livestock.

Upon delivery, the livestock are penned or marked in a way to maintain the identity of each individual owner. Operators usually follow a consistent order in sale by species. That is, hogs may be sold first, followed by sheep, and then cattle. Within a given specie, most auctions follow the practice of presenting livestock for sale in the order in which they were received. Some auctions, however, have a considerably greater time lag from delivery to sale than do others, and this can be a factor in weight shrinkage.

Auction operators usually sort an owner's livestock for size, grade, or other characteristics to obtain uniformity as the animals are presented in the sale ring. This practice is intended to enhance sale of the entire lot. The price discovery in auction markets is by public bidding (practically all auctions in the U.S. have adopted ascending, or English, bidding) in response to an auctioneer's chant. As the animals arrive in the ring, it is common practice for the manager, or his representative to provide a starting bid. Although this is not the custom in all parts of the United States, it does speed up movement through the ring. The starter attempts to put the initial price just slightly below what he thinks the livestock will sell for. To the extent he is able to judge this value, his ploy obviates the necessity of needless bidding. Following the auctioneer's chant, bidding progresses to higher levels until no one is willing to advance the last offer, and the livestock is sold to the highest bidder. Depending upon local custom and/or class of livestock involved, the selling may be done on a per head basis or by weight.

Several different procedures are followed in obtaining sale weight. Many modern auctions are constructed so that the scale platform acts as the sale ring. In addition, many have circuitry to an electronic display that exhibits total weight, number of head, and average weight in full view of the audience. Some markets, however, locate the scales on the "in" side of the sale ring, and livestock are weighed prior to entering the ring. In this case, the weight can be announced or flashed on a lighted sign. This eliminates the need for buyers estimating weight. It is not uncommon, however, where the scale is located on the "out" side, for the operator to "catch" the weight of a draft of animals or a part of a draft prior to final sale so that bidders will have an estimate of average weight while bidding. In this case, however, the official weight is taken after sale. At some markets, weights are taken as livestock is unloaded at delivery to the auction, although this is not common practice in the midwest.

After the livestock are sold, they are penned for loading out. Large-volume buyers who wish their purchases penned by sex, weight, grade, or other charcteristics, may specify how they wish each draft penned as the livestock leaves the sale ring.

The Packers and Stockyards Act regulations allow auction operators to purchase livestock that otherwise would sell at a price below what would be considered a competitively established level for that particular class, grade, and weight of animal at that time. This practice, known as "market support," is designed to provide a degree of price protection to sellers at times when buying activity is slack. A Kansas study (Beaton and McCoy 1970) based on 1965 data indicated that market support affected only 3.7 percent of the livestock handled. This study showed that auctions averaged a loss on the livestock bought in their market support activities. The losses ranged from approximately 12 cents per animal unit in smaller auctions to 7 cents in the larger auctions when the losses were spread over all livestock handled.

Other means of price protection also are available to consignors. One method is to set up a reservation price with the auction operator prior to sale; this price may be noted on the ticket accompanying the livestock into the sale ring. A reservation price means that if bids do not reach that price the livestock are not sold. Another method is for the consignor to declare "no sale" at the time the auctioneer has received the last bid. This necessitates the consignor or his representative being present during the sale. A third alternative—one definitely frowned upon—is for the consignor to bid on his own livestock or arrange for a cohort to do so. This is known as "by-bidding." Charges assessed for "no-sale" livestock vary, depending on the policy of particular auction operators (Able and Broadbent, 1952).

Costs of marketing at an auction are essentially the same as at a terminal, although slight differences obtain among states. The major items are commission and yardage. Lesser deductions may be made for such items as insurance, feed, state inspection, state fee, National Livestock and Meat Board, and brand inspection, depending upon the particular state. A considerable variation exists among auctions in the determination of commission charges. Some auctions assess commission on a per-head basis, others on a percentage of the proceeds, and some on a combination of the two.[2]

An innovation in auction marketing is the electronic auction. Telephone auctions, commonly known as Tel-O-Auctions or Teleauctions, have been in use for many years in the U.S. and other countries. These represent a simple form of electronic marketing and consist of an interlocking system of telephone conference-call set-ups whereby, as in other forms of electronic markets, traders in geographically separated locations can bid on livestock as described over the system. The livestock may be assembled at selected points or left on the producer's farm. Sorting and grading must be very precise because buyers are bidding on description—sight-unseen. They must therefore have confidence in the grading system (see Chap. 14).

A further refinement of electronic auctions is the use of a video screen so that prospective buyers can view the livestock. In contrast to telephone auctions where the livestock is assembled at a particular place and buyers may be widely separated, use of video requires that the buyers assemble while the cattle may be left at widely separated farms and ranches. Although this approach has been tested, it has not been widely used.

Another innovation in livestock marketing is auctioning slaughter cattle on a carcass basis. This custom has not progressed beyond the experimental stage in the United States (Brown and Thomas, 1970) but has been used on a limited scale in Ontario, Canada. Bidding proceeds on an agreed-upon base grade (in the U.S., that was Choice, Yield 3). After the animals have been slaughtered, price differentials are applied to the extent that quality and yield grade deviate from the base. Although this method has the potential of improving pricing efficiency it has not been accepted in the United States at this time.

Regulation and Supervision.   Auctions handling livestock that move interstate are considered to be public markets. They are posted and fall under the jurisdiction of the Packers and Stockyards Act. The ap-

---

[2]As a result of a series of nationwide public hearings in 1978, the administration of Packers and Stockyards recommended that all public market selling commissions be on a per-head basis only. A 1982 survey of Illinois producers, however, indicated that the percentage of the proceeds method is still in use in that state (Sarhan and Kunda, 1982).

plicable provisions are those discussed previously under terminal markets. Marketing charges, once established, cannot be changed without following procedures set out by P&S. Scales must be tested twice a year. The auction must (1) refrain from trade practices that limit or restrict competition, (2) must carry bond to help assure payment to patrons, and (3) report annually all transactions and payments.

Auctions not regulated and supervised under P&S may be regulated under state provisions. Many states require bonding to help assure payment to consignors. Many states require health inspection by qualified veterinarians, but few auctions assume any responsibility or grant any warranty regarding health or condition of livestock sold. Many auctions plainly display a sign disclaiming guarantees of any kind. In addition, it is common in case of an animal in doubtful condition for the auctioneer to declare that the animal is being sold "as is."

Before discussing the other types of indirect marketing, let us summarize the following important differences between terminal and auction markets:

Item	Terminals	Auctions
Number	Few (24 in 1982)	Many (1,781 in 1982)
Location	Concentrated in Midwestern states	Spread throughout the U.S.
Days/week open	7	1–2
Days/week operating	6	1–2
Commission agents	More than one	One
Can company trade?	No	Yes
Price discovery	Private treaty	Open public bidding

Board Selling and Call Markets

Board selling and call markets share many features with both terminal and auction markets. Board selling is a marketing system that lists all consigned livestock and certain market information on a marketing board. Details of handling and managing the animals are specified before the bid dates. Potential buyers can easily evaluate offers in order to decide whether to bid or not. Price discovery may take place through public bidding and/or sealed bids. Livestock under this system remain on the farm until sold since selling is done by description. Board sales can be held anywhere (e.g., a hotel or a county extension office) since the animals do not have to be present.

Call markets are contracting programs that have been used in grain trading. The Minneapolis Grain Exchange introduced them for the first time for trading hogs in 1982 (*National Hog Farmer*, November

1982). Under the call-market arrangements, sellers of livestock agree to deliver on a future day (from several weeks to several months in the future) at a specified price a standard quantity of animals (e.g., 7,500 lb) with a specified range of weight and meeting a certain quality. In contrast with futures-market contracts (discussed in Chap. 13), both parties in a call-market arrangement can be known to each other and delivery always takes place. There is no margin money requirement in a call-market contract, and specifications can be altered if sellers and buyers agree to do so. Sellers and buyers are represented by a commission firm operating on the Exchange. Offrings, bids, and terms of trade are listed for all traders or their representatives to evaluate. A series of offers, counter-offers, and revisions proceeds in the same manner as in a terminal or auction market. Following successful negotiations, a contract is signed which includes the final terms agreed upon (e.g., price, discounts, time, and place of delivery). Livestock remains on the farm until delivery day. Upon delivery, buyers pay the commission firm, which in turn pays the seller, after deducting expenses just as in a terminal market. Unlike terminals, call markets provide sellers with the advantage of knowing the price in advance. Furthermore, since livestock move directly from the farm to buyer's location, marketing costs and stress on animals are reduced.

Country Commission-man

The term "country commission-man" is not well established in marketing literature, but such agents do exist. A country commission-man simply is a commission agent who operates in the country rather than at an established market to represent producers in the sale of their livestock. This may be a case of the proposition that "if producers will not take their livestock to the commission-man, then the commission-man will go to the producer." It also probably is a recognition on the part of some producers that selling is a specialized function and that they would rather specialize in other aspects of production than attempt to be a jack-of-all-trades.

These commission-men tend to operate in areas of highly concentrated production such as are found in the cattle feeding areas of the Milo Belt, Colorado, Arizona, and California. They travel with packer buyers to the feedlots. Final transactions may be made at the feedlot or elsewhere.

This movement has not been underway long enough to know if it will develop into a significant proposition. It would appear to have merit for producers, large and small, who need the service. On the other hand, it is of doubtful feasibility where production is widely scattered over a large area.

Order Buyers

Order buyers act as agents or intermediaries to fill orders for livestock of certain specifications that they have received from clients. The specifications normally detail weight and grade. Some orders specify maximum price; others leave price to the discretion of the order buyer. Good order buyers, however, attempt to fill their orders at the lowest price possible consistent with getting that order filled. This, of course, is what keeps an order buyer in business. He works in the interest of the purchaser.

Order buyers operate at terminal markets and at auctions. They also will buy from dealers, from local markets, and directly from farmers and ranchers in the country. Many buyers are specialists in a particular class of livestock, and many operate at only one type of market. Specialists in buying slaughter cattle, slaughter hogs, and slaughter lambs are found at most terminals, purchasing for packers located at distant points. Feeder-cattle specialists also operate at terminals and, as mentioned earlier, commission agents act as order buyers at terminals when requested by patrons. Commercial feedlots utilize the services of order buyers at all types of markets. The demand for feeder cattle to stock the feedlot industry has created problems in filling these orders.

Many slaughter lambs are bought by order buyers for forwarding to packers. Since the number of packers who slaughter lambs has gradually declined, buying has become more scattered and lambs must be shipped longer distances. Many hogs are bought on order at midwestern markets for shipment to the West Coast and other points.

The true order buyer does not take title to the livestock he handles but instead merely acts as agent for the purchaser. The order buyer typically is authorized by the purchaser to draw a draft on the purchaser's bank in payment for the livestock. His reimbursement is a fee for the services performed—in most cases, a flat rate per head, which varies by class of animal. Some order buyers mix dealer operations with their order buying (i.e., they sometimes buy livestock outright, take title, and attempt to sell at a higher price for profit). There are no regulations to prevent individuals or firms from engaging in both activities simultaneously. There are no regulations to prevent the filling of an order with personally owned livestock. Most purchasers, however, prefer to deal with order buyers who stick strictly to order buying. The mixing of dealer and order-buying activities tends to diminish the confidence of purchasers. Experience has shown that one of the biggest problems of livestock growers and finishers is the purchase of stocker and feeder animals. Order buyers of feeder livestock with widely accepted reputation are much in demand.

Bargaining Associations

Bargaining associations are organizations set up with the express purpose of bargaining for producers in the sale of their products or purchase of inputs. Bargaining often covers terms of trade in addition to price. For a number of years, milk producers in Federal Order Milk Markets have had an organization for bargaining with milk handlers and processors. Federal Order Markets were set up under the Marketing Agreement Act of 1937. The Federal enabling act applies to certain commodities only. Livestock, meat, and wool are not included in the federal act.

Some states have statutes authorizing market orders and agreements for specified commodities, but, again, most states do not include livestock, meat, or wool. Colorado authorized a marketing order for lambs in 1969, but it was discontinued in 1970.

Bargaining associations are not limited to governmentally sponsored organizations; there are also privately organized bargaining associations. Probably the best known example that includes livestock in its operation is the National Farmers Organization, organized in 1955 and commonly known as NFO. The NFO is a farmer organization that bargains with packers in the sale of members' slaughter livestock. It operates as a cooperative under provisions of the Capper-Volsted Act, which authorizes farmers to organize and bargain collectively. Members pay an annual membership fee and agree to turn over to the organization the job of bargaining for price and other considerations.

The NFO gained wide attention and some notoriety during several "withholding" actions. These were attempts to use withholding tactics as a leverage in negotiating contracts with packers. Early attempts were not successful in forcing the signing of contracts. Subsequently, it has been reported that contracts have been signed, but the organization has not revealed the extent of its contracts nor the terms.

It is generally held among economists that the withholding approach used by NFO (the withholding of a perishable or at least semiperishable product like finished livestock, after the livestock have been produced and are ready for market) does not give the leverage needed for effective bargaining power. Withholding at this point results in even greater tonnages to be marketed at the end of the withholding since additional weight is gained during the interim.

It is possible, however, that some packers are willing to enter into contract if, in return, the association guarantees scheduled delivery of uniform weight and grade of livestock. Such a contract would reduce the packer's procurement costs, which would make possible a higher paying price. Effective withholding, however, necessitates the power to control production, Private, voluntarily organized bargaining associations have problems in maintaining the necessary discipline to gain production control. If some members abide by an organization's production control plan, a powerful incentive develops for individuals to drop out of the association and increase production. It is difficult for a private organization to enforce stringent enough penalities to prevent this from happening. Nevertheless, the desire and enthusiasm for bargaining power among producers has gained considerable momentum in recent years. This is an area that will attract increasing attention. It is a complex problem. From an organizational standpoint, the trend toward fewer and bigger farm operators enhances the possibility of forming bargaining associations. The number of livestock producers, however, is still relatively large. Production is widely dispersed and producers have not exhibited a complete unanimity of interest.

Antitrust decisions indicate a recognition that farmers legally have the power to form collective bargaining associations (Clodius, 1962). At the same time, these decisions make it fairly clear that undue enhancement of prices would be construed as a violation of antitrust laws. Even if a bargaining association legally gained sufficient control to raise prices above otherwise prevailing levels, economic limits still would exist on the extent to which this power could be exercised-long term. Unduly high prices would tend to encourage consumers to switch to substitute products.

DIRECT MARKETING

As used in this discussion, direct marketing is the marketing of livestock without the services of an intermediary (i.e., without the services of commission agents, order buyers, auctioneers, or personnel of a bargaining association).

Historically, direct marketing has been defined as the use of any channel, or channels, which by-pass terminal markets. This definition is too restrictive for many purposes. The range of markets that would be included in the nonterminal classification still would require subclassification to differentiate markets within that group. From the producer's standpoint, it appears that the chief point of distinction is whether he himself performs the functions of selling and buying or whether he engages the services of someone else.

Outlets Used in Direct Marketing

For those who desire to use direct marketing, a number of alternative channels for both feeder livestock and slaughter livestock are available. The types of markets within this group can be subclassified into two categories. On the one hand, operators deliver livestock to an established place of business where the price is generally on a "take it or leave it" basis. Such outlets include:

1. Direct sale to packing plants
2. Direct sale to packer buying stations
3. Direct sale in local markets, including concentration yards and locally owned and operated stockyards

Only limited opportunities are available for bargaining over price at these market outlets. On the other hand, there are outlets where the operators do not have an established place of business, as follows:

1. Country packer buyers
2. Country dealers
3. Order buyers

These marketers circulate among producers (usually in a given area), visit their premises, view their livestock, and transact business on the spot or elsewhere. Here price, weighing conditions, and delivery time are negotiated. If delivery is delayed, written contracts often are drawn up to specify terms of the trade. In addition to the above outlets used in direct marketing, producers may deal directly with other producers. This often is the case with breeding stock and is a common occurrence with feeder livestock.

These market outlets were defined earlier. At this point, those outlets in most prevalent use will be briefly discussed.

Direct Sale to Packing Plant. Such sales occur when producers haul their livestock to a packing plant, and sale is made upon arrival. The sale may be live grade and weight or carcass grade and weight. Most packing plants are prepared to buy livestock on a live basis upon delivery. The price is established basically by the plant management. Producers, of course, may call or visit the plant to ascertain paying prices, but bargaining is limited.

Packer Buying Stations. Packer buying stations are simply outlying yards owned and operated by packing firms as assembly points. Buying stations are competitive devices designed to attract receipts since they are more convenient for producers located in the vicinity of the station. Trucking expense and shrinkage are usually lower for short-distance hauling. Pricing arrangements at buying stations are similar to those of plant purchases, although discounts may be applied to offset the firm's absorption of trucking and shrinkage losses and possible feed expense—depending upon the degree of competition encountered with other packers.

Local Markets.   Local markets include locally owned stockyards and concentration yards. Historically, a difference existed in that concentration yards were granted certain privileges by railraods in assembling and forwarding hogs by rail.

Concentration yards developed primarily in the Corn Belt, but with the advent of truck transportation, their importance has declined. It is worth noting, however, that the granting of through-rail rates on livestock that are unloaded at a point, sorted, reloaded, and forwarded to another point can on occasion be an important consideration. In transportation parlance, this is known as "transit privilege" or feed-in-transit privilege. It is also applied to products other than livestock. Grain may be unloaded, stored for a time and/or milled into various products. The products then reloaded and shipped to another destination at an additional charge, which is the balance of the through-rate. Through-rate is the rate that would have applied had the grain moved directly from point of original loading directly to the final destination. Without the transit privilege, the sum of the two rates (from origin to point of unloading and from this point to final destination) invariably is greater than the through-rate. Transit privilege is applicable to cattle, which may be unloaded for grazing, reloaded at the end of the gazing season, and forwarded to another point (Riley *et al.*, 1952). In this case, the balance of the through-rate applies just to the original weight. Gain added from grazing may pay the applicable flat rate from point of reloading to final destination. Although use of the privilege is not as prevalent as in past years, it can amount to important savings in freight charges when applicable.

Locally operated stockyards are apparently more common in southern, southeastern, and eastern states than elsewhere. Many auctions in other parts of the country, however, act as local markets on off-auction days. For example, a day or two of the week may be specified for purchasing hogs. The hogs are bought outright by the auction operator upon delivery, i.e., he acts as a dealer. The auction operator may or may not have a standing agreement for sale to a packer. If he has such an agreement, he is performing the function of a packer buying station. A Kansas study (Beaton and McCoy, 1970) showed that local market (and dealer) operations of auction firms, from a profit standpoint, were just about a break-even proposition.

Country Packer Buyers. Many, and perhaps most, of the larger packers employ buyers who travel over designated areas buying livestock directly from farms and commercial feedlots. Some larger packers have well organized and equipped buying systems. Some have a head buyer's office with two-way radio communication so that instant instructions may be relayed regarding current market conditions, plant needs, relative availability of livestock as observed by various buyers and other contacts, and pricing instructions. Such a system permits a high degree of coordination in a firm's procurement objectives.

The development and growth of commercial feedlots provide a concentration of livestock that attracts packer buyers. Small producers are at a relative disadvantage not only in the reluctance of country packer buyers to visit their yards, but with their limited number of head their bargaining power is less than that of large operators.

Country Dealers. Country dealers are usually one-man operations, although a few are regional and even interregional in scope (for example, Heinhold markets and IPLA). Livestock are bought outright, the dealer taking title and attempting to resell at a profit. Smaller dealers operate in a relatively local area without an established place of business; however, they usually have holding and sorting pens. There were 6,033 dealers and other buyers in the U.S. at the end of 1984 (Table 7.2). Dealers are found in all parts of the country but concentrated in the major livestock producing regions, particularly the North Central states. According to the part of the country, local terminology may label them as truck buyers, traveling buyers, traders, speculators, scalpers, or pinhookers. In spite of the somewhat derogatory connotation of some of these labels, country dealers have survived all the changes of the U.S. marketing system. They serve the basic function of assembling livestock—brining together odd head and small lots into larger, more uniform, more marketable lots. The larger regional and inter-regional operators, of course, deal in numbers by the carlot.

In early U.S. history, relatively large lots were needed for droving. With the development of railroads, larger lots (carlots) could be shipped at lower rates than less-than-carlots. Dealers thrived in these circumstances. In a countermove, producers formed shipping associations whereby several producers could ship together in carlots and qualify for the lower rates. Development of truck transportation quickly changed this situation. Shipping associations waned. Dealers, however, simply changed with the times. Many purchased trucks and either went into strictly hauling operations or a combination dealer and hauling operation. With the expansion of auction markets, local dealers added auction buying and selling to their country operations. As is the case with terminal-market dealers, these country dealers provide a market at all times. They tend to keep geographically separated markets in line by arbitrage operations. Dealers are constantly looking for opportunities to buy in one market and resell in another. One market will not remain out-of-line long before dealers start buying in the low-priced market and reselling in the high-priced market.

Dealers handle all classes of livestock, but their activity is substantially greater in feeder livestock (particularly feeder cattle and feeder lambs) than in slaughter livestock. All types of markets are used by dealers in disposing of their purchases. They sell in the market that appears most advantageous whether it be a producer, order buyer, local market, auction, terminal, or packer.

Many studies have been made by researchers on dealer operations in various states. Unfortunately, no comprehensive national studies have been made, and most state reports are out-of-date. A regional study covering the North Central Region in 1956 (Newberg, 1963) provides the latest information on dealer activities in the Midwest. At that time, there were 5,401 dealers in the North Central Region—down from 9,880 in 1940. This study showed that " . . . most dealers had volumes below 2,000 animal units per year and half of them had volumes of less than 1,000 animal units per year" (Newberg and Hart, 1963).

Many dealers carry on some order buying along with their dealer activities, and those with the proper facilities mix in some local market operations as well. Newberg and Hart (1963) showed that dealers commonly had other occupational interests, farming being the most common, trucking second, and auctioneering third.

Livestock dealers who handle livestock that move in interstate trade are under regulations by the Packers and Stockyards Act. They must register with the USDA and file bond when dealing on their own account. Dealers who maintain scales for interstate livestock must operate those scales and have them tested like any other market under P&S. In addition, dealers are prohibited by P&S regulations from using unfair, discriminatory, or deceptive trade practices and must maintain records of transactions carried on for their own account (USDA, 1963).

Order Buyers.   Order buyers buy livestock but do not take title. They merely act as agents in buying for another party and receive reimbursement in the form of a fee (or commission). Order buyers, therefore, provide an outlet for direct sales by producers.

Data are not available on the extent of producer sales to order buyers. In former years, sale of slaughter livestock was probably almost nil. Order buyers have long played an important role, however, in furnishing a connecting link in market channels for feeder cattle and feeder lambs. With the expansion in commercial cattle feedlots and a similar, but less extensive, trend in hog feeding, it is probable that order buyers are buying directly from these operators just as packer buyers are. The trend in the size of feeding units and the tendency for these operators to market directly indicates tht order buyers will of necessity go directly to producers to fill their orders.

Feeder-cattle and feeder-lamb order buyers for years have dealt directly with producers, especially in the range states. Although data are not available on the extent of this activity, the increasing demand for feeder cattle will tend to expand its use in the future.

Other Producers. On a local basis, direct sales among producers have always been common practice. In former years, it was not a customary practice for farm cattle feeders to go beyond their local area to buy replacement stock, although some larger operators did travel to range areas and deal directly with ranchers. The increased demand for feeder cattle resulting from commercial feedlot expansion has precipitated changes in feeder-cattle procurement by both commercial feedlot operators and farm feeders. Commercial feedlot operators attempt to buy directly from producers as well as through other channels. Most farm feeders depend upon order buyers, but some significant moves of another sort are under way.

The American Farm Bureau Federation (AFBF) in 1960 established an affiliate—the American Agricultural Marketing Association. Then individual states at their option set up state marketing associations. The purpoe of these is " . . . to assist producers of agricultural commodities to organize their market power, when the need and desire exists. The AFBF established this affiliate because it recognizes the marketing of farm products by negotiating contracts with the buyer of the agricultural products will be a dominant factor in the future" (Shuman, 1963). Early efforts of this organization were directed at fruits and vegetables. As experience was gained, it moved into some areas of livestock marketing. It is not known to have affected contracts in livestock marketing at this time, but it has organized a feeder cattle marketing program. For example, the Kansas Marketing Association, through contracts with affiliates in southeastern states, buys and transports feeder cattle to Kansas for its members. This type of activity, and other modifications, are likely to increase as the trend toward direct marketing increases. The National Farmers Organization operates collection points and acts as bargaining agent for its members.

A 1976 nationwide survey of beef cattle producers showed that contracting the sale of feeder cattle and calves varies among regions and from year to year (Boykin et al., 1980). The survey indicated that only 2.5 percent of the operators sold cattle and calves under contract in 1976. The highest proportions were in the West (6.5 percent) and the lowest in the North Central Region (0.3 percent). Given the record inventories in 1976 and low prices, it appears that producers were unwilling to enter into contractual arrangements in the hope that they might be able to obtain higher prices than were offered. In comparison, the survey indicated that contracting of stocker-feeder cattle was more popular, as indicated by the fact that 20 percent of the operators contracted such cattle for sale in some regions.

Direct Marketing of Live Versus Carcass Grade and Weight

Two major arrangements are practiced in direct marketing of slaughter livestock: (1) sale of live grade and weight, and (2) sale on carcass grade and weight. The latter is also commonly known as rail grade and weight, "on the rail," or "in the meat." Live-grade-and-weight trading is an arrangement whereby price is negotiated on the basis of live animals. Whatever grading is done is estimated from an inspection of the live animal. Weight and carcass yields are estimated on the basis of live animals. Weight is estimated at the time price bargaining is taking place. For sales made by weight instead of by the head, however, the pay weight is a scale weight (sometimes reduced by a pencil shrink, which will be discussed later).

In sharp contrast, the price by carcass grade and weight is not finally determined until the animals have been slaughtered. Pay weight is taken from the weight of the carcass as it hangs on the rail. The carcass is graded either by a packing-plant employee or a government grader. Fill is no factor since weight is based on the carcass. Price is established from a predetermined scale of prices based on weight and grade. This method requires each carcass to be identified by producer ownership. Hog carcass identity can be maintained rather successfully by tattooing if carcasses are not skinned. Cattle and sheep carcasses can be tagged, but there is some risk of tags becoming lost. The same problem occurs when hog carcasses are skinned, which is the practice in the more modern plants. Either procedure necessitates a cost not incurred in live selling. Additional record keeping for settlement purposes also adds to cost.

Grading by packing-plant employees has raised the question of possible bias, as has weighing on packing-plant scales by plant employees. Objections have also been raised to the delay in payment occasioned by the delay in final settlement until the livestock have been slaughtered, weighed, and graded. Some firms, however, give an advance payment upon delivery of the animals. It is obvious in carcass-grade-and-weight selling that practically no opportunity exists for bargaining after the livestock have been delivered and slaughtered. Bargaining must precede delivery.

Due to lack of uniformity among packers in carcass-grade-and-weight buying procedure, the USDA in 1968 established regulations as follows:

1. Packers must divulge to sellers, either orally or in writing, terms of the purchase contract prior to sale.
2. Identity of each carcass must be maintained.
3. Sufficient records must be maintained to verify settlement with producers.
4. Purchase and payment must be made on the basis of carcass prices.
5. Weight must be established on the hot carcass (not chilled).
6. All hooks, rollers, gambles, and other equipment must be uniform in weight for each species and only this weight be deducted as tare.
7. Payment may be made on USDA grades or other grades, but if the latter, the packer must furnish written specifications.
8. Carcasses must be graded no later than the close of the second business day following slaughter.

These regulations, although somewhat obnoxious to many packers, have established some needed uniformity among them and permit better comparison of carcass price offers than formerly was the case.

Research results, although not completely unanimous, have indicated that this method may improve pricing efficiency (Engelman *et al.*, 1953; Luby, 1977; Schneidau *et al.;* 1977). If the price applied to various grades and weights truly reflects market value, each producer would receive true value for his livestock. Each animal would be valued separately (not an average grade and weight for an entire lot). Thus, a producer would receive a differential for the more desirable grade and weight animals. Presumably, such a differential would encourage production of the more desirable animals and discourage production of those less desirable.

Meyer and Lang (1980) conducted a study of carcass-based marketing of cattle and hogs to identify obstacles to increased use of this method. Obstacles and benefits were identified through preliminary discussions with producers and packers and researchers. Producers and packers were then asked to indicate the degree of importance of these obstacles as well as to indicate and rank possible advantages. Packers identified the following four potential obstacles, in order of importance, to carcass-based procurement:

1. Maintaining carcass identity during slaughter
2. Difficulty in computing carcass value and payment
3. Costs associated with additional grading
4. Limiting of method to producer-packer trades excludes traders from alternative marketing channels such as order buyers and organized markets.

Potential benefits from packer's view (ranked) were as follows:

1. Aid in quality control
2. Reduced risk of over-payment
3. Reduced net buying costs
4. Reduced net prices paid for livestock

According to livestock producers, the following are the most important obstacles for marketing on carcass basis:

1. The need to commit livestock for sale before value is determined
2. The inability to compare prices before selling
3. Delay in payment
4. Lack of confidence in accuracy of grading at the plant.

Most producers agreed that this method is beneficial in providing useful information for their production practices. The majority believed that carcass-based marketing makes payment more fair and increases net returns. The results of the survey suggested that many producers were aware of the full benefits of this method. The researchers concluded that, "These findings suggest that the major emphasis of any effort to increase the use of carcass-based marketing would logically be focused on producer education and assistance in decision making." They further concluded that "Because they are willing to increase their purchases on a carcass basis, packers might make changes to increase producers' acceptance of the method. Partial payment on delivery could reduce the producers' concerns about delayed payment. Standardization and/or simplification of carcass-based systems for hogs would facilitate price comparisons and perhaps reduce producers' hesitation to commit their animals before value is determined."

A study of grade-and-yield marketing of hogs was carried out in 1982 (USDA 1984). Reported findings and conclusions are similar to those in the above study. The USDA study, however, was more specific in terms of the negative impact on producers of packers' arbitrarily establishing standards for grade and yield and in questioning the accuracy of estimating carcass weight from live weight.

It is possible, of course, to sort live animals and apply price differentials according to grade and weight, a practice followed to some extent in all types of direct and indirect markets. Commission agents and auction operators normally do some sorting. It is standard procedure for buyers to cut, or attempt to cut, less desirable animals from a lot and apply a price discount. Two restrictions, however, limit the extent of sorting on a live basis. First, it is generally agreed that grading of carcasses is more precise than grading on the hoof (Naive et al., 1957). Second, market agents and buyers are reluctant to make extensive sorts. A common argument is that sorting, while possibly resulting in higher prices for some animals, will at the same time necessitate lower prices for others, so that the average price may be no better than selling unsorted. This argument ignores the issue of pricing efficiency. While the arguments pro and con go on, producers have shown a tendency to increase direct marketing.

Table 7.6 shows the number and percentage of packer purchases by carcass grade and weight in recent years. The most significant increase occurred in cattle. In 1963, only 8 percent of the cattle (for all packers) was purchased by this arrangement. By 1976, the proportion had increased to slightly more than 23 percent and in 1984, to 31.2 percent. Smaller increases are shown in carcass grade and weight purchases of calves, hogs, and sheep.

Controversial Issues in Direct Marketing

It is impossible to state unequivocally whether a producer should use direct marketing. It is possible, however, to state some criteria upon which producers can make a decision. As mentioned earlier, the critical consideration is net return. Net return is gross return less marketing costs. Involved here are livestock prices, out-of-pocket costs, and noncash costs. Out-of-pocket costs such as commission, yardage, trucking, etc., are relatively easy to determine. In direct marketing, commission, yardage, and other marketing costs as enumerated on published market "tariffs" are avoided. Trucking may be less in direct marketing or

Table 7.6. Livestock Purchased on Carcass Grade and Weight By Type of Packer, 1965, 1970, and 1975-1984.

	Cattle			Calves		
	Total purchases	Grade and weight purchases		Total purchases	Grade and weight purchases	
	(1,000 hd)	(1,000 hd)	(% of total)	(1,000 hd)	(1,000 hd)	(% of total)
10 Major Packers						
1965	9,668	1,240	12.8	2,359	186	7.9
1970	11,091	2,323	20.9	742	51	6.9
1975	11,280	3,654	32.4	597	175	29.3
1976	12,751	3,847	30.2	617	149	24.2
1977	13,199	3,211	24.3	535	120	22.4
1978	12,820	3,663	28.6	291	69	23.7
1979	12,594	3,655	29.0	209	71	34.0
1980	13,560	4,719	34.8	28	25	89.3
1981	14,501	4,244	29.3	33	32	97.0
1982	15,538	5,898	38.0	23	22	95.7
1983	16,081	6,737	41.9	1	0	0
1984	16,500	6,081	36.9	1	0	0
Other Packers						
1965	20,184	2,143	10.6	4,492	128	2.9
1970	21,107	3,686	17.5	3,178	127	4.0
1975	24,605	5,081	20.7	3,873	223	5.8
1976	24,504	4,840	19.8	4,257	259	6.1
1977	25,012	5,636	22.5	4,120	306	7.4
1978	24,275	5,785	23.8	3,374	316	9.4
1979	18,426	4,781	25.9	2,238	363	16.2
1980	17,837	4,229	23.7	2,173	422	19.4
1981	17,577	4,605	26.2	2,235	360	20.2
1982	16,887	4,684	27.7	2,491	537	21.6
1983	17,417	5,073	29.1	2,545	573	22.5
1984	18,039	4,683	26.0	2,823	862	30.5
All Packers						
1965	29,852	3,383	11.3	6,851	314	4.6
1970	32,198	6,009	18.7	3,902	178	4.6
1975	35,891	8,735	24.3	4,470	408	9.1
1976	37,255	8,687	23.3	4,874	408	8.4
1977	38,211	8,847	23.2	4,655	426	9.2
1978	37,095	9,448	25.5	3,665	385	10.5
1979	31,020	8,436	27.2	2,447	434	17.7
1980	31,397	8,949	28.5	2,20	447	20.3
1981	32,078	8,850	27.6	2,268	392	17.3
1982	32,425	10,582	32.6	2,514	559	22.2
1983	33,498	11,810	35.3	2,546.	573	22.5
1984	34,539	10,764	31.2	2,824	862	30.5

(*continued*)

Table 7.6 (continued)

	Hogs			Sheep & Lambs		
	Total purchases	Grade and weight purchases		Total purchases	Grade and weight purchases	
	(1,000 hd)	(1,000 hd)	(% of total)	(1,000 hd)	(1,000 hd)	(% of total)
10 Major Packers						
1965	39,877	1,453	3.6	8,169	379	4.6
1970	39,023	2,776	7.1	5,544	567	10.2
1975	32,631	4,108	14.7	4,150	468	11.3
1976	33,779	5,598	16.6	3,350	381	11.4
1977	36,654	5,243	14.3	2,995	277	9.2
1978	40,396	6,438	15.9	2,612	75	2.9
1979	44,633	7,554	16.9	2,601	307	11.8
1980	43,624	7,209	16.5	2,890	292	10.1
1981	40,514	8,950	22.0	2,862	101	3.5
1982	35,394	7,528	21.3	3,169	287	9.1
1983	31,810	6,984	22.0	3,088	338	10.1
1984	35,639	7,556	21.2	2,935	392	13.4
Other Packers						
1965	34,262	498	1.4	4,850	277	5.7
1970	41,823	1,108	2.7	4,087	380	9.3
1975	35,445	1,247	3.5	3,573	345	9.7
1976	34,842	1,574	4.5	3,198	242	7.6
1977	38,289	1,435	3.7	3,021	250	8.3
1978	33,382	1,271	3.8	2,496	442	17.7
1979	37,997	1,928	5.1	1,194	873	39.8
1980	49,365	2,770	5.6	2,559	1,250	48.8
1981	45,385	1,826	4.0	2,586	927	35.8
1982	46,681	4,160	8.9	2,508	1,356	54.1
1983	46,862	4,471	9.5	2,919	1,422	48.7
1984	46,655	4,290	9.2	3,547	935	27.8
All Packers						
1965	74,139	1,942	2.6	13,019	656	5.0
1970	80,846	3,884	4.8	9,631	947	9.8
1975	68,076	6,048	8.9	7,723	813	10.5
1976	68,621	7,172	10.5	6,548	623	9.5
1977	74,943	6,678	8.9	6,016	527	8.8
1978	73,778	7,709	10.4	5,108	517	10.1
1979	82,630	9,482	11.5	4,795	1,180	24.6
1980	92,989	9,979	10.7	5,449	1,542	28.3
1981	85,899	10,776	12.5	5,448	1,028	18.9
1982	82,075	11,688	14.2	5,677	1,643	28.9
1983	78,672	11,455	14.6	6,007	1,760	29.3
1984	82,294	11,846	14.4	6,482	1,377	21.2

Source: USDA (1986).

it may be more depending upon the specified delivery point and upon whether seller or buyer provides the trucking service.

Shrinkage is a major noncash marketing cost. What is needed is the difference in shrinkage that would be incurred under direct marketing as compared to indirect. Some shrinkage is incurred regardless of the method. As will be seen in a later chapter, shrinkage is affected by a number of variables. There is research that provides guidelines, but research never applies precisely to a given farm situation. Producers with an adequate set of scales on the premises can develop applicable shrinkage standards for their particular operation over a period of several shipments.

The question of price level under direct versus indirect marketing is an unresolved controversy. Terminal market personnel and auction operators who see direct marketing as a threat to their existence have consistently opposed it, contending that producers will not get full price as a result of lack of competition when a producer deals directly with professional market personnel, such as packer buyers, order buyers, dealers, and local market operators.

Lack of Competition.   The contention that competition is lacking in direct marketing appears to rest upon the assumption that sellers, buyers, and the livestock itself must be physically present to have effective competition. Economic theory, however, does not substantiate this argument. What is needed are well-informed buyers and sellers with an adequate communication system. It may be assumed that most buyers are well-informed. Whether a producer is well-informed is largely up to him. Market news reports are available from both public and private sources. The decline in receipts at some terminal markets makes quotations from those sources less reliable than formerly. The USDA Market News Service has extended coverage to some auctions and interior markets. Some of these offices have up-to-date market information taped on an automatic telephone hookup. With direct dialing anyone can easily call, either locally or long distance, and obtain current information almost instantly. Further changes may be necessary in the future to obtain adequate information from both producers and packers on terms of direct sales.

Producers' organizations may play a greater part in the future in developing market intelligence. The National Cattlemen's Association has a market information gathering system under the name CATTLE-FAX. With this system, producers furnish information that is summarized and interpreted in a central office, then disseminated to subscriber members. The National Farmers Organization has an organizational arrangement that funnels market information to its central office. Many commercial feedlot operators subscribe to one (or more) of several available market wire services. These services provide for private installations that print out on tape almost continuous up-to-the-minute market reports. Such installations are available to individual producers who are willing to pay the price. A number of reputable research consultant market services are also available on subscription. Some of these provide continuous toll-free telephone advisory service.

These types of market news services usually exceed the capability of any one individual, but a producer obtaining such information on a subscription basis can be well-informed. Reasonably adequate communications systems are available from radio, television, telephone, teletype, etc. Improvements in electronic processing and in communications are constantly improving the availability of information. Nevertheless, it probably is true that many producers are ill-informed either through neglect or in ignorance of the availability of information. If so, they are not in position to be competitive in direct marketing. However, operators of most commercial type feedyards and many progressive farm feeders probably are as well-informed as the buyers.

Research studies have not verified the contention that direct marketing has lowered prices received by producers (USDA, 1935; Stout and Feltner, 1962).

Producers often claim a stronger competitive position in direct marketing at their premises, in that they know what the terms of the transaction are before committing themselves in any way. Producers who have delivered their livestock to a market any substantial distance from home are just about committed to sell. Technically, they may have a reservation price and may take the stock back, or to another market if dissatisfied, but from a practical standpoint this usually is not feasible. It may be more feasible at local auctions, but even there it is not common practice.

Lower Quality at Terminals. On occasion, opponents of direct marketing have argued that direct buyers take the higher quality stock, leaving the lower quality to be marketed at terminals, and since direct purchase prices are often based on terminal prices, lower quality animals are setting the standards. No recent studies are available to test this statement. It was tested, however, in 1935 (USDA, 1935). The results of the study showed no evidence of a difference in quality of hogs marketed at public (terminal) markets and interior markets. The latter represented direct markets. The same study found no difference in quality of hogs marketed at the Chicago terminal and hogs sold direct to packers.

Although information is not available on the current situation, past studies have shown that producers usually tend to be relatively firmly opinionated in regard to market preferences. A 1956 study (Newberg, 1959) covering the entire North Central Region revealed that "four-fifths of the farmers interviewed indicated that in selling livestock they had only one outlet where they sold all their major class."

Noncash Marketing Costs. Out-of-pocket marketing costs are less in direct marketing than in indirect since no comission and yardage are charged. Opponents of direct marketing claim, however, that producers particularly overlook the importance of shrinkage concessions. Most producers would argue that shrinkage is less in direct sales, but this issue has several ramifications. It is not uncommon for buyers to attempt to get a concession that livestock be kept off feed and water for a period, usually overnight, and in addition that producers apply a "pencil shrink." Pencil shrink is an agreed-upon percentage reduction from the scale weight in arriving at a pay weight. If the scales happen to be located some distance from the producer's premises, the actual shrink (from an overnight stand, loading, hauling, unloading, and weighing) can be considerable. Then, if a pencil shrink is applied, the combined shrinkage concession may be more than producers realize. Only by the installation of adequate scales on the premises will a producer know the shrinkage.

Many producers of slaughter livestock apparently have not been convinced that direct marketing is detrimental to their interest since the number and proportion of cattle and hogs marketed direct continues to increase. Table 7.7 shows direct packer purchases for recent years. Although the number of sheep purchased direct by packers has declined in recent years, the proportion has increased as numbers purchased at terminals have declined; numbers purchased at auctions have not changed greatly (Table 7.4) except for a noticeable decline in indirect auction purchases in 1976.

COOPERATIVE LIVESTOCK MARKETING

Cooperative marketing associations are recognized as a special form of business organization whereby producers own and operate the business for their mutual benefit. Two factors have been largely responsible for the development of cooperatives: dissatisfaction with services available from existing market agencies and dissatisfaction with the marketing charges of existing agencies. In 1922, the U.S. legislature enacted the Capper-Volstead Act in recognition of farm producers' disadvantage with other sectors of the economy in the marketing process.

Table 7.7. Direct Purchases by Packers, Including All Except Terminal Market and
Auction Purchases, 1960-1984.

Year	Cattle (1,000 hd)	(%)	Calves (1,000 hd)	(%)	Hogs (1,000 hd)	(%)	Sheep (1,000 hd)	(%)
1960	8,420	38.6	2,572	42.5	47,104	61.1	6,654	54.0
1965	13,455	45.1	2,351	34.3	46,613	62.9	8,127	62.4
1970	21,014	65.3	1,332	34.0	55,398	68.5	6,986	72.5
1971	22,134	68.6	1,099	32.4	62,956	69.3	7,245	74.0
1972	23,150	72.2	875	31.6	58,686	70.4	7,285	74.3
1973	23,085	73.5	712	31.1	53,992	70.9	6,409	72.4
1974	23,007	71.2	735	28.4	54,176	69.8	6,644	74.9
1975	23,930	67.4	1,539	34.1	49,395	71.8	5,809	74.1
1976	25,508	67.6	1,508	30.9	48,984	71.2	5,039	74.2
1977	26,903	69.8	1,632	34.4	54,284	72.5	4,652	76.7
1978	27,541	73.9	1,488	39.0	54,456	72.8	4,029	78.9
1979	24,881	77.7	1,080	41.9	61,554	74.9	4,013	81.6
1980	23,729	77.1	971	43.8	71,268	76.7	4,388	80.5
1981	24,822	77.4	969	42.7	67,334	78.4	4,250	78.0
1982	25,311	78.1	1,075	42.8	64,879	79.0	4,617	81.3
1983	25,005	77.6	1,231	48.4	60,436	76.8	4,948	82.4
1984	27,174	78.7	1,418	50.2	68,175	82.8	5,113	78.9

Source: USDA (1986 and earlier issues).

Among other things, this Act made it clear that farm producers had the right to organize cooperative marketing associations without violating existing antitrust laws.[3] A number of states also have statutes recognizing cooperatives as a special form of business activity. Cooperatives may be incorporated or non-incorporated like other businesses. In a cooperative, however, the profits (referred to by co-ops as "savings") ordinarily are distributed back to the members on the basis of patronage. This is in contrast to other forms of business that distribute profits on the basis of ownership or investment.

Long before enactment of the statutes authorizing cooperatives, farmers had banded together in cooperative ventures, including several forms of livestock marketing cooperatives. In colonial days, co-ops were formed for importation of purebred cattle. Droving often involved informal cooperation.

Shipping Associations

The first cooperative shipping associations were formed during the 1880s to counteract excessive margins taken by local dealers and as a

[3] Clodius (1962) and Nourse (1962) point out that the mere fact of being a cooperative does not protect an association from antitrust laws if the association unduly enhances price by trade restraint activities.

means of assembling livestock in lots large enough to gain the advantage of carlot rail-freight rates. By combining shipments, scattered local producers could qualify for carlot rates. In addition, this allowed them to send their livestock to the more competitive terminal markets and proved to be a sound educational process since producers became aware of market conditions beyond their immediate locality.

The formation of shipping associations spread throughout the heavy producing region of the Midwest, reaching a peak during the 1920s. For the most part, they were concerned with assembly and forwarding stock to terminal markets, not engaged in buying and selling. Livestock in the shipments were consigned to established private-commission firms for sale at the terminals. Opposition was encountered at some terminals when sorting and maintenance of identity for individual shippers presented some problems, but this was not a controlling factor. The movement was reversed by technological developments that largely removed the need. Truck transportation and road improvements opened the way for smaller shipments. Improved communications permitted wider and more accurate dissemination of market news. Development of artificial refrigeration and improved transportation were instrumental in decentralization of the packing industry. Cooperative shipping associations as originally organized and operated are largely a thing of the past. However, from a functional standpoint, the National Farmers Organization assembly points are performing some of the original services.

Terminal Market Commission Firms

Another achievement in cooperative livestock marketing was the formation fo terminal-market commission firms. Part of the stimulus came from the resistance of established private agencies (noncooperative) to shipping association activity. In addition, there was dissatisfaction with commission charges and distrust of private commission-firms. With shipping associations as a source of shipments, it was logical for producers to carry integration an additional step and organize their own terminal commission agency.

Initially, the opposition was intense and several early attempts failed. Established commission firms opposed cooperatives for fear of losing business. Yard dealers objected because the cooperatives formed stocker and feeder divisions that completed movement of one producer's stock back to another producer without movement through a dealer. Feelings were high enough for many packers and order buyers to boycott the early cooperative commission firms.

Some success had been attained by World War I. The Equity Cooperative Exchange had been established at South St. Paul, Minnesota, and the Farmers Union at several markets, but the breakthrough occurred during the 1920s. A conference called by the American Farm Bureau Federation in 1921 resulted in a marketing strategy, which, among other things, called for the establishment of terminal-market commission firms with stocker and feeder divisions, shipping associations, and a national livestock producers' organization. An outgrowth of this was the formation of the National Live Stock Producers Association. Affiliated commission agencies with stocker and feeder divisions were organized at a number of terminals.

Some mergers have since occurred among the affiliates and some have ceased operation, but most still are in operation. Other cooperative commission firms also are in operation. Although opposition has not entirely disappeared, the cooperatives are generally accepted and are often the most enthusiastic advocates of terminal markets. The number of co-op commission firms reached a peak in the early 1930s. The decline since that time is associated primarily with the decline of livestock marketing at terminals, a development that has also affected noncooperative commission firms. In spite of the decline, cooperatives are still a viable factor at terminal markets. Ward *et al.* (1978) reported that 10 percent of commission firms at terminal markets in 1975 were cooperatives and that they handled 20 percent of the livestock at those markets. In some instances, the terminal agencies have branched out into local operations. An example of this is the Producers Livestock Marketing Association, a merged association of terminal commission firms in St. Joseph, Missouri, and Omaha, Nebraska, which also operates an auction market in central Nebraska. Other examples are the Producers Live Stock Association of Columbus, Ohio, which represents a merger of three terminal commission firms and has a number of country branches operating auctions and local markets, and the Interstate Producers Livestock Association (IPLA), a Farm Bureau affiliate with headquarters in Peoria, Illinois, and operations in Illinois, Iowa, and Missouri.

Meat Packing

From time to time, cooperatives have ventured into meat packing. Fox (1957) reported that of 17 attempts between 1914 and 1920 all failed. Failures were attributed to " . . . lack of operating capital and member support, poor facilities, inadequate volume of livestock, inexperienced and unskilled management, keen competition and unsatisfactory sales outlets." Although a number of later attempts failed, there have been some notable successes. Chapter 9 presents more discussion on cooperative meat packing.

Other Cooperative Activities

A number of livestock auctions, concentration yards, buying stations, and country commission and dealer operations are carried out by producer cooperative associations. Cooperatives have assumed leadership in the use of livestock teleauctions in the United States. Nationwide, there are more than 500 cooperatives involved in livestock and livestock products, including many cooperatively operated feedlots and a substantial number of cooperative sow-farrowing units located primarily in midwestern and plains states (Ward et al., 1978). The American Farm Bureau Federation is engaged, through its affiliates, in feeder-cattle procurement for its members. National Farmers Organization operations, already noted as a bargaining association, is another example of cooperative livestock marketing.

An area of growth in cooperative livestock marketing in recent years has been sales of specialized feeder cattle and feeder pigs. All parts of the country have experienced growth in this area, but southeastern states have been particularly active. In 1967, 200 southeastern auctions were engaged in cooperative livestock activities. The principle activity of 182 of them was marketing livestock, and 138 of these were devoted exclusively to sales of specialized feeder cattle and feeder pigs (Haas 1970).

Most specialized feeder-livestock sales use the auction method where livestock is pooled and ownership commingled. In pooling, animals are sorted by weight, grade, and other physcial characteristics, making possible the sale of larger lots of uniform quality. Producers are paid for the weight of their particular animals from the pooled price received for the entire lot.

Cooperatives have a long, and somewhat turbulent, history of marketing wool in the United States. Early attempts date back to the 1840s (Ward et al., 1978). After a number of early failures, a period of successful operations brought 40 percent of the U.S. shorn wool through cooperatives during World War II. Wool marketing is carried out primarily by local pools, which in turn are affiliated with regional cooperatives, most of which operate on pooling arrangements.

The Future of Cooperative Livestock Marketing

Cooperatives have never attained a dominant status in marketing of livestock on a national scale. In localized areas, however, cooperative influence has been felt, and the effect has been beneficial to producers. Early shipping associations enhanced the bargaining position of isolated producers in relation to local dealers and local market operators. At the same time, they provided some relief in transportation costs.

Upon passage of the Packers and Stockyards Act (1921), terminal-market commission firms supported enforcement of the provisions that alleviated unfair and discriminatory practices. These same agencies were instrumental in providing production and marketing credit, fostering improvements in market news services and grade standards, sponsoring research, and in carrying out various educational activities designed to improve quantity and quality of livestock produced.

From the standpoint of marketing efficiency, cooperatives have the dual objective of improving both operational and pricing efficiency. Results of improved operational efficiency are easier to measure and appear to have been the chief pursuit of most cooperative endeavors. These have taken the form of reduced marketing costs—coming back to producers as patronage refunds. Mehren (1965) has stated that "probably the three keys to co-op success have proved to be: keen sensitivity to changing needs of the market; willingness of members to unite in a common front and commit themselves to a common program of action; aggressive, alert, efficient farmer leadership and professional management."

Ward (1977) suggests an integrated cattle marketing system where "The cooperative performs two interrelated functions: (1) assists cattlemen who want to integrate forward as far as feeder cattle growing, cattle feeding, or cattle slaughtering, and (2) markets cattle and beef for its members." This proposal provides for flexibility on the part of the producer in deciding whether, when, and how far to integrate his individual operation but places marketing responsibility in the cooperative.

There are indications that because of changes in farming and livestock production in the U.S. traditional local cooperatives are evolving into larger and sometimes regional operations, a development that will influence cooperatives' role in livestock and meat marketing. Future cooperatives are likely to offer more, and new, services, including market information and trading assistance. Success in the future will depend upon how well changes are anticipated and how well programs are implemented that benefit producer members.

REFERENCES

Abel, H., and Broadbent, D. A. 1952. Trade in western livestock at auctions. Utah Agr. Expt. Sta. Bull. 352.

Armstrong, J. H. 1976. Hog marketing now and in the future. Swine Conference for the American Farm Bureau Federation, St. Louis, Mo., Jan.

Beaton, N. J., and McCoy, J. H. 1970. Economic characteristics of Kansas livestock auctions. Kansas Agr. Expt. Sta. Bull. 537.

Black, W. E., and Uvacek, E. 1972. Alternative systems for marketing Texas livestock. Texas Agr. Ext. Serv. *Food Fiber Economics* 1, No. 7.

Boykin, C. B., *et al.* 1980. Structural Characteristics of Beef Cattle Raising in the United States, USDA, ESCS, Agr. Econ. Rept. No. 450.

Bowen, C. C., and Thomas, P. R. 1970. Auction selling of slaughter cattle on a carcass basis. Ohio Coop. Ext. Serv. Bull. 510.

Broadbent, E. E. 1970. Are we willing to adjust? *In* Long-Run Adjustments in the Livestock and Meat Industry: Implications and Alternatives, edited by T. Stout. Ohio Agr. Res. Develop. Center, Res. Bull. 1037. Also, North Central Regional Publ. 199.

Broadbent, E. E., and Perkinson, S. R. 1971. Operational efficiency of Illinois country hog markets. Illinois Agr. Expt. Sta. Bull. 110.

Chambliss, R. L., and Bell, J. B. 1974. Selling feeder cattle in commingled lots: A pilot study of pooling in livestock auction markets. Virginia Polytechnic Institute, Agr. Econ. Res. Rept. 12.

Clodius, R. L. 1962. Lesson from recent antitrust decisions. *J. Farm Econ.*, Dec.: 1603–1610.

Cramer, C. L. 1958. Why the early week market? Missouri Agr. Expt. Sta. Bull. 712. Also, North Central Regional Publ. 91.

Eckert, A. R. 1965. Prices, motivations and efficiency in price determination in Nebraska livestock auction markets. Univ. Nebraska, Dept. Agr. Econ. Rept. 40.

Engelman, G. *et al.* 1953. Relative accuracy of pricing butcher hogs on foot and by carcass weight and grade. Minn. Agr. Expt. Sta. Tech. Bull. 208.

Engleman, G., and Pence, B. S. 1975. Livestock Auction Markets in the United States. USDA, Market Res. Rept. 223.

Farris, D. E., and Couvillion, W. C. 1975. Vertical coordination of beef in the south. Southern Cooperative Series, Bull. 192.

Farris, D. E., and Dietrich, R. A. 1975. Opportunities in cattle marketing. Texas Agr. Expt. Sta. Dir. 77-1, SP-1.

Forker, O. D., *et al.* eds. 1976. Marketing alternative for agriculture, is there a better way? Cornell University, Nat'l Public Policy Educational Committee Publication No. 7, Nov.

Foweler, S. H. 1961. The Marketing of Livestock and Meat, 2nd ed. Interstate Printers and Publishers, Danville, Il.

Fox R. L. 1957. Farmer's meat packing enterprises in the United States. USDA Farmers Coop. Serv. Gen. Rept. 29.

Fox, R. L. 1965. Livestock and wool cooperatives. *In* Farmer cooperatives in the United States. USDA Farmer Coop. Serv. Bull. 1.

Gee, K., and Magleby, R. 1976. Characteristics of Sheep Production in the Western United States. USDA Agr. Econ. Rept. 345.

Hass, J. T. 1970. Livestock cooperatives in the southeast. USDA Farmer Coop. Serv. Res. Rept. 13.

Hass, J. T., *et al.* 1977. Marketing slaughter cows and calves in the Northeast. USDA Farmer Coop. Serv. FCS Res. Rept. 36.

Hass, J. T., and Hogland, J. A. 1980. Need for cooperative hog processing in ten midwestern states. USDA, Agr. Coop. Serv. Staff Paper.

Hawkins, M. H., *et al.* 1972. Development and operation of the Alberta hog producers marketing board. Univ. of Alberta, Dept. of Agr. Econ. and Rural Soc. Bull. 12.

Holder, D. L. 1974. A tele-o-auction for marketing lambs. USDA Farmer Coop. Serv. FCS Special Report No. 4.

Holder, D. L. 1977. Cooperative marketing alternatives for sheep and lamb producers. USDA. Farmers Coop. Serv. Marketing Res. Rept. No. 1081, Aug.

Johnson, R. D. 1972. An economic evaluation of alternative marketing methods for feed cattle. Nebraska Agr. Expt. Sta. SB 520.

Lowe, J. C. 1968. Hog marketing by teletype. Manitoba Dept. of Agr. Publ. No. 471. Winnipeg, Oct.

Luby, P. 1977. Communication and pricing—What we know and what we need to know. *In* Long Run Adjustments in the Livestock and Meat Industry: Implications and Alternatives, edited by T. T. Stout. Ohio Agr. Res. and Develop. Center. Res. Bull. 1037.

McCoy, J. H., *et al.* 1975 Feeder cattle pricing at Kansas and Nebraska auctions. Kansas Agr. Expt. Sta. Bull. 582.

Mehren, G. L. 1965. Potential for cooperatives in livestock. Proc. Stockholders' and Directors' meeting. Nat. Live Stock Producers Assoc., Chicago, March.

Meyer, A. L., and Lang, M. G. 1980. Carcass-based marketing of cattle and hogs. Purdue Univ. Dept. of Agr. Econ., Agr. Expt. Sta., Sta. Bull. No. 300.

Naive, J. J., *et al.* 1957. Accuracy of estimating live grades and dressing percentages of slaughter hogs. Indiana Agr. Sta. Bull. 650.

Newberg, R. R. 1959. Livestock marketing in the North Central Region. I. Where farmers and ranchers buy and sell. Ohio Agr. Expt. Sta. Res Bull. 846. Also North Central Regional Publ. 104.

Newberg, R. R. 1963. Livestock marketing in the North Central Region. II. Channels through which livestock moves from farm to final destination. Ohio Agr. Expt. Sta. Res. Bull. 932. Also, North Central Regional Publ. 141.

Newberg, R. R., and Hart, S. P. 1963. Livestock marketing in the North Central Region. IV. Dealers and local markets. Ohio Agr. Expt. Sta. Res. Bull. 962. Also, North Central Regional Publ. 150.

Nourse, E. 1962. Lessons from recent anti-trust decisions. J. Farm Econ. Dec.: 1614–1623.

Phillips, V. B., and Engleman, G. 1958. Market outlets for livestock producers. USDA Agr. Marketing Serv. Marketing Res. Rept. 216.

Powers, M. J., and Bendt, D. R. 1968. Livestock marketing in the Upper Missouri River Basin. II. The Sioux City Stockyards—facilities and costs of operation. S. Dakota Agr. Expt. Sta. Bull. 548. Also, North Central Regional Publ. 188.

Riley, H. M., *et al.* 1952. Feed-in-transit privilege in marketing livestock. Kansas Agr. Expt. Sta. Circ. 288.

Sarhan, M. E., and Kunda, E. L. 1982. Livestock Auction Markets in Illinois. Dept. of Agr. Econ., Univ. of Illinois, AE 4538.

Schneidau, R. *et al.* 1977. Implementing Improved Pricing Accuracy—Hogs and Pork. *In* Long Run Adjustments in the Livestock and Meat Industry: Implications and Alternatives, edited by T. T. Stout. Ohio Agr. Res. and Develop. Center, Res. Bull. 1037.

Shuman, C. B. 1963. Best interest of farmers lies in working to form own supply-management program. *In* Selected Papers on Marketing. Am. Meat Inst., Chicago.

Stout, T. T., and Feltner, R. L. 1962. A note on spatial pricing accuracy and price relationships in the market for slaughter hogs. *J. Farm Econ.* 44: 213–219.

USDA. 1935. The direct marketing of hogs. USDA Bur. Agr. Econ. Misc. Publ. 222.

USDA. 1963. The Packers and Stockyards Act as it applies to livestock dealers. USDA, P&S Admin., Agr. Marketing Serv. 319, June 1963.

USDA. 1970. Packers and Stockyards Resume, USDA, P&S Admin. 8, No. 13, Dec.

USDA. 1972. Pork marketing report—a team study. USDA Farmer Coop. Serv. (unnumbered), Sept.

USDA. 1977. Packers and Stockyards Resume. USDA, P&S Admin., vol. 15, Dec.

USDA. 1978. Meat animals production, disposition, income. USDA, Econ. Stat. and Coop. Serv. MtAn. 1-1 (78) April.

USDA. 1979. 1977 Marketing channel survey, Channels used for marketing farm commodities in selected states. ESCS; SpCr-7.

USDA. 1984. Meat animals production, disposition, income—1983 Summary.

USDA. 1984. Grade and yield marketing hogs. Packers and Stockyards Administration, a team study (unnumbered).

USDA. 1986. Packers and Stockyards Resume. P&S Admin. Stat. Rept. No. 86-1.

Van Arsdall, R. N., and Nelson, K. E. 1984. U.S. Hog Industry. USDA, ERS, Agr. Econ. Rept. No. 511.

Via, J. E., and Hass, J. T. 1976. Increasing efficiency in a country hog marketing system. Maryland Agr. Expt. Sta. MP 883.

Ward, C. E. 1977. Contract integrated, cooperative cattle marketing system. USDA. Farmer Coop. Serv. Marketing Res. Rept. No. 1078.

Ward, C. E. et al. 1978. Livestock and wool cooperatives. USDA. Farmer Coop. Serv. Bull. I.

Wohlgenant, M. K., and Greer, R. C. 1974. An evaluation of selling alternatives for Montana pork producers. Montana Agr. Expt. Sta. Bull. 675.

Williams, W. F., and Stout, T. T. 1964. *Economics of the Livestock-Meat Industry.* New York: Macmillan Co.

8

Meat Packing and Processing: History, Classification, and Structure

The purpose of this chapter is to describe the present structure and characteristics of the U. S. meat industry, give a brief review of its history, and examine current important public issues. The term "meat packer" as used in the meat industry refers both to firms involved in the slaughtering of live animals and those involved in both slaughtering and processing. The term "meat processors" refers to establishments engaged in breaking carcasses into primal and subprimal cuts as well as manufacturing meat products, but not one that slaughters live animals.[1]

The meat packing and processing industry has been, and will continue to be, characterized by continuous change in location, organization, and technology. Understanding the history and early developments that led to these changes is an important first step in analyzing the present state of the industry and projecting future developments.

HISTORICAL OVERVIEW

Recorded history indicates that early meat packing was limited to livestock slaughtering and meat preservation, using primitive methods such as smoking, pickling, and packing in barrels. Packed meat was commonly traded as early as the mid 1600s between individual merchants in the American colonies and the British West Indies. The first commercial meat packing plant was established in Springfield, Massachusetts, in 1662 (Clemen, 1923). The industry continued to grow but was not organized or relatively well developed until 1742, when the Faneuil Hall meat market was established in Boston and the first set of regulations was developed. A large slaughter plant was built in the same area. Success of the meat market necessitated growth of the

---

[1]Meat processors include sausage makers, canners, boners, and makers of frozen meat speciality portions.

packing industry, which provided a ready market outlet for livestock producers.

As settlements spread westward and into the Ohio Valley following the War of Independence, a new era in livestock production and meat packing began. Slaughtering was limited to winter months prior to the use of natural ice. Cincinnati was the center of activity because of its location in relation to production and transportation means, particularly the Ohio River. The first operation was established in 1818 and Cincinnati became known as "Porkopolis." The industry grew and spread westward and southward into Kentucky and Illinois and then beyond.

By the mid-1850s three more factors had drastically changed the size and nature of the meat packing industry: (1) the expanded domestic demand for meat, particularly during the Civil War; (2) the opening of export markets, especially in England, which necessitated a change in methods used by American packers; and (3) the introduction of natural ice in 1857, which changed the industry from seasonal (winter) to a year-round operation.

Refrigeration by natural ice dates as early as 1000 B.C. but was not practiced commercially until the nineteenth century. Natural ice was quarried (sawed) in large blocks from frozen lakes and ponds, stored in "ice houses" or "ice cellars"—packed in sawdust—and used for summer refrigeration. The earliest known use of natural ice for cooling rail cars was an 1851 shipment of butter in a wooden box car insulated with sawdust. Soon thereafter it was used in rail shipments of meat from Chicago and other inland points to the East Coast. Its use extended well into the twentieth century but was gradually replaced by artifically produced ice. Although that development had its beginnings in the late 1800s, the conversion was not completed until well into the 1900s. After more than 100 years of development, mechanical refrigeration began to replace natural ice in a big way following World War II. It is now dominant in packing house chilling facilities and the transportation of meat.

The introduction and utilization of mechanical refrigeration was the most important factor in revolutionizing the meat packing industry. It reduced the cost of operations by allowing for better utilization of facilities. The volume of meat produced thus increased to meet expanding demand. Prior to effective refrigeration, moveover, and the geographical spread of both pioneer settlements and the livestock industry, livestock was produced, or shipped and slaughtered, near the point of consumption. Thus, the early era of the meat packing industry can be characterized as being decentralized. The development of railroads following the westward and southward spread of human populations

218 LIVESTOCK AND MEAT MARKETING

and animal production in the mid-1800s made the establishment of large assembly yards possible. The livestock-slaughtering industry took advantage of readily available supplies of livestock at centralized terminal markets. As more of these large multistory, multispecies plants were built, the industry became increasingly centralized and remained so until World War I.

During this era, mechanical power and large business organizations enhanced the industry's efficiency and economic growth and power. The industry had become concentrated around large terminal stockyards, with only a few large corporate plants shipping meat to farflung points of consumption. Allegations of monopoly power and anticompetitive practices began to be directed against the industry. Public scrutiny and involvement (besides sanitation) began in 1888, when the U.S. Senate authorized a study that confirmed alleged collusion and other monopolistic practices in the transportation, production, and distribution of meat, but no direct corrective action was taken. A 1904 investigation showed that no undue profits were being made by packers in holding cattle prices low but at the same time pointed to unsanitary conditions in some operations and this led to the enactment of the Federal Meat Inspection Act of 1906. Later, in response to President Wilson's request to investigate the food industry, the Federal Trade Commission (FTC) issued a report in 1919 that stated that the "Big Five" packers (Armour, Cudahy, Morris, Swift, and Wilson) held a dominant position in the meat packing industry.

The Justice Department proceeded to prosecute these five companies under the Sherman Antitrust Act, but the case was settled out of court in 1920 with the famous Packers Consent Decree. Although not admitting guilt, the five agreed to refrain from activities (including ownership) in livestock, food manufacturing, and retailing. They also agreed to submit to continued jurisdiction of the U. S. courts and to accept new provisions to preserve the intent of the decree. This action forced them to liquidate many of their interests. One of the big five (Morris) was acquired by another packer (Armour) in 1923.[2]

The 1917 FTC investigation also led to enactment of the Packers and Stockyards Act of 1921, which brought regulation of the livestock and meat industries under continuing responsibility of a specific government agency—the Packers and Stockyards Administration of the U. S. Department of Agriculture.

---

[2]The decree was modified in December 1971, January 1975, and January 1980. A petition was filed on October 16, 1981 by Swift Independent Packing Company (SIPCO) to modify the decree. Citing structural changes in the meat industry since early 1960s and lack of effectiveness of the decree, a senior U.S. District Judge abolished the Packer Consent Decree on November 23, 1981.

After World War I, the importance of centralized terminal markets began to deteriorate, and direct marketing of livestock started to grow. These developments coincided with structural changes in the whole-sale and retail segments of the meat economy, which was influenced by several important changes—for example, improved roads, introduction of refrigerated trucks, better communications technology, and the development of accepted grades and standards. Independent packers could now build specialized slaughter plants near sources of livestock supply. The industry was becoming decentralized again and moving toward less concentration, as a result of both the Consent Decree and the previously mentioned factors.

The period following World War II saw rapid movement toward decentralization and specialization in livestock slaughter. The 1960s and 1970s brought substantial technological changes in both the production/feeding and slaughter/processing industries. The trend was toward bigness in an attempt to capture the economies of scale in these industries. New and more efficient plants were built farther west in the Western Corn Belt and Plains, where the rapidly expanding commercial feeding industry was centered. Several new firms came on the scene in the 1960s and 1970s, introducing new technology (including boxed meat) and employing low-cost labor. Some of these new firms expanded at a very rapid rate, catching up and surpassing the "old line" packers in output.

During the decade of the 1970s, concerns again arose over the matter of increasing concentration, particularly in regard to steer and heifer slaughter (Williams, 1979). The industry in the early 1980s may be described as dominated by a few firms with decentralized plants near the sources of livestock supply, but centrally controlled. Allegations of questionable economic practices continue, with recent emphasis on the rapid gains of particular firms, conglomerate involvement in meat packing, and wholesale meat pricing.

CLASSIFICATION OF LIVESTOCK SLAUGHTERING AND MEAT PROCESSING

Livestock-slaughtering and meat-processing plants may be classified according to one or a combination of the following classfications: (1) type of inspection, (2) size of plant, and (3) scope of operation. In addition, other designations are used to refer to specialization in terms of operations (e.g., shipper type) or location (e.g., area, such as West Coast packer). Livestock slaughtering by farmers is classed as "farm slaughter" in contrast to "commercial slaughter"; however, custom slaughtering in commercial plants for farmers is considered commercial slaughter.[3]

Classification by Type of Inspection

Classifying slaughtering and processing plants according to type of inspection is among the most commonly used methods. Under this system plants are designated as "Federally Inspected" (FI), "State Inspected" (SI), or "Exempt" (EX).

Federally Inspected Plants. Federal government regulations requiring inspection and monitoring of meat and meat products dates back to 1890 when the Meat Inspection Act was enacted and was primarily concerned with the export market. The updated Federal Meat Inspection Act of 1906, however, required Federal inspection of plants involved in interstate or international shipment of meat and meat products and all meat sold under government contracts.

The purpose of this and subsequent Acts was to assure the consuming public that live animals as well as meat products had been monitored to ensure their being free of disease and any harmful ingredients and that the meat was safe and wholesome to consume. The USDA Food Safety and Quality Service (FSQS), renamed Food Safety and Inspection Service (FSIS) in 1982, administers the Federal inspection program. Federal inspection is provided at no direct cost to firms operating during routine working hours. The USDA charges for overtime, weekends, and holidays.

State Inspected Plants. The U.S. Wholesome Meat Act of 1967 required plants shipping meat intrastate to conform to the standards of the Federal inspection program or be federally inspected. State inspected plants are not permitted to ship meat out of the state in which they are located.[4]

Exempt Plants. Such plants are very small and not involved in commercial trade; they custom slaughter a few heads per week for individuals.

Table 8.1 presents the number of livestock slaughtered and meat production in the United States in 1982 and 1984 by type of inspection and species. The data indicate that 92 percent of the cattle, 88 percent

---

[3]Prior to 1966, custom slaughtering in plants for farmers was included in farm slaughter.
[4]There were several attempts in the U.S. Congress to eliminate this requirement and thus allow all inspected plants to engage in interstate trading.

Table 6.1. Livestock Slaughter and Meat Production in the U.S., by Species and Type of Slaughter, 1982 and 1984.

Species, kinds of meat, and class of slaughter	1982				1984			
	Head slaughtered		Meat production		Head slaughtered		Meat production	
	(1000)	(% of total)	(Mil. kg*)	(% of total)	(1000)	(% of total)	(Mil. kg*)	(% of total)
Cattle/Beef								
Fed. Insp.	33,907	93.8	9,677	94.7	35,880	94.7	10,210	95.4
Other Com.	1,937	5.4	468	4.6	1,702	4.5	411	3.8
Farm	315	.8	77	.7	310	.8	82	.8
Total	36,158	100.0	10,222	100.0	37,892	100.0	10,703	100.0
Calves/Veal								
Fed. Insp.	2,729	87.9	155	76.1	3,030	90.0	185	82.6
Other Com.	292	9.4	37	18.3	267	7.9	32	14.3
Farm	85	2.7	11	5.6	70	2.1	7	3.1
Total	3,106	100.0	203	100.0	3,367	100.0	224	100.0
Hogs/Pork								
Fed. Insp.	79,328	95.8	6,195	96.0	82,478	96.3	6,478	96.4
Other Com.	2,861	3.4	210	3.2	2,690	3.1	199	3.0
Farm	654	.8	49	.8	473	.6	42	.6
Total	82,844	100.0	6,454	100.0	85,641	100.0	6,719	100.0
Sheep/Lambs—Lambs and Mutton								
Fed. Insp.	6,273	94.4	157	95.0	6,549	94.9	164	94.8
Other Com.	175	2.6	4	2.5	210	3.0	5	2.9
Farm	194	3.0	4	2.5	141	2.1	4	2.3
Total	6,643	100.0	165	100.0	6,900	100.0	173	100.0

Source: USDA (1983 and 1985A) and AMI (1985).
*Converted to kilograms from pounds and rounded by the authors.

of the calves, 96 percent of the hogs, and 94 percent of the sheep and lambs were slaughtered in federally inspected plants during 1982. These percentages were slightly higher in 1984. Other commercial plants (state inspected and custom slaughter for farm use) and farm slaughter accounted for the remaining slaughter.

The percentages of total beef, pork, and lamb and mutton produced in federally inspected plants are similar to percentages of cattle, hogs, and lamb and sheep slaughtered. However, veal production in federally inspected plants as a percent of the total commercial slaughter was less than the percentage of number of head. This fact was due primarily to the greater average liveweight of calves slaughtered in other commercial plants.

Classification by Size of Plant

Slaughtering and processing plants may be classified according to size—i.e., number of head slaughtered, or total liveweight, handled annually. Many terms have been used to designate plants according to size. Most of the federally inspected, and some nonfederally inspected, plants are classified as "large"; such plants slaughter 907,194 kg liveweight (2 million lb) or more annually (these are also known as wholesale slaughterers). Plants that slaughter less than 907,194 kg liveweight but more than 136,079 kg (300,000 lb) are designated as "medium size" (also known as "local slaughterers"), whereas plants that slaughter less than 136,079 kg annually (300,000 lb) are designated as small. Data on very small (butchers') plants are not collected and, when available, are often incomplete.

The USDA publishes data on federally inspected plants according to size groups and the number of head slaughtered. The number of intervals and their size differs from specie to specie. Table 8.2 presents the number, by size groups, of federally inspected plants and the percentages of total cattle, calves, hogs, and sheep and lambs slaughtered in these plants in 1981 and 1984. The figures clearly show that a relatively small number of large plants accounted for most of the slaughter. For example, 136 plants in the 50,000 head and over group (9 percent of all FI plants) accounted for about 88 percent of all cattle slaughtered under Federal inspection in 1984. During the same year, there were 922 plants in the less than 1,000 head group, accounting for about 62 percent of the number of plants but slaughtering less than 1 percent of the cattle. Plants at the upper end of the range of size groups accounted for most of the calves, hogs, and sheep and lambs slaughtered during both 1981 and 1984 (Table 8.2).

Table 8.2.   Number of Federally Inspected (FI) Plants and Percentages of Total Head Slaughtered, by Species and Size Group, U.S. 1981 and 1984.

Species and size group	1981			1984		
	Number of plants	% of plants*	% of total head slaughtered	Number of plants	% of plants*	% of total head slaughtered*
Cattle						
Under 1,000	964	62.0	1.0	922	61.5	0.9
1,000– 9,999	315	20.3	3.1	313	20.9	2.6
10,000–49,999	147	9.4	11.6	129	8.6	9.0
50,000–99,999	49	3.2	10.9	53	3.5	10.7
100,000–249,999	47	3.0	22.8	47	3.1	20.6
250,000–499,999	22	1.4	24.6	20	1.3	19.6
500,000 and over	11	1.7	26.0	16	1.1	36.6
Total	1,555	100.0	100.0	1,500	100.0	100.0
Calves						
Under 100	622	75.8	0.4	645	75.5	0.3
100–9999	84	10.2	1.0	94	11.0	1.0
1,000–9,999	66	8.0	9.9	52	6.1	6.2
10,000 and over	49	6.0	88.7	63	7.4	92.5
Total	821	100.0	100.0	854	100.0	100.0
Hogs						
Under 1,000	899	64.8	0.3	894	66.7	0.3
1,000–9,999	269	19.4	0.9	241	18.0	0.9
10,000–99,999	110	7.9	4.0	107	8.0	4.3
100,000–249,999	23	1.7	4.2	26	1.9	5.7
250,000–499,999	26	1.8	11.3	19	1.4	8.2
500,000–999,999	23	1.7	19.6	21	1.6	19.3
1,000,000–1,499,999	28	2.0	38.7	20	1.5	29.7
1,500,000 and over	10	0.7	21.0	13	0.9	31.6
Total	1,388	100.0	100.0	1,341	100.0	100.0
Sheep and Lambs						
Under 100	717	72.4	0.3	703	68.0	0.3
100–999	205	20.7	1.0	252	24.4	1.1
1,000–9,999	41	4.2	2.3	49	4.7	2.3
10,000 and over	27	2.7	96.4	30	2.9	96.3
Total	990	100.0	100.0	1,034	100.0	100.0

Source: USDA (1982 and 1985A).
*Percentages were calculated by the authors.

CLASSIFICATION BY SCOPE OF OPERATION

Firms in the meat packing and processing industry may also be classified according to their scope of operation and sales distribution. Most of the large firms—IBP, Inc. (formerly, Iowa Beef Processors, Inc.); EXCEL (formerly, MBPXL), ConAgra, Wilson, Swift, Armour, and others—are multiplant operations. Their slaughtering and processing facilities are located near supply sources in many states. They have national distribution systems and often are involved in promotion and advertising. All these firms are referred to as "national" packers.

If a scope of operation and sales distribution is limited to, or concentrated in, a specific region, firms are classified as "regional" packers. Those with limited scope in terms of operation (often a single plant) and distribution (selling locally) are classified as "local" packers. Regional and local packers are sometimes referred to as "independent" packers (Williams and Stout, 1964).

LIVESTOCK SLAUGHTERING AND MEAT PRODUCTION

Slaughtering

Annual livestock slaughter in the U.S. is highly correlated with the demand for meat and the particular phase in the price/production cycles. Tables 8.3 and 8.4 present the total number of head slaughtered of various species from 1960 to 1984. Figure 8.1 shows graphically the total number slaughtered by class of livestock. These data indicate that the total number of cattle and hogs slaughtered has increased by 46 and 12 percent respectively, between 1960 and 1984, whereas the number of sheep and lambs and calves slaughtered decreased drastically. The numbers shown in Tables 8.3 and 8.4 suggest that farm slaughter for all species has declined over time, with sheep and lamb slaughter showing the smallest relative decrease.

Figures 8.2, 8.3, 8.4, and 8.5, respectively, show the leading states in commercial slaughter of cattle, calves, hogs, and sheep and lambs in the U.S. in 1984.[5] This slaughter geography, in terms of numbers slaughtered, is a reflection of the current location of inventory. The top 10 states accounted for 75.7 percent of all commercial cattle slaughter, 82.7 percent of the calves, 72.1 percent of the hogs, and 93.6 percent of the sheep and lambs slaughtered during 1984. The ranking of the

---

[5]Farm slaughter was excluded since it accounted for a very small percentage of the total; inclusion would not alter the ranking of leading states.

Table 8.3. Cattle and Calf Slaughter in the U.S., 1960–19784 (1,000 Head).

Year	Cattle Commer-cial*	Farm	Total†	Calves Commer-cial*	Farm	Total†
1960	25,224	802	26,026	8,255	386	8,611
1961	25,635	836	26,471	7,701	379	8,080
1962	26,083	828	26,911	7,494	363	7,857
1963	27,232	838	28,070	6,833	371	7,204
1964	30,818	860	31,678	7,254	378	7,632
1965	32,347	824	33,171	7,420	368	7,788
1966	33,727	444	34,171	6,647	214	6,861
1967	33,869	426	34,295	5,919	188	6,107
1968	35,026	388	35,576	5,443	170	5,613
1969	35,237	339	35,353	4,863	146	5,009
1970	35,025	331	35,356	4,072	131	4,203
1971	35,585	320	35,905	3,689	136	3,825
1972	35,779	355	36,134	3,053	148	3,201
1973	33,687	415	34,102	2,249	155	2,404
1974	36,812	541	37,353	2,987	188	3,175
1975	40,911	553	41,464	5,209	197	5,406
1976	42,654	545	43,199	5,350	177	5,527
1977	41,856	525	42,381	5,517	175	5,692
1978	39,552	418	39,970	4,170	132	4,302
1979	33,678	327	34,005	2,824	103	2,927
1980	33,807	310	34,117	2,588	91	2,679
1981	34,953	312	35,265	2,798	88	2,886
1982	35,843	315	36,158	3,021	85	3,106
1983	36,649	325	36,974	3,077	85	3,162
1984	37,582	310	37,892	3,297	70	3,367
‡	149	39	146	40	18	39

Source: USDA (1985A and earlier issues).
*Commercial slaughter includes federally inspected and other commercial.
†Totals for 1970–72 are for 48 states and are based on unrounded numbers.
‡1984 as a percentage of 1960.

top 10 states 'and their share of the U.S. total number of livestock slaughtered is given in Table 8.5 for 1965 and 1984.

The leading livestock-slaughtering states shifted positions in the 1940s and again during the 1960s and 1970s. Iowa was the leading cattle-slaughtering state in 1965, followed by California, Nebraska, and Texas. In 1984, Texas was the top-ranking cattle-slaughtering state and Kansas advanced to the second position, whereas Nebraska remained in third place, and Iowa dropped to fourth. The ten leading states accounted for 64.4 percent of all commercial cattle slaughtered in 1965 and for 75.7 percent in 1984, an indication of greater concentration in the location of feeding and slaughtering establishments.

Table 8.4. Hog, Sheep, and Lambs Slaughtered in the U.S., 1960–1984 (1,000 Head).

Year	Hogs Commercial*	Farm	Total†	Sheep and Lambs Commercial*	Farm	Total†
1960	79,036	5,160	84,196	15,899	340	16,239
1961	77,335	4,635	81,970	17,190	347	17,537
1962	79,334	4,090	83,424	16,837	331	17,168
1963	83,324	3,793	87,117	15,822	325	16,147
1964	83,018	3,266	86,284	14,595	300	14,895
1965	73,784	2,610	76,394	13,006	294	13,300
1966	74,011	1,314	75,325	12,737	267	13,003
1967	82,124	1,297	83,421	12,791	244	13,034
1968	85,160	1,241	86,401	11,884	235	12,119
1969	83,838	1,120	84,958	10,691	232	10,923
1970	85,817	1,235	87,052	10,552	249	10,801
1971	94,438	1,210	95,648	10,729	236	10,965
1972	84,707	1,158	85,685	10,301	224	10,525
1973	76,795	1,095	77,890	9,597	202	9,799
1974	81,762	1,321	83,083	8,847	217	9,064
1975	68,687	1,193	69,880	7,835	212	8,047
1976	73,784	1,175	74,959	6,714	197	6,911
1977	77,303	1,139	78,442	6,356	199	6,555
1978	77,315	1,102	78,417	5,369	174	5,543
1979	89,099	1,080	90,179	5,017	172	5,189
1980	96,074	1,100	97,174	5,579	165	5,742
1981	91,575	900	92,475	6,008	189	6,197
1982	82,190	654	82,844	6,449	194	6,643
1983	87,584	500	88,084	6,619	173	6,792
1984	85,168	473	85,641	6,759	141	6,900
‡	108	9	102	43	41	42

Source: USDA (1985A and earlier issues).
*Commercial slaughter includes federally inspected and other commercial.
†Totals for 1970–72 are for 48 states and are based on unrounded numbers.
‡1984 as a percentage of 1960.

The ten leading states in calf slaughter accounted for 69.9 percent of all commercial calf slaughtered in 1965 and 82.7 percent in 1984. New York remained the top-ranking state in calf slaughtered (12.5 percent in 1965 and 19.2 percent in 1984) followed by Wisconsin and Pennsylvania. Texas was the fourth ranking state in number of calves slaughtered during both years. The heavy concentration of calf slaughter in these states is a direct reflection of density of both production and consumption locations.

Leading hog-slaughtering states were located primarily in the Corn Belt. Comparing 1965 and 1984 rankings indicates that Iowa's position as the number one hog-slaughtering state was stable, accounting

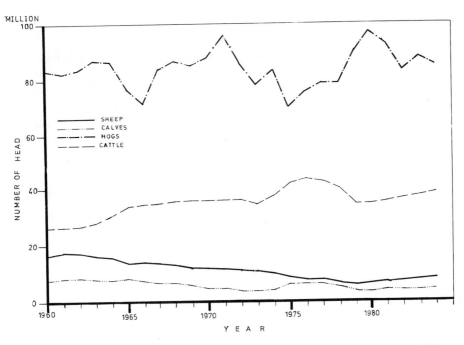

Fig. 8.1. Livestock slaughter in the United States: Number by species, 1960–1984. (Plotted by authors from USDA data.)

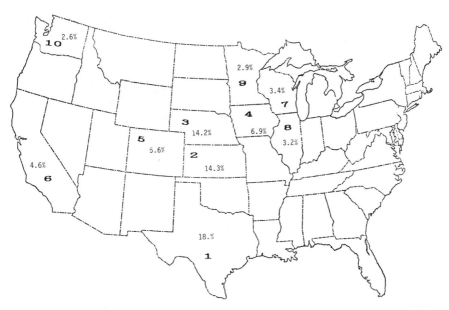

Fig. 8.2. Ten leading states in commercial cattle slaughtering, by percentage of U.S. total, 1984. (Based on data in USDA, 1985A.)

227

Fig. 8.3. Ten leading states in commercial calves slaughtering, by percentage of U.S. total, 1984. (Based on data in USDA, 1985A.)

Fig. 8.4. Ten leading states in commercial hogs slaughtering, by percentage of U.S. total, 1984. (Based on data in USDA, 1985A.)

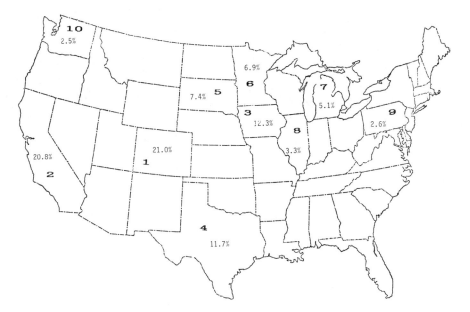

Fig. 8.5.   Ten leading states in commercial sheep and lamb slaughtering, by percentage of U.S. total, 1984. (Based on data in USDA, 1985A.)

for 20.9 percent of the U.S. commercial hog slaughtering in 1965 and 24.5 percent in 1984. Illinois was in the second position, followed by Minnesota and Michigan. The ten leading states accounted for 66.3 percent of all commercial hog slaughtering in 1965 and 72.1 percent in 1984.

California was the top sheep-and-lamb-slaughtering state in 1965, followed by Colorado, Texas, and New Jersey. In 1984, however, Colorado was the leading state, followed by California, Iowa, and Texas, whereas New Jersey dropped out of the top ten states. Table 8.5 indicates that sheep and lamb slaughtering remained heavily concentrated in a few states near the heavy lamb and mutton consumption centers.

Table 8.6 shows the percentages of federally inspected slaughter, by class, for the 1970–1983 period. Although many changes have taken place within species in terms of the relative importance of various types of animals slaughtered in the period of the 1930s to 1960s, it appears that the relative importance of various types within a species—aside from the impact of cyclical influence—stabilized during the 1970s. For example, Table 8.6 indicates that proportionately more cows and heifers were slaughtered during the liquidation phase of the last cattle cycle.

Table 8.5. Leading States in Commercial Slaughter, By Species and Share of Total, 1965 and 1984.

Rank	Cattle State	% of U.S.	Calves State	% of U.S.	Hogs State	% of U.S.	Sheep and Lambs State	% of U.S.
					1965			
1	Iowa	12.3	N.Y.	12.5	Iowa	20.9	Calif.	15.7
2	Calif.	9.3	Wisc.	11.6	Minn.	7.1	Col.	12.1
3	Nebr.	8.9	Penn.	8.7	Ohio	6.4	Texas	9.5
4	Texas	7.4	Texas	8.0	Ill.	6.3	N. J.	7.8
5	Minn.	5.0	Iowa	5.8	Ind.	5.5	Iowa	7.1
6	Ill.	4.8	N. J.	5.5	Nebr.	4.7	Utah	6.6
7	Kansas	4.6	Calif.	5.2	Mo.	4.2	Nebr.	6.1
8	Col.	4.4	Ill.	4.9	Wisc.	4.1	Ill.	6.0
9	Ohio	3.9	Tenn.	4.0	Penn.	3.9	Minn.	5.9
10	Wisc.	3.8	La.	3.7	Tenn.	3.2	Kansas	2.9
Total Ten		64.4		69.9		66.3		79.7
					1984			
1	Texas	18.0	N. Y.	19.2	Iowa	24.5	Col.	21.0
2	Kansas	14.3	Wisc.	12.6	Ill.	8.5	Calif.	20.8
3	Nebr.	14.2	Penn.	8.7	Minn.	6.7	Iowa	12.3
4	Iowa	6.9	Texas	8.2	Mich.	6.3	Texas	11.7
5	Col.	5.6	Calif.	8.1	Nebr.	4.8	S. Dak.	7.4
6	Calif.	4.6	Ill.	5.8	Va.	4.7	Minn.	6.9
7	Wisc.	3.4	Ind.	5.7	Ohio	4.6	Mich.	5.1
8	Ill.	3.2	N. Eng.*	5.6	Ind.	4.1	Ill.	3.3
9	Minn.	2.9	La.	4.7	Mo.	4.0	Penn.	2.6
10	Wash.	2.6	Fla.	4.1	S. Dak.	3.9	Wash.	2.5
Total Ten		75.7		82.7		72.1		93.6

Source: Derived from USDA (1985A and earlier issues).
*New England includes Connecticut, Maine, Massachusetts, New Hampshire, Rhode Island, and Vermont.

Table 8.6. Livestock Slaughter: Composition of Federally Inspected Slaughter, by Species and Class, U.S. 1970-1983.*

| Year[†] | Cattle (%) | | | | Hogs (%) | | | Sheep and Lambs (%) | |
	Steers	Heifers	Cows	Bulls and Stags	Barrow and Guilts	Sows	Stags and Boars	Lambs and Yearlings	Sheep
1970	53.9	27.0	17.4	1.7	92.9	6.4	0.7	92.9	7.1
1971	54.1	26.2	17.9	1.8	93.0	6.2	0.8	92.0	8.0
1972	55.0	26.5	16.7	1.8	93.2	5.9	0.9	93.2	6.8
1973	54.4	25.1	18.5	2.0	93.2	5.8	1.0	91.2	8.8
1974	53.5	23.9	20.4	2.2	92.2	6.9	0.9	93.3	6.7
1975	43.6	25.5	28.2	2.7	93.5	5.6	0.9	92.6	7.4
1976	44.3	28.5	24.9	2.3	94.4	4.8	0.8	93.6	6.4
1977	46.2	28.1	23.6	2.1	93.4	5.5	1.1	92.0	8.0
1978	46.9	29.7	21.4	2.0	93.8	5.2	1.0	93.1	6.9
1979	51.6	28.9	17.6	1.9	93.4	5.6	1.0	93.1	6.9
1980	50.7	28.4	18.7	2.2	93.2	5.6	1.2	92.7	7.3
1981	50.1	28.7	19.0	2.2	93.5	5.3	1.2	93.1	6.9
1982	48.2	29.0	20.5	2.3	93.8	5.0	1.2	92.8	7.2
1983	47.7	29.4	20.7	2.2	93.6	5.3	1.1	92.5	7.5

Source: USDA (1984).
*Data for 1970–72 are for 48 states.
[†]Yearly percentage obtained by weighting monthly percentages by numbers of animals slaughtered under Federal inspection.

Meat Production

Production of red meat in the U.S.—the primary output of the slaughtering and processing industry—increased by 156 percent between 1920 and 1984. The increase in production was primarily the result of increased demand and an expanding livestock-feeding industry associated with increased feed-grain production. Table 8.7 presents trends in production of red meat by species for selected years during the 1920–1984 period.

In 1920 6,955 million kg of red meat, in carcass-weight equivalent, were produced in the United States. Beef accounted for 41.1 percent of this total; veal, 5.5 percent; pork (excluding lard), 49.9 percent; and lamb and mutton, 3.5 percent of the total production. Lard production totaled about 888 million kg. Pork production exceeded beef production until 1953 (except for 1935), when beef production accounted for 50.3 percent of all red meat, whereas pork accounted for only 40.5 percent of the 11,198.5 kg produced. Beef production has risen sharply since the 1950s, accounting for as high as 65.6 percent of all red meat in 1976, whereas pork production has remained fairly stable, aside from cyclical impacts. Veal production was stable until the mid-1960s and has declined sharply since then. Lamb and muttom production has declined steadily since 1920, with a few exceptions, reaching its lowest level in 1979. The 1984 percentages of beef, veal, pork, and lamb and mutton were 60.0, 1.3, 37.7, and 1 percent, respectively, of the total red meat production. By 1984, total lard production had declined to 425 million kg, about 48 percent of the 1920 level.

THE STRUCTURE AND STRUCTURAL CHANGES OF THE MEAT INDUSTRY

The term "structure" as used in this book refers to certain characteristics of the industry that are believed to affect its conduct and performance within the existing economic, social, and political environments. Specifically, the following characteristics will be considered in this chapter:

1. Number and location of firms
2. Size of plants and their distribution
3. Concentration
4. Specialization and integration

Table 8.7. Red Meat and Lard Production in the United States, by Species for Selected Years.*

Year	Beef (Mil. kg)	Beef % of total	Veal (Mil. kg)	Veal % of total	Pork† (Mil. kg)	Pork % of total	Lamb and Mutton (Mil. kg)	Lamb and Mutton % of total	Total red meat (Mil. kg)	Lard (Mil. kg)
1920	2860	41.1	382	5.5	3469	49.9	244	3.5	6955	888
1925	3120	41.4	449	6.0	3687	49.0	274	3.6	7529	977
1930	2684	36.9	360	5.0	3847	53.0	374	5.1	7266	1010
1935	2997	45.8	464	7.1	2685	41.0	398	6.1	6544	579
1940	3255	37.6	445	5.1	4556	52.7	398	4.6	8653	1038
1945	4661	43.4	755	7.0	4852	45.2	478	4.4	10746	937
1950	4325	43.2	558	5.6	4860	48.5	271	2.7	10013	1193
1952	4377	42.0	530	5.1	5229	50.1	294	2.8	10430	1307
1953	5628	50.3	701	6.2	4539	40.5	331	3.0	11199	1068
1954	5880	51.4	747	6.5	4477	39.2	333	2.9	11437	1057
1955	6155	50.4	716	5.9	4985	40.9	344	2.8	12200	1207
1960	6692	52.3	503	3.9	5265	41.1	348	2.7	12808	1162
1961	6952	53.6	474	3.6	5175	39.9	377	2.9	12978	1140
1962	6951	52.9	460	3.5	5365	40.8	367	2.8	13143	1121
1963	7464	53.8	421	3.0	5637	40.7	349	2.5	13872	1122
1964	8372	56.4	460	3.1	5676	38.3	324	2.2	14831	1122
1965	8495	59.4	463	3.2	5054	35.3	295	2.1	14306	928
1966	8948	60.5	413	2.8	5143	34.7	295	2.0	14799	875

(continued)

Table 8.7. (continued)

Year	Beef (Mil. kg)	Beef % of total	Veal (Mil. kg)	Veal % of total	Pork[†] (Mil. kg)	Pork[†] % of total	Lamb and Mutton (Mil. kg)	Lamb and Mutton % of total	Total red meat (Mil. kg)	Lard (Mil. kg)
1967	9171	59.1	359	2.3	5707	36.7	293	1.9	15530	942
1968	9471	59.2	333	2.1	5926	37.0	273	1.7	16003	935
1969	9597	59.9	305	1.9	5876	36.6	250	1.6	16028	864
1970	9821	59.8	267	1.6	6090	37.1	250	1.5	16428	867
1971	9919	57.9	248	1.4	6706	39.2	252	1.5	17124	889
1972	10152	60.5	208	1.2	6177	36.8	246	1.5	16783	707
1973	9651	61.0	162	1.0	5784	36.5	233	1.5	15830	568
1974	10495	61.1	220	1.3	6262	36.4	211	1.2	17189	620
1975	10875	65.2	396	2.4	5218	31.3	186	1.1	16675	459
1976	11780	65.6	387	2.2	5631	31.3	168	0.9	17966	481
1977	11467	64.9	378	2.1	5678	32.1	159	0.9	17682	470
1978	10996	62.8	287	1.6	5075	34.7	140	0.9	17498	456
1979	9728	57.0	197	1.1	7008	41.1	133	0.8	17066	524
1980	9818	55.6	181	1.0	7537	42.6	144	0.8	17680	552
1981	10156	57.4	198	1.1	7201	40.7	153	0.8	17708	529
1982	10225	60.0	201	1.2	6458	37.8	165	1.0	17045	417
1983	10542	59.2	203	1.1	6899	38.7	171	1.0	17815	444
1984	10703	60.0	225	1.3	6719	37.7	172	1.0	17819	425

Source: USDA (1984 and earlier issues), and AMI (1985).
*Units are carcass-weight equivalent and exclude edible offal. Converted from pounds to kilograms and rounded by the authors.
†Reported as packer style beginning January 1977.

5. Product differentiation and promotion
6. Patterns of entry and exit in the industry.

Some of these characteristics have been discussed earlier in general terms. This section, however, provides more detailed information and a breakdown of aggregated statistics.

The relative importance of federally inspected plants was demonstrated in Tables 8.1 and 8.2. Table 8.8 traces the changes in proportions of total number of livestock slaughtered under federal inspection in the U.S. since 1960. It is clear from this data that the trend has been

able 8.8. Livestock Slaughtered and Red Meat Produced in Federally Inspected Plants as a
ercent of Total Slaughter, by Species, 1960–1984*

Year	Cattle/Beef (% of no.)	Cattle/Beef % of production	Calves/Veal (% of no.)	Calves/Veal (% of production	Hogs/Pork[†] (% of no.)	Hogs/Pork[†] % of production	Sheep and Lambs/ Lamb and Mutton (% of no.)	Sheep and Lambs/ Lamb and Mutton (% of production
960	75	78	61	56	79	79	86	87
961	75	79	62	56	80	80	86	86
962	76	78	63	57	81	82	86	86
963	77	80	63	55	82	83	86	87
964	79	82	63	54	83	84	87	87
965	80	82	65	56	83	84	88	88
966	80	82	65	54	85	85	89	89
967	81	83	66	53	85	86	88	89
968	84	86	69	57	87	87	90	91
969	86	87	73	59	89	89	92	92
970	87	88	72	57	90	90	93	93
971	88	89	73	59	91	91	94	94
972	89	90	76	62	92	92	94	95
973	89	91	75	59	93	93	94	95
974	89	90	74	58	93	93	94	95
975	89	90	72	57	93	93	94	94
976	90	91	80	66	94	94	94	94
977	91	92	83	68	94	94	94	94
978	92	93	84	71	95	95	93	94
979	93	94	85	73	95	95	93	94
980	93	94	86	74	95	95	93	94
981	93	94	86	74	95	95	93	94
982	94	95	88	76	96	96	94	95
983	94	95	89	78	96	96	94	95
984	95	95	90	82	96	96	95	95

Source: Derived from USDA (1984 and earlier issues) and AMI (1985).
*Computed by authors as follows: Percent FI = number of head divided by total commercial plus farm slaughter times 100.
Excluding lard; plus beginning 1977 as packer style.

toward more livestock slaughtering under Federal inspection.[6] In 1960, for example, federally inspected plants slaughtered 75 percent of all cattle, 61 percent of the calves, 79 percent of all hogs, and 86 percent of all sheep and lambs. The percentages in 1984 were 95, 90, 96, and 95 percent, respectively.

The percentages of meat production in federally inspected plants are similar to the respective percentages of number of animals slaughtered, except for veal production and calf slaughter. The difference is due primarily to the generally lighter average weight of calves slaughtered under Federal inspection as compared to the average weight of calves in other commercial or farm slaughter. Thus, veal production under Federal inspection accounts for a smaller percentage of the total than the number of calves slaughtered would indicate.

Number and Location of Slaughtering and Processing Plants

Because of the availability and completeness of data on federally inspected plants and the fact that the majority of livestock slaughtering and meat processing is done under Federal inspection, the emphasis here will be placed on these federally inspected operations. The structure of FI firms provides an adequate presentation of the entire livestock-slaughtering and meat-processing industry.

The number and the location of plants slaughtering and processing livestock and livestock products have changed over time. There are two main sources for information on the number of plants in the U.S.: USDA regular and special reports and the U.S. Department of Commerce Census of Manufacturers. The two agencies use slightly different definition and classification systems. Thus, number will depend on which data source is used and may not be similar.[7] Table 8.9 presents the number of slaughter establishments, by region, in the U.S. in 1965, 1970, 1975, and 1985, as reported by USDA. The number of commercial plants (large and medium) decreased from 3,144 plants on March 1 1960, to 2,978 on March 1, 1965. During 1960, about 17 percent (530 plants) were federally inspected compared to 571 FI plants—about 19 percent—of the total, in 1965. On March 1, 1970, of the 7,172 commercial slaughtering plants in the U.S., 726, or 10 percent, were under Federal inspection. By 1975, the number of FI plants more than doubled—

---

[6]It should be pointed out that the percentages shown in Table 8.7 would not show any measurable change if farm slaughter were excluded from calculations. This is because of the small, and declining, number of animals slaughtered on farms.
[7]See footnotes in Table 8.9 and 8.10 for USDA and U.S. Department of Commerce's definitions and classifications of plants.

to 1,485 plants—accounting for 24 percent of the 6,087 commercial slaughtering establishments. The increase in the number of FI plants after 1970 may be explained by their changing from nonFederal and Federal inspection after enactment of the U.S. Wholesome Meat Act in 1967. On January 1, 1985, the number of plants in the U.S. was 5,433, including 1,608, or 30 percent, federally inspected.

In comparison, the U.S. Department of Commerce census data indicate that the number of establishments primarily engaged in slaughtering (referred to as "packing plants" in the census) increased sharply from about 1,400 plants in 1939 to more than 2,000 following World War II. By 1958, the census showed 2,810 packing plants. The number rose to a peak of 2,992 plants in 1963 and then decreased during 1967 (to 2,697 plants) and 1972 (to 2,475 plants), but again rose to 2,590 in 1977. The difference between these trends and the USDA statistics is due primarily to differences in definition.

The number of meat-processing plants (those engaged in prepared meat but not slaughter) is also reported by the Census of Manufacturers (Table 8.10). The U.S. had 1,494 processing plants in 1958. The number dropped to 1,374 in 1967 and to 1,311 in 1972 and then rose slightly in 1977 to 1,345 plants.

Regional distribution of slaughtering and processing plants may also be observed from the data in Tables 8.9 and 8.10. Plants tend to locate in livestock-producing areas. For example, in 1975, 1,025 of the 2,978 slaughtering plants in the U.S.—about 34 percent—were located in the North Central Region, with more of these located in the eastern part of that region. The North Atlantic States had the second largest number of plants, followed by the Mountain and Pacific Regions. By 1985, the North Central Region remained the dominant slaughtering region, with a total of 2,496 commercial plants—about 46 percent of the 5,433 plants in the U.S. However, there was a signficant shift to the western part of the region (1,471 plants, or 59 percent of the region's total), with a 300 percent increase in numbers between 1965 and 1985. The number of plants has also increased in all other regions since 1965, but the North Atlantic, Mountain, and Pacific Regions have experienced the smallest increase in commercial plants since 1965 (Table 8.9).

The number of plants under Federal inspection has risen in all regions since 1965, the greatest increase occurring after 1970 (Table 8.9). There were regional differences in the number and rate of increase of these FI plants. Although the FI plants in the U.S. have increased by 182 percent since 1965, the North Atlantic and East South Central Regions have showed the greatest increase—490 and 537 percent, respectively, between 1965 and 1985. The increase from 125 FI plants in

Table 8.9. Number and Regional Distribution of Commercial Slaughtering Establishments in the U.S., Selected Years.*

State/region	1965			1970			1975			1985		
	FI†	Other‡	All	FI†	Other‡	All	FI†	Other‡	All	FI†	Other‡	All
North Atlantic§												
Total	86	430	516	86	805	891	417	307	724	427	178	605
%	17	83	100	10	90	100	58	42	100	71	29	100
South Atlantic#												
Total	41	342	383	55	599	654	77	548	625	102	562	664
%	11	89	100	8	92	100	12	88	100	15	85	100
East North Central												
Illinois	35	73	108	35	245	280	37	210	247	29	184	213
Indiana	14	79	93	14	228	242	21	145	166	21	147	168
Michigan	5	169	174	10	191	201	18	156	174	94	55	149
Ohio	35	196	231	39	319	358	39	282	321	33	250	283
Wisconsin	19	32	51	21	237	258	21	208	229	17	195	212
Total	108	549	657	119	1220	1339	136	1001	1137	194	831	1025
%	16	84	100	9	91	100	12	88	100	19	81	100
West North Central												
Iowa	31	19	50	41	474	515	47	339	386	32	312	344
Kansas	19	111	130	22	232	254	26	178	204	21	175	196
Minnesota	15	30	45	17	358	275	62	273	335	52	199	251
Missouri	18	38	56	22	331	353	128	137	265	116	140	256
Nebraska	33	28	61	34	231	265	78	131	209	59	155	214
N. Dakota	2	9	11	3	76	79	34	67	101	26	52	78
S. Dakota	7	8	15	9	154	163	9	129	138	10	122	132
Total	125	243	368	148	1856	2004	384	1254	1638	316	1155	1471
%	34	66	100	7	93	100	31	69	100	21	79	100

238

North Central Region												
Total	233	792	1025	267	3076	3343	520	2255	2775	510	1986	2496
%	23	77	100	8	92	100	19	81	100	20	80	100
East South Central*												
Total	33	147	180	41	454	495	85	360	445	140	386	526
%	18	82	100	8	92	100	19	81	100	27	73	100
West South Central												
Texas	37	175	212	67	520	587	82	465	547	68	253	321
Other††	10	186	196	23	544	567	32	372	404	88	274	362
Total	47	361	408	90	1064	1154	114	837	951	156	527	683
%	12	88	100	8	92	100	12	88	100	23	77	100
Mountain and Pacific												
Arizona	2	18	20	6	28	34	7	34	41	9	26	35
California	60	50	110	69	22	91	69	14	83	54	—	54
Colorado	17	28	45	23	59	82	21	45	66	42	20	62
Idaho	7	46	53	10	61	71	9	49	58	34	16	50
Montana	6	27	33	6	58	64	33	18	51	29	26	55
Other‡‡	39	166	205	73	220	293	133	135	268	105	108	213
Total	131	335	466	187	448	635	272	295	567	273	196	469
%	28	72	100	29	71	100	48	52	100	58	42	100
Total U.S.§§												
Total	571	2407	2978	726	6446	7172	1485	4602	6087	1608	3835	5433
%	19	81	100	10	90	100	24	76	100	30	70	100

Source: USDA (1985A and earlier issues).

*Includes plants with an output of 136,079 kg liveweight or more annually. Numbers are as of Mar. 1 before 1978 and as of Jan. 1 thereafter and include establishments engaged in slaughtering and further processing—i.e., boning and breaking as well as curing, canning, and making other products.

†All sizes of federally inspected operations.

‡All other commercial non-FI.

§Includes Maine, New Hampshire, Vermont, Massachusetts, Rhode Island, Connecticut, New York, New Jersey, and Pennsylvania.

#Includes Maryland, Delaware, Virginia, West Virginia, North Carolina, South Carolina, Georgia, and Florida.

**Includes Kentucky, Tennessee, Alabama, and Mississippi.

††Includes Arkansas, Oklahoma, and Louisiana.

‡‡Nevada, New Mexico, Oregon, Utah, Washington, Wyoming, and Hawaii.

§§Excluding Alaska.

Table 8.10. Number and Regional Distribution of Meat-Processing Plants, U.S. Census Years 1958, 1967, 1972, and 1977.*

Region	1958		1967		1972		1977†	
	(Number)	(%)	(Number)	(%)	(Number)	(%)	(Number)	(%)
North Atlantic	511	34.2	443	32.2	394	30.0	361	26.8
South Atlantic	162	10.8	155	11.3	167	12.7	160	11.9
E. North Central	382	25.6	337	24.5	308	23.5	293	21.8
W. North Central	96	6.4	95	6.9	95	7.3	110	8.2
E. South Central	49	3.3	63	4.6	69	5.3	68	5.1
W. South Central	84	5.6	97	7.1	89	6.8	122	9.1
Mountain–Pacific	210	14.1	184	13.4	189	14.4	159	11.8
Other	—	—	—	—	—	—	72	5.3
U.S. Total	1,494	100.0	1,374	100.0	1,311	100.0	1,345	100.0

Source: U.S. Department of Commerce (1981 and earlier issues).
*Comprises establishments primarily engaged in manufacture of sausages, cured meats, smoked meats, canned meats, frozen meats, natural sausage casings, and other prepared meats and meat specialties from purchases carcasses and other materials. Meat plants operated by slaughtering firms as separate establishments are also included.
†Figures that might disclose information of individual companies or geographic regions were withheld by Bureau of Census but were included in U.S. total.

the West North Central in 1965 to 316 plants in 1985 accounted for most of the 119-percent increase in the entire North Central Region.

Regional distribution of meat-processing plants, as defined by the U.S. Department of Commerce, is heavily concentrated in the North Atlantic Region, followed by the North Central Region, particularly the eastern part (Table 8.10). For example, in 1958, 34.2 percent of the processing plants were located in the North Atlantic Region, 32 percent in the North Central Region, and 14.1 percent in the Mountain-Pacific Region. In 1977, the North Atlantic Region still accounted for 26.8 percent, whereas the North Central Region had 30 percent (21.8 percent in the eastern part and 8.2 percent in the western part). Most of the meat-processing plants are located near large population centers, i.e., near consumption locations.

SIZE OF PLANTS AND THEIR DISTRIBUTION

The average size of plants in terms of number of livestock slaughtered, meat production, or other measures may be used as an indication of the size characteristics of the industry as a whole. Because the meat industry is still dominated by a large number of small plants, however, such average information would not provide meaningful presentation of the actual situation. It is more useful to use multiple size categories and examine the distribution of plants (or firms) in each size interval. An earlier discussion (e.g., Table 8.2) provided information on the size distribution of FI plants in 1981 and 1984. It was shown that during these two years a small number of large plants accounted for most of the livestock slaughtered.

Size by Annual Slaughter

In a study of the federally inspected slaughtering industry, Baker (1976) examined the distribution of plant sizes for each of the four species during 1970, 1972, and 1973 and gave some historical data from 1950 on. Tables 8.11 and 8.12 summarize Baker's findings. The largest number of FI cattle-slaughtering plants were concentrated in the middle-size classes, i.e., those slaughtering between 6,250 to 50,000 head annually. The distribution shifted toward a larger number of smaller-size classes from 1970 on, after several states eliminated their state inspection programs. This suggests that most of the previously state-inspected plants were small operations. Baker's report shows

Table 8.11. Percentages of Federally Inspected Cattle and Calf Slaughtering Plants in Various Size Groups, U.S., Selected Years.

Year	Size group (1,000-head annual slaughter)									
	Less than 0.75	0.75–1.5	1.5–3.1	3.1–6.25	6.25–12.5	12.5–25	25–50	50–100	100–200	200 or more
	Cattle (%)									
1950	7.0	2.4	4.1	10.7	16.8	23.1	19.4	10.0	4.6	1.9
1954	6.7	2.3	3.0	5.5	12.4	20.5	23.0	17.0	6.4	3.2
1962	5.9	2.3	3.7	5.5	11.6	18.9	26.1	17.7	5.9	2.4
1970	15.8	2.8	4.8	8.2	10.9	14.6	16.1	14.4	7.0	5.4
1972	53.8	5.7	4.3	4.2	4.9	7.0	6.5	7.5	3.4	2.7
1973	42.4	11.0	8.1	5.4	5.7	6.2	7.2	7.8	3.4	2.8
	Calves (%)									
1950	28.0	11.7	12.0	9.8	11.7	9.5	8.1	4.7	4.5*	
1954	31.6	7.3	11.1	9.1	9.4	10.8	7.6	6.7	6.4*	
1962	35.4	9.6	8.7	7.5	8.4	10.9	9.9	5.9	3.7*	
1970	37.8	9.5	7.4	7.8	7.8	8.5	11.7	5.0	4.5*	
1972	76.5	3.7	4.1	5.0	2.4	2.4	3.3	1.4	1.2*	
1973	80.2	2.6	5.3	3.2	2.8	1.5	2.5	1.9*		

Source: Derived from Baker (1976).
*May include plants of larger size but not disclosed for confidentiality.

Table 8.12. Percentages of Federally Inspected Hog and Sheep and Lamb Slaughtering Plants in Various Size Groups, U.S., Selected Years.

Year		Size group (1,000-head annual slaughter)											
	Less than 0.56	0.75–1.5	1.12–2.25	2.25–4.5	4.5–9	9–18.8	18.8–37.5	37.5–75	75–125	125–2500	250–500	500–1000	1000 or more
						Hogs							
1950	7.8	1.0	3.7	4.1	5.4	6.4	9.5	12.9	9.5	17.0	11.2	8.1	3.4
1954	9.8	1.4	4.0	5.1	5.4	6.2	4.3	12.7	9.4	19.2	10.9	8.0	3.6
1962	9.5	3.4	2.3	5.0	4.2	6.1	3.8	7.6	8.4	14.9	19.5	8.8	6.5
1970	31.1	5.3	3.4	5.7	4.1	6.9	5.5	6.6	3.6	5.7	9.4	8.4	4.3
1972	59.7	6.6	4.9	3.0	3.2	3.1	4.0	2.6	0.6	3.0	3.6	3.6	2.1
1973	53.9	9.8	5.7	3.8	4.5	3.5	3.0	2.3	1.1	3.7	3.2	3.7	1.8

Year		Size group (1,000-head annual slaughter)									
	Less than 0.75	0.75–1.5	1.5–3.1	3.1–6.25	6.25–12.5	12.5–25	25–50	50–100	100–200	200–400	400 or more
					Sheep and Lambs (%)						
1950	40.3	5.2	7.5	4.7	5.9	5.9	7.1	8.3	9.1	4.8	1.2
1954	42.2	4.4	4.4	4.9	2.2	5.8	6.7	7.1	8.5	12.0	1.8
1962	47.8	5.4	5.4	2.4	4.9	1.0	3.9	5.8	8.3	12.2	2.9
1970	69.4	4.2	3.5	2.3	2.3	3.1	1.6	1.6	3.9	5.4	2.7
1972	85.3	1.9	1.7	1.9	1.2	1.4	1.0	1.0	1.2	1.9	1.5
1973	86.5	2.6	0.6	2.2	1.2	0.9	1.2	0.6	1.1	1.9	1.2

Source: Derived from Baker (1976).

that the large-size cattle plants did increase from 1950 on, but at slower rates than the smaller class (Table 8.11).

Plants slaughtering calves declined in numbers until 1970, then increased. The smaller-size category, slaughtering less than 750 head annually, accounted for 28 percent of all FI calf-slaughtering plants in 1950, 37.8 percent in 1970, and more than 80 percent in 1973. The decline in the percentage of plants in the two largest-size categories (50,000 to 100,000 and 100,000 to 200,000) is probably a reflection of the increased number of calves fed and the general decline in the size of dairy herds.

Baker reported a decrease in the number of hog plants from 1950 to 1962, then an increase from 1970 to 1973. The hog-slaughtering industry is characterized by a moderate number of large-volume plants and numerous small ones. Table 8.12 indicates that very small FI plants (slaughtering less than 560 hogs annually) accounted for less than 8 percent of all plants in 1950, 31.1 percent in 1970, and 53.9 percent in 1973 (similar to the information in Table 8.2 for 1981 and 1984). The percentage of plants in large sizes has declined over time, including a large drop in the percentage of plants slaughtering more than one million hogs annually in 1970–1973. Table 8.2 shows that this size category accounted for less than 3 percent of all plants in 1981 and 1982 and slaughtered about 60 percent of all hogs.

The percentage distribution of sheep plants is shown in the bottom portion of Table 8.12. The data indicate a shift toward the very small plant size (slaughtering less than 750 sheep and lambs annually), whereas most of the other size categories have proportionately decreased. Baker reported an increase in the number of the largest category, but, because of the spectacular increase in the number of small FI plants, the proportion of large plants has actually declined.

In an exhaustive study of the beef industry, Williams (1979) reported that plants slaughtering steers and heifers decreased in numbers between 1970 and 1977. The largest reduction was in the smaller-size categories. For example, the number of plants slaughtering 1,000 head or less annually dropped by 40 percent. Plants slaughtering fewer than 50,000 head a year accounted for 85.5 percent of all FI steer and heifer plants in 1970. By 1977, the number of plants in this size category had decreased by about 33 percent (from 835 to 561 plants). In comparison, the number of plants slaughtering more than 50,000 head annually increased from 142 plants in 1970 to 150 plants in 1977. Although no plants slaughtered more than 500,000 steers and heifers in 1970, three plants were reported in this size category in 1972, seven in 1977, and 12 plants in 1982 (Nelson 1985).

Size by Employment and Value Added

The size of plants and their distribution may also be viewed in terms of the number of employees, or value added by manufacture. The U.S. Bureau of Census reports employment and value-added information for both meat-packing and meat-processing plants. Tables 8.13 and 8.14 summarize this information for 1967 and 1977.

The Census information suggests that in 1967, at one extreme, about 43.4 percent of all meat-packing plants employed one to four employ-

Table 8.13. Employment Size and Value Added of Meat-Packing (Primarily Slaughtering) Establishments in the U.S., 1967 and 1977 Census Years.

Employ-ment size group	Number of employees	Establishments		Value added by manu-facturer	
(No. of employees)	(1,000)	(Number)	(% of total)	(Mil. $)†	% of value added
		1967			
1–4	1.7	1,170	43.4	32.5	1.5
5–9	1.8	281	10.4	39.6	1.8
10–19	4.1	291	10.8	56.5	2.5
20–49	13.3	420	15.6	189.7	8.5
50–99	15.3	221	8.2	224.5	10.1
100–249	24.7	169	6.3	323.0	14.6
250–499	29.6	84	3.1	412.1	18.6
500–999	22.1	30	1.1	261.2	11.8
1,000–2,499	31.7	23	0.9	356.2	16.0
2,500 or more	26.1	8	0.2	325.2	14.6
Total	170.4	2,697	100.0	2,220.5	100.0
		1977			
1–4	2.0	1,268	49.0	42.7	1.1
5–9	2.2	330	12.7	42.3	1.1
10–19	3.4	255	9.9	81.0	2.0
20–49	8.4	256	9.9	224.0	5.6
50–99	13.4	191	7.3	407.0	10.1
100–249	21.8	149	5.7	652.8	16.3
250–499	28.3	79	3.1	689.8	17.2
500–999	28.0	40	1.5	762.6	19.0
1,000–2,499	25.5	18	0.7	694.2	17.3
2,500 or more	13.3	4	0.2	413.7	10.3
Total	146.3	2,590	100.0	4,010.1	100.0

Source: U.S. Department of Commerce (1970 and 1981).
*Includes all full-time and part-time employees on payroll during all the reported pay period.
†Value added is the adjusted total value of the manufactured product and receipt for services rendered (i.e., value of shipment) less cost of materials, supplies, containers, fuel, purchased electricity, and contract work.

Table 8.14.   Employment Size and Value Added of Meat Processing Establishments in the U.S., 1967 and 1977 Census Years.

Employment size group	Number of employees	Establishments		Value added by manufacturer	
(No. of employees)	(1,000)	(Number)	(% of total)	(Mil. $)[†]	% of value added
1967					
1–4	0.8	466	33.9	11.1	1.5
5–9	1.2	180	13.1	16.2	2.2
10–19	2.4	167	12.2	26.6	3.6
20–49	8.9	289	21.0	110.8	14.9
50–99	9.1	129	9.4	130.9	17.6
100–249	15.8	104	7.6	215.8	29.1
250–499	9.7	28	2.0	139.0	18.7
500–999	6.6	10	0.7	92.1	12.4
1,000–2,499	‡	1	0.1	‡	‡
Total	54.5	1,374	100.0	742.5	100.0
1977					
1–4	0.7	428	31.8	14.7	0.7
5–9	1.3	182	13.5	32.0	1.6
10–19	2.3	165	12.3	59.8	2.9
20–49	7.8	239	17.8	224.9	11.0
50–99	10.1	146	10.8	246.3	12.1
100–249	19.6	129	9.6	632.0	31.0
250–499	15.2	44	3.3	522.6	25.6
500–999	8.0	11	0.8	306.6	15.1
1,000–2,499	‡	1	0.1	‡	‡
Total	65.0	1,345	100.0	2,039.0	100.0

Source: U.S. Department of Commerce (1970 and 1981).
*Includes all full-time and part-time employees on payroll during all the reported pay period.
†Value added is the adjusted total value of the manufactured product and receipt for services rendered (i.e., value of shipment) less cost of materials, supplies, containers, fuel, purchased electricity, and contract work.
‡Withheld by the Census Bureau to avoid disclosing individual operations.

ees, whereas only eight plants, or 0.2 percent of all establishments, employed 2,500 or more full and part-time workers. Plants employing 100 or more workers accounted for 79 percent of total employment but only 11.6 percent of the number of plants (Table 8.13). By 1977, the number and percentage of the total of the very small plants (employing one to four workers) had increased and accounted for 49 percent of all packing plants. Those employing 2,500 or more workers decreased from eight to four plants but accounted for the same proportion of plants as in 1967 (i.e., 0.2 percent). In 1977, plants employing 100 or more workers accounted for 11.2 percent of all plants but 79.9 percent of total employment.

A small number of plants, as might be expected, accounted for most of the value added by manufacture.[8] On one extreme, the large number of very small plants (one to four workers) accounted for about 1.5 percent of the industry's total value added in 1967 and for 1.1 percent in 1977. By contrast, the very large plants (2,500 or more workers) accounted for 14.6 percent of the packing industry's value added in 1967 and dropped to 10.3 percent in 1977. Aggregating total value added by packing plants employing 100 or more workers indicates that such plants accounted for 75.6 percent of the industry's value added in 1967 and 80.1 percent in 1977 (Table 8.13).

The preceding discussion clearly suggests that the meat-packing industry is still dominated by a large number of small plants, a moderate number of medium-sized plants, and a small number of large plants. It appears that technological changes, especially labor-saving methods, have enabled large-scale plants to slaughter/fabricate most of the nation's livestock.

The Bureau of Census also reports the various employment-size groups for the meat-processing industry. Table 8.14 gives information similar to that in Table 8.13, but for the meat-processing industry. This data suggests that the structural characteristics of the meat-processing industry in terms of the number and size of distribution plants and the contribution to value added by various size groups, are similar to those of the slaughtering industry; that is, large numbers of small plants employ few workers and account for a small proportion of the industry's value added while a small number of large plants employ most of the labor force and account for the bulk of the value added.

CONCENTRATION IN THE MEAT INDUSTRY

Microeconomic firm theory suggests that if the market organization of an industry is characterized by less than perfect competition, resource misallocation will result, as well as reduced quantity and higher prices and profits. The theory also suggests that input-market imperfection would lead to depressed prices for sellers (e.g., livestock producers) and a better-than-average profit for buyers.

Economists, however, recognize that the perfect competition model is a theoretical, never attainable, abstract of the real world, though it

---

[8]See footnote in Table 8.13 for Census definition of value added.

may serve as a guideline for public policy. The perfectly competitive market is used as a benchmark against which an existing situation is compared to measure its deviation from the perfectly competitive model.

Concentration is one of the important tools used to examine degree of competition and to determine whether a company, or small number of companies, may have a monopoly or monopsony power. The term "concentration" in this chapter, then, refers to the ownership or control of a large portion of livestock slaughtering and meat processing by a small absolute number, or proportion, of companies in the entire industry. A large body of literature investigating the theoretical and empirical application of the concentration concept exists. For example, see Bain (1968), U.S. House of Representatives (1978), and General Accounting Office (1978).

A commonly used measure of concentration is the concentration ratio CRn, which is calculated by dividing the total market share of n firms by the total industry output. The number of firms, n, may be 1, 2, 3, 4, or any other number, but the most frequently used ratio is CR4, i.e., the "four-firm concentration ratio." The ratio may be calculated for a state, a region, or a nation. Any trend that might show higher CRn ratios is of great concern because of the possibility of reduced competition.

Bain (1968) suggested classifying the type of industry according to the following CR4 ratios:

Type of industry	CR4 (percent of output controlled by the top four firms)
Very highly concentrated oligopoly	75
Highly concentrated oligopolies	65
Moderately concentrated oligopolies	50
Low-grade oligopolies	35
Unconcentrated industries	Below 35

Although economists differ as to the level of concentration that may indicate the possibility of an industry's deviation from a competitive structure, many agree that monopoly, or monopsony, power may appear if the CR4 rises over 40. Some analysts argue that, although concentration ratios might serve a useful purpose in detecting potential monopolistic or monopsonistic power, other apsects of market structure should be considered. For example, the condition of entry, demand characteristics, and product differentiation would supplement the CRn

status in determining the potential behavior of an industry in the market place. Some economists also suggest that the relevant concentration ratio should be calculated for a state or a region where it is often higher than a national ratio would suggest. Such an argument is especially important in the livestock-slaughtering industry where, as will be shown later, there is some empirical evidence for it.

Historically speaking, the meat industry evolved into a less concentrated industry following the 1920 Consent Decree. Other developments (transportation, communication, technology, and grading) also influenced the evolution of independent single-species firms and the trend toward decentralization of the industry, as well as a decline in national concentration, as measured by CR4. Both the U.S. Department of Agriculture and the Bureau of Census provide information on concentration in the meat-packing and meat-processing industry.

Four-firm concentration ratios (CR4) have been reported by the USDA for commercial livestock slaughtering (CR5 before 1923, when Armour acquired Morris). Table 8.15 presents the concentration ratios for cattle, calves, hogs, and sheep for selected years from 1920 to 1950 and for the 1960–1978 period. In 1920, the five largest firms accounted for 49 percent of cattle slaughter, 34.4 percent of calf, 43.8 percent of hog, and 61.8 percent of sheep slaughter.[9] By 1960, the percentages of total commercial slaughter by the big four firms dropped to 23.5 percent of cattle, 29.0 percent of calves, and 34.9 percent of hogs. The drop in the CR4 for sheep was very small, as the four largest firms still slaughtered 54.7 percent of all sheep. The four-firm concentration continued a slight downward trend or remained about the same for cattle during the 1960s and most of the 1970s (see Table 8.15). There is some concern, however, that rapid growth in processing technology and the increasing size of new plants as well as the increasing number of mergers might alter this situation, as evidenced by an increase in the CR4 for cattle and calves since the mid-1970s. The CR4 for hog slaughter showed a fairly constant decline for 1920 to 1960, with only minor variations since then. Concentration in sheep slaughter has declined in an irregular trend during the 1920–1980 period. Compared to the 1920–1940 CR4, the national concentration in the 1980s has declined substantially for all species except for calf slaughter. In 1980, the four largest firms accounted for 39.4 percent of commercial cattle slaughter, 34.0 percent of calves, 32.4 percent of hogs, and 48.2 percent of sheep. It should be pointed out that there have been changes in the

---

[9]The term "firm" as used here refers to companies operating more than one plant at one or more locations.

Table 8.15. Percentage of U.S. Commercial Livestock Slaughter Accounted for by the Top Four Firms, By Species, Selected Years.*

Year	Cattle (%)	Calves (%)	Hogs (%)	Sheep (%)
1920	49.0	34.4	43.8	61.8
1930	48.5	45.5	37.5	68.1
1940	43.1	45.6	44.3	66.1
1950	36.4	35.4	40.9	63.6
1960	23.5	29.0	34.9	54.7
1961	24.2	30.1	33.7	54.7
1962	23.7	28.2	34.4	55.4
1963	22.9	29.1	33.8	54.5
1964	22.6	32.1	34.9	56.8
1965	23.0	32.4	35.2	57.8
1966	22.4	30.4	31.7	59.0
1967	22.2	30.2	29.8	58.1
1968	21.5	29.0	30.1	54.2
1969	23.0	27.3	33.5	60.4
1970	21.3	23.8	31.5	53.1
1971	21.4	21.6	31.8	53.2
1972	24.5	22.6	32.0	56.5
1973	24.5	23.3	33.2	56.2
1974	23.8	27.1	34.5	55.6
1975	22.2	28.4	33.0	57.5
1976	22.1	27.8	34.6	53.0
1977	21.9	29.2	33.7	55.4
1978	24.3	30.0	35.5	59.3
1979	29.3	33.5	36.5	65.5
1980	31.3	35.8	34.8	57.3
1981	34.2	35.3	35.5	57.9
1982	35.4	33.4	35.9	49.5
1983	39.4	34.0	32.4	48.2

Source: 1920–1971 from U.S. House of Representatives (1979) and 1972–1982 from Nelson (1985).
*Data for 1920 include the "Big Five" (Armour, Cudahy, Morris, Swift, and Wilson); they became the "Big Four" in 1923 when Armour acquired Morris.

firms constituting the top four. Also, the top four firms may differ from species to species.

The national concentration ratios do not appear to warrant major concern about the competitiveness of the meat industry. However, since competition for livestock occurs in relatively limited geographical locations, the ratios for individual states or regions appear to be more meaningful in the assessment of potential excessive concentration. Some economists have suggested that excessive concentration, coupled with increased use of direct marketing methods for livestock procurement, may influence prices and other terms of trade in favor of particular firms. Aspelin and Engleman (1976) state that "The meat packing industry tends to be highly oligopolistic at the state level—much more so than it is nationally. Four ranking firms account for 65 percent or more of slaughter for different species at the state level in most cases. . . . "

Tables 8.16 and 8.17 provide information on slaughter concentration ratios by type of livestock and by region in selected states during 1972 and 1982. The tables show the percentage share of the top four firms in commercial slaughter. The data indicate that the share of commercial livestock slaughter of the top four firms was higher in 1982 than in 1972. Table 8.17 indicates that their share of commercial slaughter of steers and heifers, cows and bulls, hogs, and sheep and lambs accounted for a much higher percentage of commercial slaughter in many states than the national percentage.

Williams (1979) reported to the U.S. Congress on the growing concentration problem in steer and heifer slaughtering. Several U.S. Department of Agriculture studies supported Williams' findings in general and provided additional information on steer and heifer slaughter concentration ratios in individual states. Table 8.18 presents a comparison of shares of steer and heifer slaughter by the top four firms in each of the 23 leading fed-cattle-producing states in 1970 and 1978. The data show that the CR4 in the 23 states was 66.3 percent in 1978 compared to only 54.8 percent in 1970. In 1978, the individual state's CR4 ranged from as low as 26.5 percent in Calfornia to 100 percent in Montana and North Dakota. Twelve of the 23 states showed a CR4 of more than 80 percent. According to the classification developed by Bain (1968), the U.S. Department of Agriculture concluded that steer

Table 8.16. Percentage of P&S Steer and Heifer, Cow and Bull, and Hog Slaughter Within Selected Regions Accounted for by the Top Four Firms, 1972 and 1982.

Region	Steers and Heifers		Cows and Bulls		Hogs	
	1972 (%)	1982 (%)	1972 (%)	1982 (%)	1972 (%)	1982 (%)
North Atlantic	61.66	80.92	21.40	34.36	68.33	75.60
East N. Central	26.17	45.60	39.75	54.09	36.00	39.52
West N. Central	44.98	58.36	31.34	31.71	53.46	60.46
South Atlantic	40.96	48.27	38.40	50.07	44.94	54.97
South Central	46.62	78.90	37.59	53.97	43.47	51.85
Southern Plains	51.29	81.84	34.99	40.59	59.37	75.32
Mountain	48.77	65.98	43.52	60.75	78.75	81.71
Pacific	15.72	49.26	24.25	37.67	87.73	93.27
Alaska and Hawaii	0	96.44	0	94.83	0	0

Source: Nelson (1985).

Table 8.17. Percentage of P&S Steer and Heifer, Cow and Bull, and Hog Slaughter Within Selected States Accounted for by Top Four Firms, 1972 and 1982.*

Region	Steers and Heifers		Cows and Bulls		Hogs	
	1972 (%)	1982 (%)	1972 (%)	1982 (%)	1972 (%)	1982 (%)
Arizona	89.18	98.76	*	*	*	*
California	19.11	41.39	35.82	52.48	*	*
Colorado	66.38	99.22	*	*	*	*
Florida	*	*	81.18	87.26	*	*
Georgia	*	*	79.81	97.26	71.01	85.12
Idaho	82.51	95.92	*	*	*	*
Illinois	61.47	84.79	*	*	67.95	77.92
Indiana	80.95	87.72	*	*	82.19	98.82
Iowa	66.56	85.06	79.91	96.59	47.11	62.08
Kansas	72.86	92.36	*	*	95.02	99.43
Kentucky	*	*	85.15	98.25	*	*
Michigan	52.94	69.49	76.35	88.15	*	*
Minnesota	72.86	97.27	75.41	90.89	99.98	99.56
Mississippi	*	*	87.55	98.24	*	*
Missouri	84.77	97.99	*	*	95.44	98.33
Montana	95.69	97.63	*	*	*	*
Nebraska	43.46	62.12	62.43	82.92	99.10	99.53
New Mexico	98.38	100.00	*	*	*	*
New York	*	*	35.88	72.35	*	*
N. Carolina	*	*	*	*	84.75	92.76
N. Dakota	100.00	100.0	*	*	*	*
Ohio	42.08	62.39	*	*	53.11	64.68
Oklahoma	79.99	94.14	67.29	82.36	*	*
Oregon	64.62	73.64	*	*	*	*
Pennsylvania	77.49	86.92	46.22	66.11	*	*
S. Dakota	94.75	98.79	99.31	94.97	*	*
Tennessee	*	*	61.83	88.39	*	*
Texas	52.17	81.94	41.31	45.14	*	*
Washington	73.40	98.87	*	*	*	*
Wisconsin	90.14	98.54	67.12	88.28	*	*

Source: Nelson (1985).
*Asterisks indicate that percentage was not calculated.

and heifer slaughtering in the 23 leading states (slaughtering more than 95.1 percent of the U.S. total) appeared to be highly concentrated. In a study prepared for the American Meat Institute (AMI, 1980), however, this conclusion was challenged. The AMI report argued that the USDA study incorrectly interpreted the CR4 of 66.3 percent share of slaughter in the 23 states because the top four firms differ among the states. They supported this argument by citing data derived from the 1979 study by Williams, which showed that only in two regions did the CR4 rise above 45 percent. The AMI report concluded that even a high CR4 does not necessarily mean a lack of competition and lower prices for animals, as some have alleged.

Ward (1982) suggested that increased concentration is a natural result of the higher market shares for large low-cost firms, since these firms are better able to bid for limited supplies of livestock in some areas, compared to high-cost (smaller) firms. He also discussed the impact of concentration on cattle producers and beef consumers. Ward refuted the findings of the U.S. House Committee on Small Business reports, which concluded that concentration in the beef packing industry was responsible for 30 percent of the increase in retail beef prices between 1970 and 1978.

The U.S. Department of Commerce Census data provide some information on the concentration in the slaughtering and processing industries. The Census concentration data are based on aggregated percentages of value added to the slaughtering of all livestock accounted for by the top four (CR4) and eight (CR8) firms. The census data are in general agreement with the USDA reports, i.e., they show a downward trend in national concentration in the slaughtering industry from the 1940s on.[10] This trend was observed when either of the above concentration ratios was considered. The census also provided a separate CR4, CR8, and CR20 for the meat-processing industry. Data showed that the aggregate percentages of value added by the manufacture remained relatively unchanged from the 1950s on when any of the specified ratios were used (see Table 8.18).

SPECIALIZATION AND INTEGRATION

Specialization and integration are important features in the discussion of the structure of the meat industry. These elements may be concerned with the operational and organizational characteristics of either an individual firm or the entire industry.

Specialization in the Meat Industry

In common usage, the term "specialization" is used by meat packers to refer to a firm's involvement in few or no nonmeat products; however, specialization within the meat business is also observed. There are two

---

[10]Notice that although USDA data are based on number of livestock slaughtered, Census data are based on the value added in slaughtering and processing. Although the two are not exactly comparable, they show similar trends.

Table 8.18. U.S. Census Four-, Eight-, and Twenty-Firm Concentration Ratios in the Meat Packing and Processing Industries, Selected Census Years.

Year	Percent of value accounted for by firm ranking		
	One to four largest firms (CR 4)	One to eight largest firms (CR 8)	One to twenty largest firms (CR 20)
	Meat Packing		
1954	39	51	60
1958	34	46	57
1963	31	42	54
1972	22	37	51
1977	19	37	49
	Meat Processing		
1954	16	24	35
1958	17	25	36
1963	16	23	35
1972	19	26	38
1977	23	30	39

Source: U.S. Department of Commerce (1980 and earlier census year issues).

aspects to packing-plant specialization—horizontal and vertical. Horizontal specialization refers to the degree of diversification in the number of different species slaughtered or processed by a firm. Vertical specialization, on the other hand, refers to the number, or extent, of functions performed by a firm beyond the slaughtering of livestock. The fewer the number of species slaughtered, the more horizontally specialized the operation. Similarly, the fewer the processing functions or activities performed, the more vertically specialized the operation. A plant that slaughters only one species and sells the carcasses is highly specialized in both ways; this is the so-called "kill and chill" packing plant.

Horizontal Specialization

When livestock marketing was highly centralized and most of the slaughtering was done near, or at, the terminal markets, large slaughtering firms had multistory–multispecies plants. The trend toward decentralization of the meat industry, however, was accompanied by an increasing tendency for horizontal specialization by firms, i.e., slaughtering few (usually one) species. During the same time, the industry tended to become less specialized vertically; i.e., many slaughtering firms became involved in processing operations, and some firms became specialized in processing only (Anthony and Egerston, 1966).

The USDA and the U.S. Department of Commerce Census of Manufacturing provide some useful information on these tendencies. For example, Table 8.19 provides USDA data showing that a very high percentage of the nation's FI plants slaughter cattle (84 percent in 1950 and 93 percent in 1984, reaching a high of 96 percent in 1976) and hogs (58 percent in 1950 and 83 percent in 1984). FI plants handling calves, although larger in number, were proportionately less in 1984, with 53 percent of FI plants, than in 1950, with 67 percent. The number of plants slaughtering sheep and lambs increased during this period but accounted for proportionately less of all plants until early 1970, then increased to about 64 percent of all FI plants in 1984.

A study on the industry's horizontal specialization was carried out by Baker (1976). He reported that more plants slaughtered cattle than any other species during 1970, 1972, and 1973. Table 8.20 presents more detailed data on horizontal specialization in FI plants during this three-year period. Baker also reported that the largest number of cattle plants did not slaughter cattle exclusively. For example, of 1,272 plants slaughtering cattle and other species, only 286 (22 percent) slaughtered cattle exclusively in 1973.

Baker indicated that plants highly specialized horizontally were usually larger and more modern than multispecies plants. Large, highly specialized cattle plants were usually located in the North Central Region and the Mountain States, whereas plants handling sheep only were located in the Southwest and Pacific and Northwest States. Plants handling hogs only were usually located in the North Central Region. It should be pointed out that Baker's report may have underestimated the degree of horizontal specialization, since many of the plants listed as slaughtering multispecies may have killed one species almost exclusively with only a few head of others while reporting to the USDA all species slaughtered, regardless of the number killed.

A contemporary source of information on the tendency toward higher horizontal specialization in the meat industry is the data on the top slaughtering and processing firms in the U.S. that is published annually in *Meat Industry*, a meat trade magazine. For example, the 1983 issue shows that of the nation's 25 leading red meat firms, four did not slaughter any livestock; eleven slaughtered one species; five slaughtered two; three slaughtered three; and only two plants slaughtered all four classes (cattle, calves, sheep, and hogs)[11].

---

[11]These firms had 120 plants and are ranked according to their 1983 annual sales from all operations.

Table 8.19. Number of Federally Inspected Plants and Percentages Slaughtered, By Species, U.S., Selected Years.*

Year	Number of FI slaughter plants	Number and percentage of FI plants that slaughter[†]							
		Cattle		Calves		Hogs		Sheep and lambs	
		(Number)	(%)	(Number)	(%)	(Number)	(%)	(Number)	(%)
1950	456	383	84.0	306	67.0	264	58.0	201	44.0
1955	496	438	88.0	342	69.0	277	56.0	225	45.0
1960	527	487	92.0	321	61.0	269	51.0	216	41.0
1965	596	513	86.0	256	43.0	262	44.0	182	31.0
1970	726	671	92.0	248	34.0	438	60.0	248	34.0
1973	1,364	1,272	93.0	531	39.0	844	62.0	633	46.0
1976	1,741	1,665	96.0	897	52.0	1,322	76.0	878	50.0
1980	1,627	1,411	87.0	742	46.0	1,235	76.0	849	52.0
1982	1,688	1,506	89.0	836	50.0	1,344	80.0	986	58.0
1984	1,608	1,500	93.0	854	53.0	1,341	83.0	1,034	64.0

Source: USDA (1985A and earlier issues).
*Number as of June 30 for 1950–1965, Mar. 1 for 1970–76, and Jan. 1 for 1980–1984.
†Plants that slaughtered each species sometimes during the calendar year, a number that may exceed the number of plants on a certain date. Percentages were calculated by the authors.

Table 8.20. Number of Federally Inspected Slaughter Plants, by Specialization, U.S., Selected Years.

Kind of plant	1970	1972 (Number)	1973
Cattle only	221	320	286
Cattle and other species	450	1,038	986
Total	671	1,358	1,272
Calves only	4	6	8
Calves and other species	244	487	523
Total	248	493	531
Hogs only	100	142	147
Hogs and other species	338	889	884
Total	438	1,031	1,091
Sheep and lambs only	10	16	15
Sheep and other species	248	567	633
Total	258	583	648

Source: Baker (1976).

VERTICAL SPECIALIZATION

The concept of vertical specialization is similar to that of vertical integration—i.e., the control by ownership or contract over successive stages of production or marketing. Slaughtering and processing are successive stages in meat production. Meat can be processed by a firm in the plant where slaughtering takes place; it can be shipped to a specialized processing plant owned by the same firm; or it can be sold to another firm for processing. The less processing done by a plant, the more specialized is that plant.

There are a limited number of studies on vertical specialization. In one of the most comprehensive, though not most recent, Anthony and Egerston (1966) reported that " ... a rather high proportion of the slaughter plants were doing only limited amount of processing. Half of the slaughter plants which engage in meat processing activities processed only an average of 14 percent of their slaughter production." In a related study Anthony (1966) stated that "Fifty percent of the slaughter plants processed less than 1/2 of their output. A fairly large number of FI slaughter plants (32 percent) processed more than they slaughtered; that is, they acquired meat for processing from other plants. The average processing of these plants was 333 percent of their slaughter."

Recent data indicate that about one-fifth of all FI slaughtering plants are engaged in operations other than slaughtering, a relatively higher percentage than in earlier years.

Meat Industry also publishes the types of operations performed by the leading firms. The information in Table 8.21 shows that the majority of the top 10 firms are engaged in a large number of different functions (including slaughter). It should be pointed out that while the percentage of the number of FI plants engaged in both slaughtering and processing may appear low, the capacity of such plants is very large; i.e., they handle a proportionately high volume. This conclusion is reinforced by the substantial increase in recent years in boxed beef (and pork) production, requiring processing beyond the carcass form by a relatively small number of firms.

The Department of Commerce's Census of Manufacturers (1981) data on specialization in the livestock slaughtering and meat-processing industry in 1977 show that there were 496 plants specializing in

Table 8.21. **Top Ten Meat Packers and Processors Based on Net Sales in 1983.**

Rank	Company	Net Sale (Mil. $)	No. of employees	No. of plants	Types of operation*
1	IBP, Inc.	6,100	15,000	12	a, c, d, f, i
2	Swift Ind. Pack Co.	2,540	7,000	14	a, b, c, d, e, f, g, i
3	Excel Corp.	2,300	4,900	7	a, c, i
4	Wilson Foods Corp.	2,177	8,600	9	d, e, f, g, i
5	Armour Food Co.	1,900	5,700	18	a, b, c, d, e, f, g, h, i
6	John Morrell & Co.	1,738	4,500	3	a, b, c, d, e, f, g, i
7	Swift & Co. (Esmark)	1,685	7,000	28	g, h, i
8	Oscar Mayer & Co.	1,533	13,300	9	d, e, g, h, i
9	Geo. Hormel & Co.	1,418	6,700	16	a, b, c, d, e, f, g, i
10	Monfort of Col.	1,300	3,700	4	a, b, c, g, i

Source: Nelson (1985) and Meat Industry (1984).
*Types of operation:
a = Beef slaughter
b = Beef boning
c = Boxed beef
d = Pork slaughter
e = Pork boning
f = Boxed pork
g = Portion control
h = Poultry slaughter and processing
i = Other operations

beef slaughtering (19.2 percent of all plants). Of these, 354 plants, or 71 percent of all beef plants, had specialization ratios of 75 percent or more; i.e., 75 percent or more of their total shipment was fresh beef. In 25 plants, veal was the primary class slaughtered; of these, about 60 percent were highly specialized, with 75 percent or more of their shipment being veal. For lamb and mutton, there were 13 specialized plants, of which eight, or 61.5 percent, had specialization ratios of 75 percent or more. During this year there were 112 plants with pork as their primary product; one-half of these plants had a specialization ratio of 75 percent or more. The information on the meat-processing industry during the 1977 census year shows that of the 122 processing plants reporting pork as their primary product, about 64 percent were highly specialized; i.e., 75 percent or more of their total shipments were processed, frozen, or cured pork. There were 301 specialized sausage plants, of which 246, or 81.8 percent, were specialized to the extent of 75 percent or more of their total primary and secondary shipments. Canned meat plants stood at 34, with 73.5 percent of these classified as highly specialized. These data suggest that the meat-processing industry is highly specialized.

Many of the factors that encouraged the trend toward more specialization in slaughter and meat processing are likely to continue. For example, the decentralization of the industry as a result of improvement in transportation and communication appears likely to continue; i.e., slaughter plants will continue to concentrate around areas of livestock production, whereas processing plants will be near consumption centers (e.g., large cities). With the existing technology, economies in construction costs, labor specialization, sales specialization, and the many advantages of maintaining current locations of slaughter and processing, the current degree of specialization will be maintained and may even increase.

INTEGRATION IN THE MEAT INDUSTRY

The term "integration" is defined as the act of bringing together, or incorporating, parts into a whole. Integration in the livestock–meat economy has been a consideration for many years but has been given increasing attention since the end of World War II. The most important reasons for the recent emphasis on integration in agriculture, including the meat industry, are the continuing increase in capital requirements, risk, and uncertainty with regard to prices and demand.

Firms use integration as an instrument to improve efficiency through lowering or distributing risk; adding a scarce resource, especially capital; improving production methods; controlling quality; leveling out seasonal supplies; and developing an effective marketing system. There are three basic forms of integration: vertical, horizonal, and conglomerate. Examples of each type exist in the meat industry, as will now be discussed.

Vertical Integration

Vertical integration combines two or more successive stages in the production, processing, and distribution of a commodity under single ownership or control; to this extent, it is similar to the concept of vertical specialization. A vertically integrated (coordinated) business can achieve more efficiency than would be possible if each unit operated separately. There are two types of vertical integration: forward and backward. Forward vertical integration is the carrying out of additional stages in the upper end (relative to a traditional firm's activities) of the production–marketing system. For example, a slaughtering firm expanding its operation to include processing (and other functions) is integrated forward. On the other hand, backward integration occurs when additional activities in the lower end (relative to a traditional firm's activities) of the system are performed by a firm. For example, the carrying out of feeding (or ownership) of livestock by a slaughtering firm is integrating backward. As indicated earlier, large capital requirements and the desire to reduce risk and uncertainty, as well as the advantages of large efficient operations, served as the incentives for vertical integration in the meat industry.

Vertical integration may be achieved through ownership, expansion, contracts, cooperation, and joint ventures. Vertical integration usually involves the use of new technology and tends to improve market efficiency. Public concern over possible anticompetitive conduct remains minimal as long as the size of an individually integrated firm remains relatively similar to that of its competitors and as long as each firm controls a relatively small portion of the market. If any of these conditions is violated, an antitrust situation arises, with the possibility that monopoly power may force competitors out of the market. Such a situation would generate serious public concern.

In the meat industry, the movement toward forward integration— e.g., further processing by slaughters—is viewed with less public concern than backward integration—e.g., cattle feeding by packers. The reason for these different views stems from the fact that fabrication and further processing are activities that are widely expected to be performed by packers. This attitude coupled with the potential uses of high technology and their positive impact on market efficiency have allowed many slaughterers to integrate into processing and distribution with very little public concern.

Forward Vertical Integration

For a long time, most of the pork-slaughtering plants have done all, or most of, their own processing. Hayenga (1979) indicated that the pork-slaughtering/processing subsector is characterized by firms engaged in slaughtering and processing. The main products of these firms are fresh subprimal cuts, fresh hams and bellies, and other processed pork products.

Historically, however, little or no processing was performed by packers who slaughtered cattle and sheep. During the 1950s and the 1960s, new single-species slaughter plants replaced the multispecies giants of earlier years. Swinging carcass beef (and lamb) was the order of the industry. In the late 1960s and early 1970s, a new generation of plants was introduced, and with them a new technology in processing beyond the carcass level, i.e., movement towards forward vertical integration. Boxed beef—i.e., cutting the carcass at the slaughter plant into primal, subprimal, or (in some cases) retail cuts and then boxing these products in vacuum packages—tended to revolutionize not only the beef but the entire meat industry.

Although the concept of boxing was not originated by Iowa Beef Processors (IBP, Inc.), this firm started the first large-scale boxing operation in 1967, and the rest of the industry soon followed suit. Output of boxed beef has grown rapidly ever since, and IBP, Inc. has emerged as a giant in boxing beef. The rapid growth in boxed-beef output is attributed to its cost, handling, and storability advantages compared to carcass, or swinging, beef. Cothern (1978) stated that "This concept reduced the geographic integrity of isolated markets since products could be shipped longer distances more cheaply and also could be held for longer periods of time in cold storage."

The production of boxed beef in 1976 was about 14 percent of the total beef production in the U.S. The largest firm at that time—IBP, Inc.—accounted for 39 percent of the 1.9 billion kg (4.1 billion lb) of boxed beef produced that year (Hayenga, 1978). Nelson (1985) reported that about 2.95 billion kg (6.5 billion lb) were produced in 1982, utilizing 14.8 million carcasses (or head of steers and heifers slaughtered). This amount represented about 58 percent of all steers and heifers slaughtered under Federal inspection during 1982. The four largest firms accounted for 65.8 percent of all boxed-beef production. The information on the operations performed by packers in Table 8.21

supports the fact about the rapid growth in boxing beef.[12] It is estimated that more than 85 percent of all beef poundage received by retailers in 1982 from packers/processors or their own cutting facilities
was in vacuum-pack boxed form. It appears that the trend towards
more boxed-meat production will continue as long as substantial economies are involved.

Recent concern about the rapid growth in boxed meat, particularly
beef, is focused on the impact on the market structure of this form of
forward integration and its potential for monopoly power. Some of
these issues will be discussed later under product differentiation and
promotion.[13]

Backward Vertical Integration

Backward integration from packing into feeding (particularly cattle)
has raised concern over possible anticompetitive practices. Aspelin
and Engleman (1966) identified two ways the growth of packer feeding
might affect the livestock industry: (1) packer feeding might essentially replace producer feeding, resulting in a decline in producers' income and inefficient use of existing facilities, and (2) packer feeding
might have an impact on the existing structure of marketing, including
pricing and competition.

Packer feeding of livestock has remained relatively slight during the
last 20 years, with moderate increases during favorable economic conditions. Table 8.22 shows the number of packers feeding cattle and
calves and the number of head fed for the 1960–1983 period. Also
shown is their feeding as a percentage of the total number of fed cattle
marketed. Table 8.23 shows the number of firms and volume of hogs
and sheep and lambs fed during selected years. These data indicate
that a small number of large packers are involved in livestock feeding
but that the volume fed, nationally, is relatively small. It should be
pointed out that these data are for livestock fed by or for meat packers.
Thus, in addition to outright ownership of feedlots by meat packers,
the data include livestock fed on contractural arrangements between
meat packers and feeders. The relative importance of packer feeding

---

[12]Simpson (1980) reported tha a survey of meat packers in the Southeast showed that
the majority of plants are involved in further processing of carcasses before marketing
(86 percent of the pork and 74 percent of the beef was sold in processed form).
[13]Integration forward by packers/processors into retailing has been minimal in the past.
Several factors were responsible. For example, (1) the 1920 Consent decree prohibited
the big five packers from retailing, (2) lack of experience and desire by those not prohibited under the decree to enter into and compete as retailing, and (3) the large amount
of capital and human resources required to operate retail outlets.

Table 8.22. Number of Packers Feeding Cattle and Number of Cattle and Calves Fed Compared with Total Fed-Cattle Marketings in U.S., 1960–1983.

Year	No. of packers feeding	No. of cattle fed by packers* (1,000 hd)	Fed cattle marketings in U.S.† (1,000 hd)	Packer feeding as percentage of fed marketings (%)
1960	166	907	13,496	6.7
1961	207	979	14,545	6.7
1962	216	1,051	15,365	6.8
1963	212	1,256	16,844	7.5
1964	191	1,217	18,216	6.7
1965	205	1,391	18,851	7.4
1966	203	1,598	20,551	7.8
1967	199	1,718	21,847	7.9
1968	175	1,602	23,668	6.8
1969	155	1,885	24,911	7.6
1970	141	1,740	25,725	6.8
1971	123	1,652	26,127	6.3
1972	117	1,621	27,728	5.8
1973	108	1,612	26,083	6.2
1974	115	1,565	23,994	6.5
1975	113	1,420	21,260	6.7
1976	103	1,723	25,125	6.9
1977	104	1,576	25,969	6.1
1978	92	1,542	27,850	5.5
1979	88	1,383	25,566	5.4
1980	76	955	24,004	4.0
1981	70	1,191	23,818	5.0
1982	72	912	24,902	3.7
1983	66	1,005	25,752	3.9

Source: USDA (1985B).
*Packer feeding includes cattle and calves fed by and for meat packers and transferred from feedlot for slaughter during the reporting year.
†Fed cattle marketing is the calculated commercial slaughter of fed steers and heifers for the U.S. as published by the USDA.

varies among regions and may be different within a region (Table 8.24). Therefore, while feeding by or for packers may appear relatively small at the national level, a substantial volume may be involved in some states.

Aspelin and Engleman (1966) investigated the effect on prices of packer feeding by one slaughterer at a leading terminal market in 1962, concluding that

packer feeding was about 3% of cattle slaughter by packers located near the market. The primary packer-feeder in the area fed about 10% of its cattle

Table 8.23. Sheep, Lambs, and Hogs Fed by or for U.S. Meat Packers During Selected Years.

	Sheep and lambs		Hogs	
		Head fed		Head fed
Year	No. of firms	(1,000)	No. of firms	(1,000)
1960	24	826	24	20
1965	20	826	23	43
1970	13	1,234	17	65
1975	7	1,019	11	82
1976	7	1,064	13	166
1977	8	701	9	109
1978	8	775	11	90
1979	10	677	12	88
1980	8	504	7	58
1981	5	228	9	105
1982	5	103	8	42
1983	4	335	6	68

Source: USDA (1985B and earlier issues).

slaughter. Data on movement of cattle by weeks throughout the year did not show evidence that shipments of packer-fed cattle consistently offset fluctuations in the receipts of cattle on the local (terminal) market. Apparently, packer-fed shipments did not serve to stablize the market supply to any great extent.

The statistical analysis indicated that packer feeding had significant depressive effects on weekly average prices at the terminal market, relative to prices at other terminals. Price effects were within the range of $0.25–$0.50 per cwt on the weekly average price for choice steers at the market. According

Table 8.24. Cattle and Calves Fed by or for U.S. Meat Packers, by Region During Selected Years.

	Number (1,000 head) during				
Region	1970	1974	1978	1980	1983
E. N. Central	46	19	29	11	9
W. N. Central	290	393	175	73	60
South Atlantic	40	34	64	17	32
South Central	53	25	10	4	10
Southern Plains	259	158	94	150	166
Mountain	601	681	774	485	496
Pacific	370	229	323	329	384
All Others*	83	44	20	12	3
U.S. Total	1,740	1,584	1,487	1,082	1,991

Source: USDA (1985B and earlier issues).
*"Other" includes all states with less than 500 head fed by packers, regardless of region, and feeding at location unknown.

to the mathematical analysis, a given increase in packer-fed supplies transferred to plant had more than ten times as much effect upon the local price for choice steers as did the same increase in market supplies of choice steers.

A major criticism leveled at this study was the limited sample upon which it was based, i.e., one packer and one market. Nevertheless, it called attention to a public concern over the expansion in packer feeding. Although this was the first attempt at quantitative analysis of the effect on prices of packer feeding, it was followed by a number of articles of a subjective nature. The following summary draws heavily from one such article.

Various motives undoubtedly exist for packer feeding. Farris (1967) suggests the following:

1. A more even supply of cattle may increase plant operating efficiency. Receipts fluctuate from seasonal factors and erratically from day to day and week to week. If livestock are not available, plants are shut down—an expensive proposition because of the high fixed costs in plant and equipment. Packers can reduce fixed cost per unit of output by continuous operation. Labor also has a minimum fixed cost in that unions are guaranteed a minimum week's pay whether or not livestock is available.
2. Livestock procurement costs may be lowered. Fewer livestock buyers are needed and transportation costs can be reduced if cattle are fed near the plant by the packer.
3. Risks may be reduced. The packer can control not only numbers but also quality of livestock and thereby meet specifications of meat purchasers. In addition, price risk may be reduced by strengthening the packer's bargaining position in buying livestock—especially during periods when supplies of particular grades are scarce.
4. New organizational and technological innovations may be discovered. By being actively engaged in feeding, a packer may increase his knowledge of that aspect of the industry and participate in the development of new technology.
5. Implementation of new developments may occur rapidly. Access to funds may permit packers to implement new developments more rapidly than farmers or commercial feeders.
6. Public policy usually sanctions freedom of enterprise. Livestock producers have integrated forward into meat packing, even though the extent is limited. This in itself could be grounds for arguing the case for packers' backward integration. There is merit in consistency in public policy.

Farris (1967) also recognizes some potential problems associated with packer feeding:

1. Market price manipulation may be possible. Vertical integration may provide a means of altering the market structure and in turn allow a business conduct not possible under purely competitive conditions. A packing firm able to dominate purchases at a particular location could exercise some control over prices. According to Farris, "The packer practice of negotiating for larger numbers of cattle several days in advance of shipment from the feedlot may also give packers opportunities to use such cattle in affecting paying prices."

2. The pricing process may be affected by the reduced proportion of cattle bought and sold in the marketing channel. Prices in established markets are widely publicized and used. Reduction in transactions at these markets erodes the base upon which they are established.

3. The organizational structure of agricultural production may be adversely affected. Since packer feeding is usually large-scale, its expansion may adversely affect the family-farm type of feeding operations. The same observation can be made about economical large-scale feedlots in general.

4. Packer feeding may bring unfair competition to specialized producers. This is an extension of No. 3 above. Since packers have earning from other interests that could be used to cover losses in feeding operations, it has been suggested that losses could be sustained for extended periods in a given area to the detriment of specialized feeders. It also has been suggested that packers could destabilize supplies and enhance price swings. This point, as well as several others mentioned above, prompted the National Commission on Food Marketing to propose the public reporting of activities of large, diverse firms engaged in feeding.

5. The total volume of cattle fed may be higher if packers feed, leading to depressed producer prices. Historically, variations in production have been associated with profit levels. It seems likely this will continue to be the case, whether feeding is done by packers or others.

The advocates of this type of business coordination point to its advantages in terms of increased market efficiency and lowering and distributing risk. Opponents, on the other hand, emphasize its anticompetitive aspects, including its potential impact on the structure—i.e., the possible replacement of many small, independent businesses by large organizations. Some also argue that extensive packer feeding may raise the possibility of pricing problems, including price manipulation; also, that if total volume of fed livestock increases with packer feeding, the overall price level and producers' income may be depressed.

As a result of the possible adverse impact of packer feeding of livestock, many proposals for legislation to control, or regulate, feeding by packers have been advanced, but more have not been enacted.[14] In 1974, the USDA imposed regulations to prohibit packers, or their officers or agents, from owning, operating, controlling, financing, or participating in the management of custom feedlots. Packers were permitted to own and operate their own feedlots, however, as long as no custom feeding was practiced. In May 1982, the USDA announced that the government intended to revise this eight-year-old policy. They proposed to replace the ban with a "policy statement" encouraging packers to consult with the USDA's Packers and Stockyards Administration before entering into custom feeding in order to prevent any violation of the law and to avoid possible conflict of interest. The reverse in the USDA ban was based, in part, on the results of a recent study of pricing for fed steers and heifers that concluded that no evidence existed of actual, or potential for, anticompetition (Williamson et al., 1982).

Another dimension of backward integration may occur from the retail level of the market system. Several food distribution and retail firms have integrated backward into slaughtering and/or feeding. For example, Kroger, Winn Dixie, Acme Markets, American Stores, Beatrice Foods, and Consolidated Foods operate, or have operated, slaughtering and processing facilities. The important motives of such backward integration are the desire to control other stages in the production–marketing system that could provide stability of supply, quality control, and the possibility of establishing brand names or eventually product differentiation through advertising. Retailer feeding of livestock was limited from 1971 to 1977, however, and no retailers have been involved in feeding livestock since 1977.

Farris (1967) commented on the public policy considerations as follows:

In considering policy alternatives toward packer feeding, it may be possible to adopt a course which would avoid the undesirable possibilities associated

---

[14]Engleman (1974) suggested that a packer custom feeder can transfer livestock (e.g., cattle) to its slaughtering operation at a lower price than competing packers. Thus, it is possible that such firms may use this market strength to the detriment of competing firms, a customer, or owner of the livestock. He also indicated that small firms with limited capital may not be able to establish a custom-feeding operation; thus, unfair

with the practice, yet preserve its efficiency, flexibility and potential for technological gain. One alternative would be to permit packers to feed or have custom-fed for them a certain proportion of their slaughter capacity. Analysis of various considerations would be necessary to ascertain what prohibition would best minimize adverse side effects while retaining efficiency advantages of packer feeding. Without better factual knowledge, it may be desirable to place increased emphasis on supervising market practices of integrated firms more closely, while determining whether it would be in the public interest to restrict vertical integration.

Horizontal Integration

Many large packers are integrated horizontally by pursuing management and operational control over slaughtering and/or processing facilities at different locations. This horizontal integration is achieved through a number of means, among them ownership, lease arrangements, and merger. As with most cases of horizontal integration, the purpose is to capture the benefits of economies in the procurement and marketing of products, to maintain a certain market share, to prevent competitors from entering the market in certain locations, to attempt to increase profit with larger volume, finally, to add operational flexibility during times of insufficient supply of raw material (i.e., livestock) or labor contract disputes.

Of the top 100 firms in the meat industry, 72 owned or operated more than one plant in 1983 (*Meat Industry,* 1984). Table 8.21 shows the number of plants that year for each of the top ten meat packers/processors; all had more than one plant, ranging from three up to 28 plants. It should be pointed out that the size of plants varies substantially among firms. For example, most of the IBP, Inc., plants (12 in 1983) and EXCEL (7 in 1983) were very large, whereas several of the 28 Swift & Company plants were relatively small. The top ten firms owned or operated 120 plants throughout the United States but, as shown earlier, these were concentrated near leading livestock-producing regions.

The major public concern with horizontal integration by packers is its potential impact on concentration and thus the creation of an anticompetitive environment. To illustrate, a 1970 Consent Decree prohibited IPB, Inc., from acquiring any plants in four states—Iowa, Nebraska, Minnesota, or South Dakota—until 1980. The U.S. Justice Department contended that the acquisition could lead to less competition. A similar attempt in 1977, however, failed to block a joint venture between IBP, Inc., and a group of feeders in the Pacific Northwest

(Washington, Oregon, Idaho, and Montana). The arrangement allows IBP, Inc., to operate large plants in the region.[15]

Conglomerate Integration

When a firm invests in industries unrelated to its own, a case of conglomerate integration is at hand. Conglomeration in the meat industry may occur through the meat packers' initiative—i.e., meat packers' investing (diversifying) in industries not related to meat—or the initative may come from outside—i.e., nonmeat business investing in the meat industry. This type of integration has become popular since the 1950s.

During the 1960s and 1970s, several meat-packing firms either diversified into other industries, merged with business unrelated to meat packing, or been acquired by conglomerate businesses. It is believed by most economists that the major reasons for conglomeration are to improve financial position, reduce risk, and gain tax advantages. Examples of conglomerate mergers that exist, or have existed, are the following: (1) Armour, by Greyhound; (2) Cudahy, by General Host; (3) John Morrell, by United Brands; (4) Wilson, by Ling Tempco Vaught (LTV), a merger reversed in 1981; and (5) Iowa Beef Processors, which, acquired by Occidental Petroleum in 1981, changed its name to IBP, Inc., in 1982. During the mid-1980s, the pace of mergers and acquisitions increased to the extent that any tabulation of changes became out-of-date rather quickly. Three companies emerged as dominant in the field, i.e., IBP Inc., Cargill, Inc., and ConAgra.

PRODUCT DIFFERENTIATION AND PROMOTION

The ability to differentiate products and the extent to which differentiation is accomplished are important aspects of an industry's structure (and its performance). Differentiating a product is the process by which similar products, in physical and utility terms, are made to be viewed as nonidentical by consumers. Without product differentiation a single price prevails in the market place (adjusted for time and place). Only when products are differentiated in the minds of buyers may two or more prices be observed.

---

[15]Although this joint venture is discussed as an example of horizontal integration—i.e., adding to IBP's slaughtering capacity by adding to the number of plants it operates— it may also be viewed as a backward vertical integration to gain control over a large volume of fed cattle supplied by the other party in the arrangement.

Product differentiation in the fresh meat market is considered by many as negligible. This view is due, in part, to the wide acceptance of Federal grade standards. Fresh meat, however, may be differentiated at the wholesale level by creating a bundle of services to accompany the products. Thus, a packer may establish a long-term agreement with a buyer and include certain attractive features, such as a reasonable payment schedule and lower costs for a special operation (e.g., trimming). Still other packers may establish their own cutting, trimming, or other special processing methods in order to differentiate their meat. Examples of the latter are Swift and Wilson. These firms have initiated aggressive advertising programs to promote their own brand-name fresh meat, and their strategy has recently appeared to be more market- rather than production-oriented. During the 1980s a number of efforts were initiated by packers, individual producers, a breed association, and the National Pork Producers Association to brand retail cuts of fresh meat. Time will be required to determine their success.

The processed meat sector exhibits a different situation. Production of processed meat allows for the application of available technology in developing distinctive products such as spiced meat, with flavor, color, texture, and packaging convenience. Processors are usually more successful than packers in their efforts to differentiate their products through various types of promotion of national brands through advertising, e.g., Oscar Mayer. The National Commission on Food Marketing study (NCFM, 1966) indicated that approximately 1 percent of total sales by the eight largest firms were spent on advertising. Expenditures on new product development were low (less than 0.4 percent of sales by the largest four firms in 1965 and less than 0.1 percent by the second largest four). The report stated the following:

Processed items—such as bacon, hams, sausage, and luncheon meats—are labeled with the packer or retailer name. A number of variations exist in product composition, packaging and branding, and these frequently differ among firms. Some packers have promoted their brands enough to influence consumers. As a result, in some sections of the country highly advertised brands sell at higher prices then unadvertised brands.

. . . Two thirds or more of fresh beef, veal, lamb and pork was sold unbranded by packers. But less than 10% of cured pork items and processed meats was sold unbranded by most groups of packers.

On branded items, the packers' brands predominated. Less than 5% of the cured and processed meat sold by the largest 4 packers carried the customers' labels. However, the second largest 4 packers and other reporting packers sold around 10% of their cured and processed meats under customer labels. Customer branded meats were sold chiefly to large retail chains.

Recent public concern focused on the tendency by large firms (with some degree of market power) to outspend smaller firms in advertising and special service provided, thus creating a competitive advantage by differentiating essentially the same products. Heavy advertising and promotion is considered a major source of market power for large firms and may be considered an obstacle to the existence of new, or small firms.

In addition to packers' and processors' product differentiation activities, meat is promoted by various livestock and meat trade organizations. The purpose of these promotion programs is to affect consumer's willingness to purchase red meat as opposed to other meats such as poultry and fish, regardless of the source of the meat. Such promotion programs (e.g., by the National Livestock and Meat Board) should not have an impact on the individual firm's market share (or power) except to the extent that large firms would be expected to benefit proportionately more than smaller firms if the campaign to increase red meat consumption is successful.

ENTRY AND EXIT

As in most industries, many small (and some large) firms enter and exit the meat industry each year. Entry refers to the establishment of a slaughter and/or processing operation by a business unit (e.g., a single firm or a cooperative). Exit is defined as discontinuing such activities by the operators. In general, any comparison of the number of plants, as reported by the USDA from year to year, would tend to underestimate the extent of entry and exit. This estimate is low because these numbers are reported as of a specific date each year and do not reflect during-the-year movements.

Studies have shown different patterns of entry and exit among regions. For example, more plants exited in the West during the 1950–1962 period than in other regions (Anthony, 1966). Approximately 30 percent of the packing plants in the United States went out of business between 1969 and 1979. During the same decade, about 50 percent of the members in the Western States Meat Packers Association (representing about 85 percent of all packers in the region) also exited (U. S. Congress, Committee on Small Business, 1979).

The relatively high proportion of firms entering and leaving the industry may suggest that it is easy to enter and/or exit. There are many barriers to entry, however, that give an advantage to large established firms over potential entrants. Probably the most obvious entry barrier is the large investment required to build and operate a modern plant capable of capturing all, or most, of the economies enjoyed by large-scale firms. In addition, new entrants must compete with existing established firms (which might have overcapacity plants) for a limited supply of livestock (Williams, 1979).

Another barrier to entry is the ability of established firms to create perceived differences among similar products—i.e., product differentiation through advertising. As indicated earlier, such an ability leads to greater market power. In many instances, small existing firms in the meat packing industry, as well as new ones wishing to enter, face a major barrier. Since smaller firms usually operate smaller and often less efficient plants than large established ones, advertising becomes very costly. To the extent that product differentiation and national-brand advertising for processed meats entail greater budget costs, entry into meat processing is more difficult than into slaughtering. There are several possible explanations for this observation, which has been supported by Anthony (1966) and the National Commission on Food Marketing (1966) studies. Processors have been able to brand and differentiate their products more successfully than packers have been able to differentiate fresh meat. A newcomer in processing, therefore, has the problem of winning over customers who may already have preferences for a particular brand. Another possible factor is that processors in general tend to be located near areas of heavy consumption that, geographically speaking, remain relatively stable. Livestock production, on the other hand, and particularly finished cattle production, has shifted its focus considerably, and new packing plants have tended to follow.

It should be noted that these analyses included only federally inspected plants. As was apparent in an earlier section on packing plant classification, FI plants are considerably larger in average size and slaughter a substantially larger percentage of livestock than do non-FI plants. In commenting on the possible implications of this situation to the entire industry, Anthony (1966) states: "Far more complete data are available for meat packers operating under Federal inspection than for those not receiving this service. As a result, most evidence presented in this report pertains directly to this sector of the meat packing industry as a whole as it is represented by the federally inspected sector. Because of the importance of the federally inspected sector, the necessary assumption that it is representative is not especially damaging. Nevertheless, the conclusions possible from the evidence presented are limited." A comparable qualification is appropriate for conclusions regarding the meat-processing industry.

Ward (1977) suggested that with more plant specialized in species killed and operations performed, there appear to be some exit barriers, because of the lack of potential buyers during difficult economic times. The disappearances from the rankings published by the *Meat Industry* support this statement. For example, while the profit conditions and other problems during the late 1970s and early 1980s might suggest that many firms would exit, only five firms disappeared from the top 100 packers between 1981 and 1982; three of these went out of business and the other two were bought by other packers or organized under new names and operation.

REFERENCES

American Meat Institute. 1980. An economic analysis of the structure of the U.S. meat packing industry. Prepared for AMI by Schnittker Associates, Washington, D.C.

American Meat Institute. 1985. MEATFACTS: A statistical summary about America's largest food industry. AMI 1985 edition.

Anthony, W. E. 1966. Structural changes in the federally inspected livestock slaughter industry 1950–62. USDA ERS, Agr. Econ. Rept. 83, Revised Feb.

Anthony, W. E., and Egertson, K. E. 1966. Decentralization in the livestock slaughter industry. USDA ERS, Suppl. Agr. Econ. Rept. 83.

Aspelin, A., and Engelman, G. 1966. Packer feeding of cattle, its volume and significance. USDA, C&MS Marketing Res. Rept. 776.

Aspelin, A., and Engelman, G. 1976. National oligopoly and local oligopsony in the meat packing industry. USDA, P&S Administration (unpublished).

Bain, J. S. 1968. *Industrial Organization.* 2nd ed. New York: John Wiley & Sons, Inc.

Baker, Allen J. 1976. Federally Inspected Livestock Slaughter by Size and Type of Slaughter. USDA, ERS, Statistical Bulletin No. 549, May.

Butz, D. E., and Baker, G. L. 1960. *The Changing Structure of the Meat Economy.* Harvard Univ. Graduate School Business Admin., Boston.

Clemen, R. A. 1923. The American Livestock and Meat Industry, Ronald Press, New York.

Committee on Small Business, House of Representatives. 1978. Small business problems in the marketing of meat and other commodities (Part 1—Meat Marketing). Hearings before the Subcommittee on SBA and SBIC Authority and General Small Business Problems.

Committee on Small Business, U.S. House of Representatives. 1980. Small business problems in the marketing of meat and other commodities: Part 7—Monopoly effects on producers and consumers. U.S. Government Printing Office, Washington, D.C.

Cothern, James H. 1978. Technological change, market power and beef product pricing practices. The small business in the marketing of meat and other commodities: Part 1—Meat marketing. Hearings before the Small Business Committee, U.S. House of Representatives. U.S. Government Printing Office, Washington, D.C.

Farris, P. L. 1967. Economic evaluation of cattle feeding by meat packers. Econ. Marketing Inform. Indiania Farmers, May 4–5.

General Accounting Office. 1978. Beef marketing: Issues and concerns. Study by the staff of the U.S. General Accounting Office. Washington, D.C.

Hayenga, M. L. 1978. Vertical coordination in the beef industry: Packer, retailer, and HRI linkages. University of Wisconsin, Madison, NC Project 117, WP-35.

Hayenga, M. L. 1979. Pork pricing systems: The importance and economic impacts of formula pricing. University of Wisconsin, Madison, NC Project 117, WP-37.

Meat Industry. 1984. *Meat Industry Magazine's* 6th Top 100 Packers. *The Meat Industry Magazine,* July.

National Commission on Food Marketing. 1966. Organization and competition in the livestock and meat industry. Natl. Comm. Food Marketing Tech. Study 1.

Nelson, K. E. 1985. Issues and developments in the U.S. meatpacking industry. USDA, ERS Staff Rept No. AGES 850502.

Simpson, James R., and Sullivan, G. M. 1980. Report to regional livestock marketing committee, S-116 on survey of meat packing plants in the Southeastern United States. Paper presented at the S-116 Technical Committee Meeting, Atlanta, Oct. 28.

USDA. 1984. Livestock and meat statistics, 1983. USDA, ERS, Statistical Bulletin No. 715. Also, Nos. 33 and 522, supplement issues for earlier years.

USDA. 1985A. Livestock slaughter, 1984 summary. USDA, Crop Reporting Board, SRS MtAn 1-2-1(85).

USDA. 1985B. Packer and stockyard's statistical resume, 1983 reporting year. P&S Administration, Statistical Reports No. 85-1.

U.S. Department of Commerce. 1981 and earlier issues. Census of Manufacturers, Industry Series: Meat products. Bureau of Census.

U.S. Department of Commerce. 1981 and selected issues. Census of Manufacturers, Special Report Series: Concentration ratios in manufacturing industries. Bureau of Census.

Ward, Clement E. 1977. Vertical coordination of cattle feeding and slaughtering in the cattle and beef subsector. Univ. of Wisconsin, Madison, NC Project 117, WP-14.

Ward, Clement E. 1982. Feedlot and packer concentration—Current status, courses, implications, and alternatives. Department of Agr. Econ. Paper A.E. 8209, Oklahoma State University.

Williams, W. F., and Stout, T. T. 1964. *Economics of the livestock-meat industry.* New York: The Macmillan Company.

Williams, W. F. 1979. The changing structure of the beef packing industry. Study prepared for the Committe on Small Business, U.S. House of Representatives. *In* Small business problems in the marketing of meat and other commodities (Part 4—Changing structure of the beef packing industry). U.S. Government Printing Office.

Williamson, J.C., *et al.* 1982. Geographic markets and prices for fed steers and heifers. USDA, P&S Admin., P&S Research Report No.82-1, Washington, D.C.

9

Meat Packing and Processing—Operation, Earnings, and Future

Livestock slaughter and processing plants, which are raw-material-oriented, differ widely in size as well as type. With today's economic conditions and new developments in technology, the exigencies of competition and survival require a high degree of operational efficiency. Regardless of size and type of operation, all meat packers and processors are involved in similar activities regarding plant operation, raw-material procurement (i.e., livestock and/or carcasses or other forms of input), and marketing of the various product. Therefore, although small and medium-size plants can achieve a certain degree of efficiency, economies in volume, labor utilization, and marketing are primarily found in the larger plants.

There are also some similarities in type, if not in magnitude, of problems facing individual firms. General economic, social, legal, and technological problems affect the entire industry. The type of ownership, level of costs, and realized income from meat packing differ among firms and help shape their relative position in the economy as well as their future direction.

This chapter will present a brief discussion of the various subdivisions of the meat-packing industry as well as the procurement activities of individual firms. it will examine past trends, major problem areas, and current costs and earnings in the industry as well as take a look into the future. The bases on which packers make marketing decisions will be discussed. The sale and distribution of meat and meat products by packers—basically speaking, the wholesaling of meat—will be presented in Chap. 10.

SUBDIVISIONS OF THE MEAT INDUSTRY

As discussed in the preceding chapter, the meat industry is composed of a large number of firms, which may perform only one or a great many operations. The firms range in size from pygmies to giants. The industry includes specialized and nonspecialized slaughterers/processors as well as nonslaughtering establishments of all types. Wholesalers are that part of the industry which performs all the necessary functions to move meat and meat products from packers and processors to retailers, institutions, and export markets. Wholesaling may be performed by either independent wholesale organizations, packers/processors, or agents.

In order to gain a practical understanding of the structure and operation of the meat industry, it is important to examine the different industry components to find out who the actors are and what the function of each is. A member of the meat industry is basically defined as any entity that slaughters, processes, sells, or distributes meat and meat products. Among these, however, distinct subdivisions can be identified. Sarhan and Albanos (1985) have categorized the various subdivisions in the beef and pork trades (Figs. 9.1 and 9.2).

Beef Industry Subdivision

For the purpose of this section, the beef industry is divided into two categories: Slaughterers and nonslaughterers.

Cattle Slaughterers. Cattle slaughterers are further divided into two groups: (1) slaughterers of U.S. Good or better cattle, and (2) slaughterers of U.S. Canner, Cutter, and Utility grade cattle. These two groups are usually distinct since most firms specialize in slaughtering a particular class of cattle. Often these firms are also engaged in processing the carcasses they have slaughtered and may also perform some or all of the wholesale functions.

Slaughterers of U.S. Good and Better Animals. This group is engaged in the slaughtering of fed cattle and sells its products either in boxed or loose form.

1. *Good or Better Boxed Beef Forms.* The term "boxed beef" as used here refers to the breakdown of beef carcasses into small parts that are put under vacuum in tough plastic bags, which in turn are put in boxes for shipment. Three boxed beef forms should be distinguished:
   (a) Boxed beef carcasses
   (b) Boxed vacuum-packed primal cuts
   (c) Boxed vacuum-packed standard beef cuts.
   Chapter 10 discusses in detail these three types. Boxed beef is usually wholesale-traded to retailers and institutions.
2. *Good or Better Nonboxed Beef Forms.* In addition to boxed beef, the slaughterers of U.S. Good or better cattle produce a variety of

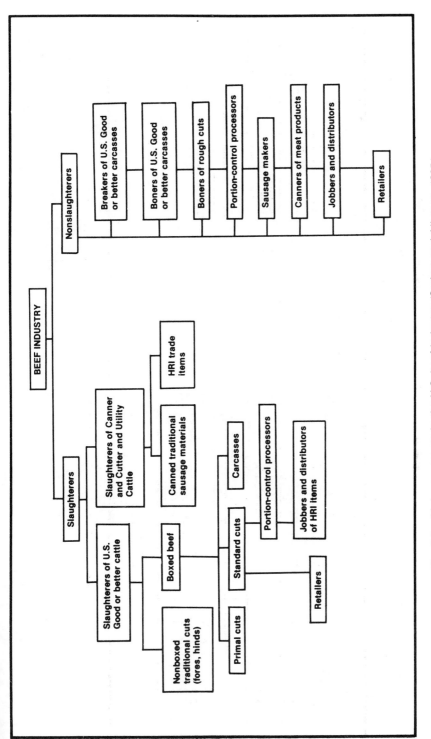

Fig. 9.1. Major segments in the U.S. beef industry. (Sarhan and Albanos, 1985.)

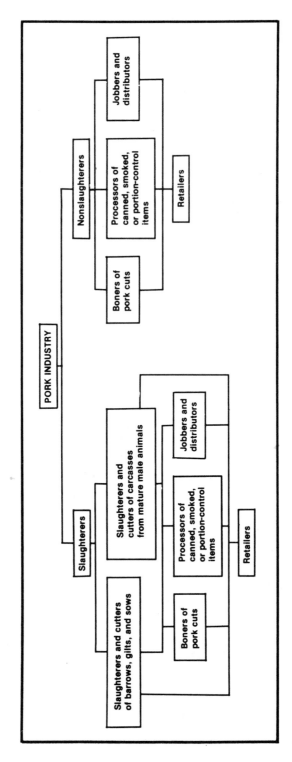

Fig. 9.2. Major segments in the U.S. pork industry. (Sarhan and Albanos, 1985.)

nonvacuum-packed beef items. These include carcasses, fores, hinds, and various primal cuts, i.e., the traditional beef cuts that have been used by the meat industry for many years. The primary outlets for these items are retailers and other packers-wholesalers as well as independent wholesalers.

Slaughterers of Canner and Cutter and Utility Cattle. This group of firms slaughters animals producing lean carcasses which are boned and further processed and usually used in canned meats and sausage items. Some of the major cuts are tenderized and used in the Hotel, Restaurant and Institutional trade (HRI).

Cattle Nonslaughterers. In addition to cattle slaughterers, the beef trade includes processors and wholesalers/distributers. These subgroups consist of the following:

1. Breakers of U.S. Good or better carcasses
2. Boners of U.S. Good or better carcasses
3. Boners of rough cuts for sausage materials
4. Portion control processors
5. Sausage makers
6. Canners of meat products
7. Jobbers and distributors

The first three of these seven subgroups can function either as separate organizations or as an integrated unit performing all three functions. They also may produce manufacturing beef by removing bones from certain primal cuts. Groups four through seven may do the actual processing of the products and/or distribute them to retailers, other wholesalers, or the HRI outlets.

Pork Industry Subdivisions

Firms in the pork industry may be classified into slaughterers and nonslaughterers.

Hog Slaughterers. Hog slaughtering firms may be classified into two distinct types: (1) slaughterers of barrows, gilts, and sows; and (2) slaughterers of mature male animals.

Slaughterers and Cutters of Barrows, Gilts, and Sow Carcasses. This group slaughters hogs and either sells split pork sides to another plant to divide into primal cuts or itself performs the cutting, processing, boxing, and other further processing (e.g., preparing hams and picnics). The remaining products resulting from carcass division are either sold to other plants or used on site for sausage materials.

Slaughterers and Cutters of Carcasses from Mature Male Hogs. This group slaughters mature male hogs and cuts the carcasses into primals (which are usually defatted); and it either removes the bones and sells the resulting manufacturing pork or sells the primals to a pork processor. The products so derived are usually processed into highly seasoned items. Meat from mature male animals is usually low in fat, and moisture is desired by an increasing number of trades and consumers.

Hog Nonslaughterers. This group may be divided into three categories: (1) boners of pork cuts; (2) processors of canned, smoked, or portion control items; and (3) jobbers and distributors.

Boners of Pork Cuts. This group may be divided into (1) those firms handling mature male carcasses, and (2) those handling other classes of pork carcasses. The output takes the form of fabricated pork items and sausage materials.

Pork boners vary in size in terms of the volume of product produced and the number of workers. For example, industry sources indicate that the number of workers may be as high as 300 for large operations to as low as six or fewer employees in small ones. Regardless of size, the main function of boners is to remove the bones from large primal cuts and produce sausage materials (usually lean contents). They may further fabricate certain primals into cuts to be sold to processors, e.g., Canadian backs.

Processors of Canned, Smoked, or Portion Control Items. This group of firms takes the raw materials (e.g., primals) and further processes them into products such as canned hams, bacon, sausage, and smoked ham. They also process fresh cuts into "portion control items" (meat cut into uniform portions for individual servings) and sell them to the HRI trade—e.g., flanked steaks.

Jobbers and Distributors. These two subgroups can function as one or as separate traders. Jobbers are engaged in the distribution of processed-pork items as well as boxed-primal-pork items. Although distributors also perform these functions, they usually handle portion control items and deal primarily with the food service industry.

THE MEAT PACKING PLANT

The type and extent of specialization of a plant determine the type of equipment and operations carried out. Some plants only kill, others kill and chill, whereas some kill, chill, and process either fresh or cured meats. Many plants are also involved in rendering and by-product activities.

All plants require enough land to accommodate the facility, parking lot, and truck loading–unloading space. A slaughter plant consists of (1) a livestock-receiving facility, which includes scales and corrals; (2) a kill floor and a dressing area; (3) chill-and-holding coolers; (4) an offal workup area; (5) an equipment-cleaning and maintenance area; (6) a waste-treatment facility; (7) an employee dressing-and-welfare area; and (8) office space.

Slaughter plants involved in fresh-meat processing (i.e., breaking, boning, boxing, etc.) require additional equipment and areas for processing. Plants that only process carcasses into fresh meat cuts do not need a kill floor or the associated space and equipment. If meat is processed beyond fresh cuts—i.e., through curing, sausage making, etc.— additional equipment and facilities will be required.

The typical plant is staffed by two types of manpower—office and production. Office manpower includes a manager, assistant manager (for most plants), production supervisor, engineer, financial officer, livestock procurement and scheduling person(s), sales person(s), and one or more secretary/receptionist(s). Several of the office functions may be performed by one individual, especially in smaller operations. Production labor includes kill-floor workers (in plants that slaughter), processing labor, and loading workers.

Studies have shown that economies of size exist in meat-packing and processing plants. For example, several studies have indicated that slaughtering and processing plants experience a decreasing average cost per head as the number killed per hour increased or as the level of utilization and capacity increased (Logan, 1966; Cothern, 1978A and 1978B; Sarhan, 1977; Burst and Kuehn, 1979; and Farris and Mathia, 1981). It should be noted, however, that economies are sensitive to the degree of plant utilization as well as to plant scale. With levels of less than 100-percent capacity, the increase in actual cost of plant operation may offset most of the economies of scale.

PLANT OPERATIONS

The following discussion concerns operations performed in plants that both slaughter and process. Although the operations are discussed for cattle plants and briefly for hog plants (or a plant handling both species), similar operations are performed when other species are considered.[1]

---

[1]The discussion in this section is based on information from Romans and Ziegler (1974), Hammons and Miller (1961), Hammons (1966), and Kropf and Breidenstein (1975).

Cattle Slaughtering and Processing Operations

The operations involved in slaughtering and/or processing are usually performed in a certain sequence, but the volume involved and the equipment used may slightly alter established procedures. Cattle received by a packer are kept in holding pens. It is usually recommended that livestock be kept off feed at least 24 hours before slaughter. Studies have indicated that fasted animals bleed out more thoroughly, produce brighter carcasses, and are easier to dress. Following are the steps in plant operation:

1. *Driving:* This, the first operation, involves moving animals from the holding pen through a chute into the immobilization pen.
2. *Stunning:* Cattle are immoblized to eliminate slaughtering pain to the animal and to gain safety and efficiency for workers. Stunning is done by a compressing gun, a rifle, or other electrical, mechanical, or chemical methods meeting the provisions of the humane slaughter acts. (Kosher killing is exempt).
3. *Sticking and Skinning:* Stunned animals are shackled by their hind legs and hoisted off the floor; an incision is then made and the slaughtered animal is left to bleed. In Kosher slaughter, unstunned animals are hoisted and a cut is made across the throat. Bled animals move (usually on a rail) to the beginning of the "disassembly" line, where the head is removed (leaving the neck on the carcass). the hide is then removed in several steps that include the use of hide-pulling devices or a skinning knife.
4. *Eviscerating:* This step involves separation of the paunch and intestines after opening the thorasic and abdominal cavities. The liver, heart, lungs, and other parts are also removed.
5. *Splitting:* Splitting, or halving, the carcass through the center of the backbone is done by a power saw or a large cleaver. A scribe saw may then be used to improve the appearance of the wholesale cuts. The spinal cord is also removed. The splitting of the forequarters and vein removal are completed before the meat is ready for chilling.
6. *Washing, Pinning, Shrouding, and Chilling:* Carcasses are washed with cold or lukewarm water to remove blood, chopped tissue, and bone dust from the inside and outside to prevent bacterial growth. Pinning is a practice used to improve the appearance of the carcass in the neck area (by making the chuck seem thicker-necked). Prior to chilling, the sides are covered with wet shrouds, or cloths. Shrouding smoothes the external fat and absorbs remaining blood. Many packers have discontinued the shrouding practice, especially if the

meat is to be fabricated at the plant. The meat is then placed in the chill room for about 24 hours. If the meat has been shrouded, the cloths are removed after chilling and the inspection stamps applied. Carcasses are then removed from the chilling room to the holding cooler where they remain until sold.

7. *Breaking, Boning, and Fabricating:* These operations are performed by packers on a part or all of the chilled carcasses. The sides are ribbed by a saw and a knife into two parts each (four quarters per animal) between the twelfth and thirteenth ribs. The quarters are then broken into primals and subprimal cuts. This process is usually done in breaking and boning rooms, where the bones are removed and the meat is cut into various wholesale cuts. After fabrication (i.e., primal, subprimal, and portion-controlled cutting) has been performed in most modern plants, meat is vacuum-packed in heavy plastic bags and placed in boxes to be kept in holding coolers until sold.

8. *Loading Operation:* When the meat is sold and ready for shipping, the carcasses, or boxes, are moved from the holding cooler to the loading dock. There they are weighed and loaded into refrigerated trucks.

9. *Other operations:* Many plants are also involved in rendering operations, hide curing, and the development and preparation of several by-products.

Hog Slaughtering and Processing Operations

The driving, stunning, and bleeding steps in hog slaughtering are similar to those described for cattle slaughtering. After bleeding, however, hogs go through a scalding in hot water to loosen hair; a sharp scraper is used to remove hair, dirt, and bristles; then washing completes the outer carcass cleaning. An alternative to scalding is skinning the hog, using a skinning rack and knife.

Head removal, evisceration, and splitting follow. Splitting is performed using a power saw to split the carcass down the center of the backbone. The viscera and carcass are inspected for disease. In a kill and chill plant, the split carcass is washed to remove blood and then placed in the chill room with no further cutting or processing, until sold. Some plants, however, may perform some by-product processing such as rendering, processing inedible offal, and/or drying blood.

Most hog-slaughtering plants are involved to some extent in pork fabrication and some meat processing, either in addition to the kill-chill function or as their sole operation. Fabrication involves breakdown of carcasses into fresh primal and subprimal cuts and marketing them as fresh boxed pork (with or without use of vacuum-packed bags). Further processing involves smoking, curing, making sausage loaves, and other operations. Sold products are weighed and moved from the holding cooler into refrigerated trucks for shipping.

Procurement Practices

Packers' demand for livestock and carcasses is a function of wholesale and retail demand for meat and other products; i.e., it is a derived demand. Therefore, a firm must determine the demand for meat and its by-products before making a decision on the number, type, and quality of animals or carcasses to purchase. In addition, the decision-maker has to consider not only general economic conditions but also competitors' prices. Once the demand for products has been translated into demand for livestock or carcasses, the firm must consider the price of the raw material and the cost of performing various operations. The firm will usually attempt to purchase raw materials at a price that will maximize its returns, given that certain constraints are met (e.g., capacity and ability to sell).

The procurement process involves making a decision on the source, or method, of purchasing livestock, carcasses, and other products, and determining a pricing strategy. These decisions are made at two levels; (1) the firm's headquarters, and (2) the field (or country) level. The remaining part of this section will examine the procurement process and present in some detail the steps involved in developing a pricing strategy.

Sources and Methods of Raw Material Procurement.   Meatpackers procure both live animals and meat. Packer's demand for live animals depends on the potential market for meat and its byproducts. Sometimes, packers may procure meat instead of live animals to meet final demand.

Meat Procurement.   The meat procured by packers and processors from other packers and processors consists of fresh beef, pork, or lamb carcasses and, in some cases, wholesale primal cuts. Carcass or primal procurement occurs at slaughtering and processing plants because of a shortage (or surplus) caused by physical as well as market conditions. For example, a firm that slaughters cattle may produce some carcasses that do not meet grade and weight specifications for its fabrication and boxing operations. This firm will sell such carcasses and buy others that fit its needs. Another situation where packers, especially multiplant firms, procure carcasses (even when they are capable of slaughtering the required number of animals themselves) arises when the cost is lower for carcasses delivered to specific locations from sources other than their own. Also, meat processors must buy a large number of carcasses or primals if they have little or no slaughter capacity.

Carcass (and primal cut) buyers rely on internal and external sources of information on prices and other market conditions. They obtain up-to-date information on the demand for their products and act accordingly with livestock buyers if the firm is involved in slaughtering. Packers and processors use private and public market information, which will be discussed subsequently in this chapter and also in Chap. 10.

Livestock Procurement. Livestock sources vary according to location, firm size, type of livestock, and other factors. Most packers employ salaried buyers and locate them at terminal markets, auction barns, and at their own country buying stations. Buyers also travel to feedlots and farms to purchase livestock. In addition, order buyers and commission firms are utilized by packers.

The U.S. Department of Agriculture (Packers and Stockyards Administration) collects and publishes annual information, by state, on the different market outlets used by packers to purchase livestock for slaughter. The published data show procurement by state where the livestock is slaughtered and therefore do not entirely represent the marketing by producers.

Terminal and auction markets were the major sources of livestock until the 1950s, at which time the number of terminal markets, and the volume of livestock sold through such outlets, declined sharply. The drop in importance of these markets coincided with an increase in direct marketing methods. Table 9.1 shows the percentages of different species of livestock purchased by packers through different methods during the years 1970 through 1984. Table 9.2 presents the percentages of packer purchases of livestock by source and packer size group in 1970 and in 1984. The Packer and Stockyards Administration statistics (not shown in these tables) indicate that the pattern of packers' procurement differs among states and regions of the country. For example, in 1984, packers in the North Atlantic region purchased 27.8 percent of their slaughter cattle directly, compared to 83.4 percent in the West North Central, 90.3 percent in the Mountain region, and 78.7 percent in the entire U.S. During the same year, direct purchases of hogs accounted for 48.2 percent of packers' purchases in the North Atlantic, 87.9 percent in the West North Central, 88.1 percent in the Mountain region, and 82.8 percent in the U.S. as a whole.

Table 9.2 indicates that during 1970, and even more so during 1984, the 10 largest packers obtained more of their livestock directly (from farmers, country dealers, etc.) than smaller packers did. For example,

Table 9.1. Percentages of Livestock Purchased by U.S. Packers Through Different Market Outlets, 1970-1984.*

Year	Direct and dealers (%)	Termi-nals (%)	Auctions (%)	Direct and dealers (%)	Termi-nals (%)	Auctions (%)
	All Cattle†			Calves		
1970	65.3	18.4	16.3	34.0	11.4	54.6
1971	68.6	15.9	15.5	32.4	8.6	59.0
1972	72.2	13.2	14.6	31.6	7.7	60.7
1973	73.0	11.9	15.1	30.9	8.2	60.9
1974	69.6	13.9	16.4	30.4	6.5	63.1
1975	65.9	14.4	19.7	32.4	8.3	59.3
1976	66.3	12.9	20.8	30.0	7.7	62.3
1977	69.4	12.0	18.6	35.5	7.2	57.2
1978	73.9	10.6	15.5	39.0	8.9	52.1
1979	77.7	8.7	13.7	41.9	6.5	51.6
1980	77.1	8.6	14.3	43.8	6.4	49.9
1981	77.4	8.1	14.5	42.7	9.0	48.2
1982	78.1	7.0	14.9	42.8	4.3	52.9
1983	76.6	7.1	15.3	48.4	4.5	47.2
1984	78.7	6.6	14.7	50.2	2.9	46.9
	Hogs			Sheep and lambs		
1970	68.5	17.1	14.3	72.5	15.1	12.4
1971	69.3	16.9	13.8	74.0	13.7	12.4
1972	70.4	16.3	13.3	74.3	13.7	12.0
1973	70.3	17.3	12.4	72.9	12.3	14.7
1974	70.0	17.6	12.4	75.1	11.5	13.5
1975	71.6	16.3	12.1	74.4	10.0	15.6
1976	71.5	17.1	11.5	75.2	9.8	15.0
1977	71.7	15.6	12.7	75.5	11.0	13.2
1978	72.8	15.8	11.5	78.9	9.9	11.1
1979	74.9	14.9	10.3	81.6	9.1	9.3
1980	76.7	13.5	9.8	80.5	7.6	12.0
1981	78.4	11.6	10.0	78.0	7.0	15.0
1982	79.0	12.0	8.9	81.3	7.7	11.0
1983	76.8	14.2	9.0	82.4	6.0	11.6
1984	82.8	10.3	6.8	78.9	8.9	12.2

Source: USDA (1986 and earlier issues).
*Pecentages are calculated from unrounded numbers. Total percentages may not add to 100 because of rounding.
†All cattle include steers, heifers, cows, and bulls.

in 1984, 93.2 percent of the cattle, 100.0 percent of the calves, 87.9 percent of the hogs, and 91.5 percent of the sheep and lambs were purchased directly by the largest 10 packers. In comparison, other (smaller) packers directly purchased 65.4, 50.2, 79.0, and 68.4 percent of their cattle, calves, hogs, and sheep and lambs, respectively (Table 9.2).

Table 9.2. Percentages of Packer Purchases from Different Market Outlets by Packer Size Group, 1970 and 1984.

	1970				1984			
	Cattle (%)	Calves (%)	Hogs (%)	Sheep (%)	Cattle (%)	Calves (%)	Hogs (%)	Sheep (%)
Ten Largest Packers*								
Direct, country dealers, etc.	79.6	35.6	78.9	76.9	93.2	100.0	87.9	91.5
Terminal markets	13.9	15.3	15.9	14.7	4.6	0.0	8.7	4.9
Auction markets	6.5	49.2	5.4	8.4	2.2	0.0	3.4	3.6
Other Packers*								
Direct, country dealers, etc.	57.8	33.7	59.0	78.2	65.4	50.2	79.0	68.4
Terminal markets	20.7	10.3	18.4	11.6	8.4	2.9	11.6	12.2
Auction markets	21.5	56.0	22.6	10.2	26.2	46.9	9.4	19.4
All Packers								
Direct, country dealers, etc.	65.3	34.0	68.5	72.5	78.7	50.2	82.8	78.9
Terminal markets	18.4	11.4	17.1	15.1	6.6	2.9	10.3	8.9
Auction markets	16.3	54.6	14.3	12.4	14.7	46.9	6.8	12.2

Source: USDA (1986 and earlier issues).
*Based on the total dressed weight of all livestock slaughtered.
†Including slaughtering food chains.

Terminal markets were more important sources than auctions for all but calves purchased by the 10 largest packers. The reverse was observed for smaller packers; i.e., auction markets were relatively more important than terminals during these two years. Still, these two sources accounted for only a small percentage of total procurement. Thus, it appears that direct purchasing of livestock is the most prevalent method used by most packers, especially large firms. Direct marketing, as defined by the USDA, includes purchasing from farmers off the farm, feedlots, or at country points from individual country dealers or organizations such as cooperatives (e.g., Interstate Producers Livestock Association, IPLA) or corporations (e.g., Hienold markets).

Firms purchase their livestock from within a relatively small radius of their facilities. Density of livestock production, operating costs, and competition determine how far beyond the traditional distance a firm would be willing to go to procure animals. For example, cattle are traditionally purchased from within a 100-mile radius of a plant, but some are purchased from as far away as 300 miles. Under some supply and seasonal conditions, cattle may be purchased from locations 500 to 1,000 miles from a plant for a smaller total cost (livestock and transportation) than from their normal procurement area (Ward, 1979). Similar practices are found in hog and sheep procurement; i.e., the normal procurement area is usually small—only a few counties or a state—but purchasing from farther distances is possible.

Packers-fed livestock, and possibly production under contract, can provide additional sources of livestock for slaughter. Multiple-plant packers also transfer carcasses and other products from plant to plant, according to their needs. These self-owned or controlled sources provide a firm with control over the quality and quantity of its raw materials.

Pricing Strategy.   Firms use all available internal and external market and cost information to determine pricing strategy. This strategy is kept flexible in order to allow for feedback from the market during the purchasing day, and adjustments are usually made. As a rule, packers purchase raw material several days in advance of delivery.

Pricing strategy for carcass procurement is relatively simple since it involves no more than gathering all internal and external information on demand, prices, and competitors' actions. A long-term relationship between traders often exists and the type of carcass (or other meat form) needed is known and traded on a formula basis (using one of the market news services). Most of these transactions can be completed over the telephone.

Livestock procurement involves more steps than carcass procurement, for it requires constant communication between the headquarters-level head buyer and field-level salaried employees (or order buyers). Livestock may be purchased on a live or carcass basis. Decisions at headquarters are made by the head buyer on volume, quality, and base price. To arrive at the right price to pay for livestock, the head buyer usually considers the firm's individual needs against market conditions, value of the carcass, value of by-products, price competition among packers, slaughtering/processing costs, transportation costs, plant capacity, and shrinkage (both live animal and cooler). Ward (1979) discussed the steps involved in the process of arriving at a daily pricing policy (or buy order) by beef packers.

COOPERATIVE MEAT PACKING

The meat-packing industry consists of firms owned primarily by corporate owners, partnerships, and individuals, including family corporations. As indicated earlier, several large meat firms have been purchased by conglomerates. An alternative to these traditional types of ownership or operation of packing plants is the "cooperatives." Interest in cooperatives in the red-meat industry originated from the concern of livestock producers about the future survival of family-size operations (USDA, 1978). Although the involvement of cooperatives in meat packing may be only one phase of a totally vertically integrated system (i.e., from breeding stock to retailing) this section will be concerned with that phase alone.

Producers engage in cooperative meat packing in order to maintain control and ownership of their livestock further down the line in the marketing channel and to take part of the additional profits from the slaughtering–processing functions. There are five approaches to cooperative meat packing (Holder and Hogeland, 1982), as follows:

1. *Custom Meat Packing:* The cooperative contracts with one or more plants to slaughter/process their members' livestock and pays a fee based on the number slaughtered. Although no investment capital is required under this alternative, operating capital is needed.
2. *Joint Venture:* This alternative is a partnership between the cooperative and an existing meat packer. The cooperative (e.g., several individuals and feedlots) provides livestock to the plant(s), and the packer is responsible for selling the meat. After expenses are paid, the net profits (or losses) are shared according to an agreed-upon plan.
3. *Leasing:* The cooperative leases an existing plant and takes full responsibility for management, operation, and marketing. Risk is borne entirely by the cooperative. Leasing requires less investment capital than building a new plant and allows the cooperative to acquire an ongoing operation.

4. *Purchasing an Existing Plant:* This alternative allows the cooperative more control over the management of the operation but requires more investment capital than the previous alternatives.
5. *Building a New Plant:* This alternative gives the cooperative flexibility and control over location, exact size, specifications, and manpower. One of the major advantages of a new plant is the opportunity to use the latest technology and equipment. The investment capital needed, however, would be the largest of any of these approaches. Management and labor must be hired, workers must be trained, and markets must be developed.

Although cooperative meat packing has been thought of and practiced for a long time, most attempts by cooperatives to enter into meat packing have not been successful. Fox (1957) reported that because of the lack of operating capital, insufficient livestock, and inexperienced management, all 17 attempts between 1914 and 1920 failed. Some more recent attempts, however, have succeeded, for example, Shen-Valley Meat packers, Farmland Industries (though its beef operation at Garden City, Kansas was forced to close in 1980 when IBP, Inc. and EXCEL built very large plants nearby), and Sterling Colorado Beef Company.[2]

Ward (1981) conducted a case study of the experience of the Sterling Colorado Beef Company with cooperative meat packing. The company was formed in 1966 by a few large cattle feeders but did not operate as a cooperative until 1976. Members committed a minimum volume to be delivered and received premiums if they delivered the desired type of animal. The study indicated that 94 percent of the members said they had benefited from the cooperative in two basic areas: having a guaranteed market outlet and receiving a fair price for their animals. Nevertheless, this plant was acquired by Cargill Inc. in the mid-1980s.

EXPENSES AND EARNINGS IN THE MEAT INDUSTRY

Expenses

The single most important cost item in the meat industry is the cost of livestock and other raw materials—about 80 percent of all expenses. Table 9.3 shows the American Meat Institute's (AMI) aggregate esti-

---

[2]Two other examples may be cited: (1) Land O'Lake (a cooperative) acquired Spencer Beef (a meat packing/processing operation with plants in several states) and within a relatively short time was acquired by Cargill Inc.; and (2) IBP, Inc. operates two large plants in agreement with the Northwest Feeders Cooperative, located in the Pacific Northwest Region, in what appears to be a successful, but controversial, joint venture, beginning in 1977.

Table 9.3. Estimated Costs and Percentage Distribution by Cost Category in the U.S. Meat Industry, 1970, 1975, 1980, and 1984.

Cost item	1970	1975	1980	1984
	(Cost in Mil. $)			
Livestock and raw materials	18,840	28,950	37,575	49,475
Operating costs				
Wages and salaries	2,310	2,830	3,761	3,495
Employee benefits	480	749	1,153	1,067
Interest	81	138	165	151
Depreciation	181	243	306	357
Rents	73	103	109	154
Taxes*	59	78	77	63
Supplies and containers	775	1,165	1,574	1,620
All other expenses	1,135	1,720	2,387	2,816
Total operating costs†	5,094	7,026	9,528	9,723
TOTAL COSTS	23,934	35,976	47,103	59,198
	(Percent distribution‡)			
Livestock and raw materials	78.7	80.4	79.8	83.5
Operating costs				
Wages and salaries	9.7	7.9	8.0	5.9
Employee benefits	2.0	2.1	2.4	1.8
Interest	0.3	0.4	0.3	0.3
Depreciation	0.8	0.7	0.7	0.6
Rents	0.3	0.3	0.2	0.1
Taxes*	0.2	0.2	0.2	0.1
Supplies and containers	3.2	3.2	3.3	2.7
All other expenses	4.8	4.8	5.0	4.8
Total operating costs†	21.3	19.6	20.2	16.5
TOTAL COSTS	100.0	100.0	100.0	100.0

Source: American Meat Institute (1985) and earlier issues.
*Other than Social Security and income taxes.
†These totals include the non meat operations of the firms classified as meat-packing companies.
‡These are percentages of total cost, including raw materials, accounted for by each cost item.

mated costs, by category, in 1970, 1975, 1980, and 1984, both in dollars and as a percentage of total costs.

Operating costs include all but the costs of raw materials. The largest components of the operating costs for an individual plant, as well as for the industry, are wages and salaries, and if employees' benefits are added, labor costs constitute almost 10 percent of total costs and account for about 50 percent of combined operating costs. It should be pointed out that these are aggregate industry figures. Individual firms may experience different cost structures. For example, in larger firms, labor costs may be proportionally less than in smaller firms, usually as a result of better management and more mechanization.

Interest expenses have maintained relatively the same proportion of costs despite the rise and fall in interest rates in recent years. The tax share of total costs has remained relatively small—about 0.2 percent of total cost—and this became even smaller in 1984. Depreciation has accounted for about 3.2 to 3.7 percent of operating costs and less than 0.8 percent of total costs. The relative importance of rents, supplies, and other expenses remained at about the same level during the years shown in Table 9.3.

Although the meat industry remains relatively labor-intensive, recent technological innovations and improvements in plant organization and management have resulted in improvements in efficiency and labor productivity. Williams (1979) reported that new developments in the beef industry (primarily large-scale, highly automated slaughter-process plants) have improved plant efficiency to the extent that an estimated cost reduction of 5 to 6 cents per pound in processing and distribution of beef was possible.

During the 1950s and most of the 1960s, labor union contracts and the relatively slow rate of improvement in technology made labor productivity (measured in terms of the Census-reported value-added per man hour) relatively small in the meat industry compared to other food-processing industries. The U.S. Department of Agriculture, however, reported an increase of 35 percent in labor productivity in the meat industry between 1967 and 1979 (USDA, 1981). In comparison, the improvement over the same period was 53 percent in the dairy industry and 32 percent for the entire food industry.

Because of the magnitude of labor costs relative to other costs, an increase in labor productivity would result in greater overall efficiency and savings than in other cost items. Maximum labor efficiency, however, could be obtained only if the design of the plant, wage rates, and level of technological advances were appropriate.

Earnings

Earnings and financial ratios in the meat industry have been reported by the AMI since 1947. The U.S. Department of Agriculture reported similar information from 1926 to 1946. These data are based on confidential information from major firms and are supplemented by information from government and private sources. Table 9.4 presents sales, earnings, and financial ratios in the meat industry during selected years from 1950 to 1984.

Table 9.4. Earnings and Financial Ratios of the U.S. Meat Packing Industry in Selected Years, 1950–1984.

Year	Total sales (Mil. $)	Earnings before income taxes (Mil. $)	Income taxes (Mil. $)	Net earnings (Mil. $)	Net Earnings as Percent of		
					Sales (%)	Total assets (%)	Net worth (%)
1950	10,050	NA	NA	89	0.89	5.10	7.27
1955	11,075	NA	NA	105	0.95	5.10	7.78
1960	13,225	212	102	110	0.83	4.31	6.67
1965	17,125	229	100	129	0.83	4.44	6.93
1970	24,400	466	222	244	1.00	5.61	9.96
1975	36,650	674	294	380	1.00	5.15	10.63
1980	47,925	822	342	480	1.00	6.21	12.15
1981	48,525	630	287	343	0.70	5.23	9.30
1982	49,500	772	344	428	0.90	5.70	11.70
1983	48,50	720	325	395	0.80	5.01	9.90
1984	49,475	727	308	419	0.80	5.37	10.30

Sources: American Meat Institute (1985) and earlier issues.

Total sales, estimated at $10.0 billion in 1950, were a little under $48 billion in 1980 and $49.5 billion in 1984. Net earnings rose from $89 million in 1950 to $244 million in 1970, to $480 million in 1980, but fell to $419.0 million in 1984. These figures are for the entire industry, i.e., all meat packers and meat processors.

Earning ratios in the meat industry (as shown in Table 9.4) have historically been low compared to other industries. Net earnings to sales, which averaged less than 1 percent in the 1950s and 1960s, were 1.00 percent in 1975, 1 percent in 1980, and 0.80 percent in 1984. This low ratio is a direct reflection of the high-volume nature of the meat industry, a fact evidenced by the high sales-to-asset ratios (also reported by the AMI) that measure the turnover rate. This ratio has historically stood at more than 5 compared to ratios of less than 2 in most other industries. Earnings-to-asset ratios ranged from 4.31 in 1960 to 6.21 in 1980, whereas earnings to net worth averaged 6.67 in 1960 and 12.15 in 1980 and were estimated at 10.30 percent in 1984 (Table 9.4).

These ratios represent averages for the entire industry. Substantial variation exists, however, among firms and size groups. Data in Table 9.5 show various financial ratios calculated by the AMI from a survey of 148 companies (100 meat packers and 48 meat processors), which accounted for 57 percent of the commercial cattle slaughter and 72 percent of the commercial hog slaughter in the U.S. during 1982. The table presents the ratios according to firm size and type and also shows

Table 9.5. Earning Ratios in the Meat Industry by Company Classification, the Entire Industry, and Other Industries in the United States in 1984.

Company classification/industry	Net earnings to Sale (%)	Net earnings to assets (%)	Net earnings to net worth (%)	Sales to total assets (%)
Meat packing*				
14 national packers	0.67	3.99	8.05	5.93
37 regional packers	1.17	8.16	15.00	7.07
49 local packers	1.32	6.86	12.13	5.21
AVERAGE 100 PACKERS	0.78	4.74	9.38	6.09
Meat processing				
48 firms	2.97	8.40	12.81	2.82
Meat industry†	0.85	5.37	10.33	6.34
Durable goods	4.41	5.68	12.02	1.29
Nondurable goods	4.79	5.92	12.33	1.24
Total manufacturing	4.61	5.81	12.18	1.26

Source: American Meat Institute (1985).
*National Packers include companies with annual sales of $500 million or more; regional packers include companies with annual sales of $50 million to $500 million; local packers sell less than $50 million annually. Sales-to-assets ratio for regional packers is based on 36 firms.
†Meat-packing industry includes meat packers and meat processors.

the ratios in durable and nondurable industries as well as total manufacturing industries in 1982. Participating meat processors experienced higher ratios in each category compared to meat packers (except sales-to-total-assets and earnings-to-net-worth for regional packers; see Table 9.5). Average net-earnings-to-assets and net-earnings-to-net-worth of processors were higher than the meat industry average, and also higher than the figures for the durable and nondurable industries. For example, in 1984, the average net-earnings-to-net-worth ratio was 9.38 for packers in the sample; 12.81 for processors; 10.33 for the entire meat industry; 12.02 for durable goods; 12.33 for nondurable goods; and 12.18 for total manufacturing.

An earlier study (National Commission on Foods 1966) showed a wide range of financial ratios from year to year, beginning in 1947, and between the first and second largest firms. With few exceptions, earning ratios for the four firms ranking 5 to 8 were higher than for those ranking 1 to 4, probably because of the large sales volume and total assets of the larger firms. Variations within these size groups also exist, and the ratios may have been more favorable for the top firms than the average group ratios indicate.

The low rate of earnings-to-sales may be explained by the high turnover, e.g., sales-to-asset ratios as shown in Table 9.5. The relatively low ratios of earnings-to-assets and earnings-to-net-worth, however, may be the result of problems within the meat industry itself. Its excess capacity, which has existed for many years and is likely to continue, tends to increase both unit and total operating costs and thus reduces net earnings.[3] One of the major factors for this excess capacity is the cyclical nature of livestock supplies. An excess capacity may be necessary in order to handle peak supplies, but many plants remain underutilized in periods of short supplies. This factor, coupled with constant competition for limited livestock, leads to increased product and operating costs and hence inadequately low financial ratios.[4]

A higher rate of technological advancement, as indicated by the replacement of old plants by new, more specialized, efficient ones in recent years, suggests that operational efficiency will cotninue to be enhanced. Recent improvement in the meat industry's relative financial ratios among other industries may hold.

PROBLEMS OF THE MEAT INDUSTRY

Individual firms may experience the various problems that face the meat industry and attempt to solve them in different ways. The major problems fall into the following general categories: (1) pricing, (2) labor wage differentials, (3) economic conditions, (4) procurement of raw materials, (5) product development, (6) government intervention, and (7) image.

Pricing Problems

Meat pricing methods at the wholesale level are discussed in detail in Chap. 10. Problems associated with formula pricing became the focus of public and industry concern in recent years as a result of widespread

---

[3]For example, Baker (1976) reported an average of 80-percent capacity utilization for specialized cattle slaughter between 1970 and 1973. Williams (1979) indicated some serious excess steer and heifer slaughter capacity in many areas. Haverkamp (1981) estimated that average utilization of hog slaughter capacity was 80 percent during 1971–81, ranging from 64 percent in 1975 to 94 percent in 1980. Simpson (1980) reported that, in a survey of meat packers in the Southwest, participants indicated that only 49 percent of their cattle and 56 percent of their hog slaughter capacity were utilized during 1977.
[4]Some economists, and many in the meat industry, suggest that these relatively low ratios are indicative of a highly competitive industry compared to other food and nonfood industries. Such judgments are difficult to evaluate without taking the industry's structure (e.g., concentration) into consideration.

use of this method. Formula pricing, also known as market basis pricing, necessitates the use of negotiated published prices as a base. A large part of wholesale meat transactions are on a market basis, though such transactions are not involved in price determination. Two private reporting services, "The Yellow Sheet" and "The Meat Sheet," and the public "USDA Market News" service report only a small fraction of the "negotiated" prices. Thus, it appears that a sizable portion of all meat transactions are based on a thinly reported market that may or may not reflect the true forces of supply and demand. Accurate, timely, and sufficient price and market information is necessary not only in establishing meat prices but also in determining livestock prices, and thus is involved in guiding production. The lack of this type of information and potential abuses of current reporting services are major concerns for the industry.

Labor Wage Differentials

Although labor costs for the entire industry have increased along with inflation, the differentiated costs among packers that perform the same services have created a serious adjustment problem. Many large old-line firms have been using the Food and Commercial Workers Union's master contract (and that of its predecessor, the Amalgamated Meat Cutters and Butcher Workmen). These master agreements usually committed the firms to pay the same wages and benefits at all locations where the firms operated. On the other hand, several new firms (e.g., IBP, Inc.) have since either obtained preferential wage agreements or operated with nonunion labor. Thus, firms with unfavorable master agreements found it difficult to compete with nonmaster firms with lower labor costs. The former either closed some plants, left the business entirely, or attempted to renegotiate labor contracts.

Faced with the closing of many plants and high unemployment during the early 1980s, most unions were willing to accept reductions in wages and fringe benefits and forego previously agreed-upon wage increases in return for job security with several old-line and new firms. Although several firms have closed some of their plants because of high labor costs, many have reopened these plants after negotiating their labor agreement. Some plants were reopened by the same firm, or by other firms, using nonunion, lower-cost labor. The problem of varying labor costs at different plants in a relatively labor-intensive industry is not easy to solve. Cooperation and understanding between labor union and firm management are needed to overcome this situation.

Economic Conditions

Unfavorable economic conditions (in addition to labor cost differentials) cause many problems to firms in all size categories, especially old-line and small ones (which are generally inefficient). Adverse economic conditions such as low economic growth; decline in consumers' real income, high interest rates, sizable operating capital requirements, and escalating energy costs, present great problems to individual firms and the industry as a whole. National and regional concentration of new and efficient plants may also present economic problems to smaller or inefficient firms.

Procurement of New Materials

Problems arising from the availability and location of livestock and/or carcasses are not only frequent but may lead to possible inefficiency in the market system. Seasonal and cyclical fluctuations in the number of livestock may require firms to operate plants at less than optimal utilization of capacity.

Shift in the location of livestock feeding may also present a supply problem in areas where the number of livestock has been reduced. For example, as the cattle-feeding industry moved westward, fewer cattle became available in the eastern part of the Corn Belt, and many packing plants were closed.

The requirement for prompt cash settlement for livestock and meat purchases may present cash flow problems to many firms. Extreme weather conditions and the operational efficiency of the livestock and meat-market system may also cause procurement problems.

Product Development and Technology

Problems in this area include those brought about by quality control, new product development, new slaughtering and processing methods, utilization of by-products, and estimation of consumer behavior and demand.

Government Intervention

This category involves problems created by, or associated with, government regulations. The meat industry must abide by local, state, and Federal regulations and laws. Problems span from sanitation concerns and safety at the plants, to the proper ingredients and composition of a product, to grading and standardization, to almost every aspect of procurement, and to production and marketing.

Image Problems

The meat industry faces some image or status problems related to its marketing methods, its integrity, and the quality and health aspects of its products. The distrust that appears to exist between packers and retailers on one hand and producers on the other has been one of the factors causing this image problem. Publicity about some recent court cases has been damaging. Controversy over the use of nitrite and growth hormones, the alleged association of animal fat with heart and other health concerns, animal welfare, vegetarian movements, and proper labeling of mechanically separated meat have all added to image problems and, to some degree, will continue to be problems the meat industry must deal with.

OUTLOOK FOR THE FUTURE

Many forces that have affected the meat industry in the past—some external and some internal—are likely to affect its future. Major external forces are (1) the consumer demand for meat, processed meat, and other products of the meat industry; (2) technological development; and (3) institutional factors. The most important internal forces are (1) industry structure, including competition and concentration; (2) changes at the retail and wholesale levels; (3) changes in procurement methods and type of raw materials required; and (4) changes in livestock production. This section will provide a brief look at future directions these forces may take.

External Forces

Demand Factors. Rising real income and increasing population in the past have increased both the per-capita and total meat consumption in the U.S. Consumption of meat in the future will be determined by the same factors as in the past, i.e. those related to income, population growth, and taste and preferences, as well as new factors such as animal welfare and vegetarian movements. There are some indications that *change* in total red-meat consumption will be greater than *change* in per-capita consumption, which might show a small or a modest increase, if at all. The availability of large quantities of poultry, fish, and meat substitutes at relatively attractive prices may further keep any future rate of growth in both per-capita and total red-meat consumption relatively low. If taste and preferences, influenced by health and economic factors, shift away from red meat toward other products, both per-capita and total red-meat consumption may decline. At present, however, there is no indication that such a shift will take place on a large scale.

Following World War II, demand for beef increased substantially while demand for veal and lamb declined and demand for pork remained relatively constant. Most noticeable was the increased demand for grain-fed beef. More recently, such factors as increased eating away from home and consumer discrimination against beef with a high fat content could indicate a major shift in demand towards ungraded, leaner beef. Some individuals and groups in the livestock industry are promoting bull meat, which contains less fat. The relatively constant demand for pork has been heavily associated with urbanization and hence the emergence of diet-and-health-minded consumers, who have encouraged the production of leaner pork.

Thus, it appears that in spite of the vegetarian and other similar movements, consumer taste and preferences are likely to in the near future change toward a different type of red meat (e.g., leaner) rather than away from it altogether. Consumer nutrition knowledge, coupled with changes in tastes and life style, will probably change the output mix of the meat industry, especially beef, in the 1980s and 1990s, more towards portion-control, lean, and partially-cooked-at-the-plant cuts. The phenomenal expansion in the food service industry in recent years is likely to continue. More meat will be consumed away from home, and meat packers/processors must be ready to accommodate the supply type, and quality required by this market.

The export market for meat, meat products, and by-products such as tallow and hides should be considered an important outlet for the industry's output. Potential markets, especially those with rapid economic growth rates, should be identified, and an industry-wide promotional program should be carried out, probably with the support and cooperation of the Federal government. To summarize, the meat packing and processing industry will probably expand, increase its level of capacity utilization, and make the adjustments needed to accommodate any future larger, and possibly different, demand for fresh and processed meat in both domestic and international markets.

Technological Development. Changes in technology have occurred in both slaughtering and processing. From early innovations in transportation and refrigeration to recent developments in slaughtering methods and the introduction of the concept of "boxed meat," the meat industry has undergone continual changes. Although it is difficult to predict the rate of technological development in the future, some current developments will probably continue, and, as a result of the continuous search for better methods, new technologies will evolve.

It is likely that the growth of the boxed beef industry will continue, with portion control items and partially cooked cuts becoming more important. Sectioned and formed meats are another potential development area. New and less costly ways to package meats will be developed. Techniques for curing and preserving meats, including extending the shelf life of fresh meat with lower time and energy costs, will be sought and/or perfected. Current methods of mechanically deboning (or separating) meat will be improved, and these meats will be used by meat processors in a manner acceptable to consumers.

Other innovations that will become more important include electrical stimulation; delayed chilling; blade tenderization; cooler aging; enzyme tenderization; tumbling; and hot boning. The major purpose of these technologies is to improve in an economical way the tenderness, flavor, juiciness, and color of meat, particularly beef. Several of these techniques are most effective in transforming forage-fed, or other lesser quality, beef into more desirable meat. Such technological developments will affect not only the productivity but also the structure and future of both the livestock feeding and meat industries.

Institutional Factors.   For many years the meat industry has been subjected to various forms of government regulations and supervision that proved necessary to protect the health and welfare of the public (and also of the animals) and to preserve and promote the competitiveness of the market. The extent and nature of such institutional actions will continue to affect the structure and direction of the meat industry in the future.

One law which, if passed, would have a substantial effect on market structure is the one introduced in the U.S. Congress to limit the size, market share, and retail activities of meat packers. Another possible law that could affect pricing efficiency in the meat industry is one requiring mandatory reporting of wholesale prices.

Any change in the official Federal grading system, meat inspection, pollution control, import and export laws, Packers and Stockyards Administration regulations, and other aspects of government supervision, regulation, or services will affect the opreational and pricing efficiency as well as the structure of the meat industry. In addition, the relationships between labor unions and meat packers, processors, and retailers (an outside factor) will also have an impact on the location, activities, and survival of many firms in the industry.

Internal Forces

Industry Structure. Economies in construction and transportation will continue to encourage the location of slaughtering plants close to livestock supply and processing plants near population centers. Thus, the decentralization that has existed for many years will likely continue. In terms of volume, federally inspected plants will continue to dominate the industry. Legislation to revise inspection, with procedures giving certain establishments more responsibilities, will probably continue to be promoted by some in both government and industry.

The number of large, efficient plants is likely to increase, whereas smaller, more inefficient firms may find it more difficult to compete and thus may either leave the industry or merge with, and be modernized by, larger firms or conglomerates. Firms will become more specialized vertically and horizontally, and both backward and forward integration will continue. Packers and suppliers of livestock will increase their informal coordination, but it is doubtful that major formal integration will occur as in the poultry industry.

Other specific structural changes will include continuing growth of the boxed-beef industry, which will be more concentrated, with larger plants dominating the slaughtering/fabrication process; the result will be relatively fewer, small, slaughter-only operations. This development, if it occurs, will in turn limit the supply of carcasses to firms engaged in breaking and fabrication, possibly forcing some of them out of business. Vacuum-packed pork and lamb operations will become more important. The recent abolition of the 1920 Consent Decree may encourage some packers to engage in activities formerly prohibited.

The expected increase in the number of large plants as a result of the economy of scale, as well as increased meat fabrication at the slaughter plant, suggests that large firms with sufficient internal and external capital and the ability to use advertising and other means to differentiate their products will continue to have a competitive edge over smaller firms. Such barriers would exclude new firms from entering into competition and further increase concentration, even as inefficient existing firms make their exit. Greater concentration may not be desirable, and legislation may be required to safeguard producer and public interests by preserving competition.

Changes at the Wholesale and Retail Levels. Significant changes have occurred at the wholesale and retail levels since World War II. The decline in the importance of packers' branch houses and the increase in direct shipping to retail outlets or central cutting and warehouse facilities will continue. These changes have been a direct result of improvements in transportation, communication, and meat preservation, all of them forces that will be major factors in future development, along with the structural changes and technological developments in the meat and meat distribution industries.

Large chain stores will continue to purchase a sizable volume of their meats directly from plants or packers' sales offices, i.e., packers that perform the wholesale function. Boxed meat received at stores or central warehouse facilities will constitute a greater portion of the total meat procured, whereas a smaller volume will be received in carcass form.

Direct purchase from the source of supply eliminates the middleman and may cut marketing costs to both packers and retailers. Many large chains, the majority of smaller food stores, and some packers, however, will continue to use the services of intermediary, i.e., independent wholesalers. Thus, it appears that independent wholesalers, who perform functions between meat firms and retailers; service the HRI trade; and facilitate marketing of exports, will continue to play an important role in meat distribution.

Growth in the number and importance of commercial food service outlets has changed the structure of meat retailing in the past 20 years. Packers and wholesalers will have to provide necessary procurement functions to meet demand specifications and volume both for this sector and for institutions.

Changes in Procurement of Raw Materials. The decline in importance of organized livestock markets—e.g., terminals and some auctions—will persist, whereas direct procurement methods will remain dominant. Pressure on some existing livestock markets resulting from small volume and idle facilities will force them out of business and further increase the relative importance of direct methods.

Cooperatives may play a larger role in the future as a source of slaughter livestock in a coordinated system with independent packers or through the ownership, or control, of packing plants.

Another potential source of livestock supplies is through individuals or organizations contracting with packers for future delivery, with the emphasis on carcass-basis rather than live-basis purchasing. This aspect will give packers more control over the volume, kind, timing, and quality of livestock produced. Packer feeding—i.e. backward integration—would also continue to provide livestock supplies, and any changes in the Packers and Stockyards Administration regulation of packers' involvement in livestock feeding would affect the volume procured from owned-controlled operations.

Large packers/processors will continue to purchase carcasses from other packers for boxed-meat production. The majority of beef and pork firms will obtain these carcasses from their own slaughtering units, but some purchasing from slaughter-only operations will probably continue, though on a smaller scale.

The potential advantages of electronic marketing as an alternative trading mechanism seem to be great. The meat industry will probably recognize the advantages of using such systems in both raw-material procurement and product marketing.

Changes in Livestock Production. Vertical coordination in the meat industry would reduce, to some extent, packers' supply-and-demand adjustment problems. Past changes in technology and in the structure of the agricultural sector have had a substantial impact on the structure of the meat industry. Future changes in these areas, as well as changes in production in response to changes at the consumer level (e.g., leaner animals), government taxes, and other policies, will also have important impacts on the meat industry.

The movement toward fewer and larger capital-intensive livestock production units is likely to continue, but most livestock will still be produced by small producers during the 1980s and into the 1990s. Many of the producers will be involved in some formal or informal arrangements in order to improve their bargaining positions, including the possibility of moving into meat packing and processing. The meat industry must adjust in order to face new situations and problems of dealing with larger individual production units or types of producers' organizations.

REFERENCES

American Meat Institute. 1985. Annual Financial Review of the Meat Packing Industry 1984. AMI, Washington, D.C.

American Meat Institute. Selected Years. Financial Facts About the Meat Packing Industry. AMI, Washington, D.C.

Baker, A. J. 1976. Federally inspected livestock slaughter by size and type of slaughter. USDA, ERS Stat. Bull. 549.

Burst, R. L., and Kuehn, J. P. 1979. The feasibility of establishing low volume beef slaughtering-processing plants in West Virginia. West Virginia Univ. Bull. 666.

Cothern, J. H.; Peard, R. M.; and Weeks, J. L. 1978A. Economies of scale in beef processing and portion control operations, Northern California; 1976. Div. of Agr. Sciences. University of California Leaflet 21027.

Cothern, J. H.; Peard, R. M.,; and Weeks, J. L. 1978B. Economies of scale in beef slaughtering, Northern California: 1976. Div. of Agr. Sciences. University of California Leaflet 21040.

Farris, D. E., and Mathia, G. A. 1981. Economics and operations of pork slaughter plants and markets for Texas hogs. Dept. of Agr. Econ., Texas A&M University, Departmental Information Report No. 81-3.

Fox, R. L. 1957. Farmers' meat packing enterprises in the United States. USDA Farmers Coop. Serv. Gen. Report No. 29.

Hammons, D. R. 1966. Hog Slaughtering and dressing systems. USDA, AMS, Marketing Research Report No. 755.

Hammons, D. R., and Miller, J. E. 1961. Improving methods and facilities for cattle slaughtering plants in the Southwest. USDA, AMS, Marketing Research Report No. 436.

Haverkamp, L. J. 1981. What can farmers and market agencies do to ensure slaughter plants availability. Paper presented at the Livestock Marketing Conference, American Farm Bureau Federation, Park Ridge, Ill.

Holder, D. L., and Hogeland, J. A. 1982. Cooperative lamb slaughtering in the Northeast. USDA, ACS, Research Report No. 14.

Kropf, D., and Breidenstein, B. 1975. Beef operations in the meat industry. The American Meat Institute.

Romans, J. R., and Ziegler, P. T. 1977. *The Meat We Eat.* 11th ed. Danville, Ill.: The Interstate Printers & Publishers, Inc.

Sarhan, M. E. 1977. Economic analysis of livestock production, processing and marketing systems for the Navajo Indian Irrigation Project, Part II: Production and financial analyses. Winrock International Center Report, Arkansas.

Sarhan, M. E., and Albanas, W. 1985. U.S. meat industry: Components, wholesale pricing and market reporting. Univ. of Illinois, Agr. Exp. Sta., AERR Report No. 198.

Simpson, J. R., and Sullivan, G. M. 1980. Report to Regional Livestock Marketing Committee S-116 on survey of meat packing plants in the Southeastern United States. Paper presented at the S-116 Technical Committee Meeting, Atlanta.

USDA. 1981. Development in farm to retail price spreads for food products in 1980. ERS, Agr. Econ. Report No. 465.

USDA. 1986. Packers and stockyards resume. P&S Administration Statistical Report No. 86-1 and earlier issues. Washington, D. C.

USDA. 1978. The future role of cooperatives in the red meats industry. Marketing Research Report 1089.

Ward, C. E. 1979. Slaughter-cattle pricing and procurement practices of meatpackers. USDA, ESS, Agr. Info. Bull. No. 432.

Ward, C. E. 1981. Cooperative marketing: Lessons learned from Sterling Colorado Beef Company. USDA, ACS, Research Report No 6.

Williams, W. F. 1979. The changing structure of the beef packing industry. Study prepared for the Committee on Small Business, U.S. House of Representatives. *In* Small business problems in the marketing of meat and other commodities (Part 4—Changing structure of the beef packing industry). U.S. Government Printing Office.

10

Meat Marketing—Wholesale

Previous chapters have examined the routes and means by which live animals are moved to the point of slaughter, but meat in the packing plant must reach an ultimate user to attain its full economic value. Between the packing house and the consumer lies a vast and complex system of market channels. Three things complicate this system: (1) the quantities involved are enormous, (2) the distances of movement are great, and (3) the products have a relatively high degree of perishability.

U. S. consumers in 1984 were provided 18.7 billion kilograms (41.26 billion pounds) of red meat (including net import/exports)—an average of approximately 76.8 kilograms (169.4 pounds) for every man, woman, and child in the country. The bulk of this meat, however, is not produced in close proximity to areas of heavy population. Consumers are concentrated on the East Coast, around the Great Lakes, on the West Coast, and more recently in the so-called Sun Belt. Meat production is concentrated in the Corn Belt and the Central and Southern Plains states.

Under present economic conditions and with the present state of technology, fresh meat is not stored for any appreciable length of time but moved rapidly through market channels into the hands of consumers. Although great strides have been made in its preservation (refrigeration revolutionized the distribution and merchandizing of meat), refrigerated meat must nevertheless be moved into consumption in a matter of days. Freezing, freeze drying, drying, and various methods of curing increase its storability in varying degrees. For certain cuts of pork (hams, bellies, and shoulders), freezing and curing are used extensively—partly to take advantage of seasonal price trends. Vacuum-bagged, boxed beef can be held three to four weeks, but in terms of total meat production, and particularly in the case of beef and lamb, storage is not a major factor. Market channels move the relatively perishable product from packers, to processors, to retailers and food service outlets. Significant changes have occurred, and are still occurring, in this system.

OVERVIEW AND EVOLUTION OF THE PRESENT WHOLESALE MEAT SYSTEM

The wholesale meat trade as described in this chapter has evolved from the simple and limited system of early colonial days into the advanced, complex, but efficient system of today. Many factors and forces—social, structural, and technological—have shaped the system over the years.

As discussed in earlier chapters, most of the livestock slaughtering, processing, and selling during early colonial days was done by farmers. Most of the products were consumed by farm families, and any marketable surplus was sold and consumed locally. During the era of limited trade with the British in the West Indies (mid 1600s), some local merchants evolved and traded locally, performing both wholesale and retail functions. Meat packing was seasonal and limited to the late fall and winter months with some meat preserved for summer consumption.

During the second half of the 1800s, the introduction of ice packing and refrigeration transformed the industry to a year-round business and opened distant domestic and export markets. A more organized and clearly defined meat-distribution system was a necessity. The need for enormous purchases by the government during the Civil War further helped shape the wholesale distribution system. Some wholesalers were involved in both wholesaling and retailing, but most sold only to retailers and institutions, which, in turn, sold to consumers.

Local butchers received meat from large national packers through the branch houses of the latter (which were made possible by the introduction of refrigeration and improvement in transportation and communications) or from small local meat-packing establishments. Buyers usually inspected both fresh and processed meats before purchasing, and the price was discovered in face-to-face negotiations. The wholesale meat trade remained much the same until World War I, at which time the class of wholesalers known as merchant, or independent, wholesalers emerged. By this time the importance of retailing by the slaughterers had dropped, and the independent wholesalers constituted an important linkage between packers and retail establishments, providing both marketing and processing services. National packers continued to market their products through branch houses, either direct from the plant or by railroad routes, which were replaced in the 1940s by truck routes.

As the commercial (hotels and restaurants) and noncommercial (institutions) trade (often referred to collectively as the food service industry) grew and meat processors evolved as a separate subsector of the meat industry, the expansion and/or need for other types of whole-salers emerged. The classes of independent wholesalers known as breakers, boners, purveyors, brokers, and jobbers became familiar and provided important services to both suppliers and retailers. Agent wholesalers such as brokers and commission firms also increased their role from the 1930s through the 1950s, whereas packer branches declined in number and their sales dropped.

One of the most important factors affecting the wholesale trade since World War II was the change in the structure and methods of the food retail business, including meat. Few food-retailing firms continued slaughtering operations, but many became involved in wholesale functions as a part of integrated operations. For example, they moved into buying directly from packers and processors for delivery to their stores or warehouses. Many chains, especially large ones, operated central cutting and/or processing facilities. These developments were associated with the decline in the relative importance of packer branch houses and the increase in the number and importance of independent wholesalers. Technological improvements in processing and packaging at the plant or at the retailer's warehouse increased at the same time that the concept of supermarkets and self-service showed substantial growth, and a whole new type of retailing–wholesaling relationship evolved.

By the middle 1950s and through the 1970s the meat industry and wholesale distribution entered a new era. Small butcher shops—those ordinarily purchasing less than one carload of meat at one time—almost disappeared and were replaced by meat departments in chain stores and supermarkets that purchased in large volumes. Grading, brand names, and improvement in communication technology changed the method of wholesaling from a personal, relatively costly, business to selling by description by phone, thus reinforcing the national nature of the meat market. The carload as a unit of trade and the role of merchant wholesalers became even more important.

During the 1970s and into the 1980s many packers became involved in further processing (i.e., the vertically integrated kind), and the concept of vacuum-packed meat products became firmly established. Retailers still have central cutting facilities, but a large proportion of meat, including beef, is shipped in boxed form directly from the plant to retailers' stores or warehouses in primal, subprimal, or portion-control cuts. This practice suggests that a shift away from relying on independent wholesalers (e.g. breakers and boners) has occurred.

Baker and Duewer (1983) examined meat movement in six southern metro areas and found that more meat is now being sold directly from packers to final outlets. Wholesalers, otherwise decreasing in number, were found to be adjusting to the change in the distribution system by expanding their product lines as well as their normal business zone. The percentages of meat moving through various channels in the six southern metro areas were as follows:

Type	Beef (%)	Pork (%)
Packers sales offices	26	50
Purveyors	22	7
Processors	14	10
Other wholesalers	32	33

New developments in computer technology have generated interest in the potentials of electronic-communication technology in meat pricing and trading. Adoption of such trading mechanisms by the meat industry at the wholesale level will have a far-reaching impact on the structure and future of the entire livestock and meat sector.

Figure 10.1 is a generalized diagram of the major channels of meat distribution. A cell is shown for by-products simply to call attention to the fact that the output of a packing plant consists of more than meat. The actual distribution of meat is also considerably more com-

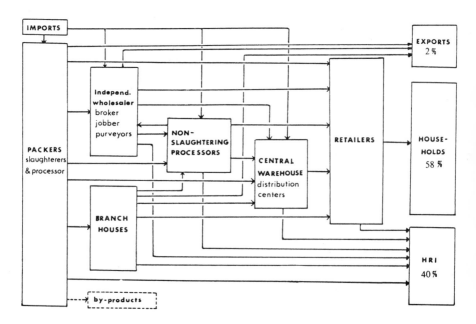

Fig. 10.1.   Meat marketing channels.

plex than that indicated. For example, the cell labeled "Independent wholesalers" does not do justice to the many types of wholesalers nor to the functions they perform. Involved here are the handling of fresh, cured, and processed meat; the cutting of caracasses into primal, sub-primal, and portion-control cuts; boning; buying outright versus simply acting as agent; peddling; etc. Some retail establishments (and some restaurant chains) also operate slaughtering and processing facilities, and some packers also operate retail establishments. Trade among packers and among processors may go direct or through agents. Sometimes more than one agent may handle a given lot of meat (either physically or by title) as it is transferred from one point in the distribution system to another.

In general, the transfer of title—i.e., the buying and selling—can be classified as either a wholesale or retail operation. To a large extent, the cuts of meat involved in these transfers can also be classified as wholesale or retail, but this distinction is gradually losing the universality it once had. Where, at one time, all of the cutting into retail cuts was done in the retail store, a strong trend is underway to move that function to earlier points in market channels. A major factor preventing its movement all the way back to the packer and processor level is lack of an acceptable method of preservation of the retail cut.

WHOLESALING DEFINED

Wholesaling is a vital linkage in the marketing process but difficult to define in precise terms. The difficulty is due to the wide variation in operating procedures and functions performed by wholesale firms or individual wholesalers. The term "wholesaling" as used here refers to the activities of firms or individuals involved in the functions performed between meat packers, processors, retailers, other merchants, institutions, and export markets, with very limited or no contact with ultimate consumers. Thus, wholesalers may be any entity performing one or more of such functions. Depending on their relative position in the market chain, wholesalers may perform functions for those preceding or following them. The definition given here does not exclude performing wholesale functions as a part of an integrated operation, e.g. a packer doing his own wholesaling.

Why the Need for Meat Wholesalers?

Wholesalers are needed to link the meat-production segment and the retail, institutional, and export markets. Although direct marketing from packers and processors to ultimate users is possible, there are many reasons that limit this type of trade. For one thing, meat production is decentralized and slaughtering is located near livestock supplies whereas the human population is concentrated elsewhere—on the East and West Coasts, the Great Lakes, and the Sun Belt States. Meat and meat products must therefore be moved from surplus to deficit areas. Moreover, because of the perishability of the products and the limited cooler and holding capacity at the plants, this movement must be carried out in a timely, systematic, and orderly manner. Wholesaling offers market services that are often not available to small or independent packers. For example, since smaller packers often have problems making contact with purchasers in distant markets, there is a real need for independent (or merchant) wholesalers, brokers, and jobbers to perform the necessary functions. Wholesaling may also be needed because some packers may not permit anyone other than wholesalers to purchase products from them, and these in turn will sell to retailers or other outlets.

Specific Functions Performed by Wholesalers

Wholesalers perform all the functions necessary to move meat and meat products from packers (point of slaughter) and processors to retail outlets, to HRI outlets, and for export. These functions must be performed by one or more members of the system, i.e., an independent wholesaler, packer, processor, or agent.

The following are possible functions of a wholesaler:

1. Own and transfer title to meat and meat products without performing any manufacturing functions
2. Own and transfer title to meat after performing one or more manufacturing functions such as breaking and boning
3. Deliver meat, utilizing owned or hired transportation means
4. Provide market and/or technical information to clients
5. Act as agent, for a fee, to facilitate buying and selling without taking title or possession of the product
6. Extend credit to clients, i.e. financing functions
7. Participate in promotion programs

What is the Size of the Wholesale Trade?

This question is hard to answer precisely because of the lack of detailed data, the presence of retrading, and because of the multiplicity of functions performed by different types of wholesalers. An indication of the size of the wholesale sector is found, however, in the possible transactions involved.

The 1984 U. S. commercial red-meat production of more than 17.68 billion kilograms (39.98 billion lb) included 10.62 billion kilograms of beef (60.0 percent); 6.68 billion kilograms of pork, excluding lard (37.8 percent); 217 million kilograms of veal (1.2 percent); and 169 million kilograms of lamb and mutton (1.0 percent). These figures may be translated into an annual (or daily) number of possible carloads of meat. Assuming 18,144 kilograms (40,000 lb) per truck and 252 working days per year, the above quantities would be equivalent to 975,000 carloads annually, divided as follows: 585,300 carloads of beef (2,322 carloads daily); 368,200 carloads of pork (1,460 carloads daily); 12,000 carloads of veal (47 carloads daily); and 9,500 carloads of lamb and mutton (37 carloads daily).

These figures may overestimate the actual number of carloads of meat traded because many packing plants are involved in further processing. Such operations reduce the total weight shipped, the reduction depending on the species and type of operations performed.

Products of all kinds must be moved through the market system to the ultimate user. In addition to fresh/frozen and processed meats, a substantial volume of variety meats and edible and inedible byproducts are traded, thus adding to the total volume. Also, some of the fresh meat, meat products, and byproducts are retraded once or more among packers and other wholesalers before reaching their final destination, transactions that also add, of course, to the volume that must be moved. Thus, the number of carloads shown here is not unrealistic.

STRUCTURAL CHARACTERISTICS OF THE WHOLESALE TRADE

Wholesale Traded Products

Wholesale traded products include processed meats[1] as well as fresh meat. For a number of years the National Livestock and Meat Board has prepared charts of wholesale (and retail) cuts of beef (Fig. 10.2), veal (Fig. 10.3), pork (Fig. 10.4), and lamb (Fig. 10.5) that generally

---

[1]*Processed meat* includes such items as bologna, luncheon meats, cured meat, smoked meat, and ground and comminuted meats, even though the later may be in the fresh state. The term *sausage* carries a double meaning. It is used to indicate fresh ground pork but also is used as a general term to include all prepared meats of the bologna luncheon-meat types, cured and smoked sausage, etc. The word *processing,* when used in the term *central processing unit,* also has another meaning from that which might be

WHOLESALE CUTS OF BEEF AND THEIR BONE STRUCTURE

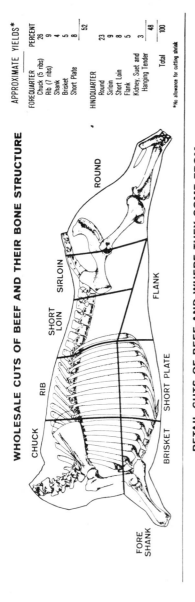

APPROXIMATE	YIELDS*
FOREQUARTER	**PERCENT**
Chuck (5 ribs)	26
Rib (7 ribs)	9
Shank	4
Brisket	5
Short Plate	8
	52
HINDQUARTER	
Round	23
Sirloin	9
Short Loin	8
Flank	5
Kidney, Suet and Hanging Tender	3
	48
Total	100

*No allowance for cutting shrink

CHUCK   RIB   SHORT LOIN   SIRLOIN   ROUND

FORE SHANK   BRISKET   SHORT PLATE   FLANK

RETAIL CUTS OF BEEF AND WHERE THEY COME FROM

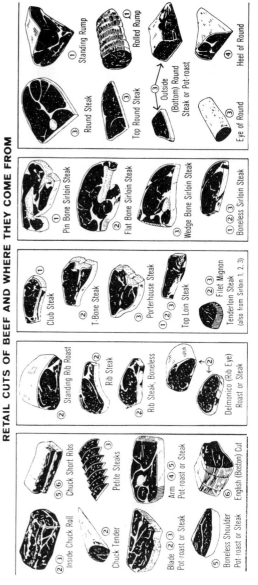

② ③ Inside Chuck Roll

② Chuck Tender

⑤ ⑥ Chuck Short Ribs

③ Petite Steaks

Blade ② ③ Pot-roast or Steak

Arm ④ ⑤ Pot-roast or Steak

⑤ Boneless Shoulder Pot-roast or Steak

⑥ English (Boston) Cut

② Standing Rib Roast

② Rib Steak

② Rib Steak, Boneless

Delmonico (Rib Eye) Roast or Steak ① ② →

① Club Steak

② T-Bone Steak

③ Porterhouse Steak

① ② ③ Top Loin Steak

② ③ Filet Mignon Tenderloin Steak (also from Sirloin 1, 2, 3)

① Pin Bone Sirloin Steak

② Flat Bone Sirloin Steak

③ Wedge Bone Sirloin Steak

① ② ③ Boneless Sirloin Steak

③ Round Steak

③ Top Round Steak

Outside (Bottom) Round Steak or Pot-roast

③ Eye of Round

Standing Rump

Rolled Rump ①

④ Heel of Round

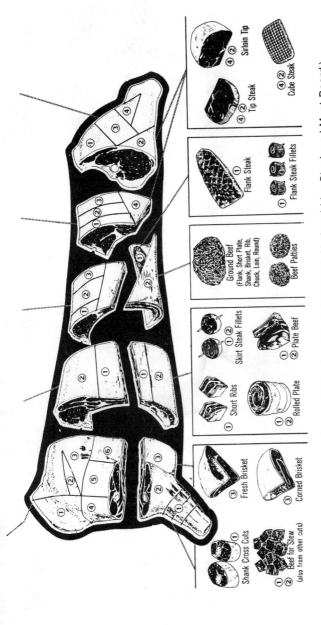

Fig. 10.2. Wholesale and retail cuts of beef. (Courtesy, National Live Stock and Meat Board.)

Shank Cross Cuts ① ② Beef for Stew
(also from other cuts)

③ Fresh Brisket
③ Corned Brisket

① Short Ribs
① ② Rolled Plate

① ② Skirt Steak Fillets
② Plate Beef

Ground Beef
(Flank, Short Plate, Shank, Brisket, Rib, Chuck, Loin, Round)

Beef Patties

① Flank Steak
① ② Flank Steak Fillets

④ ② Tip Steak
④ ② Sirloin Tip
④ ② Cube Steak

WHOLESALE CUTS OF VEAL AND THEIR BONE STRUCTURE

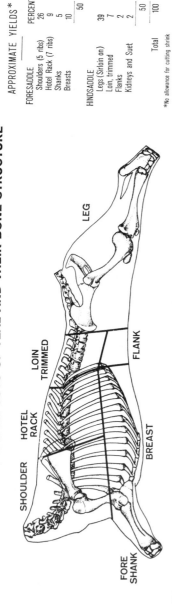

APPROXIMATE YIELDS*

	PERCENT
FORESADDLE	
Shoulders (5 ribs)	26
Hotel Rack (7 ribs)	9
Shanks	5
Breasts	10
	50
HINDSADDLE	
Legs (Sirloin on)	39
Loin, trimmed	7
Flanks	2
Kidneys and Suet	2
	50
Total	100

*No allowance for cutting shrink

SHOULDER HOTEL RACK LOIN TRIMMED

LEG

FLANK

BREAST

FORE SHANK

RETAIL CUTS OF VEAL AND WHERE THEY COME FROM

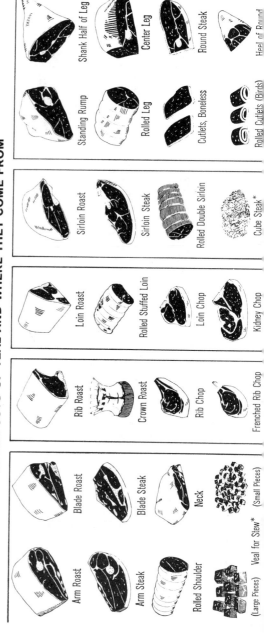

Arm Roast   Blade Roast

Arm Steak   Blade Steak

Rolled Shoulder   Neck

(Large Pieces)   Veal for Stew*   (Small Pieces)

Rib Roast

Crown Roast

Rib Chop

Frenched Rib Chop

Loin Roast

Rolled Stuffed Loin

Loin Chop

Kidney Chop

Sirloin Roast

Sirloin Steak

Rolled Double Sirloin

Cube Steak*

Shank Half of Leg

Center Leg

Round Steak

Heel of Round

Standing Rump

Rolled Leg

Cutlets, Boneless

Rolled Cutlets (Birds)

314

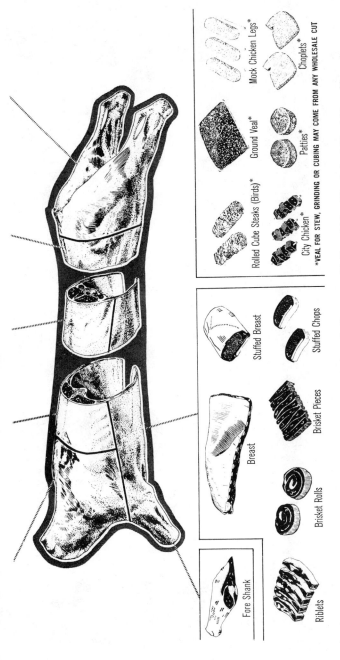

Fig. 10.3. Wholesale and retail cuts of veal. (Courtesy, National Live Stock and Meat Board.)

Fore Shank

Riblets

Breast

Brisket Rolls

Brisket Pieces

Stuffed Breast

Stuffed Chops

Rolled Cube Steaks (Birds)*

City Chicken*

*VEAL FOR STEW, GRINDING OR CUBING MAY COME FROM ANY WHOLESALE CUT

Ground Veal*

Patties*

Mock Chicken Legs*

Choplets*

315

WHOLESALE CUTS OF PORK AND THEIR BONE STRUCTURE

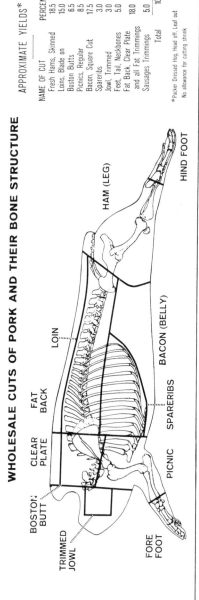

BOSTON
BUTT

CLEAR
PLATE

FAT
BACK

LOIN

TRIMMED
JOWL

PICNIC

SPARERIBS

BACON (BELLY)

HAM (LEG)

FORE
FOOT

HIND FOOT

RETAIL CUTS OF PORK AND WHERE THEY COME FROM

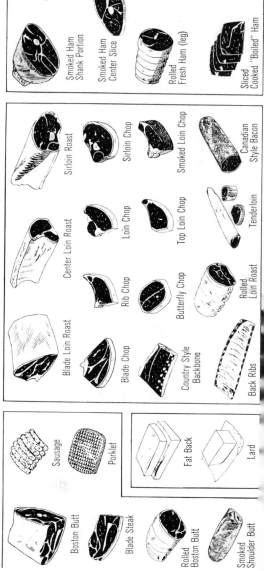

Smoked Ham
Shank Portion

Smoked Ham
Butt Portion

Smoked Ham
Center Slice

Rolled
Fresh Ham (leg)

Smoked Ham
Boneless Roll

Canned Ham

Sliced
Cooked "Boiled" Ham

Blade Loin Roast

Center Loin Roast

Sirloin Roast

Blade Chop

Rib Chop

Loin Chop

Sirloin Chop

Smoked Loin Chop

Country Style
Backbone

Butterfly Chop

Top Loin Chop

Tenderloin

Canadian
Style Bacon

Back Ribs

Rolled
Loin Roast

Sausage

Porklet

Boston Butt

Blade Steak

Rolled
Boston Butt

Smoked
Shoulder Butt

Fat Back

Lard

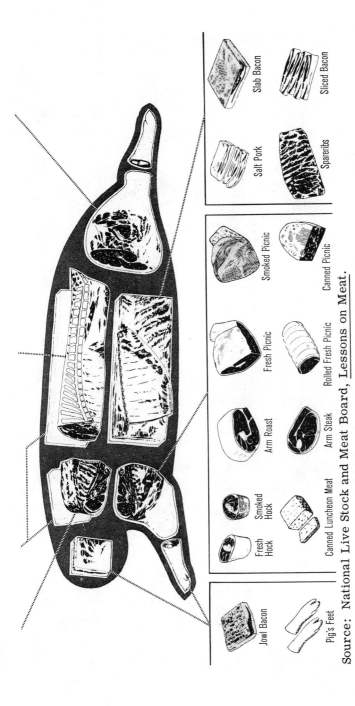

Fig. 10.4. Wholesale and retail cuts of pork. (Courtesy, National Live Stock and Meat Board.)

Source: National Live Stock and Meat Board, Lessons on Meat.

Slab Bacon

Sliced Bacon

Salt Pork

Spareribs

Smoked Picnic

Canned Picnic

Fresh Picnic

Rolled Fresh Picnic

Arm Roast

Arm Steak

Fresh Hock

Smoked Hock

Canned Luncheon Meat

Jowl Bacon

Pig's Feet

WHOLESALE CUTS OF LAMB AND THEIR BONE STRUCTURE

RETAIL CUTS OF LAMB AND WHERE THEY COME FROM

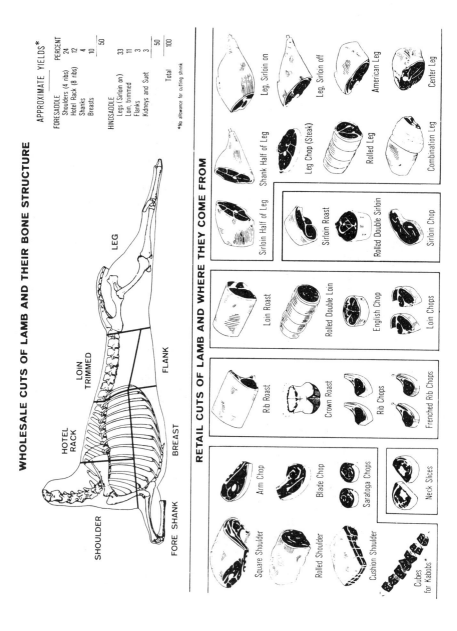

APPROXIMATE YIELDS*	PERCENT
FORESADDLE	
Shoulders (4 ribs)	24
Hotel Rack (8 ribs)	12
Shanks	4
Breasts	10
	50
HINDSADDLE	
Legs (Sirloin on)	33
Loin, trimmed	11
Flanks	3
Kidneys and Suet	3
	50
Total	100

*No allowance for cutting shank

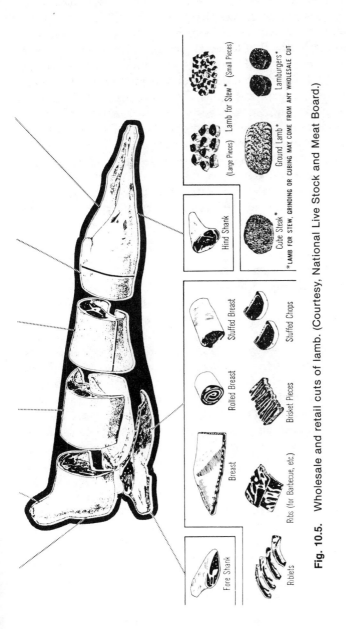

Fig. 10.5. Wholesale and retail cuts of lamb. (Courtesy, National Live Stock and Meat Board.)

correspond to the primal cuts of trade terminology. A standardized cutting, however, has not been accepted nationwide. Wholesale trade is also carried on in sides and quarters of beef, and in entire carcasses (unsplit) of veal and lamb. Wholesale shipments of carcass pork may be either "packer style" (head and leaf fat removed, jowls still attached, and carcass divided into halves) or "shipper style" (head and leaf fat attached and carcass not split). The latter constitutes only a minor fraction of pork shipments. A considerable quantity of portion-control cuts is traded on a wholesale basis to the HRI trade, and, to a limited extent, retail cuts are wholesaled to retailers. This type of activity is carried on by wholesalers who specialize in breaking down to portion cuts and retail cuts. Wholesale meat products differ from specie to specie as well as in their size, cutting method, and the form in which they are traded. The various standards established by official (USDA) and trade groups (e.g., the National Association of Meat Purveyors) facilitate common understanding of wholesale cuts traded in separate markets and among diverse groups of users.

In earlier days, larger packers built "full-line" plants—i.e., plants in which all species and classes of livestock were slaughtered. Many also had a "sausage kitchen" in the same establishment where smoking, curing and manufacturing of processed meat took place. Others did nothing but slaughtering. For some years the trend has been away from full-line plants and away from combination slaughtering and manufacturing of processed meats. Now, many are simply kill-and-chill plants that ship sides or quarters, although, as mentioned, a drastic shift to more cutting, boxing, and further processing at the packer/processor level, particularily of beef, has been under way since the mid 1970s. Because of its extreme importance to the wholesale industry, the concept of boxed beef will now be discussed in more detail.

What is Boxed Beef?

The term "boxed beef," taken literally, may refer to any wrapped or unwrapped beef products placed in boxes for shipment. Although this definition is technically correct, the term "boxed beef" as used here refers to beef carcasses broken down into primal or subprimal cuts;

---

implied in the above definition of processed meat. A central processing unit is one in which meat is broken down by a central unit of a larger operating unit, e.g., of a chain of retail stores or restaurants. To make the situation even more confusing, wholesalers who engage in the breaking down of carcasses to wholesale cuts or retail cuts are known as *fabricators*. This is a misnomer, as the word *fabricate* ordinarily refers to an assembly process, whereas the cutting of meat is *disassembly*. However, there is no confusion in the meat trade where these terms are commonly used and well understood.

packaged under vacuum in tough, leakproof, transparent plastic bags, and finally placed in boxes and shipped. Most of the big packers are also big boxed-beef producers, though many medium-size and small packers are likewise involved.

There are three basic forms of vacuum-packed boxed beef; (1) vacuum-packed boxed-beef carcasses, (2) vacuum-packed primal beef cuts, and (3) vacuum-packed standard beef cuts. There follows a brief definition of each of these (Sarhan and Albanos, 1985):

Vacuum-Packed Boxed-Beef Carcasses

This form of boxed beef refers to packaging the divided carcass into a number of boxes and selling it as a whole carcass unit. The unit, for example, may include nine boxes: two boxes of chucks, one box of ribs, two boxes of loins, two boxes of round, one box of ground beef, and one box of thin meat. There are some variations in the number of boxes and the specification of products sold by any one packer as well as among packers. The important point to emphasize here is that buyers (mostly retailers and independent wholesalers) must take all nine boxes if they purchase boxed beef under this option.

Vacuum-Packed Primal Beef Cuts

This category of boxed beef evolved from buyers' preference for purchasing selected meat items (e.g., certain primal cuts) from the nine boxes (or any other number) of boxed carcasses described above. A market has developed for individual items such as chuck, rounds, and loins. Each boxed item is priced separately, and buyers (mostly retailers) may choose one or more.

Vacuum-Packed Standard Beef Cuts

This type of boxed beef is similar to the vacuum-packed primals except that the meat is cut according to certain published specifications (e.g., those published by the National Association of Meat Purveyors in the Meat Buyers Guide. Products are purchased and priced individually (usually by retailers or institutions) and require less trimming when processed into retail cuts.

Why the Interest in Boxed Beef?

Until the middle 1960s, most beef was distributed in carcass (sides and quarters) loose/hanging form. The major factor behind the trend towards more centrally fabricated boxed beef by both packers and retailers has been its efficiency potential compared to the traditional methods of meat production and distribution. Although boxed beef may cost more per pound (at the packer and retail levels), it is preferred by the majority of traders because it is easier to handle than carcasses or primals, has longer meat-case life and lower in-store-cutting labor cost, reduces waste, and offers flexibility in promotion. A national survey by the USDA's Packers and Stockyards Administration (USDA, 1982) indicated that boxed beef accounted for 49 percent of total federally inspected steer and heifer slaughter in 1979. If the boxing done by central cutting facilities and some wholesalers were included, the percentages would be much higher. Industry sources indicate that more than 80 percent of all beef received by final outlets in the mid 1980s was in the form of boxed beef.

Figure 10.1 indicates wholesale movement from packers to various outlets (some linkages are not shown). Tables 10.1 and 10.2 show types of wholesale distributors and their potential outlets. No attempt will be made here to give a completely detailed description of the wholesaling of meat. Those interested in more information should consult Fowler (1961), Ives (1966), and Williams and Stout (1964).

What goes on in this complex network of marketing may seem rather remote to the average livestock producer. In terms of distance, many of these transactions are far removed from the feedlot scene, but they

Table 10.1. Outlets Used By Wholesale Red Meat Distributors and Their Relative Importance, U.S., 1977.

Type of outlet	Packer sales branches and offices	Merchant wholesalers	Merchant agents
	Percent of Sales		
Institutional, Industrial, Commercial, etc.[a]	6.7	19.3	21.5
Consumers and farmers	0.1	1.0	0.2
Retailers[b]	64.8	46.3	27.7
Wholesale organizations[c]	21.9	29.2	46.6
Government[d]	4.2	1.8	1.1
Export[e]	2.3	2.4	3.0

Source: U.S. Department of Commerce (1981).
[a]Also included are sales to food processors, restaurants and service businesses.
[b]Includes retailers of all types who normally buy for resale to home consumers.
[c]Includes organizations that normally purchase for resale at wholesale and also includes agents acting for others.
[d]Includes sales to the Federal, state, and local government agencies, including the military.
[e]Includes sales made direct to foreign countries or through their agents in the U.S.

Table 10.2. Types of Red Mea' Wholesale Distributors and Their Potential Outlets.

Type of Wholesaler	Potential Customers[a]															
	A	B	C	D	E	F	G	H	I	J	K	L	M	N	O	P
Packers																
Plant	x	x	x		x	x	x	x	x	x	x	x	x	x	x	x
Branches		x	x	x	x		x	x	x	x	x		x	x	x	x
Sales offices	x	x	x	x	x	x	x	x	x	x	x	x	x		x	x
Truck routes		x	x				x	x	x	x			x		x	x
Processors																
Plant			x					x	x	x	x	x	x	x	x	x
Sales offices			x					x	x	x	x	x	x	x	x	x
Portion controllers			x				x	x	x	x	x	x	x	x		x
Purveyors								x	x	x		x	x	x		x
Jobbers			x					x	x	x		x	x	x		x
Peddlers			x						x	x					x	x
Retailers																
Retail stores																
Central warehouse			x										x		x	x
Independent wholesalers																
Breakers	x	x	x	x	x	x	x	x	x	x	x	x	x	x		
Boners		x	x	x	x	x	x	x	x	x	x	x	x	x	x	x
Agents/trading firms																
Brokers/comm. fm.	x	x	x	x	x	x	x	x	x							
Speculators	x	x	x	x	x	x	x	x	x	x	x	x	x	x		x
Trading firms	x	x	x	x	x	x	x	x	x	x	x	x		x		x

[a] A = packers; B = processors; C = retail stores; D = retail warehouse; E = breakers; F = boners; G = portion controllers; H = purveyors; I = jobbers; J = peddlers; K = brokers; L = commission men/firms; M = government; N = export markets; O = consumers; and P = food service.

323

are vitally important nevertheless. It is within this network that wholesale prices come to be generated. What the packer gets at wholesale largely determines what he can pay for slaugher livestock. The producer who intends to do his own marketing must have an acquaintance with the wholesale market—its methods and procedures, any changes that may be taking place, and sources of price quotations. Livestock sales made on the carcass grade-and-weight basis are related directly to wholesale carcass prices. Sales made on the live grade-and-weight basis are only one step removed from the wholesale carcass market.

PACKER BRANCH HOUSES

Packer branch houses are satellite-warehouse processing and distribution centers owned and operated by a parent packing firm; they are located in relatively large population centers away from the packing plant(s). Basically, a branch house is a sales and distribution activity involving a considerable amount of carcass breaking, processing, smoking, and curing. In the hey-day of big packers (before decentralization of the packing industry got underway in the 1920s and 1930s), it was the major channel of distribution to larger cities. Meat was moved from packing plants to branch houses in car and truck lots, then from branch houses to retailers, independent wholesalers, hotels and restaurants, processors, and, in minor quantities, to export.

The U.S. Census of Wholesale Trade (1981) provides the latest data available on branch house, jobber, and broker operations. According to U.S. census reports, the number of branch houses dropped from 1157 in 1929 to 522 in 1958. A slight increase occurred in the following decade and then a further decline took place (Table 10.3). In dollar amount, shipments and sales were substantially higher in 1977 than in 1929. Higher meat prices have held up the dollar volume. The National Commission of Food Marketing (1966) reported that "only about 14% of meat was handled by branch houses in 1963, compared with 30% in 1939." The decline in the branch house system is attributed largely to increases in direct sales by packers to large chain retailers; large operators began to by-pass intermediate steps between packer and retailer. The greater adaptability and flexibility of truck transportation made direct deliveries more feasible and economical. Increasing operational costs in large cities, particularly labor, also have been factors in the decline of branch houses.

Table 10.3. Wholesale Red-Meat Distributors: Number of and Value of Sales, by Type, for Selected Census Years, 1929-1977, U.S.

Census year	Packer sales branches and offices		Merchant wholesalers (jobbers)		Merchandise agents (brokers)		All establishments[a]	
	(Number)	(%)	(Number)	(%)[b]	(Number)	(%)[b]	(Number)	(%)[b]
			Establishments					
1929	1,157	32.9	2,22}	63.4	130	3.7	3,512	100.0
1939	924	26.0	2,552	71.7	84	2.3	3,560	100.0
1948	756	18.8	3,200	79.7	58	1.5	4,014	100.0
1958	522	10.1	4,482	86.9	154	3.0	5,158	100.0
1967	616	10.6	5,041	86.6	163	2.8	5,820	100.0
1972	464	8.4	4,847	87.2	245	4.4	5,556	100.0
1977	435	8.5	4,443	86.7	247	4.8	5,125	100.0
			Shipments and Sales, in current Million[c]					
1929	1,923	69.7	690	25.0	145	5.3	2,758	100.0
1939	1,076	62.8	520	30.4	116	6.8	1,712	100.0
1948	2,717	51.5	1,977	37.5	577	11.0	5,527	100.0
1958	2,263	33.5	3,891	57.5	609	9.0	6,763	100.0
1967	2,811	25.4	7,395	66.9	853	7.7	11,059	100.0
1972	4,251	23.2	12,611	68.8	1,471	8.0	18,333	100.0
1977	5,843	23.4	17,487	69.9	1,681	6.7	25,011	100.0

Source: U.S. Department of Commerce (selected census years).
[a]An establishment is a single location in which business is conducted; companies often consist of more than one establishment.
[b]Calculated by authors from data in this table.
[c]Sales include merchandise sold for cash or credit by establishments primarily engaged in wholesale trade. Total sales do not include credit charges.

PACKER DIRECT SALES

Concurrent with branch-house decline has been an increase in direct wholesale selling at the packing-plant level, partly because of the desire and ability of large retail chains to deal directly with sources of supply of wholesale meat, partly because of the packers' desire to cut out costly branch-house operations, and finally because of increased use of Federal grades and specification buying, which facilitate buying by telephone. In regard to the latter point, some large buyers still buy by inspection (rather than description) in order to take advantage of certain specifications not pinpointed by Federal grade standards.

Direct plant sales are accomplished by plant sales departments, car and truck route salesmen, and the maintenance of sales offices in cities away from the location of packing plants.

Plant Sales

Practically every larger packer and many medium-sized ones maintain a carlot sales department, and practically all handle less than carlot sales. Carlot sales departments deal directly with large buyers—primarily retail chains. The shipments move by refrigerated boxcar or truck directly to the buyer's warehouse or processing center. Local sales of less than carlot quantities are handled either by buyers visiting the plant to make selection or by salesmen taking local orders.

Car and Truck Routes

In that range of territory outside of local sales and not covered by either branch houses or sales offices away from the plant, sales less than carlot are handled by car and truck routes branching out from the plant. Usually, orders are taken by route salesmen who make rounds of retail stores, restaurants, hotels, and institutions. Orders are relayed back to the plant, and deliveries are made periodically—possibly several times a week by truck or rail. Trucks have the decided advantage of door delivery. Trucks and refrigerated cars are loaded so that the last order in will be the first to come out, and so on down the route. The optimization of routing a fleet of trucks in a manner that will minimize delivery costs is a problem that lends itself well to mathematical programming. Significant savings can often be made by access to solutions of this type.

Packer Sales Offices

Many packers are too small to maintain branch houses, and some larger ones prefer not to operate any. At the same time, some in both categories want to handle sales without going through an intermediary. One way of doing this is to establish sales offices in cities away from the plant. These offices take orders and solicit orders, catering primarily to larger customers. They perform the selling function of branch houses but do not physically handle the meat. Orders are relayed back to the plant, and shipments are made directly from packing plant to purchaser.

INDEPENDENT WHOLESALERS

Many packers by choice or necessity engage the services of an intermediary in selling their products. Small independent packers located in production areas great distances from high-consumption areas often do not have the connections or facilities for direct sales. Others prefer to emphasize plant-production aspects and hire experts, so-to-speak, to do the marketing associated with the buying and selling of carcasses and wholesale cuts. A multitude of other activities is performed by independent operators who function in channels between the packers and retailers, HRI buyers, and the export trade. Among these activities are breaking (or fabricating), boning, freezing, processing, etc.

A major distinction can be made within this group of intermediaries on whether the intermediary buys the meat outright (takes title) or simply acts as an agent on a commission basis. By following a strict definition, the former can be classified as jobbers and the latter as brokers. In the meat trade, the term jobber is ordinarily used in a narrower sense; however, there is some ambiguity in its meaning. In general, the term "jobber" is used to indicate the type of outlet used by a packer rather than the method of operation. In this discussion, jobber will be used in the broader sense—i.e., an independent wholesaler who buys (takes title) and resells, hopefully at a profit. Within this general classification, reference will be made to various specialities that are related to the activities performed. By the same token, it is possible to indicate specialities, or subclassifications, within the broker class.

Wholesaling operations have grown substantially in recent years, as shown in Table 10.3. The number of meat-wholesaler jobbers about doubled between 1929 and 1977. During the same time, the value of shipments and sales by jobbers increased more than 25 times. This was a period of relatively rapid fragmentation of the packing industry and rapid expansion in both chain retail operations and the food service trade (HRI). The latter is directly related to the enormous growth of franchised motel and restaurant chains. Important also has been the growth in institutional feeding—e.g., educational dormitories, other state institutions, and factory and store cafeterias. These types of buyers not only purchase large quantities, but want regular delivery of uniform quality meat. Many of them are discriminating buyers with substantial bargaining power.

A series of cold and hot wars following World War II also necessitated large meat purchases for military installations. Military requirements have tapered off since termination of U.S. involvement in Vietnam, but that outlet still utilizes large quantities of meat. Military purchases are usually made on contract bids as are governmental school lunch and welfare purchases.

Under these circumstances, many packers find it advantageous either to sell their meat to a jobber and let him take it from there or to employ the services of a broker to act as their agent for a fee. The expansion in independent wholesaling activities in recent years seems to attest to the fact that wholesaling is a complicated, competitive aspect of the meat business and that there is a place for specialists in the performance of wholesaling functions.

Jobbers

As mentioned, the term "jobber" is used here to mean a meat wholesaler who takes title (he buys the products and resells) hoping to make a profit. It has already been mentioned that some of these operators deal in carcass meat, some in wholesale cuts, and others in retail and HRI cuts. Some specialize in breaking (fabricating); others in boning, freezing, etc. Data in Table 10.3 indicate that jobbers handle a significant volume of meat. One type of specialist within this group deserving of particular mention is the "purveyor." This term is usually restricted to meat wholesalers who deal almost exclusively with the food service industry. Particular purveyors often limit their clientele to a specific segment of that industry. For example, some handle only the very highest quality meat and deal exclusively with high class hotels, restaurants, night clubs, and steamship lines. Others cater to franchised motel chains, etc. Purveyors with long-established reputations are among the most discriminating buyers. Ives (1966) reports that "this specialized type of wholesaling has had its greatest growth during and since World War II, coincident with the growth of food service establishments in these years."

Boners specialize in the preparation of boneless meat. This, primarily, is lower grade beef that moves on through channels to processors, the military, and retailers.

The meat "peddler" is another independent jobber. Other terms used for this operator are "wagon or truck jobber" and "truck distributor." The peddler is a small operator, often consisting of only one man who does the buying, selling, and delivering. The importance of peddlers has declined along with the decline in neighborhood meat retailers and neighborhood grocery stores.

Brokers

The meat broker and live cattle broker perform similar functions at different levels in the marketing system. By definition, a broker acts as agent for the principals to a transaction. He facilitates transfer of title by bringing the seller and buyer together on terms of trade but does not take title in his own name. His reimbursement is a fee (a commission) usually paid by the seller.

Some packers without direct sales organizations prefer the use of brokers rather than selling to jobbers. Under any type of wholesaling arrangement, it is not unusual for shifting demand and supply conditions to leave packers and processors in distress situations at times. In such cases, brokers may be called upon to assist in moving the meat.

Although brokers are not involved in the movement of a major fraction of the total meat supply (see Table 10.3), they are an important link in the system for certain packers and under certain conditions. Motts (1959) reported that brokers handle less than 5 percent of the total meat supply. The National Commission on Food Marketing (1966), in a sample of packers and processors, found a range from 9 to 27 percent, depending upon type of product and type of firm.

WHOLESALE PRICING

Meat pricing at the wholesale level long has been somewhat of a mystery to producers. Unlike live animal markets, where the producer is on more or less familiar ground, there are no public markets for wholesale meat[2] such as auctions or terminals where transactions can be ob-

---

[2]In early days, there were public markets; e.g., Boston's Faneuil Hall was erected in 1742 for trading in provisions. Other large cities followed with provisions markets. Even when operating, however, quotations from these markets were largely unavailable to producers. In those days, packers were concerned primarily with packing operations and left merchandising of meat up to wholesalers. As packers established branch houses, public meat markets largely disappeared.

served. Public and private sources have published quotations of wholesale prices for some time, but the quotations themselves give no insight into the pricing mechanism, and many smaller producers are not even aware of the sources of such quotations.

Wholesale meat prices are important not only to packers and retailers but to livestock producers and consumers as well. Packers determine the prices they can pay for live animals based on expected or going market prices. Thus, producer prices are closely related to wholesale meat prices. On the other hand, wholesale prices influence retail prices and eventually affect the quantity demanded by consumers. It is because of this significant and sensitive role played by wholesale meat prices that their accuracy and integrity are of utmost importance.

Basically, pricing of meat at wholesale is done either by formula or negotiation. There are, of course, variations in both of these approaches.

Negotiated Prices

A negotiated trade is defined as a transaction where all terms of trade (delivery, quality, quantity, and price of a specific type and/or part of meat) are agreed upon at the same time. This simply is private bargaining between seller and buyer. It is analogous to private treaty in live animal marketing in that principals to the transaction rely on knowledge of the product, familiarity with current market conditions, and expertise in bargaining. The negotiation may take place by telephone based on stipulated specifications, or purchasers (or their representatives) may personally inspect and select meat in the wholesaler's cooler.

The prices retailers are willing to pay for wholesale meat is a reflection of consumer demand. In other words, retailer demand is a derived demand—derived from consumer demand. The prices at which wholesalers are willing to sell is a reflection of the costs they have incurred in obtaining the meat. Costs of a packer-wholesaler are reflected in the costs of live animals and are a derived supply. Under competitive conditions, prices are expected to tend toward an equilibrium of the supply-demand situation. It is not surprising that stable equilibrium conditions are not found in the real world as supply and demand conditions are constantly changing and assumptions of a perfectly competitive market are constantly upset. The crux of this multistep approach to pricing is well-informed buyers and sellers with at least approximate equality in bargaining power. Sarhan and Albanos (1985) outlined the following steps involved in the negotiation process.

1. *Review published market prices.* This is the starting point for most buyers and sellers, i.e.; they check the daily "market price" and use it as a base, to which several adjustments are applied.
2. *Evaluate price trends.* Published prices are adjusted accordingly.
3. *Evaluate daily market supply (offerings).* A large number of offerings indicates a large supply and suggests that the market might be weak; thus, prices would be adjusted downward. Fewer than normal offerings signal a tight supply and price adjustments would be upward, at least for the immediate future. The manner in which suppliers approach traders gives the first indication of whether the published market price is realistic or to be changed.
4. *Evaluate market demand.* No matter how attractive the offerings may seem, traders should buy only when there is demand for the product, i.e., there is a high chance that it can be sold. If meat inventory indicates little or no movement of a particular item, traders are usually reluctant to buy at the market price, if at all. On the other hand, if they are about to "special" an item, they are more eager to buy.
5. *Review the potential supply situation.* Slaughter rates are commonly used as an indicator of meat supply and traders have learned to use them as a rule of thumb in estimating meat supply.
6. *Study short-and long-term weather information.* In the short term, adverse weather can influence the immediate slaughter rates and consequently the short-term (e.g., next week's) supply. Weather can be an important factor in traders' buying and selling decisions, particularly during winter months or hot summers. Long-term weather forecasts may be used as an indicator of long-term supply. For example, weather affects grain supply, which in turn affects feed prices and can influence producers' decisions concerning feeding and, eventually, the actual supply of livestock.

Although traders may not follow these steps in the given order, all these variables, as well as others such as meat quality and firm operating costs, enter the price discovery process. It should be pointed out that although supply factors affect all traders in a similar manner, demand factors vary among traders according to their particular situation. The published price is the base from which adjustments are made to arrive at bid/offer price in these negotiated trades.

Prior to the 1920s and 1930s, the packing industry was highly concentrated in the hands of a relatively few big packers, whereas meat retailing was highly decentralized in a large number of relatively small firms. Under these conditions, there is little question that the balance of bargaining power lay with the packer-wholesalers. That situation has changed. Development of large retail chains and cooperative and voluntary wholesale buying arrangements among independent retailers have shifted the balance of bargaining power. There has been a great deal of conjecture about the implications of the present situation, but a study by the National Commission on Food Marketing in reports issued in 1966 failed to develop evidence of undue market power of any sector in the food economy.

Offer and Acceptance Pricing. One variation of negotiated pricing that usually merits special attention is "offer and acceptance pricing." Large-volume buyers under this arrangement invite wholesalers (packers, independent wholesalers, processors, etc.) to make offers on orders in which the purchaser sets forth rather rigid specifications. Specifications include such things as grade (may be both quality and yield), sex, weight (range per cut), and terms of delivery. Sales by specification normally carry the agreement or understanding that any product that does not meet the specifications upon delivery may be rejected by the purchaser. This possibility can leave the supplier in a serious situation. Unofficial reports indicate, however, that only a small fraction of shipments is rejected.

Upon receipt of offers from several prospective suppliers, the purchaser compares offering prices. Other things being equal, the lowest price will be accepted. Some would argue that such an arrangement can scarcely be classed as negotiation. There is often discussion and some negotiation, however, particularly on deviations from the specifications.

Offer and acceptance pricing ranks high in operational efficiency. Very little cost is involved in a transaction. When buying is accomplished on specification, the transaction can be consummated by telephone. Salary and travel expenses of personnel who otherwise would personally select carcasses or cuts are averted. Sellers are relieved of some expense in attending to these buyers.

From the standpoint of the mechanics of operation, this method also has the potential for a high degree of pricing efficiency. Specifications can be quite rigid. The crucial point is how well price differentials among meats of various specifications reflect their real differences to final users. Sellers whose offers are rejected are left somewhat in the dark by not knowing the extent to which their offer may have exceeded the acceptance price. For the system to work effectively over a period of time, sellers need to have either invitations from alternative buyers or alternative outlets. The degree of competition in this respect has a direct bearing on price level of offers made. If enough time is allowed for the delivery of the product, suppliers conceivably could push equivalent acceptance prices back to live animal prices—a possibility, of course, that could work either way on the level of livestock prices.

Formula Pricing

Formula-priced transactions are defined as those where delivery, quality, quantity, and other terms of trade, except price, are agreed upon at one time, with the price to be established at a specified future date (usually the day prior to shipping date). The price is determined by applying a formula to a base price, published by a specific market reporting service, for the particular product being traded.

One common-carlot carcass-beef quotation is for the River Markets (i.e., Omaha, Sioux city, St. Paul, St. Joseph, Kansas City). For example, using a published price quotation as the base, traders adjust by formula to arrive at prices applicable to, say, New York, Boston, Omaha, Kansas City, Denver, etc. A typical example of formula pricing would be the case of a Kansas City packer agreeing to deliver a carlot of carcass beef (meeting certain specifications) to Boston on a continuing basis at one of the market quotations (or some agreed upon amount under or over the published price) for beef of agreed specifications—plus transportation cost from Kansas City to Boston. Formula pricing also is used for pricing cattle sold on carcass grade. One typical arrangement here is for a packer (say a Great Plains packer) and nearby commercial feedlot manager to agree that cattle delivered two weeks hence will be priced "in the meat" at, say, $2 under the market news service quotation on the day the cattle are delivered and slaughtered. Feedlot managers, as a rule, are not enthusiastic about this approach to pricing cattle, but, during periods of over-supply and draggy cattle markets, packers sometimes insist on it.

NEGOTIATED VERSUS FORMULA PRICING

Although it is possible for all transactions to be enacted on a negotiated basis, formula-based pricing is possible only for that portion of market transactions that have to depend on negotiated trades to establish a prevailing market price. It is not known exactly what proportions of wholesale meat are traded on negotiated and formula bases, although estimates are available. The National Commission on Food Marketing found in a 1965 survey that of the meat packers and processors responding, 41 percent of beef and veal, 24 percent of lamb and mutton, 41 percent of fresh and frozen pork, 29 percent of cured hams, picnics, and bacon, and 20 percent of other processed meat transactions (involving the most important customers) were determined by formula pricing. "In nearly all cases the quotation source was the Yellow Sheet" (National Commission of Food Marketing 1966). In an Ohio study, Stout *et al.* (1968) found that "All 24 firms employed formula prices in purchasing some or all of their fresh meats." The U.S. Congress Committee on Small business (1978) estimated that 70 to 90 percent of all meat is traded on a formula basis. Hayenga (1978 and 1979) and a USDA report (1978), however, cited recent evidence, based upon industry surveys, which suggests these estimates are too high and that considerable variation exists by firm, product, and geographic region.

Fresh beef is sold by slaughterers in two forms: as carcasses or as cut and packaged boxed beef. Boxed beef, a large and growing portion of the fresh beef trade, is largely priced on a negotiated basis. Differences in packaging, processing, and specifications have made formula pricing boxed beef a relatively difficult procedure, at least until recently. A study by the P&S of boxed-beef pricing (USDA, 1982) concluded that "prices for about 85 percent of all boxed beef included in this study were determined through negotiation at the time of sale. In contrast, 35 packing plants surveyed by USDA in 1977 sold 70 percent of their steer and heifer carcasses on a formula basis." Formula pricing is popular among small- and medium-sized packers and retailers. Hayenga (1978) reported that the HRI trade tends to purchase beef on a formula basis, with several notable exceptions that are based on longer term, cost-plus price agreement. Hayenga (1979) reported the results of a survey of the pork industry that indicated that approximately 60 percent of all pork was sold as fresh, of which 50 percent was sold on a negotiated basis, 40 percent on a formula basis, and the remaining 10 percent based on daily price lists. Over 90 percent of processed pork was traded with prices based on price lists[3].

The General Accounting Office (1978), Hayenga (1978 and 1979), and USDA (1978) found regional differences in the relative proportion of negotiated and formula transactions. The most notable difference is West Coast pricing, which typically relies upon negotiations—often the offer and acceptance method—for fresh beef and pork. The evidence indicates that a negotiated price is used almost exclusively by West coast retailers in filling their normal meat requirements. In the East, meat is normally traded on a formula basis, predominantly for beef and almost exclusively for pork. Pricing methods in the Central

---

[3]Price lists are usually published by packers/suppliers of products that can be differentiated. The lists are distributed to traders and adjusted as frequently as market conditions warrant. This pricing method reflects suppliers' costs of raw materials, plus target margin. It is used mostly for processed pork products.

states defy general classification in either method; some firms base their trades on formula pricing, some negotiate, and others use a combination of the two, changing their practice to reflect short-term market characteristics.

Sources of Wholesale Market Information

Price and other market information are important for both negotiated and formula trades. Wholesale meat prices are reported primarily by three market news services: (1) *The Yellow Sheet*, published by the National Provisioner's Daily Market and News Service; (2) *The Meat Sheet*, also known as *The Pink Sheet*, published by the Meat Sheet—The Total Price Report; and (3) *Market News*, published by the United States Department of Agriculture. These services provide wholesale prices for carcass, primal, subprimal, and processed cuts of pork, beef, and lamb, along with other related information and commentary. Although all three are similar in many respects, there are also some differences.

The Yellow Sheet is privately owned, published five days per week, and mailed to paid subscribers at the end of each working day. Subscribers may also purchase the service's market information during the day through wire service or telephone. It was first published in 1927 for pork, with beef prices added in 1940. The General Accounting Office (1977) reported that the Yellow Sheet is the dominant information service. The reported prices are closing quotations as confirmed through daily telephone contact with sellers, buyers, and brokers by the services's reporters. The Yellow Sheet does not identify the type of trade—i.e., packer to packer, packer to processor—nor are prices reported for ungraded steer and heifer carcasses. The volume traded at quoted prices is not reported. The National Provisioner claims that only freely competitive transactions are used in the quotations and that each is verified. This claim, however, is disputed by some in the meat industry.

The Meat Sheet, also a privately owned service, was first published in 1974 in Elmhurst, Ill. The Meat Sheet is mailed at the end of each trading day to paid subscribers, who may also receive the information during the day through telex, wire or telephone. The information gathering procedure is similar to that used by the Yellow Sheet, i.e., daily telephone contacts are established with market participants. Market information is provided, however, in a different format and more comprehensive manner. The high, low, and closing prices for each day are reported and, if available, the reported volume traded is indicated in tons for each category. If no trades can be confirmed for the day, the symbol "O" appears in the tonnage column. The prices and transactions are identified and separated into packer-to-packer or packer-to-processor categories with price ranges, closing price, and tonnage reported for each. Information is also reported for ungraded steer and heifer carcasses and for selected boxed-beef items.

The USDA Market News, a public service, has been published since 1916. Information is made available for ten wholesale meat-marketing areas, originating from nine locations: Des Moines, Iowa; Princeton, New Jersey; Los Angeles and Martinez, California; Greely, Colorado; Moses Lake, Washington; and San Antonio, Fort Worth, and Houston, Texas. Information is disseminated through printed press, radio and television, the USDA Leased Wire Service, and a 24-hour telephone service. A weekly report is mailed, at a subscription fee, providing the number of carloads and prices for both graded and ungraded carcasses as well as some boxed-beef items. Packer-to-packer trades are identified if they are outside the general market range.

CONTROVERSY OVER ADEQUACY OF MARKET INFORMATION AND FORMULA PRICING

For many years, concern has been expressed that a large percentage of negotiated meat trades in the U.S. has not been reported to market news services. A USDA study (1978) found that during the month of July 1977, only 1.7 percent and 1.6 percent of all federally inspected steer and heifer slaughter, respectively, were reported to the Yellow Sheet and the Meat Sheet. Although the majority of boxed beef is sold on a negotiated basis, prices are reported for only a small fraction of the trade. Controversy over the accuracy and adequacy of market information supplied by marketing reporting services and the relatively small size of the negotiated-transactions base resulted in an investigation by the U.S. House of Representatives Committee on Small Business. It led the Secretary of Agriculture to appoint a Meat Pricing Task Force in 1978 to examine the facts, particularly those pertaining to beef. A wide range of conclusions and policy alternatives resulted from these investigations. For example, the Committee on Small Business (1978) concluded that: (1) the negotiated market is diminishing, (2) wholesale prices are possibly subject to manipulation, (3) the Yellow Sheet is not effectively serving the industry, and (4) the free market has deteriorated and is close to being eliminated. The Committee recommended measures designed to regulate and improve the performance of market information services and suggested researching the feasibility of a centralized market system for beef. On the other hand, the USDA's Meat Pricing Task Force (1979) proposed a set of policies directed at improvement of the system and focused on voluntary measures rather than regulatory solutions. Major recommendations were to (1) preserve an adequate volume of negotiated trading through the development of electronic marketing, or (2) obtain more adequate reporting within the present trading system.

Several economists who studied the situation reached somewhat different conclusions. Williams (1978) perceived the central issue as being not the performance of the reporting services but rather formula pricing on a forward-contrasting basis. Williams agrees that the use of formula pricing results in a "thin" market; a considerable portion of the market is insulated from use as a source of price information. Thus, Williams has advocated an outright ban on formula pricing. In a paper prepared for the Meat Pricing Task Force, he stated:

> There is nothing inherently wrong with forward contracting through use of a formula, but when the formula is tied directly to prices to be reported in the future by a major private or public price reporting service, serious problems arise. These would be much the same regardless of whether the formulas were based on the Yellow Sheet, the Meat Sheet, both of these, or the USDA meat reporting service. Use of any basis, other than a market price report (futures prices, for example), would solve many problems.
>
> Forward formula pricing tied to a major price report, and particularly where this report is the pricing 'Bible' of the industry, is potentially self-destructive. To the extent that it exists, it destroys usable sources of information on prices. Formula prices based on prices to be reported in the future by any major reporting source cannot be used by any of the reporting services, private or public, as a source of current pricing information.
>
> The problem, then, is that the reportable population of wholesale prices has been shrinking and, in many instances, has now reached the point where it is non-existent. No price can be reported at the time of sale on a forward formula pricing because no price exists. When a price finally is assigned, this cannot be used because it is bolted tightly to a reported price of the industries' pricing Bible.

Somewhat different conclusions and policy alternatives were suggested by Breimyer (1978), who saw the question as being not one of a "thin" market but, rather, the absence of the will, by market participants, to report market information. He conceded the need for mandatory price reporting and suggested conducting more research before an attempt is made at government legislation. Cothern (1978) favored the extension and strengthening of the USDA Market News as a way to provide better market information.

Earlier, the National Food Commission (1965) concluded that use of

formula pricing was increasing and mentioned several important implications of its use. These include the possibilities that (1) formula pricing tends to perpetuate geographic price patterns unrepresentative of
changing supply and demand conditions, (2) prices used as base prices
are subject to manipulation by trade interests, and (3) base prices accurately reflect equilibrium supply-demand conditions. The same issues
remain in the 1980s.

Does Formula Pricing Perpetuate Geographic Patterns?   The reasoning here is that if prices today are based on yesterday's closing price,
and if yesterday's prices were based on the previous day's closing
price, and so on—it is then conceivable that the pattern of prices would
remain fixed for the market being reported even though supply and
demand conditions had changed. Furthermore, if all, or most, meat
were formula-priced day after day, the continuing day-by-day quotation of price reporting services (i.e., Yellow Sheet, Meat Sheet, USDA)
would not adequately reflect changing supply and demand conditions.
The reasoning is logical. It would appear that the price level would
remain fixed under these circumstances. The record shows, however,
that geographic price relationships have not remained fixed and that
the price level has indeed varied. There are several apparent explanations for this. Not all meat is traded on a formula basis. Some of the
prices collected in assembling market service quotations undoubtedly
come from negotiated sales. Furthermore, some negotiation takes
place even when the base price is used as the point at which bargaining
starts. There is no evidence at this time that formula pricing has per-
petuated geographic patterns, although this could not be ruled out as
a possibility if greater use were made of it on a strict basis.

Can Formula Pricing Be Manipulated?   The nature of formula pricing
invites concern about market efficiency and possible manipulation.
Formula prices are based upon prices that are reported voluntarily, and
the reporting mechanism involves personal discretion on the part of
the market information service. For example, it is not known exactly
what should be considered the "right" price for reporting services: the
daily average, the low, the high, or the closing price.

Thus, some market participants and industry observers have hypothesized that firms could use market reporting services to affect
prices in manners advantageous to themselves and detrimental to
other market participants, including consumers and producers. The
power of firms to affect prices is believed, by some, to be strengthened
through two imperfections in the information reported: (1) the small
percentage of total volume reported, and (2) the ambiguous and some-

times incomplete transactions for which data are reported. Although allegations of this nature have failed to be substantiated in courts of law, some industry sources insist that manipulation has occurred and is still occurring. In a discussion of the beef marketing system, De-Graff (1960) stated the following:

No one organization involved in processing or distributing beef is big enough or powerful enough to dominate the market or to dictate prices in the market. The reasons why this is true center on two points. First, beef, like any major food, has a nationwide market. Prices among the regions and localities of the country are closely tied together by competitive forces, by highly developed transportation, and by effective market news services, both public and private. . . .

Second, in order to control such a market, or prices in such a market, it would be necessary to accomplish what is impossible for any food industry firm, or indeed any group of firms. It would be necessary to have a large measure of control over the following: (a) the wants and preferences of consumers; (b) the availability and price of substitute products; (c) the level and distribution of consumer incomes; and (d) a substantial part of the supply of the product involved. . . .

There are, of course, always possibilities of monopoly attempts or of collusion in any one market area. They seldom get far or last long. . . .

Comments by Williams (1979) indicate that the Yellow Sheet is vulnerable to manipulation. Once established, he stated, formula pricing introduces incentives for manipulation. In his statement before the Meat Pricing Task Force, he concluded that

If the price a seller will receive or a buyer will pay depends entirely on what the Yellow Sheet or some other sheet is to report next Wednesday or another particular day, then strong incentives will exist to influence that price. The stakes are high. Temptation to influence the outcome is there and, considering human nature, some will succumb to that temptation. Not all of the prices need to be influenced to affect trading activity at wholesale, on the futures market and in the live market. A significant alteration in wholesale prices reported for YG.3 Choice steers alone can alter conditions drastically.

Four alleged manipulation schemes employed by some traders to maximize their profit were described in Congressional Hearings, government reports and in the news media: Packer-to-packer highball, packer-to-packer lowball, high-low split, and savings on the sly. In the packer-to-packer highball scheme, a packer is committed to a sizable number of formula sales on a specified future date based on one of the reporting services published price on that day. On the day before shipping he allegedly enters the market and negotiates a small transaction with another packer to fill an alleged shortage. The negotiated price is purposefully set above the prevailing market price and is promptly reported to the reporting service. When published, it becomes the base for the seller's transactions, thereby allowing the seller to reap more profit than if settlement had been made on the previous market price. The packer-to-packer lowball scheme is similar to the highball scheme except that it is allegedly used to lower wholesale price quotations on the days a packer is expected to purchase cattle based on one of the market reporting services' quotation. The high-low split scheme involves an agreement between a packer and a processor to split a large-volume transaction into two lots with two differrent prices. The money exchanged is the agreed-upon overall average, but only the high or low price is reported to the market reporting service, depending on the purpose of the participants' action. Savings on the sly scheme is simply a transaction where the parties agree not to report the price, which could be higher or lower than the prevailing market price depending on the purpose of the scheme, to any of the marketing reporting services. Although certain conditions and incentives may exist for manipulation, there apparently is a lack of any clear-cut evidence that manipulation has actually occurred. The extent to which the Yellow Sheet is used seems to indicate a substantial degree of confidence in its reliability.

Do Formula-Generated Prices Accurately Reflect Equilibrium Prices? As long as base prices are derived from prices determined in a freely competitive market, and as long as the price reporting agency, whether private or public, obtains an adequate sample of prices, then they could be said to reflect equilibrium prices. Both the National Provisioner and USDA contend that a sufficient volume of competitively determined sales are made to reflect the market accurately (Williams, 1970). Current trends in market structure, however, indicate that the number and volume of trades meeting the preceding requirements is becoming smaller. If this trend continues, and there is reason to believe that it will, it is probable that at some point this approach will not represent an equilibrium situation nor adequately reflect the major movement of meat in wholesale channels.

Implications with Respect to Market Efficiency. There is no question that formula pricing is very efficient from an operational standpoint. It utilizes a minimum of time and manpower. One or two persons could purchase all of the meat requirements for a national retail food chain by phone. The same situation applies at the packer–processor level. This is probably a major reason why retailers and wholesalers alike appear to be satisfied with formula pricing.

From the standpoint of pricing efficiency, the system depends upon competition to establish prices that reflect true supply and demand conditions. This requires bona fide negotiated prices as the source of price-reporting-services quotations. Although questions have been raised about the adequacy of reported prices, there is, as yet, no clear-cut evidence to the contrary.

Meat marketing and pricing methods in the future will not be completely new, but rather based on the existing systems, with some modifications to utilize the latest technologies. The shift that has taken place in recent years, coupled with advancements in computer and communication technology, suggests that some adjustments in trading and market reporting appears to be imminent. Forces that have caused public concern will probably continue in the future. There are a number of alternatives available to the meat industry to alleviate public concern over wholesale meat pricing. The industry may decide to maintain, but improve, the existing system. Improvement could be accomplished by increasing the base of reported transactions and by reporting information in a more comprehensive manner. Another option would be to take advantage of available technology and actively use an electronic marketing system, such as an improved version of the Computer Assisted Trading System (CATS) that was tested in 1981, for trading and reporting purposes. Still another option would be to maintain current trading methods but use functions provided by an electronic marketing system to improve market information and reporting. The results and feedback from the CATS pilot test (Sarhan and Nelson, 1983) suggested two by-products of particular interest: (1) market information on bids and offerings, and (2) price reporting.

REFERENCES

Armstrong, J. H. 1968. Cattle and beef buying, selling and pricing handbook. Indiana Coop. Ext. Serv. May.

Baker, A. J., and Duewer, L. A. 1983. Meat distribution patterns in six southern Metro Areas. USDA, ERS, Agr. Econ. Rept. No. 498.

Breimyer, H. F. 1978. Statement before the Subcommittee on SBA and SBIC Authority and General Small Business Problems. *In* The Committee on Small Business, Small Business Problems in the Marketing of Meat and Other Commodities: Part 1— Meat Marketing. U. S. Government Printing Office. Washington, D.C.

Butz, D. E., and Baker, G. L. 1960. The changing structure of the meat economy. Res. Div., Harvard Business School.

Cothern, James H. 1978. Technological change, market power and beef product pricing practices. *In* The Committee on Small Business, Small Business Problems in the Marketing of Meat and Other Commodities: Part 1—Meat Marketing. U. S. Government Printing Office. Washington, D.C.

De Graff, H. 1960. *Beef Production and Distribution.* Norman, OK: University of Oklahoma Press.

Dietrich, R. A., and Williams, W. F. 1959. Meat distribution in the Los Angeles Area. USDA Agr. Marketing Res. Rept. 347.

Duewer, L. A. 1984. Changing trends in the red meat distribution system. USDA, ERS, Agr. Econ. Rept. No. 509.

Fowler, S. H. 1961. *The marketing of Livestock and Meat.* 2nd ed. Danville, Ill.: Interstate Printers & Publishers.

General Accounting Office. 1977. Marketing meat: Are there any impediments to free trade? Study by the staff of the U.S. General Accounting Office. Washington, D.C.

General Accounting Office. 1978. Beef Marketing: Issues and Concerns. Study by the staff of the U.S. General Accounting Office. Washington, D.C.

Hayenga, M. L. 1978. Vertical Coordination in the Beef Industry: Packer, Retailer, and HRI Linkages. University of Wisconsin, Madison, NC Project 117, WP-35.

Hayenga, M. L. 1979. Pork pricing systems: The importance and economic impacts of formula pricing. University of Wisconsin, Madison, NC Project 117, WP-37.

Ives, J. R. 1966. The Livestock and Meat Economy of the United States. Am. Meat Inst., Chicago.

Kolmer, L., et al. 1959. Consumer marketing handbook I. Meat. Iowa Coop Ext. Serv. Nov.

Motts, G. N. 1959. Marketing handbook for Michigan livestock, meat and wool. Mich. Agr. Expt. Sta. Spec. Bull 426.

National Commission on Food Marketing. 1966. Organization and competition in the livestock and meat industry. Natl. Comm. Food Marketing Tech. Study 1. Govt. Printing Office, Washington, D.C.

Price, J. F., and Snell, J. G. 1965. Meat processing handbook. Mich. Coop Ext. Serv. Sept.

Sarhan, M. E., and Nelson, K. E. 1983. Evaluation of the pilot test of the Computer Assisted Trading System, CATS, for wholesale meat in the United States. Univ. of Illinois. Dept. of Agr. Econ. AE-4553.

Sarhan, M. E., and Albanas, W. 1985. U.S. meat industry: Components, wholesale pricing and market reporting. Univ. of Illinois, Agr. Exp. Sta., AERR Report No. 198.

Stout, T. T., and Hawkins, M. H. 1968. Implications of changes in the methods of wholesaling meat products. *Am. J. Agr. Econ. 50:*660–675.

Stout, T. T., Hawkins, M. H., and Marion, B. W. 1968. Meat procurement and distribution by Ohio grocery chains and affiliated wholesalers. Ohio Agr. Develop. Center Res. Bull. 1014.

USDA. 1969. Feasibility of a physical distribution system model for evaluating improvements in the cattle and fresh beef industry. USDA Agr. Res. Serv. 52–36.

USDA. 1978. Beef Pricing Report. USDA, P & S Administration.

USDA. 1979. Report to the Secretary's Meat Pricing Task Force. USDA, Washington, D.C.

USDA. 1982. Boxed beef: Production, pricing and distribution 1979. USDA, P & S Admin. P & S Resume. Vol. XIX No. 10.

U.S. Department of Commerce. 1975. Census of Manufactures 1972. U.S. Department of Comm., Bur. of Census, Vol. 1.

U.S. Department of Commerce. 1981. Census of Wholesale Trade. U.S. Department of Comm., Bur. of Census. Also earlier issues.

U.S. House of Representatives. 1978. The Committee on Small Business, Small Business Problems in the Marketing of Meat and Other Commodities: Part 4—Meat Pricing. U.S. Government Printing Office. Washington, D.C.

Williams, W. F. 1958. Structural changes in the meat wholesaling industry. *J. Farm Econ.* 40:315–329.

Williams, W. F. 1970. Implications of developments in the pricing structure of the livestock–meat economy. *In* Long-run adjustments in the livestock and meat industry: Implications and alternatives. Ohio Agr. Res. Develop. Center, Res. Bull. 1037. Also, North Central Regional Publ. 199.

Williams, W. F. 1978. Statement before the Subcommittee on SBA and SBIC Authority and General Small Business Problem of the Committee on Small Business. *In* The Committee on Small Business, Small Business Problems in the Marketing of Meat and Other Commodities: Part 4—Meat Pricing. U.S. Government Printing Office. Washington, D.C.

Williams, W. F., and Stout, T. T. 1964. *Economics of the Livestock–Meat Industry.* New York: Macmillan Co.

11

Meat Marketing—Retail

Production, slaughter, processing, wholesaling—these functions would serve no purpose and the product would have no value without the final step—that is, getting the meat into the hands of consumers. In the United States, some 98 percent of total meat production is consumed domestically; the remaining 2 percent is exported. Most domestically consumed meat is channeled through retail outlets, but an increasing fraction goes through HRI outlets. It is estimated that 55 percent of consumer expenditures on beef and 30 percent on pork in 1981 were through the food service industry. In evaluating the retail trade, it should be noted that smaller units of the HRI trade obtain meat supplies from retail stores. It has been estimated that some one-quarter of all HRI purchases are supplied by retailers.

In 1984, farm slaughter, once an important source of meat, amounted to less than 1 percent of the total. In this chapter, we will use developments in, and characteristics of, grocery sales as proxies for meat sale. This is appropriate since meat represents the single most important food item, and because changes in meat sales parallel total grocery sales. Table 11.1 indicates that meat generates about 21 percent of all retail sales. Meat generated approximately 28 percent of all food sales in grocery stores in 1981. Beef is reported to be the largest single grocery sales item. Total fresh meat sales amounted to $27 billion in 1984. The value of processed meats would increase that by a substantial amount.

DEVELOPMENTS IN FOOD RETAILING

Significant changes have occurred in food retailing during the past 70 years and particularly since the 1930s. Two major developments are closely associated with these changes—the development of the chain system[1] and the development of the supermarket. These were not simultaneous. The chain system came first, resulting in a rapid increase in the number of stores. This was followed by development of the

---

[1]Chains are defined as firms with 11 or more stores.

Table 11.1. Value and Percentage of Meat Sold in Grocery Stores, By Type of Meat, 1972, 1976, and 1981.

Item	1972	1976	1981
		Million $	
Fresh meat, poultry, and provisions sales*	20,084	29,109	46,920
		Percent	
Meat sales as a percentage of total store sales	21.53	21.07	21.23
Beef, fresh	40.00	39.00	45.00
Lamb, fresh	3.00	2.00	2.00
Pork, fresh	8.00	9.00	9.00
Veal, fresh	3.00	3.00	1.00
Poultry	12.00	11.00	12.00
Provisions*	34.00	36.00	31.00
TOTAL	100.00	100.00	100.00

Source: Duewer (1984).
*Provisions are cured meats and sausage products.

supermarket, which resulted in a consolidation and reduction in store numbers. The total volume of business expanded greatly during this period. Figure 11.1 illustrates the trend in the number of stores and sales for the period 1940 to 1982. Sales of grocery stores in 1982 was $252 billion compared with $101.7 billion in 1972—a real growth of 147.8 percent (Table 11.2).

Retail Chains

The origin of corporate retail chains dates back to 1859 with organization of the A&P Tea Company (DeGraff 1960). Early development of chains was almost entirely a matter of horizontal integration, and the emphasis was on the number of stores rather than size of individual units. "Between 1910 and 1930, chains grew from 2,000 to 45,000 stores and encompassed 1/3 of one of the nation's largest industries. The speed and scope of this development was alarming to businessmen as well as the public" (National Commission on Food Marketing 1966).

Early chain activity also centered on the economics of obtaining supplies. Primarily, it was one of integrating wholesaling operations and retailing under one management. This was vertical integration—the control of successive stages in production and marketing channels. Some chains rather quickly went one step further and brought process-

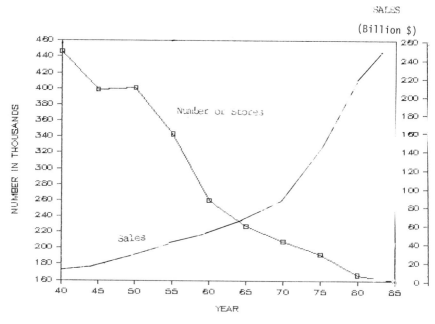

Fig. 11.1 Number of grocery stores and annual sales, 1940–1982. [Plotted by authors from data in Duewer (1984).]

ing operations under their management.[2] Thus, significant gains were made in operational efficiency, and these were reflected in prices lower than those of competing nonchain stores. Management was able to standardize, coordinate, and control activities that previously were under widely scattered, independent operations. Operational efficiency was not the only source of economic strength, however, perhaps of even greater significance was the gain in bargaining power that came with mass purchasing. This enabled the chains to obtain price concessions from suppliers that small, independent operators could not obtain. Chain purchasing departments dealt directly with packers for meat supplies, entirely by-passing established wholesale agencies.

Rapid expansion of chain activity placed small, independent meat markets and grocery stores under severe competition. The situation was aggravated by widespread economic depression during the 1930s when many were absorbed by the chains. The small business operators

---

[2]As will be noted later, meat processing by retailers has been undertaken on only a limited scale. Most extensive processing is in dairy products, fruits, vegetables, and bakery products.

Table 11.2. Number and Sales of Grocery Stores, By Type of Store.[a]

Year	Independent		Total	Chain	Grand total
	Affiliated	Unaffiliated			
		Stores, No.			
1940	108,750	296,250	405,000	41,350	446,350
1945	94,000	271,000	365,000	33,400	398,400
1950	122,000	253,000	375,000	25,700	400,700
1955	101,000	223,000	324,500	18,000	343,300
1960	84,000	156,000	240,000	20,050	260,050
1965	76,000	128,200	204,200	22,850	227,050
1970	69,400	104,700	174,100	34,200	208,300

	Independent	Chain	Convenience	Total
		Stores, No.		
1975	143,730	23,080	25,000	191,810
1980	112,600	18,700	35,800	165,100
1981	108,130	19,070	37,800	165,000
1982	104,970	18,330	38,700	162,000

	Independent		Total	Chain	Grand total
	Affiliated	Unaffiliated			
		Annual Sales (Billion $)			
1940	2.740	3.090	5.830	3.180	9.010
1945	4.700	5.300	10.000	5.350	15.350
1950	8.900	8.050	16.950	10.140	27.090
1955	15.500	9.655	25.155	14.260	39.415
1960	25.400	6.750	32.150	19.550	51.700
1965	31.800	6.100	37.900	27.205	64.925
1970	39.390	6.950	46.340	42.075	88.415

	Independent	Chain	Convenience	Total
		Annual Sales (Billion $)		
1975	70.300	66.750	5.480	142.530
1980	105.285	103.115	12.400	220.800
1981	106.875	119.905	14.120	240.900
1982	111.318	125.582	15.100	252.000

Source: Duewer (1984).
[a]Reporting of data changed in 1973 as indicated by new headings. Chaines before 1952 were defined as firms operating four or more stores, the minimum was changed to 11 stores after 1952.
[b]Excluding sales of gasoline.

did not give up without a struggle. They agitated for, and obtained, legislation designed to thwart unfair competition. The Robinson-Patman Act passed in 1936 reflected the failure of the earlier Clayton Act to restrain discriminatory practices. The Robinson-Patman Act contained provisions aimed at preventing price concession to some (the large) buyers and not to others, as well as other discriminatory trade practices that allegedly gave advantages to large purchasers. Many states also imposed taxes and regulatory strictures on chain operations. Nevertheless, expansion of chains continued.

Supermarkets

Although early chain activity centered on economies in procuring supplies, it soon became apparent to grocers that economies also were available by possible changes in selling. A major development from this line of thinking was the supermarket. The supermarket idea—large volume, low cost, and mass retailing—actually originated among independent operators, but it was adopted almost immediately by the chains. Where previously the emphasis had been put on the number of outlets, a shift began during the 1930s to fewer and larger outlets. The emphasis shifted to volume—not just to volume per se, but to the economies of size that came with volume. In addition, such innovations as self-service, cash-and-carry, and standardized accounting and operating procedures came into prominence.

Economies in both purchasing and sales allowed large-volume operators to reduce margins. The small, independent specialized meat markets, as well as grocery stores, were at a serious competitive disadvantage, and their numbers declined sharply. Although the small, independent meat market all but vanished, independent grocers (including meat departments) did not give up.

To counteract corporate chains, the independents made two major adaptations: (1) independent wholesalers sponsored the development of voluntary chain arrangements that gave independent retailers advantages of large-scale purchasing and many associated services, and (2) retailers formed cooperative wholesale purchasing and servicing organizations. In the former, a large wholesaler takes on many of the purchasing and servicing functions of the centralized purchasing department of a corporte chain, sometimes including many kinds of assistance for its members in operation and management of retail stores. The cooperative chain differs in that the independent retailers organize, own, and operate the wholesale agency for the benefit of its members. It would be a mistake to visualize all independent retailers as small operations. Many of them are large supermarkets—just as large as corporate supermarkets but with fewer stores. Many of the independents, however, own and operate more than one supermarket. There also are many superettes in the independent system, both voluntary and cooperative. "Supermarkets" are defined as stores with sales of $2 million or more annually; those with $1 million to $2 million are

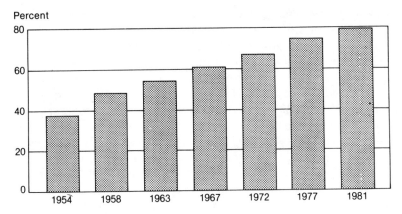

Fig. 11.2 Share of grocery store sales accounted for by supermarkets. [Courtesy, Duewer (1984).]

classed as "superettes"; and stores with less than $1 million annual sales are considered small.[3]

Development of chain operations and expansion of supermarkets were restricted during World War II. Immediately upon termination of the war, however, expansion continued at an accelerated rate. "The rapid post-war adoption of the supermarket came at the expense of many thousands or small grocery stores. The number of grocery stores operated by single-store firms dropped by more than 130,000 between 1948 and 1963. Stores with annual sales less than $5,000 dropped 86%" (National Commission on Food Marketing, 1966). Figure 11.2 indicates the growth in supermarket sales.

Recent developments in food retailing that are relevant to the meat industry are (1) the discount store, (2) the convenience store, (3) central cutting and packaging, and (4) the foodservice industry, including "fast foods."

Discount Houses

The discount house in a sense is a throw-back to the notion of early supermarket operation. Basically, they feature high-volume, limited-service, low-cost, and low-price merchandising and usually carry a wide

---

[3] Until the mid 1970s, supermarkets were defined as stores with annual sales of $1 million or more. Those with annual sales below $1 million are classed as small stores. Both inflation and expanding store size necessitated the change in the amount of annual sales needed for a store to be classed as a supermarket.

variety of goods. Some carry no food at all. Some carry food but only a limited selection of meat items, whereas others carry a full line of meat. Many discounters are organized as corporate chains.

Perhaps the best evidence that discounting has made inroads on established food retailers is found in the fact that established firms responded by adopting discount tactics themselves. For example, it was reported that in 1969, 47 percent of the chain supermarkets and 27 percent of independent supermarkets were discounting, and, furthermore, that the meat departments in 19 percent of the supermarkets and 22 percent of the superettes were discount pricing meat (Anon., 1971). In 1977, the extent of discounting among chain supermarkets remained at 47 percent, whereas 31 percent of independent supermarkets were using a discount policy (Anon., 1978B).

The practice of discounting created some repercussions throughout the retail industry. In 1972, A&P initiated a discount program known as WEO ("Where Economy Originates"). Retaliatory price cuts by competitors were associated, at least in part, with reduced earnings for the industry for several years (Parker 1975). The severity of price cuts was then apparently relaxed somewhat. Wide adoption of discounting, if that were continued, probably would defeat its purpose. A considerable range exists in the price elasticity of demand for individual foods, but the elasticity for the food total is relatively low—as indicated in an earlier chapter.

Discounting is not limited to retailing. For example, in 1969, it was reported that 33 percent of grocery wholesalers discounted prices (Anon., 1971B). In 1977, the proportion was 39 percent (Anon., 1978C).

Convenience Stores

Convenience stores are relatively small installations in carefully selected locations with potential for a large volume of traffic. They feature long hours of operation and a reasonably wide range of items with a limited number of lines of any particular item. Attempts are made to keep operating costs as low as possible, but prices usually run higher than in discount or supermarket operations. The emphasis is on convenience in location, service, and items carried.

The neighborhood grocery stores that survived the chain-supermarket revolution are, in essence, convenience stores, but the recent movement is not a revival of such stores. Some are independently owned and operated, but corporate chain systems dominate the field.

There were 500 convenience stores operating in 1957. That number has increased sharply, reaching 8,000 in 1967, 20,300 in 1973, 30,000 in 1977, and 38,700 in 1982 (Duewer, 1984). This growth is shown in

Tables 11.2 and 11.3. In a 25-year period, the movement has grown from virtually nothing to more than 38,000 stores with 6 percent of all grocery sales in 1982 (Table 11.4). There appears to be no doubt of continued growth. The extent of growth probably will be closely associated with trends in the affluence of consumers. Additional convenience stores will be built if patronage is forthcoming. Capital investments per unit are small compared to those for supermarkets.

Traub and Odland (1979) evaluated the impact of convenience foods on national food sales and expenditures. The result of their study showed that convenience products represented about half of the sales of food purchased for consumption at home. Of 166 products examined, 58 percent had a higher cost per serving than the fresh, or home-

Table 11.3.   Distribution of Grocery Store Numbers and Annual Sales, By Size of Store.

Year	Small	Superette	Supermarket	Convenience	Total
			Size		
			Store Numbers, percent		
1965[a]	73.5	12.5	14.0	NA[b]	100.00
1970[a]	65.5	16.1	18.40	NA	100.00
1975[c]	63.8	6.7	16.5	13.0	100.00
1980[d]	57.7	NA	20.9	21.4	100.00
1981[e]	54.7	5.0	17.4	22.9	100.00
1982[e]	53.2	5.0	17.9	23.9	100.00
			Annual Sales, percent		
1965[a]	16.3	13.0	70.7	NA	100.00
1970[a]	11.7	12.9	75.4	NA	100.00
1975[c]	15.6	7.7	72.4	4.3	100.00
1980[d]	17.1	NA	77.3	5.6	100.00
1981[e]	18.2	4.8	71.2	5.8	100.00
1982[e]	17.7	4.6	71.7	6.0	100.00
			Store Numbers, No.		
1982	86,130	8,220	28,950	38,700	162,000
			Annual Sales (Billion $)		
1982	44,535	11,665	180,700	15,100	252,000

Source: Duewer (1984).
[a]Small—sales less than $150,000; superette—sales from $150,000 to $500,000 annually; supermarket—sales of $500,000 or more annually.
[b]NA = Not available.
[c]Small—sales less than $500,000; superette—sales from $500,000 to $1 million annually; supermarket—sales of $1 million or more annually.
[d]Small—sales less than $1 million; supermarket—sales of $1 million or more annually.
[e]Small—sales less than $1 million; superette—sales from $1 million to $2 million annually; supermarket—sales of $2 million or more annually.

Table 11.4. Number and Percentage of Grocery Stores, By Type of Store and Sales Volume, 1982.

Type of store and sales volume	Stores		Total sales	
	No.	Percent	Million $	Percent
Supermarkets[a]	28,950	17.9	180,700	71.7
Chains	17,480	10.8	124,382	49.4
$2,000,000 to $3,999,999	3,665	2.3	10,995	4.4
$4,000,000 to $7,999,999	9,810	6.1	60,822	24.1
$8,000,000 to $11,999,999	2,340	1.4	23,400	9.3
$12,000,000 and over	1,665	1.0	29,165	11.6
Independent	11,470	7.1	56,318	22.3
$2,000,000 to $3,999,999	6,675	4.1	20,693	8.2
$4,000,000 to $7,999,999	3,650	2.3	21,016	8.3
$8,000,000 to $11,999,999	720	0.4	7,171	2.8
$12,000 and over	425	0.3	7,438	3.0
Supermarket-style[b]	8,220	5.0	11,665	4.6
Chain	850	0.5	1,200	0.5
Independent	7,370	4.5	10,465	4.1
Other stores[c]	86,130	53.2	44,535	17.7
Convenience stores	38,700	23.9	15,100	6.0
All stores	162,000	100.00	252,000	100.00
By affiliation:				
Independent	104,970	64.8	111,318	44.2
Chain	18,330	11.3	125,582	49.8
Convenience[d]	38,700	23.9	15,100	6.0

Source: Duewer (1984), based on data from the U.S. Department of Commerce and the 1966–83 Annual Report of the Grocery Industry published in *Progressive Grocer*.
[a]Supermarkets are defined as firms with at least $2 million annual sales.
[b]Annual sales of $1 million to $1,999,999.
[c]Annual sales of less than $1 million.
[d]Excludes sales of gasoline.

prepared, version, 24 percent cost less, and 18 percent cost about the same. They indicated, however, that when fuel cost and value of time spent in preparation of meals are considered, 60 percent were less expensive.

In 1970, processed meat was handled by 97 percent of convenience stores and fresh meat by 20 percent, but the selection of cuts was limited. Under present methods of operation, convenience stores on a per store basis are not major outlets for meat. Nevertheless, given a continued expansion in the number of stores, the aggregate quantity of meat can become increasingly important. The kind of research being carried out at major land grant universities in the technology of production and marketing of frozen fresh meat is particularly relevant to convenience stores. Wider consumer acceptance of frozen meat would enhance convenience store sales.

Central Cutting and Packaging

Central cutting and packaging is the use of a central unit consisting of cold storage, cutting, packaging, and delivery facilities for the servicing of a number of retail outlets. Centralized warehousing and breaking has been customary for many years for large-chain metropolitan operations. The extension to retail cutting and wrapping is of more recent origin. Centralized cutting and packaging for retail appears to be increasing, but at this time certain factors are retarding its full acceptance. For example, although there has been some improvement in meat-processing technology, present packaging techniques do not allow fresh beef to maintain a long-lasting bloom. The irregular sizes of packaged cuts are difficult to pack and handle, moreover, without breaking the packages—necessitating some rewrapping. Lack of standardization in cutting is a bottleneck to extensive centralization, not in a given metropolitan area, but as the area under consideration widens. Certain areas have become accustomed to particular methods of cutting and to the use of names for particular cuts that would not readily move in other areas.

Nevertheless, centralized cutting permits a greater degree of specialization in the use of labor, and more efficient techniques that reduce labor costs. Its widespread adoption probably would result in a decrease in the number of meat cutters needed for a given volume of meat, resulting in labor union reluctance. The farther centralized cutting and wrapping can be carried back in meat-marketing channels, the greater will be the savings in transportation. Elimination of bone and waste fat would reduce the tonnage of shipments by some 20 to 25 percent, and, hence, an approximately equivalent reduction in freight costs.

As noted in the previous section, the freezing of fresh meat appears to be particularly adapted to centralized cutting and packaging—if techniques can be perfected, that is, to maintain the bloom and acceptable appearance of the packaged meat. Past research results indicate that this can be done, as witness the improvements in vacuum-packed boxed beef and pork.

Centralized cutting and wrapping has been used successfully by some retailers for a number of years. Though its progress has been relatively slow, there is a distinct trend toward further cutting at the packer-breaker level.

"Warehouse" Type Retail Food Stores

Warehouse-type outlets may very well approach the ultimate in no-frills retailing. With an objective of minimizing costs and associated margins, they usually operate out of an unpretentious-looking building. Aisle space is frequently crowded. Shelf space for canned products may consist of stacked containers in which the goods were received. In some instances, customers have to mark prices on individual items as they are placed in the shopping cart, bring their own paper bags or boxes, and do their own bagging and/or boxing at the check-out counter. Many warehouse retail stores feature generic labeled products (i.e., cans and packages without a brand name). In general, the selection of meat cuts, the consistency of meat quality, its packaging, and display follow somewhat less rigid standards than in top level super-markets, but there are exceptions. Computer-assisted check-out is growing in acceptance at this type store, as well as in other types. The emphasis in warehouse retail stores, as it were, is on economy at any cost.

The Food Service Industry

The Food Service Industry, also referred to here as the Hotel, Restaurant, and Institutional trade (HRI), consists of more than 500,000 establishments and comprises an important market for livestock products. The industry is divided into two parts: public eating places and the institutional area. Public eating places are establishments operating for the purpose of making a profit and may be a separate entity or part of a larger facility. The institutional area of the food service industry includes operations providing supportive, and often nonprofit, service organizations, such as hospitals, sanitoriums, and schools.

Public eating places account for 75 percent of the retail value of all food consumed away from home (Duewer, 1984). Seventy-five percent of these establishments are separate outlets, with revenues generated primarily from the sale of prepared meals and snacks. These separate eating places account for 56 percent of the retail value of all food consumed away from home. That percentage probably also holds for meat (Duewer, 1984). The remaining 25 percent of the public eating places are part of larger facilities (e.g., a coffee shop in a department store or a snack bar in a bowling alley).

Expenditures for food eaten away from home in 1982 were estimated at $137 billion—about 39 percent of the total value of food consumed during the year. In comparison, the figures were $20 billion in 1960, $39 billion in 1970, and $67 billion in 1975. Unofficial reports indicate that the value of food eaten away from home is now approaching 50 percent. Van Dress (1982) indicated that beef represented 7.1 percent of all food service purchased by weight, whereas pork represented 2.4 percent. These figures exclude meats contained in mixed foods such as soups and prepared sandwiches. The menu speciality of most food service outlets is usually either a meat product or contains meat as an ingredient (Fig. 11.3).

The rapid growth in the HRI trade since the early sixties was in response to rising income, change in life style, demographic factors, and the large number of women being employed outside the home. Van Dress (1982) stated that "growth in number and revenue of away-from-home eating was spurred by rising incomes, a more mobile population, and trends toward convenience eating, and the increase in franchising and multiunit firms." The most dramatic growth has been in the "fast-food" part of the public-eating segment of the HRI trade. In terms of (constant) dollar sales of eating places, fast-food sales increased by 224 percent between 1967 and 1982, compared to a 21 percent increase for the HRI as a whole (Duewer, 1984).

"Fast foods" are one of the latest developments in food retailing. Fast foods are fully prepared, eat-in or carry-out foods ready for con-

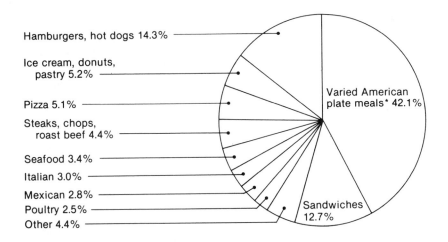

Figures may not add to 100% because of rounding.
*Usually a meat, poultry, or fish entree, a vegetable or grain, and a salad or serving of fruit.

Fig. 11.3 Establishments with food service: Distribution by menu speciality, United States, 1979. [Courtesy, Duewer (1984).]

sumption without additional preparation. For years, larger grocery stores have operated delicatessen departments that carry such meat items as luncheon meats, bacon, and canned hams. Some of these delicatessens might also feature ribs and chicken cooked in the store and sold warm. However, it usually remains for the consumer to cut, serve, and furnish accessory items.

Retail food operators recently have noted, with some envy, the acceptance and expansion of franchised, chain-operated, ready-to-eat food establishments (such as Kentucky Fried Chicken, McDonalds, etc). Some experimentation is currently going on to adapt this type of outlet to retail grocery stores, possibly as a separate department. No data are published regularly on the volume of meat moving through current franchised establishments, but there is no question that it is significant. It appears likely that retail grocers will attempt to capture some of this market. If this happens, it will put the retailers more directly into the HRI trade but is not likely to change meat-marketing channels or methods. Added outlets with promotional activity to match, however, could increase the demand for meat.

STRUCTURAL CHARACTERISTICS

In previous sections, it was noted that food retailing changed from an industry of predominantly small, independent operators to one typified by chain operations with large supermarkets during the past 60 to 70 years. Mergers, purchases, and extensive new construction were used by chains in their expansion activities. Integration, both horizontal and vertical, was used extensively in expansion and market control. One important structural change is the decline in the number of small stores and the increase in the average size per store. Data in Table 11.5 indicate that the share of total grocery sales accounted for by single-store firms fell from 51.8 percent in 1954 to 28.6 percent in 1977. During the same period, sales of firms with 101 or more stores rose from 29.4 to 40.7 percent. Many firms developed their own brand names and through advertising and promotion attempted to differentiate their products from those of competitors. Capital requirements for establishing a new store rose to heights that could not be attained by small firms.

There are certain characteristics associated with the structure of an industry that are presumed to have some effect on the conduct or behavior of firms in setting price and product policies. These, in turn, are presumed to bear some relationship to the performance of the firms and of the industry as a whole. In other words, under structural condi-

Table 11.5. Shares of Total Grocery Store Sales Accounted for by Firms of Various Sizes.

Size of firm, number of stores	Census years					
	1954	1958	1963	1967	1972	1977
	percent					
1	51.8	47.0	43.1	38.8	32.2	28.6
2 or 3	4.8	4.8	5.0	5.0	5.1	5.1
4 or 5	1.6	1.9	1.9	1.8	2.5	2.9
6-10	2.4	2.4	2.9	3.0	3.2	3.7
11-25	3.6	3.3	4.2	5.2	4.8	5.7
26-50	4.0	4.4	3.2	4.1	6.1	6.1
51-100	2.4	4.0	5.2	6.0	6.5	7.1
101 or more	29.4	32.2	34.5	36.1	39.6	40.7
Total	100.00	100.00	100.00	100.00	100.00	100.00

Source: Duewer (1984), based on U.S. Department of Commerce Census data.

tions that permit the attainment of a relatively high degree of bargaining power, it might be hypothesized that firms would be able to buy inputs at prices relatively low compared to the costs of production. If the same conditions existed in the selling area, selling prices might be set relatively high in comparison to costs. Under these circumstances, the resulting performances would yield profits in excess of those under more highly competitive conditions.

As evidenced by legislation designed to restrict monopolistic tendencies and unfair and discriminatory practices (e.g., the Sherman Act, Clayton Act, Robinson–Patman Act) and investigations by such bodies as the Federal Trade Commission and the Justice Department, the trend in the food industry to display these characteristics was a matter of serious social concern. This concern extends not only to small, independent retailers but also to farmers and ranchers, as well as to consumers in general. The Federal Trade Commission has investigated various aspects of food retailing from time to time. Congressional staff and Congressional Commissions also carry out studies (e.g., the U.S. Congress 1964 National Commission on Food Marketing, an exhaustive study at that time).

Degree of Concentration in Food Retailing

The degree of "concentration" in an industry is indicated by the size distribution of firms in that industry. One measurement of concentration is the "market share." This is determined by calculating the percentage of an industry's business done by the four (or eight, or twelve, or ?) largest firms. The larger the proportion of business done by a given number of firms, the greater the degree of concentration in that industry. It is usually hypothesized that the greater the degree of concentration, the greater the possibility of firms' enhancing their economic or market power. Industries dominated by a relatively few firms (e.g., U.S. automobile or steel manufacturers) presumably have a greater degree of control over price and product policy than an industry of many firms with none large enough to claim any dominance (e.g., farming). It may be noted that the mere existence of a high degree of concentration does not in itself provide proof that firms in fact utilize the economic power they may have, but the calculation of market shares is usually a first step in structural analysis. If it can be shown that concentration is relatively low, this factor can usually be eliminated as a source of undue market power.

Earlier discussion in this chapter indicated a tendency toward concentration in the food-retailing industry. It was pointed out that as a result of the chain and supermarket movements the trend has been toward fewer and bigger firms. "The rate of expansion of the chain store movement reached its peak in the early 1930s when stores belonging to chains totaled about 80,000. By this time the chain organizations had encompassed 1/3 of the nations's retail food business" (National Commission on Food Marketing, 1966). Chain store movement was followed by expansion in supermarkets. "Between the late 1940s and late 1950s, retail chain organizations and groups of affiliated independents expanded rapidly. . . . The supermarket movement progressed from 28% of the grocery store business going to supermarkets in 1948, to 69% in 1963. [The proportion increased to 71.7 percent by 1982; see Table 11.4.] The late 1950s and early 1960s marked a change in behavior and growth patterns in most markets in the United States. The replacement of small stores by supermarkets in most areas slowed considerably. . . . Thus on the whole, a saturation point was reached, with supermarkets doing 2/3 of the grocery business. The other 1/3 went through convenience stores and other small stores" (National Commission on Food Marketing, 1966). The number of convenience stores has expanded rapidly in recent years; this has slowed considerably the rate of decline in the total number of stores. Table 11.2 indicates that the downward trend in the number of stores has continued since the 1940s. The average sales per store increased rapidly, from $20,186 in 1940 to $198,808 in 1960, and reached more than $1.55 million in 1982, a tenfold increase in real terms (i.e., after adjusting for inflation) between 1940 and 1982 (Duewer, 1984)

The growth of affiliated independent grocers (affiliated in wholesale purchasing under either voluntary or cooperative arrangements) has roughly paralleled that of the chains since 1948. This, together with the expansion of convenience stores, has tended to neutralize the impact of growth in established chains.

The market share at the national level of the four largest grocery chains remained relatively consistent, at 20 to 22 percent, from the late 1940s to the 1960s. As shown in Table 11.6, the market share for the four leading chains dropped to 17.5 percent in 1972 and stood at 16.7 percent in 1981. Although the market share for the four and eight largest firms has dropped since 1958, the share of the 20 leading chains rose from 34 to 36 percent, suggesting that the remaining 12 firms experienced most of the growth during the period. There are no absolute standards for evaluating whether a concentration ratio of that magnitude is excessive. Bain (1959) suggested that a ratio of less than 35 percent could be considered unconcentrated. It is generally agreed, however, that measures of concentration at local levels are more meaningful than those at the national level. Shoppers of consumer goods are more or less limited in access to retail outlets, and grocery shoppers frequently are the most limited. In a study of meat marketing operations in three Standard Metropolitan Statistical Areas (SMSAs) of Texas in 1979, Clary et al. (1981) stated that "retail grocery marketing at the SMSA level is more concentrated than at the national level. However, the general trend of declining domination by the top four firms is observed at the SMSA level as at the national level. The four-firm concentration in Lubbock increased through 1972. Concentration then decreased substantially from 1972 to 1979 in Lubbock, as other firms entered the market and existing firms, other than the top four, increased their sales."

A report by the Federal Trade Commission (U.S. Department of Commerce 1975) reported that the market share of the four largest food retailers in metropolitan areas averaged more than 50 percent, and that food chains holding the largest market shares had higher gross margins and higher net profits than stores with lower market shares. Bain (1959) classified sellers with a 50 percent market share as moderately concentrated.

Table 11.6. Market Shares of 20 Leading Grocery Chains.

Rank of chains	Share of Total Grocery Store Sales							
	1954	1958	1963	1967	1972	1977	1980	1981
					Percent			
4 largest	20.9	21.7	20.0	19.0	17.5	17.4	17.1	16.7
8 largest	25.4	27.5	26.6	25.7	24.4	24.4	25.6	25.3
20 largest	29.9	34.1	34.0	34.4	34.8	34.5	36.6	36.5

Source: Duewer (1984), based on data from U.S. Department of Commerce and American Institute of Food Distribution.

Vertical Integration

Vertical integration is the control of successive stages of production or marketing—usually by ownership or contracts. Vertical integration in meat marketing by retailers would be classed as "backward integration." Successive backward stages, if carried all the way, would include wholesaling, processing, slaughtering, feedlot finishing, growing, and primary cow-calf operations. Vertical integration by retailers is not a major factor in the meat-marketing system. Studies by the National Commission on Food Marketing (1966), although indicating a slightly increasing trend, showed that purchases of hogs for slaughter amounted to less than 1/2 of 1 percent of commercial slaughter and that purchases of sheep were 3 to 3 1/2 percent. USDA's 1982 P & S Resume showed only one retailer feeding cattle and none feeding calves, hogs, or sheep in 1977, and no livestock feeding by retailers was reported thereafter.

During a period of uncertain and unstable economic conditions in 1973, some retailers purchased livestock and engaged packers to slaughter and process them on a custom basis. That was done primarily out of necessity rather than by choice, as price ceilings on meat, consumer boycotts, and rapid inflation had disrupted normal market channels. Although not classed as vertical integration, direct transactions between retailer buyers and packers (and processors) in effect integrate the wholesaling stage by eliminating it.

Among the motives for backward integration is the possibility of establishing a brand name and thereby effecting product differentiation. This, of course, is possible in processed meats, but to date, has limited application to fresh meat. As noted in the following section, contracting for production under "private label" is, in effect, vertical integration.

Differentiation of Product

In a perfectly competitive market situation, it is impossible for firms to establish and capitalize on brand names. This is an axiom of competitive theory. That corporate chains and affiliated independents have been able to establish brand names attests to the fact that competition is something less than the competitive norm.

Food retailers, as in many other industries, have several major options in distributing branded products, among them: (1) They can own outright the manufacturing and processing facilities that enable them to establish their own brand names, manufacture to their own specifications, and carry out their own advertising and promotional activities. (2) They can contract with an established manufacturer for production under their (the retailer's) own "private label." In this case, the retailer dictates the specifications of the product and carries out the advertising and promotion. (3) They can handle products manufactured and branded by an independent manufacturer or processor. Larger, well-established manufacturers carry out extensive promotional and advertising activities. Retailers, ordinarily, simply handle these products without advertising. (4) A fourth category is the same as the third except that the manufacturer does no advertising, and neither, ordinarily, does the retailer.

Although large retail chains have successfully differentiated many products under their own labels, success with differentiating fresh meat has been limited. In the case of fresh meats, a common approach is to select a word label other than one of USDA's official grade names (i.e., prime, choice, good, etc.) but carrying some other connotation of quality. Within the beef sector, some particular cattle breeders have attempted to differentiate their product on a quality basis. Distinctive packaging has not been a major factor in differentiating fresh meats.

Processed meats are more adapted to branding, as this opens the possibility of distinctive flavor, color, texture, packaging, etc. No recent studies have been made in this area, but the National Commission on Food Marketing showed substantial differentiation of such products as bacon and wieners by retailers.

Barriers to Entry

Market structure theory holds that established firms in an industry with relatively high barriers to the entry of new firms may behave differently (in price and product policies) from firms in an industry with low barriers to entry. Technically, "barrier to entry" is defined as the price or cost advantage held by established firms in an industry relative to potential new entrants (Bain 1956).

Prior to chain and supermarket developments, food retailing was considered an industry with relatively low barriers to entry, thus accounting for the numerous neighborhood "pa and ma" grocery stores. The Food Commission states: "There are strong indications, however, that post-World War II developments in food retailing have brought about a significant change in entry conditions. First, there have been dramatic organizational changes in food retailing, which themselves suggest alterations in the condition of entry. Second, various parts of this study have developed evidence which sheds light directly on the changing conditions of entry."

Organizational changes have resulted in declining numbers of stores, increasing average size of stores, increasing capital requirements for starting new stores, and declining profits for small-volume stores relative to supermarkets. Small retailers are at a disadvantage in obtaining desirable locations in competition with chains and affiliated groups. Most of the desirable locations are now found in shopping centers, and developers give preference to established firms. Advertising rates favor large-scale operators, and trading stamp companies prefer to have exclusive agreements with larger retailers. As already discussed, the concentration associated with corporate chain and affiliated groups give them more bargaining power and price concessions in their buying programs. Vertically integrated buying arrangements and the advantages gained from the conglomerate aspects of geographically large chain operations give large-scale operators advantages that are, in effect, barriers to entry by new firms.

The relevance of indicated barriers to entry in food retailing is the same for meats as for most other food products. Relatively high barriers to entry give firms in large chain operations the ability to exercise some control over pricing products. Retail meat prices are considerably more rigid than either wholesale meat prices or live animal prices. The points discussed in this section on structural characteristics (degree of concentration, vertical integration, differentiation of products, and barriers to entry) at least partially explain the basis upon which retailers derive the market power to exercise price control. These actions affect marketing margins and profit rates of large retailers.

RETAIL PRICING

Retailers have one common problem, whether they be chain or independent operator, supermarket or small store. Each has operating expenses that must be covered to stay in business. In addition, retailers hope to make a profit.

The pricing of processed meats differs little from that of nonmeat merchandise since the product sold can be identified with the product bought at wholesale. A predetermined margin can be applied to the wholesale cost to determine a target retail selling price. In practice, this is not as simple as it may appear if the price of each item is to cover expenses that might be allocated to particular items, or even to particular departments, within a store. The allocation of some expenses to particular items is difficult.

The pricing of fresh meat, however, is considerably more complicated than that of processed meat, particularly if the meat is bought in wholesale cuts that must be fabricated (broken down) into retail cuts. In this process, some shrinkage (weight loss) inevitably occurs since bone may be removed and fat may be trimmed away, and the salvage value of bone and fat is negligible. This may be called "cutting shrinkage." In addition, a so-called "store shrinkage" must be expected because of weight loss in spoilage, rewrapping damaged packages, pilferage, and returns by dissatisfied customers. These shrinkages are costs that must be covered, and it makes little difference whether they are included in operating expenses or listed separately.

Figures 10.2, 10.3, 10.4, and 10.5 show the numerous retail cuts derived from various wholesale cuts. Retailers may buy sides, quarters, primal, subprimal wholesale cuts, or boxed retail items. The extent of fabrication by the retailer, the extent of cutting shrinkage, and the amount of salvage will vary with the type of wholesale cut. Probably of greater importance, however, is the variation in the quantity of saleable meat from carcass to carcass.

Thus, in retailing fresh meat, received in nonretail cuts form, the individual items (cuts) sold at retail are different from the items purchased at wholesale, and the quantity sold at retail is different from the quantity purchased at wholesale.

It is well known that although some retail cuts are more preferred than others, yet all must move into the channels of consumption at a fairly uniform rate. This means that individual cuts must be priced at differential rates per pound, with the more desirable cuts commanding higher prices than the less desirable cuts. The aggregate weighted-average price per pound for *all* retail cuts derived from the wholesale cut must cover all expenses (including shrinkage) and yield a profit, if a profit is to be attained.

Table 11.7 illustrates several aspects of the retailer's problem in merchandising meat but should not be construed as representative for all 600-lb choice-steer carcasses.[4] It should be immediately apparent that the total value of the carcass to the retailer is dependent, not only upon retail price per pound, but also upon the cut-out. "Cut-out" is defined as the quantity of saleable meat obtained from a wholesale cut. In this example, the wholesale cut is an entire carcass. Cut-out has long been recognized as an extremely important factor in meat marketing. Two carcasses of identical weight and quality grade can yield significantly different quantities of saleable meat. This characteristic prompted the adoption of official USDA yield grades in June, 1965. Other things being equal, carcasses with higher cut-out have higher value. Among the variables that affect cut-out are conformation of the animal, degree of finish, weight of the carcass, sex, method of cutting, and degree of

---

[4]Actually, a carcass can, and usually does, yield a greater variety of retail cuts than shown in Table 11.7, which makes the pricing problem more complicated than indicated.

Table 11.7. Example of Cut-Out, Retail Prices, and Retail Value of Choice 600-lb Steer Carcass.

	Cut-out per 600-lb carcass (lb)	Retail price ($)	Retail value ($)
Steak			
Sirloin	34	3.19	108.46
Porterhouse	11	3.89	42.79
T-bone	13	3.69	47.97
Club	9	4.69	42.21
Round	36	2.49	89.64
Flank	2	4.29	8.58
Roasts			
Standing rib	29	3.99	115.71
Rolled rib	10	4.59	45.90
Rump roast	28	2.59	72.52
Arm chuck	28	2.39	66.92
Blade chuck	70	1.39	97.30
Boston pot roast	16	2.89	46.24
Heel of round	16	2.39	38.24
Other			
Brisket	11	2.19	24.09
Short ribs	15	1.59	23.85
Plate	18	1.59	28.62
Boneless neck	14	1.39	19.46
Stew meat	10	2.29	22.90
Shank	7	1.69	11.83
Hamburger	69	1.59	109.71
Kidney	2	0.69	1.38
Retail weight average price, and retail value	448	2.38	1,064.32
Salvage (bone and fat)	130	0.085	11.05
Cutting shrink	22	—	—
Total weight and value	600	—	1,075.37
Store shrink (3.25%)			34.95
Realized gross			1,040.42
Cost (wholesale)			812.50
Gross margin			227.92
Percentage gross margin			21.9

trim. By rigid specifications, careful selection of wholesale cuts, and standardization of cutting procedures, a retailer can narrow the range of cut-out obtained, but, under present conditions, he cannot hold this factor completely constant.

Table 11.7 also ilustrates differential pricing among various cuts. Prices are shown to range from 69 cents to $4.69 per lb. The average retail price per pound of meat in this example was $1,040.42 divided by 600, or $2.38. The wholesale cost was $1.35 per lb. In this case, the gross margin was $227.92 which amounted to 21.9 percent ($227.92

divided by 1,040.42 times 100) of the retail value. The percentage gross margin shown is slightly above the national average for retail meat departments, although better managers are reported to set a target of 25 percent (Anon. 1969).

If detailed research information were available on the demand for each retail cut, retailers would be able to adjust prices in a manner to maximize profits. Since this information is not available, retailers have had to discover market clearing prices through trial-and-error pricing. Operating on a continuous basis, they can readily observe those cuts that move slowly and adjust prices downward to speed up the movement before spoilage occurs or before those cuts have to be converted to a different form. Steaks and roasts can be converted to ground beef, for example, but this is not the way to stay in business. If certain cuts move out rapidly, this is a signal that prices can be raised.

Retailers are constrained to some extent in pricing policies by their competitors' actions, particularly in price raises, but also to a lesser degree in price cuts. A retailer who raises prices above those of his competitors on cuts of a given quality is likely to lose customers. A retailer who cuts prices may expect retaliation by competitors, and his actions could precipitate a price war. The latter is not likely, however, in the normal course of price adjustments that are designed merely to keep the usual volume of meat moving into consumption.

Approaches to Retail Pricing

Several different approaches are used by retailers in establishing selling prices, among them:

1. A method used by many large operators is known as "percentage gross margin."[5] Here the retailer calculates an average weighted selling price such that the gross margin over wholesale cost is some predetermined percentage of the selling price. In the example provided in Table 11.7, the gross margin was 21.9 percent. As mentioned earlier, the retailer may set up a target gross margin of, say, 25 percent but the margin actually realized will depend upon the cut-out and prices obtained for the various cuts. The calculation of a predetermined percentage gross margin is simple if the retailer knows (a) the cost of the meat laid into his retail outlet, and (b) the

---

[5]Percentage gross margin is synonymous with percentage gross profit. It also follows that absolute gross margin is synonymous with absolute gross profit. Absolute gross margin or absolute gross profit is expressed in cents per pound rather than as a percentage.

cut-out of the retail product. Let us say the delivered cost of a side of beef is $1.35 per lb and that 1.41 pounds of carcass beef yields 1 pound of retail beef. The average retail price that would give a 25-percent gross margin is obtained by the algebraic expression:

$$x = (\$1.35 \times 1.41) + 0.25\,x$$
$$x = \$2.532$$

where x = retail price.

Of course, the retailer still would be faced with the problem of pricing individual cuts to yield an average of $2.53 per lb.

2. Some retailers use a "percentage mark-up" over wholesale cost. One study indicated this to be the most widely used method among retailers in the North Central States (Forstad, 1955). The National Commission on Food Marketing (1966) stated that "of the many operating measures utilized in food retailing, (percentage) gross margin is probably the most frequently used." It is obvious that any given absolute gross margin would comprise a higher percentage of wholesale cost than of retail value. Assume that the cost and cut-out are identical with those in the example above and that the retailer desires a percentage mark-up of 33 percent. Retail price can be calculated from the following simple arithmetic expression:

Retail price = ($1.35 × 1.41) + 0.33($1.35 × 1.41)
Retail price = $2.53

3. A third approach to retail pricing is "cents-per-pound mark-up" over wholesale cost.

4. Smaller retailers sometimes simply use a prepared "retail meat pricing chart." These charts are available from various agencies and usually have a similar format. The chart is a table set up in such a way that the retailer locates a column corresponding to his wholesale cost (per side of beef, for example), or he may use a column corresponding to his average desired selling price. The retailer then simply follows down that column to successive rows that show him suggested retail prices for the various retail cuts that may be derived from the side. The suggested retail prices are such that their weighted average will equal either the average wholesale cost or average desired selling price as selected at the column heading. Such charts are based on a standardized cut-out of the various cuts of meat. Earlier comments indicate the weakness of accepting an average cut-out without knowing carcass specifications and cutting and trimming specifications. Even established retailers who work hard at maintaining such specifications periodically run cut-out tests to keep their operations in line. The chart prices, while possibly appro-

priate for a particular area at a particular time, may not agree with consumer preferences in another location or at a different time. In spite of their weaknesses, however, price charts may well serve as guides; if up-dated and made specific to particular locations, they can be very helpful.

5. A fifth approach, one that cannot be ignored by any retailer, is to be guided by the prices of competitors. As with the pricing chart, this method ignores possible differences in cut-out that result from differences in specifications of wholesale cuts ordered by competitors, differences in cutting methods, and differences in trimming specifications. Undoubtedly, most retailers take note of prices charged by their competitors. Stout et al. (1968), in a study restricted to a sample of Ohio retailers, reported, "Product pricing procedures reflected the intensely competitive nature of meat retailing. All firms, with costs and margin goals firmly in mind, priced products within the restrictive framework permitted by competitors' prices. Although net profit goals, product mix, cut-out test results, volume and turnover, brand loyalty, and other factors entered into the pricing decisions, competitors' prices were the dominant consideration."

Meat Price Specials

The complications of retail meat pricing are further compounded by the use of "special" sales—substantial short-term (week-end or early week) price reductions, usually accompanied by intensive advertising and in-store promotion. Price cuts in a "special" may amount to 10 percent off regular prices (Tongue, 1963). The evidence indicates that consumers do in fact respond to specials. William Tongue (1963) presented data showing that a beef special raised the tonnage of beef from about 20 percent of weekly store meat sales to 60 to 65 percent, smoked meats from about 1 to 41 percent and poultry from about 9 to 29 percent. DeGraff (1960) reported data from the National Association of Food Chains that indicated a smaller but nevertheless significant response. The retailer knows that a price reduction will cut his gross returns per unit, but as long as the margin still yields a positive profit he hopes the increased volume will maintain, if not improve, his net earnings.

Livestock producers have questioned the effect of meat price specials on livestock prices. No definitive research studies are available on this subject. Tongue (1963) and DeGraff (1960) both attempt to show that, logically speaking, meat price specials may be expected to benefit the livestock industry. The reasoning, in part, is that specials result in increased volume of sale, thus necessitating larger purchases at whole-sale, which, in turn, would be expected to add strength to the wholesale market. Somewhat contrary to this line of reasoning is an opinion that packers, eager to obtain the large volume of meat sales that go with a large chain special, may be willing to grant price concessions rather than hold for higher prices. Neither of these hypotheses has been veri-fied by empirical analysis.

FROZEN FOOD LOCKERS AND PROVISIONERS

Sales by frozen-food purveyors and the use of lockers, including home freezers, are classed as retail activity in that both patron and owners are final consumers. The widespread use of home freezers is an impor-tant stimulant to the demand for meat.

The commercial frozen-food locker industry, including combination slaughter–locker plants, began in the early 1900s, had its greatest pe-riod of growth during the 1930s and 1940s, and reached a peak during the early 1950s. Numbers have declined since that time, coincident with an increase in use of home freezers. Most refrigerators currently on the market have a freezing compartment, which adds greatly to total home-freezing capacity. Many households also have a separate freezer unit. The availability of home freezers is closely associated with consumer response to meat price specials. Housewives often stock-up on specials, using home freezers for storage.

As noted above, many small locker plants have gone out of business since the early 1950s. It is reported that many of those still remaining are experiencing difficulties in complying with the U.S. Wholesome Meat Act of 1967 and associated state requirements. As a result, an acceleration is expected in the rate of decline of this class of frozen-food locker plant.

Of relatively recent origin is the freezer provisioner—a specialized food-service firm that contracts with households to supply frozen foods, including meat. This type of operator is oriented directly toward supplying owners of home freezers. Some firms handle freezers as well as frozen food, whereas others handle only food. Various services are provided, including cutting, wrapping, sharp freezing, house delivery, and financing. At present, only a relatively small fraction of total meat consumed is obtained in this manner. Future growth in this segment of the meat industry will depend largely on the degree to which the quality of meat delivered conforms to expectations of consumers and the level of prices offered as compared to supermarket prices.

REFERENCES

Anon. 1969. Meat marketing trends and practices. *Food Topics.* Jan., pp. 64–67.

Anon. 1971. Grocery business annual report—1971. *Progressive Grocer.* Apr., p. 68.

Anon. 1978 A. Grocery industry report for 1977. *Progressive Grocer,* Apr., p. 55.

Anon. 1978 B. Grocery industry report for 1977. *Progressive Grocer,* Apr., p. 82.

Anon. 1978 C. Grocery industry report for 1977. *Progressive Grocer,* Apr., p. 84.

Anon. 1978 D. Grocery industry report for 1977. *Progressive Grocer,* Apr., p. 144.

Bain, J. S. 1956. *Barriers to New Competition.* Cambridge, Mass.: Harvard University Press.

Bain, J. S. 1969. *Industrial Organization.* New York: John Wiley & Sons, pp. 124–133.

Butz, D., and Baker, G. L. 1960. The changing structure of the meat economy. Harvard Univ., Div. Res., Graduate School Business Admin.

Clary, G. M.; Dietrich, R. A.; and Farris, D. E. 1981. Meat marketing operations in Dallas-Ft. Worth, Houston, and Lubbock. Texas Agr. Exp. Sta. Mp-1497, College Station.

DeGraff, H. 1960. *Beef Production and Distribution.* Norman, OK: University of Oklahoma Press.

DeLoach, D. P. 1960. Changes in food retailing. Washington Agr. Expt. Sta. Bull. 619.

Duewer, Lawrence A. 1984. Changing trends in the red meat distribution system. USDA, ERS, Agr. Econ. Rept. No. 509.

Dyer, L. W. 1985. Meat talk. *Progressive Grocer.* Sept. p. 219.

Federal Trade Commission. 1960. Economic inquiry into food marketing. I. Concentration and integration in retailing. Federal Trade Comm. Staff Rept., U.S. Govt. Printing Office, Washington, D.C.

Forstad, E. C. 1955. Retailing meat in the north central states. Indiana Agr. Expt. Sta. Bull. 622.

Harrison, T. G. 1962. How we developed our meat program. *Food Merchandising.* Feb., p. 36.

Leiman, M. 1967. Food retailing by discount houses. USDA Agr. Marketing Serv., Marketing Res. Rept. 785.

Leiman, M., and Kriesberg, M. 1962. Food retailing by discount houses. *In* Marketing and Transportation Situation. USDA Econ. Res. Serv. MTS-114.

Mueller, W. F., and Garoian, L. 1960. Changes in market structure of grocery retailing, 1940–58. Wisconsin Agr. Expt. Sta. Res. Rept. 5.

Mueller, W. F., and Garoian, L. 1961. *Changes in Market Structure of Grocery Retailing.* Madison, WI: University of Wisconsin Press.

National Commission on Food Marketing. 1966. Organization and competition in food retailing. Natl. Comm. Food Marketing Tech. Study 7, U.S. Govt. Printing Office, Washington, D.C.

Nix, J. E. 1978. Retail meat prices in perspective. USDA Econ. Stat. and Coop. Ser. ESCS-23, May.

Parker, R. C. 1975. Economic report on food chain profits. Federal Trade Commission. Staff Report (unnumbered), p. 19.

Stout, T. T.; Hawkins, M. H.; and Marion, B. W. 1968. Meat procurement and distribution by Ohio grocery chains and affiliated wholesalers. Ohio Agr. Res. Develop. Center Res. Bull. 1014.

Tongue, W. W. 1963. Week-end specials pay off at retail level and increase overall consumption of meat. Proc. 58th Annual Meeting Am. Meat Inst., Chicago, Sept. 22–25.

Traub, Larry G., and Odland, D. D. 1979. Convenience Foods and Home-Prepared foods. USDA, ESCS, Agr. Econ. Rept. No. 429.

U.S. Department of Commerce. 1971. 1967 Census of retail trade. U.S. Dept. of Comm. Summary and Subject Statistics, vol. 1, U.S. Gov't. Printing Office, Washington, D.C.

U.S. Department of Commerce. 1975. 1972 Census of retail trade. U.S. Dept. of Comm., Summary and Subject Statistics, vol. 1, U.S. Gov't. Printing Office, Washington, D.C.

USDA. 1977. Packers and stockyards resume, USDA. Packers and Stockyards Administration, vol. XV, No. 3 Dec.

Van Dress, M. G. 1982. The foodservice industry, structure, organization, and use of food, equipment, and supplies. USDA, ERS, Statistical Bull. No. 690.

12

Electronic Marketing of Livestock and Meat

The United States' agricultural marketing system is very large and complex. Although it has been performing the necessary functions of moving farm products from producers, transforming raw products to consumer goods, and channeling them into the retail end of the market, there are some problems.

Concern about the degree of market competition and efficiency is expressed by producers, consumers, and policy makers. This concern is related to the decline in the traditional large central markets and the lack of sufficient access by producers to large numbers of buyers for their products.

The decline of organized markets coupled with increased direct contracting and formula trading has resulted in "thin market" or "thinly reported market" problems. "Thin markets" commonly refer to markets characterized by low volume and a relatively small number of negotiated transactions per unit of time.[1] Prices in thin markets are usually erratic and do not necessarily reflect the true forces of supply and demand or the true value of traded commodities. Such prices may also be subject to manipulation because traders become aware of their ability to affect the market price.

As organized markets continued to decline and as direct and formula trading continued to increase, the thin market problems have become more important. Under such conditions, which make it difficult to maintain a viable, competitive market, many pricing and production-marketing coordination problems arise. Lack of sufficient, accurate market information may put small traders in a disadvantageous situation in a marketplace where larger traders have the edge. One suggested solution to some pricing and competition problems is to "thicken" the market. This objective may be accomplished through increasing the volume traded in an organized market to the point that

---

[1]Thinly reported markets may actually have sufficient number of negotiated trades to reflect supply and demand conditions; however, prices and other terms of trade are not reported to market news services.

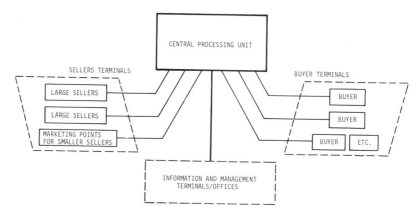

Fig. 12.1. Example of computer network configuration for electronic marketing. [Courtesy, Sarhan and Nelson (1983).]

prices do reflect actual supply and demand and are also readily available. Various means could be used, but probably the most innovative and potentially promising method is an electronic or computerized trading floor, referred to here as "electronic marketing."

The first documented electronic marketing, known as "Selevision," was used to remote-market Florida citrus fruits in the mid 1940s (Henderson, 1984). Real interest in electronic marketing began in the early 1960s, however, when the first modern teletype auction was developed in Canada to market Ontario hogs. Some successful telephone auctions for livestock were developed in the U.S. in the 1960s, but it was not until the late 1970s that several industry groups and the USDA initiated electronic-marketing pilot projects.

ELECTRONIC MARKETING—THE CONCEPT, TYPES, AND FEATURES

What is Electronic Marketing?

Electronic marketing is a trading system that utilizes electronic devices such as telephones, a teletype network, or a computer-terminals network for communication between buyers and sellers not physically present at one location (Fig. 12.1). Electronic marketing separates the negotiating function from the physical transfer of the product or commodity. It is capable of showing the offers and bids of each seller and buyer and of moving products directly, or nearly so, from sellers to buyers. The system is open to all buyers and sellers regardless of their location and is capable of providing instant market information to all traders. Price discovery is centralized and thus creates a highly competitive market environment among the large number of buyers and sellers necessary for a high degree of pricing accuracy. This is clearly an ideal system that is technologically possible and economically efficient.[2]

Types of Electronic Marketing

Although the concept of electronic marketing is not new, more advanced forms of telecommunications and data processing were introduced in the mid 1970s. Bell et al. (1983) and Henderson et al. (1976) identified five basic types of electronic markets: (1) manual clearinghouse, (2) telephone auctions, (3) teletype auctions, (4) computer networks, and (5) video auctions. All five systems provide basically the same service but differ in the degree of sophistication in terms of procedures and equipment.

Manual Clearinghouse.   The manual clearing house—the most basic form of electronic marketing—involves the use of regular telephones to list bids and offers of products at a central sales office. Market personnel at the central sales office sort bids and offers, match trades, and inform buyers and sellers of the quantity and price and other terms of trade. Delivery is arranged after trades are completed and products are transported directly to buyers.

Telephone Auctions.   These, also known as "teleauctions" or "Tele-O-Auctions," are primarily a form of conference telephone calls that were first introduced in the United States in Virginia in 1962 and were used to sell slaughter hogs. This simple method involves simultaneous two-way communication between bidders scattered over wide geographical areas by means of a regular conference telephone call connecting them with an auctioneer who is located at a central sales office (e.g., at a producer cooperative headquarters). The auction procedure

---

[2]It is important to distinguish between *electronic marketing* and *computerized information systems*. Electronic marketing includes the sales negotiation as an integral part of the system and price establishment occurs within the overall process. On the other hand, computerized market information systems use electronic devices to compile and disseminate information on sales, offerings, purchase requirements and/or prices, and other terms of trade *subsequent to* actual transactions. That is, prices are established in private negotiations as an adjunct to the system, not a part of it. In electronic marketing, the computer acts as a communication manager and may perform numerous marketing functions. Market information is only a byproduct of computer marketing.

is similar to regular auctions except that bidders and animals are not all in the same location. Selling is by description, usually off the farm, on the basis of specific known grades and standards. Commingling is possible to form large and uniform lots at local yards. Livestock movement from sellers to buyers and the financial settlement follows successful completion of a trade. Use of telephone conferences is still popular for selling feeder pigs, feeder and slaughter cattle, market hogs, and lambs.

Teletype Auctions. This system was first used to market slaughter hogs in Ontario, Canada in 1961 and is still used there and in other provinces. Teletype systems are similar to telephone auctions except that each buyer has direct communication through a teletype buying machine connected to a central computer instead of through voice communication with an auctioneer. Typically, a Dutch (regressive) auction method is used. Livestock may be assembled at a certain location prior to sale. Selling is by description, and the computer acts as the auctioneer, with automatic selling tape changing the price at prespecified time intervals.

Computer Networks. Computer networks—the more innovative and most advanced of electronic marketing methods—were first introduced in 1975 when Plains Cotton Cooperative Association of Lubbock, Texas developed TELCOT to sell cotton. Other computerized systems have been developed since. Computerized systems consist of hardware and software. The hardware usually consists of a central computer, a number of televisionlike devices (commonly referred to as Video Display Terminals, VDT), a keyboard, and printers at each participating site. The central computer and terminals at the various locations are linked together via the telephone system (Fig. 12.1). The exact configuration of equipment depends on the type of communications system used and the computer program utilized (i.e., software). Software refers to the computer programs or instructions that tell the computer what to do in terms of how products are described and listed and how negotiations will be conducted.

Video Auctions. This form of electronic marketing uses video tapes of livestock that is still on farms and ranches to sell in a competitive environment. It was first used to sell cattle in Oregon in 1975. Video marketing involves assembling potential buyers to view tapes and review information provided by sellers and then engage in a traditional auction. Buyers may be assembled in one location (e.g., a hotel or agricultural extension office) or at several locations where video tapes are simultaneously reviewed, all buyers being interconnected through a telephone conference call (i.e., a combination of teleauction and video auctions). Delivery of sold livestock follows the sale. Most video auctions sell feeder cattle, but other species are also sold.

Henderson (1984) suggested that while the concept of electronic marketing includes all the above variations, only computerized sytems that utilize open, competitive price-discovery methods capable of handling large number of traders and transactions simultaneously have the capacity to contribute substantially to the improvement of the pricing and operational efficiency of the market. Furthermore, computerized systems are capable of utilizing advances in computer and communication technology.

Features and Functions of Electronic Marketing

The specific form of communications system and operational procedures in an electronic marketing system may vary in design and organization, but all systems share similar operational features and provide similar functions. All electronic marketing systems have five features in common: (1) organized trading, (2) centralized sales negotiation, (3) remote market access, (4) selling by description, and (5) post-sale shipment of traded commodities (Henderson, 1982).

A complete electronic marketing system has five functions: (1) listing, (2) dissemination, (3) trading, (4) reporting, and (5) clearinghouse. Before using an electronic marketing system, traders must have identification numbers; these are either given to the system's operator or entered on the computer.

Listing.   Sellers describe the commodity (or product) being offered according to standard grades (third-party graders or inspectors are usually assigned). In the case of livestock, grading may be done at the farm or ranch or at a local assembly location where commingling may occur to form large loads prior to sale. Buyers may also list orders or bids to buy certain items consistent with the standard grades and descriptions.

Dissemination.   Bids and offerings are disseminated to potential traders at remote locations through two-way communications for easy access by traders.

Trading.   Utilizing the same communications medium, buyers bid against each other (auction system) or negotiate with sellers (private negotiation system) until acceptable terms, or stalemate, is reached. It should be pointed out that negotiation methods range from relatively simple manual methods to complex ones. Auction methods usually allow for "no sale" and/or "firm price" options.

Reporting. Statistics compiled from completed transactions are summarized and placed in public files for all traders to review. This market information is a by-product of actual trading on the system.

Clearinghouse. The system performs the recording and confirming of transactions and invoicing. It may also involve issuing checks to sellers.

SUGGESTED ADVANTAGES AND DISADVANTAGES OF ELECTRONIC MARKETING

Advantages

The principal advantage of electronic marketing is the potential gain in market efficiency. This is especially important in markets with many and dispersed sellers and buyers where gathering of large volumes of market information is possible. A properly organized and operated electronic marketing system has the potential to improve both pricing and operational efficiency. In other words, by centralizing price discovery and decentralizing the direct flow of products, it may reduce marketing costs and increase competition by preserving the advantages associated with central markets. Bell et al. (1983) and Purcell and Williamson (1980) identified the following six advantages of electronic marketing:

Improved Market Access. Buyers, regardless of their size or geographical area, can have access to any participating market because their physical presence is not required. Large numbers of potential market participants means increased competition, which suggests that producers are more likely to receive the "true" market value of their livestock. This advantage is particularly important to small and more geographically remote producers.

Lower Costs to Individual Buyers. Since buyers do not have to be physically present at sales barns, farms, or terminals, the electronic system will reduce their costs of livestock procurement.

Higher Market Operational Efficiency. Electronic markets allow buyers to enter the process without investment in physical facilities. When livestock are graded, grouped, and offered in uniform lots but moved only after successful negotiations are complete, the time and costs of selling can be reduced considerably. Reducing the transportation costs of cross-hauling and multiple handling also adds to the system's efficiency.

Greater Pricing Accuracy. There is some evidence that electronic marketing is capable of improving pricing accuracy, as measured in terms of its ability to differentiate prices to reflect differences in transportation, transformation, storage, and quality.

Improved Market Information. Electronic markets are capable of processing and providing more complete market information in a rapid and timely manner. Because trading is by description, detailed information on commodities and product characteristics, volume and prices are made available to large numbers of traders simultaneously.

Improved Condition of Livestock. With reduced handling and movement, livestock should reach buyers with less delay and fewer bruises, smaller shrink, and in overall better condition.

In addition to these advantages, some observers suggest that electronic trading, by promoting overall market efficiency, may limit government regulation. Also, such systems tend to equalize market power by providing similar information to all participants regardless of size (this would be viewed as a disadvantage by large traders, who normally have access to more and more timely market information). Other advantages include providing auxiliary services, e.g. farm management and accounting services.

Disadvantages

The following list of suggested disadvantages of electronic marketing was provided by participants in a 1980 Electronic Marketing Seminar held in Dallas (Sporleder, ed., 1980). It should be pointed out, however, that several of these items were shown to be groundless after several pilot projects were conducted:

1. Objection to untraditional change.
2. Product differentiation in meat may not fit standard terminology.
3. Perishability of meat limits the use of wide trading areas.

4. Antitrust problems may result.
5. Cost-effectiveness has not been assured.
6. Problems in description or specification of product or animal.
7. Validity of contracts must be assured.
8. Costs may be too high for an unproven system.
9. A monopoly system may be required, thus inviting government regulations.
10. A dual marketing system during the start-up of an electronic marketing system may lead to insufficient volume to make costs reasonable.
11. An electronic system may fail to recognize the importance of non-price factors.
12. Some participants in the current system will be excluded.
13. Personal interchange is lacking.

CONDITIONS IMPORTANT TO THE SUCCESS OF ELECTRONIC MARKETING

The several conditions for a successful electronic marketing system may be grouped into two categories, as follows: (1) conditions basic to a commodity or industry, and (2) conditions established by the design and operation of the system itself.

Conditions Basic to the Commodity or Industry

These are the conditions that must pre-exist within an industry. Henderson et al. (1976) and Henderson (1982) suggested four such conditions, here to be defined and discussed briefly.

Potentially Competitive Markets. The potential for a competitive system must exist. Situations involving a market power imbalance (between buyers and sellers) are open to the possibility of an electronic marketing system, provided that the powerful side will accept such a system. Electronic marketing offers few advantages where one or a few traders dominate the market.

Traders' Interest. Traders must perceive a need for an alternative (probably more competitive) market system. They must be willing to trade by description and abide by the rules.

Accurately Describable Commodities. Items to be traded must be describable in meaningful and consistent terms. In addition, they must remain stable from the time they are described until they are sold and delivered.

High Volume and Frequent Trading. Candidate commodities must be produced and traded in relatively large volume. Frequency of trading should be high in order to provide for market liquidity.

Conditions Established by the Design and Operation of the System

Henderson et al. (1976) suggested that the following conditions should be created within the marketing system itself in order to achieve successful implementation:

Trader Education. Electronic marketing is new and "out of tradition" to most producers, and thus educational programs are essential to help them understand the working and potential benefits of such a system and enhance the probability of their accepting it.

Performance Guarantees. The system must earn traders' confidence and provide for market and fiscal integrity. Contracts, bonding, penalties, clear and enforced rules, and government regulations and assistance are ways to accomplish this.

Grading Systems. One of the critical elements in the success of electronic trading is the ability to describe satisfactorily the product being traded. The development and use of meaningful grades and standards and a method of third-party inspection are essential to assure the success of electronic marketing.

High Actual Volume Trading. The system must achieve a high volume of actual trades to ensure price accuracy and market efficiency. High volume may be achieved by voluntary or mandatory methods.

In addition to the above conditions, Henderson (1982) stated the following:

A good measure of indomitable and innovative spirit is an essential ingredient in the successful development and implementation of electronic markets at this point in time, partly because there is no clear cut pattern to follow for success and partly because those with vested interests in the current system have much reason to argue that it can't be done and to discourage its use by whatever means possible. Because development costs are often high and because competitive reaction demands a good measure of staying power, this entrepreneurial spirit must be backed by adequate venture capital. An undercapitalized electronic trading venture, as is true of most commercial innovations, is likely to wither before it can be fully and fairly tested in the marketplace.

EXAMPLES OF COMPUTERIZED MARKETING SYSTEMS

A number of computerized marketing systems are now being used or have been pilot-tested but are currently not operating. Examples of computerized systems currently in operation include TELCOT's cotton trading system; the Egg Clearinghouse, Inc. (ECI); and the National Marketing Association, Inc. (NMA), which evolved from a pilot project developed in Virginia to sell slaughter cows and later modified to include lambs. In the late 1970s and early 1980s, USDA provided funds to several states to develop and pilot-test electronic marketing methods for livestock and meat. Three systems were pilot-tested in the early 1980s: (1) CATTLEX—Cattle Exchange—was developed by Texas A&M University for feeder cattle; (2) HAMS—the Hog Accelerated Marketing System—was developed in Ohio to market slaughter hogs; and (3) CATS—Computer Assisted Trading System for wholesale meat was developed by the American Meat Exchange and tested by the University of Illinois. In order to illustrate the operational procedures of electronic marketing, a brief description of the features and operation of these three systems is presented.

CATTLEX—Cattle Exchange

CATTLEX is a computerized cash and contract marketing system for feeder cattle developed by Texas A&M University in cooperation with the Texas Department of Agriculture and with funding from USDA. The system was pilot-tested from September 3, 1980 to November 20, 1981. The trading was conducted through centralized remote-access using the English-auction bidding system. The system network consisted of a central computer and a number of terminals placed at different locations in Texas and one in New Mexico. The number of locations increased from 14 when the test began operation to 29 by midsummer 1981. Terminals were located at selected feedlots, auction markets, order buyers' offices, and one producers' cooperative. Cattle were offered either on cash sales or contract basis. Cash sales were for delivery within 14 days of the day a lot was initially listed, whereas contract sales were for delivery more than two weeks in the future. Sellers had the right to set the exact delivery date for both options.

Listing Procedures on CATTLEX. The first step in trading on CATTLEX was to list cattle for sale by completing a "Certificate of Agreement for Sale of Cattle." The certificate included information supplied by the cattle owner and certified by a third-party grader. Request to list cattle on the system was then submitted to the system's operator or auction market management either in person or over the telephone. Auction prices were for cattle either on the ranch or delivered to a specified location. In addition to owner information about the cattle, sellers submitted a no-sale (or reservation) price for the cash market offerings and a sale price for contract offerings. Owners of the cattle paid a listing fee. Following the request to list cattle for sale, animals were graded, either on the farm—for lots of 40,000 lb (truckload or larger)—but after delivery to auction or an assembly point for smaller lots—10,000 to 40,000 lb. A weight-adjustment scale was used to reflect price differentials and deviations from prespecified payweight ranges. The information provided by the seller along with the grader's assessment/comments were entered into a catalog of lot listing on the computer (Table 12.1), which was made available to all potential buyers. The eight-digit lot number (shown in the first column of Table 12.1) gives potential buyers a summary of basic information. The first three digits indicate the location of the listing terminal; digits four and five give the sequential week of the year; and the last three digits indicate the total number of lots listed from that terminal that week.

Reviewing the Information Before Bidding. A potential buyer could survey one or all lots listed, and, furthermore, the system allowed traders to examine (sort) lots in certain locations or according to several sorting factors (Table 12.2). Potential bidders could access more information about a particular lot by simply entering into the computer terminal the lot number following the statement, "Detail listing for," which is shown at the bottom of the screen in Table 12.1. In response to such a request, the system would retrieve a display similar to the simulated ones shown in Tables 12.3 and 12.4.

Auctioning Procedures on CATTLEX. Table 12.5 shows a simulated screen of the CATTLEX auction system as viewed by traders on the VTD. A total of 16 lots are shown on each full screen—eight above and eight below the starred-line. Those above the asterisks are lots currently being auctioned and the eight below are those that have already been auctioned. The VDT display rotates automatically every two minutes with the last line disappearing as a new line (i.e., lot) appears on top. At the end of 16 minutes, the highest bidder with a price at least equal to the no-sale price buys the lot. It should be pointed out that a particular individual's entry in the column headed "MY BID" in Table 12.5 is displayed only to that individual, thus allowing him to compare his bid with that of others as shown in the column headed "HIGH

Table 12.1. Example of VDT Display to Buyers Showing Catalog Display of Offerings for a Particular Day.

Welcome to Tamu Cattlex
Listing for the Sale of 06/23/80

Lot	Sale	No. Head	Ave Wt.	S[a]	D[b]	Co.[c]	A[d] G	USDA Grade	Common Name	Time On
00212014	1	27	401	S	D	015	SY	MED 2	Hereford	1100
00112007	2	25	686	S	D	213	ST	MED 1	CB # 2	1102
00212001	3	25	335	H	D	089	NC	MED 2	CB # 1.5	1104
00112013	e	180	650	S	C	423	LY	MED 1	OKIE # 1	
00112011	4	80	600	H	R	257	FY	MED 2	CB # 2	1106
00212003	5	35	659	S	D	015	SY	LRG 1	Okie # 1	1108
00112017	6	73	525	H	R	073	NC	LRG 2	Okie # 1	1110
00112009	7	88	372	H	D	213	SY	SML 1	Okie # 2	1112
00112026	e	430	500	H	C	041	FY	MED 2	Hereford	
00112020	8	40	484	H	D	213	NC	MED 1	Hereford	1114
00112010	e	175	475	S	C	423	NC	MED 1	Okie # 1.5	
00212005	9	175	300	S	R	089	SY	SML 2	Okie # 3	1116
00112012	10	44	448	H	D	213	NC	MED 1	Hereford	1118
00112025	11	38	634	S	D	213	FY	MED 2	Ang # 2	1120
00112018	12	49	468	S	D	213	NC	MED 1	Okie # 1	1122
00212012	13	50	825	H	R	285	LY	LRG 1	Okie # 1	1124
00112019	14	35	676	H	D	213	SY	LRG 1	Okie # 1	1126
00112016	15	90	800	S	R	213	LY	MED 1	Okie # 1	1128

Detail Listing for[f]

Source: Sporleder and Davis (1981).

[a] S = Steers; H = Heifers.
[b] Entries in this column indicate delivery options: D = delivered to assembly point; R = ranch cattle; and C = contract cattle.
[c] Code number for county where cattle are located.
[d] Age (see Table 12.2).
[e] Contract cattle are not assigned a sale number or a "time on" because they are not offered over the auction, but on a separate screen.
[f] This statement at the bottom of the screen allows buyers to call up another screen for detailed description of a particular lot by simply typing the lot number into the VDT's keyboard.

Table 12.2. Sorting Factors Used on Cattlex System.

Factor	Categories	Description
Lot Size	1	30 head or less
	2	31–60 head
	3	61–90 head
	4	91 head or more
Sex	S	Steers
	H	Heifers
	B	Bulls
Weight	1	Under 400 lb
	2	401–500 lb
	3	501–600 lb
	4	601–700 lb
	5	701 lb and over
Grade	L	Large—1, 2, 3
	M	Medium—1, 2, 3
	S	Small—1, 2, 3
Age	NC	New crop (less than 10 months)
	SY	Short yearlings (9–12 months)
	FY	Full yearlings (12–14 months)
	LY	Long yearlings (15–18 months)
	ST	Short two (19–23 months)
	LT	Long two (24 months and over)

Source: Derived from Sporleder and Davis (1983).

Table 12.3. Example of VDT Display to Buyers for Feeder Cattle Showing Data for Cattle Delivered to Assembly Point.

DELIVERED LOT NO: 00223015
NO. OF CATTLE: 45
GRADER NO. 18
DATE DESCRIBED: 5 JUN 80

LOCATION: SEALY AUCTION
TIME AND DATE OF DELIVERY: 1430:4
  JUN 80
FOB DELIVERY LOCATION: SEALY
  AUCTION
WEIGHING LOCATION: 0915 SEALY
  AUCTION

DESCRIPTION
SEX: 45 STEERS
AGE: LY
PREDOMINANT GRADE:
  COMMON NAME: #1 OKIE
  USDA GRADE: MEDUM—2
FLESH CONDITION: MEDIUM
% SHRINK: 2

PREDOMINANT BREED: 3/4 ENGLISH
  1/4 BRAHMAN
EST. WEIGHT RANGE: 650–740
PAY WEIGHT: 666
IDENTIFICATION: EAR TAGS

****
GRADER COMMENT: PASTURE CATTLE
****

OWNER SUPPLIED INFORMATION: ON RYE GRASS 45 DAYS PRIOR TO
  LISTING. ALL MALES WERE KNIFE CASTRATED. PARASITE
  CONTROL: GRUBS TREATED WITH WARBEX. FALL 1978, CYANAMID
  (MANUFACTURER).

Source: Sporleder and Davis (1981).

Table 12.4. Example of VDT Display To Buyers for Feeder Cattle Showing Data for Cattle Still on Ranch.

RANCH LOT NO: 00523146	CATTLE LOCATION: WALLER COUNTY
NO. OF CATTLE: 80	PROPOSED TIME & DATE OF DELIVERY: 830:9 JUN 80
GRADER NO: 18	FOB DELIVERY LOCATION: SEALY AUCTION
DATE DESCRIBED: 1 JUN 80	WEIGHING LOCATION: 0915 SEALY AUCTION
DESCRIPTION	PREDOMINANT BREED: 3/4 ENGLISH
SEX: 80 STEERS	1/4 BRAHMAN
AGE: LY	EST. WEIGHT RANGE: 650–740
PREDOMINANT GRADE:	PAY WEIGHT: 680
COMMON NAME: #1.5 OKIE	IDENTIFICATION: BRANDED
USDA GRADE: MEDIUM–2	
FLESH CONDITION: MEDIUM	
WEIGHING CONDITIONS: OVER-	
NIGHT STAND, ON TRUCK	
% SHRINK: .02	

3 + 3.75 − 4 + 6.25 − 5 + 10.5 − 6 + 7.75 − 7 + 5.50 − 8 MAY STEERS
GRADER COMMENT: PASTURE CATTLE

****

OWNER SUPPLIED INORMATION: ON RYE GRASS 45 DAYS PRIOR TO LISTING. ALL MALES WERE KNIFE CASTRATED. PARASITE CONTROL: GRUBS TREATED WITH WARBEX. FALL 1978, CYANAMID (MANUFACTURER).

Source: Sporleder and Davis (1981).

BID." The eight lots shown below the starred-line represent recent sales and prices paid. Whenever, after 16 minutes, the highest bid is below the owner's no-sale price, the lot is registered as a counteroffer, shown on the screen as C.O. (Sale number 067 in Table 12.5 is an example). For C.O. lots, the seller has two minutes either to accept or to reject the highest bid. If rejected, the lot is offered again the next day.

Selling procedures for contract cattle is simpler because the first bidder with a price equal to or greater than a seller's prespecified offer price purchases the lot.

Procedures After the Sale. Buyers of cattle are required to make a margin deposit on the lots purchased. Final adjustments for the transaction are made on the delivery day. The third-party grader makes final adjustments and computations, and the information is entered on the computer. Buyers pay buying terminals, and sellers receive the money

Table 12.5. Example of VDT Display to One Buyer Showing Current Cattlex Auction Market.

WELCOME TO TAMU CATTLEX

11:15 AM   FUTURES: MAR 81.27   APR 82.40   MAY 82.17   AUG 82.60   VOL 2,201

CURRENT AUCTION MARKET   TIME 11:31   FEB 22

LOT NUMBER	NO. HEAD	S X	AVE WT	D R	CO.	A G	USDA GRADE	COMMON NAME	SAL NO.	HIGH BID	MY BID	TIME OFF
00208015	55	S	776	D	232	LY	MED2	# 1.5 Okie	076	83.70	83.00	1146
00508108	25	S	552	D	035	NC	MRD 3	# 2 CB	075	86.60		1144
00808031	31	H	414	D	248	NC	SML 2	# 2 Okie	074	80.25		1142
00908002	22	S	672	D	152	LY	MED 3	# 1 C.B.	073	82.85	82.85	1140
00308017	170	S	650	R	080	FY	MED 1	# 1 ANGUS	072	87.75	86.95	1138
00508071	44	S	583	D	035	LY	MED 2	# 2 Okie	071	83.30		1136
00508133	325	S	700	R	035	LY	LRG 2	# 2 Okie	070	88.00	87.25	1134
00808026	35	S	812	D	248	ST	MED 3	# 2 Herfd	069	81.90		1132
**********	**********	**********	**********	**********	**********	**********	**********	**********	**********	**********	**********	**********
01208028	82	S	725	R	172	LY	MED 2	Angus Choc.	068	86.20	86.20	1130
00508038	32	S	621	D	035	LY	MED 2	# 1.5 Okie	067	C.O.		1128
00108062	27	S	506	D	011	FY	MED 2	# 2 Okie	066	86.00		1126
01308015	61	S	529	D	033	LY	MED 1	# 1.5 Okie	065	86.25		1124
00708019	75	H	482	D	088	NC	SML 2	# 3 C.B.	064	80.20		1122
00608023	53	S	666	D	010	FY	MED 1	# 1 Okie	063	85.75		1120
00408011	240	S	750	R	204	LY	MED 2	# 2 C.B.	062	87.75		1118
00108041	29	S	612	D	011	LY	LRG 2	# 2 Okie	061	85.45		1116

SAL No. ----   AUTH NO. ----   BID PRICE $---:   83.00
                                                                   076

Source: Sporleder and Davis (1981).

from listing terminals. Settlement between terminals is made through a wire transfer of funds to and from a specified financial institution.

HAMS—Hog Accelerated Marketing System

HAMS—an acronym for Hog Accelerated Marketing System—was jointly developed and initiated by the Ohio State University, the Ohio Department of Agriculture, and the Ohio Producers Livestock Association (PLA). Planning for the development began in 1978; actual trading on the system was conducted between October 23, 1980 and June 12, 1981. The system's network included a central computer (a Hewlett-Packard 3000 minicomputer), a set of computer terminals, and leased telephone lines. The system functions included auctioning, accounting, communications, and reporting.

HAMS Operation. Sellers used computer terminals (located at 17 PLA yards and at several large farms in Ohio) to communicate with 17 meat-packing plants with buying terminals in seven states: Ohio, Pennsylvania, New York, Maryland, Virginia, Tennessee, and Kentucky. A buying terminal was also set up with a large order buyer in Ohio.

Farmers used the system to list hogs for sale and to acquire market information. All hogs were inspected, graded, and sorted by a HAMS representative prior to the sale. Information on description, grades, location, and numbers were stored on the computer and made available to potential buyers upon demand.

Hogs were sold either while on farms (for larger lots) or from a local yard (for small consignments). The computer used the stored information to conduct auction bidding on the hogs listed for sale. HAMS also was designed to provide a firm offer option.

Product descriptions were based on a modified USDA grading system with five grade categories: $1+$, 1, $1-$, $2+$, and $2-$. These grades were based on fat thickness and degree of muscling (the grades were correlated with hog value in terms of the percent of lean cuts expected from the hog carcass). In addition to the standardized grades, buyers had access to other information such as hair color, number of hogs available, and their location.

To illustrate the selling procedures on HAMS, assume that a buyer accessed the system to obtain information on current trading activities (i.e., to monitor the market). Table 12.6 is a simulated display of the information he would see on his computer's VDT.

At this time on that date, the trader would see that bidding had been completed for lot number C001 and that that lot had been sold on a

Table 12.6. Example of a Competitive Offer Screen on Hams.

YOUR BID PRICE IS $33.25

HIGHEST BID $33.50

Live $/Cwt.	Carcass $/Cwt.	Lot no.	Location	Head	Avg wt.	Total wt. 1,000	Handle	Composition No.	(Grade)	No. of Reds
$35.00[a]		C001	3 – Easton	200	220	44.0	Hines	100 (1+)	100 (1 –)	0
→ [b]		C002	2 – Mt. Ver.	50	200	10.0	White	50 (2+)		50
		C003	1 – Wash.	175	225	39.4	Smith	100 (1 –)	75 (2+)	25
		C004	1 – Wash.	200	220	44.0	Baldy	100 (1+)	100 (1 –)	39
		.	.	.	.	.		.	.	.
.		.	.	.	.	.		.	.	.
.		.	.	.	.	.		.	.	.
		C015	1 – Mary.	75	230	17.2	Comm.	40 (2+)	35 (2 –)	35

Source: Baldwin (1980).
[a]The $ sign indicates that these lots have been sold; all remaining lots are available for sale.
[b]The → (arrow) signifies that this lot is in the selling mode; all remaining lots are to be sold.

Table 12.7. Example of VDT Display of the Inspection Screen For Lot Number C004 on Hams.

HANDLE: BALDY		LOCATION: Washington C.H.	DEL 3	TOTAL WT. 44
GRADE	NUMBER	AVG. WT.	WT. RANGE	RED
1 +	100	220	210–230	0
1	100	220	210–230	39
	TOTAL NO. 200		AVG. WT.	220
			WT. RANGE	200–230
			NUMBER OF REDS	39

COMMENTS: WEIGHT ON FARM

Source: Baldwin (1980).

liveweight basis for $35.00/cwt. Lot number C002 was currently in the bidding process, whereas lots C003 through C015 were in the queue awaiting bidding to begin. New lots were added consecutively to the bottom of the display, and, when a full screen was reached, the topmost item rotated off to the public-information file.

If, at this time, the trader was interested in bidding on lot number C004, he could acquire detailed information by accessing an inspection screen, which would display all available data on this lot at his terminal screen (Table 12.7), including information prerecorded by the third-party grader and data provided by the seller under the general comment section.

If the trader elected to bid on lot C004 after reviewing the data, he could do so (1) by typing price increments onto the screen and hitting the enter button on the terminal's keyboard, or (2) by activating the enter button, which in this case automatically increased the bid by some specified amount (e.g., 10 cents/cwt). After the final bid, the computer recorded the price and issued the comment to the buyer, "You bought it" or "Lot already sold."

The trader could also buy hogs on a firm offer basis. He could acquire market information on each firm offer lot in the same manner as in the auction case, i.e., by accessing the desired lot's inspection screen. If he elected to buy any lot on the firm offer screen, he typed in the lot number and pressed the big button on the terminal's keyboard (Table 12.8). The computer would then inform him if he had bought the lot or if it had already been sold.

Trading on HAMS was terminated after 31 weeks of operation. The original project plan stipulated that trading should not continue beyond that period unless there was clear evidence that it could become

Table 12.8. Example of a Firm Offer VDT Display Screen on Hams.

LOT NUMBER TO BUY ( )

Live $/Cwt.	Carcass $/Cwt.	Lot no.	Location	Head	Avg wt.	Total wt. 1,000	Handle	Composition		No. of Reds
								No.	(Grade)	
$39.75[a]		F001	3 – WASH.	200	220	44.0	Baldy	100 (1+)	100 (1–)	0
$38.75[a]		F002	2 – Wil.	50	210	10.5	Ash	50 (2+)		25
.	.	.	.	.	.	.		.	.	.
.	.	.	.	.	.	.		.	.	.
.	.	.	.	.	.	.		.	.	.
		F015	2-Spfd.	100	215		Spring	100(1)		0

Source: Baldwin (1980).

[a]The $ sign indicates that these lots have been sold; all remaining lots are available for sale.

self-supporting. That would have required tripling the volume traded on the system, which was unlikely without the participation of other organizations.

CATS—Computer Assisted Trading System

The Computer-Assisted Trading System, CATS, was an electronic marketing system for trading meat at the wholesale level that was developed by the American Meat Exchange (AME), a private company with the same ownership as the *Meat Sheet*, with technical assistance provided by the General Electric Information Services Company (GEISCO), a subsidiary of General Electric. The hardware consisted of a central computer and a network of remote-access terminals (Video Display Terminals, VDT), a keyboard console, and printers located in participating meat-traders' offices in various locations. *Traders* accessed CATS via a local telephone or toll-free WATTS line that linked them to the computer complex. CATS was tested nationwide from June 15, 1981 until November 16, 1981.

CATS offered several features that provided users with flexibility with respect to conditions and terms of trade while preserving traditional trading methods. Specifically, it had the following features:

Regional Pricing. The national market was divided into ten regions. Prices were quoted on a delivered basis in nine of these and on an F.O.B. basis in the tenth, i.e., the River Region (see p. 333). Thus, it allowed for regional price difference while preserving the widely used River Region base price. Provisions were made to reduce confusion over multiple-zone traders by issuing the same public ID number to single-zone traders listed in several regions.

Multiple Time Frames. The system provided three alternative time frames (spot, intermediate, and long-term) for delivery of products and permitted users to specify different prices for each period.

Product Identification and Differentiation. The system took into consideration the different cutting methods and specifications recognized in the current markets. The National Association of Meat Purveyors' (NAMP) Meat Buyer Guide was used to identify products. Both carcasses and boxed items were offered.

Traders' Identity. Each trader was identified by a company name and a USDA establishment number on all public bids and offerings, but not on transaction listings or summaries.

Private Negotiation. Unlike CATTLEX and HAMS, the price discovery on CATS was achieved through private negotiation among traders. The computer assisted traders in negotiating trades, but the final acceptance of refusal of the trade remained with traders, not the computer. The identity of traders who completed transactions remained private. The private negotiation method was used in order to reflect the known and acceptable market practices at the time.

CATS' operation involved five functions: input, inquiry, trading, summarization, and reporting. Input was the first step a user encountered with CATS and involved interactive data entry and editing through the user's computer terminal, date (by region), and price. A trader's ID was automatically entered by CATS. All entries were validated according to preestablished editing rules. Once verified, this information was made available to other eligible traders. Inquiry provided users with on-line information and allowed them to review selected bids and/or offerings (Table 12.9) or available market information by region, time frame, and item (Table 12.10). Negotiation involved establishing and conducting private negotiations between potential traders. Each trader had the option to accept, reject, or enter another counter offer or bid at any time. The process continued until a transaction was either consummated or a withdrawal was made (Table 12.11 shows a simulated screen of the negotiation process). Consummated transactions were placed in a confirmed transaction data-base file to be used for inquiry and reporting purposes. A printed confirmation was produced at each trader's terminal for completed transactions. Summarization involved consolidation of daily transactions into a summary file for reporting purposes. CATS generated six different types of reports that contained information of use to users. These reports, which could be accessed by entering the appropriate command, were: bids listing, offers listing, transaction listing, transaction summary, confirmation of trade, and a daily four o'clock report.

SOME EMPIRICAL RESULTS OF ELECTRONIC MARKETING PROJECTS

Analyses of the results from several electronic marketing projects and feedback from livestock and meat industries suggest that electronic marketing appears to have much to offer in terms of pricing and operational efficiency. Because of the small share of the market captured by electronic marketing systems during the test period, however, only limited analyses were possible. Nevertheless, Schrader (1984) indicated

Table 12.9   Example of VDT Display of CATS Bids Listings. [a]

| 06/19/81 | 13:25 CST | | | | BIDS LISTING | | | PAGE 1 | | |

SELECTION CRITERIA: REGION = CHGO, ME, SE, E   TIME = SPOT,IM   ITEM = 100SY36/7

REG MKT	TIME FRAME	ITEM	QTY (000)	D/S DATE[b]	PRICE	COMPANY NAME	ESTAB. ID	TIME CST	PUB[c] ID
ME	SPOT	100SY36/7	80	06/20D	111.00	MTMART	915	08:15	35154
ME	SPOT	100SY36/7	20	06/19D	111.50	OBMART	137	08:21	35178
E	IM	100SY36/7	40	06/24D	112.00	CEMART	896	09.00	35199
CHGO	SPOT	100SY36/7	80	06/19D	112.50	EPROCS	177	09.13	35219
ME	SPOT	100SY36/7	90	06/20D	111.00	DBUYER	429	09.46	35242
SE	IM	100SY36/7	40	06/26D	111.50	WHLSLT	978	10.48	35294
.	.	.	.	.	.	.	.	.	.
.	.	.	.	.	.	.	.	.	.
.	.	.	.	.	.	.	.	.	.

Source: Sarhan and Nelson (1983).
[a]Dots on the bottom of the simulated screen means that the actual list of information is longer than shown.
[b]For River Region trades—i.e., F.O.B. trades—delivery date is the same as shipping date and an S instead of D (for delivery) appears following the date.
[c]This public ID is assigned to the bids by the system when they are entered for public showing.

Table 12.10. Example of a VDT Display of a CATS Negotiation Screen.

NEGOTIATION: 61382820–02[a] 06/19/81   13:30 CST   STATUS: ACCEPT[b]

ITEM: 100SY36/7

QYT (000): 40   PRICE = 111.75   REGION = ME   DEL:0620   SPOT TERMS = NET7

SHIP-TO: BILL-TO: SHIP-FROM:

DEMO BYR CO DEMO BYR CO MEAT SELLER

2409 VINE ST   2409 VINE ST   1980 UNION ST
INDIANAPO-   INDIANAPO-   COLUMBUS, OH
LIS, IN 46204   LIS, IN 46204   43215

PREMIUMS AND DISCOUNTS:

TRIM + 1.000

SDD + 0.150

REMARKS:

1 DELIVER IN A.M. ONLY

CHANGE?[c]

Source: Sarhan and Nelson (1983).
[a]Following the eight-digit negotiation number is a (02), which indicates that this is round two in the negotiation process.
[b]The status has presumably changed from blank during round one to "Accept" in round two.
[c]The CHANGE? command at the bottom of the screen allows traders to make any changes.

Table 12.11. Example of VDT Display of CATS Transaction Summary Screen.

06/19/81   13:30 CST   TRANSACTION SUMMARY   PAGE[a]

SELECTION CRITERIA: ITEM = 100SY36/7;   REGION = CHGO, SE, ME;
TIME = SPOT, IM

REG MKT	TIME FRAME	ITEM	VOLUME (000)	HIGH	LOW	LAST	WGTD AVG.[1]
CHGO	IM	100SY36/7	160	113.00	111.50	112.00	112.370
ME	IM	100SY36/7	200	113.75	111.00	112.00	111.750
ME	SPOT	100SY36/7	80	113.25	112.00	113.00	111.675
SE	IM	100SY36/7	120	113.00	111.50	112.25	112.250
CHGO	SPOT	100SY36/7	200	112.50	111.50	111.75	110.200
CHGO	IM	100SY36/7	120	112.75	110.75	111.50	111.350
E	SPOT	100SY36/7	40	112.00	110.00	111.75	110.000

Source: Sarhan and Nelson (1983).
[a]WGTD AVG. = Weighted average price with weights being the relative volume traded at each price. For example, the $112.370 price (first line) was calculated as follows:

$$\left(\frac{40}{160} \times 111.50\right) + \left(\frac{80}{160} \times 113.00\right) + \left(\frac{40}{160} \times 112.00\right) = 112.375$$

that experience with ECI, CATTLEX, and HAMS suggested that prices on electronic systems tended to be higher than other market methods. Sporleder (1984) discussed the impact of electronic marketing on the structure of agricultural markets. His analysis suggested that electronic marketing could result in larger geographic procurement areas, which, in turn, could enhance buyers' competition in disparate submarkets. Results from all operational and experimental electronic marketing suggested that per-unit marketing costs could be lower than those achieved by conventional methods, provided that a minimal volume is traded on the system. A brief discussion of the specific experiences with CATTLEX, HAMS, and CATS follows.

CATTLEX Experiences

A total of 18,453 cattle were listed on CATTLEX during the pilot test period. Of this total, 40 percent were on ranch basis, 49 percent on contract basis, and 11 percent were listed under the delivery option. Only 12.8 percent of all cattle listed were actually sold during the pilot test. Proportionally more steers were sold than heifers. Sporleder (1983) suggested a number of reasons for the high proportion of no-sale: (1) the general decline in the feeder–stocker market during the test period, (2) the blind no-sale price option, intended to allow producers to participate in the pricing process, gave sellers the flexibility to "test" the market and obtain information from CATTLEX while reserving, or selling through, alternative methods, (3) informal information suggested that some cattle moved into custom feedlots rather than selling in the cash market, i.e., sellers speculated that potentially high fed-cattle prices would offset additional feeding costs, and (4) only a small number of potential producers participated in the pilot for want of convenient access to the system.

Statistical analysis indicated that there was some difference between price fluctuation (variability) in CATTLEX and conventional markets. However, Sporleder (1983) suggested that because of the small volume traded on CATTLEX, the full impact on price variability was unclear. The results also suggested that prices of cattle sold on CATTLEX were significantly higher than prices in Amarillo, the competitive market used for comparison, even after adjusting for transportation costs.

HAMS Experiences

During the 31-week period of trading on HAMS, 189,735 hogs were marketed, about 1,300 head per day or only 36 percent of the estimated minimum cost-effective volume of 3,600 head (Henderson and Baldwin, 1981). Costs ranged from $2.10 to $3.10 per head compared to $1.40 to $1.50 in conventional auctions and $1.75 to $2.00 in terminals. It was estimated that if 3,600 head per day were to be marketed, the total marketing costs (excluding transportation) would amount to $1.25 to $1.50 per head.

During the pilot test period, almost all hogs came from clientele of PLA. Other producers, those who had not traditionally marketed through the cooperative, did not participate. Henderson and Baldwin (1981) suggested a combination of factors for this reluctance, including unwillingness to disrupt normal sales channels, anticooperative bias, and competitive reaction by other marketing organization.

There were an average of 6.4 buyers per day on the market, compared to one or two buyers in the conventional system. Fourteen of the packers were active, and as many as ten were active bidders on some lots. Packers purchased 60 percent of all lots during the first four months and about 50 percent during the last part of the trading period. Data shows that competition was high among buyers.

Prices obtained on HAMS were compared with Peoria market prices in order to evaluate HAMS impact on competition. Traditionally, Ohio's prices have been $0.80 to $1.10/$cwt$ below Peoria's. HAMS prices averaged only 18 cents below Peoria's, with prices higher on HAMS during 9 of the 31 weeks. A gross price gain of 70 cents/cwt was obtained, reflecting lower buyer costs and greater competition. During the five weeks immediately following the termination of HAMS experimental project, Ohio's hog prices returned to their historic relationships vis-a-vis Peoria and were even below the pre-HAMS level.

HAMS also allowed for price differentials based on differences in hog quality and terms of delivery. The 1+ grades were sold at a premium (about 27 cents/cwt) compared to grade 1 hogs, whereas lower quality grades were discounted. Large lots (50 head and more), as well as hogs sold directly on the farm, sold at higher prices. Hogs listed early in the day sold at higher prices (about 20 cents/cwt) than hogs listed later because early listing allowed packers to meet their daily kill. The decline in the number of "early hogs" eliminated this advantage by the end of the project.

CATS EXPERIENCES

When trading on CATS began, there were 13 companies committed to the system. Two of the 13 participants were retailers, and the remaining 11 were meat packers and wholesalers. Two more retailers joined the test two weeks after its initiation. An additional pork slaughterer/ processor joined the pilot after 18 weeks. Participants represented a large geographical area, and several were national packers or retailers.

There were 220 beef and pork items available to CATS users during the pilot. Participants placed items from all but one category—cow carcasses; none of the participants were cow carcass suppliers (Sarhan and Nelson, 1983).

During the 23-week CATS operation, 109 transactions were completed, involving 117 carloads of 12 different meat and meat-product items. About 90 percent of all completed transactions were beef items, mostly carcasses. The most frequently traded beef item was carcass yield three Choice, weighing 600 to 800 lb. Although many boxed beef and pork items were listed, none were sold.

The CATS pilot clearly demonstrated that meat could be traded using a computerized system. Lack of complaints regarding CATS's ability to describe meat items adequately reinforced this conclusion. Furthermore, the pilot showed that traders had few or no problems using the computer equipment. Sarhan and Nelson (1983) reported that the most important lesson learned from the test was that meat industry commitment was essential for its full success. A survey of the meat industry, carried out as a part of the evaluation, indicated that the majority of traders believed that a modified CATS-type system could have great potential in the areas of market information and overall improvement of the meat-marketing system. Because of the meagerness of active participation, it was not possible to make any factual statements regarding the economic viability of the system.

REFERENCES

Baldwin, D. 1980. HAMS. *In* Proceedings, National Symposium on Electronic Marketing of Agricultural Commodities. Sporleder, T. L., ed. Texas Agr. Expt. Stat. MP–1463, pp. 74–97.

Bell, J. B., et al. 1983. Electronic Marketing, What, Why, How. Virginia Tech. and Virginia State. Virginia Coop. Exten. Serv. Pub. 448-004.

Henderson, D. R., et al. 1976. Centralized remote-access markets. *In* Marketing alternatives for agriculture. Is there a better way? Prepared for the subcommittee on agricultural production, marketing, and stabilization of prices of the committee on agriculture and forestry, U.S. Senate.

Henderson, D. R., and Baldwin, E. D. 1981. Marketing slaughter hogs by remote-access computerized auction: Theory and empirical results. Selected paper presented at the annual meeting, American Agricultural Economics Association, Clemson, S. Carolina, July 26–29.

Henderson, D. R. 1982. Electronic markets for agricultural commodities: Potentials and pitfalls. NC project 117, WP–62.

Henderson, D. R. 1984. Electronic marketing in principle and practice. *Amer. Jour. Agr. Econ.* **66,** No. 5:848–853.

Purcell, W., and Williamson, K. C. 1980. Electronic marketing: A new way to sell Virginia livestock. Virginia Polyt. Inst. and State University. Coop. Exten. Serv. VAE No. 315.

Russell, J. R., and Purcell, W. D. 1983. Determining the feasibility, design and implementation of an electronic marketing system: The experience with Electronic Marketing Association, Inc. Virginia Tech. Dept. of Agr. Econ. MB 309.

Sarhan, M. E., and Nelson, K. E. 1983. Evaluation of the pilot test of the Computer Assisted Trading System, CATS, for wholesale meat in the United States. Univ. of Illinois, Dept. of Agr. Econ. AE–4553.

Schrader, L. F. 1984. Implications of electronic trading for agricultural prices. *Amer. Jour. Agr. Econ.* **66,** No. 5:854–858.

Sporleder, T. L., ed. 1980. Proceedings, National Symposium on Electronic Marketing of Agricultural Commodities, Dallas, March 17–18. Texas Agr. Expt. Stat. MP–1463.

Sporleder, T. L., and Davis, E. E. 1981. CATTLEX: A computerized cash and contract market for feeder and stocker cattle. Operating procedures and trading techniques. Texas Agr. Expt. Sta. Texas A & M Univ., College Station.

Sporleder, T. L. 1983. An economic evaluation of a computer-based trading system for feeder and stocker cattle. Texas A & M Univ., Dept. of Agr. Econo. Unpublished report.

Sporleder, T. L. 1984. Implications of electronic trading for the structure of agricultural markets. *Amer. Jour. Agr. Econ.* **66,** No. 5:859–863.

13

Futures Markets

Interest in, and use of, livestock futures markets increased substantially during the 1970s as farmers and ranchers sought ways of improving their risk-management strategy. This is a direct reflection of concern over increasing risk, which has arisen from persistently accelerating capital and operating costs, on the one hand, and extreme product price fluctuations, on the other, the latter associated with increased but erratic exports of agricultural products and weather-induced as well as cyclical variability in domestic production. These conditions are likely to continue. Farmers and ranchers will have increasing need for means of shifting price risk. The futures market is one of several available means that can be used for this purpose.

WHAT IS A FUTURES MARKET?

A futures market is a market in which contracts are bought and sold. These are contracts in which a seller agrees to deliver and a buyer agrees to accept a specified commodity (e.g., live steers) at a future time. Terms of the contract specify: (1) commodity being traded, (2) price, (3) quantity, (4) quality, and (5) time of delivery.

Futures trading in livestock is relatively new (it did not begin until 1964), but there is another type of livestock contract, known as a "forward cash contract," that has been used for many years, and it is important to distinguish between the two. Many examples could be given of the forward cash contract, but the following is illustrative. It is not unusual for a rancher to enter into agreement with a buyer in the spring in which he sells calves to be delivered in the fall. This contract would also specify the price, time of delivery, place of delivery, etc. Obviously, this is a contract for delivery at a future date. The buyer in this contract may, if he chooses, sell the contract (his obligation to accept) to another buyer. Presumably he would take this step if the second buyer were willing to pay him something above the stated contract price in order to obtain the contract rights. Moreover, the original buyer might, sometime after entering the contract, be willing to sell to a second buyer at no premium if he had reason to believe the price would move down by the specified time of delivery.

The second buyer might be willing to pay a premium for the contract if he wanted the cattle and thought the stipulated contract price was a good buy, or if he wanted the privilege of reselling the contract to still another buyer. That opportunity can present itself on an advancing market. The original seller—the rancher—conceivably could buy back the contract (though he, too, might have to pay a premium to get it) and thus cancel out his obligation to deliver. This illustration involves a contract for future delivery, but, technically speaking, it is not a "futures market contract." It is commonly known, rather, as a "forward cash contract."

It was this sort of trading in cash contracts for the delivery of grain that prompted the organization more than a century ago of a specialized market to facilitate the trading in cash grain markets. From this emerged the concept and techniques for trading in futures contracts. The term "futures market" is reserved for a specialized market in which contracts are bought and sold under formal, regulated, conditions. Trading can be transacted only by specified people, at a specified place, during specified hours, under specified rules and regulations.

Such trades can be made only by members of the organized exchange or employees of a firm that holds membership (owns a seat) in the exchange. Memberships are limited in two ways: (1) Only a stated number are made available, and (2) ethical and financial standards must be met. Limitation of membership is no handicap to anyone who wishes to trade. It simply means that a nonmember must have a member make the trade for him, and memberships are held by brokerage firms in the business of performing this service for a fee. Moreover, trades can be made only on the "floor" of the designated exchange, but, again, this is no handicap to a nonmember who wishes to trade, as the nonmember can place his trading order through a broker by telephone. Distance from the exchange itself is thus no factor.

Terms of the contracts are standardized with respect to quantity (per contract), quality, allowable tolerances in delivery of quality other than that specified in the contract, premiums and discounts for delivery of quality other than the specified contract quality, place of delivery, time of delivery, and any other factors that affect the value of the commodity. The market exchanges have comprehensive self-regulating safeguards. In addition, they are supervised and regulated by the Commodity Futures Trading Commission (CFTC), an agency of the Federal government. Thus it is apparent that a futures market is an "organized" market.

The rancher and cattle buyer, mentioned in the cash forward contract illustration, could meet anywhere—each acting as his own agent—to draw up and sign a contract. This arrangement may be satisfactory when only a relatively few contracts are to be made and when the major objective is the actual transfer of the physical commodity (e.g., cattle) from seller to buyer. An active futures market will complete hundreds of trades each day. Although this type of market facilitates the transfer of the physical commodity, only a minor fraction of futures contracts are fulfilled by these deliveries. The futures market serves other functions that will become apparent later.

A number of futures markets are now in operation. Markets exist for trading in live slaughter cattle, live feeder cattle, live hogs, frozen pork bellies, wool, eggs, iced broilers, most grains, orange juice, sugar, coffee, onions, potatoes, cocoa, plywood, lumber, propane, copper, mercury, tin, several precious metals, foreign currencies, government securities, interest rates, financial market indices (e.g., Value Line and Standard and Poor's 500), and others. Frozen skinned hams and frozen boneless and carcass beef were traded on the futures market for a time, but trading was discontinued for want of sufficient volume.

Some markets specialize in only one or a few commodities; others handle trades in a number of commodities. Trading in livestock and/or meat is available at the Chicago Mercantile Exchange (commonly referred to as CME, the Mercantile Exchange, or simply as the "Merc"), Mid-America Commodity Exchange, Chicago Board of Trade, Minneapolis Grain Exchange, Pacific Commodity Exchange, New York Mercantile Exchange, and the Winnipeg Commodity Exchange. Wool was traded on Wool Associates of the New York Cotton Exchange until suspended in 1977. Each of these markets also handles trades in other commodities.

Like cash contracts, futures contracts specify a time for delivery (and acceptance)—a time at which the contract matures. Whereas many cash contracts specify an exact date of maturity, however, a futures contract specifies a period within a particular month (contract month) during which delivery may be made. Each exchange, through its organization, determines which months shall be specified as contract months, and also the period within the month during which delivery shall be permitted. When the Chicago Mercantile Exchange initiated trading in live cattle in November, 1964, each of the 12 months was designated as a contract month. Traders, however, centered activity primarily in contracts maturing in February, April, June, August, October, and December. In 1977, trading was reopened in the January contract. The contract delivery months for hogs are February, April, June, August, October, and December. At any given time of the year trades may be made in any one of these contract months. For example, in January of a given year, traders have a choice of making trades in any of the above contract months for that year and/or contracts that mature in the following year, as trade activity dictates. In 1984, the CFTC approved the CME's proposal to expand its listing of slaughter cattle futures contracts from six to eight. As a result, the CME allowed, beginning in August, 1984, trading for two additional deferred contracts, thus allowing traders to buy and/or sell distant futures contracts further along than was previously allowed.

Trading is done by open, verbal (as well as hand signal) bids and offers between brokers, or their representatives, on the floor of the exchange as these agents vie with each other to fill their clients' orders to the best advantage. Floor traders who trade for their own accounts also contribute to the volume of business. At any given time on an active market, some clients are attempting to sell and others are attempting to buy. Brokers with "buy" orders will, in the interest of their clients, attempt to make purchases at the lowest possible price. Likewise, brokers with "sell" orders will attempt to make sales at the highest possible price. These conflicting intentions, along with standardized contracts, standardized marketing conditions, and a well-organized system of market information, result in a highly competitive market. Commodity futures markets, along with securities markets, are considered to conform more closely to the perfectly competitive economic model than any other type of market.

In the process of "opening an account" with a broker, a client is required to sign a margin agreement, show evidence of financial responsibility, and deposit prescribed margin funds with the broker. "Margin" is the amount of "security" money a trader is required to put up in order to make a futures transaction. In a sense, the margin is equivalent to a down payment or "earnest" money. A trader in the futures market does not put up the full value of the contract—only the margin, which amounts to a relatively small fraction of the full value. The same policy is observed in many cash contracts upon signing of the contract. Full payment is made upon delivery of title. Similarly, in futures trading, if a contract is held until delivery of the commodity, full payment is required.

The initial margin is usually equal to a small percentage of the value of the contract. In addition, there is a maintenance margin, which is roughly 75 to 85 percent of the initial margin. Both margins may vary among different commodities. The actual minimum initial and maintenance margin requirements are specified by commodity exchanges, depending on what the exchange considers an adequate guarantee of performance. Margin requirements normally are higher for speculative accounts than for hedging accounts. If they choose, brokerage firms may require a higher margin than that specified by the exchange from

Table 13.1. Examples of a Margin Call and Money Withdrawal.

	Contract Price ($)	Position Value ($)	Net Capital Deposited ($)	Equity ($)
Example 1:				
Day 1	60.00	0	2,400	2,400
Day 2	60.25	+ 100	2,400	2,500
Day 3	59.00	− 400	2,400	2,000
Margin Call		− 400	2,800	2,400
Example 2:				
Day 1	60.00	0	2,400	2,400
Day 2	61.50	+ 600	2,400	3,000
Withdrawal of	$600	+ 600	1,800	2,400

all traders or a particular trader. Leuthold and Van Blokland (1981) summarized the functions of margins as follows:

First, they guarantee performance of futures contracts. Second, they provide the futures market system with money so that the clearing house can collect from traders who lose in futures trading and pay those who gain. And, third, since the initial and maintenance margins are only a fraction of the futures contract's full value, they enable customers to participate in trading without incurring too large a financial burden.

If, after having made a trade, the market price moves favorably for a trader, his margin fund simply stays on deposit with the broker (unless the trader decides to make a withdrawal) and is returned when the trade is closed out. If the market price moves unfavorably, however, the margin is used to cover losses, and before the margin fund is exhausted, the broker will call for additional margin; if this is not forthcoming, the account will be closed out by the broker.

The two examples shown in Table 13.1 illustrate the working of the margin concept.[1] Assume that a trader buys a live cattle futures contract (40,000 lb) for June delivery at $60 per cwt. Assume that the initial margin is $2,400 (i.e., 10 percent of the contract's full value), and the maintenance margin level is $2,040 (i.e., 85 percent of the initial margin). By the second day in Example 1 the price is $60.25, and the trader's equity rises by $100 to $2,500 [(60.25 × 400 cwt's/contract) − (60.00 × 400) = 100]. By the end of the third day, the price has fallen to $59.00 per cwt; the equity position now is $2,000, which is $40 below the maintenance level of $2,040. The broker makes a

---

[1]These examples are based on the discussion in Leuthold and Blokland (1981).

"margin call," and the trader, if he or she wishes to maintain the market position, must deposit $40 to bring the equity position back up to the initial $2,040 level. The trader has the option not to deposit the funds but to close the trade. In Example 2, the price jumps from $60 to $61.50, bringing the trader's equity to $3,000. The trader may withdraw the $600 surplus ($3,000 − $2,400). Because of the frequent fluctuation of futures prices, however, it may not be practical to withdraw such a small amount.

A trader never knows who it is that takes the opposite end of his transaction. As previously indicated, the transaction is executed by two brokers (or their representatives), one acting as agent for the seller, the other for the buyer. Each commodity exchange has a clearing association (clearing house) that performs a function similar to a bank clearing house. Brokerage firms hold membership in the clearing house, and all transactions are cleared through it. For every sale cleared by one broker, an identical purchase is cleared by the broker who took the opposite end of that transaction on the floor of the exchange. A client who has made a trade has an obligation to his broker, and the broker has an obligation to the clearing house. This contractual obligation is just as legal and binding as any other type of contract. An important difference, however, is that futures markets are organized in such a way that traders can easily liquidate their original position prior to maturity of the contract simply by making an offsetting trade (if the initial trade were a purchase, it can be offset by a sale, or vice versa) for the same number of contracts in the same contract month as the original trade.

Traders rarely enter the market with intentions of making or accepting delivery of the actual commodity. They liquidate their position prior to termination of trading in a given contract month. It should be emphasized, nevertheless, that however rarely it may happen, it is possible to make delivery and get delivery on a futures contract. An exception is feeder cattle futures as will be discussed later.

FUNCTIONS OF FUTURES MARKETS

Futures markets are considered to perform two basic functions: (1) price setting through speculative activity (Tomek and Gray, 1970) and (2) hedging (Working, 1962). Working and others have shown that the existence of futures markets depends basically upon hedging, which is the use of futures transactions in such a way as to offset the effects of an adverse price change in the cash market.

Any person who owns a commodity automatically assumes risks, one of the most important being that market prices may drop before the commodity is sold. Cattle feeders and hog feeders have seen potential profits vanish as market prices decline. A packer who has a commitment to supply meat to a wholesaler or retail buyer for a stipulated price may see his potential profits vanish as market prices move up. Hedging in the futures market is the transference of such price risks to other parties, usually speculators.

At any given time, prices generated in the futures market represent an aggregate consensus, primarily of speculators' analyses and opinions of future prices based upon current and foreseeable circumstances. As conditions change with the passing of time, the consensus may, and usually does, change. Although the futures market, historically viewed, has not been an accurate forecaster of future prices, this fact does not detract from its performance in hedging and price setting.

Speculation in the futures market, as implied, is the voluntary assumption of price risk. Hedging in the futures market could not adequately be accomplished without speculation. Although the interests of the livestock and meat industry are primarily centered in hedging price risk, it is important to understand at least the mechanics of speculation.

Speculation

Speculation in the futures market—the voluntary assumption of price risk—is not done for the fun of it. Speculators hope to make a profit. The concept of speculation in futures is deceptively simple, but consistent, and long-run profits are difficult to come by. No attempt will be made here to diagnose or prescribe speculative techniques or programs. Only the mechanics of speculation and its relation to hedging will be discussed.

At any given time, a speculator may, by whatever means are at his disposal, make a market analysis in which he concludes that during the next "X" days, weeks, or months the futures price for a particular commodity will move up, down, or remain unchanged. For illustrative purposes, assume that this analysis indicates that the price will move up. It is obvious that the speculator could make a profit by buying a futures contract now and reselling it later if the price does in fact rise—provided, of course, that the selling price exceeds the buying price by more than the amount of charges involved in making the trades. If the speculator's analysis had indicated that the futures market price would move down, it is equally apparent that he could make a profit by selling a futures contract now and buying it back later—again provided that the buying price drops below the selling price by an amount exceeding the charges involved in making the trades. The futures market provides the mechanism by which speculators can make such trades, but there is nothing inherent in this market that guarantees the speculator a profit. It should be perfectly obvious, moreover, that if the speculator's analysis is in error—if the market moves in the opposite direction from what his analysis showed—then he would sustain a loss.

A futures market that remains relatively stable over time is of little interest to speculators, since profit potentials arise from price changes. Historically speaking, commodity prices (i.e., livestock, grain, etc.) have fluctuated rather sharply. For example, the price of Choice 900- to 1,100-lb slaughter steers at Kansas City was $34.00 per cwt during the spring of 1970; by fall of that same year, the price was $27.00. During the same period, hog prices dropped from $30.00 to $15.00. In a four-month period beginning August 1973, slaughter steer prices dropped nearly $20.00 per cwt. Grain prices also fluctuate sharply, although government price-support programs tend to dampen the variations. Over a period of time, futures prices tend to move in the same general direction as market prices for the actual, physical commodity (the latter market is called the "cash" or "spot" market to differentiate it from the futures market).

Following are hypothetical examples of two speculative ventures: In Example A, prices move in the expected direction; in Example B, prices move opposite from the expected.

Example A. Assume that a speculator has opened an account with a broker and that on January 12 his analysis indicates that the price of October live-cattle futures will rise during the following three months. The speculator thus places an order with his broker on January 12 to buy two units of CME October cattle "at the market." The designation, "at the market," leaves it up to the broker to get the best buy possible at that time.[2] Let us say the order is executed at $58.50 per cwt. At this point (January 12), the speculator is "long" two units of October cattle. Since each contract unit, by CME specification, consists of 40,000 pounds liveweight, the total value would be

$$2 \times 40,000/100 \times \$58.50 = \$46,800.00$$

---

[2]Other types of orders are: (1) "limit order," which can be executed only at a specified (or better) price; (2) "open order," which also specifies the price, but the order stands until it is executed or cancelled; (3) "day order," which must be executed on a specified day or is automatically cancelled (unless otherwise stated, all orders are considered to be day orders); and (4) "stop (loss) order," which stipulates a price, but then, if or when the market reaches that price, a market order becomes effective.

Now assume that three months later (April 12), the speculator closes out his position. He will do this by placing an order with his broker to sell two units of CME October cattle. The broker executes the order at, say, $61.00 per cwt. This liquidates the speculator's position in October cattle, and the value of the sale would be

$$2 \times 40{,}000/100 \times \$61.00 = \$48{,}800.00$$

Gross profits would thus be $48,800.00 − 46,800.00 or $2,000.00. The broker's commission and interest on margin funds must be deducted from gross profits. Futures markets suggest commission rates and margin requirements, but individual brokerage firms have flexibility in setting the levels. We shall assume a commission of $50.00 per contract. That covers both ends of the transaction, i.e., the original purchase and subsequent sale. Commission on two contracts would thus be twice $50, or $100.00. Margin requirements are assumed to be $2,000.00 per contract for a total of $4,000.00. Interest at 10 percent for three months would be 0.10 × $4,000 × 3/12, or $100.00. Net profits then would be $2,000.00 − $100.00 − $100.00, or $1,800.00.

Example B. In this case, assume everything identical with Example A up to the point of liquidating the original position. At this point, assume that prices have declined so that the liquidation sale of two units of October cattle is made at $56.50 per cwt. Under these conditions, the sale value would be

$$2 \times 40{,}000/100 \times \$56.50 = \$45{,}200.00$$

Gross profits would be $45,200.00 − $46,800.00, or −$1,600.00. Commission charges and interest on margin money would be the same as in Example A.[3] Net profits therefore would be

$$-\$1{,}600.00 - \$100.00 - \$100.00 = -\$1{,}800.00.$$

The speculator under these circumstances would have sustained a loss of $1,800.00.

There are, of course, many other types of speculative ventures that can be undertaken in futures markets. The type illustrated here is one of the most elementary, but the two assumed outcomes will serve to

---

[3]Additional margin probably would be required, but this factor is ignored for simplification.

illustrate the place of speculation as an adjunct to hedging. Without speculation, hedgers at times would have difficulties in placing orders, as will become apparent in the following discussion.

Hedging Price Risk

Hedging price risk in the futures market is the use of futures market transactions in such a way as to offset the effect of adverse price movements in the cash market. Whether a price change is "adverse" depends upon the position one holds in the actual commodity (in the cash market). To the cattle feeder who has a pen of cattle on feed, it is clear that a price decline in cattle would be adverse. To a packer who has an agreement to deliver dressed beef carcasses at a stipulated price, but who has not yet purchased cattle for slaughter, a price rise in cattle would be adverse.

A "hedge" is accomplished by taking a position in the futures market opposite from the one held in the cash market. The cattle feeder mentioned above has "bought" the cash commodity (actual cattle). His position is then said to be "long" the cash market. To execute a hedge, he would take an opposite position (selling) in the futures market. He then is said to be "short" the futures market; in trade terminology, this would be called a "short hedge." Likewise, the position described for the packer above is said to be "short" the cash market. He would execute a hedge by taking a "long" position (buying) in the futures market. This is called a "long hedge."

How can a hedger be sure of being able to take the desired position in the futures market? Here is where speculation comes in. Any transaction requires the participation of two parties. A sale cannot be made in the futures market, or any other market, unless someone else takes the opposite side of the transaction (buys). A purchase cannot be made unless someone else sells. A hedger can never be sure that a speculator stands ready to take the opposite side of a transaction at a particular price the hedger may choose, but, in an active, viable market, he can be sure that a speculator will take the opposite side at some price. If the market has a relatively high volume of hedging and speculative activity, the hedger can be reasonably sure that a trade will be executed near the price level at which other trades are being made at that particular time. Speculators are needed to give markets the flexibility and breadth to absorb hedges without undue price reaction.

Theoretical Cash-Futures Price Relationships. For the futures market to provide an adequate hedging mechanism, two fundamental cash-futures price relationships must hold: (1) Over a period of time, cash

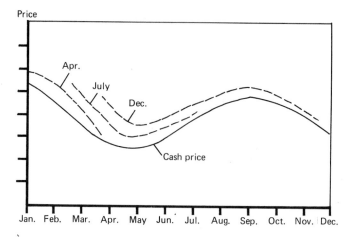

Fig. 13.1. Typical relative movements of cash and futures prices.

prices and futures prices for a given commodity must move in the same general direction, and (2) as a futures contract expires (during month of contract maturity), cash price (at par delivery points[4]) and the price of the expiring futures must come reasonably close. Figure 13.1 illustrates these relationships. The point of major concern with both these relationships is the stability and predictability of the differences between cash and futures prices. That difference is known as the "basis."

In the first instance, a hedger expects that, over time, if cash prices advance, the futures prices will advance and that if one declines, the other will decline. Erratic day-to-day or short-period deviations from this proposition may occur and not be particularly damaging, but sustained, unpredictable movements would render the futures market untenable for hedging purposes. For effective hedging, variations in the difference between the two prices (i.e., variations in the basis) must be less than variations in cash and futures prices—a relationship that has been confirmed by Leuthold (1977) and Price et al. (1978).

Futures prices, basically, are determined by traders' (primarily speculators') expectations of supply and demand conditions as deducted

[4]Par delivery points are locations designated by futures markets as points where commodities may be delivered to satisfy futures contracts at the contract prices. Prior to closing of the Chicago Stock Yards in 1971, Chicago was the par delivery point for live cattle. Currently, several markets are considered par delivery locations. Livestock may also be delivered to other, non par delivery points, but at a discount from the quoted price.

from current and anticipated conditions.[5] Current cash prices are based upon appraisal of the current supply–demand situation as conditioned by futures expectations. Thus, cash and futures prices usually react in the same direction to continuously developing supply and demand factors. Tomek and Gray (1970) state, "The element of expectations is imparted to the whole temporal constellation of price quotations, and futures prices reflect essentially no prophecy that is not reflected in the cash price and is in that sense already fulfilled." Records show that, over time, cash prices and futures prices usually move in the same general direction, though not necessarily at the same rate (Blau, 1944–1945).

The tendency for cash prices and futures prices at par delivery points to come reasonably close together at the expiration of a futures contract is based upon the fact that any point of time in the future inexorably becomes the present with the passage of time. As mentioned earlier, futures contracts can be liquidated by delivery of the actual commodity (though this is seldom consummated). The possibility of delivery sets up powerful speculative forces that prevent a wide divergence of prices at the termination of futures contracts. To use an exaggerated example, assume that as a June cattle contract approaches expiration (during the month of June), the cash price of contract-grade cattle in Omaha, Nebraska, or Sioux City, Iowa (designated par delivery points for live slaughter cattle CME contracts) is $5.00 per cwt above the futures price. A strong incentive would exist for speculators to buy futures, hold the futures until the cattle are actually delivered, and then immediately sell these cattle on the higher cash market. On the other hand, if cash prices are $5.00 below futures prices as expiration of the futures approaches, a strong incentive would exist for speculators to sell futures and, when the June contract expires, to buy some actual cattle in the relatively low-priced cash market and then deliver them in satisfaction of the futures obligation.

Thus, forces are set in motion that bring cash prices (of the contract grade) and futures prices of an expiring futures fairly close together as trading in the contract month terminates. A study of Ehrich (1969) showed that futures prices tended to converge with the average price of 1,100- to 1,300-lb Choice steers at Chicago. Of course, there are uncertainties in exact time of delivery, in exact quality that might be

---

[5]It will be shown later that the futures market has not been an accurate forecaster of each price over an extended period, but it was not organized for price-forecasting purposes.

delivered,[6] and in elapsed time between delivery and resale of the actual commodity so that cash and futures prices are not necessarily identical at contract termination; hence, use of the term "reasonably" close.[7]

Although these two fundamental price relationships hold within reasonable limits, there is a substantial amount of variability and uncertainty associated with the live animal basis, as will be discussed in a later section.

With the introduction of "cash settlement" for feeder-cattle futures contracts in 1986, forces that tend to bring the futures price and the cash price reasonably close together at expiration of a contract may not be quite so obvious as indicated above. It is stated in a CME brochure, however, that "cash and futures prices are forced to converge by setting the final futures settlement price equal to the prevailing cash price." (Chicago Mercantile Exchange, 1986).

The fact that the cash price and futures price tend to come together at futures contract maturity implies that the basis relative to the "near" futures narrows as the near futures terminate. But which futures market and which cash prices are we concerned with? Any reference to basis should be specific with respect to both points. The several markets that handle livestock and livestock products were listed earlier. Since the bulk of futures trading in these commodities at this time is done in the Chicago Mercantile Exchange, however, that market will be used in the following discussion as a source of reference for futures price quotations. There are, however, many cash markets for livestock and meat throughout the United States.

The earlier comment about cash and futures prices coming reasonably close together at contract maturity specified the cash price at par delivery points. A cattle feeder at Pampa, Texas, who sells finished cattle to a nearby packer needs to know the Pampa basis, i.e., the amount by which Pampa cash price is below (or above) the CME cattle futures price for a specified contract month. To appraise a potential hedging situation effectively, every feeder needs an understanding of the concept of "basis" and a knowledge of the actual basis of the market in which he sells relative to the futures in which he contemplates placing a hedge. The concept is simple and futures prices are relatively

---

[6]Presumably a trader who chooses to deliver actual cattle in fulfillment of a futures contract would deliver the lowest quality that meets contract specifications. However, grading live animals is somewhat subjective.

[7]Occasionally a "squeeze" develops as a contract is being closed out. Traders become anxious to get out before delivery, and futures deviate temporarily from cash prices. This, however, is a short-lived phenomenon.

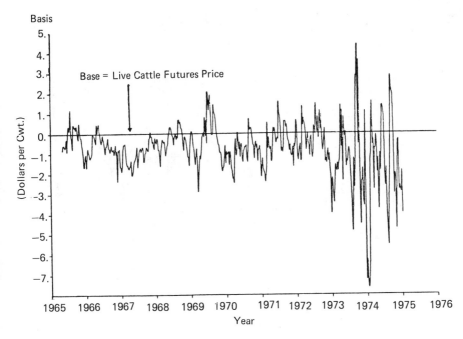

Fig. 13.2. Kansas City live-cattle basis, May, 1965–Dec. 1974.

easy to obtain. It is difficult at some local points, however, to obtain
adequate local cash prices for comparison with futures prices. Not only
are local price quotations by sex, grade, and weight often difficult to
obtain, but studies have shown that the basis varies over time. Figure
13.2 shows the Kansas City live-steer basis. Figure 13.3 shows the St.
Joseph, Mo., live-hog basis. A substantial variation has existed in the
basis over the years, with an apparent increase in variability in recent
years.

To this point we have been concerned with the locational basis, i.e.,
we have assumed that the local cash price being compared to a futures
price was for cattle of identical sex, weight, and grade as specified in
the futures contract. On occasion, livestock producers may be interested in a basis that also includes other factors, such as steers of lower
or higher grade, heifers (instead of steers), or weights and dressing
yield different from those specified in the futures contract. Hog producers may desire the basis for hogs that do not meet contract specifications. Very little empirical work is available on the applicable basis
for any of these factors at local markets, but producers often can obtain reasonable estimates from experienced producers and market personnel.

Basis

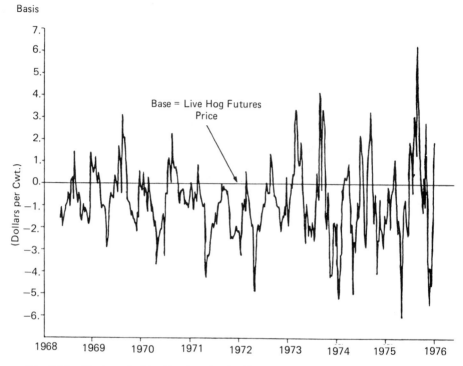

Fig. 13.3. St. Joseph, Mo. Live-hog basis, May, 1968 to Dec. 1975.

Mechanics of Hedging. Four steps can be identified in every hedging operation—two in the cash market and two in the futures market: (1) Assumption of original position in the cash market; (2) assumption of original position in the futures market; (3) liquidation of position in the cash market; and (4) liquidation of position in the futures market.

Steps 1 and 2 usually are carried out at, or about, the same time in a *traditional* hedge. At a later date, Steps 3 and 4 are also carried out at, or about, the same time in the traditional hedge. In the more modern (selective) hedging programs, exceptions are made to these generalizations (and also to most other generalizations), but for purposes of this exposition it will be assumed that transactions in Steps 3 and 4 are executed simultaneously but at a later date than Steps 1 and 2.

Steps 2 and 4 require the services of a broker. The livestock producer who contemplates hedging should "open an account" with a brokerage firm prior to the time he wishes to place the hedge. The producer also should acquaint himself with specifications of the futures contracts.

The various exchanges publish and distribute free brochures with this information. Most brokerage firms have them for distribution.

In the examples immediately following, none of the transactions are dated. This may simplify the presentation, but it also oversimplifies one problem. In executing a hedge in the futures market, it is necessary to specify the contract month in which the hedge is to be placed. In general, a hedge is placed in the contract month that coincides with the anticipated sale month of the actual commodity, or the contract month that matures next after the anticipated sale date of the actual commodity. For example, if feeder cattle are bought on Nov. 1 and are to be fed 140 days, the sale date would be March 18. Futures trading in slaughter cattle is not carried on in a March contract, so a hedge on such cattle usually would be placed in the April contract.

Examples of Hedges.   Assume in the following hypothetical examples that an account has been opened and initial margin requirements deposited with a brokerage firm at the time hedge transactions are initiated.

Example 1: "Short" Hedge of Cattle on Feed. Assume that 600-lb Medium Frame No. 1 feeder steers are purchased, fed 140 days, and sold as 1000-lb Choice slaughter steers. At the time the feeder cattle are purchased, cash prices are $58 per cwt for Choice feeders and $56 for Choice slaughter steers at the market used by the cattle feeder.

The conditions set up are elementary. It is assumed that: (1) a short hedge is executed at the same time the feeder cattle are purchased (i.e., today) and that the futures position is liquidated by an offsetting transaction at the same time the cattle are sold (i.e., 140 days after today); (2) cash and futures price movements are exactly parallel; (3) the operation is fully hedged during the entire feeding period; (4) there is no death loss; (5) there are no marketing costs in the cash market; (6) margin requirements are $1,200 per contract unit (margin requirements sometimes are less on hedge transactions than on speculative transactions), with interest on margin funds at 9 percent; and (7) the commission is $50 per contract unit.

Tables 13.2, 13.3, and 13.4 summarize hedging results under three alternative price movements: downward, 1(A); upward, 1(B); and no change, 1(C). It will be noted that the indicated net returns are identical ($1,140) under each of the three alternatives. This follows from the assumption of identically parallel movements in the cash and futures markets (i.e., the basis remains unchanged)—admittedly an unrealistic assumption, but one deliberately chosen to illustrate the point that a

Table 13.2. Hedging Example 1(A): "Short" Hedge of Cattle on Feed—Assuming Price Declines During Feeding Period.

Cash Market ($)	Futures Market ($)	Results ($)	
Today:	Today:		
(1) Buy 200 feeder steers, @ $58/cwt	(2) Sell futures contracts, five units @ $57/cwt	Loss in cash market	10,400
		Gain in futures market	12,000
Cost of feeders: 69,600		Less commission	250
Cost of gain @ $51/cwt: 40,800		Less interest on margin	210
Total cost: $110,400	Total value of sale: $114,000	Net profit	$1,140
140 days from today:	140 days from today:		
(3) Sell 200 Choice slaughter steers @ $50/cwt	(4) Buy futures contracts, five units @ $51/cwt		
Total returns: $100,000	Total purchase value: $102,000		

Table 13.3. Hedging Example 1(B): "Short" Hedge of Cattle on Feed—Assuming Price Increases During Feeding Period.

Cash Market ($)	Futures Market ($)	Results ($)
Today:	Today:	Gain in cash market: 13,600
(1) Buy 200 feeder steers, @ $58/cwt	(2) Sell futures contracts, five units @ $57/cwt	Loss in futures market 12,000
Cost of feeders: 69,600		Less commission 250
Cost of gain @ $51/cwt: 40,800		Less interest on margin 210
Total cost: $110,400	Total value of sale: $114,000	Net profit: $1,140
140 days from today:	140 days from today:	
(3) Sell 200 Choice slaughter steers @ $62/cwt	(4) Buy futures contracts, five units @ $63/cwt	
Total returns: $124,000	Total purchase value: $126,000	

Table 13.4. Hedging Example 1(C): "Short" Hedge of Cattle on Feed—Assuming Price Remains Unchanged During Feeding Period.

Cash Market ($)		Futures Market ($)		Results ($)	
Today:		Today:			
(1) Buy 200 feeder steers, @ $58/cwt		(2) Sell futures contracts, five units @ $57/cwt		Gain in cash market	1,600
				Gain in futures market	0
Cost of feeders:	69,600			Less commission	250
Cost of gain @ $51/cwt:	40,800			Less interest on margin	210
Total cost:	$110,400	Total value of sale:	$114,000	Net profit:	$1,140
140 days from today:		140 days from today:			
(3) Sell 200 Choice slaughter steers @ $56/cwt		(4) Buy futures contracts, five units @ $57/cwt			
Total returns:	$112,000	Total purchase value:	$114,000		

hedge tends to offset the effects of price change, whether the change be a decline or an advance.

Results in Table 13.2 show that the hedge provided protection against a cash price decline, the adverse price movement being offset in the futures transaction. The feeding operation would have sustained a loss of $10,400 if carried out unhedged. Under hedged conditions (as assumed), the futures market gain ($12,000) offset (in fact, more than offset) the cash market loss and resulted in a net return of $1,140.

It is apparent in Table 13.3 that a hedged feeder will forego windfall profits that would otherwise accrue from a price advance. If the operation had been unhedged, a gain of $13,600 would have been realized from cash market transactions. But with advancing prices, the futures transactions would sustain a loss of $12,000. A hedge "protects" from a favorable price movement just as it does from an adverse price movement.

If prices remain steady (unchanged), nothing is gained from a hedging operation (see Table 13.4). In fact, the commission and interest on funds tied up in margin would reduce the net return by those amounts.

In real-world hedging operations, the cash and futures markets seldom move in exactly parallel fashion. In a short hedge, if the futures price drops more than the cash price, a hedger will gain more on the futures transaction than he loses on the cash transaction. If the futures price drops less than the cash price, he will gain less on the futures transaction than is lost on the cash transaction.

In the previous examples, the futures price at initiation of the hedge (i.e., $57 per cwt "today") was indicated to be higher than the average total cost per hundredweight of the finished cattle ($110,400 ÷ 2,000 cwt = $55.20 per cwt). The latter is known as the "break-even" price. This situation was deliberately built into Examples 1(A), 1(B), and 1(C). Real-world market conditions are not always that accommodating. At times, the futures price is less than the "break-even" price. When this situation exists, the execution of a hedge usually results in a net loss, as illustrated in Table 13.5, where it is assumed that cash prices decline during the feeding period and the result is a net loss of $4,860.

It needs to be emphasized that hedging in itself does not guarantee a profit. A hedge only sets the selling price. In this sense, it can be used as a forward pricing device. If that price is above the break-even price, a profit is indicated, but if it is below the break-even price, a loss is to be expected. It will be noticed that the reference to profit and loss in this last sentence is qualified. This is necessary because if cash and futures prices do not move in a parallel manner—i.e., if the basis does

Table 13.5. Hedging Example 1(D): "Short" Hedge of Cattle on Feed—Assuming Futures Price At Initiation of Hedge is Below Break-Even Price.

Cash Market ($)		Futures Market ($)		Results ($)	
Today:		Today:			
(1) Buy 200 feeder steers, @ $58/cwt		(2) Sell futures contracts, five units @ $54/cwt		Gain in cash market	3,600
				Loss in futures market	8,000
Cost of feeders:	69,600			Less commission	250
Cost of gain @ $51/cwt:	40,800			Less interest on margin	210
Total cost:	$110,400	Total value of sale:	$108,000	Net loss:	$4,860
Break-even price					
$110,400/2,000 cwt = $55.20/cwt					
140 days from today:		140 days from today:			
(3) Sell 200 Choice slaughter steers @ $57/cwt		(4) Buy futures contracts, five units @ $58/cwt			
Total returns:	$114,000	Total purchase value:	$116,000		

not remain constant—then profits (or losses) will vary as mentioned in the paragraph immediately preceding.

In each of the four examples (Tables 13.2, 13.3, 13.4, and 13.5), it can be seen that the assumed cash sale price of the cattle was $1 below the liquidation price of the futures. That is, the basis was minus $1 at the time the transactions were closed out. This conforms to the earlier statement that cash prices and futures prices "tend to come reasonably close together at par delivery points at contract maturity." The basis tends toward an amount equal to delivery costs. At non-par delivery points, freight costs add to the basis. Furthermore, it usually is not possible (and, in fact, is not desirable) to attempt to liquidate the hedge during the final days of a terminating contract, at which time cash and futures prices are expected to approach each other. A hedge usually is liquidated as the cattle are sold, and they may be sold prior to maturity of the contract month in which the hedge is placed. The basis is less predictable at such times than it is near contract termination.

The principles and mechanics used by a producer in hedging feeder cattle and hogs on feed are similar to those explained for hedging slaughter cattle. No explicit examples will be given.

Example 2: "Short" Hedge of Hogs Bought on Contract. Packers (or other buyers, such as IPLA or country dealers) at times buy hogs from producers on forward cash contract before the hogs are finished out. Terms of the contract call for delivery when the hogs are finished, but the price may be set upon signing the contract.

A primary reason packers (or other buyers) enter such contracts is to line up supplies in advance. Producers may be willing to contract to reduce price uncertainty. The producer may prefer such a cash contract in lieu of hedging in the futures market. The packer in this situation may want protection against a price decline. Why? If hog prices decline, this packer's competitors will be able to obtain their kill at prices lower than the contract price to which this packer is committed. In sale of the meat, then, this packer would be at a disadvantage.

By hedging in the futures market, the packer can shift this price risk. Upon signing the cash contract, the packer assumes a *"long"* position in the *cash market*. He can hedge this position by taking an opposite (*"short"*) position in the *futures market*. Table 13.6 illustrates the results of a hedge in which a contract price was set at $44 per cwt on July 1 but the cash price had dropped to $40 per cwt upon delivery, Sept. 20. Market sale weight is assumed to be 200 lb per head. A contract unit is 30,000 lb liveweight. The commission is calculated at $40 per unit (round-turn) and the margin requirements (for a hedged transaction) at $750 per unit with interest at 9 percent.

Table 13.6. Hedging Example 2: "Short" Hedge of Hogs Bought by Packer on Contract—Assuming Price Declines $4 Per CWT in Cash Hog Market.

Cash Market ($)		Futures Market ($)		Results ($)	
On July 1:		On July 1:		Contract cost of hogs	$26,400
(1) Packer contracts 300 hogs for Sept. 20 delivery @ $44/cwt		(2) Sell Oct. futures contracts, two units @ $45.50/cwt		Less gain in futures market	$2,400
				Plus commission	80
				Plus interest on margin	30
Total value of contract:	$26,400	Total value of sale:	$27,300	Net cost to packer:	$24,110
On September 20:		On September 20:			
(3) Hogs are delivered to packer who pays contract of $44/cwt, but cash price has dropped to $40/cwt		(4) Packer buys Oct. futures, two units @ $41.50/cwt			
Total market value:	$24,000	Total purchase value:	$24,900		

The results in Table 13.6 show that gains in the futures transaction offset declines in the cash market price. The packer's net cost would be $24,100. The cost unhedged would have been $26,400. In this example, the gain in the futures market would have offset the $2,400 decline in cash value. In a sense, the $80 commission and $30 interest on margin could be classed as insurance premiums against the price decline in the cash market.

Cross Hedging Meat in Livestock Futures Market

The food service industry, such as restaurants and institutions, as well as wholesale meat traders and retailers, operate in a common environment of risk and volatile dressed-meat prices. Coupled with large inventories and many contractual commitments, this environment can create budgeting and management problems. In order to survive under these, and other adverse economic conditions, members of the meat industry must be able to develop a sound business strategy to cope with risk.

Several methods have been adopted, or suggested, to deal with risk and uncertainty. A firm, for example, may elect to ignore the risk element altogether and accept it as a part of its daily operation. Or a firm may enter into contractual arrangements, possibly with several trading partners. This type of forward contracting, however, has its limitations and potential problems. For example, it may be difficult to secure long-term forward contracts of any size when the general price trend is upward. A third method that has been suggested, but not widely used, is to cross hedge meats, including meat cuts, in the livestock futures market.

"Cross hedging" is the buying (selling) of some cash commodity while simultaneously selling (buying) a futures contract for a different, yet related, commodity. A beef trader may cross hedge carcasses, or certain beef cuts, with live cattle futures. This is a likely combination because prices for such items would presumably move, or have a close correlation with, cattle prices. A number of meat traders are successfully engaging in cross hedging, but the majority of traders feel uneasy with this option and do not utilize it. The limited use of cross hedging is due in part to a lack of understanding of its workings and potential benefits, which, in turn, is due to the unavailability of reliable, easy-to-understand, easy-to-use information.

Economists have devoted relatively little attention to formulating models and explaining the practical application of cross hedging. Hayenga (1979) explored the behavior of a food-manufacturing firm in the procurement of inputs in an imperfect market structure. He pointed out that, because agricultural commodity prices have become more volatile in recent years, making sound procurement decisions is now more important. In the case of fresh meat, he noticed a great aversion to being at a competitive disadvantage in commodity procurement mistakes and perceived a need to cross hedge fresh meat inventories, to keep such inventories at a minimum level, and to keep open forward positions only if a great profit potential exists. Anderson and Danthine (1981) took a very theoretical approach to cross hedging. Their study highlighted a portfolio strategy and suggested that cash and futures trading are never perfect substitutes. They used a mean-variance utility formulation to find the optimum market position that minimizes risk and maximizes returns. They found that the amount to hedge in a particular contract depends upon the relationship between cash and futures prices.

Hayenga and Dipietre (1982A) analyzed the possibility of cross hedging 15 wholesale beef products with the live-cattle futures contract. They showed that it is not necessary for meat and live cattle prices to move together so long as price changes are proportional, and thus predictable. A simple econometric model was used to investigate the correlation between the two prices. The coefficients of determination values obtained were very high, indicating that meats and live-cattle prices are closely related. They concluded that live cattle futures contracts may be used as a risk-reduction tool when dealing with large inventories or forward sales of beef.

In another study concerned with pork products, Hayenga and Dipietre (1982B) developed a hedging strategy that included the appropriate ratio of pork to live hog quantity to be hedged, as well as basis calculations. The econometric model's results showed a very high R^2, thus favoring a cross hedging program. Using the standard error of forecasting (SEF) to indicate the level of the basis risk borne by the hedger, however, the results showed that for some pork items cross hedging might increase rather than decrease risk.

In a 1981 study, Ginn concluded that cross hedging of several domestic fabricated meat cuts in live-cattle futures was feasible. He outlined, and gave examples of, a procedure to implement such a strategy. Using two statistical methods, Miller and Luke (1982) analyzed the results of hedging top sirloin butt prices in the live-cattle futures market. Using historical data, they found that risk could be reduced without reducing the mean return. This conclusion proved to be true for either method of estimation. They concluded that cross hedging could be useful in the meat industry.

Example 3: "Long" Hedge of Forward Beef Sales. Packers, at times, enter contracts with large retail and wholesale buyers for the sale of meat of certain specifications—to be delivered at some specified later date—the price being established at negotiation of the contract. If the packer has already bought the livestock, he knows the cost and can price the meat accordingly. On the other hand, if he has not yet bought the livestock, he could, if he chose, enter the contract, price the meat, and utilize the futures market to protect himself from an advance in livestock prices.

Unofficial reports indicate that this type of hedge is seldom used by packers, but the possibility merits a brief presentation. Flour millers have long used such hedges in contracting for delivery and pricing flour before actually purchasing the wheat from which the flour was to be milled.

In this example, assume that (1) the meat sold under contract is 72,000 lb of USDA Choice-steer beef carcasses weighing 600 lb each at a contract price of $90 per cwt with delivery in 60 days; (2) the packer has not yet bought cattle to fill the contract; and (3) cattle prices advance $3 per cwt by the time cattle are purchased. The price risk of such a meat sale could conceivably be hedged in either beef-carcass futures or live-cattle futures. Futures markets have been established for beef carcasses but have never attracted sufficient volume for effective hedging. It is relatively easy to translate carcass requirements into live-cattle requirements, however, and a high correlation exists between wholesale-carcass prices and live-cattle prices. The sale of beef carcasses, therefore, can be cross hedged in the live-cattle futures. Commission and margin costs for live-cattle futures hedging transactions are calculated at $50 and $1,200, respectively, per contract unit.

Table 13.7 illustrates how this contract sale could be hedged by a purchase in live-cattle futures. The $3 advance in cash live-cattle prices is assumed to be matched by an equivalent advance in the futures market, so that the additional cost of cattle would be offset by a gain in the futures market. Unhedged, the $3-per-cwt advance in the cash market would have resulted in an additional cost of $3,600 to the packer. Since this would be offset by the hedge, the only additional cost would be $200, the cost of commission, and the interest on margin. As in the previous example, this can be looked upon as a premium for price risk insurance.

This same type hedge could be used by large retailers in (1) advertising programs where retail prices are announced before wholesale meat purchase contracts have been made, or (2) fixing the purchase price of wholesale meat at a time when market analysis shows the likelihood of advancing prices. In both instances, the risk is one of advancing prices, and the initial step in the futures market would be to take a long position, a position that would be liquidated as actual supplies

Table 13.7. Hedging Example 3: "Long" Hedge of Forward Sale of Beef—Assuming Price Advance of $3 Per CWT in Cash Cattle Market.

Cash Market ($)		Futures Market ($)		Results ($)	
Today:		Today:		Loss on cash market	3,600
(1) Sell 72,000 lb Choice beef on contract @ $90/cwt [equivalent to 120 head of steers (1,000 lb each) @ $56/cwtᵃ]		(2) Buy futures contracts, three units @ $54/cwt		Gain on futures market	3,600
				Less commission	150
				Less interest on margin	50
Total value of sale:	$67,200	Total purchase value:	$68,400	Net cost:	$200
56 days from today:		56 days from today:			
(3) Buy 120 Choice steers @ $59/cwt		(4) Sell futures contracts, three units @ $60/cwt			
Total cost:	$70,800	Total sale value:	$72,000		

ᵃ$56 per cwt is considered to be the live-weight equivalent of dressed cost.

were purchased in the cash wholesale meat market. In actuality, there is little evidence that retailers use such hedges. In most cases, they are able to obtain a firm agreement on meat prices prior to advertising, and, as a matter of operating policy, retail prices (with the exception of specials) are held relatively steady compared to wholesale meat and live animal prices.

Example 4: Hedging Feed Costs. Feed cost is a principal component of the total cost of finishing livestock, and the major share of feed cost in grain cost. A livestock feeder who purchases grain for feeding can, if he chooses, use the futures market to protect himself against a rise in grain prices. Attention is called to an earlier assertion that hedging livestock prices does not in itself guarantee a profit. Likewise, the hedging of feed prices does not in itself guarantee a profit. Hedging grain prices, in effect, sets the price of grain and can be effected at the start of the feeding period (or earlier). Whether or not a feeder chooses to hedge will depend on (1) whether the current grain futures prices permit him to set (lock in) prices that are favorable, and (2) the feeder's analysis of whether grain prices are likely to rise. Corn futures are available, and corn is actively traded, but lack of interest in grain sorghum futures resulted in their abandonment. Since cash prices of corn and grain sorghum are closely correlated, a feeder who desires price protection in grain sorghum can hedge by using corn futures.

Explicit, step-by-step procedures will not be shown for this example. Since the risk to be avoided is a rise in grain prices, a long hedge (a purchase of futures) against grain requirements is called for. A feeder should (1) calculate his grain requirements, (2) place a hedge by purchasing futures, and then (3), as grain is purchased on the cash grain market, liquidate an equivalent quantity of futures, hold the remainder until additional grain is purchased, and finally liquidate more futures.

Soybean meal and some other feed ingredients may be hedged in futures markets in a like manner.

Use of a Hedge Worksheet. It must be emphasized, again, that hedging in itself does not guarantee a profit. Before a hedge is executed, each hedging situation should be evaluated by an analysis of estimated costs and estimated returns to labor, management, and profit. Profit is defined here as an amount over and above an acceptable return to labor and management; in other words, any return to labor and management is considered as a cost to be covered before profits are calculated. Some operators may prefer to place a zero value on labor and management and consider everything over operating costs as profit; this option is up to the individual.

Table 13.8 is the authors' version of a worksheet designed to evalu-

Table 13.8. Hedge Worksheet for Cattle.

Buy _____ lb _____ feeder _____ ; feed _____ days; sell _____ lb _____ slaughter cattle
    (Grade)   (Steers   (Grade)
                    or heifers)

A. Estimated Costs:

    (1) Cost of feeder per head (_____ lb @ $ _____)....................$_____
    (2)Cost of gain:
        (a) Feed costs per head...............................$_____
        (b) Nonfeed costs per head.........................$_____
        (c) Total cost of gain per head [line (2a) + line (2b)]..........$_____
    (3) Marketing costs per head (in cash market).......................$_____
    (4) Hedging costs per head.......................................$_____
    (5) Total all costs per head [line (1) + line (2c) + (3) + line (4)]......................$_____
    (6) Acceptable operators return per head for labor and management...............$_____
    (7) Break-even amount, total per head [line (5) + line (6)]...............$_____
    (8) Break-even price, per cwt [line (7) ÷ sale weight]................$_____

B. Estimated Hedge Selling Price:

    (9) Current Chicago futures price, _____ (month), per cwt............$_____
    (10) Basis adj. for market location differential per cwt.....................$_____
    (11) Basis adj. for grade differential per cwt...................$_____
    (12) Basis adj. for avg. livewt and dressing yield...........................$_____
    (13) Basis adj. for heifer differential per cwt...................$_____
    (14) Effective futures hedge price
        [line (9) ± line (10) ± line (11) ± line (12) − line (13)]...............$_____

C. Estimated Profit:

    (15) Est. hedged profit per cwt [line (14) − line (8)]......................$_____
    (16) Est. hedged profit per head [line (15) × sale wt]....................$_____

D. Estimated Hedged Return to Labor, Management, and Profit per Head
    (17) [line (6) + line (16)]....................... ....$_____

ate the feasibility of a hedge in terms of profit and returns to labor
and management. Even a cursory review of this worksheet reveals two
critical components: costs and basis. Costs are listed as (1) cost of
feeder cattle, (2) cost of grain, (3) marketing costs (in cash market), (4)
hedging costs, and (5) if an operator chooses to enter it, an "acceptable
operator's return to labor and management."

Basis, it will be recalled, is the difference between the applicable
cash-market price (i.e., the cash market in which the livestock will actually be sold) and the futures price. As the worksheet shows, this difference can be affected by market location, grade, sex, weight, and dres-
ing yield. If a feeder were located near a par delivery point, feeding
Choice steers of 1,050 to 1,150 pounds with a carcass yield of 61 per-

cent, each of the indicated items of basis adjustment would be minimal, for these characteristics would meet par specifications of the CME futures contract. There are costs associated with delivery, however, e.g., grading, yardage, fee for handling by firm on the yard, etc., and there will be some trucking cost regardless of how close the feedyard may be to the delivery yards. If the feeder operated near Greeley, Colo., or Lubbock, Texas, for example, he would need to enter a substantial locational differential. If he were feeding cattle of lower grade than Choice, he would need to enter a grade differential, and so on for sex and liveweight and dressing yield.

A question might be raised whether heifers can be hedged in a futures that specifies steers as the base commodity. Obviously, heifers cannot be delivered to satisfy the contract, but delivery is not anticipated. The steer futures could be used, and satisfactorily—providing cash heifer price movements generally parallel steer futures price movements, even though they occupy different absolute levels. The futures may also be used for hedging on a selective basis (even though cash and futures price movements are not parallel) if they move in a predictable pattern allowing one to determine when it is advantageous to hedge and when not to hedge.[8] Records show that slaughter steer and heifer prices for given grade and comparable weight do move in a generally parallel fashion. Deviations from parallel movements occur with variations in relative supplies, but such change occurs at a slow rate.

Worksheet Evaluation of a Cattle Feeding Hedge.   In Table 13.9, an example is shown of a completed cattle hedge work sheet. It is suggested that such an analysis be completed prior to purchasing feeder cattle. Every feeder should have a solid estimate of his cost of gain, including nonfeed costs. It is recognized that cost of gain varies with weather conditions, inherent gainability of cattle, etc., but many factors are controllable. Over a period of time, with the aid of a good set of records and efficient management, cost of gain can be estimated with an acceptable degree of accuracy. Without such an estimate the evaluation of a hedging potential is seriously handicapped.

In calculating basis adjustments, the first prerequisite is a familiar-

---

[8]This is precisely what is involved in hedging steers on a local basis. For example, a feeder at North Platte, Nebraska, does not expect his local price level to equal that at Chicago, but if the Chicago futures is to work satisfactorily as a hedging mechanism, his local cash-price movements must generally parallel futures prices or, if not parallel, then move in a predictable relationship.

Table 13.9. Hypothetical Example: Hedge Worksheet for Cattle.

Buy <u>700</u> lb <u>Choice</u> <u>feeder steers</u> feed <u>135</u> days; sell <u>1,060</u> lb <u>Choice</u> slaughter cattle
      (Grade)   (Steers   (Grade)
               or heifers)

A. Estimated Costs:

   (1) Cost of feeder per head (<u>700</u> lb @ <u>$54.00</u>)..............$378.00
   (2) Cost of gain:
      (a) Feed costs per head...............................$156.00
      (b) Nonfeed costs per head.........................$ 52.00
      (c) Total cost of gain per head [line (2a) + line (2b)]..........$208.00
   (3) Marketing costs per head (in cash market).........................$ 4.00
   (4) Heading costs per head...$ 1.80
   (5) Total all costs per head [line (1) + line (2c) + (3) + line (4)].......................$591.80
   (6) Acceptable operators return per head for labor and management................$ 12.00
   (7) Break-even amount, total per head [line (5) + line (6)]...................................$603.80
   (8) Break-even price, per cwt [line (7) ÷ sale weight]...$ 56.96

B. Estimated Hedge Selling Price:

   (9) Current Chicago futures price, April (month), per cwt.............$ 59.75
   (10) Basis adj. for market location differential per cwt....................$ −1.50
   (11) Basis adj. for grade differential per cwt.....................................$ −0.50
   (12) Basis adj. for avg. livewt and dressing yield...........................$ −
   (13) Basis adj. for heifer differential per cwt..................................$ −
   (14) Effective futures hedge price
      [line (9) ± line (10) ± line (11) ± line (12) − line (13)].............$57.75

C. Estimated Profit:

   (15) Est. hedged profit per cwt [line (14) − line (8)].....................................$ 0.79
   (16) Est. hedged profit per head [line (15) × sale wt]...................................$ 8.37

D. Estimated Hedged Return to Labor, Management, and Profit per Head

   (17) [line (6) + line (16)]..$ 20.37

*Entry for operators' labor and management is optional; each individual must decide whether to enter such a charge. If entry is made, the amount will vary with individual's objectives.

ity with futures market contract specifications. Any deviation from those specifications gives rise to variations in the basis. Items listed in lines 10, 11, 12, and 13 of the worksheet (Tables 13.8 and 13.9) indicate the major factors, but not all of these will apply in every case. Information needed for basis adjustment usually is not available in published form, but experienced producers and market personnel have satisfactory knowledge of the price effect of such factors.

In the example of Table 13.9, costs (line 5) are shown to be $591.80. Line 6 provides a space for entering an amount for the operator's labor and management. As mentioned earlier, this is a matter for each operator to decide for himself. Most operators hope to obtain some reimbursement for their labor and management. It makes little difference in some respects whether this is itemized separately or lumped in with profits. From a business standpoint, however, there is merit in setting an explicit goal for labor and management. In this example, $12 per head was entered as an acceptable return for labor and management (line 6). The total amount needed to return all costs ($591.80 plus $12.00 for labor and management) is then $603.80 (line 7). This breaks down to $56.96 per cwt (line 8), referred to as the break-even price. Note that the break-even price is calculated from "sale weight." Steers handled in a feeding program as described in this example would have to be fed to a weight of around 1,100 pounds to realize a sale weight of 1,060 pounds. This is due to weight shrinkage in marketing—either actual or "pencil" shrink.

The entry in line 9 should be the futures price for the contract month in which the hedge is placed. The current futures price assumes that a hedge could be placed at about the most recently quoted price. This would be the case ordinarily, unless the market were actively moving either up or down.

Lines 10, 11, 12, and 13 are reserved for basis adjustments, as previously described. In the example (Table 13.9), an adjustment of − $1.50 was indicated for location and − $0.50 for grade differential. Nothing was entered in line 12 because the anticipated average weight and dressing yield were assumed to be equivalent to contract specifications. Line 13 does not apply in this case since the example deals with steers. The *effective* futures hedge price (line 14) is line 9 adjusted for basis factors; in this example, it is $57.75. This immediately can be compared with the break-even price of $56.96 (line 8). When the effective futures hedge price equals or exceeds the calculated break-even price, a potentially favorable situation is indicated. In this case, it is seen in line 16 that the estimated hedge profit is $8.37 per head; in line 17, this $8.37 is then added to line 6 (acceptable operator's return to labor and management), making a total return of $20.37 per head.

Again, this is not a guaranteed return. However, if expected cash-futures price relationships hold, and if costs and bases have been accurately estimated, the estimate of line 17 will approximate feeding returns on a hedge operation.

Feeder-cattle programs may be hedged in a similar manner by use of feeder-cattle futures. Feeder-cattle growing operations, feedlot finishing, and feed procurement could be tied together in a virtually completely hedged operation by manipulating the respective futures.

Worksheet Evaluation of a Hog-Feeding Hedge. Table 13.10 illustrates worksheet evaluation of hedging a hog-feeding operation. The format used is similar to that in the previous example for cattle. In

Table 13.10. Hypothetical Example: Hedge Worksheet for Hogs.

Buy 40 lb #2 feeder pigs feed 120 days; sell 220 lb #2 slaughter hogs
    (Grade)   (Grade)

A. Estimated Costs:
   (1) Cost of feeder per head (40 lb @ $ $1.13)..............$45.00
   (2) Cost of gain:
     (a) Feed costs per head...............................$55.60
     (b) Nonfeed costs per head.........................$20.00
     (c) Total cost of gain per head [line (2a) + line (2b)].........$75.60
   (3) Marketing costs per head (in cash market).......................$ 1.50
   (4) Hedging costs per head.......................................$ 0.45
   (5) Total all costs per head [line (1) + line (2c) + (3) + line (4)].........................$122.55
   (6) Acceptable operators return per head for labor and management...............$ 2.00
   (7) Break-even amount, total per head [line (5) + line (6)]....................$124.55
   (8) Break-even price, per cwt [line (7) ÷ sale weight]....................$ 56.61

B. Estimated Hedge Selling Price:
   (9) Current Chicago futures price, June (month), per cwt..............$ 52.80
   (10) Basis adj. for market location differential per cwt....................$− 1.00
   (11) Basis adj. for grade differential per cwt...............................$−
   (12) Basis adj. for avg. weight differential per cwt.........................$−
   (13) Effective futures hedge price
     [line (9) ± line (10) ± line (11) ± line (12)]..............$51.80

C. Estimated Profit:
   (14) Est. hedged profit per cwt [line (13) − line (8)]..............................$ −4.81
   (15) Est. hedged profit per head [line (14) × sale wt]..........................$ −10.58

D. Estimated Hedged Return to Labor, Management, and Profit per Head
   (16) [line (6) + line (15)]...$ −8.58

this case, however, the relationships among costs, bases, and futures prices are intentionally set up so that the effective futures hedge price ($51.80 on line 13) is less than the break-even price ($56.61 on line 8). That situation would prevail even if nothing were entered for operator's labor and management (line 6).

In general, an evaluation that shows a negative return to labor, management, and profit (line 16) would be considered a nonhedging situation. Under such hedged conditions, the operator would expect to take a loss. Hedging still might be feasible, however, if, for some reason, an operator (or his banker) preferred to take the indicated loss rather than assume the risks of an even greater loss were the feeding operation to be carried out unhedged.

**able 13.11. Hypothetical Example: Hedge Worksheet—Maximum to Pay for 650-lb
eeder Steers.**

. Estimated Hedge Selling Price:

    (1) Current Chicago futures price, Oct. , (month) per cwt................$ 56.45
    (2) Basis adj. for market location differential per cwt......................$ −1.50
    (3) Basis adj. for grade differential per cwt..$ −0.75
    (4) Basis adj. for avg. livewt and dressing yield.............................$ −
    (5) Basis adj. for heifer differential per cwt..$ −
    (6) Effective futures hedge price
[line (1) ± line (2) ± line (3) ± line (4) − line (5)]...............$54.20

. Estimated Sale Weight per Head:

    (7) From production records...................................1,060 lb

. Estimated Market Value of Finished Cattle per Head

    (8) [line (6) × line (7)]..$574.52

. Estimated Costs (Exclusive of Feeder Animal):

    (9) Cost of gain:
       (a) Feed costs per head.....................$156.00
       (b) Nonfeed costs per head...............$ 52.00
       (c) Total cost of gain per head [line (a) + line (b)]....................................$208.00
   (10) Marketing costs per head (in cash market)...$ 4.00
   (11) Hedging costs per head...$ 1.80
   (13) Total all costs per head [line (9)(c) + line (10) + line (11)]....................$213.80
   (14) Acceptable operators return per head for labor and management........................$ 12.00
   (15) Total of [line (13) + line (14)]..$225.80

. Estimated Maximum Amount for Feeders:

   (16) Est. amount per head [line (8) − line (15)]...$348.72
   (17) Est. price per cwt [line (16) ÷ 6.50]*...$ 53.65

In general form, this term is [line (16) ÷ wt of feeder in hundredweights].

The data used in Tables 13.9 and 13.10 are hypothetical. Each feeder
should use cost and basis data pertinent to his individual situation.

Worksheet Analysis of Maximum Price to Pay for Feeder Cattle.
The futures market can be used to approximate the maximum price an
operator should pay for feeder cattle in situations where he would follow through with a hedge on the feeding operation. Table 13.11 illustrates an approach to the calculations involved.

    This analysis, like those preceding, necessitates a knowledge of costs
and bases. A number of the items estimated in Table 13.9 are identical
for this analysis, although used in a different order. The approach here
takes the "effective futures hedge price" (line 6 in Table 13.11) as the

estimated selling price of finished cattle, as would be the case if the cattle were hedged. This is in line with the earlier discussion where it was shown that a short hedge in the futures market, can establish selling price providing the appropriate basis is considered.

With selling price established, the market value of finished steers will be the product of selling price and sale weight (see line 8 of Table 13.11). By deducting all costs except that of the feeder steer itself (line 15) from market value (line 8), an estimate can be obtained of the maximum amount per head that should be paid for a feeder steer (see line 16). Division of this amount by the weight of a feeder steer gives the maximum price per hundredweight (line 17).

The format of Table 13.11 also is readily adaptable for estimating the maximum amount a hog feeder should pay for feeder pigs, providing the futures market is used for a short hedge.

It should be noted at this point that the use of this worksheet as described here is not equivalent to accepting the futures quotation as a forecast of prices. By making a sale (a short hedge) in the futures market, however, an operator can "lock-in" that price—with the qualifications mentioned earlier regarding possible variation in the basis.

Research Findings on Hedging Strategies

A critical question in evaluating the feasibility of hedging is its effect upon (1) the level of profits, and (2) the stability of profits. Other things being equal, most operators would prefer higher profits. Some may prefer more stable profits at somewhat lower average levels to higher average profits if the latter are highly variable as well. The optimum hedging program, however, would be one that increases profit level and simultaneously reduces the variability of hedged operation.

A considerable body of research literature has been developed on hedging strategies in recent years. The studies generally agree that routine hedging of every lot of cattle or hogs placed on feed will reduce the variability of profits over a period of years but will not enhance average profits. In a simulated analysis of a continuously operated cattle feedlot, Price (1976) found weekly average profits of routinely hedged operations to be $2.45 per head, whereas profits on unhedged operations were $13.82 per head. Even though variability of profits was reduced significantly, the reduction would be unacceptable by most standards. Although there are notable short-run exceptions, cattle prices have been on a general uptrend since initiation of live-cattle futures in late 1964. This fact largely accounts for the failure of routine hedging to enhance average profits. The costly and disruptive effect of numerous short-run downturns in cattle and hog prices, especially the

1973–1976 and 1982–1986 periods, has prompted the development of strategies that provide for elective hedging.

Two basic approaches to selective hedging are: (1) to develop criteria that specify *whether* to place a hedge, then, *if* a hedge is placed, to maintain it until the livestock are sold; or (2) to develop criteria that specify *whether* to place a hedge, then, *if* a hedge is placed, to use further criteria to provide for a possible lifting of the hedge (and subsequent replacing/relifting, etc.) before the livestock are sold. Several possibilities will be examined within each of those classifications.

Selective Hedge: Futures > Break-even.   This strategy specifies that a hedge will be placed only when the futures price (adjusted for basis) is greater than the calculated break-even price (calculated at the beginning of the feeding period). For those cases where the criteria for placing a hedge are not met, a feedlot operator has two alternatives: (1) feed the livestock unhedged, or (2) place no livestock on feed during that period. In a simulated commercial cattle feedlot operation covering the period May 1965–December 1974, McCoy and Price (1975) found that following this strategy using alternative (2) resulted in higher profits than unhedged operation, but the difference was statistically nonsignificant. Alternative (2) resulted in lower profits than alternative (1) if both fixed and variable costs were considered, but alternative (2) resulted in profits greater than alternative (1) if only variable costs were considered.

Selective Hedge: Futures > Cash.   This strategy specifies that a hedge will be placed only when the futures price (adjusted for basis) at the beginning of a feeding period is greater than the current cash price for contract grade cattle. Profits under this program were greater than the futures > break-even program and significantly greater than unhedged operations under alternative (1) described above. Alternative (2) produced significantly lower profits.

Selective Hedge: Futures > Break-even and Cash.   Under this strategy, a hedge is placed only when the futures price (adjusted for basis) at the beginning of a feeding period is greater than the calculated break-even price *and* at the same time is greater than the current cash price. This program produced the highest profits of the three selective hedging strategies discussed up to this point. The variance of profits under each of these three strategies was lower than the variance in profits of unhedged operations, but only in the futures > cash program was the variance significantly less than that of unhedged operations.

Selective Hedge: Flexible Application.   The selective hedge discussed previously followed the pattern that *if or when* the criteria being used specified that a hedge be placed, the hedge was not lifted until the livestock were sold. That is the traditional pattern. It sometimes is argued that if the profit margin locked in by the hedge is satisfactory at the initiation of the hedge, it ought to be good enough to stay with till the end of the feeding period. The livestock feeder with a short hedge who follows that approach, however, will forego additional profits if livestock prices turn upward after the hedge is placed. A substantial amount of research has been done on developing strategies to identify turning points in price trends so that a short hedge may be lifted once an uptrend is established and replaced if or when the trend subsequently turns downward.[9]

Among the most commonly used approaches for identifying price trends and turning points are the following: (1) quantitative price prediction models, (2) point and figure charts, (3) bar charts, and (4) moving averages. Brown and Purcell (1978) used approaches (1) and (4), both separately and in combination, to evaluate hedging programs for feeder cattle. Price and McCoy (1978) used approach (4) to evaluate hedging strategies for slaughter steers, feeder steers, and hogs. In both of these studies, flexible selective hedging produced greater profits than unhedged or traditional selective hedging. Further improvement can be expected in the development of these techniques. Brandt (1985) evaluated six quarterly price-forecasting methods using a simple hedging-strategy decision rule. The results indicate that hog producers and buyers could reduce the risk of unfavorable price movements by combining selective hedging strategies with information from a forecasting model. The results also showed that modest improvements in prices are possible under this risk management approach.

A word of caution is in order. At this stage, it is not known whether the U.S. Internal Revenue Service (IRS) will classify flexible selective hedging as a bona fide hedge for income tax reporting. In a bona fide hedge, gains and/or losses on the futures transactions are treated as ordinary gains/losses. Gains and/or losses on futures transactions that do not qualify as bona fide hedges are treated as capital gains/losses, and the length of time involved in most livestock hedges would put them in the classification of short-term capital gain/losses. Income-tax consequences of short-term capital gains/losses are considerably different from ordinary gains/losses. This may be a moot question in view of impending tax law changes.

---

[9]In the case of a long hedge, criteria are developed for lifting the hedge if the price trend turns downward and for replacing it if prices subsequently turn upward.

Problems and Characteristics of the Basis.   Basis is usually defined as the difference between futures price and cash price at a specified cash market and specified time. This definition is somewhat ambiguous since it is not apparent whether, or when, the basis is positive or negative. It is more precise to define basis as the amount by which cash price is below the futures price (i.e., negative) or above the futures price (i.e., positive). As shown in Figs. 13.2 and 13.3, the basis for cattle and hogs may be positive or negative.

In futures markets for storable commodities that are produced at one time of the year and stored for use throughout the subsequent period, a logical reason exits for hypothesizing that the futures price for a given contract month at any particular time will be above the cash price at par delivery points by the amount of storage charges that would carry the commodity to termination of the futures contract.[10] The basis at nonpar markets would include, in addition to storage, a transportation charge. In that sense, the basis for storable commodities can be construed to be a market-determined charge. Live animals in condition for slaughter are not storable. Some efforts have been made at a theoretical explanation of a cash-futures price relationship for live cattle. Skadberg and Futrell (1966) pointed out the unique differences between livestock and storable commodities; i.e., livestock change form over time, holding time is limited as livestock approach market condition, and there is no necessary tie between today's cash price and the futures price for deferred delivery. In a theoretical treatment, Paul and Wesson (1967) concluded that the difference between a futures price and the sum of feeder cattle and feed prices on the cash market is the price of feedlot services. A refinement of this approach was pursued by Ehrich (1969). Leuthold (1977) makes a good case for a proposition that the basis for nonstorable commodities is not market-determined, but rather that cash prices and futures prices of nonstorables are determined in independent markets and that the basis (the difference between them) is a residual.

Leuthold (1979) examined the factors that explain the basis variation over time for live-cattle futures. His analysis concluded that a major portion of basis variability can be explained by factors that determine and shift supply. These results confirmed the argument that the basis reflects the expected change in cash prices from the current

---

[10]A considerable body of literature exists on this aspect of cash-futures price relationships. The subject is complicated, including as it does consideration of risk premium and convenience yield as well as out-of-pocket storage costs. Periods of time when cash grain prices exceeded futures grain prices prompted the development of the theory of "inverse" carrying charges. No effort is made in this text to relate this theory to livestock and meat futures.

time until the maturity of the relevant futures contract. Price et al. (1979) measured the magnitude and variability of the live-cattle basis in four Kansas locations. The results showed that there was a statistically significant variation by location, but there were no significant differences in mean levels of the basis in delivery and nondelivery periods. However, it was also shown that there was less variance in the basis during the delivery period, which, the authors stated "may point to the desirability of (1) expanding the number of contracts to trade in each month of the year or (2) figuring a more conservative basis for cattle to be finished in a nondelivery period to reduce chances for windfall hedging losses." In 1983, Leuthold and Peterson developed and tested a model identifying the variables that affect the cash-futures price spread (basis) for hogs. The results supported their basic hypothesis, and the findings of earlier studies, that the basis is primarily a function of the factors affecting supply. The most important variables were current slaughter, expected marketing of live hogs, and cold storage.

Suffice it to say that at this stage there is not a universally accepted basis theory for livestock futures, but that does not mean that futures cannot be used for hedging. A number of studies have shown practical application of selective hedging and flexible selective hedging as described earlier, e.g., Brown and Purcell (1978), Erickson (1978), Heifner (1972), McCoy and Price (1975), McCoy and Price (1976), Price (1976), and Brandt (1985).

Do Futures Market Prices Forecast Cash Prices?

It might be argued that traders base their evaluation of futures prices on expected supply–demand conditions and that the price level at any given time represents a consensus of expected prices in the future. An almost equal case could be made that the futures price at a given time is a consensus of what the actual price will not be at termination of the contract. Specultive buyers trade on the expectation that prices will move higher and speculative sellers expect prices to move lower. Tomek and Gray (1970) state the following:

... prices of futures 6 months from maturity, 1 month from maturity, and cash prices are all 'forecasts' or 'nonforecasts' in approximately the same degree. . . .

Of course, unforeseen developments occur between futures expiration dates. The new but unpredictable information may indeed change expectations, but this is reflected in the entire constellation of prices. This in no sense implies that the expired futures was incorrectly priced before its expiration, nor therefore that the pre-existing price relationship was in error. The range of prices at a point in time is based on the information then available, but new events and information may make the forecast of the previous period incorrect.

Just and Rausser (1981) found that there is some degree of accuracy in the futures market prices as a forecasting tool of several agricultural commodities, compared to econometric models. For livestock, however, they indicated that some of the econometric forecasts are preferable. Martin and Garcia (1981) found that live-cattle futures were inadequate in forecasting cash prices. On the other hand, they found that live-hog futures performed relatively well in forecasting cash prices during stable economic conditions, but poorly during unstable conditions. Leuthold and Hartman (1980) used a semistrong form test of market efficiency to compare the performance of futures markets with econometric models in forecasting subsequent cash prices of cattle, hogs, and pork bellies. Based on the empirical results, they concluded that, at times, futures markets did not appear to utilize—or correctly use—all available information to reflect prices accurately in the future. In a 1984 study, Barton and Tomek (1984) found that forward-pricing models are poor predictors of futures price changes. They concluded that "market prices six or more months before maturity have not been especially good guides to price at maturity."

If futures prices did not move, there would be little incentive for either speculation or hedging. It is apparent that traders take a position because they believe that the price will move. Regardless of whether one accepts the theory that futures prices represent traders' best estimate of what prices actually will be at a future date, or the opposite—that it represents their judgment of what it will not be—the record clearly shows it has not been an accurate forecaster of prices. This fact, however, does not negate its usefulness as a hedging mechanism. As long as a market attracts sufficient speculation to absorb hedges without undue price reaction, it can perform the hedging function, which in actuality is a price-setting function. Price forecasting is a responsibility of the personnel who trade on the futures market, and not vice versa.

Does Futures Trading Stabilize Livestock Prices?   Observation of the record would immediately prompt the conclusion that livestock prices have not stabilized since initiation of futures trading. Price changes are reflection of changes in supply and demand. If it could be shown that the futures market tends to stabilize supply or demand (or both), then a reason would exist for suggesting that futures trading stabilizes prices. There is nothing inherent in the market, however, that tends to stabilize demand. Factors that affect demand were discussed in Chap. 3 and are beyond the scope of the futures market.

If futures prices were relatively stable and if producers in large volume used the market as a price-setting mechanism (by hedging), then the futures market would impart a degree of stability in prices. Tomek and Gray (1970) state that "for commodities such as potatoes, which lack continuous inventories, prices of distant futures are less variable than cash prices and hence producer-hedging in such markets tends to stabilize revenue." This property is yet to be shown for livestock futures. Livestock futures might continue to exist with somewhat less fluctuation than at present, but if the futures market became highly stable, it probably would disappear. Without price movement, there would be no incentive for either speculation or hedging.

Although futures may not be expected to stabilize prices, hedging can contribute to the stability of profits (McCoy and Price, 1975; McCoy and Price, 1976).

Hedging and Livestock Credit

Large-scale feeding operations require large-scale financing. Summers (1967) commented that "not long ago, most cattle loans were to farmers who had feed in their cribs and who seldom asked to borrow more than 20% of their net worth for the purchase of feeders. Today, cattle feeders are more likely to have a modern feedlot, and may have part of the facilities paid for but have a small net worth in relation to the requested loan, yet they ask us to furnish money for the cattle and the feed as well." Grain merchandisers and storage interests long have found bankers more prone to grant credit on hedged than unhedged commodities. With the inauguration of live-cattle futures, it was anticipated that cattle feeders who hedged would be in a better position to obtain credit than formerly. Theoretical considerations link credit availability to the degree of risk, and since hedging is presumed to lessen price risk, it follows that credit would be more readily available to a hedged operator.

Little work has been done to test this hypothesis. In a 1965 survey, Waldner (1965) reported that of the banks he contacted regarding loan policy on hedged cattle, " . . . no bank had a defined loan policy nor was any bank prepared to alter its customary loan policy to accommodate 'hedged' cattle." This was relatively soon after initiation of futures contracts in live cattle. In a 1968 study of South Dakota lending agencies, Powers (1968) found that hedging and forward contracting (referred to in this text as "cash contracting") had little influence on the ability of a producer to obtain a loan. If a producer qualified for a loan otherwise, however, hedging permitted an increase in the size of the loan. He found, also, that hedging had no effect on interest rates. Powers' study is summarized as follows:

The data . . . indicate that the average increases in loans on hedged livestock ranged from 12.2 to 17.5% of the value of assets. On contracted livestock the average increases ranged from 11.9 to 18.3%. All of these increases are significantly greater than zero, thus indicating that hedging and forward contracting of livestock assets do aid farmers in obtaining capital by increasing the amount loaned on given livestock assets.

With respect to interest rate, Powers commented:

. . . not a single agency which had made loans on hedged and contracted collateral reduced the interest rates on such loans . . .
There are probably three major reasons for these results. First, some of the lenders probably believe that hedging and forward contracting do not reduce their risk. . . . Second, a number of the respondents indicated that they based the interest rate on their cost of money, not on the different amounts or risk presented by farmers or firms. Third, it is quite likely that the risk reduction has been fully accounted for by the increase in the size of the loan.

Lending institutions have given substantially greater emphasis to livestock hedging in the years since the price breaks of 1973 and the 1980s. Lenders are more knowledgeable of the market than formerly, and many insist that low-equity customers hedge their livestock operations.

Harris and Baker (1980) reported the results of a mail survey of farm lenders in Illinois. The survey was designed to measure lenders' credit responses and their attitude towards hedging. Although the survey was concerned with crop farmers, the results reflect the respondents' views towards hedging in general, which could be relevant to livestock producers. The responses suggest that lenders are willing to provide more credit to farmers who pledged preharvest-hedged crops as collateral. The majority, however, indicated that hedging increased credit by no more than the amount of margin calls. Respondents also indicated that larger loans backed by hedged commodities were based on the perception that hedging reduces the risk of both borrower and lender.

RECENT DEVELOPMENTS—CERTIFICATES OF DELIVERY, CASH SETTLEMENT, AND LIVESTOCK OPTIONS

Certificate of Delivery System in Live-Cattle Futures[11]

Although, as indicated earlier, only a minor fraction of futures contracts are fulfilled by actual delivery of the commodity at stake, certain markets have experienced a sizable number of deliveries and redeliveries of live cattle. Until 1983, the delivery procedure was as follows: A seller (short) informed the CME clearing house of his intent to deliver live cattle to fulfill a futures-contract obligation (through a Notice of Intent to Deliver). The buyer (long) with the earliest placed position in the contract is assigned the notice, and the cattle are delivered to an approved location on the following business day. Often, longs had no immediate need for the cattle or took them at an inconvenient location. The frequent solution for such buyers was to go short on the futures and redeliver the same cattle on the following delivery day. The same situation could be repeated. These redeliveries caused hardship on the cattle and put them out of condition; they also involved additional costs and efforts by the livestock yards and possibly by Federal graders.

In January, 1983, the procedures for delivering slaughter cattle on a futures contract were replaced by a new procedure—called the Certificate of Delivery System. The new system was developed by the CME in cooperation with the cattle industry and was approved by the CFTC.

WHAT IS A CERTIFICATE OF DELIVERY?

The new delivery system temporarily substitutes a Certificate of Delivery for the delivery of actual live cattle until a long willing to receive physical delivery has been matched with the Certificate. The Certificate replaces the Notice of Intent to Deliver. It commits the seller (long) to deliver cattle meeting the CME contract's specifications at a specified location three business days in the future. A Certificate, if not taken by Demand or Reclaim Notices (see below for definition) between 1:30 and 3:00 P.M. on each of the first three successive business

---

[11]This discussion draws heavily from information published by the CME in 1983 following the introduction of the Certificate of Delivery system.

days, is assigned to the oldest long in the market. During the first two days, a long who was assigned the Certificate may choose not to take delivery by retendering the Certificate at a specified fee. The fees are accumulated to the Certificate and accrue to the final long who accepts the Certificate, or to the original tendering short who reclaims the Certificate. A long assigned the certificate on the third day must accept delivery of the cattle.

A "Demand Notice" feature is included in the new system that gives any long the opportunity to move to the head of the line (i.e., to step ahead of the oldest long) and accept cattle that are then delivered at a preferred location. The system also allows the original short to regain a certificate he has tendered—but which has not yet been claimed by a long—by issuing a "Reclaim Notice" after first establishing a long position in the market. A "Demand Notice" takes precedence even if it is received by a clearing house after a "Reclaim Notice."

Cash Settlement in Feeder-Cattle Futures

After a period of intensive study, the Chicago Mercantile Exchange, in the fall of 1986, inaugurated a new procedure for the settlement of feeder-cattle futures. Prior to that time, settlement by delivery of feeder cattle required actual physical delivery of medium frame No. 1 steers weighing from 575 to 700 lb. Under that arrangement, a relative shortage of deliverable cattle, redelivery problems as indicated for live (slaughter) cattle futures, and delivery at inconvenient locations led to numerous problems. The new procedure requires a cash settlement based on the average of actual cash market prices of feeder cattle weighing 600 to 800 lb (known as the U.S. Feeder Steer Price), which when fed to slaughter weight will grade 60 to 80 percent Choice beef. Physical delivery of feeder cattle is no longer possible in settlement of a futures contract. Preliminary evidence indicates this change may impart greater stability to the basis for feeder cattle as well as simplify settlement of futures contracts.

Options on Livestock Futures

Beginning on October 30, 1984, agricultural producers and other traders were allowed to buy and sell agricultural commodity options for the first time since 1936 when they were banned by the government. Slaughter cattle options were traded on that same day on the CME floor. Options on live-hogs futures also began on February 1, 1985 at the CME. Such options provide livestock producers with an additional pricing strategy and a new way of risk management, offering some different characteristics than futures.

What is an Option?   An option is a contract that gives the buyer (option holder) the right (*not*) the obligation to buy or sell a futures[12] contract at a specified price (strike price) on or before a specified date (expiration date). Option contracts are legal documents that specify the futures contract to be traded, the strike price, and the expiration date. The cost of buying the option—called the "option premium"—is a nonreturnable cost of trading that is determined by the supply-and-demand conditions of the option market. Trading in options can take place only in licensed (organized) exchanges by employees of a member firm in the same manner as futures are traded.

There are two types of options: (1) the *call option*, which conveys to its holder the right to buy futures contract(s) at a fixed (maximum) price; and (2) the *put option*, which grants the right to sell futures contract(s) to its writer at a fixed (minimum) price. The fixed price in a call or put option is called a "strike price." There is a specified date on or before which the rights must be exercised—called the "expiration date"—after which the option is worthless.

To illustrate the use of options, assume that an option seller (writer) is offering the right to sell (i.e., a put option) one December-slaughter cattle-futures contract at $60 per cwt (strike price) for $3 per cwt (premium). The total cost (option premium) is $1,200 ($3 × 40,000/100) per live-cattle futures contract. A cattle producer who buys such a put option may exercise the right to sell it for $60 at any time up to the expiration date. Assume that, in October, the December futures is trading at $50 per cwt and that the producer decides to exercise the put option, i.e., by selling a December futures contract at $60 per cwt. In order to complete the transaction, he must buy back the futures contract at $50, making $10 per cwt gross profit (or $7 net profit after subtracting the $3 premium). On the other hand, if December futures climb to $70 per cwt at the time his cattle are ready for the market, he will not exercise the option.

Livestock producers can also use the call option—the right to buy—to purchase corn futures at a specified price on or before the expiration date. If, at harvest, the price of corn is sufficiently low in the cash market, he will let the option expire. On the other hand, if the price of

---

[12]In the broad sense, options may also be used to buy and sell physical commodities. This section, however, is concerned with trading options for the underlying futures contracts.

corn at harvest is higher than the strike price, he would exercise the call option.

Unlike futures contracts, which set a fixed price, the above examples indicate that a put (call) option establishes a minimum (maximum) selling (buying) price but does not eliminate the opportunity to receive (buy at) higher (lower) market prices. Kenyon (1984) summarized this feature as follows:

Options, therefore, permit farmers to establish desired selling prices without sacrificing their potential to benefit if the prices increase after the put option is purchased. If prices rise, the option is not exercised and the farmer loses only the premium. If prices fall, the farmer can exercise the option and obtain a price higher than the market price. Thus, with a put option, a farmer eliminates downside market price risk while retaining the opportunity to benefit from higher prices.

With a call option, a farmer eliminates price risk above the exercise price while retaining the opportunity to buy at market prices below the exercise price. Hence, options provide price insurance for farmers against undesirable price changes while allowing farmers to benefit from favorable price changes.

In addition to the premium, option buyers and sellers must pay commissions to their brokers. Unlike futures trading, however, where both buyers and sellers may receive margin calls, only option sellers may receive margin calls and are required to put margin money. Buyers of options do not receive margin calls since their maximum losses are limited to the premium regardless of futures price movement. Kenyon (1984) explained the reason option sellers (writers) deposit margins and receive margin calls as follows:

Because he or she has the potential liability to provide a futures contract to the option buyer should the buyer elect to exercise the option. This margin procedure assures the option buyer that the option seller (writer) will always have sufficient funds on deposit with the clearing corporation to pay the difference between the option strike price and current market price should the buyer exercise the option. If the option price never increases, the option writer will receive no margin calls and the option will expire worthless. If the option expires out of the money, the option buyer will lose the premium and the option writer will keep the premium as payment for providing the option buyer with price insurance.

The degree to which livestock producers will use options will be largely determined by the costs involved and their understanding of the system and its benefits.

REFERENCES

Anderson, R. W., and Danthine, J. P. 1981. Cross hedging. *J. Political Econ.* 89:1182-1196.

Bailley, F., Jr. 1968. The cattle feeder and the futures market. *Banking,* pp. 57-59.

Bakken, H. H., ed. 1970. *Futures Trading in Livestock—Origins and Concepts.* Madison, W Mimir Publishers.

Barton, B. W., and Tomek, W. G. 1984. Performance of the live cattle futures contract: Basis and forward-pricing behavior. Dept. of Agr. Econ. Agr. Expt. Sta., Cornell Univ., A.E. Res. 84-3.

Blau, G. 1944-1945. Some aspects of the theory of futures trading. *Rev. Econ. Studies* 12:7.

Brandt, J. A. 1985. Forecasting and hedging: An illustration of risk reduction in the hog industry. *Amer. J. Agr. Econ. 67,* No. 1:24-31.

Brown, R. A. and Purcell, W. D. 1978. Price prediction models and related hedging programs for feeder cattle. Oklahoma Agr. Expt. Sta. Bull. B-734.

Chicago Mercantile Exchange. 1983. New Certificate of Delivery System in live cattle. 1/83/15m.

Chicago Mercantile Exchange. 1986. Cash settlement for feeder cattle futures, p.3

Ehrich, R. L. 1969. Cash-futures relationships for live beef cattle. *Am. J. Agr. Econ.,* Feb., pp. 26-40.

Erickson, S. P. 1978. Selective hedging strategies for cattle feeders. Univ. of Illinois, Dept. Agr. Econ., Illinois Agr. Econ. vol 18, No. 1, pp. 15-20.

Futrell, G. A., and Skadberug, J. M. 1966. The futures market in live beef cattle. Iowa Coop. Agr. Ext. Serv. Circ. M-1021.

Ginn, B. 1981. Guidelines and hedging concepts for cross hedging fabricated cuts on the live cattle, live hog, and broiler futures contracts. Unpublished report prepared for the CME.

Gray, R. W. 1961. The search for a risk premium. *J. Political Econ.* LXIX, No. 3:250-260.

Hayenga, M. L. 1979. Risk management in imperfect markets: Commodity procurement strategy in the food manufacturing sector. *Amer. J. Agr. Econ.* 61:361-357.

Hayenga, M. L., and Dipietre, D. D. 1982. Hedging wholesale meat prices: Analysis of basis risk. *The J. Fut. Markets* 2:131-140.

Hayenga, M. L., and Dipietre, D. D. 1982. Cross hedging wholesale pork products using live hog futures. *Amer. J. Agr. Econ.* 64:747-741.

Johnson, D. A. 1970. The use of live steer futures contracts and their effect on cattle feeding profits. M. S. Thesis, Kansas State Univ.

Harris, K. S., and Baker, C. B. 1980. Does hedging increase credit for Illinois crop farmers? *Nor. Cent. J. Agr. Econ 3,* No. 1:47-52.

Just, R. E., and Rausser, G. C., 1981. Commodity price forecasting with large-scale econometric models and the futures market. *Amer. J. of Agr. Econ 63,* No. 2:197-208.

Kenyon, D. E. 1984. Farmers' guide to trading agricultural options. USDA. Econ. Res. Serv. Agr. Info. Bull. 463.

Kimple, K. C. et al.1978. the live cattle basis at selected locations in Kansas. Kansas Agr. Expt. Sta. Bull. 621.

Leuthold, R. M. 1977. An analysis of the basis for live beef cattle. Univ. of Illinois, Dept. of Agr. Econ. Staff Paper, No. 77 E-25.

Leuthold, R. M. 1979. An analysis of the futures-cash price basis for live beef cattle. *Nor. Cent. J. Agr. Econ.* 1:47-52.

Leuthold, R. M., and Hartmann, P. A. 1980. An evaluation of the forward-pricing efficiency of livestock futures markets. *Nor. Cent. J. Agr. Econ.* 3, No. 1:71–78.

Leuthold, R. M., and Van Blokland, P. J. 1981. Futures. A guide for farmers and lenders. Using the futures market in financial planning. Univ. of Illinois. Coop. Ext. Serv. Circ. 1191.

Leuthold, R. M., and Peterson, P. E. 1983. The cash-futures price spread for live hogs. *Nor. Cent. J. Agr. Econ.* 5, No. 1:25–29.

Martin, L., and Garcia, P. 1981. The price-forecasting performance of futures markets for live cattle and hogs: A disaggregated analysis. *Amer. J. Agr. Econ.* 63, No. 2:209–215.

McCoy, J. H., and Price, R. V. 1975. Cattle hedging strategies. Kansas Agr. Expt. Sta. Bull. 591.

McCoy, J. H., and Price, R. V. 1976. Hog hedging strategies. Kansas Agr. Expt. Sta., Bull. 604.

McCoy, J. H., and Rice, R. V. 1978. Flexible selective hedging of livestock. Dept. Econ. Kansas State Univ. Unpublished data.

Miller, S. E., and Luke, D. B. 1982. Alternative techniques for cross hedging wholesale beef prices. *J. Fut. Markets.* 2:121–129.

Paul, A. B., and Wesson, W. T. 1967. Pricing feedlot services through cattle futures. USDA Agr. Econ. Res. 29, No. 2, 33–45.

Powers, M. 1968. Hedging forward contracting and agricultural credit. S. Dakota Agr. Expt. Sta. Bull. 545.

Powers, M., and Hohnson, A. C. 1968. The frozen pork belly futures market: An analysis of contract specifications and contract viability. Dept. Agr. Econ., Univ. Wisconsin Agr. Econ. Bull. 51.

Price, R. V. 1976. The effects of traditional and managed hedging strategies for cattle feeders. M.S. Thesis, Kansas State Univ.

Price, R. V. et al. 1979. Basis variability of live cattle futures at selected Kansas markets. *Nor. Cent. J. Agr. Econ.* 1, No. 2:133–139.

Schneidau, R. E. 1967. Hedging on the live hog futures market. Indiana Coop. Agr. Ext. Serv. Circ. EC-312.

Skadberg, J. M., and Futrell, G. A. 1966. An economic appraisal of futures trading in livestock. *Amer. J. Agr. Econ.* 48:1485–1489.

Summers, M. M. 1967. Hedging and how it helps reduce loan risk. *Agr. Banking Finance*, May/June, p. 32.

Tomek, W. G., and Gray, R. W., 1970. Temporal relationships among prices on commodity futures markets: Their allocative and stabilizing roles. *Amer. J. Agr. Econ.* 52, No. 3:372–380.

Waldner, S. C. 1965. Will hedging offer financing advantages? *Feedlot*, Sept., p. 54.

Working, H. 1960. Speculation on hedging markets. *Food Res. Inst. Studies* 1, No. 2:185–220.

Working, H. 1962. New concepts concerning futures markets and prices. *Am. Econ. Review* LII, No. 3:434–436.

Working, H. 1963. Futures markets under renewed attack. *Food Res. Inst. Studies* 4, No. 1:13–24.

14

Grades and Grading

Producers, slaughterers, processors, and distributors are familiar with live animal and meat grades. Market news reports utilize Federal grade nomenclature in reporting prices, and within the meat trade, both Federal and private (brands) grades are used for wholesale transactions. Consumers are exposed to Federal grades—though most know little about them (Hutchinson 1970)—and private brands through advertising media and grocery store shopping. In short, grades and grading are an integral part of livestock and meat marketing.

This chapter is concerned primarily with Federal government grades, but private brands that are based on consistent quality specifications are tantamount to private grades.

There is evidence that some consumers confuse inspection with grading (Hutchinson, 1970). The difference should be clearly understood. Both the USDA inspection mark and USDA grade mark are applied in color on meat, but that is the only similarity. Inspection is concerned with the wholesomeness of meat and meat products—such things as diseased animals, sanitation in slaughtering and processing plants, prevention of adulteration, correct labeling, etc. This is a separate and distinct activity from grading. The inspection mark stamped on a carcass is a circle, and, if the carcass passes inspection, the circle contains the abbreviations, "U.S. INSP'D & P'S'D." The grade mark, on the other hand, is a shield in which is inscribed the abbreviation USDA and also the grade name or number as the case may be. When viewed side by side the difference is obvious as shown on page 447.

DEFINITION AND PURPOSE

Grading is the segregation of items of a commodity into distinct lots, or groupings, that have a relatively high degree of uniformity in certain specified attributes associated with market preferences and valuation. The relevant attributes differ widely among commodities in number, range of variability, and susceptibility to objective measurement. Eight grades are used to cover the range in quality of steer and heifer carcasses, but only three for ready-to-cook poultry. In conjunction with

GRADE MARKS

INSPECTION MARK

← Yield grade

← Quality grade

the quality grades for beef and lamb, five separate yield, or cutability, grades (i.e., yield of boneless, closely trimmed retail cuts) are assigned. Pork grades incorporate both yield and quality considerations without separate designations for each. Poultry grades are based entirely on quality.

Quality grades in beef are basically determined on subjective considerations. Quality is based on the "eatability" or palatability characteristics of the lean meat.[1] Cutability, or yield, grades for beef are determined primarily by objective measurements. Pork carcass grades rely heavily on objective measurements to determine the expected yield of lean cuts, which is then weighed against a subjective determination of "acceptable" or "unacceptable" quality of the lean.

Even though the definition of grading may be relatively straightforward, the drawing up of standards or specifications for a system of grades is a complex problem. Some of the attributes upon which grades are based can be evaluated directly; others, only indirectly, through so-called "indicators." For example, the yield of lean cuts of pork is related to ("indicated by") backfat thickness, carcass weight, and carcass length. A great amount of research and consultation is involved in developing grade standards.

The *purpose* of grading is related to whether the grading is a private or public function. Grading is not the sole prerogative of government.

---

[1]Prior to 1976, conformation of the carcass was also a consideration in beef quality grades, but that factor was eliminated with the grade changes of that date.

Most national packers and many regional packers have private grades and grade standards. The Federal government has its own extensive system of live animal and meat grades.

The objectives of a firm in setting up private grades are only partially compatible with the objectives of a public grading system. A primary concern of a private grading system is to adequately describe the quality of the product so that trade can be conducted with a minimum of time, effort, and expense. Grade designations that fully and consistently describe a product do away with the necessity of personal inspection by buyers and permit transactions to be made by telephone, or other electronic/remote communication systems, a convenience that lessens the expense of both buyers and sellers. In this respect, private and public grading have a common purpose.

Private firms also use grades, however, to differentiate their products from those of competitors. To the extent that the products are indeed different, this grading provides an informational service that assists buyers and, if the difference commands a higher market price, the result is a matter of buyer discretion. On the other hand, if the differentiation is spurious, buyers may be misled, and the result may be individual and social loss.

From the standpoint of the public interest, a profusion of grades and grade standards is confusing. Without some official supervision of the application of specified standards, doubts and suspicions sometimes arise as to whether products are of sufficient quality. The general public also has an interest in the effect grades have on the way the market system allocates resources among alternative production possibilities.

Producers' interest in grades is associated with the degree to which grades assist them in obtaining equitable prices. Consumers are primarily interested in obtaining products commensurate with the prices they have to pay for their preferences.

In view of the multiplicity of considerations, it was deemed to be in the public interest to inaugurate a system of Federal grades and grading. At the same time, individual firms retain the privilege of using private (or house) grades, either alone or in combination with U.S. grades.

The principal purposes of government grades can be placed under the general headings of improving (1) pricing efficiency, and (2) operational efficiency.

Grades and Pricing Efficiency

As indicated in Chap. 3, pricing efficiency is concerned with such things as the accuracy, effectiveness, and speed with which a price system measures product values to buyers and reflects these values back through marketing channels to producers. Involved in this concept are issues of efficiency in (1) the allocation of resources among alternative uses, and (2) the distribution of income among producers and others involved in the various economic activities of an industry. The uniform application of an appropriate set of grades can contribute to pricing efficiency. If consumers indicate a willingness and ability to pay more (or less) for a certain quality of meat, that information must be transmitted back to producers before they can react. A market economy depends upon price differentials to relay the message, and grades provide a meaningful common language whereby the price differential can be associated with the desired (or undesired) quality characteristic.[2] It is recognized that, at a given time, price differentials among quality levels of a particular product can occur as a result of variations in relative supplies as well as variations in demand. Over a period of time, however, the pricing system is presumed to allocate resources in such a way as to optimize supplies of various qualities of the product. This is implied by the very idea of pricing efficiency.

Grades also have a place in improving efficiency in the distribution of products of varying quality among alternative uses. Differential pricing among grades enables wholesalers and retailers to move given supplies into their highest order use at prices that clear the market. Thus, Canner and Cutter grades are diverted into processed meats (i.e., relatively low order use). Prime grade steaks and roasts go to the highest class night club, hotel, restaurant, and cruise ship trade. Choice and Select grades form the primary retail cuts. As a result, total revenue from the entire supply of meat is enhanced, and increased competition tends to distribute the benefits among all sectors of the livestock and meat industry.

The use of grades can increase the degree of competition in a market by increasing the level of public knowledge. Buyers and sellers in a perfectly competitive market are assumed to possess perfect knowledge of market conditions. Grades cannot be expected to impart perfect knowledge, but their use can "enhance" the knowledge of traders. This applies not only to quality aspects but also to yield characteristics (cutability) of animal carcasses. The difference in retail sales value between adjacent yield grades of choice carcass beef—though it varies with relative supply and demand—can easily amount to $5.00 per cwt. Therefore, a knowledge of yield grades and associated value differen-

---

[2]Grades that transmit quality differentials to consumers would enhance total utility even though no price differentials existed.

tials can strengthen competition between wholesalers and retailers. Uniformity in application of adequately descriptive grades allows trade by specification (as contrasted to inspection) via telephone or wire service. This enhances competition since wholesalers and retailers can shop over wide areas. The use of uniform Federal grades permits small packers to compete with large packers in terms of quality—if not volume—of product. This also increases the degree of competition and pricing efficiency.

Grades and Operational Efficiency

Operational efficiency is concerned with the costs of marketing functions. The concern is not necessarily with reduction in total but rather per-unit marketing costs. This goal may be accomplished by marketing a given quantity of goods at lower total cost, an increased quantity at the same total cost, or an increased quantity at a less than proportionate increase in total cost.

In some circumstances, grading can improve operational efficiency, whereas in others it may have the opposite effect. Grades permit trading by specification, which can result in a reduction in transaction expenses (travel, labor, and associated costs) for both buyer and seller, compared to trading by inspection. It is generally assumed that this means a reduction in total marketing expense, which is probably correct, but the statement must be qualified. Grading does not come free. Total marketing costs will be reduced providing the reduction in transactions costs are not exceeded by costs of grading, additional telephone expenses, costs associated with possible misunderstandings, and rejection of shipments that do not meet grade specifications.

Government grading of fresh beef and lamb has largely forestalled the advertising of private grades. As a result, the advertising bill is undoubtedly less than it would be otherwise and, this reduction in marketing cost can be construed as a gain in operational efficiency.[3] The mid-1980s was marked by an increase in packers' attempts to differentiate their products by private grading, a movement whose impact remains to be determined.

Federal grading also has had an impact on decentralization and specialization in the packing and processing industries. Use of Federal grades permitted small packers to compete with large operations, and

---

[3]This is not to be construed as an indictment of all advertising, but brand name advertising designed to alter consumers' preferences to match the characteristics of a product or to develop fictitious differences among products can result in social costs from misallocation of resources (see Farris, 1960).

smaller independent packers led the way in decentralization. This trend was followed by a decline in the number of small local packers. The opening of plants near livestock production centers contributes to cost reduction in a number of ways. Under the prevailing freight rate structure, transportation costs are less for dressed meat than for live animals. Operating costs are often less at interior points than at terminal locations, moreover, because of lower wage rates, taxes, utility rates, etc.

Specialization is also enhanced since grading permits more accurate description and identification of products. Specialization in products is complemented by specialization in labor, equipment, plant layout, and work techniques, which, in turn, contribute to cost reduction and operational efficiency.

DEVELOPMENT OF LIVESTOCK AND MEAT GRADES

During earlier periods a variety of market terms evolved in particular localities that were more or less descriptive of certain characteristics of livestock. Associated with the expansion of the large terminal markets of that era was the private publication of market prices that relied on local class and quality terminology. This, of course, marked a significant advance over having no published quotations at all, and the reports were undoubtedly useful to livestock interests. However, weaknesses were apparent, among them a lack of uniformity in terminology and standards among markets. A price quotation on "native cattle," for example, had limited meaning when the specifications for "native cattle" varied from one market to the next, or when some markets did not use the classification of "native cattle" at all.

In many cases, an accepted term did not necessarily mean the same thing to different users at a given market. Such conditions are symptomatic of growing pains in any developing economy. Trade in meat is handicapped to the extent that buyers must physically inspect all lots of animals, and market price quotations cannot serve their full potential of usefulness.

The handicaps of this situation were apparent for many years, and some pioneering efforts were at last made to develop uniform grades and standards. The Agricultural Experiment Station of Illinois was a leader in this area. Between the years 1901 and 1908, a series of investigations were made of actual conditions and ways and means to improve them. Five Illinois bulletins were isssued with the following titles: "The Market Classes of Horses," 1901; "Market Classes and

Grades of Cattle, with Suggestions for Interpreting Market Quotations," 1902; "Market Classes and Grades of Swine," 1904; "Market Classes and Grades of Horses and Mules," 1908; and "Market Classes and Grades of Sheep," 1908. These studies did not precipitate immediate governmental action, but a movement soon developed for official market news reporting. The ensuing debates over the implementation of market reporting could not be separated from the consideration of official grades, because the lack of uniformity in local grade names and specifications rendered them unsatisfactory for reporting purposes. In response to this situation (and also for other reasons), the USDA established an Office of Markets in 1913.[4]

The Office of Markets began developing official grades for live animals and meat about 1915 (Dowell and Bjorka, 1941). The work done at Illinois provided a starting point, but vested interests in local grades and lack of agreement on grade standards were serious obstacles to obtaining a consensus. Nevertheless, unofficial and unpublished grade specifications were drawn up and began to be used for market reporting of meat prices in 1916. Responsibility for developing grade standards and implementing their use has shifted from one office to another within USDA, usually after an administrative reorganization. Current responsibility for live animal and carcass grades lies with the Agricultural Marketing Service.

Derivation of an acceptable and adequate set of grade standards requires an enormous effort. Information must be obtained from all interested parties to determine the attributes that impart value to a product. There are differences of opinion on this point among producers, packers, processors, wholesalers, retailers, and consumers. Even when a consensus can be obtained, problems arise in selecting the indicators for measuring these attributes in live animals and meat, especially when only subjective measures are usable. The USDA held many conferences and hearings with all interested parties, including agricultural college personnel. Research was conducted and encouraged at colleges, and a considerable amount of experimentation was carried out using unofficial and tentative standards before any grades were officially promulgated. This work did not come to an end with the establishment of official grade names and standards. Over any period of time, changes occur in the quality of a product, in consumer preferences, in trade practices, etc. Continuous change requires continuous review of grade standards and revision or amendment as the occasion demands. Figure 14.1 shows the steps and precautionary measures involved setting up standards.

---

[4]Over the years, the Federal grading service has been under a succession of different offices as a result of renaming, merging, and reorganizing.

The application of uniform grades requires some prior classification and subclassification of livestock. In the case of live animal grades, an obvious first classification is by specie—cattle, hogs, and sheep. Beyond that, for official grading purposes, livestock are segregated according to use—i.e., slaughter or feeder. Within use categories, a further breakdown, referred to officially as *class*, is made on the basis of sex condition. Grades are then applied to the class.[5]

The various specie and use categories of livestock with their designated classes are as follows: (A) Slaughter cattle—steers, heifers, cows, bullocks, and bulls. (B) Feeder cattle—same as slaughter cattle except that bulls are not graded. (C) Slaughter swine—barrows, gilts, sows, boars, and stags (boars and stags are not graded). (D) Feeder pigs—same as slaughter swine (except sows, boars, and stags are not graded). (E) Slaughter lambs, yearlings, and sheep—ram, ewe, and wether (these class names are used in conjunction with age groupings, i.e., lambs, yearlings, and sheep). (F) Feeder lambs, yearlings, and sheep—ewe and wether (in the case of feeder sheep, only the ewe class applies).

In addition to grades for live animals, it was found necessary to have grades for carcass meat. The first grades for dressed beef were formulated in 1916. "They provided the basis for uniformly reporting the dressed beef markets according to grades, which work was inaugurated as a national service early in 1917" (USDA 1965A). These beef grades enjoyed an unofficial, tentative status until 1926, but in the meantime a number of revisions were made as experience and usage dictated. Use of the grades also spread beyond market reporting. "The tentative standards, although designed primarily for meat market reporting, were put to further practical test in numerous ways. During World War I they were used in the selection of beef for the Army, Navy, and Allies. Later they were included in the specifications of the Emergency Fleet Corporation for the purchase of its beef supplies. Soon thereafter they were incorporated in the specifications of many commercial concerns, including steamship lines, restaurants, hotels, dining car services, and hospitals" (USDA 1965A).

Official grades were promulgated for carcass beef on June 3, 1926. These Federal grades have been used on a voluntary basis from the beginning, except during World War II and the Korean Conflict when they were mandatory for all FI plants handling beef, veal, calf, and lamb. The voluntary stamping of graded beef became available in 1927.[6] For a brief period at the beginning, grading costs were paid by

---

[5]Some classes are designated and defined but not graded.
[6]For a comprehensive analysis of issues involved in the early days of grade development and marking of beef, see Rhodes (1960). Some opposing views are presented by Williams (1960).

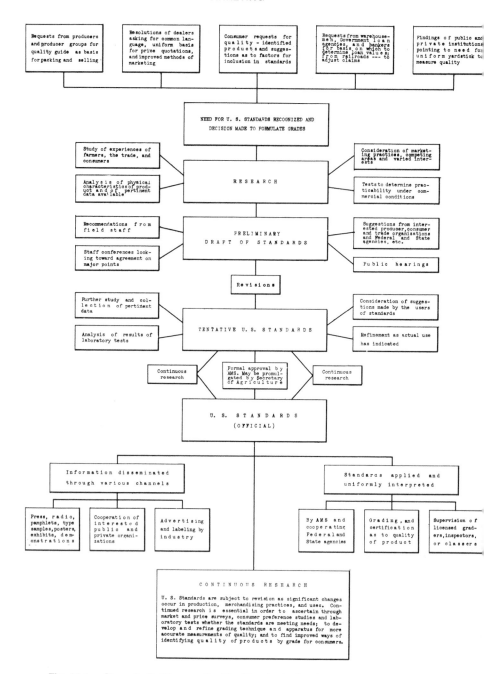

Fig. 14.1.   Steps in Setting up Quality Standards for Farm Products. (From USDA.)

the Federal government, but since that time costs have been paid by the parties who request the service.

Eight changes (amendments or revisions) have been made in the official beef grades—in 1939, 1941, 1949, 1950, 1956, 1965, 1973, 1976 and 1987. The 1965 revision not only changed quality standards but added standards for "cutability" as well. Cutability is the consideration of the percentage of trimmed, boneless, major retail cuts that can be derived from a carcass. Cutability has been recognized as an important value-determining characteristic for a number of years, and standards for it were proposed and tested over a one-year trial period beginning July 1, 1962. With some modifications, it was made official in 1965. A new class designated as "Bullock" (bullocks are young bulls) was added in the 1973 revision. This class was the result of research that showed young bulls to be superior to steers in rate and efficiency of gain. Prior to 1973, meat from these animals was designated as "bull" beef. Consumer bias against that designation was considered a deterrent to its acceptance. A conviction remains among some that the term "bullock" is also a deterrent, but at the time of the revision the official position was that enough difference existed between the respective palatabilities of young bull and steer beef that the grading system should differentiate them and "bullock" was selected as an appropriate term.

A revision in beef carcass grades was announced to become effective in April 1975, but legal procedings delayed its implementation until February 1976. Major changes were: (1) A reduction was made in marbling requirements for the Prime and Choice grades for all but the youngest cattle; (2) marbling requirements for the Good grade were increased for young cattle and decreased for older cattle; (3) conformation was removed as a factor in quality grades; and (4) yield grading was made mandatory on all carcasses that are quality graded. Previously, carcasses could be quality graded, yield graded, or given both designations. In 1987 Good grade was renamed Select.

Changes in slaughter cattle grades have usually paralleled those of carcass beef, but the timing has varied slightly, as shown in Table 14.1.

The development of other dressed meat grades (veal and calf carcasses; pork carcasses; and lamb, yearling mutton, and mutton carcasses) as well as grades of live, slaughter, and feeder animals followed a comparable course of formulation, tentative adoption, official promulgation, and subsequent amendment. Comments here will be limited to a few major changes; details may be found elsewhere.[7]

---

[7]Details of grade specifications and changes are published in USDA Service and Regulatory Announcements, which are issued with each amendment and revision. Rules are also published in the Federal Register.

Table 14.1. Changes in USDA Grades for Slaughter Cattle.*

1918	Tentative 1928	Published 1928	1939	1950	Official 1956	1966†	1975	1976ª	1987
Adopted for market reporting									
Prime		Prime	Prime	Prime‡	Prime‡	Prime‡	Prime	Prime	Prime
Choice		Choice	Choice	Choice	Choice	Choice	Choice	Choice	Choice
Good		Good	Good	Good	Good	Good	Good	Good	Select
Medium		Medium	Medium		Standard	Standard	Standard	Standard	Standard
				Commercial	Commercial	Commercial	Commercial	Commercial	Commercial
Common		Common	Common	Utility	Utility	Utility	Utility	Utility	Utility
Cutter		Cutter	Cutter	Cutter	Cutter	Cutter	Cutter	Cutter	Cutter
Low Cutter									
Canner		Canner	Canner	Canner	Canner	Canner	Canner	Canner	Canner

Source: USDA.

*Area of spaces occupied by grade names is not intended to be proportional to the relative importance of grades.

†Reduced marbling requirements in quality grades and added five yield grades (Nos. 1, 2, 3, 4, and 5) to identify differences in cutability.

‡Only steers and heifers eligible for Prime grade.

ª"Bullock" added as classification for young bulls; but provided for only five grades: Prime, Choice, Good, Standard, and Utility.

Reduced marbling requirements for Prime and Choice grades for all but the youngest cattle; increased marbling requirements for Good grade for young cattle and decreased them for older cattle; removed conformation as a factor in quality grades; and yield grading was made mandatory if quality grade used.

During the period of tentative feeder cattle grades, the grouping was referred to as "Feeder and Stocker Cattle." Although "stocker" is a commonly used term in the cattle trade, it is no longer used in official grade standards. The term "feeder" is intended to include those formerly classed as "stockers and feeders." Table 14.2 illustrates changes in the grade names for feeder cattle, which, until the 1979 change, corresponded to those for slaughter cattle except for the bottom two grades. Grade terminology and change for vealers and slaughter calves are shown in Table 14.3.

Several major changes have been made in slaughter barrow and gilt grades. In 1952, the formerly tentative Choice grade (meat type) was divided into two grades and renamed Choice No. 1 and Choice No. 2; the former Choice grade (fat type) was renamed Choice No. 3 (Table 14.4). These changes represented a significant recognition of preference for leaner, meat-type pork and the importance of yield of lean cuts. The changes in 1968 were designed to reflect improvements in quality that could not be properly evaluated under previous standards. Minimum requirements for backfat thickness were eliminated for U.S. No. 1 grade, and a new U.S. No. 1 grade was specified for superior carcasses, which had been graded either U.S. No. 1 or Medium under previous standards. Under the revision, most of the former U.S. Nos. 1, 2, and 3 were renamed U.S. Nos. 2, 3, and 4, respectively, whereas the former Medium and Cull grades were renamed Utility. The term "Utility" now has a generally uniform meaning in the grade pattern of all species. In

Table 14.2. Changes in USDA Grades for Feeder Cattle.*

Tentative				Official		
1925	1934	1938	1942	1964	1979	
					Frame	Thickness
		Fancy	Fancy	Prime†	Large	1
		Choice	Choice	Choice	Large	2
		Good	Good	Good	Large	3
				Standard	Medium	1
		Medium	Medium		Medium	2
				Commercial	Medium	3
		Plain	Common	Utility	Small	1
		Inferior	Inferior	Inferior	Small	2
					Small	3

Source: USDA
*Area of spaces occupied by grade names is not intended to be proportional to the relative importance of grades.
†Only steers and heifers were eligible for Prime grade.

Table 14.3. Changes in USDA Grades for Vealers and Slaughter Calves.*

Tentative	Official		
1926	1928	1951	1956
	Prime		
		Prime	Prime
	Choice		
	Good	Choice	Choice
		Good	Good
	Medium		
		Commercial	Standard
	Common	Utility	Utility
	Cull	Cull	Cull

Source: USDA (1957).
*Area of spaces occupied by grade names is not intended to be proportional to the relative importance of grades.

a 1985 amendment, the prior grade names remained unchanged, but carcass length was dropped as a grade factor. Depth of backfat was retained as a primary factor, and degree of muscling was introduced as a modifying factor. Feeder pig grades are of relatively recent origin, and, as for other species, their development has reflected an attempt to keep feeder grades comparable to slaughter grades (Table 14.5).

The development of lamb grades has had a particularly stormy history. A major source of difficulty arose from the use of a single set of standards to evaluate diverse types of lamb: " . . . western lambs, bred for their ability to use sparse ranges or mountain pastures and for their wool, are different from native lambs" (Fienup et al., 1963). Although Federal grade standards recognized differences arising from stages of maturity, they did not differentiate among lambs produced in various geographical locations. Western lamb producers felt that early official standards discriminated against their lambs, and, in 1959, several sheep industry groups requested a suspension of Federal grading. "Much of the pressure on Federal grades for lamb in 1959 arose out of a disagreement over the quality levels that were included in U. S. Choice. Federal standards for lamb were designed on the basis of meat-type characteristics more prominent in native lambs. A smaller proportion of western than native lambs met conformation standards for U. S. Choice prior to the 1960 revision. In attempt to qualify for U. S. Choice by improving quality to offset a lack of conformation, many lambs were fed to heavier weights and discounted in price. . . . The lower conformation requirements in the new standards (1960) increased the proportion of western lambs grading U.S. Choice" (Fienup et al., 1963).

Table 14.4. Changes in USDA Grades for Slaughter Barrows and Gilts.*

Formulated	Tentative			Official		
1918	1930	1940	1952†	1955	1968‡	1985¶
Formulated for use in market reporting	Choice (meat-type)		Choice No. 1	U.S. No. 1	U.S. No. 1 / U.S. No. 2	U.S. No. 1 / U.S. No. 2
			Choice No. 2	U.S. No. 2	U.S. No. 3	U.S. No. 3
	Choice (fat-type)		Choice No. 3	U.S. No. 3	U.S. No. 4	U.S. No. 4
	Good					
	Medium		Medium	Medium		
	Cull		Cull	Cull	U.S. Utility	U.S. Utility

Source: USDA (1968B and 1985).

*Area of spaces occupied by grade names is not intended to be proportional to the relative importance of grades.

†Former tentative Choice (meat-type) subdivided and renamed Choice No. 1 and Choice No. 2; former tentative Choice (fat-type) renamed Choice No. 3.

‡U.S. No. 1 in 1968 was a new classification for superior carcasses. Former U.S. Nos. 1, 2, and 3 renamed U.S. Nos. 2, 3, and 4, respectively. Former Medium and Cull grade names dropped. Utility added for barrows and gilts with characteristics that indicate carcass lean of unacceptable quality. Four numbered grades based on expected combined carcass yield of the four lean cuts were added.

¶Grade names remained unchanged in 1985 revision. Carcass length was dropped as a grade factor. Backfat thickness was retained as a major factor and degree of muscling was introduced as a modifying factor.

Table 14.5.   Changes in USDA Grades for Feeder Pigs.*

Tentative	Official	
1940	1966	1969
		U.S. No. 1
	U.S. No. 1	
	U.S. No. 2	U.S. No. 2
		U.S. No. 3
	U.S. No. 3	U.S. No. 4
	Medium	U.S. Utility
	Cull	U.S. Cull

Source: USDA (1969A).
*Area of spaces occupied by grade names is not intended to be proportional to the relative importance of grades.

A major change in 1969 was the establishment of yield grades for lamb. A chronological picture of changes in slaughter lamb, yearling, and sheep grades is shown in Table 14.6. Thus, cutability (yield of retail cuts) now is an integral factor in the grade standards of cattle, hogs, and lamb. Subsequent changes in 1982 and 1984 were designed to clarify quality characteristics.

Table 14.6.   Changes in USDA Grades for Slaughter Lambs, Yearlings, and Sheep.*

Formulated 1917	Tentative			Official			
	1936	1940	1951	1957[†]	1960[‡]	1969[¶]	1984
Formulated for use in market reporting	Choice or No. 1	Prime	Prime[#]	Prime[#]	Prime[#]	Prime[#]	Prime**
		Choice					
	Good or No. 2						
		Good	Choice	Choice	Choice	Choice	Choice
	Medium or No. 3						
		Medium	Good	Good	Good	Good	Good
	Plain No. 4						
		Common	Utility	Utility	Utility	Utility	Utility
	Cull No. 5						
		Cull	Cull	Cull	Cull	Cull	Cull

Sources: USDA (1969) and Federal Register (1984A).

*Area of spaces occupied by grade names is not intended to be proportional to the relative importance of grades.
[†]No grade name changes. Quality requirements for Prime and Choice reduced for more mature lambs. Quality requirements for Good lambs increased slightly.
[‡]No grade name changes. Quality and conformation requirements lowered for Prime and Choice. Limit placed on the extent superior quality may compensate for deficient conformation.
[¶]Yield grades (No. 1, 2, 3, 4, and 5) added to pre-existing quality grades.
[#]Slaughter sheep older than yearlings not eligible for Prime grade.
**Cull grade for slaughter lambs and yearlings dropped.

For centuries, wool has been an important product of the sheep industry. For much of the world's history, the wool produced by sheep was more important than the meat. That generally was the situation in early America and, to a limited extent, continues to be in some parts of the world. Meat is the primary product of the U.S. sheep industry, but wool can make the difference between profit and loss since it constitutes approximately 10 percent of the sales from a ewe flock.

The fiber market distinguishes wool from wool top, and separate grades have been developed for each. "Wool" is defined as the fiber from the fleece of sheep. "Wool top" consists of continuous untwisted strands of scoured wool fibers from which the shorter fibers, or "noils," have been removed by combing.

Grade standards for wool were first promulgated in 1926. The basic grade factor was fiber diameter (i.e., fineness) as determined by visual inspection. Twelve grades were established. Revisions were proposed in 1955 and in 1963 but were not adopted. In the revised standards of 1966, the major changes were as follows: (1) Four grades were added—two intermediate degrees of fineness and an additional grade at each end of the range of specified diameters (the latter two grades are open-ended in that they encompass all degrees of fineness outside those specified in the 14 intermediate grades; see the following section entitled *Annotation of Grade Standards*). (2) Provision was made for objective measurement of fiber diameter (in addition to visual determination). (3) Recognition of the distribution of various fiber diameters in a fleece, or group of fleeces (as represented by the standard deviation from the average diameter of a sample fiber).

Official USDA standards for wool top were also established in 1926. At that time the number of grades was increased to 12, corresponding to the range in recognized fiber diameters in official USDA wool grades. The following changes have since occurred:

Since 1926, the wool top standards have been revised three times. In 1940, a grade 62s was added and average fiber diameter and fiber diameter distribution specifications were issued for eight of the 13 grades. These revised standards also provided that grade could be determined either by inspection—visual comparison of samples with practical forms of the official grade standards—or by measurement of samples. In 1955, a grade 54s was added, bringing the total to 14 grades. During that year, all grades were assigned average fiber diameter and fiber diameter distribution specifications. Until 1955, grades were determined by either the inspection or measurement method. At this time, however, an addition to the standards provided that in cases where these methods resulted in different grades, the grade determined by measurement would prevail.

The current wool top standards became effective January 11, 1969. On that date two new grades, 'Finer than Grade 80s' and 'Coarser than Grade 36s,' were added. A dual grade designation was also provided for wool top in which the average fiber diameter and fiber diameter distribution do not meet the requirements of the same grade" (USDA 1971).

ANNOTATION OF GRADE STANDARDS[8]

In the previous section, a brief designation was given of historical developments of the U.S. grading system. In this section, emphasis will be on standards currently in use. Both aspects are important. Knowledge of the background of grade development affords a better understanding of how and why the system evolved. This type of information is helpful, if not essential, in formulating the further amendments that will inevitably come. Readers interested in greater detail on development are referred to the references at the end of this chapter.

A general knowledge of current grade standards is essential to everyone engaged in livestock and meat marketing. As mentioned in earlier chapters, extensive use is made of official USDA grades in wholesale meat marketing, even though grading is strictly voluntary. Many large retail chain buyers insist on USDA-graded meat in their wholesale purchasing program. Many retailers carry through by using grade labels on retail cuts. Recently, however, many retailers began purchasing ungraded (so-called "no-roll") beef in response to growing consumer demand for leaner meat than the current grading system promotes.

Live-animal grades are not officially applied in marketing livestock, but the USDA Market News Service publishes price quotations by grade. In direct selling by carcass grade and weight, USDA standards may or may not be used (some packers insist on using their own grading system; others rely on USDA grades). An intelligent interpretation of price quotations calls for some understanding of official grades. Selling (or buying) by carcass grade and weight, or involvement in the wholesale meat trade, demands a knowledge of grade standards. But a knowledge of grades and grading is also important in buying and selling by liveweight methods. Packer buyers are experienced in estimating the potential carcass grade of live animals. Producers also need to be able to estimate grade if they are going to get a price commensurate with the quality and cutability attributes of their livestock. In developing a breeding herd, it is imperative to be able to select stock

---

[8]Materials in this section draw heavily upon USDA publications giving official U.S. grade standards and a series of USDA market bulletins that present a more popularized version of grade information.

for herd improvement, which also means improvement in the grade of animal produced.

No attempt will be made here to present the methods and techniques of actual grading. This complex activity requires extensive study and training. An attempt will be made, however, to point out the attributes, or characteristics, of live animals and meat upon which grades are based, as well as the indicators used in evaluating these attributes.

This section will discuss both carcass and live-animal grades. Separate standards have been established and published for carcass and live-animal grades, but a high correspondence exists between them. Historically, carcass grades have been established first and slaughter-animal grades then made to conform to them. Feeder-animal grades are also made to conform to slaughter-animal grades. For example, a U.S. No. 1 feeder pig is evaluated on its potential for feeding into a U.S. No. 1 slaughter hog, which has the potential of producing a U.S. No. 1 carcass.

It is apparent that some of the indicators used to evaluate a carcass may be different, and presumably more precise in application, from those used on the live animal, but the basic attributes that give the carcass value and utility are the same as those of the live animal.

Carcass Beef

Grades of carcass beef are based on a separate evaluation of two general considerations: (1) palatability characteristics of the lean, which is referred to as "quality," and (2) the indicated percentage of trimmed, boneless, major retail cuts, which is referred to as "yield grade" or "cutability." Prior to 1976, quality grades included a consideration of "conformation." Conformation is the build, shape, and outline or contour of an animal and its different primal parts. Conformation formerly was used as an indicator of (1) carcass yield relative to live weight, (2) yield of primal cuts from a carcass, and (3) the percentage of lean, fat, and bone in a carcass. Dropping of that factor was a reversion to previous standards. "In previous grade standards for beef and in the standards for grades of other kinds of meat, the Department uses the term 'quality' to refer only to the palatability-indicating characteristics of the lean, without reference to conformation" (USDA 1965A).

Standards are established for eight quality grades: Prime, Choice, Select, Standard, Commercial, Utility, Cutter, and Canner. Five cutability (or yield) grades have been defined: Nos. 1, 2, 3, 4, and 5, with No. 1 representing the highest cutability. Not all classes are eligible for every quality grade. Cows are not eligible for Prime grade, and, in addition, bull beef is not quality graded. Bullocks are excluded from Commercial, Cutter, and Canner grades. All classes are eligible for all yield grades.

Steer, heifer, and cow carcasses are graded and stamped with no reference to sex condition. Separate grade standards are provided for bull and bullock carcasses, and, when the carcasses are grade stamped, they are also stamped "BULL" or "BULLOCK" as the case may be. As mentioned earlier, the bullock classification was provided in 1973 to designate young bull beef, which had previously been marked as bull beef. At the same time, the term "stag" was eliminated, and beef formerly in that class was redesignated as bullock or bull depending on its evidence of skeletal maturity.

Prior to the revision of 1976, quality and yield grades were separate considerations. Although grading is not mandatory, the 1976 revision stipulated that, if a carcass is quality graded, it must also be yield graded, and that it must carry both stamp marks. Although the standards for both quality and cutability are defined primarily for carcass beef, the quality standards apply also to certain wholesale and primal cuts—forequarters, hindquarters, rounds, loins, short loins, loin ends, ribs, and chuck. Portions of primal cuts may also be graded if still attached to the primal cut. Although the original grade is not designated as a retail grade, retailers do retain it in cuts fabricated from wholesale and primal cuts. In addition to carcasses, cutability grades may be applied to hindquarters, forequarters, ribs, loins, and short ribs, but not to rounds and chucks.

Carcass Quality Factors. The quality grade of a beef carcass is based on the palatability-indicating characteristics of the lean. Determination of the quality of the lean is accomplished by considering the de-

QUALITY GRADE MARKS

gree of its marbling and firmness in conjunction with its maturity. Maturity is determined by evaluating the size, shape, and ossification of the bones and cartilages and by the color of the lean. The term "marbling" refers to the flecks of fat interspersed among muscle fibers in the lean. The degree of marbling is considered to be positively associated with flavor, tenderness, juiciness, and palatability in general. Marbling requirements for a given grade increase with maturity. Seven different degrees of marbling and five different maturity groupings are recognized in the application of grade standards. Figure 14.2 illustrates the relationship between marbling, maturity, and quality.[9] Marbling requirements for bottom USDA Choice vary from a minimum of the range set up for the "small" degree of marbling found in the youngest animals to a maximum set up for the "modest" degree found in the second stage of maturity. Prime, Choice, Select, and Standard grades are limited to beef from relatively young animals.

Carcass Yield Grade, or "Cutability," Factors.   Official grade standards provide for five cutability groupings in recognition that carcasses of identical quality grade and weight can have substantial difference in value as a result of differences in the percentage of closely trimmed, boneless retail cuts obtainable from the carcasses. These groupings—called "yield" grades—are numbered 1 through 5, with No. 1 having the highest percentage of retail cuts and No. 5 the lowest.

---

[9]Based on the perception that there is a need to respond to the growing demand for leaner beef, and on the belief that existing grades tend to discourage producers from producing leaner animals, the National Cattlemen's Association (NCA) petitioned the USDA to consider changes from the 1976 standards. Other groups provided USDA with recommendations and suggestions. On December 29, 1981 USDA announced a proposal to revise the official U.S. standards for grades of carcass beef and slaughter cattle and scheduled five public hearings on the proposal. The proposal called for the following changes: (1) Reduce the minimum marbling requirements for the Prime, Choice, and Good grades in "A maturity" to "minimum moderate," "typical slight," and "minimum traces," respectively. (2) Grade Utility all young beef not meeting minimum requirements for the Good grade. (3) Eliminate the Standard grade. (4) Double the rate of increase in marbling requirement in "B maturity," and increase marbling to maturity ratio from 1:1 to 2:1. (5) Change quality grade requirements for bullock beef so they would still be the same as those for steer, heifer, and cow beef in "A maturity" while bullock beef would still be identified for class. (6) Change the standards for grades for slaughter cattle to reflect proposed changes in carcasses. (7) Maintain the existing yield grade standards. The proposal generated wide interest among diverse groups. Strong opposition by consumers, retailers, and local and regional producer groups was expressed throughout the hearings and in the media. Opponents expressed concern that the proposed change would lead to lowering the quality of beef and could lead to consumer confusion and decreased demand for beef. On September 20, 1982, USDA, citing insufficient public and meat industry support, withdrew its proposal. Various groups have since been discussing the possibility of developing a new system that would reflect consumer preferences but be acceptable by the majority of concerned groups.

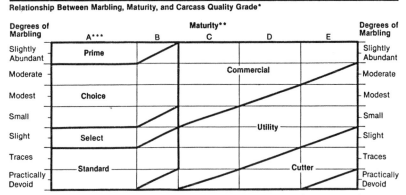

Relationship Between Marbling, Maturity, and Carcass Quality Grade*

*Assumes that firmness of lean is comparably developed with the degree of marbling and that the carcass is not a "dark cutter."
**Maturity increases from left to right (A through E).
***The A maturity portion of the Figure is the only portion applicable to bullock carcasses.

Fig. 14.2. Relationship Between Marbling, Maturity, and Carcass Quality Grades of Beef. (*Federal Register, 1984B.*) (Good changed to Select by authors.)

Value, of course, varies with the level of market prices, but $10.00 per cwt of carcass is not unusual.

The chief factors that account for variation in yield of retail cuts are (1) the amount of fat that must be trimmed, and (2) the thickness and fullness of the muscling. Extensive research has shown that four indicators highly correlated with yield are: (1) the amount of external fat; (2) the amount of kidney, pelvic, and heart fat; (3) the area of the rib eye muscle; and (4) the carcass weight. The following mathematical equation for calculating yield grade shows relationships among the four factors:

YIELD GRADE MARKS

$$Y.G. = 2.50 + 2.50\ X1 + 0.20\ X2 - 0.32\ X3 + 0.0038\ X4$$

where:

Y.G. = yield grade
X1 = backfat thickness; in inches
X2 = kidney/pelvic/heart (KPH) fat, in percent of hot carcass weight.
X3 = ribeye area, in square inches
X4 = hot carcass weight, in pounds

The result is expressed as a whole number (any fractional part is dropped). A simpler means of evaluating objective measurements is by use of a slide-rule type of device, designed by the Livestock Division, Consumer and Marketing Service, USDA, called the Beef Carcass Yield Grade Finder.

Under a USDA proposal, the kidney/pelvic/heart (KPH) fat would not be considered in determining yield grade.

In contrast to quality-grade indicators, all of these yield factors can be measured objectively. Although of great help in developing yield-grade standards, in application actual measurement is unnecessary. Descriptions given in the standards (USDA 1965A) "facilitate the subjective determination of the cutability group without making detailed measurements and computations. The cutability group for most beef carcasses can be determined accurately on the basis of a visual appraisal."

The establishment of yield grades culminated a long period of discussion and research. It had been known for a number of years, of course, that differences existed in cutability. Consequently, large wholesale buyers, including buyers for large chains, personally selected carcasses when buying from packers. Many still do this to meet the more exact specifications of both yield and quality grades, but, as will be pointed out subsequently, a rapid growth has occurred in the use of yield grades since their inauguration in 1965.

Figure 14.3 illustrates the economic significance of the variation in yield grades. During mid–1985, the carcass price of yield grade 2 averaged about $15.00 per cwt over yield grade 4. That would amount to $105.00 on a 700-lb carcass. At the same time, there was a relatively minor price difference between yield grade 2 and yield grade 3, which together comprised approximately 90 percent of federally inspected steer and heifer slaughter. About 3.5 percent was yield grade 1.

Slaughter Cattle

The term "slaughter cattle" does not include vealers and slaughter calves. Special efforts have been made to have grades for slaughter

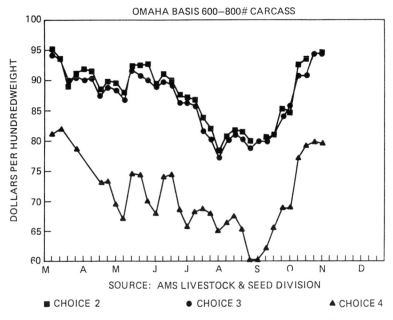

Fig. 14.3. Relationship Between Yield Grades, Beef, 1985. (USDA, 1985.)

animals conform directly to the grades of carcasses produced from the live animals. Eight quality grades and five yield grades, identical in name with carcass grades, have been established for slaughter cattle. Eligibility of the various classes for particular grades are identical for both live animals and carcasses.

Quality Grade Factors.   Slaughter-cattle quality grades are based on factors related to the palatability of the lean. In evaluating quality, attention is directed primarily to finish, i.e., fatness of the animal (its amount and distribution), muscling (its firmness and fullness), and physical characteristics associated with maturity. By necessity, appraisal of finish is achieved primarily by observable characteristics of the external finish.

From the standpoint of maturity, approximate maximum age limits for steers and heifers are 42 months for Prime and Choice, and 48 months for Select and Standard. After 48 months of age, Commercial grade applies. No age limits are recognized for any class in the Utility, Cutter, and Canner grades.

Yield Grade Factors.   The factors used in establishing yield grades for slaughter cattle are identical with those used for carcass beef—i.e., thickness of fat over ribeye; percentage of kidney, pelvic, and heart fat; carcass weight; and area of the ribeye muscle. These characteristics cannot be measured directly. They can be estimated and the yield calculated by equation, but the USDA advises the following:

... a more practical method of appraising slaughter cattle for yield grade is to use only two factors normally considered in evaluating live cattle-muscling and fatness.
    In the latter approach, ... [the] evaluation of the thickness and fullness of muscling in relation to skeletal size largely accounts for the effects of two of the factors—area of ribeye, and carcass weight. By the same token, an appraisal of the degree of external fatness largely accounts for the effects of thickness of fat over the ribeye and the percentage of kidney, pelvic, and heart fat (USDA 1966B).

Veal and Calf Carcasses

Veal and calf production has been decreasing for a number of years. In 1984, it amounted to only 479 million pounds, or only 2 percent of a total of 23,895 million pounds of beef, veal, and calf commercial slaughter. Nevertheless, veal and calf production are important in some areas.
    The basic factor that differentiates veal, calf, and beef is maturity, and the three respective sets of standards designed for grading are intended to represent the entire range in bovine maturity. For grading purposes, veal, calf, and beef carcasses are distinguished "primarily on the basis of the color of the lean, although such factors as texture of the lean; character of the fat; color, shape, size and ossification of the bones and cartilages; and the general contour of the carcass are also given consideration. Typical veal carcasses have a grayish pink color of lean that is very smooth and velvety in texture and they also have a slightly soft, pliable character of fat and marrow, and very red rib bones. By contrast, typical calf carcasses have a grayish red color of lean, a flakier type of fat, and somewhat wider rib bones with less pronounced evidences of red color (USDA, 1982A). Color of the lean in beef carcasses becomes progressively darker red with increasing maturity.

GRADE AND CLASS MARK

Official grade standards recognize three classes of veal and calf carcasses on the following basis of sex—steers, heifers, and bulls. Standards are established for six grades: Prime, Choice, Good, Standard Utility, and Cull. Each class is eligible for the full range in grades. In addition to the grade stamp, veal and calf are also stamped "VEAL" or "CALF." Select grade does not apply to veal or calf.

Yield grades have not been established for veal and calf carcasses. "Veal and calf carcasses are graded on a composite evaluation of two general grade factors—conformation and quality. These factors are concerned with the proportions of lean, fat and bone in the carcass and the quality of the lean" (USDA 1982A). Without explicitly using the term "cutability," this factor is recognized—primarily in the consideration of conformation. Quality of the lean is identified by considering the color, texture, firmness, and marbling of the lean.

Vealers and Slaughter Calves

According to the USDA (1957): "The basis for differentiation between vealers and calves is made primarily on age and certain evidence of type of feeding. Typical vealers are less than three months of age and have subsisted largely on milk . . . they have the characteristic trimness of middle. . . . Calves are usually between three and eight months of age, have subsisted partially or entirely on feeds other than milk for a substantial period of time, and have developed the heavier middles and physical characteristics associated with maturity beyond the vealer stage."

The three classes of vealers and calves are steers, heifers, and bulls. Eligible grades for each class are Prime, Choice, Good, Standard, Utility, and Cull. Grade is determined by a composite evaluation of conformation, finish, and quality. "Conformation refers to the general body proportions . . . and to the ratio of meat to bone . . . Finish refers to the fatness of the animal . . . Quality in the slaughter animal refers to the refinement of hair, hide and bone and to the smoothness and symmetry of the body. Quality is also associated with carcass yield and the proportion of meat to bone" (USDA, 1957). Thus, it becomes apparent that the yield of lean meat (as well as carcass yield) is inherent in the grade standards by considerations of conformation, finish, and quality. The intent of evaluating quality of the meat is explicit in the statement that "the quality, quantity, and distribution of finish are all closely associated with the palatability and quality of the meat" (USDA, 1957). Figure 14.4 illustrates the quality grade of various degrees of dispersion of fat particles within the muscle structure, sometimes

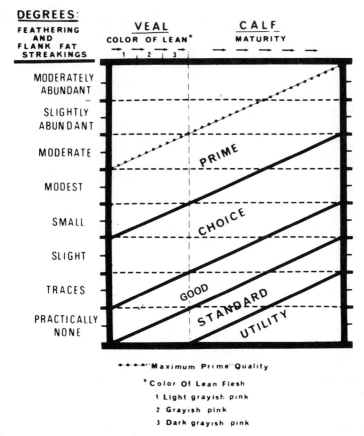

Fig. 14.4. Quality Grade Equivalent of Various Degrees of Feathering and Flank Fat Streakings in Relation to Color of Lean (Veal) or Maturity (Calf). (*Federal Register, 1984B.*)

called feathering, and flank fat streakings in relation to color of lean (veal) and maturity (calf).

Feeder Cattle

The official distinction between feeder cattle and slaughter cattle lies in the intended use. Feeder cattle are intended for further feeding (growing or finishing) before slaughter. It is recognized that some so-called "two-way" cattle do not fit exclusively into the feeder or slaughter classification, but this is no obstacle to grading. Any cattle may be graded for slaughter purposes—based on slaughter-grade standards. However, if used as feeder animals, cattle will be graded on feeder-cattle grade standards.

Grades of feeder cattle are related to slaughter-cattle grades in that the primary characteristics considered are those that affect the logical slaughter potential of the feeder animals as beef.

The introduction of so-called "exotic breeds' into the U.S. and the wide adoption of cross-breeding programs rendered the feeder-cattle-grade standards of 1964 somewhat obsolete. New USDA feeder-cattle-grading standards were introduced in 1979. The new, two-pronged grade standards are based on frame size and thickness (indicated by a muscle score). Three categories of muscling—numbered 1, 2, and 3—are used, and these are closely related to yield grade. Three frame sizes—large, medium, and small—are used. Thus, there are nine grade combinations of frame size and thickness under the existing system. Frame size is related to the length of feeding period and is considered an indicator of the final weight at which an animal reaches the Choice quality grade.

Pork Carcasses—Barrows and Gilts

Market classes of pork carcasses are defined as barrows, gilts, sows, boars, and stags. The following comments, however, will be limited to barrows and gilts. In grade standards (and in market prices), no distinction is made between barrows and gilts. Specified grades are U.S. Nos. 1, 2, 3, 4, and Utility. According to USDA revisions (Federal Register, 1984C), effective in 1985, "grades for barrow and gilt carcasses are based on two general considerations: (1) quality—which includes characteristics of the lean and fat, and (2) the expected yield of the four lean cuts (ham, loin, picnic shoulder, and Boston butt)." From the standpoint of quality, two general levels are specified: "acceptable" and "unacceptable." By direct observation of a cut surface, acceptability is based on considerations of firmness, marbling, and color. Indirect indicators are firmness of fat and lean, feathering between the ribs, and color. The degree of external fatness, as such, is not considered in

evaluating the quality of the lean (USDA 1982A). Suitability of the belly for bacon (in terms of thickness) also is considered in quality evaluation, as is "softness" and "oiliness" of the carcass. Carcasses with an unacceptable quality of lean, and/or bellies that are too thin, and/or carcasses that are soft and oily are graded U.S. Utility.

If a carcass qualifies as acceptable in quality of lean and belly thickness, and is not soft and oily, then it is graded U.S. No. 1, 2, 3, or 4 " ... entirely on the expected carcass yields of the four lean cuts. ... " (USDA, 1984C). Carcasses graded U.S. No. 1 are expected to yield 60.4 percent or more of the four lean cuts, based on chilled carcass weight; U.S. No. 2 carcasses, 57.4 to 60.3 percent; U.S. No. 3 carcasses, 54.4 to 57.3 percent; and U.S. No. 4 carcasses, less than 57.4 percent. Yields of the four lean cuts are determined by considering two characteristis: (1) the backfat thickness over the last rib, and (2) the degree of muscling (thickness of muscling in relation to skeletal size). Carcass length was dropped as a grade factor in the 1985 amendment.

The grade of a barrow or gilt carcass is determined according to the following USDA equation (Federal Register 1984C):

$$\text{Carcass Grade} = [4.0 \times \text{backfat thickness over last rib (in inches)}] - [1.0 \times \text{muscling score}]$$

To apply this equation, muscling should be scored as follows: inferior = 1, average = 2, and superior = 3.

Basically, grades for pork carcasses, like those for beef carcasses, are designed to evaluate both quality and yield. The significance of quality and yield considerations to the livestock and meat industry follows the same pattern discussed under the section on beef carcasses.

Slaughter Hogs

The classes of slaughter hogs and associated grade names are identical with the classes and grades of swine carcasses discussed in the previous section.

Standards used in grading slaughter animals are consistent with those used in grading carcasses (a U.S. No. 1 slaughter barrow or gilt is expected to produce a U.S. No. 1 carcass, and so on through the other grades). The same attributes are evaluated in the live animal as in the carcass: (1) quality of the lean, and (2) yield of the four lean cuts. As was the case with carcasses, quality of the slaughter animal includes, in addition to the quality of the lean meat per se, a consideration of belly thickness as an indicator of its adequacy for bacon production and a determination of whether the carcass will be soft and oily. "Since carcass indices of lean quality are not directly evident in barrows and gilts, some other factors in which differences can be noted must be used to evaluate quality. Therefore, the amount and distribution of external finish, and indications of firmness of fat and muscle are used as quality-indicating factors" (Federal Register, 1984C).

Slaughter barrows and gilts that do not meet standards of acceptable quality are graded Utility. Those that meet the standards are assigned grade U.S. Nos. 1, 2, 3, or 4 on the basis of expected combined carcass yield of the four lean cuts, with U.S. No. 1 representing the highest yield.

Feeder Pigs

Following revision in grade standards for pork carcasses and slaughter swine in 1968, grade standards for feeder pigs were revised in 1969 to keep feeder-pig grades consistent with slaughter-swine and pork-carcass grades. Official standards do not differentiate between barrow, gilt, or boar pigs, but it is assumed that boar pigs will be castrated prior to the development of secondary physical characteristics of a boar. Since sows, stags, and mature boars are seldom used as feeders, they play no part in the following discussion. The criteria upon which feeder pigs are evaluated are comparable to those for feeder cattle, namely, logical slaughter potential and "thriftiness." As pointed out by USDA (1969), "the logical slaughter potential of a thrifty feeder pig is expected slaughter grade at a market weight of 220 lb after a normal feeding period. . . . Thriftiness in a feeder pig is its apparent ability to gain weight rapidly and efficiently." Designated grades for feeder pigs are U.S. Nos. 1, 2, 3, and 4 on the basis of logical slaughter potential.

An indication of slaughter potential is derived by a composite evaluation of the development of the muscular and skeletal systems. Indicators of thriftiness are relative size for age, health, and other general characteristics.

Lamb, Yearling Mutton, and Mutton Carcasses

Revision of the grade standards for lamb, yearling mutton, and mutton carcasses in 1969 included establishment of explicit yield grades. This change followed a lengthy period of discussion, conferences, and research. As was the case with other meats, not all interests agreed to the change, but USDA investigations indicated a consensus in favor of it. An amendment in 1982 further clarified quality characteristics.

The groupings of lambs, yearlings, and sheep (which produce the previously mentioned carcasses) are based on age or maturity differences—characterized by differences in development of the muscular and skeletal systems. Grading of carcasses as enunciated by USDA in 1984 (Federal Register 1984A) is as follows:

The grade of an ovine carcass [is] based on separate evaluations of two general considerations: palatability-indicating characteristics of the lean and conformation, herein referred to as quality; and the estimated percent of closely trimmed, boneless, major retail cuts to be derived from the carcass, herein referred to as yield. However, the grade of an ovine carcass when applied by Federal meat graders may consist of an identification for the quality grade, the yield grade, or a combination of both quality and yield grades. In previous grade standards for ovine carcasses, the department used the term 'quality' to refer only to the palatability-indicating characteristics of the lean without reference to conformation. Its use herein to include consideration of conformation is not intended to imply that variations in conformation are either directly or indirectly related to differences in palatability.

The relevant retail cuts are from the leg, loin, hotel rack, and shoulder.

The definitions of such terms as "quality of the lean" and "conformation," as well as the indicators used to evaluate them, are consistent with those used in grading beef carcasses. Quality grades specified for lamb and yearling mutton are Prime, Choice, Good, and Utility. Mutton carcasses, however, are not eligible for Prime grade but are subject to the additional lower Cull grade. In addition to the grade stamp, yearling mutton and mutton are stamped "YEARLING MUTTON" or "MUTTON," as the case may be.

QUALITY GRADE MARKS

Five yield grades—numbered 1 through 5—cover the range of cutability, with Yield Grade 1 indicating the highest yield. "A carcass which is typical of its yield grade would be expected to yield 3.5% more in total retail cuts than the next lower yield grade, when USDA cutting and trimming methods are followed" (USDA, 1970C). Variations in yield are attributed primarily to the same two considerations pertaining to beef carcasses—namely, the amount of fat trimmed off in making retail cuts and the thickness and fullness or muscling.

The yield grade of an ovine carcass, or side, is determined on the basis of the following equation (USDA 1982B):

$$Y.G. = 1.66 - 0.05\ X1 + 0.25\ X2 + 6.66\ X3$$

where:

Y.G. = yield grade
X1 = leg-conformation grade code
X2 = kidney and pelvic fat, in percent
X3 = adjusted fat thickness over ribeye, in inches

Any fractional part of a yield grade is dropped in this calculation, and the result is reported as a whole number. "Leg conformation" is the evaluation used in quality grading; it is expressed as a coded number ranging from 1 to 15, with 15 being the most desirable (i.e., the conformation applicable to high Prime). The amount of external fat, an indicator of retail trim, can be measured but also accurately estimated. Kidney and pelvic fat cannot be measured without removal from the carcass; this too, however, can be evaluated subjectively with an acceptable degree of accuracy. Figure 14.5 illustrates the relationship between flank-fat streakings, maturity, and quality of sheep carcasses.

Yield grades are applicable to wholesale and primal cuts as well as to carcasses.

Slaughter Lambs, Yearlings, and Sheep

As for other species, USDA (Federal Register, 1984A) specifies that "grades of slaughter ovines are intended to be directly related to the

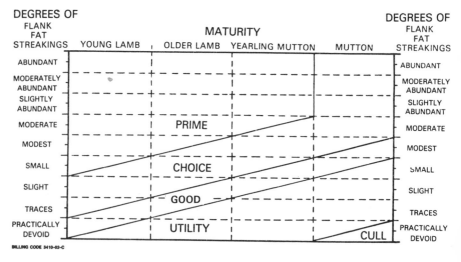

Fig. 14.5. Relationship between Flank Fat Steakings, Maturity, and Quality of Lamb and Mutton. (*Federal Register, 1982.*)

grades of the carcasses they produce. To accomplish this, these slaughter ovine grade standards are based on factors which are directly related to the quality grades and the yield grades of ovine carcasses." Quality grade names and yield designations for the live animals are identical with those for carcasses. The factors upon which live quality and yield grades are based, also are consistent with those of carcass grades. The presence of the fleece, however, makes evaluation more difficult and necessitates handling as well as visual observation.

Wool and Wool Top

Grades of wool are indicated by "numerical designations of fineness based on average fiber diameter and variation of fiber diameter" (USDA, 1966). Grades of wool top are similarly defined as a "numerical designation of wool top fineness based on average fiber diameter and fiber diameter dispersion" (USDA, 1971). Official specifications for each provide for two methods of determining grade: (1) by measurement, and (2) by visual inspection. Both methods are official, but if the grade determined by inspection for a given lot differs from the grade determined by measurement, then the grade determined by measurement prevails.

Grading by visual inspection may appropriately be classified as an art. Skilled and experienced commercial graders can, almost instantaneously, grade fleeces that to an amateur might appear identical. Specifications for official sampling, measuring, and grading are spelled out in detail (USDA, 1966C and USDA, 1971). The following (from USDA, 1966C), is a summary of the official standards of the United States for grades of wool:

Sec. 31.0 *Official grades.* The official grades of wool shall be those established in Secs. 31.1 through 31.16, provided, however, that the wool which qualifies for any of the grades in Secs. 31.1 through 31.15 on the basis of its average fiber diameter shall be reduced in grade to the next coarser grade if its standard deviation in fiber diameter exceeds the maximum specified for the grade to which the average fiber diameter corresponds.

Sec. 31.1 *Finer than grade 80's.* Wool with an average fiber diameter of 17.69 microns or less and a standard deviation in fiber diameter of 3.59 microns or less.

Sec. 31.2 *Grade 80's.* Wool with an average fiber diameter of 17.70 to 19.14 microns, inclusive, and a standard deviation in fiber diameter of 4.09 microns or less.

Sec. 31.3 *Grade 70's.* Wool with an average fiber diameter of

19.15 to 20.59 microns, inclusive, and a standard deviation in fiber diameter of 4.59 microns or less.

Sec. 31.4 *Grade 64's.* Wool with an average fiber diameter of 20.60 to 22.04 microns, inclusive, and a standard deviation in fiber diameter of 5.19 microns or less.

Sec. 31.5 *Grade 62's.* Wool with an average fiber diameter of 22.05 to 23.49 microns, inclusive, and a standard deviation in fiber diameter of 5.89 microns or less.

Sec. 31.6 *Grade 60's.* Wool with an average fiber diameter of 23.50 to 24.94 microns, inclusive, and a standard deviation in fiber diameter of 6.49 microns or less.

Sec. 31.7 *Grade 58's.* Wool with an average fiber diameter of 24.95 to 26.39 microns, inclusive, and a standard deviation in fiber diameter of 7.09 microns or less.

Sec. 31.8 *Grade 56's.* Wool with an average fiber diameter of 26.40 to 27.84 microns, inclusive, and a standard deviation in fiber diameter of 7.59 microns or less.

Sec. 31.9 *Grade 54's.* Wool with an average fiber diameter of 27.85 to 29.29 microns, inclusive, and a standard deviation in fiber diameter of 8.19 microns or less.

Sec. 31.10 *Grade 50's.* Wool with an average fiber diameter of 29.30 to 30.99 microns, inclusive, and a standard deviation in fiber diameter of 8.69 microns or less.

Sec. 31.11 *Grade 48's.* Wool with an average fiber diameter of 31.00 to 32.69 microns, inclusive, and a standard deviation in fiber diameter of 9.09 microns or less.

Sec. 31.12 *Grade 46's.* Wool with an average fiber diameter of 32.70 to 34.39 microns, inclusive, and a standard deviation in fiber diameter of 9.59 microns or less.

Sec. 31.13 *Grade 44's.* Wool with an average fiber diameter of 34.40 to 36.19 microns, inclusive, and a standard deviation in fiber diameter of 10.90 microns or less.

Sec. 31.14 *Grade 40's* Wool with an average fiber diameter of 36.20 to 38.09 microns, inclusive, and a standard deviation in fiber diameter of 10.69 microns or less.

Sec. 31.15 *Grade 36's.* Wool with an average fiber diameter of 38.10 to 40.20 microns, inclusive, and a standard deviation in fiber diameter of 11.19 microns or less.

Sec. 31.16 *Coarser than grade 36's.* Wool with an average fiber diameter of 40.21 microns or more.

Official U.S. wool top grades and associated standards are shown in Table 14.7.

Table 14.7. Wool Top Grades and Specifications.

| Grade | Average fiber diameter range, microns | Fiber diameter distribution, percent* | | | | | | | | Number of fibers required per test† |
		25 Microns and under, min.	30 Microns and under, min.	40 Microns and under, min.	25.1 Microns and over, max.	30.1 Microns and over, max.	40.1 Microns and over, max.	50.1 Microns and over, max.	60.1 Microns and over, max.	
Finer than 80s..	Under 18.10	95	—	—	5	1	—	—	—	400
80s	18.10–19.59	91	—	—	9	1	—	—	—	400
70s	19.60–21.09	83	—	—	17	3	—	—	—	400
64s	21.10–22.59	—	92	—	—	8	1	—	—	600
62s	22.60–24.09	—	86	—	—	14	1.5	—	—	800
60s	24.10–25.59	—	80	—	—	20	2	—	—	800
58s	25.60–27.09	—	72	—	—	28	—	1	—	1,000
56s	27.10–28.59	—	62	—	—	38	—	1	—	1,200
54s	28.60–30.09	—	54	—	—	46	—	2	—	1,400
50s	30.10–31.79	—	44	—	—	56	—	2	—	1,600
48s	31.80–33.49	—	—	75	—	—	25	1	1	1,800
46s	33.50–35.19	—	—	68	—	—	32	1	1	2,000
44s	35.20–37.09	—	—	62	—	—	38	—	2	2,200
40s	37.10–38.99	—	—	54	—	—	46	—	3	2,400
36s	39.00–41.29	—	—	44	—	—	56	—	4	2,600
Coarser than 36s	over 41.29	—	—	—	—	—	—	—	—	2,600

Source: USDA (1971).

*The second maximum percent shown for any grade is a part of, and not in addition to, the first maximum percent. In each grade, the maximum percent and the first maximum percent total 100 percent.

†Research has shown that when wools of average uniformity in fiber diameter are measured, the prescribed number of fibers to measure per test will result in confidence limits of the mean ranging from approximately ±0.4 to ±0.5 micron at a probability of 95 percent.

TRENDS IN USE OF FEDERAL GRADES

Federal grading has been on a voluntary basis except during World War II and the Korean War. The service was not readily accepted at the beginning, although a slight annual increase was evident. The normal reluctance in the industry to accept something new was further strengthened by the expense involved since packers had to pay for the cost of grading. In addition, some packers had vested interests in their own private grading systems and viewed Federal grades as detrimental to their interests. Following World War II, the proportion of graded meat dropped significantly, but not to its former level. The same thing happened following the Korean War. Since the latter war, the trend toward grading of beef and lamb steadily increased until the 1976 beef grade revision, which specified that any beef carcasses quality graded must also be yield graded. This ruling resulted in a decrease in quality grading, but the proportion of commercial carcass beef graded in 1984 was approximately 50 percent. Yield grading of beef increased rapidly following the initiation of the service in 1965, and the grade revision of 1976 gave it a sharp boost. Quality grading and yield grading both facilitate the marketing function and will continue in general usage.

IMPROVEMENTS IN GRADES
OF LIVESTOCK PRODUCED

An efficiently operating market system is presumed to price products over a period of time in a manner that reflects changing demand-and-supply characteristics. Theoretically, prices on less preferred products will tend to decline, and production of those products also will tend to decline, the reverse is expected on the more preferred products. Grades and grading provide a means of imparting knowledge that presumably tends to make the system more efficient. The pork market provides evidence that this has occurred in spite of much criticism and impatience with the rate of change.

Long-run wholesale pork prices show a clear-cut increasing trend for the four major lean cuts as a percentage of live hog values, whereas the price of lard has declined. This is the consumer's way of saying, through the marketing system, that they prefer lean pork. Data in Table 14.8 indicate that producers have received the message. Through breeding and feeding programs, average lard production has declined. The trend has been underway for decades, but, in just the 23-year period of Table 14.8, lard production per cwt of hogs slaughtered dropped from 14.1 pounds in 1959 to 6 pounds in 1976 and to 4.6 pounds in

Table 14.8. Changes in Selected Characteristics of Hogs Slaughtered Under Federal Inspection, 1959, 1969, 1976, and 1983.

Characteristic	1959	1969	1976	1983
Lard per cwt, lb	14.1	9.7	6.0	4.6
Lard per animal, lb	33.7	23.2	14.4	11.2
Pork per animal*, lb	149.8	161.9	172.4	178.8
Average dressed weight, lb	183.5	185.1	186.8	190.0[†]
Liveweight, lb	239.5	239.5	238.0	243.0
Dressing yield, %	76.6	77.3	78.4	78.2[†]

Sources: USDA (1977 and 1984).
*Pounds of pork per animal calculated.
[†]Adjusted for shipper-style carcass.

1983—a 67-percent decline. The pounds of pork produced per animal increased from 149.8 in 1959 to 178.8 in 1983, with average liveweight remaining essentially unchanged until the 1980s, when it increased slightly. This type of information indicates general improvement in production of meat-type hogs and indirectly suggests that improvements have been made in the grade of hogs, but it does not show changes within the grouping of generally acceptable hogs.

Data are not regularly collected on hog slaughter by grade, since the wholesale trade makes little use of pork grades. However, the USDA has made special studies of the percentage of barrow and gilt carcasses in each of the various grades, and these show a substantial increase in the percentage of U.S. No. 1 carcasses and a substantial decrease in the percentage of U.S. No. 3 carcasses. For example, 96 percent of the hog carcasses graded in 1980 were U.S. No. 1 and No. 2.

Data on the distribution of beef by grade has been collected for a number of years. Changes in grade standards have affected the historical grade distribution, several of them tending to increase the proportion of beef graded Choice. However, even when grade standard changes are accounted for, there is an apparent increase in the proportion of beef graded Choice and a decrease in beef graded Standard. The proportion graded Good held fairly stable until the revision of 1976, then dropped as a result. There are indications that grade use varies among stores and geographical locations. Beef packers usually request grading only for those carcasses from young cattle that qualify for the top four grades: Prime, Choice, Select, and Standard. In 1984, 93 percent of all carcass beef was graded Choice, 3 percent Prime, and 4 percent other grades (AMI, 1985). In response to the current strong demand for leaner beef, retailers are procuring large quantities of carcasses with less marbling than in USDA's Choice grade. Ungraded, "no roll" carcasses are given a generic quality designation or a store label.

An example of how a change in standards can affect distribution by grade is found in the case of lamb. A revision in 1960 relaxed the requirements for Prime grade. As a result, "Prime increased from 1% in 1959 marketing year (March through the following February) to 16% in 1960 and 12% in 1961. . . . Good dropped from 11% in 1959 to 3% in 1960 and 1961. Choice dropped from 87% in 1959 to 81% in 1960 and 82% in 1961" (Fineup et al., 1963). However, in the case of lamb, other factors, such as cut-out of retail cuts, tend to confirm a genuine improvement in the quality of lamb produced.

Factors other than the use of grades has probably had an effect on grade improvement, but grades and grading provide a means for improving market efficiency, and an efficient market tends to induce the production of preferred products. The evidence clearly indicates that this has happened and that the use of grades has undoubtedly been a beneficial contribution.

CONSUMER PREFERENCES AND KNOWLEDGE OF MEAT GRADES

In most discussions concerned with grades and grading, it usually is assumed (explicitly or implicitly) that (1) consumers prefer one grade to another, (2) they are able to distinguish among grades, and (3) they act accordingly. Numerous studies have been made to test hypotheses along these lines. This section is not intended to be a comprehensive review of the results but rather to point up some generalizations derived from such studies. The area of consumer preference involves many subjective considerations that are exceedingly complex, and study results have not been entirely consistent.

Consumer preference studies ordinarily are not designed to determine whether consumers can grade meat (place meat of various characteristics in the correct grade). There is clear evidence that consumers are not well-informed about grade names, let alone grade standards. Consumer preference studies are more concerned with a determination of the attributes in meat that consumers prefer and in their ability to differentiate between meats possessing varying degrees of those attributes.

Consumer evaluation of meat is largely based on (1) visual preferences, and (2) sensory preferences—but these are not mutually exclusive. Other possible considerations are situational factors and imaginary differences. In studies of visual preferences, consumers usually are shown photographs of cuts of meat (sometimes actual cuts of meat are used) so selected as to suggest differences between grades and/or within grades. In most of these studies, consumers have usually indicated a preference for leaner cuts whether the meat be beef, pork, or lamb (Branson, 1957; Perdue, et al., 1958; Rhodes, et al., 1955; Seltzer, 1955; Stevens et al., 1956).

With beef, the leaner-appearing cuts are the so-called "lower" grades—Commercial, Standard, and Good (Select). A first reaction might be that consumers are irrational, but a more considered judgment is that studies asking consumers' preferences within a range from Commercial to Prime places the respondent in a position not experienced in actual buying.

Most stores carry only one grade of beef—usually Choice, or its equivalent, if not officially graded.[10] The only alternative consumers have in this situation (and the only experience) is selection within the given grade. Many consumers select the leaner-appearing cuts to avoid trimming waste, with the expectation that eating quality will be relatively uniform. When confronted with Prime grade, which has the appearance of more fat, and Good (Select), Standard, and Commercial, which appear to be leaner in that order (even though trim specifications may be comparable), many consumers seem to follow the pattern of selecting the leaner, which in these circumstances are cuts of different quality. In this situation, decisions based on visual appearance are rational.

When it comes to sensory tests (eating tests), consumers tend to show a preference for Prime and Choice grades of beef. Kiehl and Rhodes (1956) reported that "the eating preference patterns contradict the visual preferences found by many researchers, including ourselves. Many visual preferences have been made for the leaner grades at equal prices or some even with price differentials against the leaner cuts. Eating preferences were very rarely for the leaner grades."

Ikerd et al. (1971), in a semantic differential factor analysis of the consumer image of pork, found that "The overall image of pork indicated by the study was that pork was wholesome and healthy, low in purchase cost, practical, tasty, and generally acceptable. However, it was considered lacking in stimulative quality and pork was considered to be fatter than consumers desired."

---

[10]Some stores carry other USDA grades, but few advertise the fact. During parts of the 1973–76 period, when grain prices were high and fed beef supplies relatively scarce, many stores experimented with the equivalent of "good" grade beef sold under their own brand name. That practice dwindled subsequently when grain prices dropped and the volume of choice beef increased. However, with a growing demand for leaner beef, many stores have returned to the practice of selling own-brand of less-than choice (leaner) beef.

Consumer studies of pork have shown a consistent preference for lean cuts; however, a substantial variation was apparent among the studies on the degree of preference (Birmingham et al., 1954; Nauman et al., 1959; Stevenson and Schneider, 1959; Trotter and Engelman, 1959; Vrooman, 1962).

Several studies have shown that consumers, by and large, are not familiar with grade names and often confuse inspection with grading. In a study including beefsteak and bacon (along with other nonmeat items), Hutchinson (1970) found that 90 percent of the persons interviewed said "yes" to the question, "Is there a government grade for beafsteak?" and a like percentage said they usually bought government-graded beefsteak. Some skepticism arises, however, when 70 and 81 percent, respectively, of the respondents answered "yes" to the same questions for bacon. Bacon is not sold by government grade. The author (Hutchinson, 1970) commented that "possibly a halo effect exists; the consumer reasons that since some beef is graded, all meat is graded. When asked to identify the shape of the USDA grade mark, 21.5 percent correctly identified the shield-shaped mark, but 29.5 percent said it was a circle, indicating a high probability that they were confusing the inspection mark with the grade mark."

In summary remarks, Hutchinson (1970) stated, "Most U.S. consumers know little about federal grades for the foods they buy, but those who are aware of grades say they find them helpful in buying decisions . . . the use of both adjective and letter grades for different food items apparently was not confusing."

With reference to data collected in a study of opinions about meats, Weidenhamer et al. (1968) reported that "homemakers are indeed confused about inspection and grading. Although virtually all respondents reported that the meat they buy is inspected and that beef is graded, half of the respondents stated that pork is graded; and a considerable number ascribed functions of grading to inspection, and vice versa. A question, therefore, arises about which statements regarding these functions were made on the basis of knowledge, which were based on assumptions, and which stemmed from misrepresentations—such as may be fostered by the way some stores or packers indicate that the meats they sell are inspected or graded." These authors found homemakers were not well informed on grade names. When confronted with a list of 10 grade names for beef—including five correct grade names and five spurious grade names—respondents included one spurious grade name among the three most frequently mentioned.

Despite inconsistencies among studies and lack of pronounced consensus among consumers on some attributes of meat, consumer preference studies will continue to serve an extremely useful purpose. They have pointed up some identifiable preferences such as that for leaner cuts and a positive relationship between marbling and palatability. Probably of importance equal to any positive results was the revelation that quality is an extremely complex subject. Meat itself is a complex product. Nevertheless, intelligent improvement in grade standards necessitates continued study of quality attributes that consumers can identify with reasonable accuracy and consistency. The ordering of preferences should be immaterial to researchers and public agencies involved in developing grade standards. If consumers were to prefer Standard grade beef over Select, and Select over Choice, this is the consumers' prerogative. From a grading standpoint, it is important for the grades to be based on characteristics that allow consumers to differentiate between grades, regardless of the order of preference.

ADDITIONAL USDA MEAT SERVICES

The USDA provides two additional services closely related to its grading services; (1) the Meat Acceptance Service, and (2) the Carcass Data Service. Both are voluntary, provided upon request, and paid for by users of the service.

Meat Acceptance Service

The Meat Acceptance Service is a service provided for large institutional buyers of meat (hospitals, steamship lines, government institutions, restaurant chains, etc.). Under this program, which began about 1960, an official USDA grader will certify that meat and meat products are in compliance with the purchaser's specifications. As an assist in the program, USDA has prepared a series of Institutional Meat Purchase Specifications (IMPS) covering some 300 fresh, cured, and processed meat and meat products. The specifications were developed in conjunction with members of the meat trade and define in detail such things as kind of cut, quality grade, size and weight of cut, and style of trim. If the predesigned "specs" do not meet a particular buyer's need, USDA will cooperate in drawing up specifications that meet that buyer's need.

Detailed specifications put a buyer in a position to ask suppliers for bids, thus facilitating the "bid and acceptance" method of purchasing mentioned in Chap. 10. After the purchaser has accepted a bid, a USDA grader examines and then accepts and certifies the shipment should it meet the specifications.

Purchasers and suppliers must make prior arrangements for the ser-

ACCEPTANCE STAMPS

vice, and the USDA is reimbursed for its costs. Normally, the supplier pays the cost, which is presumably recovered in a price mark-up of the meat.

This service can benefit both purchaser and supplier. The purchaser is provided with (1) assistance, if necessary, in determining specifications that will meet his particular needs, and (2) professional assistance that relieves him of employing experts to do the buying (buying can be done by "bid and acceptance") and to examine the shipment upon arrival. The service's official certification also assures the supplier that his shipment will not be rejected upon arrival.

Accepted meat is stamped, either directly on the meat itself if individually possible or on the carton containing meat products that cannot be stamped individually. The stamps used are shown here. Meat that can be individually stamped bears the insignia shown here. Cartons that are stamped bear both stamps. The letters "AC" in this example identify the grader who accepted the product.

Beef Carcass Data Service

For a number of years, cow-calf producers and feedlot operators have indicated an interest in obtaining data on the carcass characteristics of their cattle after slaughter. This is vital information for a cow-herd operator engaged in a herd improvement program. It is equally vital to a feedlot operator's feeding program. In a very direct way, this type of information enters into their marketing programs. Both classes of producers had experienced difficulties in obtaining it prior to the initiation of this service. Keeping track of the identity of animals during growing, finishing, and slaughtering is a difficult job. Without some agreement with packers and graders, producers (and feeders) had problems in lining up all the necessary arrangements. During the early 1960s, the USDA made attempts to alleviate the latter difficulty.

This was a program designated the Beef Carcass Evaluation Service. Packers were informed of it and graders were instructed to cooperate.

It was the producer's responsibility to make arrangements with a packer and Federal grader to place an identification on each animal. After slaughter, the grader had to fill out a form giving carcass characteristics and relay it to the producer.

The program worked, but, from the producer's standpoint, making arrangements was cumbersome and sometimes frustrating. Participation was limited in spite of the need and desire for carcass information.

In an effort to improve the service, USDA in early 1970 initiated a revised program on an experimental basis—renamed the Beef Carcass Data Service. Under the new setup, producers can purchase bright orange-colored USDA ear tags with identification marks—not directly from USDA, but from a cooperating organization that acts as a participating agency. This may be a cattle producer or feeder association, an agricultural organization, a state department of agriculture, etc. A cow-herd operator can tag his calves or a feedlot operator can tag his feeders, and—if the ear tag does not become lost or removed—that animal will be positively identified when it reaches a packing plant, even though it may have passed through several different ownerships and may have been transported far from the home ranch or feedlot. Producers have no further responsibilities. Prearrangements have been made with USDA inspectors and graders whereby the inspector will remove the tag from the ear on the slaughter floor and attach it to the carcass. The grader at the plant will examine the carcass for quality grade and yield grade along with such relevant details as the evaluation of marbling, backfat thickness, ribeye area, kidney, pelvic, and heart fat, and carcass weight. This data, along with tag number, will be forwarded to a clearing center, which forwards it to the cooperating organization, which, in turn, delivers it to the tag owner.

REFERENCES

Abraham, H. C. 1977. Grades of fed beef carcasses. USDA. Agr. Mktg. Serv. Mktg. Res. Rept. No. 1073.

Agnew, D. B. 1969. Improvements in grades of hogs slaughtered from 1960–61 to 1967–68. USDA Econ. Res. Serv., Mktg. Res. Rept. 849.

American Meat Institute, 1985. Meatfacts. A statistical summary about America's largest food industry. AMI, Washington, D. C.

Birmingham, E. B., et al. 1954. Fatness of pork in relation to consumer preference. Missouri Agr. Expt. Sta. Bull. 549.

Branson, R. E. 1957. The consumer market for beef. Texas Agr. Expt. Sta. Bull. 856.

Clemen, R. A. 1923. *The American Livestock and Meat Industry*. New York: Ronald Press Co.

Dowell, A. A., and Bjorka, K. 1941. *Livestock Marketing*. New York: McGraw-Hill Book Co.

Farris, P. L. 1960. Uniform grades and standards, product differentiation and product development. *J. Farm Econ.*, Feb., pp. 854–863.

Federal Register, 1984A. Standards for grades of slaughter lambs, yearlings, and sheep; final rule. **49**, No. 200:43035–43039.

Federal Register, 1984B. Standards for grades of carcass beef and standards for grades of slaughter cattle; proposed rule. **49**, No. 218:44724–44737.

Federal Register, 1984C. Standards for grades of barrow and gilt carcasses, and standards for grades of slaughter barrows and gilts; final rule. **49**, No. 242:48669–48676.

Fienup, D. F., et al. 1963. Economic effects of U.S. grades for lamb. USDA Econ. Res. Serv. Agr. Econ. Rept. 25.

Hendrix, J., et al. 1963. Consumer acceptance of pork chops. Missouri Agr. Expt. Sta. Res. Bull. 834.

Hutchinson, T. Q. 1970. Consumers' knowledge and use of government grades for selected food items. USDA Econ. Res. Serv. Mktg. Res. Rept. 876.

Ikerd, J. E., et al. 1971. The Consumer image of pork. Missouri Agr. Expt. Sta. Res. Bull. 978.

Kiehl, E. R., and Rhodes, V. J. 1956. Techniques in consumer preference research, *J. Farm Econ.* 38, No. 5:1335–1345.

Nauman, H. D., et al. 1959. A large merchandising experiment with selected pork cuts. Missouri Agr. Expt. Sta. Res. Bull. 711.

Perdue, E. J., et al. 1958. Some results from a pilot investigation of consumer preferences for beef. Oklahoma Agr. Expt. Sta. Process. Ser. P-304.

Rhodes, V. J. 1960. How the marking of beef grades was obtained. *J. Farm Econ.* 42, No. 1:133–151.

Rhodes, V. J., et al. 1955. Visual preference for grades of retail cuts. Missouri Agr. Expt. Sta. Res. Bull. 583.

Rhodes, V. J., et al. 1956. Consumer preferences and beef grades. Missouri Agr. Expt. Sta. Res. Bull. 612.

Seltzer, R. E. 1955. Consumer preferences for beef. Ariz. Agr. Expt. Sta. Res. Bull. 267.

Stevens, I. M., et al. 1956. Beef consumer use and preference. Wyoming Agr. Expt. Sta. Res. Bull. 343.

Stevenson J., and Schneider, V. 1959. Consumer reaction to price differentials for meat-type pork. Econ. Marketing Inform. Indiana Farmers Oct. 30.

Trotter, C., and Engelman, G. 1959. Consumer response to graded pork. Penn. Agr. Expt. Sta. Res. Bull. 650.

USDA. 1956. Official United States standards for grades of vealers and slaughter calves. USDA Agr. Mktg. Serv. Regulatory Announcements 114.

USDA. 1957. Official United States standards for grades of vealers and slaughter calves. USDA Agr. Mktg. Serv. Regulatory Announcements 113.

USDA. 1965A. Official United States standards for grades of carcass beef. USDA Consumer Mktg. Serv. Regulatory Announcements 99.

USDA. 1965B. Official United States standards for grades of feeder cattle. USDA Consumer Mktg. Serv. Regulatory Announcements 183.

USDA. 1966A. Official United States standards for grades of veal and calf carcasses. USDA Agr. Marketing Serv. Regulatory Announcements 113.

USDA. 1966B. Official United States standards for grades of Slaughter cattle. USDA Agr. Mktg. Serv. Regulatory Announcements 112.

USDA. 1966C. Official United States standards for grades of wool. USDA Consumer and Mktg. Serv. SRA—C & MS, No. 135.

USDA. 1968A. Official United States standards for grades of barrow and gilt carcasses. USDA Consumer Mktg. Serv. Reprinted in Federal Register.

USDA. 1968B. Official United States standards for grades of slaughter barrows and gilts. USDA Agr. Mktg. Serv. Regulatory Announcements 172.

USDA. 1968C. USDA yield grades for beef. USDA Consumer Marketing Serv. Mktg. Bull. 45.

USDA. 1969A. Official United States standards for grades of feeder pigs. USDA Consumer Mktg. Serv. Regulatory Announcements 189.

USDA. 1969B. Official United States standards for grades of lamb, yearling mutton, and mutton carcasses; slaughter lambs, yearlings and sheep. USDA Agr. Mktg. Serv. Regulatory Announcements 168.

USDA. 1970A. USDA grades for pork carcasses. USDA Consumer Marketing Serv. Mktg. Bull. 49.

USDA. 1970B. USDA grades for slaughter swine and feeder pigs. USDA Consumer Mktg. Serv. Mktg. Bull. 51.

USDA. 1970C. USDA yield grades for lamb. USDA Consumer Mktg. Serv. Mktg. Bull. 52.

USDA. 1971. USDA grade standards for wool top. USDA Consumer and Mktg. Serv. Mktg. Bull. No. 53.

USDA. 1975A. Official United States standards for grade of slaughter cattle. USDA Agr. Mktg. Serv. (Unnumbered).

USDA, 1975B. Official United States standards for grades of carcass beef. USDA Food Safety and Quality Serv. (Unnumbered).

USDA. 1977. Livestock and meat statistics. USDA Stat. Rept. Serv. Supp. for 1976 to Stat. Bull. No. 333.

USDA. 1978. Livestock, meat, wool market news. USDA Agr. Mktg. Serv. Vol. 46. No. 22.

USDA. 1982A. Meats, prepared meats, and products (grading, certification and standards). USDA Agr. Mktg. Serv. (Title 7 includes amendments through Jan. 1, 1982.)

USDA. 1982B. Official United States standards for grades of lamb, yearling mutton, and mutton carcasses. USDA Agr. Mktg. Serv. (Unnumbered).

USDA. 1984. Livestock and meat statistics. USDA, ERS. Stat. Bull. No. 715.

USDA. 1985. Livestock, meat, wool market news. USDA Agr. Mktg. Serv. Vol. 53. No. 44.

Vrooman, C. W. 1952. Consumer report on pork production. Oregon Agr. Expt. Sta. Bull. 521.

Weidenhamer, Margaret et al. 1968. Homemakers' opinions about selected meats—a preliminary report. USDA Statist. Reporting Serv. SRS-12.

Williams, W. F. 1960. Note on how the marking of beef grades was obtained. *J. Farm Econ.* 42, No. 4:878–886.

15

Market Intelligence

It became increasingly evident during the agricultural crisis of the 1980s that success in farming or ranching requires more than technical production equipment and skill. The fruits of efficient production can be lost by inadequate market information. Just as production knowledge and practices have become more and more sophisticated, so has product marketing. Market information is available, but one must be familiar with the sources, obtain the information, and devote some time to its study and analysis. To meet this challenge, many producers allocate part of their time to market analysis as rigorously as they pursue technological production developments.

In a competitive market economy, the bargaining position of buyers and sellers is conditioned by the degree to which they are informed. The classical economic concept of a perfectly competitive market assumes perfect knowledge—a goal, of course, that is unattainable. Traditionally, agricultural producers have been labelled as "price takers." Part of this reputation stems from lack of effective organization but part also from lack of market information, which, in a systematic sense, may be called market intelligence.

There has always been a need for market information, but the urgency has increased with the trend toward more and more direct marketing. Livestock producers now deal directly with professional buyers in the sale of finished stock and often with professional sellers in the purchase of feeder stock. The concept of competition implies a notion of rivalry, or struggle, and a large share of that struggle is in keeping at least as well informed as other parties. Other parties include competitors in the industry as well as participants in buying and selling transactions. No single person or firm could possibly observe enough to keep abreast of the ever-changing economic and political forces that shape nationwide and worldwide markets. U.S. livestock and meat markets, like many other native markets, are affected by the supply-demand trends, import–export regulations, and public-policy decisions not only of this country but of Australia, New Zealand, Argentina, Canada, Ireland, the Common Market Countries, and many others. Private sources gather and disseminate much information, but it was recognized at an early stage that government services were justified not only from the standpoint of practicality, but also as a matter of public interest.

MARKET DIMENSIONS

Market intelligence needs may be considered in two general dimensions: (1) the short run, and (2) the long run. It is impossible to specify short and long run in weeks, months, or years, but, in general, the short run is concerned with marketing to best advantage a production output that is virtually complete in quantity and quality already (i.e., essentially no time remains for altering the product). The long run envisions enough time to adjust production programs, the latter, coincidentally, being related to marketing programs. The time required for such changes is greater in cow–calf operations than for sow herds and is something else again for a calf wintering program.

A feeder with a pen of livestock that is about finished out and ready for sale needs to know current price levels for his class, grade, and weight of livestock (implied here is the ability to evaluate grade). He needs to know variations in relevant prices among alternative market outlets. Information on current conditions of supply and demand and market movements help him size up the current market situation, although as an individual he has no control over them. The market intelligence needed in this short-run situation is sometimes referred to as "price and sales information," or as "market news."

The position a producer finds himself in at a given time, however, is, in part, determined by decisions he and others had made some months earlier—i.e., when he bought feeder animals, outlined his feeding program, or initiated a breeding program. It was then that the wheels were set in motion that largely determined the quantity and quality of livestock that would be available at later dates. Information is needed to assist producers in making wise planning decisions in this longer run context. This type of information is also needed by packers, processors, cold-storage interests, wholesalers, and retailers. Consumers, too, have an interest, in that better informed market participants make for a more efficient market system, which, in turn, allows consumer demands to guide production. The informational needs in this situation call for data and analyses that project probable supply and demand conditions—information that attempts to look ahead rather than at the present moment. This type of market intelligence often is referred to as "outlook and situation information" and is construed to include analyses of changing consumer preferences.

DEVELOPMENT OF INFORMATION SERVICES

The history of meat and livestock market reporting in the United States is almost as old as the livestock industry itself.[1] The earliest sources of market information were newspaper quotations of prices for provisions (lard, tallow, and salted, pickled, and smoked meats). The press, then as now, recognized the newsworthiness of market reports. The reporting of live-animal prices followed that of meat prices by a considerable number of years. The export sale of provisions gave that market a semblance of organization long before enough consistency was generated in live markets to warrant price reports.

Private market reporting grew with the industry largely in the form of newpapers, magazines, trade publications, and publications sponsored by organized markets. Some of the problems inherent in these reports were mentioned in Chap. 14 (Grading). The heterogeneity and inconsistency in use of terms, both within given markets and between markets, seriously handicapped the interpretation of reports.

In addition, the need for basic industry data was also recognized at an early date. The merits of turning this job over to the Federal government were evident from the start,[2] although the beginnings were on an elementary scale. The first Census of Agriculture was taken in 1840 by the U. S. Office of Patents. In later years, responsibility for census enumeration was placed in the Bureau of Census, U. S. Department of Commerce. Early census data did not provide any information of immediate application to the marketing of livestock, but it established the Federal government as the data collecting and disseminating agency. Subsequent organization of the U. S. Department of Agriculture in 1862 placed additional agricultural data collection, interpretation, and dissemination in that branch of the Federal government. Its early efforts were directed at increasing production, rather than improving marketing.

Producer dissatisfaction with market conditions was particularly evident during the latter half of the 1800s and the first decade of the 1900s. Producers, then as now, were troubled by the difference between prices received at the farm and prices charged at retail, and deficiencies in market price reporting were indicated to be one of the major problems. During this period, many conferences were held and investigations were carried out. Among the spokesmen for producers, Henry C.

---

[1]Three excellent accounts of the early historical development of market information are Dowell and Bjorks (1941), USDA (1969A), and Smeby (1961).
[2]For further discussion of the public role in collection and dissemination of prices of agricultural commodities, see Henderson et al. (1983).

Wallace—editor of *Wallace's Farmer*—stands out. Wallace was also the secretary of a farmers' organization, the Corn Belt Meat Producers Association. This organization, together with another—the American National Live Stock Association—carried on active campaigns in attempts to alleviate what were considered detrimental market reporting practices. The accusations ranged from inadequate and inaccurate reporting to deliberate misrepresentation. Henry Wallace participated in the conferences, carried on discussions in his magazine, and stimulated interest in producer organizations. During the fall of 1915 he published an editorial in which he presented, in some detail, suggestions for investigating the situation and for establishing a Federal market reporting service.

A logical branch of government for doing marketing work was already in existence at that time, although it was relatively new. The USDA Office of Markets had been established in 1913, and within it a Division of Livestock, Meats, and Wool in early 1915. As a result of studies made by that office and guided extensively by Wallace's work, the Federal government in 1915 set up arrangements for collecting market information. Congress appropriated $65,000 in 1916 for collection and dissemination of information on the number and grade of livestock being produced; prices, receipts, and shipments by class and grade at central markets; prices of meat and meat products; and the amount of meat in storage. At administrative discretion, however, the initial emphasis was on meat and lard. The first Federal report on meat marketing was issued in December, 1916; the first livestock marketing report, eighteen months later. These early market reports were limited to prices and market conditions at a few central markets.

By this time, tentative grades had been established on meat and livestock, so that for the first time a uniform language was available for use in price quotations. Although the original emphasis was on meat market reporting, this gradually changed over the years. By the early 1940s, major attention was on the live-animal market. As the trend toward direct marketing picked up momentum, particularly after World War II, interest again shifted to the meat trade. Direct selling, especially by the carcass grade and weight method, necessitates a good knowledge of conditions in the wholesale meat market. At the present time, interest being high in the live-animal market, the Market News Reporting Service attempts to maintain a balanced reporting of meat, livestock, and wool markets.

Market reporting, as carried on by the Market News Reporting Service, is primarily aimed at reporting current prices, movements, and market conditions, that is, to serve short-run informational needs. Many states also carry out market reporting functions—some in cooperation with the Federal service, others entirely as a state effort. Private firms and agencies pursue continued efforts in this area. Newspapers, radio and TV stations, farm magazines, farm organizations, commission firms, auction operators, and private market agencies expend an enormous amount of energy in providing market intelligence to all sectors of the livestock and meat trade. Many are engaged in dissemination of market news only, using the data collected by government agencies as their major source, but there are exceptions. The *National Provisioner's* "Yellow Sheet" and the *Meat Sheet*, also known as the "Pink Sheet," are compilations of privately collected information on the wholesale meat market. The American National Cattleman's Association's "CATTLE-FAX" depends largely on privately collected data and its interpretation. Several well-established private research-consulting firms that specialize in livestock are primarily market analysts who make use of data generally available to the public.

Comprehensive work in the collection of situation and outlook type information began shortly after that for market news. Following World War I, and continuing to the present, there has been a profound interest in knowing the forces behind market trends. The vast amount of data needed for this type of analysis requires government services. Involved here, in addition to livestock and meat data and feed supplies, are such things as population (by age classifications), incomes (distributed by income levels), prices and supplies of products that compete with meats, trends in consumer preferences, imports, exports, etc. As mentioned earlier, a start on this type of information was made in 1840 in the first agricultural census. The agricultural census, however, does not collect nearly all the information needed, and, furthermore, it is taken only at five-year intervals. In certain data series, the census serves an extremely useful purpose as a benchmark against which to check data collected from other sources, but by itself is inadequate for outlook and situation analysis since many of these require annual, quarterly, and monthly data. Although some work was done in this area earlier, the USDA began to place particular emphasis on it after World War II. The office with this responsibility has undergone several name changes over the years; currently, major data collection is done by the Crop Reporting Board (CRB) of the Statistical Reporting Service (SRS) and the Livestock Division of the Agricultural Marketing Service (AMS). In addition, the Economic Research Service (ERS) collects and publishes several statistical reports on domestic and international trade and prices.

Analysis and interpretation of livestock and meat marketing data is performed by many governmental agencies. Of particular interest are the Livestock and Poultry Situation and Outlook, the Cotton and Wool Situation and Outlook, and the Fats and Oils Situation and Outlook, published regularly by the Commodity Economics Division of ERS.

PUBLIC AGENCIES AND INSTITUTIONS

Federal-State Market News Reporting Service, AMS, USDA[3]

The Market News Reporting Service is an arm of the Agricultural Marketing Service within the USDA hierarchy. Individual states may at their option cooperate with the Federal agency in activities within their respective states.

The major responsibility of the Federal–State Market News Reporting Service is collection and dissemination of current, unbiased market information. The agency gathers data on many agricultural products, but this discussion will be limited to those activities that report prices, market conditions, and current supplies and demand for livestock, meat, and wool at selected markets throughout the United States.

Organizational Features.   The Market News Reporting Service cooperates, when arrangements can be made, with state marketing agencies in setting up Federal–State offices. In other instances, the Federal service maintains offices not associated with state agencies. In the 1980s, there are more than 25 state marketing agencies cooperating with the Federal agency, and more than 60 livestock, meat, and wool field offices are maintained throughout the United States. These provide coverage of most terminal livestock markets and major auctions. Information is collected on direct sales of livestock from major areas. Data on meat sales are collected from 10 trading areas in the Midwest, Colorado, Texas, the East Coast, and the West Coast. Wool and mohair marketing data are obtained from 14 areas, with the primary office located in Denver. Arrangements have also been made for the collection and dissemination of data on offal sales, daily slaughter estimates, weekly meat production estimates, daily pork cut-out values, and beef cut-out values.

The Market News Reporting Service attempts to keep pace with changing times, but this is a continuing problem. Funds and personnel are limited, and lapses typically occur before changes can be made. The

---

[3]Much of the material in this section was furnished by Dr. Paul M. Fuller, Chief, Livestock Market News Branch, Agricultural Marketing Service, USDA.

situation was relatively simple when terminals dominated the market scene since a single reporter could personally cover these highly concentrated activities. Because of the expansion in auctions and direct marketing, however, the opposite situation prevails. Maintaining the established standards of excellence within fund restrictions has limited the reporting of auction sales to the major markets. The expansion in direct selling of livestock has presented still another problem. Direct sales from farms are widely scattered and usually nonobservable, private transactions. Sales out of commercial feedlots are somewhat more concentrated, but adequate coverage is still a problem. Direct sales of slaughter livestock, of course, involve packing plants that, in effect, are points of concentration, but decentralization of the packing industry presents a widely scattered pattern, and there is no legal compulsion for buyers and sellers to divulge purchase and sale information. This fact points up an important aspect of the entire governmental marketing intelligence system. Market News Reporting Service depends primarily upon *voluntary* cooperation of all segments of the industry in gathering information and also of the news media in disseminating it.[4]

At scheduled times, the assembled market information is fed into a leased teletypewriter system for dissemination to the press, radio, television, and trade sources. There are about 100 automatic self-answering, taped, telephone reports. In addition, mimeographed and printed reports are sent by mail.

Operational Features.   The method of operation is conditioned by the type of market being covered. At most markets, trained professional reporters personally observe sales, interview buyers and sellers, and check receipts and movements that have a bearing on supplies and demand. Where sales are sparse or distances too great, information is gathered by telephone and teletypewriter, with some follow-up personal contacts and inspection of sales records.

Terminal Markets.   Experienced market reporters are stationed at most terminal markets. These individuals are capable livestock graders who tour the yards during trading hours to interview buyers and sellers and observe sales, including both private treaty and auction sales (at those terminals with auction facilities). Reporters have working relationships with market personnel that permit discussions not afforded general market visitors. Actual transactions are ordinarily

---

[4]Some data collected by regulatory agencies—e.g., the Meat Inspection division and the Packers and Stockyards, USDA—are mandatory and find use in certain aspects of marketing, but these agencies are not a part of the Market News Reporting Service.

private affairs between buyer and seller, but this confidence is usually shared with market reporters. Reporters realize, however, that market personnel may sometimes attempt to bias the report for personal gain. An experienced reporter can recognize this and make appropriate adjustments.

Three reports are issued each day at terminals: (1) early morning, (2) mid-session, and (3) market closing. These reports are flashed over the wire network to other livestock markets and the news media. In some cases, the reporter may also broadcast directly over a local radio station. The early morning report consists of an estimate of that day's receipts, an evaluation of opening price trends, and observations of early sales. Once this report has been filed, the reporter returns to the yards for observations that will comprise the mid-session report. By mid-session, a substantive report can be made on receipts, price trends, and quotations for the bulk of sales by class, grade, and weight. Further observations and checks give indications of possible late changes that go into the closing report.

Auction Markets. Reporters take a position at auction markets that permits an unrestricted view of the sales ring. They record sale prices and evaluations of the grade and condition of the animals on a prepared form. They can often observe weights on the auction scales. Reporters are trained to recognize when not all lots are uniform in grade and other value factors and make the appropriate adjustments. A local report is issued for each sale, and a summary is forwarded to an appropriate central office for dissemination on a statewide or area basis.

Direct Livestock Sales. Information is assembled on direct sales of slaughter cattle, feeder cattle, hogs, and sheep from 26 major market areas. Contract sales are covered as well as current transactions. Much information is gathered by telephone and teletypewriter, but also at feedlots, packing plants, and ranches. Reports are issued daily, semiweekly, or weekly, depending upon trading volume.

Wholesale Meat Market. Wholesale prices on carcass and primal cuts are reported daily from selected points, including the Midwest, Colorado, Texas, the East Coast, and the West Coast. A relatively recent addition is the collection and reporting of prices on fabricated cuts of beef (wholesale and oven-ready cuts prepared by packers). Chief reliance in this operation is placed on telephone interviews. A comprehensive meat and other livestock products report, mailed daily on a subscription basis, was initiated in March, 1986.

Wool and Mohair. A weekly wool market report is issued from Denver. An experienced reporter collects information by telephone and by visiting with ranchers and local market agents.

Other Products. The Market News Reporting Service also reports a weekly hide and offal value, which is released from Princeton. Daily estimates also are made on pork and beef cut-out values. Pork cut-out is the combined value of pork cuts, based on prices of 150-lb and 180-lb hog carcasses graded U. S. No. 1 through U. S. No. 4. The beef cut-out value is based on the combined value of beef cuts from Choice, yield 3,600 to 700-lb carcasses.

In addition to strict adherence to official grade terminology, the Market News Reporting Service is uniform in its use of terms to describe market conditions. Following are the commonly used terms and their meaning (USDA 1975):

MARKET—A term with several meanings:
 A geographic location where a commodity is traded.
 The price, or price level, at which a commodity is traded.
 To sell (verb).

MARKET ACTIVITY—The pace at which sales are being made.
ACTIVE—Available supplies (offerings) are readily clearing the market.
MODERATE—Available supplies (offerings) are clearing the market at a reasonable rate.
SLOW—Available supplies (offerings) are not readily clearing the market.
INACTIVE—Sales are intermittent with few buyers and sellers.

PRICE TREND—The direction in which prices are moving in relation to trading in the previous reporting period(s).
HIGHER—The majority of sales are at prices measurably higher than the previous trading session.
FIRM—Prices are tending higher, but not measurably so.
STEADY—Prices are unchanged from previous trading session.
WEAK—Prices are tending lower, but not measurably so.
LOWER—Prices for most sales are measurably lower than the previous trading session.

SUPPLY/OFFERING—The quantity of a particular item available for current trading.
HEAVY—When the volume of supplies is above average for the market being reported.
MODERATE—When volume of supplies is average for the market being reported.
LIGHT—When the volume of supplies is below average for the market being reported.

DEMAND—The desire to possess a commodity coupled with the willingness and ability to pay.

VERY GOOD—Offerings or supplies are rapidly absorbed.

GOOD—Firm confidence on the part of buyers that general market conditions are good. Trading is more active than normal.

MODERATE—Average buyer interest and trading.

LIGHT—Demand is below average.

VERY LIGHT—Few buyers are interested in trading.

MOSTLY—The majority of sales or volume.

UNDERTONE—The situation or sense of direction is unsettled market situation.

Market News Reports. The Market News Reporting Service has a system of satellite and leased wire facilities over which reports are made available to communications media (Fig. 15.1). Not all office locations are concerned with livestock, meat, and wool information, but the network is nevertheless available for transmission of reports. Kansas City is a critical relay point, connecting the network of the eastern half of the nation with Mountain, Southwest, and West Coast market points. Although the widest and most rapid dissemination occurs over the wire network, Market News Reporting Service also makes extensive use of mimeographed, mailed reports.

Each week, summarized data from field offices are forwarded to Washington to be compiled in a weekly publication entitled *Livestock Meat and Wool Market News*. This publication should be on the "must" list for most livestock producers and market personnel, containing, as it does, not only relatively up-to-date data for selected markets, but also digests of current releases and reports, including outlook and situation reports issued by other government agencies.

Special mention should also be made of a valuable improvement in market news reporting—the automatic, taped, self-answering telephone service. These devices accept long distance as well as local calls, are updated several times during each day, and are available on a 24-hour basis.

The estimated daily slaughter under Federal inspection is released at 2:30 P.M. Eastern time for cattle, calves, hogs, and sheep. The actual slaughter by class and specie is available two weeks later, and live and dressed weight information three weeks later. The weekly total meat production is released each Friday afternoon.

Livestock market news reporters have also been designated as the officials to prepare appropriate specifications for the settlement of futures and Commodity Credit Corporation contracts.

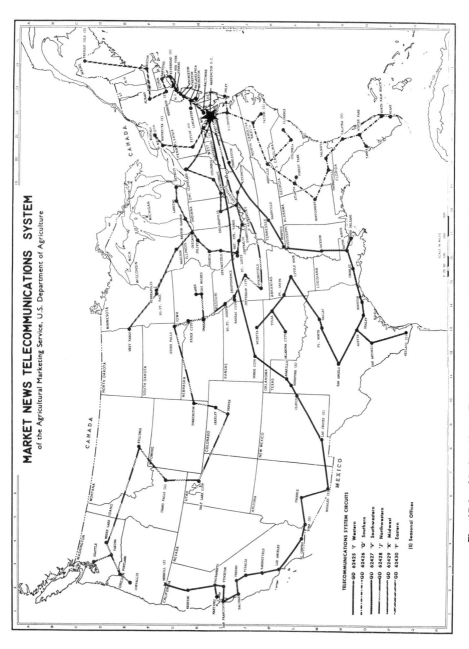

Fig. 15.1. Market News Telecommunications Network, 1985. (Courtesy of USDA,

STATISTICAL REPORTING SERVICE, SRS, USDA

The USDA's Statistical Reporting Service (SRS) is headquartered in Washington, D. C., and maintains 44 State Statistical Offices (SSOs) to serve the 50 states. Most state offices are joint Federal–State endeavors (USDA 1983). SRS, through its Crop Reporting Board (CRB), is responsible for data gathering as contrasted with analysis and interpretation. Most data are collected by state Agricultural Statistics Offices formerly referred to as the Crop and Livestock Reporting Service. The information is forwarded to a Washington office of the Crop Reporting Board, where, in closed door sessions, the board reviews state and other aggregated compilations prior to release. SRS issues about 300 national and 9,000 state reports each year that cover about 120 crops and 45 livestock items. The number, coverage, and title of reports, however, is under almost constant review and change.

Vast amounts of data are collected on all aspects of crops and livestock, including such general categories as production, distribution, storage, inventories, average prices received by farmers, values, animals slaughtered, meat production, etc. Most of these data are related to marketing.

The type of data collected and schedules of distribution make this market-related information particularly adapted for outlook and situation analyses. The research and analysis functions, however, are usually carried out by other agencies. The Crop Reporting Board makes the data available not only to other governmental agencies but also to the public. Many of the findings have considerable newsworthiness (without further analysis) and are widely disseminated by the media. Reports are released according to a fixed schedule on specified dates throughout the year. Security measures are strict to prevent premature access to estimates. It should be understood, however, that this is not the same up-to-the-minute price and market condition information reported by the Market News Reporting Service.

Relevant SRS publications are the following:

1. *Cattle*—January 1, _____ (Jan.), and July 1, _____ (July) Reports number of cattle and calves on farms by class and by state (Jan. only), and annual calf crop. The July report gives the national inventory only.
2. *Cattle and Calves on Feed*—(Jan., Apr., July, Oct.) Reports number on feed at beginning of each quarter for important feeding states; number by class and by weight group for leading states; and number of grain-fed cattle marketed.
3. *Cattle and Calves on Feed*—(Monthly) Reports number on feed

at beginning of each month for seven important feeding states and number of grain-fed cattle marketed.

4. *Hogs and Pigs*—(June) Reports inventory of hogs and pigs on farms June 1, an estimate of spring pig-crop farrowings that year, and an estimate of intended farrowings for the following fall pig crop for the U.S.

5. *Hogs and Pigs*—(Dec.) Reports inventory of hogs and pigs on farms Dec. 1, an estimate of fall pig-crop farrowings that year, and an estimate of intended farrowings for the following spring pig crop, by states.

6. *Hogs and Pigs*—(Mar., June, Sept., Dec.) Provides quarterly estimates of farrowings and inventory for important hog-producing states.

7. *Sheep and Goats*, January 1, _____—(Feb.) Reports number of sheep and lambs on farms Jan. 1, by class and by state. Gives lamb crop and sheep and lambs on feed for important sheep states. Also gives Texas' inventory of goats.

8. *Sheep and Lambs on Feed*, January 1, _____—(Jan.) Reports inventory of sheep and lambs January, and number of sheep on feed, by weight classification and by state for important lamb-feeding states.

9. *Wool Production and Value,*_____—(Apr.) Reports number of breeding ewes, lamb crop, and wool and mohair production by state.

10. *Meat Animals—Farm Production, Disposition and Income*_____—(Apr.) Gives data on indicated items, by state.

11. *Livestock Slaughter*—(Monthly and annual) Gives number of head and live weight of cattle, calves, hogs, sheep, and lambs slaughtered in commercial plants, by state; meat production, by species, and lard production for the United States.

Economic Research Service, ERS, USDA

In addition to the reports just listed, which are published by USDA's SRS, the Economics Research Service (ERS) issues, about mid-year, an annual summary of livestock and meat data for the previous year, along with a historical series for several prior years. Each year, adjustments and corrections are made in the data of prior years, if necessary. This publication is entitled *Livestock and Meat Statistics* and contains a wealth of basic market-related data. Prior to 1957, these data were published under the title, *Livestock Market News Service Statistics and Related Data.*

The Commodity Economics Division of ERS basically is responsible for the analysis and interpretation of data in a situation–outlook framework. One of its major activities is the analysis of livestock, meat, and wool data. It also issues a publication entitled *Livestock and Poultry Situation and Outlook* about six times a year, and about four times each year it issues *Cotton and Wool Situation and Outlook.* These situation reports periodically include special articles analyzing currently relevant problems in the livestock and meat industry.

This agency goes beyond the presentation of data, its activities including production, demand, and price projections—though these are somewhat guarded. Retail meat price compilations are given in each issue of the *Livestock and Poultry Situation and Outlook,* and data, with commentary, are also given on imports and exports of livestock and meat. Other relevant publications emanating from this agency are the *Feed Situation and Outlook* and the *Fats and Oil Situation and Outlook.*

These "situation" reports are recommended as another "must" among government publications for livestock and meat industry personnel with an interest in the market situation.

Although not directed specifically at livestock and meat concerns, ERS's *Agricultural Outlook* (monthly) contains much relevant statistical data, along with descriptive features of current interest.

State Activities

It was mentioned previously that some states cooperate with the Federal government in operation of the Market News Reporting Service. Most important agricultural states carry on additional work under a department, division, or office of marketing. Among the major livestock-producing states, these agencies conduct a variety of programs associated with the marketing of livestock, meat, and wool. No attempt will be made here to enumerate individual state activities, but some of the general areas include promotional programs designed to increase meat consumption, programs designed to improve both the quantity and the quality of products produced, collection and dissemination of market news not covered by the Federal service, and preparation and dissemination of outlook-type information.

Colleges and Universities

Most land grant colleges and universities in important livestock-producing states are actively engaged in work related to livestock and meat marketing, an activity shared by personnel in the Agricultural Experiment Station and the Cooperative Agricultural Extension Service. The major responsibility of the former is research; of the latter, dissemination of information. In most cases, these activities are closely coordinated. In some, the personnel hold joint appointments and often serve under joint administrative arrangements. Research activities cover every facet of marketing. Virtually no effort is expended to *collect* marketing news, but substantial effort is devoted to the preparation and dissemination of outlook and situation type information, including both on-campus and off-campus conferences and meetings, radio and television programs, and published materials. A number of colleges and universities have a long history of work in livestock marketing and regularly issue publications (monthly or weekly) devoted in full or in part to analyses designed to assist producers in both short- and long-run marketing decisions.

Commodity Futures Trading Commission

The Commodity Futures Trading Commission (CFTC)—established by the U.S. Congress in 1974, initially on a temporary basis—has been given the responsibility of supervising and regulating activities in the futures markets. CFTC replaced the Commodity Exchange Authority, which had been under the USDA. Although the basic functions of CFTC are supervisory and regulatory, it collects a substantial amount of data on futures trading that is made available to market analysts.

PRIVATE FIRMS, AGENCIES, AND ORGANIZATIONS

Newspapers, Radio, and Television

The management of news media usually respond to the interests of subscribers, listeners, and viewers, but that response is conditioned by the degree of interest shown, the availability of materials with which to satisfy the interest, and personal considerations. Since livestock producers continually request more and improved market information, there is no question about their interest, but that message is not always conveyed to media management. News media, generally speaking, are not organized to collect market infomation and must depend upon other sources. The Federal–State Market News Reporting Service has attempted to fill this need by making releases available through news wire services.

The available materials are utilized in varying degrees of coverage (from zero to full) by newspapers, radio, and television stations. Many areas lack adequate local newspaper accounts, and some of the more remote areas have problems with radio and television reception, yet these media often are listed by producers as being among their most important sources of information (Bohlen and Beal, 1967; Roberts, 1959). In most important livestock producing areas, certain newspapers, radio stations, and television stations have developed a respected reputation for livestock market reporting. These sources usually are known among local producers and market personnel or can be easily determined by inquiry from experienced stockmen or market representatives.

Farm and Trade Magazines

Farm magazines have been cited as one of the most important sources of livestock marketing information, and a large number of magazines cater to the livestock clientele (Roberts, 1959). Their coverage ranges all the way from general farm subjects to those devoted to a single aspect (such as feeding), a single specie, or even to a particular breed. The latter, however, are ordinarily less market oriented than others. Some magazines regularly devote a section to livestock marketing, and some utilize the services of special contributing editors or correspondents. Others include special articles at irregular intervals.

Trade magazines are oriented to the problems and issues of particular sectors of the industry; these may be commodity groups, such as wool or meat, or functional groups, such as wholesalers or retailers. The following magazines are cited simply as examples of the variety of interest groups: *Beef, Farm Journal, Farm Quarterly, Feedlot Management, National Hog Farmer, National Livestock Producer, Beef Digest, National Provisioner, Successful Farming, Progressive Farmer, Western Livestock Journal, Western Meat Industry, Progressive Grocer, Super Market News, Farm Futures, Meat Industry,* and *Commodities.*

Market Agencies

Many market agencies—i.e., commission firms, auction markets, and related organizations (such as livestock market foundations found at some terminals)—prepare and distribute market information. In most cases, emphasis is placed upon prices and market conditions of the particular market where the agency is located. A common form of presentation is the weekly market newsletter or card. Auctions and foundations often sponsor radio and television broadcasts.

Market agencies are frank in acknowledging a dual purpose in their market reporting activities, as follows: (1) a desire to provide information service, and (2) a determination to use this information as a competitive tool in market promotion and solicitation of business. From a business standpoint, both objectives are perfectly legitimate and tend to increase the degree of competition in the marketing system as long as the information is accurate and the methods of presentation are fair.

Personnel of progressive market agencies also personally visit the farms and ranches of customers and potential customers and participate in field programs. Again, these may have promotional and solicitation aspects, but at the same time they can be informational.

Market Analysis and Price Reporting Firms

A number of market analysis firms make a business of selling market information—usually on a subscription basis. This class of agency tends to be more specific in its forecasts and recommendations than most public agencies. A wide variety of services and reports are offered, ranging from monthly letters to daily private-wire reports and continuous toll-free-telephone advisory service. The frequency of reporting, extent of market coverage, and degree of analytical sophistication of the firm are usually reflected in the price charged. The following is in no sense a complete listing; the firms named are simply examples of this type of service: *Doanes Agricultural Digest, Kiplinger Agricultural Letter, National Provisioner's Daily Market and News Service* (the Yellow Sheet), *Meat Sheet* (the Pink Sheet), *The Helming Group, Farmers Grain and Livestock, Inc., Livestock Research Institute, Top Farmers Market News, Professional Cattle Consultants, Commodity News Service,* and *Reuters Limited.*

The Yellow Sheet and the Meat Sheet differ from the others listed here in two major respects. First, their coverage is devoted primarily to wholesale meat prices, whereas the others are concerned primarily with livestock. Second, they basically report market prices rather than perform analyses. They are unique examples of private firms in the area of price reporting in the livestock-meat industry complex—a field otherwise almost exclusively in the domain of public agencies. Both "Sheets" are mailed daily to paid subscribers by first class mail. In addition, subscribers may obtain, at extra cost, their market information through telephone or wire service. More innovative dissemination methods of market information include remote copier service, recorded telephone summaries, telex messages, and telephone interface with a central computer by way of computer terminals.

An important byproduct of the Computer Assisted Trading System (CATS) for wholesale meat and other types of electronic marketing pilot-tested in the early 1980's was market information. It appears that computer communications will play an important role in market reporting.

Industry Organizations

Producers Associations. The interest of producer organizations in livestock marketing dates back many decades. The Grange considered marketing problems a major issue shortly after the Civil War. Efforts of the Corn Belt Meat Producers Association and the American National Livestock Association to promote market news reporting have been mentioned. Every major farm organization has long been concerned with various aspects of marketing. Until recently, the efforts of producer organizations have been directed almost exclusively at public policy issues. Several such issues were mentioned in earlier chapters—monopolistic trade practices and the establishment of Federal grade standards. Within recent years, however, several producer organizations have taken a more direct approach to markeing problems in an attempt to shift the balance of bargaining power to producers.

Two of these organizations, both of which use privately developed market intelligence systems as a basic tool, merit special attention. They are the National Cattlemen's Association and the National Farmers Organization (NFO). The National Cattlemen's Association set up a separate corporation—Cattle Marketing Information Services, Inc. (CMIS)—to operate their service, appropriately dubbed "CATTLE-FAX." Both CMIS and NFO have developed systems for determining, on a relatively local basis, the number of livestock on feed, potential supplies at future dates, together with current prices, market conditions, and other market factors. In addition to data collected from its own members, each has access to and summarizes a great amount of market information made available by many other sources. This, however, is about as far as the similarity goes.

NFO is entirely a centralized operation. Information is funneled into a central office where it is used in contract negotiation with packers and other selling operations for the membership. CMIS assembles, analyzes,and interprets its information centrally but transmits it by telephone and by mail back to its members for their individual use (or for local pooled arrangements) in negotiating direct sales to packers. CATTLE-FAX subscribers pay a monthly fee—a fixed minimum plus a charge per head, up to a stipulated maximum total fee. The CATTLE-FAX service would be rather expensive for a single farm-sized cattle feeder, but pooled arrangements can be set up that allow several small operators to share the cost of an installation located in a bank or business establishment convenient to the group. NFO's cost is included in membership dues.

A number of other producer organizations are active in marketing work and provide varying degrees of market information but usually on substantially smaller scales than the two mentioned. The following are cited merely as additional examples (with no elaboration on their programs). The American Farm Bureau Federation (which sponsors the American Marketing Association), the American Sheep Producers Council, The Mid West Wool Association, The National Swine Producers Council, and the National Livestock Producers Association.

A variety of other industry organizations with interest in market information exists at different levels of the total livestock–meat marketing system. Only four will be cited here. The American Meat Institute (AMI) is mentioned as representative of the packer–processor sector of the industry: the Super Market Institute, Inc., and the National Association of Retail Grocers as representative of retailers: and the National Livestock and Meat Board, which cuts across all levels of the marketing system.

American Meat Institute.   A group of meat packers met in 1906 and organized the American Meat Packers Association. The name was changed to the Institute of American Meat Packers in 1919 and to the American Meat Institute (AMI) in 1940. Membership in AMI is composed of packers, processors, and associate members. Its major activities include sponsorship of research and educational and promotional programs. Although the AMI may be classed as a trade organization with primary allegiance to its members, its declared objectives and multidimentional program of activities are of direct and indirect benefit to the entire livestock–meat economy. The central office of this organization maintains a section devoted to continuous development of market information. Among its releases are *Financial Facts About the Meat Packing Industry, MEATFACTS,* and a weekly report. The *Financial Facts*, an annual, draws heavily from data collected directly by AMI and not available from any other source. Supplemented by government information, these original data are then made available to the public. *MEATFACTS* presents an annual statistical summary about the meat industry and draws heavily from the USDA and U.S. Department of Commerce data. The weekly release primarily is an AMI staff summary and interpretation of currently relevant government releases; its distribution is limited to members of the Institute. In 1966, the AMI, under authorship of its then Vice President and Director of Marketing, J. Russel Ives, published a book-length treatise entitled *The Livestock and Meat Economy of the United States*. This is a comprehensive treatment of the economic aspects of livestock production, meat packing, processing, wholesaling, and retailing.

Super Market Institute and National Association of Retail Grocers. These are trade organizations oriented primarily to the interest of their members. The National Association of Retail Grocers has a long history with food retailers, having been organized in 1893. The Super Market Institute was organized in 1937, concurrently with the rapid expansion in supermarkets. Both carry an extensive informational program covering all phases of retail operation. The Super Market Institute is somewhat unique in that it maintains a well-stocked and up-to-date library of informational materials on all aspects of food retailing.

National Livestock and Meat Board (NLMB). The NLMB is an industrywide organization whose directorate includes representatives (through organizations) from all sectors of the livestock–meat economy—livestock producers, market agencies, packers, processors, wholesalers, retailers, and eating establishments. Producer groups, however, hold about half the directorate positions. The NLMB was organized in 1923 as a nonprofit, nongovernmental service association. Its major activities are (1) sponsorship of research, (2) assembling of information, (3) carrying out of educational programs, and (4) promotion of meat, meat products, and merchandising techniques. Over the years, this organization has financed a wide variety of research ranging from highly technical characteristics of meat to applied techniques in marketing.

From an organizational standpoint, NLMB operates separate beef, pork, lamb, and sausage promotion programs under their respective Beef Industry Council, Pork Committee, Lamb Committee, and Sausage Council. The program of NLMB is financed through contributions by livestock producers in cooperation with participating marketing firms and meat packers. In the case of direct sales, marketing firms and packers assemble the funds from producer sales and forward them to NLMB. Upon a producer's request, however, the money is returned to him. It is estimated that contributions are made on about 45 percent of all livestock marketed and slaughtered. The Board also receives some direct contributions from organizations. The beef Promotion and Research Act incorporated into the 1985 Farm Bill provided enabling legislation whereby the livestock/meat industry set up a mandatory checkoff for producer marketing. Its continuance, however, depends upon a producer referendum. If continued, this will provide substantially additional funds for beef promotion and research.

The Board's informational and educational activities are directed primarily at the promotion of meat and, on the whole, are consumer-oriented. Demonstrations in meat cutting, merchandising, and cooking are performed by permanently employed specialists. A wide variety of charts, pamphlets, brochures, and visual aids are prepared by the Board's own experts (marketing specialists, nutritionists, home economists) and made available to communications media, professional groups (doctors, food specialists, food journalists), educational institutions, the meat trade, etc. Considerable effort is directed, on the one hand, toward meat merchandising, and, on the other, toward professional groups whose members are in a position to recommend meat as a food item or influence consumer attitudes toward meat.

REFERENCES

Anon. 1965. A half century of Federal Market News. *Am. Cattle Producer*, June, p. 15.

Bohlen, J. M., and Beal, G. M. 1967. Dissemination of farm market news and its importance in decision making. Iowa Agr. Expt. Sta. Res. Bull. 533.

Dietrich, R. A. 1967. Price information and meat marketing in Texas and Oklahoma. USDA Econ. Res. Serv. (in cooperation with Texas Agr. Expt. Sta. and Oklahoma Agr. Expt. Sta.) Agr. Econ. Res. Rept. 115.

Dowell, A. A., and Bjorka, K. 1941. *Livestock Marketing*. New York: McGraw-Hill Book Co.

Engleman, G. 1956. The role of livestock market news in a free pricing economy. Paper presented to Beef Cattle Breeders' and Herdsmen's Short Course, Univ. Florida, Gainesville.

Henderson, Dennis R., et al. 1983. Public price reporting. *In* Federal Marketing Programs in Agriculture, Issues and Options. Edited by W. J. Armbruster et al. Danville, IL.: The Interstate Printers & Publishers, Inc.

Newell, S. R. 1954. Reporting supplies and markets. USDA Yearbook Agr.

Phillips, V. B. 1961. Price formation and pricing efficiency in marketing agricultural products: The role of market news and grade standards. *Proc. 26th Ann. Conf. Natl. Assoc. Sci. Teachers*, Washington, D. C., April.

Pierce, J. C. (Undated.) The Livestock Division—its programs—its aims. USDA Consumer Marketing Serv. (unnumbered).

Roberts, W. P. 1959. Economics information for stockmen; where to find it. Wyoming Agr. Expt. Sta. Bull. 363.

Seufferle, C. H. 1960. Livestock marketing information. Nevada Agr. Expt. Sta. Cir. 28.

Smeby, A. B. 1961. History of livestock, meat, wool market news. USDA (unnumbered).

Straszheim, R. E. 1968. The how and why of government crop and livestock reports. Econ. Marketing Information, Indiana Farmers. Agr. Staff, Purdue Univ., June 28.

USDA. 1969A. The story of U.S. agricultural estimates. USDA Statist. Reporting Serv. Misc Publ. 1088.

USDA. 1969B. Market news keeps pace with livestock industry. USDA Consumer Marketing Serv., Agr. Marketing, July 4–5.

USDA. 1970A. The market news service on livestock, meat and wool. USDA Consumer Marketing Serv. Marketing Bull. 50.

USDA. 1970B. Federal–State market news reports—A directory of services available. USDA Consumer Marketing Serv. 21. Rev. Nov.

USDA. 1975. Glossary of terms. USDA Agr. Mktg. Serv. AMS–566.

USDA. 1983. Scope and Methods of the Statistical Reporting Service, USDA, SRS Misc., Publ. 1308.

Uvacek, E. Jr., and Goodwin, J. (Undated.) Interpreting livestock and meat market news. Southern Coop. Ext. Serv. Marketing Publ. 69–3.

Wasson, C. R. 1954. The market's nervous system. USDA Yearbook Agr.

16

Regulatory and
Inspection Measures

The livestock–meat industry is faced with a rather wide array of governmental regulations. Not all were set up specifically for the control of marketing problems (in fact, most were not), but all affect either directly or indirectly various aspects of the marketing system. As in other government regulations—whether they be for traffic control, drug control, antilittering, registration of firearms, property zoning, licensing, etc.—the basic justification for control (or restriction) of individual liberties is enhancement of the general welfare. General welfare is a broad term construed to include such concerns as health, economic well-being, social conditions, aesthetic values, humane consideration, etc. These do not represent static situations since human values change over time, technological and economic developments introduce new factors, and new knowledge is gained through study and research. Thus, the establishment of regulatory measures is not a once-and-for-all event; further changes may be expected. As stated by Brooks (1954), "The regulation of marketing is designed to promote the public welfare and, therefore, is to be modified or altered from time to time to meet the changing needs of the nation."

MEAT INSPECTION

Meat inspection is concerned with the wholesomeness, cleanliness, and truthfulness in labeling of meat and meat products. During the agrarian era when people slaughtered their own livestock, processed the meat, and consumed it themselves, there was little public concern about wholesomeness and sanitation; responsibility was left to individuals. The philosophy of individual responsibility carried over to commerce as the economy moved into the commercial era. The prevailing doctrine was *caveat emptor,* or "let the buyer beware." Some states and cities acted on behalf of the public with food inspection laws, however, and did so long before the Federal government. Nevertheless, forces were underway that finally led to action by the Federal government.

The first Federal move was prompted by problems in the export trade. By the late 1800s, the United States had a substantial export market in both pork products and beef, but there was stiff opposition from foreign countries on economic and political grounds, plus allegations of diseased beef and trichinosis from the consumption of U.S. pork. A number of countries imposed import restrictions that had a crippling effect on the U.S. meat industry (Clemen, 1923).

Loss of these markets aroused producers and packers to the extent that an act of Congress in 1890 required "the certification of certain meats processed for exportation. In 1891 and 1895 Congress extended meat inspection to partial protection of domestic consumers by requiring inspection of animals for disease before slaughter" (Crawford, 1954).

This act proved inadequate for full protection, however, and was followed by the Meat Inspection Act of 1906. One of the most influential factors for reform at that time as a description by Upton Sinclair of conditions in Chicago packing plants. This appeared in his 1906 novel *The Jungle* and received wide publicity in newspapers and magazines. Whether the report was fact or fiction, it aroused intense public attention and emotion.

The 1906 act maintained the antemortem inspection and added a compulsory postmortem inspection along with other features that substantially strengthened its effectiveness. The standards and procedures of the 1906 act set the pattern for meat inspection to this day. A major change, however, was made in 1967. Prior to 1967, authority for Federal meat inspection was limited only to meat that moved in interstate or foreign commerce. This left authority for inspection of meat moving in intrastate trade up to the individual states. The result was a hodgepodge of state and municipal regulations with adequate inspection in some states and none at all in others.

Even though nearly 85 percent of the nation's meat supply was produced in federally inspected plants, Havel (1968) reported that only 5,555 of the 14,832 meat facilities operated on an intrastate basis were currently subject to state or local inspection, leaving 9,277 plants exempt from any inspection controls. Congress, over much opposition, passed the Federal Meat Inspection Act, commonly known as the Wholesome Meat Act, in December, 1967. This act specified that by Dec. 1, 1969 each state was to have in operation inspection standards and procedures for red meat at least equal to those of Federal requirements or submit to Federal inspection of meat and plants in which meat was slaughtered for sale within that state's borders.[1] Farm slaughter of meat for home consumption was excluded. Subsequently, an additional year's extension was granted for compliance.

The purpose of meat inspection is to safeguard health by (1) eliminating diseased and otherwise unwholesome meat from human consumption, (2) maintaining sanitary conditions during slaughtering and processing, (3) preventing the addition or use of harmful ingredients, and (4) preventing false or misleading labeling of meat and meat products. This important, immense assignment requires a large and well-trained group of personnel. The basic core of employees are licensed veterinarians who are assisted by trained food inspectors.

The entire regulatory process includes examination of plants before granting approval as an FI plant, antemortem and postmortem inspection of animals and carcasses, inspection of plant operations, checks on ingredients used in processing, truthfulness of labels, checks on the inspection of imported meats, and inspection of plants in foreign countries that export meat to the United States. Operators desiring Federal inspection are required to submit plans and specifications of their plants to USDA. Examination of the plans and specifications is followed by examination of the plant. If the plant meets requirements, the operator is granted an official number that appears on the stamp used to mark the meat and meat products produced. The number identifies that particular plant. Shipments of meat bearing that number can easily be traced if the need arises.

Inspection regulations prescribe that animals be examined on the premises before they are brought to the killing floor (i.e., the antemortem inspection). This applies to all species. Any animal showing obvious signs of disease or disorders that are cause for condemnation is immediately tagged "U.S. CONDEMNED." If not already dead, it must be killed by an official of the establishment and placed in a disposition tank in the presence of an inspector. As the animal is placed in the tank, the inspector removes the tag and reports the disposition. Animals showing some signs for suspicion of disease or disorder that cannot be confirmed during the antemortem inspection are tagged "U.S. SUSPECT." These animals are slaughtered separately and given an extra thorough postmortem inspection to determine whether they should be condemned or passed.

Animals that pass the antemortem inspection are cleared for slaughter. At the time of slaughter, each carcass and viscera is carefully ex-

---

[1]The Wholesome Meat Act of 1967 covered inspection of all red meats but did not apply to poultry, fish, or certain wild game animals. Poultry inspection was covered in the Poultry Products Inspection Act of 1968.

amined. If evidence of abnormal conditions exists, the carcass is tagged "U.S. RETAINED," moved from the regular line, and kept in a locked compartment pending further examination. Depending upon the results of this examination, it is either condemned or passed. Carcasses that pass inspection are stamped with a circular brand bearing the plant number and the abbreviated inscription: "U.S. INSP'D & P'S'D" (see below).

This mark is imprinted with a harmless (edible) indelible fluid at various places on a carcass so that after breaking, the mark will show on various wholesale cuts. Under certain conditions parts of a carcass may be condemned and the remainder passed.

Processed meats are marked by a circular brand on the container or package, showing the establishment (plant) number and the wording "U.S. INSPECTED AND PASSED BY DEPARTMENT OF AGRICULTURE' (see below).

Inspection continues beyond the killing floor. In the processing departments, inspectors check to see that sanitary conditions are maintained, that added ingredients meet specifications, and that labeling is truthful.[2] Unlike slaughter inspection where each animal and carcass

[2]For example, a recent regulation to control the production and labeling of cured and smoked pork products on the basis of meat protein value rather than added substances (PFF—Protein Fat-Free) was introduced by USDA in 1984 and became final and binding on April 15, 1985. Under PFF regulations, the burden and responsibility of meeting the minimum protein requirements and accuracy of labeling rest with the processing plant. USDA, through its FSIS, has the monitoring and enforcement responsibility.

is examined, not all processed products are inspected. The emphasis in processing plants is on monitoring production and operations. Periodically, samples of processed products, ingredients, containers, and wrapping materials are selected for laboratory analysis.

The meat-processing industry has taken advantage of advanced technology and quality-control systems to provide effective production control and ensure product consistency and compliance with inspection laws and regulations. In an attempt to cut the Federal government's costs and regulatory burden, USDA made use of existing industry practices and technological achievements to introduce a voluntary quality-control system, known as Total Quality Control (TQC), in September, 1980. Under this system, meat-processing plants with good quality records for cleanliness may apply for FSIS approval of the TQC program. If approved, plant inspectors continue to spot-check TQC plants by unannounced inspections and use system-generated data in addition to their own observations on wholesomeness and labeling accuracy. Some observers believe that inspectors can review a much broader scope of plant operations in a more objective manner because of the new and better data available. It should be emphasized that *only meat-processing plants* can qualify under the TQC program. Daily inspection at slaughtering plants remained unchanged.

A similar but less comprehensive quality-control system, known as Partial Quality Control (PQC), is also available. PQC is the exercise of quality control on only a single aspect of plant operation. A plant may have a number of them. When a plant changes to TQC, all of the PQCs are incorporated in the TQC.

The meat inspection service also covers imported meats. No country is permitted to ship to the United States unless its own inspection system rates at least equal to that of the United States. The export country designates and certifies which of its plants may ship to the United States. These plants are then inspected at least once a year by a USDA foreign review officer. Inspectors at U.S. ports of entry check inshipments (on a sample basis) for wholesomeness and cleanliness. Meat inspection is carried out under the Federal Meat and Poultry Inspection program, which is administered by the Food Safety and Inspection Service (FSIS), formerly the Food Safety and Quality Service (FSQS) of USDA.

Packers sometimes buy slaughter animals from producers "subject to inspection"—a practice used with animals that show some reason for possible condemnation. The agreement between packer and producer usually stipulates a price that will apply if the carcass (or part of it) passes inspection, and payment is usually withheld pending inspection. This practice has features beneficial to both producers and packers. Without it, packers would undoubtedly either reduce their offering price enough to compensate for the risk factor involved or simply refuse to buy such animals. At the same time, producers are afforded a market for animals they might not be able to sell otherwise and which they probably would hesitate to slaughter for home consumption.

In 1984, 95.5 percent of cattle, 92 percent of calves, 97 percent of hogs, and 97 percent of all sheep and lambs—together producing more than 95 percent of all red meat—were slaughtered under Federal inspection (USDA 1985). These percentages increased substantially following the Wholesome Meat Act of 1967 but have tapered off in recent years. Most plants now have USDA or equivalent inspection so that further increases will be largely from new plants.

Under provisions of the Meat Inspection Act, a series of regulations was issued in 1978 to effect a lowering of the level of sodium nitrite (or the equivalent potassium nitrite) in the production of bacon. These regulations were prompted by concern over the reported relationship between nitrosamines in fried bacon and the occurrence of cancer. Nitrites have been used for many years in bacon production for control of botulism organisms.

The cost of Federal meat inspection is borne by the Federal government—except that, when plants operate overtime, plant owners reimburse the Federal government for overtime worked by inspectors.[3] Furthermore, "the cost of preparing, equipping, and maintaining the plant to meet inspection requirements, as well as losses resulting from condemnation of animals, carcasses, or products" are also borne by the plant's owner or operator (USDA, 1984). The government publishes a guide to construction and layout of plants for operation under Federal inspection. This publication is revised to reflect past experience of both

---

[3]Overtime inspection fees in 1985 were: $21/hr for basic overtime and holiday inspection, and $35/hr for laboratory services. In 1985, in an attempt to assist in cutting Federal spending, the administration proposed a new "user fee" to be phased in over three years in order to defray the cost of the mandatory meat and poultry inspection program. Many in the meat industry and trade organizations (e.g., AMI) opposed what they called a "meat tax" proposal on the ground that it discriminates against meat and that it could erode consumer confidence in the meat inspection program. They argued that the regulated should not pay for regulations and that consumers benefit more from inspections. FSIS suggested that, although the inspections benefit consumers, they also help the industry maintain consumer confidence in products. Strong industry lobbying, supported by many in Congress, succeeded in removing the proposal from the fiscal year 1986 budget. However, some members of the meat industry still believe that the "meat tax" issue may surface in the future.

the government and industry in design, building, altering, and maintaining such plants (USDA, 1984).

It is estimated that the cost of inspection is less than one-half cent per pound of red meat. By any reasonable standards, that must be considered a very nominal cost for insurance of wholesome and clean meat. In an excellent study of the benefits of meat inspection, Roberts (1983) indicated that available information suggest the cost-effectiveness of Federal efforts in meat inspection.

FOOD, DRUG, AND COSMETICS ACT

Public concern over the wholesomeness of food during the period previously mentioned was not limited to meat. The separate Meat Inspection Act attests to the particular importance attached to meat, but concurrently with the passage of the Meat Act, Congress also enacted a Food and Drug Act. Both of these Acts were signed on the same day—June 30, 1906—by President Theodore Roosevelt. This action dealt a *coup de grace* to the doctrine of *caveat emptor*. The major purpose of the Food and Drug Act was to assure the public of wholesome, sanitary, unadulterated, and truthfully labeled foods. Changing conditions, new products, and new technology since that time necessitated changes in and strengthening of the law. This was accomplished by the Food, Drug, and Cosmetics Act of 1938, which, as amended, provides the framework of today's pure food and drug regulations. Administration of these Acts was under the Department of Agriculture from 1906 to 1940, at which time it was transferred to the Federal Security Agency. In 1953, the Federal Security Agency was reorganized and became the Department of Health, Education and Welfare (HEW), which became the Department of Health and Human Services (HHS) in the late 1970s. This agency currently administers the Act under its Food and Drug Administration (FDA).

The concurrent enactment of a separate Meat Act and a Food and Drug Act might appear to indicate Congressional intent that the Meat Act cover all aspects of regulation with respect to meat. Changing circumstances, however, have introduced new problems. The two agencies—i.e., USDA's FSIS and HHS's FDA—cooperate in some areas. One of the areas of recent mutual concern is residues in meat resulting from the use of feed additives, drugs, and pesticides. USDA inspectors test for such residues on a random sampling basis and turn findings over to the FDA for enforcement. FDA has the authority to initiate criminal prosecution of producers who market livestock containing illegal drug and hormone residues.

ANIMAL DISEASE CONTROL

Early U.S. history recorded numerous costly outbreaks of animal disease. Effective veterinary treatments were not available. Quarantines were applied in some areas to restrict the spread of disease and counter quarantines were applied in other areas as retaliatory measures. As a result, "Our system of interstate and export animal transportation was denounced as a disgrace and an outrage on the first principles of humanity. There was a growing demand for protection of the public health in connection with the meat supply" (Van Houweling, 1956). A Veterinary Division established in the USDA in 1883 was given responsibility for developing information on the prevalence of animal disease and means of controlling and eradicating disease. In 1884, Congress enacted *An Act for the Establishment of the Bureau of Animal Industry.*

Currently, authority and responsibility at the Federal level for control and eradication of animal disease is lodged in the Animal and Plant Health Inspection Service (APHIS) of USDA. Its programs are carried out in cooperation with the states.

An interaction exists between disease control and meat inspection programs. The more effective the degree of control, the fewer animals and carcasses will be condemned during inspection. Disease detection during inspection often assists in disease control because use of purchase records, brands, tags, etc., can often trace the origin back to a particular owner or locality where control measures can be applied. Disease control activities, of course, are not limited to meat inspection but are also carried out by Federal inspectors stationed at designated public markets, by state inspectors at local markets, and by veterinarians in their regular practice.

Detection is followed up by appropriate measures, depending upon the circumstances. With some diseases—e.g., foot and mouth disease— immediate disposal is called for. In other cases, movement of the animals is restricted in some way—quarantine may be imposed, treatment or immunization required, or immediate sale for slaughter ordered (as is the case with brucellosis reactors). Generalization about state restrictions is difficult because of the varying rulings among states. At federally inspected public markets, diseased animals are segregated and disposed of under supervision of an inspector. Contaminated vehicles, pens, and premises are disinfected under supervision of an inspector and the state of origin is notified. Outshipments of animals that pass inspection are certified for interstate shipments.

At the international level, a complete embargo is enforced on the importation of live animals or fresh meat from countries infected with especially dreaded diseases, such as rinderpest and foot and mouth disease. Livestock may be imported from so-called "clean" countries, but under strict inspection. Each year substantial numbers of feeder cattle are imported to the U.S. from Mexico and Canada. These cattle must come in through designated ports of entry where they are examined by U.S. inspectors.

Disease control measures of foreign countries are still a factor in U.S. livestock and meat exports. In relation to total U.S. production, the exportation of livestock is relatively small, yet it has increased substantially in recent years. Breeding cattle is by far the major item, with lesser numbers of sheep, lambs, hogs, and horses. "The major obstacle that U.S. cattle face is in meeting certain foreign requirements for Blue Tongue disease, once thought to occur only in sheep but now known to affect cattle as well" (Dobbins, 1968). The U.S. exports only a minor tonnage of meat, but overseas sales of certain products (lard, tallow, variety meats, hides, and skins) are very important to the industry. It is impractical to attempt to list detailed restrictions imposed by particular countries on the importation of U.S. products. A number of restrictions are based on presence of animal disease, some are based on hormone residues. Ostensibly, these regulations are enforced in the interest of public health, but in some cases there are strong suggestions that they are also used to control imports for economic and political reasons.

FEDERAL TRADE COMMISSION

The Federal Trade Commission (FTC) was established in 1914 by enactment of the Federal Trade Commission Act. The conditions that led to the establishment of the FTC have been discussed in earlier chapters. This was just one step in a series of governmental actions designed to curb unfair trade practices and a tendency toward monopolization of trade by big business. Prior to FTC, there had been the Interstate Commerce Commission Act (1887) and the Sherman Antitrust Act (1890). The Interstate Commerce Commission (ICC) was the first Federal regulatory agency empowered to control railroad rates and services. Its purpose was to eliminate rate discrimination among shippers and cut-throat competition among carriers. The Sherman Antitrust Act was designed to curb industrial monopoly. Both had a common purpose of restraining monopoly, but the approaches were substantially different. The ICC Act, in effect, made public utilities of the railroads. It might be noted parenthetically that a Special Studies Subcommittee of the U.S. House of Representatives, House Government Operations Committee, in a 1969 study, recommended creation of a public utility type of commission to regulate the U.S. cattle industry. Opposition in both legislative branches killed this proposal.

The approach under the Sherman Act was an effort to make competition effective by outlawing (1) certain restraints to trade, (2) monopoly, and (3) attempts to monopolize. Largely as a result of judicial difficulties in defining and interpreting terms as well as administrative apathy, Congress in 1914 tried to clarify the situation by enacting the Federal Trade Commission Act and the Clayton Act. The Clayton Act listed a series of practices that specifically were declared to be unfair and illegal. The FTC was established as the watchdog agency to determine violations. Its major role now is the investigation of unfair trade practices and the issuance of rulings. Major actions are turned over to the courts.

One of FTC's early actions was an investigation of practices in the meat-packing industry in 1917. This investigation has already been mentioned (Chap. 8) as a major factor in the Packers Consent Decree of 1920—an agreement whereby the five major packers of that time consented to abide by a number of stringent trade and operational specifications. Those packers have periodically tried to gain modifications of the Consent Decree, but the courts and Department of Justice stood firm on all original specifications until 1971. At that time, the Department of Justice agreed to an amendment freeing the remaining four concerned packers (Swift & Co., Armour & Co., Wilson & Co., and Cudahy Co.) from a restriction on production and distribution of more than 100 specified product lines. The amendment allows manufacturing and wholesaling but maintains the original restriction on retailing. As indicated earlier, the 1920 Packer's Consent Decree was abolished by a Chicago Federal judge in November, 1981.

PACKERS AND STOCKYARDS ACT

The Packers and Stockyards Act of 1921 was an attempt to provide relief for livestock producers who charged packers and market agencies with a variety of unfair and monopolistic practices. The Act was originally administered by the Packers and Stockyards (P&S) Administration—an agency directly responsible to the Secretary of Agriculture, USDA.[4] The Act consists of five Titles: Title I—definitions; Title II—

---

[4]Administrative reorganization in 1977 placed the agency under the Agricultural Marketing Service (AMS) of the USDA and dropped the word "Administration" from its title. However, this was changed again in 1980, and the original designation, i.e., Packers and Stockyards Administration, was reinstated.

antitrust provisions concerned with meat packers; Title III—unfair trade practices provisions and regulations of public stockyards; Title IV—general provisions; and Title V—provisions related to live poultry dealers and handlers (USDA, 1978). Until mid 1970s, approximately 75 percent of the P&S resources were devoted to Title III (stockyards) activities and the remaining to Title II provisions. In 1981, however, only 60 percent of P&S resources were devoted to stockyards regulations and 40 percent to packers. This shift is a reflection of the recent public concern over the change in the structure of the U.S. livestock-meat economy, including integration and concentration tendencies.

Major provisions of the Act, as they apply to particular types of markets, were discussed in Chap. 7. In general, the act is designed to regulate the business practices of those engaged in the buying and selling of livestock and meat that enter interstate and international trade. Regulations cover the activities of stockyard companies, market agencies, dealers, packer buyers, and meat packers.

With respect to livestock marketing (USDA, 1969B), the Act specifically prohibits any stockyard owner, market agency, or dealer subject to its jurisdiction from engaging in any unfair, unjustly discriminatory, or deceptive practice or device in connection with the receiving, marketing, buying, selling, feeding, watering, holding, delivery, shipment, weighing, or handling of livestock.

By definition, the term "packer" is rather broad. In addition to those who buy livestock across state lines for slaughter, "those who manufacture or prepare meats or meat food products for sale or shipment in interstate commerce are also packers, including wholesalers, fabricators, restaurant and hotel suppliers, and food chains who purchase meat in commerce for fabricating or other processing or preparation" (USDA, 1969B). Packers may not (USDA, 1969B) (1) engage in or use any unfair, unjustly discriminatory, or deceptive practice; (2) make or give any undue or unreasonable preference or advantage to any person or locality, or subject any person or locality to any undue or unreasonable prejudice or disadvantage; (3) agree or arrange with any other packer to apportion purchase or sale territories or supplies for the purpose or with the effect of restraining commerce or creating a monopoly; or (4) engage in any act for the purpose of, or with the effect of, manipulating or controlling prices, creating a monopoly, or restraining commerce.

An amendment in 1968 required that payment for livestock purchased on grade and yield basis be made on hot carcass weight. This was a much debated issue. Prior to the 1968 amendment, a wide variety of arrangements prevailed for adjusting hot weight to its cold equivalent, with resulting dissatisfaction among producers. A general feeling existed that shrinkage adjustments in calculating cold weight tended to favor the packers. The 1968 amendment provided for uniform tare adjustments for the weight of rollers, gambels, hooks, and other equipment. Presumably, carcass grade and weight arrangements are now more uniform.

Producers who have reason to believe they have suffered loss or damage from violations of the P&S Act may petition for reparations by filing a written complaint with an area supervisor or directly with the Secretary of Agriculture within 90 days of the wrongful action. Areas and locations of area offices are shown in Fig. 16.1. Some of the more commonly mentioned unfair trade practices that would justify filing a complaint are: dishonest weights, failure to pay for livestock, failure to rectify a mix-up in ownership of livestock, misrepresentation of livestock, etc. Upon receiving a complaint, P&S carries out an investigation without charge.

Under administrative authority, the P&S Administration issued a regulation in 1974 prohibiting dual ownership of packing plants and custom feedlots. Packers may own and operate feedlots for their own

Fig. 16.1.   Areas and Locations of P & S Area Offices. (Courtesy of USDA, P & S.)

livestock or may place that livestock in custom feedlots but are prohibited from owning a custom feedlot.[5]

An important amendment in 1976 assures prompt payment to producers from the sale of slaughter livestock. Producers had advocated such a law for years, but Congress did not act until the bankruptcy of a leading beef packer left Midwest cattle feeders with some $20 million of unpaid cattle sales. Under this amendment, packers who buy $500,000 or more of livestock a year must carry a bond equal to a two-day kill.[6] Buyers of slaughter livestock must pay sellers by the close of the business day following the sale, unless buyer and seller mutually agree otherwise. The law also provides that if a packer pays by check, the account receivable proceeds therefrom, and the product inventory of the packer is held in trust to cover the value of the producer's sale until the packer's check is cleared by the buyer's bank. The 1976 law applies to interstate meat wholesalers, brokers, dealers, and distributors as well as packers.

Problems have existed for some time in the sale of livestock that are under liens held by lending agencies. Under traditional law, if the livestock owner did not pay off the loan, the buyer could become liable. A Clear Title Law was incorporated into the 1985 Farm Bill to make liability more specific. It contained two options, as follows:

1. Each state may enact specific provisions for the central filing of liens (which would require a complex classification scheme), this file designed so as to provide buyers with names of lenders so that the lender's name may be listed on payment checks. If this option were not taken, then in December 1986 a second option would automatically become effective.

2. Under the second option, it is incumbent upon lenders to give prior notice to potential buyers of livestock that they have a loan on the animals and want to be listed as payee on checks at time of sale.

HUMANE TREATMENT OF LIVESTOCK

The 28-Hour Law

One of the earliest Federal laws related to the marketing of livestock was a statute enacted in 1873 intended to alleviate cruelty to livestock

---

[5]In September 1984, the P&S replaced the rule that prohibits meat packers from owning custom feedlots by a policy statement.
[6]In 1982, P&S proposed the elimination of bonding requirements for small livestock dealers (which would have included about 3,000 dealers and order buyers) with less than $500,000 annual sale. In face of widespread industry opposition, the P&S dropped the proposal.

while in transit on railroads (Dowell and Bjorka, 1941). The Act stipulated that livestock could not be kept in continuous transit more than 28 hours without a rest stop. At a maximum of 28 hours, the livestock were to be unloaded, fed, watered, and rested for at least five consecutive hours. Transportation agencies were made responsible for furnishing the necessary facilities and services. In practice, however, the facilities and services actually furnished were often inadequate. Due to aroused sentiment, the 1873 Act was replaced and another—known as the 28-Hour Law—was passed in 1906. The purpose of this Act was similar to the earlier one, but it was more specific with respect to minimum quantity of feed, cleanliness of water, and methods and procedures for handling stock during loading and unloading. In cars that were loaded with sufficient space for each animal to lie down, feeding and watering were permissible without unloading. In addition, the 1906 Act provided for an eight-hour extension, or a total of 36 hours, upon request. This law is still effective.

A limitation of time in continuous transit has economic as well as humane implications. Extended deprivation of feed, water, and rest undoubtedly results in discomfort and suffering. Prior to the Act, periods of 60 hours or more in transit were reported. However, the associated costs of such handling are important. Shrinkage, bruising, crippling, and death increase with time in transit. This law was effective in accomplishing both the intended objective of alleviating cruelty and reducing its related costs. The need for such a law is considerably diminished now. Improved, faster freight service makes it possible for many shipments to reach their destination within 36 hours, and with expeditious service, shipments from mid-country can reach either coast with only one rest stop. Trucks were not included in the provisions of the original law, but most buyers of livestock, for economic reasons, insist on a rest stop during any extended trip—whether the haul be by rail or truck.

Humane Slaughter Act

Public sentiment over alleged cruelty to livestock during slaughter reached a peak during the 1950s. Methods of handling, shackling, stunning, and killing were considered inhumane and abhorrent by some people. A campaign for modification of slaughter methods culminated in the Humane Slaughter Act of 1958. Provisions of the Act instructed the Secretary of the U.S. Department of Agriculture to prescribe humane methods and made that office responsible for their administration. Unlike many laws, this Act did not prescribe criminal penalties for noncompliance, but it did stipulate that government must purchase meat exclusively from plants using humane methods, and this was a persuasive provision. Among other features, this Act provides for keeping animals relatively calm prior to stunning, and using electrical, mechanical, or chemical methods for rendering the animals unconscious prior to killing.

As was mentioned with respect to the 28-Hour Law, humane slaughtering has economic as well as humanitarian aspects. Capital requirements for complying with the recommended mechanical methods are negligible, consisting usually of a captive bolt stunner, a small-caliber gun type of device. These devices are faster and use less labor than previous methods. The cost of electrical stunners and carbon-dioxide tunnel installations (the common chemical method) are offset by the attendant elimination of shackling and associated equipment, but probably the most important economic plus is that fewer pork carcasses suffer the bruises and damaged parts that resulted from the shackling and hanging previously required prior to the sticking of hogs.

Provisions of the Act exempted killing methods used in religious rituals such as kosher slaughtering. Even though compliance with this law is not manatory per se, it is reported that most meat is produced under approved methods.

Commodity Futures Trading Commission Act

Trading in livestock and livestock product futures is regulated under the Commodity Futures Trading Commission (CFTC), an autonomous agency of the Federal government. Trading in commodity futures has a long history. As mentioned in Chap. 13, the Chicago Board of Trade was organized in 1848. Although the market served a useful economic purpose, a number of abuses were evident from time to time in the price manipulation and undue price fluctuations associated with speculative maneuvering. Bills were introduced in Congress as early as 1884 in attempts to provide Federal supervision and regulation of trading. It was not until 1922, however, that the first law was passed—the Grain Futures Act. This Act was amended and renamed the Commodity Exchange Act in 1936.

The 1936 Act, with subsequent amendments, remained the basic law for the maintenance of fair and honest trading in commodity futures markets until the CFTC was established by congressional mandate in 1974. The commission became effective in 1975, with its major responsibility being the prevention of price manipulation and unfair trading practices—involving among other things, the regulation of registration requirements, financial standards, and trading practices. The definition of hedging was broadened from the rather narrow concept specified in the Commodity Exchange Act.

Major emphasis of the 1963 Act and subsequent amendments is placed on the detection of attempted speculative price manipulation and trading activities that distort competitive prices. Some publications on early efforts at "cornering the market" depict an action-filled, romantic situation, but, to a hedger or legitimate speculator who may be caught in a distorted market, the situation is anything but romantic.

MEAT IMPORT LAWS OF 1964 AND 1979

The question of regulating (either restricting or encouraging) the supply of meat, like any other product, raises extremely complex issues. Conflicts of interest are inherent between producers and consumers, between producers and importers, and within the producing sector itself. At the national level, the interest of a particular group may be incompatible with the overall national interest, a point that will be discussed further in Chap. 17, "International Trade." Cattle producers during the early 1960s became deeply concerned over rising imports of beef. Concern had been expressed on previous occasions, but the problem had seemed to ebb and flow without reaching major proportions. Occasionally, imports would increase to about 5 percent of total beef production, usually in response to relatively high U.S. prices, and then drop back to about 1 percent as U.S. prices declined. A nominal tariff had been imposed on livestock and meat for many years, and this, along with tariffs in general, had been reduced from a high point in the 1930s. As mentioned in an earlier section, a complete ban had been enforced for many years against the importation of fresh meat from countries infected with rinderpest and/or foot and mouth disease. The situation was different, however, in the late 1950s and early 1960s.

Long-term trends in beef imports has been upward since the mid 1950s (see Fig. 16.2). In the early 1960s, beef imports increased to more than 10 percent of total U.S. production—about twice the level of previous high points in the early 1950s. A number of factors were involved, but a major one was the discontinuance of an agreement in 1958 between Great Britain and Australia whereby Australia no longer was required to ship stipulated quantities of low-grade beef to Great Britain. The U.S. market was the most lucrative outlet in the world, and substantial quantities began coming in, not only from Australia, but from New Zealand, Ireland, and other countries. The situa-

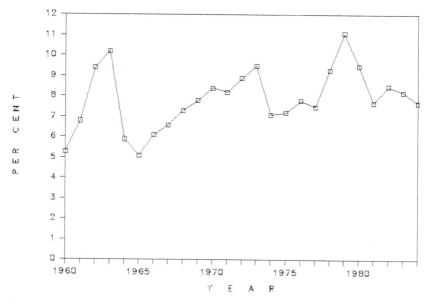

Fig. 16.2. U.S. Beef Imports as a Percentage of Total Beef Production, 1960–1984. (Plotted by authors from USDA data.)

tion was compounded by relatively high production in the United States.

Attempts were made during the late 1950s and early 1960s to control the meat import situation through voluntary agreements with major exporters. More stringent types of regulation were viewed unfavorably by State Department officials because an effort was under way to implement a broad tariff liberalization policy. Spokesmen for the cattle industry, however, did not view voluntary control as a satisfactory solution to the problem.

The Meat Import Act of 1964

After a series of hearings, Congress enacted the Meat Import Law (Public Law 88–482) in August, 1964, to become effective Jan. 1, 1965. This bill provided for import quotas, based on a formula, for fresh, chilled, and frozen beef, veal, mutton, and goat meat, including both carcass and boneless meat but not pork, lamb, or canned meats. The purpose of the law was to limit annual imports of the specified meats to a level comparable to a selected base period (1959–1963) with an annual adjustment ("growth factor") based on changes in domestic production relative to the base period.

The base quota was established as the average annual quantity imported during the base period (1959–1963), which was 725,400,000 lb (329,000 metric tons). Each year the growth factor is determined by calculating the percentage by which the estimated U.S. commercial production of the specified meats in the current calendar year and the two preceding years (i.e., a three-year moving average) exceeds (or falls short of) the average annual U.S. production during the base period. Thus, to determine the growth factor at the beginning of a given year, it is necessary to estimate production for that year. The calculated growth factor is then multiplied by the base quantity to determine the amount of increase (or decrease) in the base. This increase (or decrease) added to the base gives an adjusted base quota. With U.S. production on an increasing trend for the period following enactment, the typical annual adjustment was upward. The Act allowed a 10-percent leeway above the adjusted base quota before quotas would be applied to individual countries. Thus, a "quota trigger point" was determined at 110 percent of the adjusted base quota.

In this process, the Secretary of Agriculture is required to estimate at the beginning of each quarter year the quantity of prospective imports. If the quantity of prospective imports exceeds the trigger point, the President is required to invoke a quota on imports of these meats. In case quotas are imposed, the total import quota would be allocated among exporting countries on the basis of shares supplied by those countries during a representative period.

The law also contains provisions for extraordinary conditions, however, under which the President can suspend or increase quotas. These were as follows:

1. If he determines it necessary because of overriding economic or national security interests.
2. If the supply of meat is inadequate to meet domestic demand at reasonable prices.
3. If international agreements are entered into after enactment of the Act that have the same effect as the Act.

It is seen that the Meat Import Law provided for a flexible quota. As U.S. production increased, the quota increased. At the time it was passed, there was a considerable body of opinion that imports would never reach the trigger point. In the late 1960s, however, it became apparent that imports would reach that point unless some action were taken. In an effort to avert the necessity of invoking mandatory individual quotas, the Secretary of Agriculture, in the fall of 1968, began a program of negotiating voluntary quota agreements with exporting countries—an action based on provisions of the Agricultural Act of 1956. Among the major exporters, only Canada refused to go along with this program. Most countries abided by the agreements on direct shipments,[7] but some exported meat to Canada where it was then transshipped to the United States. These negotiations have continued until the present time (mid 1980s).

When it appeared in 1970 that the trigger point would be exceeded, President Nixon, under requirements of the act, issued a proclamation, on June 30, "to place a limitation on imports of meats covered by the Act." At the same time, the President suspended the limitation, as authorized by law, after determining that "this action was required by the overriding interest of the United States" (USDA, 1970B). Thus, it may be said that quotas were triggered but immediately rescinded. The same sequence has occurred several times in subsequent years. On two occasions when domestic meat prices increased substantially from previous levels (1973 and 1978), the President has authorized increased imports above the trigger point—ostensibly in the public interest.

Prior to 1977, substantial quantities of beef and veal were brought into the U.S. by way of Foreign Trade Zones in circumvention of import quotas. That loophole was closed by an administrative regulation in late 1976 that specified that, beginning January 1, 1977, any foreign beef or veal processed in Foreign Trade Zones, possessions, or territories and shipped into the U.S. must be included in the quota of the country of origin.

The Meat Import Act of 1979

Provisions of the Import Law of 1964 caused imports to increase when domestic production increased and decrease when domestic production decreased—with a slight lag caused by the three-year moving-average feature. Since price movements bear an inverse relationship to available supplies, the Acts tended to accentuate price swings associated with production cycles, thus causing production and price destabilization. This result has provoked several proposals to amend the law to make effects of imports contra cyclical. On December, 31, 1979, President Carter signed the Meat Import Act of 1979 (Public Law 96–177). The new law replaced all provisions of the 1964 Act but retained its intent: to provide mandated control on meat imports. In addition, the new law required that the average carcass weight of imported live cat-

---

[7]Several Central American countries were exceptions and were issued mandatory quotas.

tle (excluding breeding stock) be subtracted from production in calculating annual quotas and in arriving at base production.

As with the 1964 law, the Secretary of Agriculture is required to publish an adjusted-base import quantity for the coming year before the first day of January and to report on the status during the year. Unlike its predecessor, however, the 1979 law uses a countercyclical approach to calculate allowable meat import levels. A new average annual quantity imported during the 10-year period from 1968 to 1977 replaces the previous base quantity. The new base is 1,204.6 million pounds (546,400 metric tons). In calculating annual quotas, two factors are considered—production factors and countercyclical factors. Most imported beef is comparable to beef derived from the slaughter of domestic cows, (i.e., beef used for hamburgers and processed meats). The formula used in calculating the annual quota specifies cow beef production in determining the countercyclical adjustment. The new annual quota formula is as follows:

$$\text{Annual quota} = \left[\begin{array}{c}\text{Average}\\\text{annual}\\\text{imports}\\(1968\text{--}77)\end{array}\right] \times \left[\dfrac{\begin{array}{c}3\text{-yr moving}\\\text{average of}\\\text{domestic}\\\text{production}\end{array}}{\begin{array}{c}10\text{-yr average of}\\\text{domestic}\\\text{production}\\(1968\text{--}77)\end{array}}\right] \times \left[\dfrac{\begin{array}{c}\text{Per-capita 5-yr}\\\text{moving average of}\\\text{domestic cow beef}\\\text{production}\end{array}}{\begin{array}{c}2\text{-yr moving average}\\\text{of domestic cow beef}\\\text{production}\end{array}}\right]$$

The 1979 law gives the President limited authority to suspend any quantitative limitations in the Act by giving 30 days notice and proclaiming that his proposed action is in the best economic and/or security interest of the nation. Whereas specific quotas and presidential proclamations have been imposed only to a minor degree, existence of the law has had a considerable psychological effect on negotiations for voluntary restraint agreements with exporting countries.

POLLUTION CONTROL

Widespread public concern with environmental degradation reached major proportions during the 1960s. Livestock feedlots, with large numbers of animals in highly concentrated circumstances, give rise to air pollution from feedlot odors and water pollution from waste materials carried in water run-off.

Pollution problems are indirectly related to marketing in that regulations designed to control pollution influence the location of feedlots, which, in turn, affects transportation costs and competitive position with respect to both feed and feeder livestock procurement and sale of finished livestock.

A number of states have enacted legislation designed to protect the interests of both the public and feedlot owners. One common form of regulation is to require a license, or permit, for operation of a feedlot. Requirements for obtaining a permit vary but usually include provisions for adequate drainage and control of run-off. One of the most vexatious problems arises when housing developments expand into the vicinity of a long-established feedlot and the occupants begin to complain of feedlot odors. Protestations of both water pollution and air pollution have resulted in the closing of some commercial feedlots, notwithstanding valid permits and licenses. Concern with ecological values undoubtedly make feedlot pollution an increasing problem.

The Federal government, under authority of the U.S. Environmental Protection Agency (EPA), has extensive pollution control requirements, many of which apply to livestock feedlot operations.

REFERENCES

Acker, D. 1963. *Animal Science and Industry.* Englewood Cliffs, NJ: Prentice-Hall.

Brooks, N. 1954. The wide range of regulation. USDA Yearbook Agr.

Clemen, R. A. 1923. *The American Livestock and Meat Industry.* New York: Ronald Press.

Commodity Futures Trading Commission. 1978. Report on farmer's use of futures market and forward contracts. Commodity Futures Trading Commission (unnumbered), Feb. 15.

Crawford, C. W. 1954. The long fight for pure foods. USDA Yearbook Agr.

Dobbins, C. E. 1968. Past and prospects: U.S. livestock in export market. *USDA Foreign Agr.* 6, No. 46:1-3.

Dowell, A. A., and Bjorka, K. 1941. *Livestock Marketing.* New York: McGraw-Hill Book Co.

Fowler, S. H. 1961. *The Marketing of Livestock and Meat.* 2nd ed. Danville, IL: Interstate Printers & Publishers.

Gast, L. L. 1969. USDA's watchdog is added protection. USDA Agr. Res. Serv., Agr. Marketing, Sept. 4.

Gunderson, F. L., et al. 1963. *Food Stondards and Definitions in the United States.* New York: Academic Press.

Havel, J. T. 1966. Inspection of interstate meat in Kansas. *In* Your Government. Univ. Kansas, Sept. 15.

Johnson, A. C., Jr. 1977. Public regulation of futures trading in the United States. University of Wisconsin, Dep. of Agr. Econ. Economic Issues, No. 9.

Kauffman, R. R. 1965. Recent Developments in futures trading under the Commodity Exchange Act. USDA Commodity Exchange Authority Agr. Inform. Bull. 155.

Lee, R. F., and Harper, H. W. 1966. Meat and poultry inspection. USDA Yearbook Agr.

Roberts, Tanya. 1983. Benefit Analysis of Selected Slaughtering Meat Inspection Practices. NC. Proj. 117, WP-71, Wisc. Sept.

USDA. 1952. The inspection stamp as a guide to wholesome meat. USDA Agr. Infor. Bull. 92.

USDA. 1956. The little purple stamp. *USDA Agr. Research* 4, No. 12:4–10.

USDA. 1969A. His mission: Consumer protection. *USDA Agr. Marketing* 14, No. 11:3.

USDA. 1969B. The Packers and Stockyards Act, what it is and how it operates. USDA P&S Amin. PA-399, Rev. Aug.

USDA. 1970A. Commodity Exchange Act As Amended. USDA Commodity Exchange Authority (unnumbered), Rev. Feb.

USDA. 1970B. Livestock and meat situation. USDA Econ. Res. Serv. LMS-174.

USDA. 1971. Accurate weights, guidelines for weighing livestock. USDA Packers and Stockyards Administration, PA-986.

USDA. 1974. Regulations and statements of general policy issued under the packers and stockyards act. USDA Packers and Stockyards Administration (unnumbered), June.

USDA. 1975. Packers and Stockyards Act. USDA Packers and Stockyards Administration, PA-1019.

USDA. 1978. Packers and Stockyards Act, 1921, As Amended. USDA Packers and Stockyards Administration, Nov.

USDA. 1984. U.S. inspected meat and poultry packing plants. A guide to construction and layout. USDA, FSIS, Agr. Handbook 570, Apr.

USDA. 1985. Livestock slaughter 1984 summary. USDA, SRS, CRB, MtAn 1-2-1(85), Washington, D. C., Mar. 15.

USHEW, 1970. Requirements of the United States Food, Drug and Cosmetics Act. U.S. Health, Education, Welfare, FDA Publ. 2.

Vanhouweling, C. O. 1956. Our battle against animal diseases. USDA Yearbook Agr.

Williams, W. F., and Stout, T. T. 1964. *Economics of the Livestock-Meat Industry.* New York: Macmillan Co.

Ziegler, T. 1965. *The Meat We Eat.* Danville, IL: Interstate Printers & Publishers.

17

International Trade in Livestock, Meat and Wool

International trade in meat involves only about 6 percent of the world production, but this relatively small proportion disguises significant economic and political situations. Two particularly important economic aspects are as follows: (1) At any given time, the import–export position of a given country may deviate substantially from the average of the overall world situation; and (2) over the years, the import–export position of a country can (and does) change.

With regard to the former, the United Kingdom exports virtually no beef, but in recent years has imported nearly 40 percent of its consumption. On the other hand, Australia and New Zealand import no beef but export approximately 50 percent of their production. The United States exports substantial quantities of some products and imports others. Many of the less developed countries subsist almost entirely on their own production. Thus, to say that only 6 percent of the world's meat moves in international trade ignores the fact that some countries are highly dependent upon imports, some are highly dependent upon exports, some are dependent upon both, and others are virtually independent.

The United States furnishes a good example of a country whose import–export position has changed dramatically over time. U.S. exports of both pork and beef expanded rapidly following the Civil War. As may be seen in Figs. 17.1 and 17.2, exports reached a peak about World War I, then dropped precipitously, and have remained low since then with the exception of a brief rise during World War II and a slightly increasing trend since the early 1960s. An equally dramatic change is apparent in imports of beef, which have increased from virtually nothing prior to World War I to over 2 billion pounds (0.907 billion kg) in recent years. The U.S. became a net importer of beef since late 1940s (Fig. 17.1). Imports of pork, although much less than of beef, have picked up significantly, exceeding pork exports since the early 1950s.

Such changes over time, and differences among countries in import–export balances, prompt the question: What gives rise to international trade?

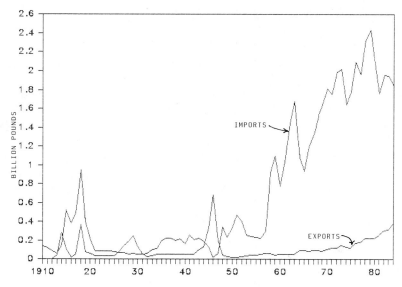

Fig. 17.1.   U.S. Beef Exports and Imports, 1910–1984. (Plotted by authors from USDA data.)

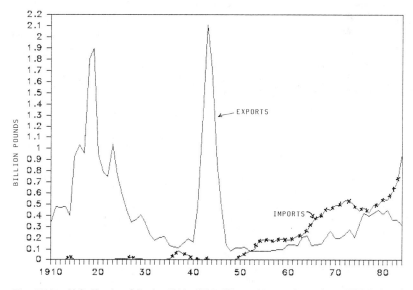

Fig. 17.2.   U.S. Trade of Pork, 1910–1984. (Plotted by authors from USDA data.)

BASES FOR INTERNATIONAL TRADE

International trade has individual as well as general welfare implications. At the national level, trade policy is governed by a mix of economic and political considerations that may vary from country to country. From the standpoint of individuals, the motive that generates trade is essentially the same whether the trade be local, regional, or international in scope. That motive is profit. In the absence of artificial restriction, an incentive exists to move goods internationally if the price in an importing country is high enough to cover production costs as well as cost of moving the product to that country and at the same time allow for a reasonable profit. From the consumer's standpoint, an incentive exists to buy imported goods when such goods can be purchased more cheaply than domestically produced products (of equal quality).

These conditions, however, are simply reflections of more basic, underlying economic conditions. Why are some countries able to produce certain products more cheaply than others? Why doesn't a single low-cost country produce the entire world's supply of a given product?

The Principle of Absolute Advantage

The United States can produce cameras, but the cost is higher than the price of cameras shipped in from Japan, for example. Japan can raise hogs, but if they want pork, it can be purchased from the United States at a price less than the cost of producing it in Japan. These blunt statements of apparent fact gloss over some difficult problems in comparing absolute costs but serve to provide an introduction to basic factors behind specialization and trade.

The following hypothetical example illustrates the gain for each country by specializing and trading. Assume that with one unit of labor and capital the United States can produce either 1000 lb of pork or 12 cameras. With an equivalent expenditure of labor and capital, Japan can produce 800 lb of pork or 20 cameras. Now, if the United States and Japan each devoted two units of labor and capital to production, and if *each* produced *both* items, the total output would be:

	Pork Production (lb)	Camera Production (No.)
United States	1000	12
Japan	800	20
Total	1800	32

On the other hand, if each devoted two units of labor and capital to production of the product in which it has an absolute advantage, the result would be as follows:

	Pork Production (lb)	Camera Production (No.)
United States	2000	—
Japan	—	40
Total	2000	40

In total production, the gain is 200 lb of pork and 8 cameras.

By trading at an exchange of 1000 lb of pork for 20 cameras, each could have pork and cameras as follows:

	Pork (lb)	Cameras (No.)
United States	1000	20
Japan	1000	20
Total	2000	40

It is apparent that in the absence of trade restrictions, each would specialize, trading would follow, and each would benefit. But what makes it possible for one country, or one area, to gain an absolute cost advantage over another? Generally speaking, the contributing factors can be classified as follows:

1. Natural phenomena, such as climate, geographic characteristics, or natural resources
2. Particular attributes or characteristics of the people
3. Capital accumulation and industrial development
4. Differing proportions of available resources relative to the demands for them

Many examples could be given where geography, climate, or natural resources give an area an absolute cost advantage in producing certain products compared to other areas. Natural phenomena are particularly important in the production of feed supplies for livestock, and feed is the primary factor in livestock production. Natural forage is usually the cheapest feed for maintaining breeding herds of cattle and ewe flocks and in producing grass-fed beef. Thus, the vast range areas of the United States, Argentina, Australia, and New Zealand have a decided absolute cost advantage over such areas as central Europe, say, in producing grass-fed cattle or maintaining breeding stock.

In addition to natural phenomena, human skills and capabilities play an important role in costs of production. Education, training, and experience vary greatly around the world. This is true in all industries, including livestock production. Custom and tradition also can be important modifying forces. In Nigeria, for example, the Fulani tribesmen are superb cattle husbandrymen. Yet the centuries-old tradition of accumulating cattle as a symbol of wealth tends to limit the off-take of their herds. Human characteristics, customs, traditions, and religious beliefs also have varying effects on the demand for goods, and particularly the demand for meat. In India, beef is not eaten by a large segment of the population. There and elsewhere, the orthodox of Islam and of the Jewish faith do not eat pork.

Capital accumulation and associated industrial development affect the costs of production directly, and, indirectly (through effects on personal income), the demand for meat and other products. The more highly developed countries have a tremendous head start on less developed countries in capital accumulation. Without this build-up, large-scale enterprises and economies of size would be impossible. Producers in countries so favored hold a competitive cost advantage over their counterparts in less developed countries.

The relative proportions of available resources also influence the way those resources may be most profitably utilized. An example in contrast would be Belgium and New Zealand. Belgium may be better suited to lamb production than New Zealand from the standpoint of soil and climate, but since Belgium has a much higher human population density, she must specialize in higher valued land-use—high-yielding grain and forage crops, industrial production, etc. New Zealand has relatively less pressure on its land and can utilize it for lamb production.

Cost differences arising from such factors are evident for many goods in many countries, and often the differences are obvious. Kansas can hardly compete with Honduras in producing bananas. Niger cannot compete with the United States in producing heavy construction equipment. Great Britain cannot produce grass-finished beef as cheaply as Argentina, and so on. Yet a comparison of costs in different countries is a tenuous undertaking, especially in the not-so-obvious cases. Differences exist in monetary units and exchange rates. The applied technology differs greatly, as does the available mix of resources and other factors. Fortunately, it is not necessary to depend upon analyses of absolute costs. Another approach is available: the determination of "comparative costs" or "comparative advantage."

The Principle of Comparative Advantage

Let the following assumptions hold for an elementary case of just two countries—the United States and a foreign country—and two products—grain-finished beef, say, and watches. There are no artificial barriers to trade (such as tariffs, quotas, exchange controls, etc.). both countries have the natural resources, manpower, skills, and capital to produce either or both products. The cost structure is such that with one unit of labor and capital, the United States can produce 1800 lb of fed beef or six watches. The foreign country, with one unit of labor and capital can produce 600 lb of fed beef or four watches. Clearly, the United States has an advantage in the production of both products, but it is apparent that its advantage in the production of beef is greater than in watches. The foreign country is at a disadvantage in both products, but its disadvantage is least in the production of watches.

Suppose, furthermore, that each country uses two units of resources in producing beef and one unit in producing watches. The total quantity produced would then be as follows:

	Beef Production (lb)	Watch Production (No.)
United States	3600	6
Foreign country	1200	4
Total	4800	10

Now let the United States specialize and devote all three units of resources to beef production and the foreign country specialize entirely in watch production. Total production would then be as follows:

	Beef Production (lb)	Watch Production (No.)
United States	5400	—
Foreign country	—	12
Total	5400	12

The United States would not be interested in trading unless it could get a watch for something less than 300 lb of beef, for it can produce a watch at that ratio of resources use (1800:6). The foreign country would not be interested in trading unless it could get more than 150 lb of beef per watch (600:4). Assume the bargaining settles at 200 lb of beef for one watch. If 1,400 lb of beef were exchanged for seven watches, the distributions of the two goods would be as follows:

	Beef (lb)	Watches (No.)
United States	4000	7
Foreign country	1400	5
Total	5400	12

Both countries in this case would benefit by specialization and trading at the indicated terms of trade, even though the United States was shown to have an advantage in the production of both products.

A generalization, referred to as the "principle of comparative advantage," emerges from this set of circumstances and may be stated as follows: Countries gain by producing the products in which they have either the greatest comparative advantage or the least comparative disadvantage.

Does this mean that certain countries would produce the entire world's supply of some products and other countries the entire supply of other products? The answer is qualified. Many countries are at such a decided disadvantage in the production of some goods that no output would be feasible. It would be advantageous for most countries to produce a variety of goods, however, particularly when transfer costs are taken into consideration. The relative cost situation also changes as any given country attempts to expand production and exploit its advantage. As production increases, unit costs eventually rise. It is unlikely, therefore, that any one country will produce the entire world's supply of a given product on the basis of comparative advantage.

Conflicting Interests in International Trade

The above are theoretical concepts—explanations of economic pressures behind international trade in a freely competitive situation. The real world, however, deviates considerably from the perfectly competitive model. For one thing, the competitive model assumes mobility of resources, and resources do not move freely within a country, let alone between countries. In spite of possible gains, governments around the world have instituted a wide array of obstacles to international trade such as tariffs, licenses, quotas, arbitrary control of exchange rates, etc. Among the reasons given for such restrictions are the protection of new industries, the shielding of established industries from the rigors of foreign competition, retaliation for another country's restrictions, and the desire to encourage domestic production (in an effort to avoid dependence upon imports in time of war or to avoid a situation of weakness in international politics).

Most countries encourage exports through such measures as domestic subsidies, overseas promotion, etc. Sometimes, they tax exports in an effort to discourage outmovements and keep the product available for domestic use, and, on occasion, they encourage imports to bolster domestic supplies. Usually, however, governments tend to restrict imports as a measure of protection for home industries. As noted in the previous chapter, the U.S. Meat Import Laws of 1964 and 1979 provided for import quotas as a protective device for the U.S. cattle industry. Similar import quotas are found in other countries. For example, meat quota policies in Japan and South Korea have provided protection to local beef production for many years.

Import restrictions may be achieved through Voluntary Export Restrictions (VERs). Under this system, exporting countries curtail shipments to an importing country to avoid those countries' protectionist measures, such as tarrifs. Allen et al. (1983) analyzed the economic and welfare effects of VERs. In the case of beef, they indicated that an exporting country can actually improve its welfare position through VERs by capturing tariff equivalent revenue (export tax). On the other hand, importing countries usually suffer a welfare loss. The empirical results of the study indicate that exporting countries adopt VERs on beef shipped to the U.S. gain about $8.3 million annually, whereas the net welfare loss to the U.S. averages $35.3 million—resulting from a $70 million benefit to producers and a $105 million loss to U.S. consumers. They concluded that "Because VERs cannot be justified by the United States with efficiency criteria, their use must be based on a desire to convert $3.00 of consumer welfare into roughly $2.00 of producer welfare while maintaining the semblance of free-trade posture."

Arguments for and against free trade center around three different points of view:

1. Its effects on particular industries—or more precisely, individuals within particular industries
2. Its effects on the general national interest, irrespective of the implications to individuals
3. Its worldwide effects, irrespective of the implications to particular countries or individuals

If "world welfare" were the goal, all barriers to trade and migration of people would be removed. Some workers in traditionally low-wage countries would be expected to move to high-wage countries. The resulting tendency for wages to even out would raise average world wages—to the benefit of some individuals but the detriment of others. If national welfare were the goal, it might be suggested that relatively cheap beef be imported from Australia. The usual argument is that consumers in general would benefit from the resulting decrease in cost of living, but another result would be a decline in cattle prices to the detriment of cattle producers. Many cattle producers also produce wheat, and the export market is vital for wheat. A given individual may find it advantageous to favor import restrictions on beef but oppose a foreign country's restrictions on wheat imports. Thus, conflicts of interest arise within an industry, between individual and national interests, and between national and world interests. These are exceedingly complex issues, having political and social as well as economic implications.

Governments have responded over the years to a multitude of pressures and considerations. Broad policy objectives set the guidelines within which specific regulations are applied to particular products. And the general policy objectives can, and do, change. In 1930, the Smoot-Hawley Tariff Act culminated a highly protectionist policy—a policy of high tariffs. This policy drew retaliatory trade restrictions from other countries, and international trade was choked off. The United States changed its policy in 1934 under the Reciprocal Trade Agreements Program, which was aimed at reducing tariffs. Liberalization of trade has been the general policy ever since, and tariffs on many products have been substantially reduced as a result. The policy, however, has met opposition whenever individual industries have felt a particular disadvantage. As mentioned, the beef cattle industry is a case in point. Swine producers are also seriously questioning the rising importation of pork.

In spite of numerous governmental impediments, large quantities of meat and substantial numbers of livestock do in fact move in international trade. In countries with advantageous cost conditions and various programs of government encouragement, there is constant pressure to export meat to favorable price markets. Changing cost structures continually alter the production/cost ratios among countries. These forces, together with supply-demand structures, continually alter the price levels. The U.S. beef industry provides an example of the effect of such changes on trade. With the opening of vast range areas during the last half of the 1800s and early decades of the 1900s, the United States possessed both an absolute and comparative advantage in grass-finished beef production. In spite of numerous health and tariff restrictions, American exporters opened a sizable market in European countries. Following World War I, trade wars, largely in a form designed to protect home industry and combat world-wide depression and unemployment, reduced most international movements. Economic recovery during and following World War II brought relative affluence to the United States, and, with it, a growing demand for grain-finished beef. This resulted in a relative shortage and increased price for the lower quality beef used in hamburgers and processed meats. In the meantime, producers in the low-cost range areas of Australia, New Zealand, Argentina, and other countries not only took over the European market but began extensive shipments of grass-finished beef into the United States. Partially instrumental in these developments were various subsidies and incentive programs that encouraged production in some of the exporting countries, but the main factors were relative costs of production and meat prices in the respective countries. Export–import activity then and now attests to the importance of the economic forces that lie behind international trade.

Meat Trade

As may be seen in Table 17.1, beef and veal comprise about 42.5 percent of the total world red-meat production, 8 percent of which enters international trade. Pork comprises 50 percent of world red-meat production, and 4 percent of it enters world trade. In contrast, lamb, mutton, and goat meat amounts to only 7.5 percent of world red-meat production, but the proportion entering world trade is almost double that of beef, or about four times as much as pork. International trade in

Table 17.1. Red Meats: Percentage of Total World Production and Percentage Moving in International Trade, 1983.

Item	Beef and veal*	Pork	Lamb, mutton, and goat meat	Total
Percentage each specie is of total world red meat production	42.5	50.00	7.50	100.00
Percentage of production moving in international trade†	7.90	4.05	15.00	6.23

Source: FAO (1984A and 1984B).
*Including buffalo meat.
†Based on quantities exported worldwide.

red meat bears little resemblance to the free trade envisioned in the competitive model. Virtually every country has restrictions of one sort or another on meat trade.

Beef. Table 17.2 shows the import–export movements of beef and veal for important producing and consuming countries. Beef exports of a country are influenced by production capacity, current weather conditions, the stage of the cattle cycle, and national economic and

Table 17.2. Beef and Veal: International Trade in Selected Countries, Average 1975–79, 1980, and 1983.*

Region and country	Avg. 1975–1979 Exports	Avg. 1975–1979 Imports	1980 Exports	1980 Imports	1983[†] Exports	1983[†] Imports
			Weight (1,000 metric tons)			
North America:						
Canada	46	101	65	80	95	95
Costa Rica	43	—	32	—	32	—
Dominican Rep.	3	—	3	—	3	—
El Salvador	4	—	2	—	2	—
Guatemala	22	—	13	—	9	—
Honduras	29	—	35	—	17	—
Mexico	30	1	1	1	8	2
Nicaragua	39	—	27	—	15	—
Panama	2	—	1	—	4	—
United States	52	916	80	946	123	893
Subtotal	270	1,018	259	1,027	308	936
South America:						
Argentina	563	—	469	—	420	—
Brazil	138	65	169	65	450	20
Colombia	17	—	12	—	18	—
Uruguay	126	1	117	—	210	—
Venezuela	—	39	—	46	—	51
Subtotal	844	105	767	111	1,098	71
Europe:						
EEC:						
Belgium/Lux.	47	53	72	45	85	40
Denmark	167	1	174	1	170	2
France	281	214	309	263	362	294
W. Germany	206	253	342	246	345	200
Greece	—	87	—	110	—	100
Ireland	291	3	382	5	280	12
Italy	15	334	70	366	50	380
Netherlands	165	86	226	125	238	55
U. Kingdom	116	466	168	397	150	310
Subtotal[‡]	1,288	1,497	1,743	1,558	1,680	1,393

Table 17.2. (*continued*)

Region and country	Avg. 1975–1979 Exports	Avg. 1975–1979 Imports	1980 Exports	1980 Imports	1983[†] Exports	1983[†] Imports
			Weight (1,000 metric tons)			
Austria	10	14	15	11	22	7
Finland	—	1	1	2	15	—
Portugal	—	30	—	13	—	—
Spain	—	55	3	17	—	20
Sweden	7	17	14	11	27	5
Switzerland	—	16	5	13	2	16
Subtotal	17	133	38	67	66	48
Bulgaria	14	9	30	1	25	1
Czechoslovakia	13	13	10	15	50	25
E. Germany	21	5	33	—	30	—
Hungary	64	10	100	5	50	—
Romania	67	1	95	5	75	1
Poland	45	23	43	35	10	40
Yugoslavia	59	29	66	75	65	30
Subtotal	283	90	377	136	305	97
USSR§	31	231	35	385	30	335
Africa:						
South Africa	19	48	12	13	—	52
Egypt	—	15	—	95	—	110
Subtotal	19	63	12	108	—	162
Asia:						
China (Taiwan)	—	12	—	17	—	20
Israel	—	40	—	32	—	55
Japan	—	129	—	174	—	185
Rep. of Korea	—	23	—	2	—	60
Philippines	—	13	—	5	—	6
Turkey	—	—	—	—	20	—
Subtotal	—	217	—	230	20	326
Oceania:						
Australia	977	—	840	—	730	—
New Zealand	352	—	346	—	355	—
Subtotal	1,329	—	1,186	—	1,085	—
Total selected countries	4,081	3,354	4,417	3,622	4,592	3,368

Souce: USDA (1983).
*Carcass weight equivalent basis.
[†]Preliminary.
[‡]Including intra-EEC trade.
§Estimated based on USSR statistics and on Trading Partner data. Reported on product weight basis.
Notice: Dash indicates no trade or trade less than 1,000 metric tons.

political policies. For many years, Argentina was the leading exporter, but, in the early 1970s, Australia emerged as the leader. Argentina's decline was related to national policies that discouraged production and trade and also to unfavorable weather. Argentina still has the capacity to produce and could regain the lead if the proper economic incentives were provided.

The rank of various countries in beef exports changes some from year to year, but typically the same six or eight countries are found near the top. In addition to Australia and Argentina, they include New Zealand, Ireland, France, the Netherlands, West Germany (the Federal Republic of Germany), Denmark, Uruguay, and Brazil. Mexico and Central American countries individually export only relatively minor quantities, but their shipments increased in the late 1970s, and collectively they have the potential for assuming a more important role in world trade. For the continent of Africa, data are available for only a few countries. Currently, African trade is relatively insignificant. Should African countries gain control over disease and improve sanitation in packing plants, however, Africa will make its presence known in the beef trade.

The United States is the major importer of beef—a position she acquired from the United Kingdom during the 1960s. During the 1975–79 period, the United Kingdom, on the average, was a strong second, followed by Italy, West Germany, the USSR, and France. It should be noted that West Germany, like several other European countries, has a sizable trade in both imports and exports of beef and veal. Generally, these are not identical products. Some countries import wholesale cuts of fresh meat, which are then processed and reshipped in the processed form. In recent years, Japan has joined the top 10 importers of beef.

Pork. Denmark, long renowned for superior quality bacon and hams, is the chief exporter of pork, and her neighbors—the Netherlands, Belgium, and Luxembourg—are also important exporters (Table 17.3). These countries have for many years carried out effective breeding, feeding, and processing programs with rigidly enforced specifications designed to produce bacon, hams, and other pork products that meet the highly discriminating British consumer standards. Five eastern European countries—East Germany, Hungary, Poland, Yugoslavia, and Romania—are likewise surplus pork producers and move substantial quantities in the international market. Ireland is one of the few European countries with a substantial net surplus of both pork and beef. The determination of these European countries to participate in international meat trade, coupled with the powerful economic forces

Table 17.3.   Pork: International Trade in Selected Countries, Average 1975-79, 1980, and 1983.*

Region and country	Avg. 1975-1979		1980		1983†	
	Exports	Imports	Exports	Imports	Exports	Imports
			Weight (1,000 metric tons)			
North America:						
Canada	53	63	117	17	170	11
Mexico	1	6	—	11	3	—
United States	126	212	114	249	92	298
Subtotal	180	281	231	277	265	309
South America:						
Brazil	7	—	—	—	4	—
Colombia	—	—	—	—	—	—
Venezuela	—	3	—	7	—	—
Subtotal	7	3	—	7	4	—
Europe:						
EEC:						
Belgium/Lux.	239	22	227	29	200	25
Denmark	556	1	683	—	740	—
France	45	240	52	289	52	330
W. Germany	32	341	63	424	90	470
Greece	—	9	—	16	—	32
Ireland	37	3	55	8	53	9
Italy	36	267	39	344	45	330
Netherlands	513	36	602	41	665	45
U. Kingdom	16	512	23	534	35	540
Subtotal‡	1,474	1,431	1,794	1,685	1,880	1,781
Austria	2	3	5	5	4	1
Finland	13	1	25	—	33	—
Portugal	—	8	—	—	—	—
Spain	1	37	1	9	1	6
Sweden	31	9	34	5	51	4
Switzerland	1	6	2	5	1	4
Subtotal	48	64	67	24	90	15
Bulgaria	24	—	19	—	20	—
Czechoslovakia	2	6	3	6	—	—
E. Germany	130	3	209	—	245	—
Hungary	50	2	92	—	150	—
Romania	61	—	60	—	75	—
Poland	92	15	98	11	30	40
Yugoslavia	31	6	29	9	40	8
Subtotal	390	32	510	26	560	48
USSR§	16	70	—	120	—	100

(continued)

Table 17.3. (*continued*)

Region and country	Avg. 1975–1979		1980		1983†	
	Exports	Imports	Exports	Imports	Exports	Imports
			Weight (1,000 metric tons)			
Asia:						
China (Taiwan)	26	—	24	—	35	—
Japan	—	174	—	155	—	210
Rep. of Korea	4	4	—	—	—	—
Philippines	—	1	—	1	1	1
Subtotal	30	179	24	156	36	211
Oceania:						
Australia	3	—	—	—	3	—
New Zealand	1	1	—	1	—	1
Subtotal	4	1	—	1	3	1
Total selected countries	2,149	2,061	2,626	2,296	2,838	2,465

Source: USDA (1983)
*Carcass weight equivalent basis.
†Preliminary.
‡Including intra-EEC trade.
§ Estimated based on USSR statistics and on Trading Partner data. Reported on product weight basis.
Notice: Dash indicates no trade or trade less than 1,000 metric tons.

alluded to earlier, is reflected in the fact that their canned bacon, ham, and other meat products may be found on the shelves of food stores throughout the United States. The United States and Canada also export significant quantities of pork products, primarily of lard, variety meats, casings, etc.

Not included in Table 17.3 are lard and other fats. The United States is the major producer, user, and exporter of these products.

The United Kingdom is the clear leader in pork imports. West Germany, the United States, Italy, and France are substantial importers, but at a significantly lower level than the U.K. Japan has emerged as an important importer in recent years. Even though the U.S. is listed as a leader in both exports and imports of pork, she imports two to three times more than she exports.

Lamb, Mutton, and Goat Meat.   Import–export movements of lamb, mutton, and goat meat are shown in Table 17.4. Goat meat is a minor fraction of the total, but it is an important food in certain countries—particularly in some Near Eastern and African countries not shown in these tabulations. New Zealand is in a class by itself in the exportation

Table 17.4. Lamb, Mutton, and Goat Meat: International Trade in Selected
Countries, Average 1975-79, 1980, and 1983.*

Region and country	Avg. 1975–1979 Exports	Avg. 1975–1979 Imports	1980 Exports	1980 Imports	1983[†] Exports	1983[†] Imports
			Weight (1,000 metric tons)			
North America:						
United States	1	15	1	15	1	9
South America:						
Argentina	35	—	18	—	22	—
Europe:						
EEC:						
Belgium/Lux.	—	13	1	17	1	10
Denmark	—	2	—	—	—	3
France	1	46	1	38	6	52
W. Germany	9	27	9	30	1	26
Greece	—	11	—	8	—	17
Ireland	11	—	16	—	17	—
Italy	—	15	—	12	—	15
Netherlands	14	2	15	2	6	1
U. Kingdom	39	226	37	191	36	205
Subtotal[‡]	74	342	79	298	67	329
Portugal	—	—	—	—	—	—
Spain	1	2	1	1	1	—
Subtotal	1	2	1	1	1	—
Bulgaria	16	1	35	1	30	1
Czechoslovakia	—	1	—	1	—	—
E. Germany	2	—	5	—	6	—
Hungary	5	1	4	—	3	—
Romania	42	—	53	—	55	—
Poland	—	—	—	—	—	—
Yugoslavia	3	—	3	—	6	—
Subtotal	68	3	100	1	100	1
USSR§	—	72	—	157	—	155
Africa:						
South Africa	—	1	—	1	—	3
Egypt	—	2	—	13	—	5
Subtotal	—	3	—	14	—	8
Asia:						
Rep. of Korea	15	16	13	13	7	7
India	4	—	3	—	20	—
Israel	—	—	—	1	—	—

(continued)

TABLE 17.4. *(continued)*

Region and country	Avg. 1975–1979 Exports	Avg. 1975–1979 Imports	1980 Exports	1980 Imports	1983† Exports	1983† Imports
			Weight (1,000 metric tons)			
Japan	—	269	—	157	—	170
Turkey	4	—	6	—	50	—
Subtotal	23	285	22	171	77	177
Oceania:						
Australia	238	—	247	—	200	—
New Zealand	406	—	450	—	592	—
Subtotal	644	—	697	—	792	—
Total selected countries	846	722	918	657	1,060	679

Source: USDA (1983)
*Carcass weight equivalent basis.
†Preliminary.
‡Including intra-EEC trade.
§Estimated based on USSR statistics and on Trading Partner data. Reported on product weight basis.
Notice: Dash indicates no trade or trade less than 1,000 metric tons.

of lamb and mutton—accounting for 50 percent or more of all international shipments. Australia is the next most important exporter. Together, these two "down under" countries move approximately 76 percent of all lamb and mutton. Nevertheless, Romania, Bulgaria, the United Kingdom, Turkey, and Argentina also export sizeable quantities.

The chief importers of lamb, mutton, and goat meat are the United Kingdom, Japan, and the USSR. Additional important importers are France, West Germany, Greece, Canada, and the United States. Interestingly enough, the increasing importance of the USSR is a relatively recent development.

Horsemeat. Horsemeat is important in the United States only as a source of pet food but it is commonly used as human food in northern European countries and in Japan. Japan is the leading importer followed by Belgium, Luxembourg, the Netherlands, and France. Argentina and Brazil are the outstanding sources of horsemeat—accounting for more than one-half of all international shipments. Other South American countries, Mexico, Canada, and Poland are likewise suppliers.

Cattle Hides and Calf and Kip Skins

Often overlooked in discussions of the livestock economy is the extensive and important trade in hides and skins. The production and availability of hides and skins parallel the production of live animals. Expanding world cattle production has increased the availability of these products, and, in spite of stiff competition from synthetics, a relatively strong world-wide demand exists for hides and skins.

Prior to the 1960s, Argentina was the leading hide exporter, but in recent years that role has been taken over by the United States, which now dominates the world's exports of hides and skins. For example, during the 1976–78 period, U.S. exports accounted for about 44 percent of total world exports—up from 35 percent in 1970. Other leading suppliers are Australia, Canada, France, West Germany, Spain, Yugoslavia, Poland, and Czechoslovakia. It should be pointed out that although Argentina was replaced by the U.S. as the world's leading exporter of hides and skins, it continues to export large quantities of finished leather goods, a form of planned integration to capture an attractive value added.

In recent years, the leading producers of calf and kip (the untanned hide of a young animal) skins have been the United States, France, Argentina, West Germany, New Zealand, Australia, and Italy. In exports, however, the leaders have been the Netherlands, France, the United States, New Zealand, and West Germany.

A major change among importers of skins has been the recent rapid rise to leadership of Spain. Other important importers are Japan, Korea, West Germany, and Italy.

Wool Trade

World wool production reached a peak in 1968, then turned downward until 1973, reached another minor peak in 1975, followed by a two-year drop. Although the trend since 1977 has been upward (Fig. 17.3), U.S. production continues its decline of many years (Table 17.5 and Fig. 17.4) despite a government incentive program designed to encourage the domestic industry. Congress enacted a law in 1954 providing for incentive payments to wool growers with the stated purpose of maintaining U.S. production at at least 300 million pounds a year—an action prompted by the belief that wool is a strategic war material. Producers, however, have not responded to the incentives. Lack of labor on the big ranches is given as a chief cause. The fact that sheep on family farms consistently return more income per dollar invested than

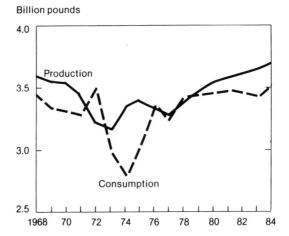

Billion pounds

Fig. 17.3. World Production and Consumption of Raw Wool, 1968–1984 (Clean Content Weight. Production Data on a Marketing Year Basis). (USDA Exten. Serv. undated.)

Table 17.5. Wool: Domestic Production, Exports and Imports of Raw Clean Wool, U.S., 1970–1983

Year	Domestic production*	Exports	Imports	Total supply[†]
		Weight (1,000 pounds)		
1970	88,158	200	152,135	241,093
1971	85,142	6,318	126,575	205,399
1972	90,762	11,224	96,639	176,177
1973	81,726	3,726	60,125	138,125
1974	73,525	4,271	26,947	96,201
1975	67,488	7,674	33,626	93,440
1976	62,197	1,130	57,463	118,530
1977	58,455	385	58,958	117,028
1978	55,082	425	50,404	105,061
1979	56,022	313	42,330	98,039
1980	56,398	304	56,483	112,577
1981	57,916	307	74,251	131,860
1982	55,755	1,351	61,421	115,825
1983[‡]	52,940	1,104	78,059	129,985

Source: USDA (1984A).
*Shorn and pulled wool. Conversion factors from grease basis to clean basis are as follows: Shorn wool production—47.7 percent from 1970–71 and 52.8 percent from 1972–1983; pulled wool production—72.9 percent from 1970–1983.
[†]Production minus exports plus imports; stocks not taken into consideration.
[‡]Preliminary.

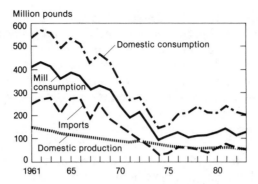

Fig. 17.4.   U.S. Production, Imports, and Consumption of Raw Wool, 1961–1983 (Clean Basis). (USDA Exten. Serv. undated.)

do other livestock has not been able to stem the drift to other livestock or to crop enterprises.

In the period following World War II, domestic demand for wool was weakened by the wide acceptance of man-made fibers (domestic and imported) and from imported wool and wool fabrics. The importation of raw wool remained at a relatively high level until the late 1960s, but then a precipitous decline set in. The same pattern applied to the foreign trade balance of wool textile products, especially apparel wool, until the early 1980s, at which time imports began to increase (Table 17.5).

Wool produced in the United States is used chiefly in the fabrication of clothing, blankets, etc. The wool used for rugs, on the other hand, is all imported. Australia and New Zealand are the chief suppliers of wool, followed by South Africa and the countries of South America.

U.S. MEAT ANIMAL IMPORTS AND EXPORTS

The economics of transporting meat compared to live animals limits the international movement of slaughter animals to trivial numbers. Small but significant movements of breeding stock take place, however, and, as far as the United States and her neighbors are concerned, varying but often substantial movements of feeder cattle.

Beef Cattle

Imports of beef cattle are shown in Table 17.6. In the past 15 years, imports of breeding cattle, including dairy as well as beef stock, have ranged from 5,640 head in 1977 to almost 25,000 head in 1970. Compared to the approximately 46 million head of breeding cows (both beef and dairy) in the United States, it can be seen that from the standpoint of total numbers, breeding cattle imports are relatively insignificant. Yet, for particular herd owners, the importation of select stock undoubtedly is of ultimate importance. Were it not for the ban on importation of cattle from areas of foot and mouth disease, the importation of breeding cattle would be larger.

Table 17.6 also shows the number of "other" cattle imported in recent years. A majority of these are feeder cattle almost entirely from Canada and Mexico, with a substantial Mexican predominance in most years. When U.S. slaughter-cattle prices are attractive, both Canada and Mexico are induced to ship in some slaughter animals.

Exports of cattle are shown in Table 17.7. The exportation of "other" (i.e., feeder) cattle reached significant numbers in the mid 1970s, followed by a precipitous decline. Most of the breeding cattle exported from the U.S. go to Canada and Mexico, but it is not unusual for annual shipments to go to 30 different countries.

Sheep and Hogs

Imports of live sheep and lambs are somewhat variable and relatively small in numbers (see Table 17.6). In the early 1960s wide publicity was given to the importation of slaughter lambs from New Zealand,

Table 17.6. United States Imports of Meat Animals, 1970–1983.

Year	Cattle (head)			Sheep and lambs	Hogs
	Breeding stock	Other cattle	Total cattle		
1970	24,762	1,142,900	1,167,662	11,716	67,832
1971	21,624	969,085	990,709	5,454	77,532
1972	17,441	1,169,035	1,186,476	13,765	89,032
1973	15,541	1,023,444	1,038,985	9,514	87,615
1974	12,082	556,189	568,271	900	196,347
1975	6,391	382,938	389,319	3,497	29,768
1976	11,225	972,619	983,844	4,607	45,577
1977	5,640	1,127,639	1,133,279	8,530	43,030
1978	9,678	1,243,062	1,252,740	11,195	202,446
1979	11,360	720,954	732,314	9,478	136,556
1980	8,503	672,266	680,769	20,518	247,288
1981	8,193	651,004	659,197	6,860	145,695
1982	7,754	996,753	1,004,507	9,286	294,937
1983	9,492	911,315	920,807	7,128	447,465

Source: USDA (1984C) for 1970–1982; USDA (1984B) for 1982 and 1983.

Table 17.7.   United States Exports of Meat Animals, 1970–1983.

| | Cattle (head) | | | | |
Year	Breeding stock	Other cattle	Total cattle	Sheep and lambs	Hogs
1970	26,323	61,714	88,037	132,856	24,845
1971	33,271	59,685	92,956	213,806	17,347
1972	40,115	63,805	103,920	159,428	12,316
1973	79,939	192,642	272,581	204,339	16,802
1974	88,509	115,871	204,380	290,659	15,801
1975	71,587	124,339	195,926	339,246	15,960
1976	58,961	145,583	204,544	244,450	10,768
1977	68,590	38,407	106,997	205,149	10,212
1978	70,761	51,447	122,208	141,778	12,717
1979	39,367	26,806	66,173	125,395	13,449
1980	24,850	40,271	65,571	123,521	16,291
1981	32,251	55,567	87,818	220,882	24,124
1982	30,411	27,098	57,509	280,644	36,830
1983	39,413	16,509	55,922	220,562	23,326

Source: USDA (1984C) for 1970–1982; USDA (1984B) for 1982 and 1983.

but the number soon dwindled. Most imports of sheep are breeding animals. Imports of hogs are also variable and normally a minor market factor. During the mid 1980s, however, substantial numbers of slaughter hogs were imported from Canada.

Exports of sheep, though small, have increased substantially during recent years (Table 17.7). World trade in live hogs is of minor importance—virtually all are breeding stock. The U.S. is not a leader in exportation of hogs. But, although the numbers are small, for particular breeders this is an important business.

MAJOR SOURCES OF U.S. MEAT
AND LIVESTOCK PRODUCT IMPORTS

Tables 17.8 and 17.9 show the chief suppliers of meat to the United States. As shown in these tables and in Fig. 17.5, beef and veal account for most of the U.S. meat imports in terms of quantity and value. In recent years, Australia alone has furnished about 45 percent of the U.S. imports of beef and veal. New Zealand supplied an additional 25 percent. Argentina, Brazil, Mexico, and Canada are all important suppliers, and the Central American countries have come up rapidly in recent years. Imports from Ireland, formerly a chief supplier, have

Table 17.8. United States Imports of Beef and Veal and of Lamb and Mutton by Country of Origin, Selected Years.

Country	Beef and veal				Lamb and mutton			
	1970	1975	1980	1983*	1970	1975	1980	1983*
	Weight (million kilograms†)							
Canada	35.56	9.70	42.82	59.15	0.27	‡	0.05	‡
Mexico	35.66	13.52	0.22	1.22	—	—	—	—
Argentina	64.00	25.50	33.48	38.46	—	—	—	—
Brazil	13.06	15.83	24.04	33.75	—	—	—	—
Denmark	0.18	1.32	1.45	0.90	—	—	—	—
W. Germany	‡	0.05	‡	‡	—	—	—	—
Poland	‡	—	—	—	—	—	—	—
Netherlands‡	‡	0.05	—	—	—	—	—	—
Ireland	31.30	3.08	4.17	4.44	—	‡	—	—
Australia	243.03	309.00	363.70	278.82	27.26	2.50	2.27	1.90
New Zealand	109.59	125.55	149.37	163.34	10.07	8.85	13.11	6.71
Other	79.02	92.80	83.50	61.73	0.05	0.32	0.05	0.22
Total:								
Product weight:								
	612.00	596.35	702.80	641.81	37.65	11.67	15.48	8.83
Carcass weight equivalents:								
	823.70	808.30	945.74	884.50	55.34	12.24	14.97	8.62

Source: USDA (1984C).
*Preliminary.
†Converted from pounds to kilograms by the authors.
‡Less than 50,000 lb (22,680 kg).
Notice: Dash indicates data not available.

dropped substantially since Ireland was admitted into the European Community trading bloc in 1973.

The bulk of imported beef is in frozen, boneless form and primarily used for processing purposes—including hamburgers. Not shown in the tables are the sizable quantities of beef produced from imported feeder cattle, which, in some years, amount to 1 million head. Although that is only about 2 ½ percent of total cattle slaughter, beef from these cattle constitutes 18 to 20 percent of total beef imports, and the bulk is block beef rather than processing beef.

Lamb and mutton imports into the United States come almost exclusively from Australia and New Zealand, and, as shown in Table 17.8, the importation of each has declined sharply—from 55 million kg in 1975-1979 to less than 9 million kg in 1983.

Canada, Denmark, Poland, and Netherlands supply most of the U.S. pork imports (Table 17.9), which principally consists of canned bacon, hams, and shoulders, except in the case of Canada.

Table 17.9. United States Imports of Pork and Total Meat by Country of Origin, Selected Years.

Country	Pork				Total meat imports*			
	1970	1975	1980	1983†	1970	1975	1980	1983†
	Weight (million kilograms‡)							
Canada	28.67	16.92	91.13	123.83	65.59	26.80	134.80	183.93
Mexico	§	—	—	—	35.65	13.51	0.22	1.59
Argentina	§	§	—	§	64.00	25.49	33.52	38.46
Brazil	—	—	—	—	13.06	15.92	24.08	33.88
Denmark	54.70	41.32	32.57	59.05	65.45	45.81	39.87	67.00
W. Germany	0.64	0.32	0.50	0.63	1.04	0.50	0.63	0.72
Poland	25.40	36.52	42.37	27.44	25.49	38.28	42.54	27.44
Nether.	39.33	31.75	4.00	10.61	39.96	31.88	4.26	11.25
Ireland	0.05	0.10	§	§	31.34	3.17	4.17	4.44
Australia	0.13	0.05	0.18	0.22	270.93	311.62	366.09	280.95
New Zealand	§	§	§	—	119.75	134.50	162.47	170.10
All other	8.75	21.50	25.80	30.03	88.58	115.30	110.35	93.00
Total:								
Product weight:	157.67	148.37	196.55	251.82	820.84	762.78	923.00	912.76
Carcass weight equivalent:	222.70	199.12	249.47	318.42	1101.77	1019.67	1208.37	1211.09

Source: USDA (1984C).
*Total meat includes quantities of other canned, prepared, or preserved meat.
†Preliminary.
‡Converted from pounds to kilograms by the authors.
§Less than 50,000 lb (22,680 kg).
Notice: Dash indicates data not available.

1,000 metric tons

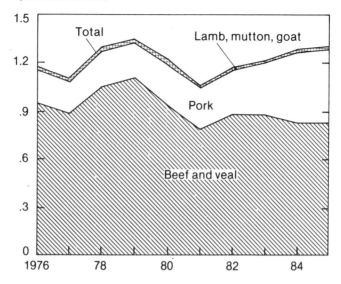

Fig. 17.5. U.S. Imports of Red Meat, 1976–1985 (Carcass-Weight Equivalent.). USDA Exten. Serv. undated.)

MAJOR DESTINATIONS OF U.S. EXPORTS

As may be seen in Tables 17.10 and 17.11, U.S. exports of meat go chiefly to its territories, but Canada and, more recently, Japan are large and expanding outlets. Historically, the largest dollar export item among livestock products has been tallow, but in recent years hides and skins have replaced tallow as the major export. Variety meats and red meats have made significant gains (Table 17.2 and Fig. 17.6), but the value of lard, casings, and mohair exports has been on a declining trend for many years.

Quantities of export items are shown in Table 17.10 and 17.11. Although the major items of U.S. export do not constitute a large fraction of the total quantity or value of livestock and meat produced, they nevertheless constitute an important fraction. Generally speaking, these are items with a low demand preference at home. Without foreign outlets, their value would be considerably less and have an adverse effect on U.S. livestock prices. In recent years, the value of livestock and livestock products exported has equalled that of imports.

Table 17.10. U.S. Exports of Beef and Veal and of Lamb and Mutton by Country of Destination, Selected Years.

Country	Beef and veal				Lamb and mutton			
	1970	1975	1980	1983*	1970	1975	1980	1983*
	Weight (million kilograms†)							
Canada	5.26	3.58	4.94	6.35	‡	0.54	0.05	0.09
Mexico	0.18	0.41	0.91	0.27	0.05	0.18	0.09	0.09
France	0.14	0.05	0.05	0.09	—	—	‡	‡
Bahamas	3.40	2.72	3.26	2.77	0.22	0.31	0.14	0.14
W. Germany	‡	0.09	0.18	0.13	—	—	—	‡
Jamaica	0.72	0.59	0.32	0.72	‡	0.05	‡	‡
Japan	0.50	8.03	34.25	60.55	—	—	‡	‡
Netherlands	0.09	0.36	0.63	0.27	—	‡	‡	—
Venezuela	‡	‡	0.45	3.00	0.05	0.05	0.05	‡
All other	2.99	4.85	14.51	18.87	0.18	0.18	0.27	0.32
Total	13.28	20.68	59.50	93.02	0.50	1.31	0.60	0.64
Carcass weight equivalent:								
Total Exports:	18.00	24.26	80.01	125.28	0.82	1.77	0.68	0.64
Shipment to territories§:	29.25	31.97	21.86	18.73	2.49	1.81	1.36	1.00
Total exports and shipments:	47.25	56.23	101.87	144.01	3.31	3.58	2.04	1.64

Source: USDA (1984C).
*Preliminary.
†Converted from pounds to kilograms by the authors.
‡Less than 50,000 lb (22,680 kg).
§ Puerto Rico and Virgin Islands.
Notice: Dash indicates data not available.

Table 17.11. U.S. Exports of Pork and Total Meat by Country of Destination, Selected Years.

Country	Pork				Total meat imports*			
	1970	1975	1980	1983†	1970	1975	1980	1983†
	Weight (million kilograms‡)							
Canada	10.66	33.80	15.10	9.57	17.64	40.18	21.36	17.05
Mexico	1.22	0.77	10.25	10.30	1.72	1.63	11.65	10.80
France	0.05	0.09	1.18	1.31	0.36	0.36	2.58	1.50
Bahamas	1.58	1.90	2.45	1.58	5.85	5.80	6.35	5.08
W. Germany	0.05	§	0.59	0.31	0.13	0.13	1.00	0.50
Jamaica	0.59	0.72	0.86	0.27	1.67	1.50	1.22	1.18
Japan	7.35	45.85	27.71	35.88	8.07	54.70	62.82	96.75
Netherlands	§	0.13	0.72	0.27	0.13	0.54	1.95	0.54
Venezuela	0.50	0.45	4.26	0.63	0.54	0.54	4.99	3.76
All other	5.76	7.43	21.09	10.66	12.70	15.65	41.18	34.25
Total	27.76	91.14	84.23	70.78	48.81	121.03	155.10	171.41
Carcass weight equivalent:								
Total Exports:	33.92	98.02	114.17	99.47	52.75	124.05	194.86	225.30
Shipment to territories″:	54.06	45.76	74.88	64.22	85.82	79.56	98.11	83.96
Total exports and shipments:	87.98	143.78	189.05	163.69	138.57	203.61	292.97	309.36

Source: USDA (1984C).
*Including sausage, bologna, and frankfurters, canned and not canned, sausage ingredients, meat and meat products not elsewhere classified.
†Preliminary.
‡Converted from pounds to kilograms by the authors.
§Less than 50,000 lb (22,680 kg).
″Puerto Rico and Virgin Islands.
Notice: Dash indicates data not available.

Table 17.12. United States Exports of Livestock Products, Selected Years.

Product	1970	1976	1980	1981	1982	1983	1984
				Value (million $)			
Live Animals:							
Cattle and calves	29.3	92.2	54.6	65.6	50.1	44.0	56.5
Hogs	2.4	0.8	6.7	9.1	13.9	10.6	8.0
Sheep	1.3	4.0	5.1	9.1	10.6	6.8	11.2
Meat							
Beef and veal	24.6	110.1	249.3	300.0	373.2	391.8	469.6
Pork	26.2	265.6	189.3	253.0	188.5	183.5	113.3
Lamb, mutton and goat	0.8	3.8	2.3	2.8	4.9	4.6	5.7
Processed*	9.7	17.6	21.2	24.5	10.4	9.0	7.7
Tallow, grease, and fat	244.1	439.1	751.6	742.6	638.4	587.2	676.1
Variety meats	69.5	151.6	300.8	306.4	398.8	324.9	329.9
Casings	13.1	25.2	21.6	20.0	19.3	19.0	17.2
Hides and Skins	144.4	518.0	682.1	691.0	744.1	786.1	1,148.4
Wool and Mohair	7.9	24.4	21.1	31.3	29.7	45.1	39.7
Total	573.3	1,652.4	2,305.7	2,405.3	2,481.9	2,412.6	2,883.3

Source: USDA (1984C) and earlier issues for 1970, 1976, 1980, 1981, 1982; and AMI (1985—compiled by the American Meat Institute from USDA data) for 1983 and 1984.
*Includes sausage, canned meats, and canned specialities.

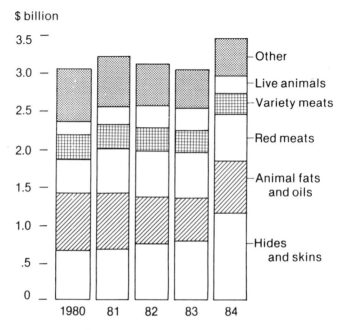

$ billion

Fig. 17.6. U.S. Exports of Livestock Products, 1980–1984. (USDA Exten. Serv. undated.)

EFFECT OF IMPORTS ON U.S. LIVESTOCK PRODUCTION AND PRICES

As pointed out in Chap. 16, rises in beef imports during the late 1950s and early 1960s were blamed for depressed cattle prices and led to enactment of the Meat Import Quota Law of 1964. Consumer concern over high meat prices in 1973 prompted the President of the United States to cancel import restrictions in view of "over-riding economic interests." The voluntary quotas negotiated during 1974–1977 allowed imports essentially at the maximum level provided under the Meat Import Quota Law. That was a period of cattle liquidation, high beef production, and disastrously low cattle prices. Cattlemen reacted with deep concern. Remedial proposals ranged from complete prohibition of imports to contracyclical quotas. The enactment of the Meat Import Act of 1979 introduced a contracyclical factor in calculating annual import quotas. Thus, it allows for liberalizing quotas during periods of cyclically declining domestic beef production on the one hand, and for imposing increasingly stricter quotas during periods of cyclically increasing domestic beef production on the other.

The major item of imported meat—frozen, boneless beef—competes directly with U.S. boned beef from cull beef and dairy cows and bulls and also competes directly with trimmings and increasingly larger portions of lean cuts from steer and heifer carcasses. Most of it is used in processed meats, including hamburger. Indirectly, imported beef competes with grain-fed beef, pork, lamb, and other foods. It is well known that one type of meat can be substituted for another meat or for an altogether different food.

In terms of the demand concepts discussed in Chap. 3, we will be concerned here with the effect that increased quantities of imported beef have, not only on identical or comparable U.S. products, but also on prices of substitute products such as grain-finished beef and pork. This involves the concepts of the price elasticity of demand, the cross elasticity of demand, and cross flexibility.

During the height of discussions over imported beef in 1963, the USDA (1963) published results of a study showing that imports of beef and veal have a greater effect on cow prices than on fed beef prices. More specifically, the study indicated that a 20-percent increase in imports (from 1962 levels) would result in a reduction of 80 to 90 cents per cwt in utility-grade cow prices. The same increase in imports would cause a 50 to 60-cents decline in Choice steer prices. It is generally recognized that, in the short run, changes in the supply of beef are the primary factor affecting prices. The USDA study showed that a 10-percent change in steer and heifer beef production for the period 1948–1962 was associated with a 13-percent change in the opposite direction of fed-cattle prices, and a 23-percent change in the opposite direction of cow prices. Furthermore, a 10-percent change in cow beef production (domestic cow beef plus imported beef) was associated with a 3-percent change in the opposite direction of fed-beef prices and a 7.5-percent change in the opposite direction of utility-grade cow prices. These are average net changes after consideration of other factors that affect prices.

Purcell (1968) estimated the effect of imported beef and veal on prices and revenue for cattle and hogs on an annual basis from 1947 to 1966; results are shown in Table 17.13. The United States was a slight net importer in 1947, but the effects were not measurable. Since 1948, the United States has been a net importer every year. According to Purcell, imports in 1963 pushed cattle and calf prices down $4.27 per cwt. This represents an aggregate average price decline for all classes of cattle and calves. Evidence from the USDA and other studies would indicate that cow prices were depressed by more than $4.27 and fed cattle prices by somewhat less. Revenues of cattle and calf producers in 1963 were off as a result of imports by almost $1.3 billion,

Table 17.13.   Estimated Effect of Net Imports of Beef and Veal on Price and Revenue for Cattle and Calves and Hogs, United States, 1947-1966.

Year	Cattle and Calves			Hogs		
	Price ($/Cwt)	Revenue* (Million $)	(%)[†]	Price ($/Cwt)	Revenue* (Million $)	(%)[†]
1947	—	—	—	—	—	—
1948	−1.01	−201.3	−3.5	−0.74	−106	−2.6
1949	−0.72	−143.6	−2.4	−0.43	−65	−1.9
1950	−1.06	−210.7	−3.4	−0.61	−97	−2.8
1951	−1.49	−271.2	−4.2	−0.98	−169	−4.5
1952	−1.25	−247.6	−3.8	−0.68	−119	−3.4
1953	−0.67	−171.4	−2.8	−0.36	−55	−1.5
1954	−0.53	−142.3	−2.3	−0.26	−39	−1.1
1955	−0.48	−133.2	−2.1	−0.16	−27	−1.0
1956	−0.29	−85.2	−1.4	−0.07	−12	−0.5
1957	−0.82	−234.1	−3.6	−0.29	−47	−1.6
1958	−2.45	−638.3	−9.1	−1.04	−170	−5.3
1959	−2.78	−714.3	−9.7	−0.85	−160	−6.1
1960	−2.02	−565.0	−7.8	−0.62	−114	−4.1
1961	−2.69	−770.0	−10.5	−0.87	−158	−5.3
1962	−3.70	−1,063.3	−13.7	−1.16	−221	−7.2
1963	−4.27	−1,292.1	−16.7	−1.17	−235	−7.9
1964	−2.59	−880.3	−11.8	−0.67	−136	−4.6
1965	−2.21	−770.3	−9.8	−0.78	−142	−3.9
1966	−2.78	−1,004.2	−12.5	−1.05	−198	−4.9

Source: Purcell (1968).
*Estimated change in revenue to primary producers in the United States attributed to net imports with actual domestic output (slaughter).
[†]Based on estimated reduction in revenue to primary producers due to imports relative to actual revenue.
[‡]Percentage increase in beef and veal due to imports (estimated cross price flexibility: −0.91).

or 16.7 percent. In 1966, the effect on cattle and calf revenues again reached $1 billion. Cross relationships are shown in the effects of beef and veal imports on the price and revenue of hogs (Table 17.13). The relatively heavy beef imports of the early 1960s depressed hog prices $1.16 to $1.17 per cwt and reduced hog revenues to farmers in 1963 by $235 million, or almost 8 percent. Thus, it is apparent why livestock producers were incensed as imports increased in the late 1950s and the early 1960s. Their concern is unabated as imports continue to press upon the quota levels provided by the Import Quota Act of 1964 and the Meat Import Act of 1979.

A series of studies during the 1970s (Graeber and Farris, 1972; Jackson, 1972; Ehrich and Usman, 1974; Freebairn and Rausser, 1975; and Folwell and Shapouri, 1976) confirmed the direction of effect as shown in earlier studies, even though the magnitude of effect was somewhat different. Davis (1977) summarized four of these studies, as shown in Table 17.14. All indicate a negative effect on cattle prices—ranging from $1.08 per cwt to $1.91 per cwt for cull cows. The effect on the price of slaughter steers is variously shown to be $0.24 per cwt and $0.60 per cwt; for feeder cattle, $1.16 per cwt; and for an aggregated "all cattle" price, $1.41 per cwt. These studies were essentially comparable in estimating the price effect for a 200-million-lb increase in imports—relative to average imports over the period studied.

In this type of analysis, results are not expected to be identical among studies. The particular statistical model and time period used can affect derived estimates. The results are consistent in indicating a substantial price impact, and, as pointed out by Davis (1977), the impact may have been even greater during those years when U.S. production was highest (and prices were relatively low). During those years, the market would have been operating beyond the point of average imports—in a relatively inelastic segment of the demand function where any incremental change in quantity would have a greater proportional effect on price than the same change would have at the point of average imports.

Two of these studies estimated the effects of imports on farm revenues. Folwell and Shapouri (1976) estimated that 1975 cattle revenues were reduced $1.6 billion from what they would have been had imports been held to 1964 levels and that 1976 cattle revenues were reduced $1.8 billion. Freebairn and Rausser's (1975) estimates were $1.1 billion and $1.5 billion for 1975 and 1976, respectively.

Jackson (1972) estimated that elimination of meat quotas in 1975 would have resulted in a 1.2-percent decrease in high-grade beef prices and a 2.5-percent decrease in low-grade beef prices at retail. At the farm level, his analysis indicated a 1.9-percent decrease in high-grade

Table 17.14. Estimated Effects of Increased Beef Imports on Cattle Prices in Dollars per Hundredweight.

Cattle classification	Study			
	Farris and Graeber*	Rausser and Freebairn[†]	Folwell and Shapouri	Ehrich and Usman[†]
	Effect ($ per cwt)			
All Cattle			−1.41	
Cull Cows	−1.91	−1.09		−1.08
Slaughter steers	−0.24	−0.60		
Feeder calves		−1.16		

Source: Davis (1977).
*Estimated at 1 lb per capita (202 million lb) increase in beef imports.
[†]Estimated at 200 million lb increase in beef imports.

beef and a 3.9-percent decrease in low-grade beef. Jackson's general conclusion was that "the quota affords only very modest protection or benefits to the U.S. beef producer. When considered in the light of side effects the quota has on domestic consumption, in terms of higher retail meat prices, and on those countries as a means of improving the income of beef producers has very little in its favor."

Nelson et al. (1980) used a linear programming model to evaluate the impact of the 1979 Meat Import Act on the optimal size of a U.S. beef herd. The model covered the five major beef-producing regions. Results indicate that the optimal least-cost U.S. cow herd would have to be bigger if all beef imports were curtailed and per-capita consumption remained at the assumed annual level of 124 pounds. The increase in cow numbers, as well as in the length of feeding period, would be necessary to offset the reduced supplies from external sources. Furthermore, the larger herd would increase average costs and corn utilization.

Holder (1981) used a stepwise regression model to examine the relative importance of prices of substitutes and their consumption (including quantities imported) on retail prices of lamb. The results suggest that if imports of lamb and mutton were eliminated, per capita consumption would decrease by 0.15 pound and the retail price would increase by 8.6 cents; live lamb prices, however, would increase by only 4.3 cents. To the extent that this model assumed imported lamb to be a perfect substitute for domestic lamb—an assumption that can be questioned on the ground that imported (frozen) lamb must normally be discounted against fresh lamb—the above results may overestimate the actual impact of restricting lamb imports.

Simpson (1982) argued that since the United States is the largest producer, consumer, and importer of beef in the world, any major changes in its import policy would not only affect the U.S. beef cattle industry but have major influence on the international beef trade and exporters' trade policy. The author simulated the impact of the U.S. Meat Import Act of 1979 on domestic beef-cattle production under two alternative scenarios: (1) with a cattle inventory cycle similar to the preceding cycle, and (2) with a slower growth of cattle inventories than in the past. Intended to simulate the impact of import quota rather than to predict actual outcome, this study concluded that the meat import bill would operate as intended—i.e., provide systematic countercyclical quota adjustment—only under the first scenario. It would have the opposite impact if inventory growth rate proved to be slower than in the last cycle. Examining the results of his simulations, Simpson concluded that "the apparent similarity of trigger levels under the two radically different projections is an indication that, despite belief to the contrary, the 1979 bill cannot be considered particularly beneficial or harmful to either the United States or exporting nations.

TRADE PROMOTIONAL ACTIVITIES

International trade is not a passive proposition. On the contrary, it is a highly competitive, aggressive contest among nations and individual firms. Although trade restrictions impede the international flow of meat and other products, most countries with exportable surpluses are actively engaged in efforts to stimulate trade. Among the tactics used are the following:

1. International trade fairs
2. Solo country exhibits
3. Trade missions
4. In-store promotions, including demonstrations, prizes, etc.
5. Promotional activities by agricultural attachés or other governmental agents stationed in foreign countries
6. Direct contact and selling by representatives of individual firms
7. Governmental manipulation of import–export regulations
8. Export subsidies
9. The use of marketing boards or comparable agencies in expediting export movements.

Recipient countries also utilize a number of devices to encourage and/or discourage imports and exports. Among the approaches used are import tariffs, export taxes, import and export licensing, exchange controls, embargoes, and import trade missions. While exporting countries are busy courting prospective importers, the importers are busy attempting to diversify their sources of supply.

Following is a summary of promotional activities of a group of selected countries.

Australia

Australia's greatest promotional expenditures are in wool marketing. She is the major contributor to the International Wool Secretariat—an international pooled effort to promote the sale and use of wool. Other principal contributors are New Zealand and South Africa. In addition, Australia maintains Trade Commissioners in a number of overseas posts and participates in trade fairs in a number of importing countries. One of its principal meat promotional agencies is the Australian Meat and Livestock Corporation (AMLC), established in 1977 to replace the Australian Meat Board. Operational funds are derived from a levy on livestock slaughtered. The Board maintains offices in New York (serving North American markets), Tokyo (serving the North Asian region), and Bahrain (serving the Middle East region). The latter office gained additional responsibilities for North Africa and various Mediterranean markets following closure of the AMLC office in London in December 1984). The central government matches AMLC funds for approved promotional proposals.

Canada

Canada's promotional efforts in agricultural products are directed primarily to wheat sales, but livestock and meat receive some attention in trade missions, trade fairs, exhibitions, and advertising and other publicity.

Denmark

Denmark carries on an aggressive overseas marketing program. Although not all of the agencies mentioned here spend equal effort on the promotion of livestock products, taken together they indicate a well-planned, comprehensive approach to overseas marketing. A Traveling Ambassador for Agriculture was appointed in 1967. A marketing office is maintained in Beirut and covers a number of Near East countries. Danish Food Centers are operated in London, Manchester, and Glasgow. These centers are partially financed by the Danish Bacon Factories Export Association. A Danish Food Festival and Danish Food Fair have operated in Japan. Denmark has also participated in various food fairs in Europe. Use is made of television and press advertising in the United Kingdom, Germany, and Japan.

Netherlands

The Netherlands also maintains a relatively extensive export marketing program. Most of the funds are derived from Marketing Board levies, but the central Ministry of Agriculture also contributes. The Netherlands participates in numerous food fairs, carries out substantial TV advertising programs, and in-store promotions. To foster the sale of breeding stock in less developed countries, the Netherlands sends experienced herdsmen to acquaint local herdsmen with the proper care and feeding of imported stock.

New Zealand

Like Australia, New Zealand is a heavy contributor to the International Wool Secretariat. New Zealand has a Wool Marketing Board, but, other than fund contributions to the Secretariat, its activities are directed primarily to domestic affairs. A Meat Board is active in promoting overseas sales of meat and meat products. The Board maintains an office in London that covers the United Kingdom and Europe. Promotional activities are also carried on by the Board in Canada and in Far Eastern countries. Activities include press and TV advertising, retail store display materials, demonstrations, and participation in food fairs. An office titled the Meat Export Department Co., Ltd., is maintained in Canada.

South Africa

South Africa is an important exporter of wool, and major emphasis is placed on that commodity. Minor amounts are spent for promotion of mohair and meat. The principal activities include trade missions, trade fairs, TV advertising, and in-store promotions.

European Economic Community

The European Economic Community (EEC), generally referred to as the Common Market, is an organization of European nations formed under the so-called Treaty of Rome of January, 1958. Under this agreement, Belgium, France, Italy, Luxembourg, the Netherlands, and West Germany formalized a comprehensive arrangement for cooperation in economic, social, and political activities. Great Britain, Denmark, and Ireland were admitted in 1973 and joined later by Greece, Spain, and Portugal. Of particular interest to international trade, the EEC plan provides for a common policy whereby barriers are to be removed (over a period of time) for trade among the signatories, but trade with outside countries is strictly regulated. A primary purpose of the regulation is the protection of EEC producers and the encouragement of local production. Consumer interests are also taken into account through various subsidy arrangements.

Imports of livestock products are permitted with varying degrees of regulation, depending upon the degree to which the particular product is competitive or complementary to the domestic production and needs of the EEC. One of the most potent means of regulating meat and livestock imports is by variable levies. By a complicated series of formulaic calculations, internal target prices are set up, and so-called "sluice-gate prices" are determined for imported products. If the selling price of a third country is less than the sluice-gate price, a levy is imposed to make up the difference. Thus, the lower the outside price, the higher the variable levy. Other restrictions include requirements for import licenses, prior deposits by importers, and quotas. In addition, health regulations and inspection and shipping requirements under the 1983's Third Country Directive (TCD) are relatively strict on imports of meat and livestock products.

EEC restrictions are more severe on fresh meats than on by-products. Since the United States does not compete actively in the fresh meat trade of EEC, the restrictions affect the United States less than other countries. Generally speaking, the EEC considers by-products obtained from the United States to be complementary to their own production and needs.

United States

The United States works actively through agricultural attachés that are stationed in most countries.

The attachés—which constitute a branch of the diplomatic corps that is organizationally tied with USDA's Foreign Agricultural Service (FAS)—not only promote U.S. products but are valuable in arranging contacts for representatives of private firms in their respective promotional activities. They also work in conjunction with private firms in arranging for displays at trade fairs and in-store displays. In addition, the agricultural attaché's office collects and makes available to interested parties information on production and trade for the country in which it is located.

The United States sends meat and livestock trade missions to foreign countries, many of which are sponsored jointly by government and private organizations such as the American Meat Institute, the National Cattlemen's Association, and various breed associations. It should also be noted that the USDA works actively with exporting countries in negotiating voluntary quotas on meat shipments to the United States.

In 1976, a group composed of beef producers, pork producers, meat packers, and others interested in the export market, organized the United States Meat Export Federation, Inc., with a major objective of expanding overseas sales of U.S. meat and meat products. Offices are maintained in Japan and Europe. The Federation is designed to coordinate export activities. Following its organization, the Federation and USDA's Foreign Agricultural Service signed an agreement to join efforts in a cooperative program of sales promotion.

An International Livestock Program (ILP) was established at Kansas State University in 1985 to provide technical assistance to countries desiring to import livestock or livestock products. The ILP provides long- and short-term courses, workshops, and seminars on various phases of livestock management, livestock development, livestock products and marketing. Programs are available both in the U.S. and abroad and encompass all livestock species (dairy, poultry, swine, sheep, goats, beef, and horses). The ultimate goal of ILP is the promotion of livestock and livestock products for export trade.

REFERENCES

Albaugh, R. 1965. The livestock and meat industry of Australia. USDA Foreign Agr. Serv. M-164.

Allen, Roy, et al. 1983. Voluntary Export Restraints as Protection Policy: The U.S. Beef Case. *Amer. J. Agr. Econ.* 65, No. 2:291–296.

American Meat Institute. 1985. MEATFACTS. A statistical summary about America's largest food industry. AMI, 1985 ed. August.

Davis, E. E. 1977. Impact of beef imports. Texas Agr. Ext. Serv. *Food and Fiber* 6, No. 7:1–3.

Decourcy, J. 1967. World production and trade: tallow and greases. USDA Foreign Agr. Serv. M-182.

Ehrich, R. L., and Usman, M. 1974. Demand and supply functions for beef imports. Wyoming Agr. Expt. Sta. Bull. 604.

Food and Agriculture Organization of the United Nations. 1984. FAO Production Yearbook, vol. 37, Rome.

Food and Agriculture Organization of the United Nations. 1984. FAO Trade Yearbook, vol. 37, Rome.

Folwell, R. J., and Shapouri, H. 1976. An econometric analysis of the U.S. beef sector. Washington State Univ., Dept Agr. Econ. Mimeographed (unnumbered).

Freebairn, J. W., and Rausser, G. C. 1975. Effects of changes in the level of U.S. beef imports. *Amer. J. Agr. Econ.* 57, 676–688.

Graeber, K. E., and Farris, D. E. 1972. Beef cattle research in Texas, 1973. Texas Agr. Expt. Sta. PR-3217.

Holder, D. L. 1981. Effect of lamb imports on the price of lamb. USDA, Livestock and meat marketing program (unpublished).

Ives, J. R. 1966. The Livestock and meat economy of the United States. Am. Meat Inst., Chicago.

Jackson, G. H. 1972. The impact of eliminating the quota on U.S. imports of beef. Cornell Univ., Dept. Agr. Econ., A. E. Res. 338.

Lege, F. M., III. 1974. Livestock exhibits throughout the world. USDA Foreign Agr. Serv. FAS M-259.

Lege, F. M., III. 1976. Guide for U.S. cattle exporters. USDA Foreign Agr. Serv. Agr. Handbook No. 217.

Lege, F. M., III. 1977. Suggested procedures for exporting breeding cattle and swine. USDA Foreign Agr. Serv. FAS M-274.

Leighton, R. I. 1970. *Economics of International Trade.* New York: McGraw-Hill Book Co.

Nelson, K. E., et al. 1980. Impact of meat imports on least cost U.S. beef production. Selected paper presented at the Annual meeting of the Amer. Agr. Econ. Assoc., Urbana, Ill., July.

Purcell, J. C. 1968. Trends and relations in the livestock-meat sector affecting prices and revenue to primary producers. Georgia Agr. Expt. Sta. Res. Bull. 35.

Simpson, J. R. 1982. The countercyclical aspects of the U.S. Meat Import Act of 1979. *Amer. Jour. Agr. Econ.* **64**, No. 3:243-248.

USDA. 1975. Foreign agriculture circular. USDA Foreign Agr. Serv. FLM. 12-75.

USDA. 1977A. Livestock and meat statistics. USDA Econ. Res. Serv. and Stat. Reporting Serv., Stat. Bull. 522.

USDA. 1977B. Handbook of agricultural charts. USDA Agr. Handbook No. 524.

USDA. 1977C. Livestock and meat. USDA Foreign Agr. Serv., FLM 3-77.

USDA. 1978. Livestock and meat situation. USDA Econ., Stat., and Co-op. Serv. LMS-220.

USDA. 1983. Livestock and poultry situation. USDA, FAS, FL&P-3-83.

USDA. 1984A. Agricultural Statistics 1984. USDA, SRS, Washington, D.C.

USDA. 1984B. U.S. agricultural trade statistical report, calendar year 1983. A supplement to foreign agricultural trade of the United States. USDA, ERS, May.

USDA. 1984C. Livestock and Meat Statistics, 1983. USDA, ERS, Stat. Bull. 715.

18

Marketing Costs

Marketing margins and costs are a matter of concern to all sectors of society—producers, processors, distributors, and consumers. Producers question the legitimacy of $0.52/lb for slaughter cattle but $4.50/lb for steak. Consumers often assume that rising retail prices are filling the pockets of producers. It is not well understood that 1 pound of retail meat is derived from substantially more than 1 pound of liveweight and that many intervening steps are required to get that liveweight from the feedlot to the retail counter. As more and more women enter the work force, the demand has increased for a retail cut with more built-in service and convenience. This chapter will not settle the issue of undue marketing costs or excess profits—a subject beyond questions of economics. It will make an attempt, however, to explain how price margins (spreads) and the market basket and marketing bill are calculated, as well as other factors associated with various aspects of marketing costs.

MARKETING SPREADS—GENERAL COMMENT

"Marketing spread" is a general term referring to the difference between the value of a product at one point in the marketing system and the value of an equivalent quantity of the same product at another point in the marketing system. Price spread may be viewed as the value added between these designated points in the marketing system, or alternatively, it may be viewed as the sum of all costs (middlemen costs) in performing whatever functions are necessary, including profits. In the case of meat, the USDA calculates two spreads: a farm (live animal)–wholesale (carcass) spread and a wholesale—retail spread. The sum of these two is the farm-retail spread. "Marketing spread" is often used synonymously with "price spread."

The marketing spread for the bundle of farm products that make up the so-called "market basket" (i.e., the farm-retail spread) has amounted to about 65 cents per consumer dollar in recent years. Commodities that require relatively little processing and other marketing services naturally have a smaller spread than those that require extensive processing.

Farmers are prone to emphasize the residual element of this figure, which shows that they receive 35 percent of the consumer's dollar spent for food. During 1945, the last year of World War II, the farmers' share was 54 percent—the highest of record dating back to 1913. The average for all nonwar years since World War II has been about 40 percent. Since 1970, it has ranged from 33 to 44 percent. As shown in Fig. 18.1, and as will be discussed later, the farmers' share of consumers' expenditures for red meat differs substantially from this average for all food products.

Farmers tend to attribute their relatively low income position to their lower share of the consumer dollar and often assume that the larger share that goes to market agencies is indicative of inefficient marketing, excessive profits, or both. Consumers, generally speaking, are far removed from the agricultural scene and most are not well acquainted with the intricacies of the marketing system. To many, it is simple logic that rising retail prices must be putting profits in farmers' pockets. This notion may be heightened by occasional publicity giving the impression that farmers are getting rich from Federal handouts for not producing.

Obviously, a considerable amount of misunderstanding exists about marketing spreads, their relation to marketing efficiency, excess mar-

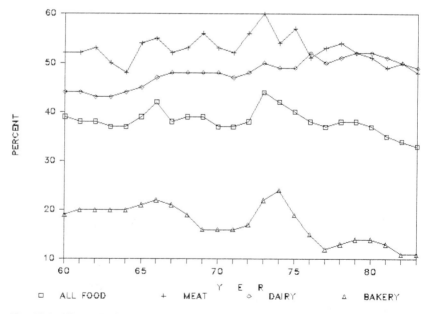

Fig. 18.1. Farmer's Share of Retail Costs for Selected Commodities, 1960–1984. (Plotted by authors from data in USDA (1984 and earliers issues).)

keting profits, retail prices, and producer profits. An understanding of the method of calculating spreads is a first step to their proper interpretation.

PRICE SPREADS FOR BEEF, PORK, AND LAMB[1]

The farm–retail price spread, by definition, is the difference between the retail price per unit of a commodity and the price received by farmers for an equivalent quantity.

The basic data needed for calculating spreads are prices and values at the retail and farm levels, but in the case of beef, pork, and lamb, interest also centers in an in-between level—i.e., the carcass or wholesale value. For meat price spreads, therefore, a determination is needed for three levels: (1) retail price; (2) wholesale or carcass value equivalent, and (3) farm value equivalent. The word "equivalent" is used because 1 pound of retail meat necessitates somewhat more than 1 pound at wholesale and even more at the farm level. The determination of retail price itself is no small matter, for a carcass has been broken down into many cuts by the time it reaches the retail counter. Each cut comprises a different volume of the carcass and each sells at a different price. Cutting methods can affect the volume of meat in various cuts so that this also must be standardized for calculation purposes. What is desired at retail, then, is a weighted average price per pound based on standardized yields of the various cuts.

Retail prices are estimated weighted averages for U.S. Choice, Yield Grade 3 beef. Prices are obtained by the Red Meat Section of the Animal Products Branch, National Economics Division, ERS, USDA. Since 1981, prices have been obtained by this agency from the Department of Labor, Bureau of Labor Statistics.

The determination of carcass value necessitates a conversion factor based on weight loss from carcass to retail. The conversion factor is associated with animal types and cutting methods. These change over time, and USDA makes adjustments as needed. A number of adjustments made in 1978 are still effective (Duewer, 1986). In the case of beef, the carcass–retail conversion factor is 1.48 (prior to 1978, it was 1.41). This means that 1.48 pounds of carcass beef is the wholesale equivalent of 1 pound at retail. A carcass-to-retail byproduct value was added for beef in 1978 to reflect the value of fat and bone trim. Begin-

---

[1]Lawrence A. Duewer, Agricultural Economist (Animal Products Branch, National Economics Division, ERS, USDA), provided much of the material in this section.

ning in 1978, beef trimmings were adjusted for fat removal (i.e., "de-fatted") in determining the amount of ground beef produced.

Live cattle prices used to be determined at the farm level. Beginning in 1978, however, the live animal price was taken at the first market level after the feedlot. Quotations are weighted uniformly to determine a live steer price. Under procedures established in 1978, the live animal–retail conversion factor is 2.40; i.e., 2.40 pounds of live animal are needed to obtain 1 pound of retail beef (formerly this factor was 2.28). This change was made to reflect changes in animal type and industry practices. Thus, to obtain the gross farm (live[2]) value, the live animal price must be multiplied by 2.40. However, gross farm value includes a valuation of farm by-products (primarily hide and offal), and this must be subtracted from gross value to arrive at net farm value. Price spreads are calculated each week and month and then aggregrated into quarterly and annual price spreads.

Assuming the following prices and values:

	¢/lb
Composite retail price	190
Wholesale carcass price	84
Farm level price	53
Farm by-product value	15
Carcass by-product value	2

a simplified hypothetical example of beef price spreads and equivalent values for a given month might be as follows:

1. Equivalent gross carcass value $84.0 \times 1.48 = 124.3$¢
2. Equivalent net carcass value $124.3 - 2.0 = 122.3$¢
3. Carcass–retail price spread $190.0 - 122.3 = 67.7$¢
4. Equivalent gross farm value $53.0 \times 2.40 = 127.2$¢
5. Equivalent net farm value $127.2 - 15.0 = 112.2$¢
6. Farm–carcass price spread $122.3 - 112.2 = 10.1$¢
7. Farm–retail price spread $190.0 - 112.2 = 77.8$¢
8. Farmers' share of beef dollar $(112.2/190.0) \times 100 = 59.1\%$

The approach in calculating pork price spreads follows the same general procedure as described for beef. Pork prices and values are determined for barrows and gilts, i.e., an average of all grades. For pork, a

---

[2]"Farm" value is the nomenclature used, although the live value is determined at the first market level. Prior to 1978, a live animal transport cost was deducted from market value to arrive at a "farm gate" value.

wholesale conversion factor of 1.06 is used to obtain a carcass value equivalent for 1 pound of pork at retail. To carcass value equivalent is applied a conversion factor of 1.70 to obtain gross farm value equivalent of 1 pound of pork at retail. And from gross farm value is deducted an allowance for pork by-products. The allowance recently was adjusted to reflect the trend toward a decreasing yield of lard.

Price spreads are no longer calculated for lamb.

Characteristics of Marketing Spreads

As previously mentioned, the total farm–retail spread is composed of two components: (1) the farm–carcass (wholesale[3]) spread, and (2) the carcass (wholesale)–retail spread. Over the years, these spreads have exhibited some common characteristics and also some that are peculiar to particular species. Although the spreads have not remained constant, they have been more stable than farm value, as may be observed in Fig. 18.2 for beef.[4] Farm value is directly related to prices received by producers. As farm price rises and falls, farm value rises and falls but the spreads tend to be more fixed. This anomaly is largely explained by the fact that the elements that comprise slaughtering, processing, wholesaling, and retailing costs (wage rates, rent, taxes, interest charges, freight rates, profits, etc.) simply do not vary in the same way that the farm price for livestock varies. The market structure under which these items are determined is subject to more institutional control than is the market for live animals.

The tendency for the farm–retail spread to remain relatively fixed results in a decline in the farmer's share of the meat dollar when farm prices fall and an increase when farm prices rise. Assume that the farm–retail spread for pork is a constant 30¢ per lb. If the farm value were also 30¢, the retail price would be 60¢ and the farmer's share would be 50 percent. If the farm value dropped to 25¢ (due, say, to increasing hog slaughter), the retail price (if it dropped the same amount) would be 55¢ and the farmer's share would be 45 percent. This disparity has been a matter of contention with producers, and what compounds their concern even more is the tendency for retail prices to be rather sticky. Retail prices do change, but usually with a lag after-farm price and wholesale price change. In the above example, if retail

---

[3]Prior to 1970, the spread between farm level price and wholesale meat price was referred to as the "farm-wholesale" spread. In the case of beef and lamb, this was changed to "farm-carcass" spread in 1970 to reflect the fact more accurately that prices and values at wholesale level are for carcasses rather than primal wholesale cuts. The term "wholesale" is still used for pork, since the prices and values used apply to wholesale pork cuts.
[4]Pork and lamb exhibit the same characteristics.

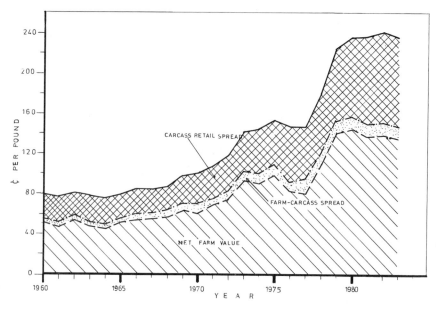

Fig. 18.2. Retail Prices, Carcass Value, and Net Farm Value of Choice Grade Beef. (Plotted by authors from USDA data.)

prices had remained at 60¢ after the farm value had dropped to 25¢, the farmer's share would have been only 42 percent, at least temporarily. The reverse happens during rising farm prices (i.e., the farmer's share tends to rise), but if farmers' reactions are an indication of their feelings, this does not seem to balance the situation. Part of the reason it does not balance out in the eyes of producers is that their share, over a period of time, has not averaged out at a constant level. As shown in Fig. 18.3, it has usually tended downward.

Over the same period, the farm–retail spreads (the costs of marketing) have trended upward for all three species of red meat (see Figs. 18.4, 18.5, and 18.6). This is a reflection of the general inflationary trend in most market input items. Freight rates were an exception until the late 1960s when that trend also turned upward. Labor is the largest single item among marketing costs, but the pronounced upward trend in hourly wage rates has been partially offset by increasing labor productivity. In spite of productivity gains, however, unit labor costs have risen substantially.

The carcass (wholesale)—retail spreads have exhibited a generally increasing trend for all three species (Figs. 18.4, 18.5, and 18.6). These, basically, reflect retail marketing costs, and, as calculated by USDA, all cutting, processing, packaging, and merchandising costs of beef and

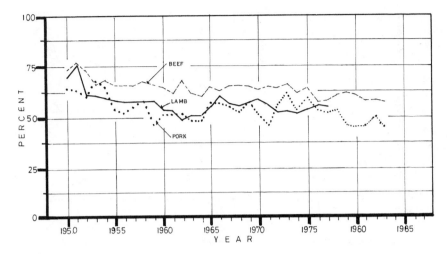

Fig. 18.3. Farmer's Share of Consumer's Meat Dollar, 1950–1983. (Plotted by authors from USDA data.)

lamb are attributed to the retail level. This practice is not entirely appropriate because more and more breaking, cutting, and processing are being done at the packer level. It does tend to explain, however, why the carcass—retail spread for beef and lamb is greater than for pork. Since pork, traditionally, has been broken into wholesale cuts and proc-

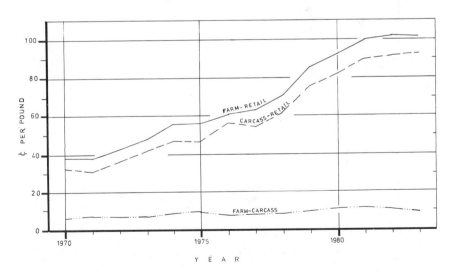

Fig. 18.4. Price Spreads for U.S. Choice Grade Beef, 1970–1984. (Plotted by authors from USDA data.)

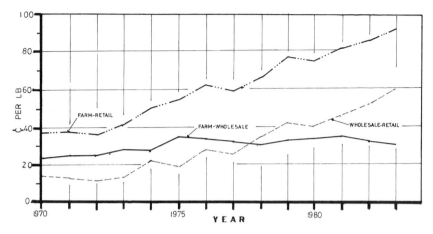

Fig. 18.5. Price Spreads for Choice Pork, 1970–1983. (Plotted by authors from USDA data.)

essed to a considerable extent by packers, the cost of doing so falls into the farm–wholesale spread. Thus, the farm–carcass (wholesale) spread is greater for pork than for beef and lamb.

The farm–carcass (wholesale) and the carcass (wholesale)–retail spreads for all species have been on an increasing trend—the sole ex-

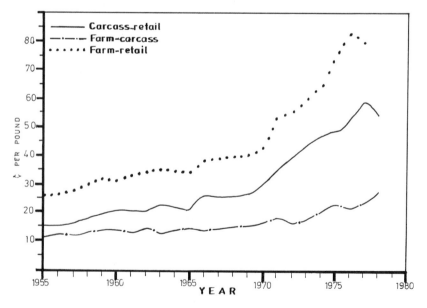

Fig. 18.6. Price Spreads for Choice Lamb, 1955–1979. (Plotted by authors from USDA data.)

ception being the farm–carcass spread for beef (Fig. 18.4). This trend is attributed to improved technology and increases in the efficiency of labor and equipment (Duewer, 1970).

IMPLICATIONS WITH RESPECT TO MARKETING EFFICIENCY

The farmer's share of the consumer's dollar spent for beef in 1983 was 57 percent; during the same time, it was less than 10 percent for canned beets. On the basis of this evidence, some persons tend to conclude that the marketing of beets must be less efficient than the marketing of beef. This is an unwarranted conclusion. Neither the farmer's share nor the absolute amount of marketing spread is adequate in itself for evaluating marketing efficiency—either operational efficiency or pricing efficiency. It has been pointed out earlier that price spreads consist of marketing and processing costs, plus profits to participating agencies. The matter of profits will be examined later. Some products simply require more marketing inputs relative to the value of the product itself than do others. This difference is apparent in the case of beets and beef where processing costs are substantially higher for beets relative to the value of the product.

Some might argue that the marketing costs of both are too high. It is assumed in a competitive economy that astute businessmen are continually looking for ways to reduce costs, but the possibility of further improvements should be a matter of continuing concern for both individual firms and the general public. The public concern is reflected in numerous governmental research and extension projects that have been designed to reduce marketing costs.

Although it would be possible to reduce the farm–retail price spread to zero (i.e., farmers could get 100 percent of the consumers' meat dollar if they slaughtered, processed, and delivered meat to the consumers' doors), this system would not necessarily be the most efficient one. In fact, it was discovered long ago that specialization and trade based on comparative advantage (as discussed in the previous chapter) would result in a greater total and per capita real income. A severe price and income squeeze on farmers during the 1970s prompted several farm groups to slaughter, process, and retail their own meat. If there were excess profits to be had in it, this approach would prevail, but in a competitive situation, economies normally accrue to specialization, which is difficult to accomplish in a farm–retail operation.

The major utility aspects affecting marketing costs and the farmer's share are place, time, and form.

Place. Transportation costs for meat could be reduced by raising beef cattle near the centers of population, of course, but this would increase other costs—feed, labor, pollution abatement, etc.—and negate the comparative advantages of production in the Milo Belt and the Corn Belt. It would be less efficient from an overall standpoint, and consumer prices would increase.

Time. Any product with a seasonal variation in production is faced with a time problem if the product should be made available to consumers uniformly throughout the year. Beets provide an excellent example of a product with a seasonality of production—the entire crop is harvested within a short period. In processed form, however, beets may be stored and made available for the remainder of the year. Although processing and storage are costly and reduce the farmer's share, this recourse cannot be classed as inefficient.

Beef is being produced more uniformly throughout the year as large commercial feedlots grow in importance. If year-round production had been attempted when the industry was composed entirely of small family farms, costs undoubtedly would have increased. Net costs probably have not increased with commercial lots since cost gains from economies of size and a more complete utilization of facilities probably offset the cost-increasing tendency of reduced summer gains. There still is some seasonality in beef production however. This means that slaughtering and processing facilities have unused capacity at times, which causes unit costs to increase and is reflected in marketing spreads and farmers' shares. To reduce this cost by completely leveling out production might increase production costs.

Cold storage is used to a greater extent with pork than beef or lamb to alleviate the time factor. This increases the marketing spread and reduces the farmer's share but again, cannot be classified as inefficiency per se.

Form. Some products require more processing (change in form) than others. Pork is subjected to more processing than beef, which goes far to explain why the farmer's share is smaller for pork than for beef. Canned beets are an extreme example of a product that requires much more processing relative to value than either pork, beef, or lamb. Again, this is not an indictment of marketing efficiency.

Reduction in Farmer's Share over Time. As pointed out earlier, the farmer's share has been on a generally declining trend. Inefficiencies cannot be completely ruled out, but studies on the market structure of the meat industry have failed to confirm any substantial degree of inefficiency. There is plenty of evidence that consumers are demanding (or merchandisers are selling them) more and more services, including such things as more trimming, more boning, better and more attractive packaging, more processing and preparation (e.g., fully cooked meats, TV dinners, etc.), more parking space, air-conditioned stores, carryout service, etc. The cost of all such items ends up in the marketing spread and reduces the farmer's percentage of the dollar spent for meat. The recent trend toward patronizing discount food stores despite their reduction in some services may be partially responsible for the recent leveling off of the farmer's share in recent years. There is no indication, however, of a slackening in the demand for built-in convenience in meat items.

Implications With Respect to Profits

Any increase in marketing profits would show up in the price spread and—everything else being equal—would result in a decrease in the farmer's share. As has been pointed out, the food industry has been subjected to a number of investigations when monopoly and undue profits were suspected. The Consent Decree was an outgrowth of one such investigation and put some restrictions on the actions of the packers involved. More recent investigations have been conducted, the most comprehensive one being the 1965 National Commission on Food Marketing, which covered the entire food industry, including a complete investigation of the livestock and meat industry. Although the Commission was critical of some aspects of the industry, it ended with a generally favorable conclusion, expressed by Brandow (1966), its executive director, as follows: The Commission concluded its study believing that the contribution of the food industry to a high and rising level of living was fully comparable with that of other leading sectors of the economy. In broadest terms, the industry is efficient and progressive. Supplied by a highly productive agriculture, manufacturers and distributors have provided consumers with a varied, abundant, and nutritious array of goods at generally reasonable prices.

Some data are available on industry profits that are adequate for comparison with other industries but cannot settle the question of what constitutes a reasonably adequate profit level. The latter requires a value judgment, and differences of opinion are to be expected. Compared to other U.S. industries, including chain food stores, the meat packing industry generally had the lowest returns. For example, the national Commission on Food Marketing (1966B) stated that profits to retail food chains were "high relative to other industries during most of the postwar period. These high levels of profits resulted from a rapid rise in popularity of the supermarket. In response to this increase in demand, many thousands of supermarkets were built. As this rapid building program caught up with demand around 1960, profits for food retailers returned to levels comparable to other industries." Meat-packing-industry profits after taxes are typically about 1 percent of sales, which is at or near the bottom of the range for major U.S. industries. As a percentage of net worth, meat-packing profits are usually less than the average for major U.S. industries—about 10 to 11 percent during the 1970s and into the 1980s.

What does price spread and farmers' share of the consumers' expenditure reveal about producers' profits? The same generalization applies here as with the packer's and retailer's profits discussed previously. By itself, the farmer's share (either at a given time or a change over time) is not an adequate indicator of the farmer's profit or its relation to that of other industries. A 30 percent share of $1.50 per retail pound of beef would represent more dollars than 50 percent of 70c per pound.

The farmer's profit position can be better evaluated by examining his returns on net worth as was done with the other sectors. Farm management records show that the livestock producer's returns are extremely unstable from year to year; over the long term, they average about 3 to 4 percent of equity. This is substantially lower than the percentage found in other sectors of the meat industry. The effect of relatively low returns has been apparent for many years as livestock production shifts into fewer and larger units—a trend that was accentuated during the farm crisis of the 1980s.

Seasonality in Price Spreads

Seasonal variation in meat production leads to a seasonal variation in prices, and this, in turn, affects price spreads. Production of pork normally drops off during mid-summer and prices rise seasonally. During this period the farm value rises and the farm–retail spread declines slightly. With a lag of about one month, retail prices rise. It may be noted, however, that the farm–retail spread and retail prices are considerably more stable than production and net farm values. Beef and lamb also exhibit seasonal tendencies. The magnitude of seasonal variations associated with beef is considerably less than that of either pork or lamb.

Price Spread Versus Gross Margin
and Profit Margin

Some confusion exists with respect to the definition of price spread, industry gross margin, and profit margin. On occasion, they have been

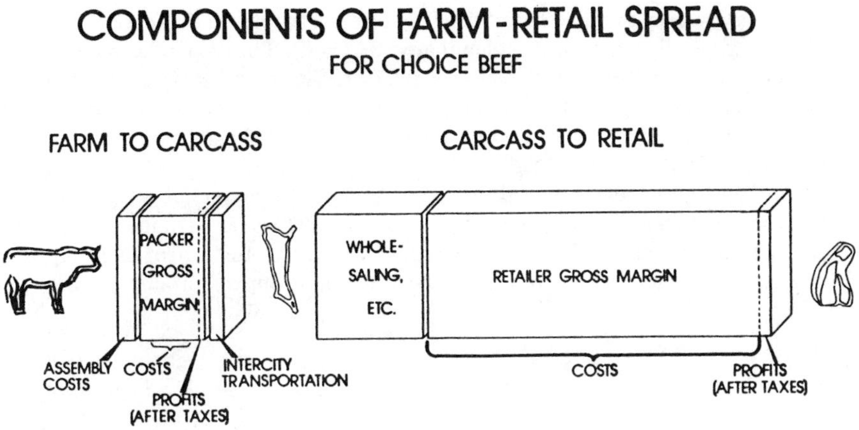

COMPONENTS OF FARM-RETAIL SPREAD
FOR CHOICE BEEF

FARM TO CARCASS   CARCASS TO RETAIL

Fig. 18.7. Schematic Comparison of Price Spread, Gross Margin, and Profit. (USDA 1975A.)

used interchangeably, but they are not equivalent, and important errors are made in using them synonymously. Figure 18.7 illustrates the basic differences among the terms.

Price spreads, gross margin, and net profit margins measure different aspects and components of the spread between what farmers receive and consumers pay.

Price spreads are normally greater than gross margins for any single marketing agency. Likewise, gross margins are greater than net profit margins (USDA, 1975A).

The farm–retail spread includes all costs and profits from assembly of the live animals (shown at the extreme left side of Fig. 18.7) to purchase of the meat at retail outlets (shown at the extreme right side of Fig. 18.7). Within that system, packer gross margin (which includes packer costs and profits) and retail gross margin (which includes retailer costs and profits) are isolated diagramatically from the other costs encompassed in USDA's spread computations.

The farm–carcass spread includes approximate charges for marketing cattle, slaughtering, and transporting the dressed carcass to the cities where consumed.

The carcass–retail spread includes not only the gross margin for retailing, but also the charges for other intermediate marketing services such as cutting carcasses into smaller portions, wholesaling, and local delivery to retail stores.

Gross margins (difference between dollars paid and dollars received) of packers and retailers, on the other hand, don't take into account all marketing functions. Rather, they represent the tab for a packer's or retailer's labor cost, packaging, overhead, other costs and any net profit. They exclude some items included in the spread, like charges for transportation and services performed by businesses other than meat packers or retailers. Because such costs are included in what they pay for beef, gross margins of these firms are smaller than the overall USDA spreads.

Profit margins, before and after taxes, are a relatively small component of the gross margin and total operating cost of a firm. They are usually expressed as a percent of total sales or of stockholder's equity for a firm or group of firms, rather than for an individual product or group of products (USDA, 1975A).

MARKET BASKET

Market basket calculations are for a "basket," or group of products, representative of average quantities of domestic, farm-originated food products purchased annually by wage earners and clerical worker families and single workers living alone. Market basket statistics have four components:

1. Retail cost—which is actually somewhat less than an average sized family's expenditure for food since the market basket does not include cost of meals away from the home, imported foods, seafoods, and foods of nonfarm origin
2. Farm value—the gross returns to farmers for the quantity of farm products equivalent to those in the market basket
3. Farm–retail spread—the difference between retail cost and farm value
4. The farmer's share.

The farm–retail market basket spread is similar in concept to the price spread in that it is an estimate of costs of marketing (assembling, processing, transporting, and distributing). In the case of the market basket, the spread is the cost for the entire quantity in the basket, whereas the price spread discussed earlier was cost for one unit of the product; for meat, it was the cost per retail pound.

Table 18.1 shows trends in the index of various components of the market basket of all farm foods, including meat, and for meat separately. Retail costs have advanced at a faster rate than farm value. The farm–retail spread has increased for the same reasons explained under price spreads. The rate of increase in the spread was higher for meat

Table 18.1. The Market Basket of Farm Food and Meat Products: Retail Cost, Farm Value, Farm to Retail Spread, and Farmer's Share of Retail Costs, 1970-1983.*

	Market basket of farm food				Market basket of meat products			
Year	Retail Cost[†]	Farm Value[‡]	Farm to Retail Spread§ (% of Index)	Farmer's Share of Retail Cost (%)	Retail Cost[†]	Farm Value[‡]	Farm to Retail Spread§ (% of Index)	Farmer's Share of Retail Cost (%)
1970	113.7	114.0	113.5	37	116.6	113.7	120.0	53
1971	115.7	114.6	116.4	37	115.5	112.1	119.3	52
1972	121.3	125.1	119.1	38	129.8	133.2	124.7	56
1973	142.3	167.9	127.2	44	160.1	179.5	137.4	60
1974	161.9	181.5	150.4	42	162.9	162.1	163.9	54
1975	173.6	187.8	165.2	40	178.3	188.3	166.5	57
1976	175.4	178.0	173.9	38	178.5	170.1	188.4	51
1977	179.2	178.5	179.6	37	174.2	169.8	179.5	53
1978	199.4	204.3	196.5	38	206.8	206.4	207.3	54
1979	222.7	226.3	220.6	38	241.9	234.6	250.4	52
1980	238.8	237.6	239.6	37	248.8	234.0	266.1	51
1981	257.1	243.0	265.4	35	257.8	235.5	284.0	49
1982	266.4	245.7	278.6	34	270.3	251.3	292.4	50
1983	268.7	240.3	285.5	33	267.2	235.8	304.0	48

Source: USDA (1984A).
*The market basket represents purchasing patterns of domestically produced farm foods in food stores by households from July 1972 through June 1974. Index: 1967 = 100%.
[†]Special index of retail prices for domestically produced foods published by the Bureau of Labor Statistics.
[‡]Gross return or payment to farmers for the farm products equivalent to foods in the market basket.
§The spread between the retail cost and farm value is an estimate of the gross margin received by marketing firms for assembling, processing, transporting, and distributing the products.

than for the basket as whole (Table 18.1). The farmer's share has exhibited a downward trend since the late 1940s. It partially recovered during the erratic price movements of the early 1970s but then returned to its former ways.

In market basket calculations, all meat is aggregated into a single figure. Of all three components, meat is by far the most important item, comprising, in recent years, about 30 percent of retail sales, 44 percent of farm value, and 20 percent of the farm–retail spread. The second and third most important food groups are fresh fruits and vegetables and dairy products, respectively. In recent years, fruits and vegetables comprised 23 percent of retail sales, 15 percent of farm value, and 28 percent of the farm–retail spread, whereas dairy products were about 17, 21, and 14 percent, respectively (USDA, 1983 and 1984A).

Market basket statistics are published quarterly and summarized annually by the USDA.

THE MARKETING BILL

The marketing bill is the total cost of marketing the entire quantity of U.S. farm-originated foods purchased by civilizians. It is the difference between consumer expenditures and farm value. Marketing bill statistics show the distribution of consumer expenditures between the marketing system and farmers, and the distribution of marketing costs among commodity groups and individual cost components such as labor, transportation, and fuel.

Since marketing costs on a per unit basis have been on an increasing trend, it is no surprise that the total marketing bill also has increased, as shown in Fig. 18.8. Out of a total marketing bill of $312 billion in 1983, the farm value was $83.6 billion; the marketing bill was the difference, or $228.4 billion (USDA, 1984A).

In dollar expenditures by consumers, the most important marketing bill item is meat—comprising about 30 percent of total expenditures.

During recent years, about one-third of the increase in the marketing bill has been due to inflation. Table 18.2 illustrates why the marketing bill has increased. The cost of energy (fuel, power, and light) has increased at a spectacular rate. Wages, materials, and rent have increased substantially, and the profit rates have also increased. Figure 18.9 shows the major components of the marketing bill in 1982. Labor costs make up the largest part of the marketing bill—33 percent of total food expenditures, approaching one-half of the costs of marketing foods. The second largest are the container and packaging costs, which

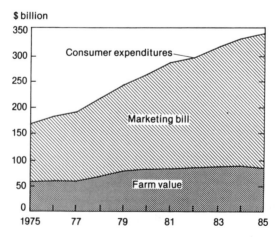

Fig. 18.8. Marketing bill, Farm value, and Expenditures for Farm Foods (For Domestic Farm Foods Purchased by Civilian Consumers for Consumption both at Home and Away from Home). (USDA Exten. Serv. undated.)

Table 18.2. Marketing Costs for Farm Food Products, 1970–1983.

Year	Labor	Packaging	Intercity Transport Rail and Truck	Fuels and Electricity Cost (Billion $)	Corporate Profits Before Taxes	Other	Total Marketing Bill
1970	32.2	8.2	5.2	2.2	3.6	23.7	75.1
1971	34.5	8.5	6.0	2.4	3.9	23.2	78.5
1972	36.6	8.9	6.1	2.5	4.0	24.3	82.4
1973	39.7	9.4	6.4	2.8	5.4	23.4	87.1
1974	44.3	11.8	7.5	3.7	6.1	24.8	98.2
1975	48.3	13.3	8.4	4.6	7.1	29.7	111.4
1976	53.8	14.5	9.1	5.0	7.6	35.0	125.0
1977	58.3	15.1	9.7	5.6	7.9	36.1	132.7
1978	66.1	16.6	10.5	6.3	9.2	38.6	147.1
1979	75.1	18.6	11.8	8.0	9.9	42.7	166.1
1980	81.7	21.1	13.0	9.9	11.0	46.7	183.4
1981	91.2	22.9	14.3	11.8	12.0	53.0	205.2
1982	96.7	23.2	14.7	12.4	13.1	55.7	215.8
1983	102.7	24.2	15.3	13.2	14.2	58.8	228.4

Source: USDA (1984A).

account for 8 percent of total food expenditures. Intercity truck and rail transportation comprise 5 percent, and profits, 5 percent. As shown in Table 18.2, the cost of each of the components of the marketing bill has increased drastically in dollar terms since 1970.

The marketing bill does not include all expenditures for food in the U.S. The Department of Commerce publishes data on personal consumption expenditures for food that include a number of items not in

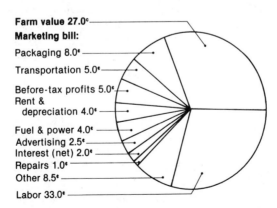

Fig. 18.9. What a Dollar Spent on Food Paid for in 1984. (USDA Ag. Exten. Serv. undated.)

the marketing bill. Among these items is food served in institutions, on airlines and dining cars, at recreational facilities, at dormitories, through vending machines, etc. For example, total food expenditures were estimated to be $329 billion in 1983 compared to consumer expenditures of $228 billion in marketing bill calculations.

FACTORS AFFECTING MARKETING COSTS AND SHARE TO FARMERS

The circumstances of an individual producer can vary considerably from the averages presented here, and the share accruing to individuals likewise can vary. The following factors affect a farmer's share:

1. *Type of livestock program.* A farmer who maintains a cow herd, retains and feeds out his own calves, sells direct to a local packer, who, in turn, sells the meat to a local retailer would receive a considerably larger share of the retail dollar than a neighbor who buys yearling feeders, finishes them out and sells to a distant packer who ships the meat to a still more distant retailer.
2. *Costs incurred and prices received.* These will vary considerably among producers. Cost control is partially a matter of management expertise. Prices paid for feeder animals and received for finished stock are related to marketing ability, but vagaries of the market can affect profits.
3. *Grade of livestock fed, particularly yield grade.* This can affect the price and quantity of meat at retail.

Examples are available from studies that illustrate varying shares of returns to producers under several different types of production and marketing programs. The results obtained are not to be construed as suggestive of average returns that producers might expect from the indicated production or marketing programs. Neither are they suggestive of the superiority of any one production or marketing program over another.

As an illustration, the results from a South Dakota report (Schulte, undated) are shown in Fig. 18.10. In this study, Example No. 1 assumes that U.S. Choice grade steer calves were raised in southeastern South Dakota, marketed as finished steers through the Sioux Falls terminal, slaughtered locally, and the Choice carcasses sold to a New York retail firm. Example No. 2 assumes that U.S. Good grade calves were raised and fed out on the same farm in southeastern South Dakota, sold through the Sioux Falls terminal to a southwestern Minnesota

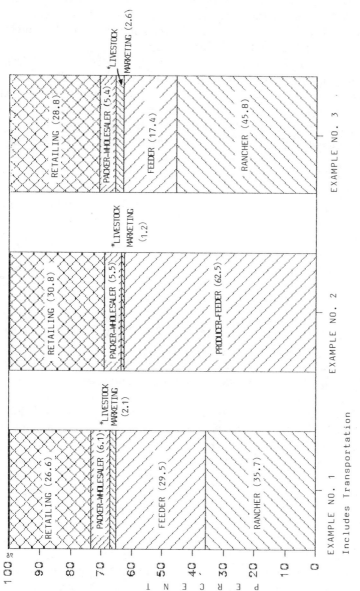

Fig. 18.10. Beef: Comparison of the Percentage of Gross Returns to Producers and Marketing Agencies. (Schulte, undated.)

packer who, in turn, sold the U.S. Good grade carcasses to a retailer in Omaha. Example No. 3 assumes that U.S. Good grade yearlings in south-central South Dakota were sold through auction to a feeder in eastern South Dakota, marketed as finished steers through the Sioux Falls terminal to a local packer who shipped the U.S. Good grade carcasses to a retail firm in Philadelphia.

The major variation in shares is in the split between the original producer (rancher or producer–feeder) and the feeder. In Example No. 2, producer and feeder are one and the same person, who therefore gets the entire 62.5 percent. The combined rancher and feeder share in Examples No. 1 and No. 3 is approximately the same, but the division between rancher and feeder is considerably different in the two examples.

Figure 18.11 shows results of a USDA study (Duewer, 1970). The beef example assumes that U.S. Good grade feeder steers from near Casper, Wyo., were marketed through the Omaha terminal to a feeder near Lincoln, Nebraska, and then sold as finished Choice grade steers through the Omaha terminal to a local packer who shipped the carcasses to a retailer in New York. The same program was assumed for 1967 and 1969. The pork example (again the same program at two different dates) assumes that hogs were raised in western Iowa, sold through the Sioux City terminal to a local packer, and that the wholesale cuts were then shipped to a retail firm in Los Angeles. In the beef example, both the rancher and the retailer shares were less in 1969 than in 1967. Most of the gain was in the feeder's share. In the pork example, both the retailer and packer–wholesaler shares declined from 1967 to 1969, with the gain going to the original producer.

These examples are presented, not to emphasize the quantities shown, but to illustrate the point that shares can vary with different programs (the South Dakota study) and that different shares can be obtained from the same program at different times (the USDA study).

Dissatisfaction exists among producers over the farmer's share, and various actions have been suggested to alleviate the situation. In some instances, farmers have set up farmer-owned cooperatives to capture a greater share of marketing profits. In a few instances, farmers have organized cooperative packing plants. Most cooperative packing ventures have failed. Although several successful plants are currently operating, they handle only a minor fraction of livestock slaughter.

Farmer organizations on occasion have indicated an interest in the ownership and operation of a national retail food chain but have not made the plunge. Generally speaking, cooperative ventures in retailing to date have been somewhat less than smashing successes. If the profit rates reported earlier in this chapter are accurate, it appears doubtful

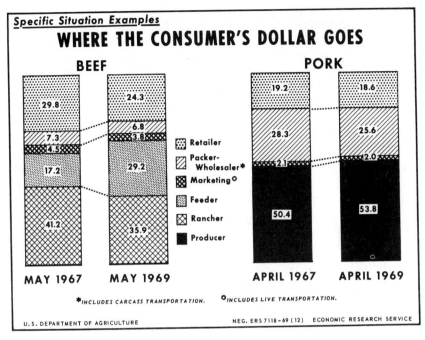

Fig. 18.11.   Where the Consumer's Dollar Goes. (USDA.)

that any significant one-shot gain can be squeezed out in favor of farmers, but this is no excuse for assuming a passive attitude toward marketing costs. Improvements undoubtedly can be made, and a series of small gains might be significant in improving a produer's position.

COMMENTS ON SELECTED ITEMS OF MARKETING COST

Live animal shrinkage, transportation, and bruise, crippling, and death losses have been selected for particular comment here. In the determination of price spreads as previously discussed, account was taken of retail "store shrinkage." In addition, cooler shrinkage was recognized, along with trimming loss, in the conversion factors used for carcass weight and live weight equivalent. Neither shrinkage in live animal weight from the feedlot to market place, however, nor bruise, crippling, or death loss was explicitly considered. Transportation costs were specifically accounted for in the spread calculations but merit additional comment. Rail and truck rates have increased more than threefold since 1969 (Fig. 18.12), and in view of possible U.S. energy shortages,

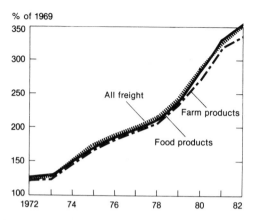

Fig. 18.12. Change in Retail Freight Rate for Agricultural Products, 1972–1982. (USDA Exten. Serv., undated.)

transportation may become an increasingly critical factor in livestock and meat shipments, as with all commodities. Transportation is significant not only in the number of dollars involved, but also as a factor in the changing structural characteristics of the livestock–meat industry. These two aspects are related.

Transportation

Early developments in transportation, and their impact upon the livestock and meat industry, were noted in previous chapters. Overland droving in eastern areas, the great cattle trails of the range area, and the era of canal building were all passed by as the railroads pushed their steel rails throughout the country. The railroad system set the pattern for concentrated and centralized livestock marketing and meat-packing locations. Then came the motor truck and highway system, which was instrumental again in reversal of the organizational structure (decentralization).

The impact of transportation development was not limited to the livestock sector. Hulbert (1920), writing at the time some of these significant changes were occurring, said, "If the great American novel is ever written, I hazard the guess that its plot will be woven around the theme of American transportation, for that has been the vital factor in the national development of the United States. Every problem in the building of the Republic has been, in the last analysis, a problem of transportation," In view of subsequent concern with social and environmental problems, undoubtedly many currently would disagree with the attachment of this degree of importance to transportation. Even in the earlier days, concurrent developments in refrigeration, communications, and implementation of grade standards were teamed with transportation as factors in changing the structure of the livestock and meat industry. There is no question, however, that the central importance of transportation lies in marketing cost reductions. Conceivably, droving could have continued as the mode of transport as production expanded to mid-continent. But at what cost? Today, cattle are droved from the southern fringes of the Sahara Desert more than 1000 miles to Lagos, Nigeria, and other west African coastal cities, but consumption is only 8 to 10 pounds per person and not many people can afford the price. Transportation alone would not solve the Nigerian problem, but it would help.

Innovations in Transportation. It is not enough simply to refer to railroads and trucks as means of transportation. Many improvements have been (and are being) made within each system that sustain a continuous competitive contest between these two types of carriers. In this contest, trucks have virtually taken over all short hauls of both livestock and meat. The truck advantage in short hauls lies in the faster time, lower cost, convenience, and flexibility, including pickup and delivery at destination. Trucks are vying for long hauls of livestock by increasing capacity, controlling temperature, and improving designs that reduce bruising and crippling and expedite loading and unloading. Cross-country, triple-deck trucks haul thousands of hogs from the Midwest to the West Coast each year. Some of these are equipped with air-conditioning units for use in hot weather; others have sprinkling or fogging devices. Triple-deck trucks are also used for lambs. Double-deck cattle trucks have been in use for a number of years.

Railroads have also made improvements with multideck cars and improved construction for greater animal comfort and reduced bruising, including such innovations as improved ventilation, suspension, coupling, and operational procedures that reduce starting and stopping jerks. More recent developments involve the use of multideck rail cars with continuous feed and water provided during the trip, making unloading for food and rest unnecessary. Most railroads now operate "express" livestock trains to speed delivery.

Some years ago railroads introduced "piggyback" hauling of loaded trucks as a countermeasure to truck competition. Piggyback use in refrigerated trucks has increased for meat and is used to some extent for live animals. Significant improvements have been made in the refrigeration capacity of rail cars, and, in long hauls, the railroads are competitive with trucks in meat transportation.

Containerization and palletization of meat shipments have progressed, but much research is still needed to perfect the techniques and maintain quality during shipment. These developments apply to both truck and railroads—and, in fact, extend to airlines and shipping lines as well. Lack of standardization in container size is a problem not only for a given mode of transportation, but especially when shipments involve different modes of transportation.

Types of Motor Carriers.   A first, broad classification of motor carriers is "for hire" and "private" truckers. Private truckers who haul their own products are subject only to state trucking regulations. For-hire truckers fall into two classes: (1) regulated carriers, which are subject to Federal regulations, and (2) unregulated carriers, or "exempt carriers," which, at the Federal level, are usually subject only to regulations concerning the type of commodities that may be hauled, safety specifications, and maximum hour limitations for drivers. The crucial aspects of exemption are freedom in rates charged and routes of operation. Historically, provisions of the Interstate Commerce Act placed regulation of transportation under the Interstate Commerce Commission (ICC). Through a series of administrative rulings, court decisions, and amendments, however, the hauling of certain commodities by truck was made exempt from Federal regulation.

The major classification of exempt commodities is unmanufactured agricultural products, which include livestock—with certain exceptions. The determination of what constitutes "manufacturing" as applied to agricultural and fishery products has been a matter of contention in establishing the list of exempt products. The exemption does not apply to railroads. Under the provisions of the Motor Carrier Act of 1980, unprocessed farm products continued to be unregulated, but other farm-related products have been added to exempt status (Hutchinson, 1981).

Within the group of regulated carriers, a distinction is made between "common carriers," which are available to the public generally, and "contract carriers," which provide services to shippers under contract. Until the passage in 1980 of the Motor Carrier and Staggers Rail Acts, regulated carriers (railroads and regulated trucks) were subject to numerous Federal restrictions including the charges, routes used, and how permits may be issued. Certain states have regulations (taxes, rates charged, safety requirements, load limits, etc.) that apply to all carriers (exempt or regulated) operating in, or through, that state. Although some regulations are still in effect, the 1980 acts were intended to encourage competetion and increase economic efficiency by providing regulated carriers with more flexibility in operation as well as in rate-setting.[5] For example, the 1980 Motor Carrier Act allows rates to fluctuate freely 10 percent above or below a reference point based on previous rates. Furthermore, it requires that ICC take into consideration future costs, a provision not allowed under the pre-1980 conditions. Although the economic deregulation of regulated trucks and railroads in 1980 gave carriers more freedom in rate setting and operating conditions, exempt carriers have greater flexibility in rates and in operation than do regulated carriers.

Comparison of Truck and Rail Rates. A regional study conducted by western states (Capener, 1969) indicated that truck rates on cattle were clearly less than rail rates on hauls of up to 200 to 300 miles (Fig. 18.13). For both feeder and slaughter cattle, the rate for interstate trucks was greater than that for rail over distances more than 300 to 400 miles. Rail rates on slaughter cattle were about 15 percent higher than rail rates on feeder cattle. Rates are important, but other factors must also be considered. Usually, some trucking is required to bring livestock to a rail loading point and take them away from the unloading point. Time in transit is also important and will be discussed later. The adequacy of rest stops is a factor in shrinkage. On this score, railroads have had better facilities than those available for trucks, but in recent years improvements have been made in privately operated rest stops.

The Back-Haul Problem. A factor contributing to livestock transport costs is difficulty in obtaining back-hauls. Established truckers often have contracts for possible return freight, but timing is a problem. At best, back-hauls are irregular, inconvenient, or seasonal. Railroads may be able to park cars in freight yards for use at their convenience, but the cars may eventually return empty. Truckers normally must return to their base of operations within a relatively short time,

---

[5]Opponents of deregulation suggested that contrary to the intent of the law, deregulation of trucks and railroads could actually reduce competition, increase rates, and deprive isolated rural areas from needed services. Some studies were carried out in the early 1980s to examine the impact of deregulation on efficiency and rates. For example, Beilock and Freeman (1984) examined the impact of deregulation on motor carriers' services to small and isolated locations in Florida. The result of a 1982 survey of 893 shippers and receivers located throughout Florida indicated a large consensus that deregulation is working well. This conclusion was based on observed lower rates, increased competition, and improved services. The study found no difference in services between different firm sizes. Another example is the investigation by Fuller et al. (1983) of the impact of the 1980 Staggers Act on railroad rates. The study concluded that the increased flexibility in rate-setting provided by the act should not yield general rate increases on export-grain movements.

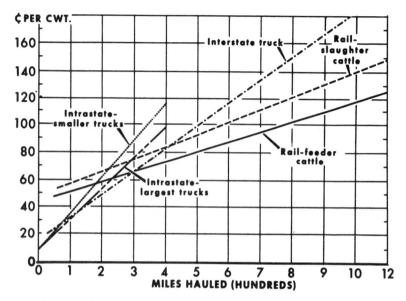

Fig. 18.13. Comparisons of Regional Rate Functions for Hauling Cattle in the West. (Capener, 1969.)

whether loaded or empty. The impact of empty returns can be illustrated by a hypothetical example. Assume that the cost of operating a diesel-powered semitrailer is $1.20 per loaded mile. If return hauls are never available, a one-way charge of $2.40 per mile would be required to break even (ignoring the fact that costs would be slightly less on the empty return). If back-hauls were available one-half the time, however, a charge of $1.80 per mile would give a monetary return equivalent to $2.40 per mile without a back-haul.

An advantage of air-conditioned trucks is their adaptability to back-hauls of perishable products. Truckers operating under exempt status have a problem in that the return load must also be an exempt product if carried for hire. This difficulty may be avoided if the trucker buys (takes title to) the cargo for the return trip. Doing so can be costly, however, unless outlets are prearranged.

Industry Location Related to Transportation Costs. The transportation rate structure plays a crucial role in industrial location. Other factors, of course, affect packing plant location, but, everything else being equal, the relationship between the cost of shipping live animals versus the cost of shipping dressed meat is a determining factor, as it is for the location of feedyards. The relationship between cost of shipping feed grain versus cost of shipping meat (or livestock) can determine where livestock will be fed.

After a period of relative stability in freight rates, an industry will develop a locational pattern compatible with that rate structure. Subsequent changes of an unequal geographical nature can disrupt the locational pattern. The flour milling industry in parts of the hard red winter-wheat area experienced such a disruption during the early 1960s following a reduction in wheat rates to Southeastern states without an equivalent reduction in flour rates. As a result, many flour mills ceased operation in the hard red winter-wheat area, and milling capacity expanded in the Southeastern states. Cattle feeding in the Milo Belt is somewhat vulnerable to the transportation rate structure since a reduction in feed-grain rates to the Southwest or West Coast areas without equivalent changes in livestock and meat rates could disrupt cattle feeding and meat packing there.

Shrinkage

"Shrinkage" is recognized as a loss of weight. Livestock typically shrink during the marketing process, and meat loses weight in marketing channels. Where livestock is sold on a liveweight basis, the number of pounds sold (or paid for) is equally as important as the price. Directly or indirectly, a reduction in weight represents a cost. When meat loses weight in marketing channels, that must be reflected as a cost. In marketing, a distinction is made between the following:

1. "Actual" shrink
2. "Pencil" shrink
3. "Cooler" shrink
4. "Cutting" shrink
5. "Store" shrink

Cooler shrink—a loss due to evaporation of moisture—usually ranges from 1.5 to 3 percent by weight. Cutting shrink is 2 to 3 percent, and store shrink, 5 to 5.5 percent. Cooler shrink, cutting shrink, and store shrink were considered in a previous chapter; this section will be devoted to live animal shrinkage, i.e., actual shrink and pencil shrink.

Actual loss in body weight may arise from excretory shrink (the emptying of the digestive and urinary tracts) and tissue shrink (a loss of body tissue). "Tissue shrink occurs on long, extended shipments or during long periods of fast. These two types of shrinkage probably occur as two distinct phases in the shrinkage process. Only in the early part of shipment do excretory and tissue shrinkage occur simultaneously. During the latter part of the shipment, tissue shrinkage is relatively more important" (Harston, 1959A).

The economic importance of tissue shrink is readily apparent. A loss in body tissue reduces carcass weight and directly affects value. If buyers (and sellers) were able to evaluate "fill" precisely and if proper allowances were always made in the agreed-upon price, excretory shrink would have no economic significance. In slaughter livestock, this would involve a precise estimate of carcass yield, and in feeder livestock, an estimate of deviation from normal fill (i.e., an "excess-fill," or the opposite, a "shrunk-out" condition). Professional marketers are able to average out these estimates over a number of lots with a high degree of accuracy. The occasional buyer or seller usually lacks comparable ability, and even the professional may be off on any given lot. In addition to impreciseness of knowledge, inequality of bargaining ability may also result in prices not adequately reflecting shrunk-out or excess-fill conditions. Therefore, excretory shrink cannot be dismissed as completely noneconomic.

Factors Related to Shrinkage. A number of studies have been made over the years in attempts to measure the extent of shrinkage and determine associated factors. Several factors have been isolated, but inconsistency in results points up the fact that shrinkage is a complex phenomenon. Efforts to derive predictive mathematical functions have, in general, been marked with a relatively low degree of accuracy. Results of the studies permit some generalizations on explanatory variables, however, and provide guidelines for manipulation of controllable variables.

Major factors that affect shrinkage are time in transit, distance hauled, degree of fill, weather conditions, weighing conditions, sex, weight of the animals, class of animals, type of feed, mode of transportation, handling procedures, preconditioning, type of feedlot shelter, rate of gain near end of feeding period, and yield grade. Most of the research on shrinkage has been concerned with liveweight shrink, but some studies—e.g., (Raikes and Tilley, 1975)—have dealt with hot-carcass shrink as well as liveweight shrink.

Time in Transit and Distance Hauled. Time in transit and distance hauled may be discussed together since these variables are highly interrelated and have the same general effect on shrinkage. Liveweight shrink has been consistently found to have a positive relationship with distance (and time) to market (Abbenhaus and Penny, 1951; Henning and Thomas, 1962; and Raikes and Tilley, 1975). Shrinkage, whether measured in pounds or percentage of body weight lost, increases with distance and time, but not at a constant rate throughout the trip. Shrinkage occurs at a faster rate during the early part of the trip, meaning that shrinkage increases at a decreasing rate with distance and time. Figure 18.14 shows the results of an Indiana study in which

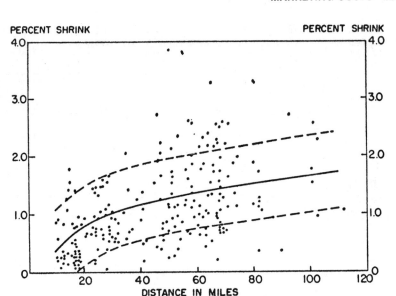

Fig. 18.14.   Farm-Weight to Sale- (or Catch-) Weight of Selected Hogs Sold at Local and Terminal Markets in Relation to Distance Traveled, Oct. 31, 1956 to Feb. 24, 1958. (Stout and Cox, 1959).

shrinkage of hogs increased throughout the distance, but the rate tapered off with distance. The same general type of relationship holds between shrinkage and time in transit and is also consistent for cattle and sheep. Of these two variables, time in transit is probably the more realistic to deal with since two different truckers, hauling identical loads over the same route, might have different times in transit. Over-the-road speeds may differ, length of meal and coffee stops may differ, etc.

The amount of shrinkage to be expected with time or distance cannot be precisely specified because other factors also enter the picture. Tables 18.3 and 18.4, however, show the results of well-planned studies of cattle and hog shrinkage. It may be noted in Table 18.3 that average shrinkage for the group was 3.9 percent for the entire 200-mile haul and that nearly one-half of this occurred during the first 25 miles. Table 18.4 again illustrates a declining rate of shrinkage for hogs, reaching a maximum of 2.76 percent when the hogs were not allowed a fill at the market.

Similar results were obtained in a study (Table 18.5) of marketing alternatives and costs for Wyoming cattle (St. Clair, 1976). He stated that "it is probable that cattle shrink nearly 2% during the first hour of the trip. After 3 hours they have shrunk 4% and after 5 hours, 5%.

Table 18.3. Percentage of Shrink for 60 Fat Cattle Between Each Check Weighing During 200-Mile Truck Haul (Total Animal Weight Equals 100%)

			Miles traveled between weighing				
Weight Class	No. Head in Each Class	Avg. Weight (lb)	0–25 (%)	25–50 (%)	50–100 (%)	100–200 (%)	Total Weight Loss (%)
Group avg.	60	1122	1.8	0.7	0.8	0.6	3.9
Under 1000	11	954	1.5	0.7	0.9	0.8	3.9
1000–1099	10	1056	2.1	0.9	0.8	0.3	4.1
1100–1199	24	1139	1.8	0.8	0.8	0.7	4.1
Over 1200	15	1263	1.9	0.5	0.7	0.5	3.6

Source: Abbenhaus (1951).

Therafter, shrinkage progresses more slowly to 8 or 8.5% after 25 to 30 hours of hauling." The Wyoming study found that shrinkage costs for 600-lb feeder cattle traveling a distance of up to 760 miles (19 hours in transit) exceed the direct cost of transportation (Table 18.5). It should be pointed out that shrinkage costs to producers depend not only on hours in transit and the amount of fillback but also on the market price at the time of sale. Therefore, a different truck transportation cost and different market prices than those used in St. Clair's study would generate different conclusions than those stated here. Producers must adjust their marketing methods accordingly. In a study comparing costs of selling feeder cattle in Montana through direct and

Table 18.4. Relationship of Length of Haul to Shrinkage of Hogs (1132 Lots; 38,303 Hogs).

	Shrinkage	
	When not fed at Market	When fed at Market
Miles hauled	(%)	(%)
0–5	1.06	*
6–15	1.12	1.03
16–25	1.39	1.24
26–35	1.75	1.51
36–45	2.06	1.79
46–55	2.50	1.99
56–65	2.68	2.03
66–75	2.76	2.08
76–85	*	2.14
86–95	*	2.16

Source: Wiley and Cox (1955).
*Sufficient data not available.

Table 18.5. Estimated Marketing Costs for Shipping 600-lb Wyoming Feeder Cattle to Markets at Various Selected Distances from the Ranch.*

Miles	Hours in Transit at 40 mph	Gross Shrink (%)	Net Shrink (Assume 35% fill-back) (%)	Market Charges Based on $4.2/hd ($/cwt)[†]	Truck Transport[‡] ($/cwt)	Cost of Shrink ($/cwt @ $35 price)§	Total Costs ($/cwt)
10	0.25	0.60	0.39	0.70	0.09	0.14	0.93
50	1.25	2.15	1.40	0.70	0.24	0.49	1.43
100	2.50	3.73	2.42	0.70	0.39	0.85	1.94
200	5.00	5.00	3.25	0.70	0.63	1.14	2.47
300	7.50	5.63	3.66	0.70	0.84	1.28	2.82
400	10.00	6.04	3.93	0.70	1.03	1.38	3.11
600	15.00	6.76	4.39	0.70	1.37	1.54	3.61
720	18.00	7.10	4.62	0.70	1.55	1.62	3.87
760	19.00	7.20	4.68	0.70	1.61	1.64	3.95
800	20.00	7.30	4.74	0.70	1.67	1.66	4.03
920	23.00	7.60	4.94	0.70	1.85	1.73	4.28
1000	25.00	7.80	5.07	0.70	1.96	1.77	4.43
1200	30.00	8.15	5.30	0.70	2.20	1.86	4.76

Source: Adapted from St. Clair (1976).
*Estimates in the table are smoothed adaptation and somewhat of a compromise between data obtained from various sources.
[†]For breakdowns of market charges at Wyoming auctions, out-of-state auctions, and terminals, see St. Clair (1976).
[‡]Transportation costs are based on a rate function fitted to the results of a survey of auction and terminal-market operators. The basic equation is as follows: $\log Y = 0.18126 + 0.70348 \log X$, where X = distance (miles) and Y = transportation charges (cents per mile).
§ The average price received for beef cattle by Wyoming farmers and ranchers during the five years, 1970–74, was $33.92/cwt.

indirect outlets, Marsh (1983) concluded "When market distance is increased, direct costs of transportation and costs of shrink are significant. Thus, the compensating prices at the auctions or terminals must increase significantly to induce a producer to forego a direct ranch sale."

Raikes and Tilley (1975) found that hot-carcass weight shrink was not significantly affected by distance.

Degree of Fill. Degree of fill refers to the extent feed and/or water are denied, or made available, to the animals both prior to shipment and at the destination. Since excretory shrink results from elimination of the digestive and urinary tracts, it stands to reason that some of this loss will be quickly regained when the animals have access to feed and water, as shown in Table 18.4. The degree of fill, however, is highly variable, depending upon:

1. Whether the animals were taken off feed prior to shipping
2. Quantity of feed and water consumed during rest stops
3. Time allowed for fill and degree of emotional distrubance during transit and during the fill periods

Some shippers claim to regain all the shrink, but instances are known where emotional disturbance have resulted in no fill at all.

Raikes and Tilley (1975) found that withholding both feed and water from slaughter steers for 12 hours prior to slaughter had a significant effect on both liveweight shrink and hot-carcass shrink. That degree of fasting resulted in an additional liveweight shrink of 2.128 percent over that of the control (nonfasted) animals, and the hot-carcass weight of the fasted steers was 7.762 pounds lower than that of the control steers. Their work and that of others suggests that withholding of feed, but not water, will not increase hot-carcass shrinkage, but that withholding both does.

Shrinkage is one variable that is at least partially controllable by a shipper. Generally speaking, it is considered desirable to do any necessary sorting several days prior to shipping, to withhold feed immediately prior to shipment, to handle the animals as quietly and gently as possible during loading (utilizing a pen and loading chute arrangement that facilitates speed with a minimum of excitement), and to minimize time in transit consistent with road conditions and general safety considerations. Time of arrival at the market will depend upon length of haul. If a public market is used, the time of arrival should be scheduled. On relatively short hauls, arrival two to three hours prior to market opening will give the animals time to settle down and quench their thirst. Then, if a sale can be made shortly after the market opens, feeding probably will not be economical (Wiley and Cox, 1955). On longer hauls, it is desirable to schedule arrival for the evening prior to the day of sale and give access to both feed and water.

Any attempt to gain excess fill is not recommended. Experienced buyers will insist on docking the price of such animals.

Weather Conditions. Shrinkage tends to increase as temperatures move from moderate levels toward either extreme of heat or cold, as illustrated in Fig. 18.15 in the case of hogs. "Extreme temperatures have an effect on fat cattle shrinkage during marketing. But other things—wind, rain, snow, humidity, and other weather conditions—seem to have more effect than temperature alone" (Harston, 1959B). In the Raikes and Tilley (1975) study, a significant relationship was shown between shrinkage and "feeding period." Feeding period re-

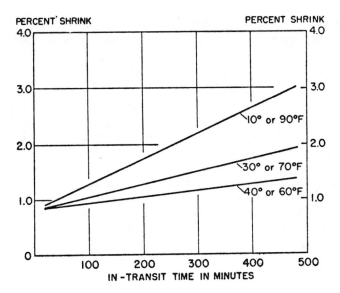

Fig. 18.15.   Effects of Variation Around 50°F Over Time on In-Transit Shrinkage of Slaughter-Weight Market Hogs, from 232 Observations. (Stout and Cox, 1959).

ferred to different time periods,[6] and the authors reasoned that weather condition was the basic factor involved. The effects of temperature extremes can be alleviated by taking such measures as properly adjusting the ventilation; covering open trucks in cold weather and using straw bedding; using wet sand for bedding and spraying and fogging during hot weather; and scheduling hauls during the best time of day (this will depend upon weather conditions).

Weighing Conditions.   Weighing conditions include such arrangements as holding livestock off water and/or feed for a specified time prior to weighing, and, in the case of feeder cattle or lambs, driving the livestock to a specified place for weighing. Since weighing conditions affect the shrinkage and hence the value of the animals, the weighing conditions need to be considered as an integral part of the bargain, along with the price. Harston (1959A) reported that overnight shrink (12-hr stand) will vary with the type of feed. Cattle off green grass, wet beet pulp, or silage will ordinarily shrink 4 percent, whereas fat cattle off concentrates will shrink about 2.5 to 3 percent if no feed and water are available. If feed and water are available, morning weights of fat

---

[6]In this study, one group of steers was marketed in May and another in October. These were the two time periods involved in the analysis.

cattle will be 2 percent less than evening weights. Range cattle not used to enclosures often shrink more than 5 percent when held in a dry lot overnight. In several respects, the considerations involved here are similar to those previously discussed under degree of fill.

Shrinkage from driving livestock will depend not only on the distance, but also on weather conditions, speed of travel, and handling procedures. Harston (1959B) reported an 8.4-percent shrink on steers from a 50-mile drive under favorable handling conditions. Under the best of conditions, such shrink would probably amount to 3 to 4 percent in a 6-to-8-mile drive.

Sex, Class, and Weight of Animals. Most studies show that heifers shrink more than steers. Harston (1959B) reported, however, that the difference was not great except during the summer when heifers shrank 11.5 lb for each 10 lb that steers shrank. Much variation occurs in comparison of sex. Bulls usually shrink a lot if there are disturbing circumstances or strange animals in nearby pens. Calves also are heavy shrinkers, largely because they are often weaned at market time. Finished cattle shrink more during the latter hours of transit (Table 18.6).

Studies relating shrinkage to weight of hogs have been inconsistent (Bjorka, 1938; Stout and Cox, 1959). In the case of cattle, Harston (1959B) reported that shrinkage was not closely related to weight except as weight is correlated with degree of fatness.

Mode of Transportation. The comparative shrinkage by truck versus rail on short hauls is irrelevant since other considerations have given trucks a virtual monopoly on short hauls. The evidence in Fig. 18.16 indicates relatively little difference between rail and truck shrinkage of cattle in long hauls—up to 30 to 40 hr in transit.

Factors other than mode of transportation easily could account for the apparent differences.

Preconditioning. Studies of the effect of preconditioning on shrinkage have been somewhat inconclusive. It appears reasonable that

Table 18.6. Comparison of Shrinkage by Fat Cattle and Feeder Cattle.

Time in Transit	Rate of Shrink	
	Fat Cattle	Feeder Cattle
(hr)	(%)	(%)
6	5.4	3.8
10–17	6.2	8.2
60	10.8	12.4

Source: Data from Harston (1959B).

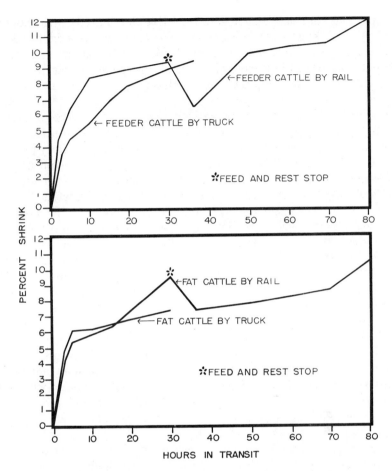

Fig. 18.16. How Shrinkage Differs When Cattle are Shipped by Truck and Rail (Feeder and Fat Cattle). (Harison, 1959B).

weaning, vaccination, castration, and other such operations cause stress. If these operations were accomplished as part of preconditioning, subsequent shrinkage would be reduced. The fact that preconditioning is not standardized, however, has probably contributed to the conflicting results. Additional research is needed to evaluate not only shrinkage, but also other economic aspects associated with preconditioning.

General Considerations. To the extent that actual shrinkage can be predicted and controlled, it becomes a bargaining issue (comparable to pencil shrink in the following section). Raikes and Tilley (1975) pointed out that packers have an incentive to require the withholding of both feed and water because the shrinkage in liveweight reduces liveweight cost more than the reduced value due to carcass weight loss. Producers with a knowledge of actual shrinkage under varying conditions however, may negotiate for an offsetting price increase.

Pencil Shrink.   Pencil shrink, as defined in Chap. 7, is a negotiated or an agreed upon deduction from scale weight in order to arrive at an appropriate pay weight. This is common practice, particularly in direct cattle sales. Normally, the deduction is specified as a percentage and may range from 2 to 5 percent, but more usually is 3 to 4 percent. The logic of pencil shrink is that some shrinkage will definitely take place and that an estimate or allowance must be made to compensate the buyer for the expected loss in weight accompanying the transaction. Everyone is aware that the same results could be obtained by adjusting the price without resorting to pencil shrink, but the custom is well established, and some buyers (and sellers) apparently believe that bargaining advantages accrue to them. The practice is here to stay unless some governmental action is taken to stop it, and, while this move has been discussed, it appears unlikely. There is nothing inherently dishonest about the practice, but if both parties are not equally informed and of equal bargaining ability, inequities can result.

In a bargaining situation, the general idea is to reach a trade-off between pencil shrink and price. An equal trade-off is one in which the price adjustment exactly offsets the pencil shrink and can be illustrated as follows: Suppose a rancher wants to realize $60.00 per cwt for his 450–lb steer calves. What price would he need if he agreed to a 4-percent pencil shrink? In the absence of pencil shrink, each calf would be worth (450/100) × $60.00, or $270.00. A pencil shrink of 4 percent would amount to a deduction of 18 lb per calf, or a pay weight of 432 lb. Thus, the trade-off price would need to be $270.00 ÷ (432/100), or $62.50 per cwt. The same result can be obtained by direct calculation, as follows:

$$\frac{60.00 + 96}{100} = \$62.50$$

Here, the 96 is the difference between 100 percent and the 4 percent pencil shrink. If the rancher decided not to bargain for a higher price to offset the effect of the 4-percent pencil shrink, but instead settled for $60.00 per cwt and also granted the shrink, he actually would have realized ($60.00) (432/450), or $57.60 per cwt for his calves. Again, this result can be obtained more simply as follows: ($60.00) (96/100) =

$57.60. The same general principles apply to any class of livestock. The differences in value received can amount to substantial sums of money.

Tables have been prepared showing the trade-off price for various levels of pencil shrink allowance and cattle price level. Two such examples are reproduced in Tables 18.7 and 18.8. These tables are derived by straight arithmetic as illustrated in the preceding examples. A glance at Table 18.8 shows that each 1-percent shrink in $50.00 calves amounts to 50¢ per cwt. Since most professional marketers have enough experience to make accurate mental estimates, few of them carry tables. The nonprofessional, occasional trader would do well either to resort to a table or to make the necessary calculations.

One aspect of the shrinkage–bargaining issue that needs special mention is the combination of pencil shrink and weighing conditions. A set of yearling steers sold with, say, a 3-percent pencil shrink are likely to sustain, after an overnight stand and a 10-mile haul before weighing, at least 5 to 6 percent actual shrinkage in addition to the pencil shrink (i.e., a total of 8 to 9 percent). This can be offset by providing an adequate consideration in the price. But, as in any other transaction in a competitive market, the "consideration" will depend upon the demand and supply conditions for livestock at the particular time in question and the astuteness and bargaining ability of the participants.

One overriding consideration in shrinkage is the desirability of having an accurate set of scales at the farm, ranch, or feedlot. Shrinkage is so variable that results of average, or unknown, conditions from other sources serve at best only as guidelines or approximations. With a good set of scales, an operator can establish shrinkage with a reasonable degree of accuracy for his particular situation. The availability of scales also serves the extremely important function of permitting an operator to check rates of gain and feed consumption for his particular, and often unique, conditions.

Bruising, Crippling, and Death Loss

Bruised carcasses are costly. In the first place, the bruised area is normally condemned and must be trimmed away; and second, the remainder of the carcass is docked because of its less appealing appearance. Cripples are docked severely on a live basis as some must be condemned and others partially condemned. Dead animals, of course, have virtually no salvage value. Livestock Conservation, Inc., a Chicago-based organization that has collected data and carried out educational programs for many years to reduce such losses, estimates that millions of dollars are lost each year. The irony of the situation is that most

Table 18.7. Shrinkage Table (Offer) Realized Prices: Dollars per Hundredweight Shrinkage Deducted.

Offer ($)	Percent Pencil Shrink				
	2%	3%	4%	6%	8%
50.00	49.00	48.50	48.00	47.00	46.00
49.75	48.75	48.26	47.76	46.77	45.77
49.50	48.51	48.02	47.52	46.53	45.54
49.25	48.27	47.77	47.28	46.29	45.31
49.00	48.02	47.53	47.04	46.06	45.08
48.75	47.77	47.29	46.80	45.83	44.85
48.50	47.53	47.04	46.56	45.59	44.62
48.25	47.29	46.80	46.32	45.35	44.39
48.00	47.04	46.56	46.08	45.12	44.16
47.75	46.79	46.32	45.84	44.89	43.93
47.50	46.55	46.08	45.60	44.65	43.70
47.25	46.31	45.83	45.36	44.41	43.47
47.00	46.06	45.59	45.12	44.18	43.24
46.75	45.81	45.35	44.88	43.95	43.01
46.50	45.57	45.10	44.64	43.71	42.78
46.25	45.33	44.86	44.40	43.47	42.55
46.00	45.08	44.62	44.16	43.24	42.32
45.75	44.83	44.38	43.92	43.01	42.09
45.50	44.59	44.14	43.68	42.77	41.86
45.25	44.35	43.89	43.44	42.53	41.63
45.00	44.10	43.65	43.20	42.30	41.40
44.75	43.85	43.31	42.96	42.07	41.17
44.50	43.61	43.16	42.72	41.83	40.94
44.25	43.37	42.92	42.48	41.59	40.71
44.00	43.12	42.68	42.24	41.36	40.48
43.75	42.87	42.44	42.00	41.13	40.25
43.50	42.63	42.20	41.76	40.89	40.02
43.25	42.39	41.95	41.52	40.65	39.79
43.00	42.14	41.71	41.28	40.42	39.56
42.75	41.89	41.47	41.04	40.19	39.33
42.50	41.65	41.22	40.80	39.95	39.10
42.25	41.41	40.98	40.56	39.71	38.87
42.00	41.16	40.74	40.32	39.48	38.64
41.75	40.91	40.50	40.08	39.25	38.41
41.50	40.67	40.26	39.84	39.01	38.18
41.25	40.43	40.01	39.60	38.77	37.95
41.00	40.18	39.77	39.36	38.54	37.72
40.75	39.93	39.53	39.12	38.31	37.49
40.50	39.69	39.28	38.88	38.07	37.26

Table 18.7. (*continued*)

Offer	Percent Pencil Shrink				
($)	2%	3%	4%	6%	8%
40.25	39.45	39.04	38.64	37.83	37.03
40.00	39.20	38.80	38.40	37.60	36.80
39.75	38.96	38.56	38.16	37.36	36.57
39.50	38.71	38.32	37.92	37.13	36.34
39.25	38.46	38.07	37.68	36.90	36.11
39.00	38.22	37.83	37.44	36.66	35.88
38.75	37.98	37.59	37.20	36.42	35.65
38.50	37.73	37.34	36.96	36.19	35.42
38.25	37.48	37.10	36.72	35.96	35.19
38.00	37.24	36.86	36.48	35.72	34.92
37.75	37.00	36.62	36.24	35.48	34.73
37.50	36.75	36.38	36.00	35.25	34.50
37.25	36.50	36.13	35.36	35.02	34.27
37.00	36.26	35.89	35.52	34.78	34.04
36.75	36.02	35.65	35.28	34.50	33.81
36.50	35.77	35.41	35.04	34.31	33.58
36.25	35.53	35.16	34.80	34.08	33.35
36.00	35.28	34.92	34.56	33.84	33.12
35.75	35.04	34.68	34.32	33.60	32.89
35.50	34.79	34.44	34.08	33.37	32.66
35.25	34.54	34.19	33.84	33.14	32.43
35.00	34.30	33.95	33.60	32.90	32.20
34.75	34.05	33.70	33.36	32.66	31.97
34.50	33.81	33.46	33.12	32.43	31.74
34.25	33.56	33.22	32.88	32.20	31.51
34.00	33.32	32.98	32.64	31.96	31.28
33.75	33.08	32.74	32.40	31.72	31.05
33.50	32.83	32.50	32.16	31.49	30.82
33.25	32.58	32.25	31.91	31.26	30.59
33.00	32.34	32.01	31.68	31.02	30.36
32.75	32.10	31.77	31.44	30.79	30.13
32.50	31.85	31.51	31.20	30.55	29.90
32.25	31.60	31.28	30.96	30.32	29.67
32.00	31.36	31.04	30.72	30.08	29.44
31.75	31.12	30.80	30.48	29.84	29.21
31.50	30.84	30.56	30.24	29.61	28.98
31.25	30.62	30.31	30.00	29.38	28.75
31.00	30.38	30.07	29.76	29.14	28.52

Source: Wellman (undated).

Table 18.8. Shrinkage Table (Asking) Prices: Dollars per Hundredweight Needed to Compensate for Shrinkage.

Asking ($)	Percent Pencil Shrink				
	2%	3%	4%	6%	8%
50.00	51.02	51.54	52.08	53.19	54.36
49.75	50.77	51.29	51.83	52.93	54.10
49.50	50.51	51.03	51.56	52.65	53.81
49.25	50.26	50.78	51.31	52.39	53.55
49.00	50.00	50.51	51.04	52.12	53.27
48.75	49.75	50.26	50.79	51.86	53.00
48.50	49.49	50.00	50.52	51.59	52.72
48.25	49.24	49.75	50.27	51.23	53.43
48.00	48.98	49.48	50.00	51.05	52.17
47.75	48.73	49.23	49.74	50.79	51.90
47.50	48.47	48.97	49.48	50.52	51.62
47.25	48.22	48.72	49.23	50.26	51.36
47.00	47.96	48.45	48.96	49.99	51.08
46.75	47.71	48.20	48.70	49.72	50.81
46.50	47.45	47.94	48.44	49.46	50.54
46.25	47.20	47.69	48.19	49.20	50.28
46.00	46.94	47.42	47.92	48.93	50.00
45.75	46.69	47.17	47.66	48.66	49.72
45.50	46.43	46.91	47.40	48.40	49.46
45.25	46.18	46.66	47.15	48.14	49.19
45.00	45.92	46.39	46.88	47.87	48.92
44.75	45.67	46.14	46.62	47.60	48.64
44.50	45.41	45.88	46.36	47.34	48.38
44.25	45.16	45.63	46.11	47.08	48.11
44.00	44.90	45.36	45.84	46.81	47.83
43.75	44.65	45.11	45.58	46.54	47.56
43.50	44.39	44.85	45.32	46.28	47.29
43.25	44.14	44.60	45.07	46.02	47.03
43.00	43.88	44.33	44.80	45.75	46.75
42.75	43.63	44.08	44.54	45.48	46.48
42.50	43.37	43.82	44.28	45.21	46.20
42.25	43.12	43.57	44.03	44.96	45.94
42.00	42.86	43.30	43.76	44.68	45.66
41.75	42.61	43.05	43.50	44.42	45.39
41.50	42.35	42.79	43.24	44.15	45.12
41.25	42.10	42.54	42.99	43.90	44.86
41.00	41.84	42.27	42.71	43.61	44.57

Table 18.8. (*continued*)

Offer ($)	Percent Pencil Shrink				
	2%	3%	4%	6%	8%
40.75	41.59	42.02	42.46	43.36	44.31
40.50	41.33	41.76	42.20	43.09	44.03
40.25	41.08	41.51	41.95	42.84	43.78
40.00	40.82	41.24	41.67	42.55	43.48
39.75	40.56	40.98	41.41	42.29	43.21
39.50	40.31	40.72	41.15	42.02	42.93
39.25	40.05	40.46	40.89	41.76	42.66
39.00	39.80	40.24	40.63	41.49	42.39
38.75	39.54	39.95	40.36	41.22	42.12
38.50	39.29	39.69	40.10	40.96	41.85
38.25	39.03	39.43	39.84	40.69	41.58
38.00	38.78	39.18	39.58	40.43	41.30
37.75	38.52	38.92	39.32	40.16	41.03
37.50	38.27	38.66	39.06	39.89	40.76
37.25	39.01	38.40	38.80	39.63	40.69
37.00	37.76	38.14	38.54	39.36	40.22
36.75	37.50	37.89	38.28	39.10	39.95
36.50	37.24	37.63	38.02	38.83	39.67
36.25	36.99	37.37	37.69	38.56	39.40
36.00	36.73	37.11	37.50	38.30	39.13
35.75	36.48	36.86	37.24	28.03	38.86
35.50	36.22	36.60	36.28	37.77	38.59
35.25	35.97	36.34	36.72	37.50	38.32
35.00	35.71	36.08	36.46	37.23	38.04
34.75	35.46	35.82	36.20	36.97	37.78
34.50	35.20	35.57	35.94	36.70	37.50
34.25	34.95	35.31	35.68	36.44	37.22
34.00	34.69	35.05	35.42	36.17	36.96
33.75	34.44	34.79	35.16	35.90	36.68
33.50	34.18	34.54	34.90	35.64	36.41
33.25	33.93	34.28	34.64	35.37	36.14
33.00	33.67	34.02	34.37	35.11	35.87
33.75	33.42	33.76	34.11	34.84	35.60
33.50	33.16	33.51	33.85	34.57	35.33
33.25	32.91	33.25	33.59	34.31	35.05
32.00	32.66	32.99	33.33	34.04	34.78

Source: Wellman (undated).

bruises occur on the higher priced cuts and much of the loss could be prevented by simple and sensible precautions.

Among the major causes of bruising are the following: overcrowding; trampling; striking with clubs, canes, or whips; kicking, prodding, and horning; fork and nail punctures; slipping; lifting sheep and lambs by the wool; and poor loading facilities.

Optimum density of loading depends somewhat on weather conditions, but too few or too many animals in a truck or rail car will increase the incidence of bruises. There is little excuse for striking animals to the extent of bruising (aside from the moral significance and the bruise losses sustained, the associated agitation and excitement will increase shrinkage). Inadequate and poorly designed pen and loading facilities can be corrected. Narrow gateways and protruding boards, nails, and sharp edges are frequent causes of bruising and can be corrected.

Many of the factors contributing to bruising also contribute to crippling and death. In addition, inadequate temperature control is a major cause of death. Improper loading density and lack of adequate partitioning together with faulty loading and unloading facilities are major causes of crippling. Most of these factors are controllable to a large degree.

Bruising, crippling, and death loss probably cannot be eliminated since accidents *will* happen, but this loss can certainly be reduced by proper precautions.

REFERENCES

Abbenhaus, C. R., and Penny, R. C. 1951. Shrink characteristics of fat cattle transported by truck. Chicago Union Stockyard and Transit Co., Chicago.

Agnew, D. B. 1973. Cost of marketing U.S. livestock through dealers and public agencies. USDA Marketing Res. Rept. No. 998.

Agnew, D. B. 1975. Trends in prices and marketing spreads for beef and pork. USDA Econ. Res. Serv., ERS 556 (Revised).

Bermettler, E. R. 1964. Interstate transportation of Nevada cattle. Univ. Wyoming, Max C. Fleischmann Coll. Agr. Bull. 234.

Beilock, Richard, and Freeman, J. 1984. Florida motor carrier deregulation: perspectives of urban and rural shipper/receivers. *Amer. J. Agr. Econ.* **66**, No 1: 91–98.

Bjorka, K. 1938. Shrinkage and dressing yields of hogs. USDA Tech. Bull. 621.

Boles, P. P. 1976. Operations of for-hire livestock trucking firms. USDA Econ. Res. Serv., Agr. Econ. Rept. No. 342.

Brandow, G. E. 1966. Implications for consumers in the work of the National Commission on Food Marketing. Proc. 44th Ann. Agr. Outlook Conf., Washington, D.C., Nov. 16.

Capener, W. N., et al. 1969. Transportation of cattle in the west. Wyoming Agr. Expt. Sta. Res. J. 25.

Casavant, K. L., and Nelson D. C. 1967. An economic analysis of the cost of operating livestock trucking firms in North Dakota. N. Dakota Agr. Expt. Sta. Agr. Econ. Rept. 55.

Duewer, L. A. 1969. Effects of specials on composite meat prices. USDA Agr. Econ. Res. Serv. 21, No. 3, 70–77.

Duewer, L. A. 1970. Price spreads for beef and pork revised series, 1949–69. USDA Econ. Res. Serv. Misc. Publ. 1174.

Duewer, L. A. 1978A. Personal correspondence. Agricultural Economist, Commodity Economics Division, Econ., Stat., and Co-op. Serv., USDA.

Duewer, L. A. 1978B. Changes in price spread measurements for beef and pork. USDA Econ., Stat., and Co-op. Serv. LMS-222,33.

Duewer, L. A. 1986. Personal telephone conference and correspondence. Agricultural Economist, National Economics Division, Econ. Res. Serv., USDA.

Fuller, Stephen, et al. 1983. Effect of railroad deregulation on export-grain rates. N. Central J. Agr. Econ. 5, No. 1: 51–63.

Harston, C. R. 1959A. Cattle shrinkage is important. Montana Agr. Expt. Sta. Circ. 220.

Harston, C. R. 1959B. Cattle shrinkage depends on where, when and what you market. Montana Agr. Expt. Sta. Circ. 221.

Harston, C. R. 1959C. Cattle shrinkage depends on how you market. Montana Agr. Expt. Sta. Circ. 222.

Harston, C. R., and Richards, J. 1965. Montana Livestock transportation. Montana Agr. Expt. Sta. Bull. 592.

Henning, G. F., and Thomas, P. R. 1962. Factors influencing the shrinkage of livestock from farm to first market. Ohio Agr. Expt. Sta. Bull. 925.

Hulbert, Archer B. 1920. The paths of Inland Commerce, vol. 21. Yale Chronicles of American Series. By permission of United States Publishers Assoc., New Rochelle, N.Y.

Hutchinson, T. Q. 1981. Motor Carrier Act of 1980. National Food Review. Summer issue.

Madsen, A. G. 1965. Calf shrinkage under auction market conditions. USDA Consumer Marketing Serv. Res. Rept. 718.

Marsh, J. M. 1977. Effects of marketing costs on livestock and meat prices for beef and pork. Montana Agr. Expt. Sta. Bull. 697.

Marsh, J. M. 1983. Comparing costs of selling Montana feeder cattle through direct and indirect markets. Montana Agr. Exp. Sta. Res. Rept. 192.

Moser, D. E. 1970. Changes in transportation and their implications for the livestock and meat industry. In Long-Run Adjustments in the Livestock and meat industry: Implications and Alternatives, edited by T. T. Stout. Ohio Agr. Res. Develop. Center Res. Bull. 1037. Also, North Central Regional Publ. 199.

National Commission on Food Marketing. 1966A. Organization and competition in the livestock and meat industry. Natl. Comm. Food Marketing Tech. Study 1, U. S. Govt. Printing Office, Washington, D.C.

National Commission on Food Marketing. 1966B. Organization and competition in food retailing. Natl. Comm. Food Marketing Tech. Study 7. U.S. Govt. Printing Office, Washington, D.C.

Raikes, R., and Tilley, D.S. 1975. Weight loss of fed steers during marketing. Amer. J. Agr. Econ. 57, No. 1: 83–89.

Schulte, W. (Undated.) Beef marketing margins and costs. S. Dakota Coop. Ext. Serv. FS-209.

Sperling, Celia. 1957. The agricultural exemption in instrastate trucking, a legislative and judicial history. USDA Agr. Marketing Serv., Marketing Res. Rept. 188.

St. Clair, J. S. 1976. Marketing alternatives and costs for Wyoming cattle. Univ. of Wyoming, Agr. Expt. Sta. Res. J. 108.

Stout, T. T., and Armstrong, J. H. 1960. What happens when hogs are fed at market? Purdue Univ. Dept. Agr. Econ., Econ. Marketing Inform. for Indiana Farmers, Mar. 30.

Stout, T. T. and Cox, C. B. 1959. Farm-to-market hog shrinkage. Indiana Agr. Expt. Sta. Res. Bull. 685.

USDA. 1975A. Price spreads and industry margins are not the same. USDA Econ. Res. Serv., ERS-607.

USDA. 1975B. Facts on farm–retail price spreads for beef and pork. USDA Econ. Res. Serv., ERS 597.

USDA. 1977. *1977 Handbook of Agricultural Charts.* USDA Handbook No. 524.

USDA. 1978. National food review. USDA Econ., Stat., and Co-op. Serv. NFR-1.

USDA. 1983. Developments in farm to retail spreads for food products in 1982. USDA, ERS, Agr. Econ. Rept. 500.

USDA, 1984A. Agricultural statistics 1984. USDA, SRS, U.S. Government Printing Office, Washington, D. C.

USDA. 1984B. Livestock and meat statistics, 1983. USDA, ERS, Stat. Bull. 715.

USDA. 1986. 1985 agricultural Chartbook enlargements. USDA, Ext. Serv.

Wellman, A. C. (undated). Dressed, live price and shrinkage tables. Nebraska Coop. Ext. Serv. EC 70–839.

Wiley, J. R., and Cox, C. B. 1955. Hog shrinkage—farm to market. Purdue Univ. Dept. Agr. Econ., Econ. Marketing Inform. for Indiana Farmers, Feb. 26.

19

Meat Substitutes and Synthetics

A rapid rise in meat prices during the early 1970s gave impetus to a development that was already well underway—the production of meat substitutes and synthetics. Meat substitutes are not new. People of certain religions and cultures have survived on meat substitutes for centuries. The U.S. livestock and meat industry, however, became interested and concerned, especially during the decade of the 1970s. Not only did the general consumer begin to balk for economic reasons, but a vegetarian subculture became more widespread as well, and reduced meat consumption (particularly fatty meats) became more commonly prescribed by the medical profession for certain cardiovascular and other diseases. Concurrent shortfalls of food and feed crops in many countries intensified the concern by questioning the wisdom of feeding scarce grain to livestock for a source of protein. A great deal of governmental and industrial effort, in the U.S. and elsewhere, was expended in technological research on meat substitutes and synthetics.

Subsequent improvement in world-wide crop production and increased meat production (associated with the liquidation phase of the cattle cycle in major cattle-producing countries) led to extreme declines in meat prices and grain prices. Concern temporarily abated over the economic urgency for meat substitutes but surfaced again in the late 1970s when meat production dropped and prices rose rapidly—a predictable reflection of the cattle cycle. The basic circumstances that precipitated livestock and meat concern are still very much in evidence. Problems have not developed to the magnitude that many feared, but the enormous potential market—about 40 billion pounds of red meat—provides a great incentive to industry for the development of substitutes and synthetics.

CLARIFICATION OF TERMS

Use of the terms "substitute" and "synthetic" in connection with agricultural products has not been entirely consistent, but, generally speaking, "substitutes" are considered to be products used in place of conventional natural-form agricultural products. The natural-form agricultural product may or may not have undergone processing.

"Synthetics," on the other hand, are products derived from raw materials of nonagricultural origin and used in place of agricultural products. Thus, substitution may involve one agricultural product for another, or it may involve a synthetic for an agricultural product. As used here, then, "synthetics" are substitutes, but not all "substitutes" are synthetic.

ASSOCIATED FACTORS

The forces that stimulate development of substitutes, both agricultural and synthetic, may be classified as economic, social, technological, and institutional. In a competitive economy, businessmen constantly are searching for ways of luring customers from competitors with better, different, or less expensive products. The overriding incentive, from the producer's standpoint, is profit. Consumer demand changes rather slowly, but nevertheless it does change. Personal disposable incomes have been increasing, giving people more and more discretionary spending power. Tastes change with affluence, fads, increases in knowledge, and changes in occupational status. An almost continuous stream of technological developments provides sources of know-how for product and market development. Shifts in the urban-rural distribution of population and intracity shifts to suburbia, or vice versa, are related to social changes that impinge upon the preferences of people for agricultural and other products. Institutional factors include governmental concern and action about the health and welfare of the general public. Recent years have witnessed an increase in governmental attention to consumer problems. Although the government still recognizes the interests of separate sectors, agriculture's influence has declined and will decline further in the future.

The impact of substitute and synthetic products on agriculture's economic position is a complex phenomenon. Each product must be viewed separately since some agricultural sectors produce substitutes themselves and other sectors utilize them in their productive processes, both of which presumably benefit those sectors. Other sectors find the demand for their products displaced by substitutes and suffer adversely. A substitute that draws its raw materials from agriculture may have little effect on agriculture as a whole, but it may alter intraagricultural relationships. For example, oleomargarine had an adverse effect on the dairy sector because of the reduction in demand for butterfat, but enhanced the demand for vegetable fats, primarily soybean oil. Presumably, one agricultural sector's loss in this case was another's gain. Expansion in use of soybean oil for oleomargarine, however, affected its availability and price for other uses. Soybean meal is a joint product that is also affected. Urea, a synthetic product used to replace part of the agriculturally based protein supplements in feeds for ruminant animals, has adversely affected the soybean and cotton sectors by reducing demand for their respective meals. Presumably, the feeders of urea (the feeding sector) derive some benefit. And it is likely that some soybean growers also feed urea so that adverse effects to one enterprise may be at least partially offset by beneficial effects to another on the same farm. Significant increases in the use of synthetic fibers have severely cut into the demand for cotton and wool, with no offsetting benefits to agriculture, and the same has happened to citrus growers as a result of the expansion of synthetic citrus drinks. Other examples could be cited, but these should be sufficient to illustrate some of the complexities and conflicts of interest within agriculture and between agricultural and nonagricultural industries.

RAW MATERIAL SOURCES

Vegetable Protein Substitutes

Major efforts to date to develop meat substitutes have centered on the use of vegetable proteins. Soybeans are the major source of raw materials, but cottonseed, peanuts, sunflower, and safflower are potential alternative sources. Soy proteins are used in two general ways: (1) as a dilutant or extender in processed meat items and in comminuted meats, and (2) as the major ingredient in a meatless meat product designed to be a total substitute with characteristics of meat and referred to as "meat analog."

Soy proteins are currently used in four forms: (1) flour and grits, (2) concentrates, (3) isolates, and (4) textured items. Flour and grits are lowest in protein content with 40 to 55 percent, while concentrates are 65 to 70 percent, isolates 90 to 97 percent, and textured products range from 50 to more than 90 percent (Manley and Gallimore, 1971). The textured products may be "extruded" or "spun." Extruded soy items are near the low end of the protein range, whereas spun proteins are near the upper end of the range. The various forms differ also in physical and chemical properties, use, and price. The spinning process, which is similar to that used in manufacturing rayon and nylon, is the most complex and costly. Extruded and spun proteins can be textured into a fibrous structure with the chewability characteristics (varying degree of tenderness, toughness, and mouth-feel) of meat. They also can be colored, flavored, and molded into characteristic forms to simulate meat. Although much improvement has been made in the meat-like characteristics of analogs, discriminating consumers usually prefer the real product. In addition to simulating the appearance, color, texture, and flavor of meat, analogs are capable of manipulation with respect to caloric content, cholesterol content, protein content, and additives of various sorts. In other words, meat analogs can be manufactured to desired specifications with complete uniformity of product and without seasonal or cyclical variation in supply. Another appealing factor is no cooking loss or shrink during meal preparation. As will be recalled from earlier chapters, large retail chain and HRI buyers are insisting on a year-round supply of uniform quality product. Meat analogs can satisfy these requirements.

Synthetic Substitutes

Among leading developments in synthetic substitutes is the use of the single-cell protein (SCP)—a microorganism (yeast, bacteria, or fungi) capable of transforming organic carbon compounds into protein. The process involves cultivation (or "feeding") of the organisms in a hydrocarbon medium, then processing the cells to reclaim the protein. Numerous sources of hydrocarbons are available, but petroleum is probably one of the most abundant. A number of petroleum firms in the United States, several western European countries, and the Soviet Union carried out extensive experiments in the 1970s to develop a practical process for commercial production. It has been pointed out that the waste gas "flared" in just one Middle Eastern country would produce the protein equivalent of about one-half the soybean acreage of the U.S. The emerging recognition of the eventual world-wide depletion of petroleum and natural gas, and the associated price increases of the 1970s, cast doubt on the feasibility of this source of protein. Other substantial sources of hydrocarbons are available, however, some of which are industrial waste and animal products. The current state of technology and the relatively successful experiments in the U.S. and in Europe leave no doubt that protein compounds can be produced by SCP. Since the late 1970s some success has been achieved, and some commercial operations are currently underway in Europe (primarily for animal feed products) and in the U.S. (focusing on human food products, generally in a powder used to fortify food products such as bakery items). Although commercial application in human food is limited at this time, it is expected to expand if or when economic conditions warrant it. Findlen (1974), in a discussion of SCP as a source of feed protein, concluded that under current costs and prices (early

1970s) the likelihood of factory-grown protein replacing natural crop-grown protein was not likely in the near future. In referring to the longer-run, he stated, "Looking ahead, however, the new protein sources could become a replacement for conventional proteins in times of crop shortfalls and high meal prices, if demand for high protein supplements in animal rations outpaces available supplies." These observations and conclusions are still valid.

COMPETITIVE CONSIDERATIONS

Meat substitutes already are on grocery store shelves in a variety of forms—imitation bacon bits or crumbles, bacon strips, products resembling beef and ham—and incorporated in processed and comminuted meats. Relatively high meat prices in 1973 induced widespread merchandising of soy-beef blend hamburger. Generally speaking this was a blend of 75-percent beef and 25-percent soy protein—textured soy flour or concentrate. Gallimore (1976) analyzed the market penetration of soy-beef-blend hamburger in a study of three retail chains with approximately 1500 stores operating in 21 major markets. Over a 46-week study period, the blends' market share was about 24 percent of all ground beef sold. In the same study, Gallimore found the following:

The demand for blend was highly elastic as the quantity of soy-beef blend sales increased on the average 1.6 to 1.8 percent for each 1 percent decrease in price. As the price of regular ground increased, more blend was sold, with the cross-elasticity ranging from 1.1 to 1.6, indicating that the blend was considered a close substitute for regular ground.

The subsequent decline in beef–soy blend sales as beef prices decreases suggests that the sale of soy proteins as meat extenders directly to consumers will be more cyclic than the sale of soy products to institutional markets.

Economics is only one of several factors, but for the majority, price is critical. "The influence of selling price was shown with beef–soy blends that sold well as long as beef sold 15 to 20 cents a pound higher than the blends; when the price differential decreased, blend sales also dropped. The drop in sales of beef–soy blends with declining beef prices indicates that consumers consider beef–soy blends less satisfactory than all beef" (Wolf, 1976).

Institutions are reported to be relatively heavy users of prepared dishes. The extent to which substitutes have replaced meat has not been precisely measured, but at this stage it is relatively minor. What happens in the future will depend upon economic considerations, consumer tastes and preferences, and the impact of groups in position to recommend or influence their consumption.

The economic considerations concern producers, consumers, and retail store operators. Retailers are interested in the total contribution of meat operation to net profit. They will not necessarily push a cheaper product if it contributes a smaller margin to net profit. Not enough experience has been gained yet to know the effect of meat substitutes on retail margins.

From the consumers' stand point, the price of substitutes compared to that of meat is one of the controlling factors, but also important is the degree to which substitutes satisfy tastes and preferences. The quantity of substitutes in labeled meat products is relatively small, and many consumers probably are unaware of its presence. According to Moede et al. (1969), Federal standards of identity permit soy protein to be used in meat products up to a 3.5-percent level. Regulations, however, do not cover all uses. Manley and Gallimore (1971) report that food served in restaurants is not subject to the same labeling and identification requirements as food sold directly to consumers.

Soy proteins can be readily incorporated into items such as stews, soups, chili, stroganoffs, etc. The least expensive of the substitutes—flour or grits—is generally used. Here the soy proteins can compete with meat and probably will be used to the limit allowed by law, even though the meat they replace in most of these products is from trimmings and the less expensive cuts. Table 19.1 shows the relative cost of net utilizable protein (NPU) from several food sources. "From the information on relative costs, it is obvious why users (at this time decision-makers in institutional kitchens) are interested in substituting soy proteins for more expensive animal proteins. If proteins from soy cost 31 cents per lb and proteins from beef cost $3.26 per lb, there is a strong incentive to substitute soy proteins in uses for which the two products are interchangeable, for example: pizza, sausage, frankfurters, meat loaf, sandwich salami, etc. Add to this the functional advantages of soy proteins (water and fat retention, improvement in keeping quality, browning effects, etc.) and soy proteins appear to have a bright future. These cost and functional advantages will no doubt do much to overcome present deterrents to acceptance identified with consumer prejudices and governmental regulations. Both these barriers are toppling much faster than most people have imagined possible" (Manley and Gallimore 1971).

The barriers did not topple to the extent implied in that study, due to a large extent to a change in price relationships associated with increased supplies of meat. On the basis of cost of net utilizable protein, however, the advantage is still with soy protein. Cyclical change in

Table 19.1.   Relative Costs of Net Utilizable Protein Coming
from Selected Food Sources.

Protein Source	Price of the Food*	Cost of the Net Utilizable Protein[+]
	($/lb)	($/lb)
Beef	0.49	3.26
Chicken	0.33	2.47
Fish	0.45	3.07
Whey (dry)	0.09	0.84
Milk	0.07	2.34
Skim milk (dry)	0.22	0.79
Eggs	0.25	2.09
Dry beans	0.07	0.65
Soybean flour	0.08	0.31
Wheat	0.03	0.41
Cottonseed flour	0.35	1.57
Rice	0.09	1.71

Source: Manley and Gallimore (1971).
*These are for wholesale, lots FOB, point of manufacture.
[+]Crude protein values from *Composition of Foods*, USDA Agr. Handbook 8. Net
utilizable protein (PUN) is the proportion of nitrogen intake that is retained in the
human body. The NPU values used to construct this table from *Amino Acid Content of Food and Biological Data on Proteins*, FAO Nutritional Studies Rep. 24.

relative meat scarcity and relatively high prices will bring this comparison into the limelight again periodically.

Attempts to substitute meat analogs for the higher priced cuts involve several considerations. (1) Textured items and isolates are more
costly to produce under the present technology than soy flour or soy
concentrate, and (2) consumers are more discriminating when the substitute is an imitation of the total product. A study based on 1967–
1968 prices reported that "the textured meat-type products made from
soy protein isolate currently available would probably need to be
priced at retail near the upper range of prices for red meat. These products are reported to have a relatively high ingredient and production
cost, and adding usual marketing markups would result in retail prices
that might range as high as those for steaks and other cuts from sir-
loins" (Moede et al., 1969). This relationship is a tenuous one, for if the
price of meat rises or the cost of meat analogs decreases, the substitutes could be competitive from a price standpoint.

Certain consumers, for religious and philosophical reasons, and others in response to transitory fads, welcome imitation meats. The extent
to which these groups may influence the total demand for meat is unknown. They probably will not have a significant effect, however, for
it is likely that most of them have been using some other substitute in

the past, and, if so, their acceptance of "meatless meat" will not affect the demand for meat.

Groups that may already have had some effect and could have considerably more in the future are those with dietary restrictions. Some members of the medical profession recommend that patients with certain cardiovascular problems reduce the intake of animal fat as a measure of control over blood cholesterol levels. Others recommend a restricted fat diet for weight control, or other reasons. Engineering control over the specifications of substitute meat products indicates that they are made to order for these situations, and cost may not be the controlling factor.

Thus, it appears that pending further cost-reducing technological developments in substitutes, the major use of soy proteins is in processed meats and prepared dishes in the hotel, restaurant and institutional trade. Institutions provide a growing market for products such as bacon bits, which can be incorporated in scrambled eggs, soups, stews, etc. The elimination of preparatory steps and the ease of storage, along with competitive prices, give soy proteins an advantage in these markets. A large potential institutional buyer of soy-added beef is the USDA's school lunch program. USDA is currently purchasing bulk beef and beef patties that contain added vegetable protein product (vpp), a fortified soy product in either a granular isolater or textured concentrate.

To date, only minor inroads have been made in the market for higher priced cuts, but increased use is expected for certain dietary purposes, and, if cost-reducing technology is developed along with improved meatlike characteristics, the general demand for genuine meat will be vulnerable. The magnitude of the potential market is so extensive that continued research and development in substitutes is to be expected.

One of the few reported tests in the household market sector was on a bacon substitute (Corkern and Dwoskin, 1970). The test product was an analog designed to simulate the texture, color, and taste of bacon in the form of bacon strips—not chips or crumbles—and was sold in a frozen state. The experiment was conducted for six months in Fort Wayne, Indiana, utilizing 40 supermarkets in national, regional, and local chains. The market test was conducted by a private research firm under contract to the manufacturer of the product, and results were published by the USDA. During the first three months (Phase I) an intensive promotional and advertising program was carried out, consisting of in-store promotion, as well as newspaper and TV advertising. During the latter three months (Phase II), the advertising was similar to that ordinarily carried on for long-established products.

Bacon analog sales amounted to 4 percent of bacon sales during

Phase I and declined to 1.3 percent of bacon sales as promotion and advertising dropped off in Phase II. Bacon sales also declined during the period of Phase II, but only one-eighth as much as the drop in bacon analog sales. A survey of purchasers showed that, "In general, users expressed a high level of satisfaction. The product's strongest attributes were ease and speed of preparation and good cooking qualities. A large proportion of the users found nothing they disliked about the product" (Corken and Dwoskin, 1970).

There was no clear evidence that bacon analog sales replaced bacon sales during the test period, but this would hardly be expected in a short, introductory period. The survey showed that many consumers were attracted by the advertised low caloric and cholesterol content, and relatively low price. On an as-served basis, the bacon analog was advertised to cost one-half as much as bacon.

Results of the test showed no adverse reaction to the product in the frozen state. "All in all, test market results, though limited, indicate a good chance for further commercial success of the bacon analog" (Corkern and Dwoskin, 1970).

In a consumer panel study of approximately 600 randomly selected urban, southern households, Mize (1972) found no adverse effect on palatability from the addition of 2 percent of soybits to ground beef. Weimer (1976) conducted taste tests under controlled laboratory conditions using regular hamburger and three ground-beef products containing textured vegetable protein (tvp). In one test, participants were told which products contained tvp. In another test, that information was withheld. In the test when knowledge of the contents was unknown, the participants indicated no difference in preference among the products, but when the products containing tvp were identified, regular hamburger was significantly preferred. From a merchandising standpoint, this indicates problems with preconceived bias and suggests the possibility of image enhancement by proper choice of label name, e.g., avoidance of use of the word *soy*.

IMPLICATIONS FOR FOOD SUPPLIES

As a matter of self-interest, the livestock and meat industries are rightfully concerned about competition from substitute and synthetic meats. A discussion of the subject, however, would be incomplete without recognition of general food-supply problems—both domestic and world-wide. People in the United States as a whole are the best fed in the world, but recent studies have shown serious inadequacies in the diets of a substantial number. And on a comparative basis the problem is infinitely more serious in less developed countries around the world.

Demographers estimate that the world population will almost double by about the year 2000. This would mean that within little more than a decade world food production will need to almost double just to maintain the present inadequate level of supplies. The problem is one not only of total quantity but also—and this is especially serious—of a lack of high protein foods. There is little doubt that the United States has the capacity to produce sufficient total food supplies for itself and, with proper economic incentives, to continue to produce sufficient animal protein for domestic needs. However, without some considerable shifts in income distribution, substantial numbers of people probably will not have the purchasing power to buy adequate supplies of animal proteins. It is certain on the world scene that the need will exist for more, and less expensive, proteins than can be furnished from animal sources.

The pressure on food supplies points up the need to consider the efficiency of protein production from alternative sources. On this score, "The production potential of single-cell proteins is fantastic. Production increases exponentially so that a 1-lb seeded culture would multiply to 2 tons of edible food (1/2 protein, 1/2 carbohydrates and fats) in 24 hr. The SCP yield from 1000 lb of petroleum is approximately 1000 lb of edible product, which compares with 500 lb of catfish, 250 lb of dressed poultry, and 75 lb of dressed beef per 1000 pounds of feed" (Swackhamer, 1969). On a conversion ratio of 7-lb-of-grain to produce 1-lb-of-beef, it would require about 39 lb of grain to produce 1 lb of animal protein.[1] Soybeans average about 37.9 percent protein (Morrison 1956). While this 37.9 figure is not all recoverable in the form of protein concentrates, insofar as technical production efficiency is an issue, it is apparent that protein production by way of animal agriculture is less efficient than by either vegetable or synthetic production.

Table 19.1 shows that, in 1970, the cost of 1 lb of protein from soybean flour was about one-tenth that of protein from beef. That ratio changes continually as relative prices of the basic commodities change, but, except in unusual circumstances, the cost advantage will be with vegetable protein. From the standpoint of palatability and preferences, it nevertheless remains to be shown that people, even in protein deficient areas, can be induced to consume a new food if that new food constitutes a significant change from traditional consumption patterns.

---

[1]This is based on a beef protein content of 17.9 percent (Moede et al, 1969).

Several commercial U.S. firms have promoted vegetable protein-fortified bottled and canned drinks with some success in less developed countries. Any gains made in vegetable or synthetic protein consumption in less developed countries would be little threat to U.S. or international meat industries. Most of the people in such countries consume less than 10 lb (4.5 kilograms) of meat per capita. Vegetable or synthetic proteins would not be a substitute, but an addition to their present meat consumption.

ALTERNATIVE LIVESTOCK-MEAT INDUSTRY REACTION

The intrusion of substitute and synthetic products into agricultural markets has prompted various reactions. When oleomargarine began to make inroads into the butter market, dairy farmers attempted to induce legal action prohibiting its manufacture and sale. When this proved ineffective, the approach was switched to taxation by individual states and attempts to prohibit its being colored yellow prior to sale. Some states adopted such measures, but all have now faded away. Agriculture has less political power now than in the days of the oleo battle, and even if farmers and ranchers had the power to induce legal restrictions on meat substitutes, the oleo experience indicates its futility.

The cotton and wool industries have given up a considerable share of their markets to substitute and synthetic fibers. After a somewhat belated start, these industries instituted concerted research efforts to develop processing technology for improved characteristics of their products in line with consumer preferences. Improvements have been made in such things as altering the shrink characteristics of wool and cotton fabrics, improving wash-and-wear characteristics, permapress, etc. Technical improvements along with concurrent marketing and merchandising innovations have been effective. Although these industries have not regained their former position in the fabric market, the market share for cotton has improved, and the long-time drop in wool production has tended to obscure an improvement in consumer preference for wool. The point to be emphasized is that the approach here has been more effective than that used with oleo.

In a protein-deficient world, the livestock and meat industries cannot make an effective case for opposing improved technology for the production of vegetable and synthetic protein foods. Public opinion would not support such a stand, and as pointed out above, it probably would be ineffective anyway. However, the following aspects warrant consideration: (1) The competitive structure necessitates continual efforts to improve the acceptance of meat and meat products through improvements in production, processing, and merchandising. The most effective competitive device is a product that satisfies consumers' tastes and preferences and that is backed up by an effective merchandising program. (2) The livestock and meat industry also has a responsibility of inducing governmental vigilance with respect to truthfulness in the labeling of substitute and synthetic products so that the public will be fully aware of their ingredients and their health-related characteristics. It cannot be assumed that all such products will equal the nutritive qualities of meat.

REFERENCES

Anon. 1968. Food from petroleum. Standard Oil Company, SPAN 8, No. 3, Fall.

Corkern, R. S., and Dwoskin, P. B. 1970. Consumer acceptance of a new bacon substitute. USDA Econ. Res. Serv. 454.

Corkern, R. S., and Poats, F. J. 1968. Synthetics and substitutes in food and non-food markets. USDA Marketing Transportation Situation, Econ. Res. Serv. MTS-171.

Ethridge, M. D. 1975. Competitive potential of synthetic meat products: Some efficiency implications of nutritional composition. Western Agr. Econ. Assn., Proceedings 48th Annual Conference, Reno, Nevada, July, 191–195.

Findlen, P. J. 1974. Factory-grown feed protein is no match for soybean meat. USDA Foreign Agr. Serv., Foreign Agr., Nov. 6–16.

Gallimore, W. W. 1972. Synthetics and substitutes for agricultural products: projections for 1980. USDA Econ. Res. Serv., Marketing Res. Rept. No. 947.

Gallimore, W. W. 1976. Estimated sale and impact of soy-beef blends in grocery stores, USDA Econ. Res. Serv., National Food Situation, NFS-155, 37–44.

Lublin, J. S. 1976. Soybean saga, revival is attempted for meat substitutes that flopped after '73. Wall Street Journal. Oct. 26, 1.

Manley, W. T., and Gallimore, W. W. 1971. Emerging product inroads into agriculture: synthetics and substitutes. Proc. 1971 Natl. Agr. Outlook Conf. Washington, D.C., Feb. 24–25.

Miner, B. D. and Gallimore, W. W. 1977. Soy protein use can increase 71% by 1985. USDA Farmer Co-op. Serv. Farm Cooperatives, July, 4–6.

Miner, B. D. 1976. Edible soy protein: Operational aspects of producing and marketing. USDA Farmer Co-op. Serv., FSC Res. Rept. 33.

Mize, J. J. 1972. Factors affecting meat purchases and consumer acceptance of ground beef at three levels with and without soya-bits. Georgia Agr. Expt. Sta., Southern Cooperative Series Bull. 173.

Moede, H. H., et al. 1969. Meat and poultry substitutes. In synthetics and Substitutes for Agricultural Products, and Compendium. USDA Econ. Res. Serv. Misc. Publ. 1141.

Morrison, F. B. 1956. Feeds and Feeding, 22nd ed. Morrison Publishing Co., Clinton, Iowa.

Swackhamer, G. L. 1969. Synthetics and substitutes: Challenge to agriculture. Federal Reserve Bank of Kansas City Monthly Rev. Mar., pp. 3–12.

USDA. 1967. Proceedings of International Conference on Soybean Protein Foods. USDA
Agr. Res. Serv. 35–71.
Weimer, J. 1976. Taste preference for hamburger containing textured vegetable protein.
USDA Econ. Res. Serv., National Food Situation, NFS–155, pp. 45–46.
Wolf, W. J. 1976. Edible soy protein, operational aspects of producing and marketing-
market growth. USDA Farmer Co-op. Serv. FSC Res. Report 33, pp. 40–45.

Index

Index

747 4194